PLATE I. RESTORATION OF AN EGYPTIAN VASE OF THE
PYRAMID AGE. (AFTER BORCHARD)

The original was wrought of gold (here yellow), inlaid with lapis
lazuli (here blue), by the goldsmith (§ 82 and Fig. 47)

# ANCIENT TIMES A HISTORY OF THE EARLY WORLD

## AN INTRODUCTION TO THE STUDY OF ANCIENT HISTORY AND THE CAREER OF EARLY MAN

BY

## JAMES HENRY BREASTED, Ph.D., LL.D.

PROFESSOR OF ORIENTAL HISTORY AND EGYPTOLOGY; CHAIRMAN
OF THE DEPARTMENT OF ORIENTAL LANGUAGES
IN THE UNIVERSITY OF CHICAGO

GINN AND COMPANY
BOSTON · NEW YORK · CHICAGO · LONDON
ATLANTA · DALLAS · COLUMBUS · SAN FRANCISCO

𝕿𝖍𝖊 𝕬𝖙𝖍𝖊𝖓𝖆𝖚𝖒 𝕻𝖗𝖊𝖘𝖘

GINN AND COMPANY · PRO-
PRIETORS · BOSTON · U.S.A.

# PREFACE

In the selection of subject matter as well as in style and diction, it has been the purpose of the author to make this book sufficiently simple to be put into the hands of first-year high-school pupils. A great deal of labor has been devoted to the mere task of clear and simple statement and arrangement. While simple enough for first-year high-school work, it nevertheless is planned to interest and stimulate all students of high-school age. In dealing with each civilization a sufficient framework of political organization and of historical events has been laid down; but *the bulk of the space has been devoted to the life of man in all its manifestations* — society, industry, commerce, religion, art, literature. These things are so presented as to make it clear how one age grows out of another, and how each civilization profits by that which has preceded it.

The story of each great race or nation is thus clearly disengaged and presented in period after period; but, nevertheless, the book purposes to present the career of man as a whole, in a connected story of expanding life and civilization from the days of the rudest stone hatchet to the Christian cathedrals of Europe, without a serious gap. A symmetrical presentation of the career of man requires adequate space for the origins of civilization and the history of the Orient, as these two subjects have been revealed by the excavations and discoveries of the last two generations, especially the last twenty-five years. The reasons for devoting more than the customary space to these subjects in this book may therefore be briefly noted.

The length of the career of man discernible by us has been enormously increased at the present day by archæological

iii

discovery, carrying back the development of human arts at least fifty, and perhaps two hundred thousand, years. Even as recorded in *written* documents, modern discovery in the Orient has placed behind the period of human history as formerly known to us another period equally long, thus doubling the length of the historic age. It cannot be said that all this vast new outlook has as yet been surveyed and briefly presented in a form intelligible to younger students as an imposing panorama of the expanding human career. The attainment of such a point of view of the career of man has been a slow process. The ancient history written by Sulpicius Severus, about 400 A.D., survived for over a thousand years, and became a respected textbook, which was in use as late as the sixteenth century. It dealt almost exclusively with the history of Rome. A mention of the battle of Marathon was its *only reference* to Greek history. The Roman colossus bulked so large that nothing earlier could be seen behind it.

Within the last few years, however, the marvelous genius of the Greeks has finally found full recognition in our historical textbooks. There is another similar step yet to be taken, and that is to discern behind Greece and Rome an additional great and important chapter of the human story and to give it adequate and interesting presentation to young readers. Probably no one outside the arcanum of the traditional classicists would question the assertion that conquests which we owe to the Orient, like the discovery of metal and the invention of alphabetic writing, were achievements of far greater importance than the details of the Peloponnesian Wars, whether estimated by their consequences to the human race or by their value as information in the mind of the modern high-school pupil. Whether such achievements are regarded as falling within the historic epoch or not is a matter of small moment. They belong to the *human career*, and as such they should find their place in the picture of that career which is presented to the younger generation.

The intelligent person of to-day desires to be so familiar with such facts as these in the rise of civilization as to possess some moderate acquaintance with the early chapters in the human career. Civilization arose in the Orient, and early Europe obtained it there. But the languages of the early Orient perished, and the ability to read them was lost many centuries ago. On the other hand, the languages of Greece and Rome were never lost, like those of the ancient Orient. In modern educational history Greek and Latin have not been suddenly recovered, and we have not had to grow accustomed to their abrupt introduction into science and education. The sudden and dramatic recovery of the earlier chapters of the human career, lying behind Greece and Rome, has created a situation to which our histories of the ancient world, as they are found in our public schools, have not yet adjusted themselves. The habit of regarding ancient history as beginning with Greece has become so fixed that it is not easily to be changed. Furthermore, the monuments and documents left us by the ancient Orient are far larger in extent than those which we have inherited from Greece and Rome together, and their enormous volume, together with their difficult systems of writing, have made it very laborious to recover and arrange the history of the Orient in form and language suitable for the high-school pupil.

In 1884 Eduard Meyer, the leading ancient historian of this generation, in his *History of Antiquity* devoted six hundred and nineteen pages to the Orient. In the third edition, still unfinished, which began to appear in 1913, the portion of the Orient thus far issued (less than half) occupies eleven hundred and fifty pages. The remainder, still unpublished, will easily bring the treatment of the Orient up to twenty-four or twenty-five hundred pages, that is, about four times its former bulk. A textbook which devotes a brief fifty- or sixty-page introduction to the Orient and begins " real history " with the Greeks is not proportioned in accordance with modern knowledge of the ancient world.

Furthermore, the value of the early oriental monuments as teaching material has as yet hardly been discerned. The highly graphic pictorial monuments and records of the East, when accompanied by proper explanations, may be made to convey to the young student the meaning and character of a contemporary historical source more vividly than any body of ancient records surviving elsewhere. When adequately explained, such records also serve to dispel that sense of complete unreality which besets the young person in studying the career of ancient man. These materials have not been employed in our schools, because they have not been available to the teacher in the current textbooks.

Finally, when we recall that the leading religion of the world — the one which still dominates Western civilization to-day — came to us out of the Orient; when we further remember that before it fell the Roman Empire was completely orientalized, it would appear to be only fair to our schools to give them books furnishing an adequate treatment of pre-Greek civilization. This does not mean to question for a moment the undeniable supremacy of Greek culture, or to give it any less space than before. The author believes that no one who reads the chapters on Greece in this survey will gain the impression that Hellas has been sacrificed to Moloch — in other words, to her oriental predecessors.

The author is convinced that the surviving monuments of the entire ancient world can be so visualized as to render ancient history a very real story even to young students, and that these monuments may be made to tell their own story with great vividness. This method he has already introduced into the ancient-history chapters of *Outlines of European History, Part I*, where it has demonstrated its availability. The same method has been employed in illustrating this ancient history. The result has been a book somewhat larger than the current textbooks on ancient history; but the excess is due to the series of illustrations. The book actually contains a text of about five hundred pages, with a " picture book " of about two hundred and fifteen pages. Teachers will do well to make the illustrations and accompanying descriptive matter part of each lesson. The references in the text to the illustrations, and the references to the text in the descriptive matter under the illustrations, if noted and used, will be found to merge text and illustrations into a unified whole. It should be noted that all references to the text are by paragraph (§) except a few references by "Section."

An elaborate system of maps has been arranged by the author for the purpose of bringing the successive epochs of history before the pupil in terms of geography. The underlying principle is the arrangement on the same plate of from two to four maps representing successive historical epochs. It is believed that these composite maps, called by the author sequence maps, will prove a powerful aid to the teacher.

The author has not found it an easy task to turn from twenty-five years of research in a laboratory of ancient history, extending from a university post in America to the frontiers of the oriental lands, and endeavor to summarize for youthful readers the facts now discernible in the career of ancient man. Under these circumstances the experience of my friend Professor James Harvey Robinson, who has done so much for the study of history in the schools of America, has been invaluable. The book owes a great deal to the inspiration of his unflagging interest and the helpfulness of his long experience in the art of simplification. It may be mentioned here that Professor Robinson's *Medieval and Modern Times* forms the continuation of this volume on ancient history. To my colleague Professor C. F. Huth also I am indebted for careful reading of the proofs, accompanied by unfailingly valuable counsel. To him, furthermore, I owe the excellent bibliography of Greece and Rome at the end of the volume. Mr. Robert I. Adriance, head of the history department of the East Orange high schools, has kindly read all the proofs. His discerning criticisms and wide knowledge have proved very valuable to the book, and his unfailing interest has been a great encouragement.

It will be noticed that some of the author's treatment of the ancient world in *Outlines of European History, Part I*, has been retained here. These portions had already been looked over by Mr. A. F. Barnard of the University High School of Chicago, and he has also very kindly read the proofs of the remainder of the volume. The chapters on the Babylonians and Assyrians have been read by Professor D. D. Luckenbill, and that on the Hebrews by Professor J. M. Powis Smith, and to their kindness I am indebted for several suggestions. The sections on early Christianity and the Church have likewise been looked over by my colleague Professor S. J. Case. To all these friends and colleagues the author would here express his sincere thanks.

It has been very gratifying to the author to be able to include in a book of this character the six charming etchings made expressly for the volume by Mr. George T. Plowman. To Mrs. William T. Brewster he is also indebted for the beautiful water color of the Plain of Argos (Plate III). Besides photographs furnished by the Egyptian Expedition of The University of Chicago, many illustrations have been contributed by foreign scholars, to whom the author would here express his thanks, especially to Bissing (Munich), Borchardt (Cairo), Déchelette now alas! a sacrifice of the great war (Roanne), Dörpfeld (Athens and Berlin), Hoernes (Vienna), Koldewey (Babylon), Montelius (Stockholm), Schaefer (Berlin), Schubart (Berlin), Steindorff (Leipzig), and some others, who have kindly furnished photographs and sketches. The author is also especially indebted to Messrs. Underwood & Underwood for permission to use their unrivaled series of Egyptian, oriental, and Mediterranean photographs as the basis for a number of sketches: Figs. 23, 122, 128, 153, 159, 163, 171, 174, 175, 176, 177, 178, 179, 189, 190, 203, 221, 260. No more vivid impressions of the places and scenes where the men of the early world lived and wrought can be obtained than by the use of these photographs in stereoscopic form. Teachers who make the Underwood stereographs a part of their equipment will find that their teaching gains enormously in effectiveness. The author desires to thank also Mr. E. K. Robinson of Ginn and Company, without whose experienced assistance and unfailing patience it would have been impossible to complete the unusual and elaborate illustrative scheme of this book. To the publishers, who have unhesitatingly supported this expensive and laborious illustrative equipment and to the remarkably skillful and efficient proofreaders and printers who have solved the numerous and extraordinary typographical difficulties involved in so large an illustrative scheme, the author would also offer his hearty thanks.

JAMES HENRY BREASTED

# CONTENTS

xi

## PART III. THE GREEKS

# LIST OF COLORED PLATES

# LIST OF MAPS

# ANCIENT TIMES

## PART I. THE EARLIEST EUROPEANS

### CHAPTER I

#### EARLY MANKIND IN EUROPE

SECTION 1. EARLIEST MAN'S IGNORANCE AND PROGRESS

We all know that our fathers and mothers never saw an aëroplane when they were children, and very few of them had ever seen an automobile. Their fathers lived during most of their lives without electric lights or telephones in their houses. Their grandfathers, our great-grandfathers, were obliged to make all long journeys in stagecoaches drawn by horses, and some of them died without ever having seen a locomotive. One after another, as they have been invented, such things have come and continue to come into the lives of men.

1. Man's gradual invention and acquirement of the possessions of life

Each device grew out of earlier inventions, and each would have been impossible without the inventions which came in before it. Thus, if we went back far enough, we would reach a point where no one could build a stagecoach or a wagon, because no one had invented a wheel or tamed a wild horse. Earlier still there were no ships and no travel or commerce by sea. There were no metal tools, for no one had ever seen any metal. Without metal tools for cutting the stone there could be no fine buildings or stone structures. It was impossible to write, for no one had invented writing, and so there were no books nor any knowledge of science. At the same time there were no schools or hospitals or churches, and no laws or government. This book is intended to tell the story of how

2. Ancient history a story of similar achievements followed by national rivalries

mankind gained all these things and built up great nations which struggled among themselves for leadership, and then weakened and fell. This story forms what we call ancient history.

**3.** Man began with nothing and with no one to teach him

If we go back far enough in the story of man, we reach a time when he possessed nothing whatever but his hands with which to protect himself, satisfy his hunger, and meet all his other needs. He must have been without speech and unable even to build a fire. There was no one to teach him anything. The earliest men who began in this situation had to learn everything for themselves by slow experience and long effort, and every tool, however simple, had to be invented.

**4.** Savages of to-day show us the life of earliest man ; the Tasmanians and what they had *failed* to learn

People so completely uncivilized as the earliest men must have been, no longer exist on earth. Nevertheless, the lowest savage tribes found by explorers at the present day are still leading a life very much like that of our early ancestors. For example, the Tasmanians, the people whom the English found on the island of Tasmania a century or so ago, wore no clothing; they had not learned how to build a roofed hut; they did not know how to make a bow and arrows, nor even to fish. They had no goats, sheep, or cows; no horses, not even a dog. They had never heard of sowing seed nor rais·ing a crop of any kind. They did not know that clay would harden in the fire, and so they had no pottery jars, jugs, or dishes for food.

**5.** The Tasmanians and what they *had* learned

Naked and houseless, the Tasmanians had learned to satisfy only a very few of man's needs. Yet that which they had learned had carried them a long way beyond the earliest men. They could kindle a fire, which kept them warm in cold weather, and over it they cooked their meat. They had learned to construct very good wooden spears, though without metal tips, for they had never heard of metal. These spears, tipped with stone, they could throw with great accuracy, and thus bring down the game they needed for food, or drive away their human enemies. They would take a flat stone and, by chipping off the edges to thin them, they could make a rude knife with which to skin and cut up the game they killed. They were also very deft in weaving cups, vessels, and baskets of bark fiber. Above all, they had a simple language, with words for all the ordinary things they used and did every day.

It was only after several hundred thousand years of savage life and slow progress that the earliest prehistoric men of Europe reached and passed beyond a stage of savagery like that of the Tasmanians just described. The Europe which formed the home of these earliest men was very different from what it is to-day. In the shadow of the lofty primeval forests which fringed the streams and clothed the wide plains, the ponderous hippopotamus wallowed along the shores of the European rivers. The fierce rhinoceros, with a horn three feet in length, charged through the

FIG. 1. FIRE-MAKING WITHOUT MATCHES, BY MODERN NATIVES OF AUSTRALIA

The outfit is very simple, consisting merely of a round, dry stick placed upright with the lower end in a hole in a dry tree-trunk lying on the ground. By turning the stick rapidly between both hands the friction finally generates sufficient heat to produce flame (§ 8)

heavy tropical growth on their banks, and vast elephants, with shaggy hair two feet long (Fig. 10, 7), wandered through the jungles behind. Myriads of bison and wild horses grazed on the uplands, and the broken glades sheltered numerous herds of deer. A moist atmosphere, warm and enervating, vibrant with the notes of many tropical birds, pervaded this prehistoric European wilderness stretching far across Europe.

**7.** Life and haunts of the earliest European; his wooden weapons and tools

FIG. 2. A GROUP OF NORTH AMERICAN INDIANS MAKING FLINT WEAPONS. (AFTER HOLMES)

The farthest Indian is prying loose a large flint stone. This is the raw material, which is then taken by the middle Indian, who crashes it down upon a rock and shatters it into fragments. One of these fragments is then taken by the nearest Indian, who holds it in his left hand while he strikes it with a stone in his right hand. These blows flake off pieces of flint, and the Indian is so skillful that he can thus shape a flint hatchet. This process of shaping the flint by blows (that is, by *percussion*) was the earliest and rudest method and produced the roughest stone tools. In the course of thousands of years two improvements followed — chipping the edge by *pressure* (Fig. 5) and sharpening the edge by *grinding* (Fig. 16, *5*)

With nothing to cover his nakedness, the early savage of Europe roamed stealthily through these tropical forests, seeking his daily food among the roots, seeds, and wild fruits wherever he could find them, and listening with keen and eager ear for the sound of small game which he might be able to lay low with his rough wooden club. Doubtless he often fled in terror as he felt the thunderous tread of the giant animals of the forest or caught dim glimpses of colossal elephants plunging through the deep vistas of the jungle. At night the hunter slept wherever the game had led him, after cutting up the flesh of his prey with a wooden knife and devouring it raw. Not knowing how to

make a fire to ward off the savage beasts, he lay trembling in
the darkness at the roar of the mighty saber-tooth tiger.

At length, however, he learned to know fire, perhaps finding
it in his jungle haunts when the lightning kindled a forest fire,
or fearing it from afar as he viewed the terrible volcanoes
along the Mediterranean. It was a great step forward when he
at last learned to produce it himself with his whirl-stick (Fig. 1).
He could then cook his food, warm his body, and harden the
tip of his wooden spear in the fire. But his dull wooden knife
he could not harden, and he sometimes found a broken stone
and used its ragged edge. When he learned to shape the stone
to suit his needs (Fig. 2), and thus to produce a rude tool or
weapon, he entered what we now call the Stone Age, more
than fifty thousand years ago.

**8.** Man learns to kindle fire and use stone

From this point on we can hold in our hands the very stone
tools and implements with which early men maintained themselves in their long struggle to survive. By the long trail of
stone implements which they left behind them we can follow
them and tell just how far they had advanced in the successive stages of their upward career; for these stages are revealed to us by their increasing skill in working stone and in
other industries which they gradually learned. We can distinguish, in the examples of their handiwork which still survive,
three successive ages, which we may call the Early Stone Age,
the Middle Stone Age, and the Late Stone Age. Let us now
observe man's progress through these three ages, one after
the other.

**9.** Career of early man traceable in surviving stone implements and other works of his hands

## Section 2. The Early Stone Age

Until a short time ago it was supposed that human history
was comparatively brief. Moreover, everyone took it for
granted that the earlier period of man's past had left no surviving traces. An old letter written in London two hundred
years ago (1714) tells how a certain apothecary discovered
the bones of an elephant in a gravel-pit near London, and, near

**10.** Modern ignorance of man's vast age until fifty years ago

FIG. 3. A FLINT FIST-
HATCHET OF THE EARLY
STONE AGE

Rough flint flakes older than
the fist-hatchet still survive
to show us man's earliest
efforts at shaping stone.
But the fist-hatchet is the
earliest well-finished type
of tool produced by man.
The original is about 9
inches long, and the drawing reduces it to less than
one third. Either end might
be used as the cutting edge,
but it was usually grasped
in the fist by the narrower
part, and never had any
handle. Handles of wood
or horn do not appear until
much later (cf. Fig. 16, 4–5).
Traces of use and wear are
sometimes found on such
fist-hatchets

by, the flint head of a spear. Although this letter was soon afterward published, with a drawing of
the spearhead, no attention was paid
to it and it was quickly forgotten.
For over a century similar discoveries. both in England and on the
Continent, met with the same fate.
It was not until some fifty years
ago, after the evidence had been
available for a century and a half,
that the eyes of scientific men were
at last opened to the fact of the
enormously long sojourn of man
upon the earth.

Long-continued excavations, especially in France, have furnished
thousands of stone tools which reveal to us the progress of the Early
Stone Age hunter after he had found
that he could chip stones. By studying the collections of such stone tools
now in the museums of Europe we
can see how the early man gradually
outgrew a variety of rudely chipped
stones and finally produced a successful stone implement (Fig. 3).
This he used for almost everything.
It was from eight to ten inches long,
narrow above and wider below, and
sufficiently sharp to enable him to
cut the roots and branches which he
used for food, to shape his wooden
fire-kindling outfit (Fig. 1), and to
hew out his heavy wooden club.

This stone implement we call a "fist-hatchet," because it was grasped in the fist, usually by the narrow end, for the hunter had not yet discovered how to attach a handle. These fist-hatchets have been found in many places in Europe as well as in other parts of the world. It is the earliest widely made and used human device which has survived to our day.

Perishing probably in great numbers, as his hazardous life went on, this savage hunter of prehistoric Europe continued for thousands of years the uncertain struggle for survival. He slowly improved his rough stone fist-hatchet, and he probably learned to make additional implements of wood, but these have of course rotted and perished, so that we know nothing of them. Of all the later possessions of man he had not yet one. The wide grainfields and the populous and prosperous communities of later Europe were still many thousands of years distant, in a future which it was even more impossible for him to foresee than our own now is for us. Single-handed he waged war upon all animals. There was not a beast which was not his foe. There was as yet no dog, no sheep or fowl, to which he might stretch out a kindly hand. The ancestor of the modern dog was then either the jackal or the fierce wolf of the forest, leaping upon the primitive hunter unawares, and those beasts which were the ancestors of our modern domestic animals were either not yet in existence in Europe or, like the horse, still wandered the forests in a wild state (cf. Fig. 12). *12. Limitations of Early Stone Age man*

At length the Early Stone Age hunter began to notice that the air of his forest home was losing its tropical warmth. Geologists have not yet found out why, but the climate grew colder, and, as the ages passed, the ice, which all the year round still overlies the region of the North Pole and the summits of the Alps, began to descend. The northern ice crept farther and farther southward until it covered England as far south as the Thames. The glaciers of the Alps moved down the Rhone valley as far as the spot where now the city of Lyons stands (see map, p. 8). On our own continent of North America *13. Coming of the ice*

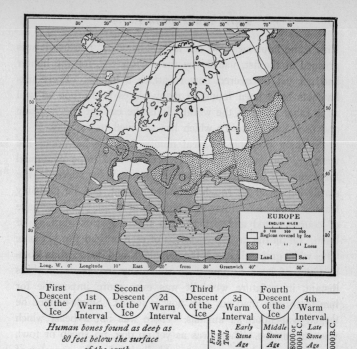

First Descent of the Ice — 1st Warm Interval — Second Descent of the Ice — 2d Warm Interval — Third Descent of the Ice — 3d Warm Interval — Fourth Descent of the Ice — 4th Warm Interval

*Human bones found as deep as 80 feet below the surface of the earth*

First Stone Tools | Early Stone Age | Middle Stone Age | 8,000 or 10,000 B.C. | Late Stone Age | 3000 B.C.

Not less than 50,000 years

### SKETCH MAP OF EUROPE IN THE ICE AGE AND DIAGRAM SHOWING FOUR SUCCESSIVE DESCENTS OF THE ICE

During the Ice Age the ice advanced and retreated four times; that is, there were four periods of cold, each followed by a long interval of warmth. These periods of cold and warmth are indicated by the falling (cold) and the rising (warmth) of the wavy line in the diagram. We are now living in the fourth warm interval. It is clear that prehistoric men began to make fist-hatchets in one of the warm intervals; but it has been very difficult for geologists and archæologists to find out *which* warm interval. Some think that it was the *second*, and if so, then men began making stone tools at least two hundred thousand years ago. Most investigators, however, now believe that stone toolmaking began early in the *third* warm interval; that is, the warm interval preceding the last advance of the ice. In this case stone toolmaking may have begun as late as fifty thousand years before Christ. But Professor Henry Fairfield Osborn, in his valuable volume *Men of the Old Stone Age*, accepts a date over one hundred and twenty-five thousand years ago for the earliest stone tools, which he also places in the *third* warm interval

8

the southern edge of the ice is marked by lines of bowlders carried and left there by the ice. Such lines of bowlders are found, for example, as far south as Long Island, and westward along the valleys of the Ohio and Missouri.

The hunter saw the glittering blue masses of glacier ice, with their crown of snow, pushing through the green of his forest abode and crushing down vast trees in many a sheltered glen or favorite hunting-ground. Many of the animals familiar to him retreated to the warmer South, and he was forced gradually to accustom himself to a cold climate. This change ended the Early Stone Age, but the rude fist-hatchet of its hunters, and the bones of the huge animals they slew, were sometimes left lying side by side in the sand and gravel far up on the valley slopes where in these prehistoric ages the rivers of France once flowed, before their deep modern beds had been eroded. And as these long-buried relics are brought forth to-day, they tell us the fascinating story of man's earliest progress in gaining control of the world about him. The coming of the ice, strange as it may seem, brought with it a new period of progress, which we call the Middle Stone Age.

14. The end of the Early Stone Age

## Section 3. The Middle Stone Age

Unable to build himself a shelter from the cold, the hunter took refuge in the limestone caves (Fig. 4), where he and his descendants continued to live for thousands of years. We can imagine him at the door of his cave, carefully chipping off the edge of his flint tools. He has left the rude old fist-hatchet far behind, for the hunter has finally discovered that by *pressure* with a hard piece of bone he can chip off a line of fine flakes along the edge of his flint tool and thus produce a much finer cutting edge (Fig. 5) than by chipping with *blows* (or *percussion*), as he formerly did. This discovery enabled him to produce a considerable variety of flint tools — chisels, drills and hammers, polishers and scrapers (Fig. 5). The new *pressure*-chipped edges

15. The industries of Middle Stone Age man; the new pressure-chipped edge, and introduction of bone and ivory implements

were sharp enough to cut and shape even bone, ivory, and especially reindeer horn. The mammoth (Fig. 10, 7) furnished the hunter with ivory, and when he needed horn he found great herds of reindeer,[1] driven southward by the ice, grazing before the entrance of his cavern (Fig. 10, 3–5).

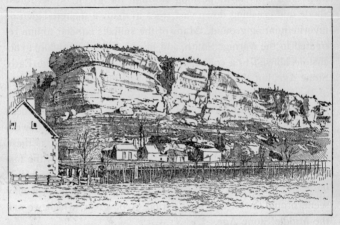

FIG. 4. CLIFFS IN THE SOUTH OF FRANCE CONTAINING CAVERNS INHABITED BY MIDDLE STONE AGE MAN

This district is filled with remains of Middle Stone Age man. The dark opening at *A* is the entrance to a famous cavern (called *Font-de-Gaume*) containing the finest wall paintings (§ 18) of the Middle Stone Age surviving in France. They are surpassed only by those of Altamira, Spain. On the floor are layers of rubbish containing human remains, as in Fig. 9. (Drawn from a photograph by Professor Osborn)

**16. The Middle Stone Age hunter's new weapons and skin clothing**

Equipped with his new and keener tools, the hunter worked out barbed ivory spear-points, which he mounted with long wooden shafts. He also discovered the bow and arrows, and he carried at his girdle a sharp flint dagger. For straightening his wooden spear-shafts and arrows he invented an ingenious shaft-straightener of reindeer horn. Another clever device of

[1] The reindeer was so plentiful in this age that French archæologists often call it the "Reindeer Age."

horn or ivory was his new throwing-stick, by which he could hurl his long spear much farther and with greater power (Figs. 6 and 7) than he could before. Fine ivory needles (Fig. 8) show that the hunter now protected himself from cold, and from the brambles of the forest wilderness with clothing made by sewing together the skins of the animals he slew.

Thus equipped, the hunter of the Middle Stone Age was a much more dangerous foe of the wild creatures than were his ancestors of the Early Stone Age. In a single cavern in Sicily modern archæologists have dug out the bones of no less than two thousand hippopotamuses which

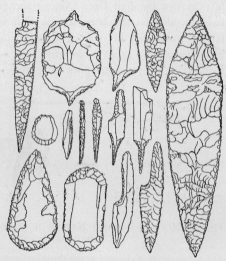

17. Life of the Middle Stone Age hunter

FIG. 5. FLINT TOOLS AND WEAPONS OF THE MIDDLE STONE AGE

From right to left they include knives, spear- and arrow-points, scrapers, drills, and various edged tools. They show great skill and precision in flaking. The fine edges have all been produced by chipping off a line of flakes along the margin, seen especially in the long piece at the right. This chipping is done by *pressure*. The brittleness of flint is such that if a hard piece of bone is pressed firmly against a flint edge, a flake of flint, often reaching far back from the edge, will snap off in response to increasing pressure. This was a great improvement over the earliest method by striking (*percussion*, Figs. 2 and 3)

these Middle Stone Age hunters killed. In France one group of such men slew so many wild horses (Fig. 10, *6*) for food that the bones which they tossed about their camp fires gathered

in masses forming a layer in some places six feet thick and
covering a space about equal to four modern city lots of
fifty by two hundred feet.   Among such deposits excavators
have found even the bone whistle with which the returning
hunter announced his coming to the hungry family waiting
in the cave (Fig. 4).   On his arrival there he found his home
surrounded by revolting piles of garbage.   Amid foul odors

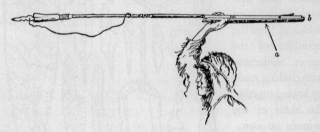

FIG. 6.   MODERN ESKIMO NATIVE HURLING A SPEAR WITH A
THROWING-STICK

The spear lies in a channel in the throwing-stick (*a*), which the hunter
grasps at one end.   At the outer end (*b*) of the throwing-stick is a hook
(cf. Fig. 7, *B*) against which the butt of the spear lies, and as the hunter
throws forward his arm, retaining the throwing-stick in his hand and
allowing the spear to go, the throwing-stick acts like an elongation of
his arm, giving great sweep and propelling power as the spear is discharged.   Modern schoolboys would not find it hard to make and use
such a throwing-stick (see § 16)

of decaying flesh this savage European crept into his cave-
dwelling at night, little realizing that, many feet beneath the
cavern floor on which he slept, lay the remains of his ancestors
in layer upon layer, the accumulations of thousands of years
(Fig. 9).

**18. Discovery of Middle Stone Age art — carvings, drawings, and paintings**   It is not a little astonishing to find that these Middle Stone
Age hunters could already carve (Fig. 7), draw (Fig. 10), and
even paint with considerable skill.   A Spanish nobleman, in-
vestigating a cavern on his estate in Northern Spain, was at
one time digging among the accumulations on the floor of the

cave, where he found flint and bone implements, when his little daughter, who was playing about in the gloom of the cavern, suddenly shouted, "Toros! toros!" ("Bulls! bulls!"). At the same time she pointed to the ceiling. The startled father, looking up, beheld a never-to-be-forgotten sight which at once interrupted his flint-digging. In a long line stretching far across the ceiling of the cavern was a vast procession of bison bulls painted in well-preserved colors on the rock. For at least ten thousand years no human eye had beheld these cave paintings of a vanished race of prehistoric men, till the eye of a child rediscovered them.

Other evidences of higher life among these early men are few indeed. Nevertheless, even these ancient men of the Middle Stone Age believed in divine beings; they already had a crude idea of the life of the soul, or of the departed person after death. Dressed in his customary ornaments, equipped at least with a few flint implements, and protected by a rough circle of stones, the departed hunter was buried in the cave beneath the hearth where he had so often shared the results of the hunt with his family. Here the bodies of these primitive men are found at the present day, lying in successive strata of refuse which continued to collect for ages, the lowest bodies sometimes far

*A   B*

**19.** Religion and life hereafter, in the Middle Stone Age

FIG. 7. A THROWING-STICK ONCE USED BY A HUNTER OF THE MIDDLE STONE AGE

Two views of the same stick, seen from front (*A*) and side (*B*). It is carved of reindeer horn to represent the head and forelegs of an ibex. Observe hook at the top of *B* for holding the butt of the spear-shaft, as in Fig. 6. The throwing-stick and the bow were man's earliest devices for propelling his weapons with speed

down at the bottom of the deep accumulations which gathered over them (Fig. 9).

**20.** Retreat of the ice; dawn of the Late Stone Age

The signs left by the ice, and still observable in Europe, would lead us to think that it slowly withdrew northward to its present latitude probably not less than some ten thousand years ago. The retreat of the ice was due to the fact that the climate again grew warmer and became what it is to-day. At this point, therefore, the men of the Middle Stone Age, whose story we have been following in France, entered upon natural conditions in Europe like those of to-day. They had, meantime, maintained steady progress in the production of tools and implements with which to carry on their struggle for existence and to wring subsistence from the world around them. That progress now carried man into the third great period of the Stone Age, which we may call the Late Stone Age.[1]

FIG. 8. IVORY NEEDLE OF THE MIDDLE STONE AGE

Such needles are found still surviving in the rubbish in the French caverns, where the wives of the prehistoric hunters lost them and failed to find them again twenty thousand years ago. They show that these women were already sewing together the skins of wild animals as clothing

## SECTION 4. THE LATE STONE AGE

**21.** Distribution of surviving remains of Late Stone Age man in Europe

The Late Stone Age remains of man's life are discovered widely distributed throughout a large part of Europe. In our study of such remains we must regard Europe as a whole, and not confine ourselves to France and its vicinity, as heretofore. Especially beside watercourses, lakes, and inlets of the

---

[1] The Stone Age periods are as follows:

Early Stone Age (stone edge made by striking, or *percussion*) } Called Paleolithic **Age**
Middle Stone Age (chipped stone edge made by *pressure*) } by archæologists.

**Late** Stone Age (stone edge made by *grinding*) } Called Neolithic Age by } archæologists.

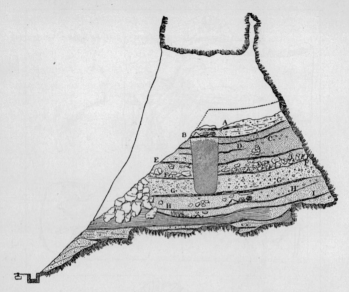

FIG. 9. A CROSS SECTION SHOWING THE LAYERS OF RUBBISH
AND THE HUMAN REMAINS IN A MIDDLE STONE AGE CAVERN
(AFTER DÉCHELETTE)

This cavern is at Grimaldi on the Italian coast of the Mediterranean,
just outside of France. The entrance is at the left and the back wall
at the right. We see the original rock floor at the bottom, and above
it the layers of accumulations, 30 feet deep (§ 17). The black lines *A*
to *I* represent layers of ashes, etc., the remains of nine successive
hearth-fires, each of which must have been kept going by the natives
for many years. The thicker (lightly shaded) layers consisted of bones
of animals, rubbish, and rocks which had fallen from the roof of the
cavern in the course of ages. The lowermost layers (below *I*) contained bones of the rhinoceros (representing a warm climate), while the
uppermost layers contained bones of the reindeer (indicating a cold
climate). Two periods, the Early and the Middle Stone Age, are thus
represented; the Early Stone Age below, the Middle Stone Age (or
Reindeer Age, § 15) above. Five burials were found by the excavators
in the layers *B*, *C*, *H*, and *I*; layer *C* contained the bodies of two
children. The lowermost burial (in *I*) was 25 feet below the surface of
the accumulations in the cave. Such prehistoric skulls and bones show
that several different races followed each other in Europe during the
Stone Age. The space required and the difficulties involved in their
discussion have compelled their omission in this volume. Hence the
successive culture stages have been presented without reference to race

15

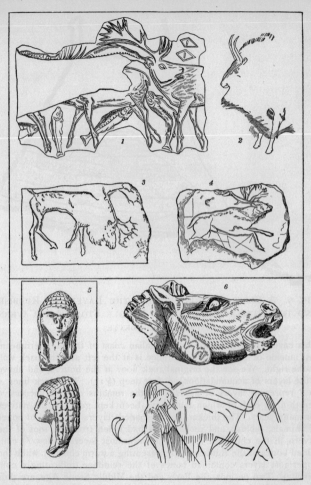

FIG. 10. CARVINGS IN IVORY (1 AND 3–7) AND IN STONE OF
CAVERN WALLS (2), MADE BY THE HUNTERS OF THE MIDDLE
STONE AGE

The oldest works of art by man, made ten or fifteen thousand years ago.
*1*, reindeer and salmon — hunter's and fisherman's talisman; *2*, bison
bull at bay; *3*, grazing reindeer; *4*, running reindeer; *5*, head of woman,
front view and profile; *6*, head of wild horse whinnying; *7*, mammoth,
showing huge tusks and long hair — an animal long since extinct

16

sea these early communities throughout most of Europe located their settlements. It is, however, impossible to determine the different races and peoples in various parts of Europe in the Late Stone Age.

The earliest of such Late Stone Age settlements are found on the shores of Denmark, where the wattle huts (Fig. 11) of the prehistoric Norsemen stretched in straggling lines far along the sea beach. We do not know the race of these earliest Norsemen, but we can see that they were both fishermen and hunters. They already possessed rude boats from which they were able to secure myriads of oysters near the shore, or even to push timidly out into deep water for other shellfish. On shore the hunter followed the wild boar and the wild bull (Fig. 12) in the neighboring forests, and brought down the waterfowl in the marshes. The air was keen — possibly a little colder than now. On their return at twilight the hunters and fishermen, crouching about the fire, devoured their prey, tossing aside the oyster shells and the bones of deer and wild boar, which formed a circle of very ill-smelling food refuse about the fire.

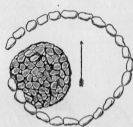

22. Earliest settlements of the Late Stone Age found in Denmark

FIG. 11. PLAN OF REMAINS OF A LATE STONE AGE HUT

The circle of stones surrounded the base of the walls. Beside the door (at the left) is a rough stone hearth, placed there in order to allow the smoke to escape through the door, chimneys having not yet been devised. The walls were of wattle (interwoven reeds), made tight by daubing with clay. The rubbish found in the circle sometimes contains patches of burned clay, bearing on one side the indented pattern of the basket-like wattle and on the other the impression of the human fingers which pressed the clay on the walls thousands of years ago. The fire which destroyed the hut baked the clay plaster to pottery

This refuse gathered in ridges parallel with the shore-line and hundreds of feet long (Fig. 13), marking the line of fires which once gleamed along the shores of prehistoric

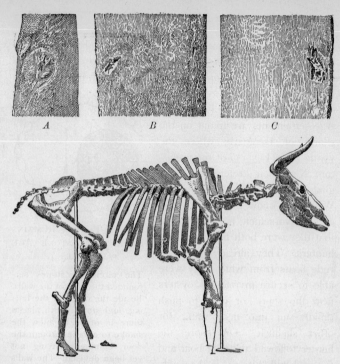

FIG. 12. SKELETON OF A WILD BULL BEARING THE MARKS OF
THE LATE STONE AGE HUNTERS' ARROWS WHICH KILLED HIM IN
THE DANISH FORESTS SOME TEN THOUSAND YEARS AGO

A Late Stone Age hunter (§ 22) shot him in the back near the spine
(see *upper* white ring on skeleton). The wound healed, leaving a scar
on the rib (*A*, above). Another hunter later shot him, and this time several arrows pierced his vitals. One of them, however, struck a rib (see
*lower* white ring on skeleton) and broke off. Both sides of this wound,
still unhealed, with the broken flint arrowhead still filling it, are shown
above in *B* and *C*. While the wounded bull was trying to swim across
a neighboring lake he died and his body sank to the bottom, and the
pursuing hunter, on reaching the lake, found no trace of him. In the
course of thousands of years the lake slowly filled up, and water 10 feet
deep was followed by dry peat of the same depth, covering the skeleton
of the bull. Here he was found some years ago (1905), and with him
were the flint arrowheads that had killed him. His skeleton, still bearing the marks of the flint arrowheads (*A*, *B*, *C*), was removed and set
up in the Museum at Copenhagen

Denmark. Each of these shell-heaps is to-day a storehouse of remains from the life of these earliest Norsemen. The shells and bones reveal how extensive was their control over the wild life about them. The marks of animal teeth on many a bone show us how the jackals of the neighboring forest crept up to gnaw the bones along the margin of the heap; and, slowly growing more and more familiar with their human neighbors,

23. The shell-heaps of Denmark and their revelations

Fig. 13. Ridge composed of the Food Refuse of Late Stone Age Man on the Coast of Denmark

The ridge on the top of the hill at the right stretches along the margin of a depression (at the left), which was once a shallow inlet of the sea but is now filled up and has become a hayfield (notice the hay wagon). Such a ridge made up chiefly of oyster shells is sometimes over half a mile long and over thirty paces wide and may contain a hundred thousand stone tools, weapons, and fragments of pottery

these wild beasts at last remained by the fireside, to become the loyal companions of man, the earliest domestic animal, which to-day we call the dog.

Bits of burned clay and broken pots, still lying in these shell-heaps, show us that these early Norsemen had already gained knowledge, probably from the South, of the hardening quality of clay when exposed to fire, and they were now able to make rude kettles of burned clay, which we call pottery, the earliest in Europe.[1] This is one of the most important

24. Industries revealed by the shell-heaps of Denmark: earliest *pottery* in Europe; *ground* stone tools

[1] Pottery was probably invented independently in many different regions of the world. The endeavor to make a water-tight, fireproof kettle by smearing a basket with clay would result in pottery when the attempt was made to heat water in it over a fire.

innovations of the Late Stone Age. Another important achievement marked the beginning of this age. This was the discovery that *the edge of a stone tool might be ground upon a whetstone*, precisely as we grind a steel tool at the present day. In the shell-heaps we find the earliest heavy stone axes with a *ground edge* (Fig. 16, 5). They made the man of the Late Stone Age vastly more successful in his control of the world about him.

**25. Tools of the Late Stone Age man**

His list of tools as he went about his work was now almost as complete as that of the modern carpenter. It included, besides the ax, likewise chisels, knives, drills, saws, and whetstones, made mostly of flint but sometimes of other hard stones. Our ancient craftsman had now learned also to attach a wooden handle by lashings around the ax-head, or even to bore a hole in the ax-head and insert the handle (Fig. 16, 5). These tools as found to-day often display a polish due to the wear which they have undergone in the hands of the user.

**26. Effectiveness of stone tools**

It is a mistake to suppose that such stone tools were wholly crude and ineffective. A recent experiment in Denmark has shown that a modern mechanic with a stone ax, although unaccustomed to the use of stone tools, was able, in ten working hours, to cut down and convert into logs twenty-six pine trees eight inches in thickness. Indeed, the *entire work of getting out the timber and building a house was done by one mechanic with stone tools in eighty-one days*. It was therefore quite possible for the men of the Late Stone Age to build comfortable dwellings and to attain a degree of civilization far above that of savages.

**27. Swiss lake-villages of the Late Stone Age**

This step, however, we are not able to follow among the shell-heaps of Denmark. The most plentiful traces of the earliest wooden houses are to be found in Switzerland, whither we must now go. Here the house-building communities of the Late Stone Age, desiring to make themselves safer from attack by man and beast, built their villages out over the Swiss lakes. They erected their dwellings upon platforms supported over the water by piles which they drove into the lake bottom. In long lines such lake-villages, or groups of *pile-dwellings*, as they are called, fringed the shores of the Swiss lakes (Fig. 14). In a few cases they grew to a considerable size. At Wangen not

FIG. 14. RESTORATION OF A SWISS LAKE-DWELLERS' SETTLEMENT

The lake-dwellers felled trees with their stone axes (Fig. 16, *5*) and cut them into piles some 20 feet long, sharpened at the lower end. These they drove several feet into the bottom of the lake, in water 8 or 10 feet deep. On a platform supported by these piles they then built their houses. The platform was connected with the shore by a bridge, which may be seen here on the right. A section of it could be removed at night for protection. The fish nets seen drying at the rail, the "dug-out" boat of the hunters who bring in the deer, and many other things have been found on the lake bottom in recent times

less than fifty thousand piles were driven into the bottom of the lake for the support of the village (see remains of such piles in Fig. 15).

In so far as we can judge, these lake-dwellers lived a life of enviable peace and prosperity. Their houses were comfort- able shelters, and they were furnished with plentiful wooden

28. Life of the Swiss lake-dwellers

furniture and implements, wooden pitchers and spoons, besides pottery dishes, bowls, and jars (Fig. 16, *1, 2, 3*). Although roughly made without the use of the potter's wheel (§ 83), and unevenly burned without an oven (Fig. 48), pottery vessels added much to the convenience of the house. The waters under the settlement teemed with fish, which were caught

FIG. 15. SURVIVING REMAINS OF A SWISS LAKE-VILLAGE

After an unusually dry season the Swiss lakes fell to a very low level in 1854, exposing the lake bottom with the remains of the piles which once supported the lake villages along the shores. They were thus discovered for the first time. On the old lake bottom, among the projecting piles, were found great quantities of implements, tools, and furniture, like those in Fig. 16, including the dugouts and nets of Fig. 14, wheat, barley, bones of domestic animals, woven flax, etc. (§ 29). There they had been lying some five thousand years. Sometimes the objects were found in two distinct layers, the lower (earlier) containing only *stone* tools, and the upper (later) containing *bronze* tools, which came into the lake-village at a later age and fell into the water on top of the layer of old stone tools already lying on the bottom of the lake (see § 329)

with a bone hook through a trapdoor in the floor of the house, or snared in nets which the possession of flax, as we shall see, enabled the lake-villagers to make.

**29. Domestication of wild grains and beginning of agriculture; flax and weaving**

While he had thus not ceased to be a fisherman and hunter, the lake-dweller now discovered other sources of food. For thousands of years the women of these early ages had gathered the seeds of wild grasses to be crushed between two stones and made into rude cakes. They now gradually learned that the growth of such wild grasses on the margins of the forest and the shores of the lake might be artificially aided.

From such beginnings it was but a step to drop the seed into the soil at the proper season, to cultivate it, and to harvest

**30. Cultivation of millet, barley, and wheat in the Late Stone Age**

FIG. 16. PART OF THE EQUIPMENT OF A LATE STONE AGE LAKE-DWELLER

This group contains the evidence for three important inventions made or received by the men of the Late Stone Age: *first*, pottery jars, like *2* and *3*, with rude decorations, the oldest baked clay in Europe, and *1*, a large kettle in which the lake-dwellers' food was cooked; *second*, ground-edged tools like *4*, a stone chisel with ground edge (§ 24), mounted in a deerhorn handle like a hatchet, or *5*, stone ax with a ground edge, and pierced with a hole for the ax handle (the houses of Fig. 14 were built with such tools); and *third*, weaving, as shown by *6*, a spinning "whorl" of baked clay, the earliest spinning wheel. When suspended by a rough thread of flax 18 to 20 inches long, it was given a whirl which made it spin in the air like a top, thus rapidly twisting the thread by which it was hanging. The thread when sufficiently twisted was wound up, and another length of 18 to 20 inches was drawn out from the unspun flax to be similarly twisted. One of these earliest spinning wheels has been found in the Swiss lakes with a spool of flaxen thread still attached. (From photograph loaned by Professor Hoernes)

the yield. When they had learned to do this, the women of these lake-dwellers were already agriculturists. The grains which they planted were barley, wheat, and some millet.[1] This

---

[1] Oats and rye, however, were still unknown, and came in much later.

new source of food was a plentiful one; more than a hundred bushels of grain were found by the excavators on the lake bottom under the vanished lake-village of Wangen. Up the hillside now stretched also the lake-dweller's little field of flax beside the growing grain. His women sat spinning flax (Fig. 16, *6*) before the door, and the rough skin clothing of their ancestors (Fig. 8) had given way to garments of woven stuff.

**31. Social effects of agriculture**

These fields were an additional reason for the permanency of the lake-dweller's home. It was necessary for him to remain near the little plantation for which his women had hoed the ground, that they might care for it and gather the grain when it ripened. As each household gradually gained an habitual right to cultivate a particular field, they came to set up a perpetual claim to it, and thus arose the ownership of land. It was to be a frequent source of trouble in the future career of man, and the chief cause of the long struggle between the rich and the poor — a struggle which was earlier unknown, when land was free to all.

**32. Domestication of sheep, goats, and cattle**

On the green Swiss uplands above the lake-villages were now feeding the descendants of the wild creatures which the Middle Stone Age hunters had pursued through the forests and mountains; for the mountain sheep and goats and the wild cattle (Fig. 12), like the dog on the shores of Denmark (§ 23), had slowly learned to dwell near man and submit to his control.[1] For a long time, however, the Late Stone Age man in Europe was still without any beast of burden. For thousands of years his ancestors of the Middle Stone Age had pursued the wild horse for food (§ 17), but had made no effort to tame and subdue the animal.[2]

---

[1] Domestication of these animals, like the cultivation of grain and flax, was much older in the Orient than in the Late Stone Age in Europe; but it is still a question just how the early Europeans received these things from the Orient. (See § 49.)

[2] The draft horse, one of the most important influences in the history of civilization, came in comparatively late, from the Northern Orient, as we shall see (§ 247).

The strong limbs of the once wild ox (Fig. 12), however, made him well adapted to draw the hoe of Late Stone Age man across the field — a hoe, to be sure, equipped with two handles (Fig. 44), which thus became the earliest plow, while the ox which was tamed to draw it became the earliest draft animal of Europe. Thus "plow culture" slowly replaced the cruder and more limited "hoe culture"[1] carried on by the women. It was at this point, therefore, that the early European passed far beyond our own North American Indians, who remained until the discovery of America entirely without draft animals, and hence practiced only "hoe culture."

Agriculture, requiring as it now did the driving and control of large draft animals, exceeded the strength of the primitive woman, and the primitive man was obliged to give up more and more of his hunting freedom and devote himself to the field. Thus the hunter of thousands of years became an agriculturist, a farmer. By this time a large part of the Late Stone Age Europeans had adopted fixed abodes, following the settled agricultural life in and around villages (§ 38).

On the other hand, the domestication of grass-eating animals, feeding on the grasslands, created not only a new industry but also a second class of men who might still follow a roving life, leading their flocks about and pasturing them where the grasslands were too poor for agriculture. Such shepherd people we call nomads, and they still exist to-day. Without any fixed dwelling places, accompanied by their wives and children, they lead a wandering life, driving their flocks from pasture to pasture. These nomad peoples took possession of the eastern grasslands stretching from the Danube eastward along the north side of the Black Sea and thence far over into Asia. Their life always remained ruder and less civilized than that of the agriculturalists and townsmen (see § 136).

[1] "Hoe culture" is the term applied to agriculture carried on by hand, without any draft animals; that is, entirely with the hoe, as contrasted with cultivation by the plow drawn by an animal.

**36.** Age-long conflict between nomads and townsmen

Thus developed side by side two methods of life—the settled, agricultural life and the wandering, nomad life. The importance of understanding these will be evident when we realize that the grasslands became the home of a numerous *unsettled* population. Thus such grasslands have become like overfilled reservoirs of nomad peoples, who have periodically overflowed and overwhelmed the towns and the agricultural settlements. Many epochs of human history can be understood only as we bear these facts in mind, especially as we shall see later Europe invaded over and over again by the hordes of intruding nomads from the eastern grasslands (§§ 370–373 and Section 99).

**37.** Buildings and architecture in Late Stone Age Europe

The *settled* communities of the Late Stone Age at last began to leave behind them more impressive monuments than pottery and stone tools. In all Europe before this there had existed only fragile houses and huts. But toward the close of the Late Stone Age the more powerful chiefs in the large settlements learned to erect great tombs, built of enormous blocks of stone. They fringe the western coast of Europe from Spain to the southern Scandinavian shores. There are at the present day no less than thirty-four hundred stone tombs of this age, some of considerable size, on the Danish island of Seeland alone. In France (Fig. 17) they exist in vast numbers and imposing size, and likewise in England. The often enormous blocks in these structures (Figs. 18, 20, and 21) were mostly left in the rough, but if cut at all, it was done with stone chisels. Such structures are not of masonry, that is, of smoothly cut stone laid with mortar. They can hardly be called works of great architecture,—a thing which did not as yet exist in Europe. We shall first meet it in the Orient (§ 95).

**38.** The earliest towns in Europe; rise of government

When we look at such buildings of the Late Stone Age still surviving, they prove to us the existence of the earliest towns in Europe. For near every great group of stone tombs there must have been a town where the people lived who built the tombs. The remains of some of these towns have been discovered, and they have been dug out from the earth covering them. Almost

all traces of them had disappeared, but enough remained to show
that they had been surrounded by walls of earth, with a ditch
on the outside and probably with a wooden stockade along the
top of the earth wall. They show us that men were learning to
live together in considerable numbers and to work together on

FIG. 17. LATE STONE AGE TOMB IN FRANCE

It was in such tombs that dead chiefs of the Late Stone Age were buried.
The stones, weighing even as much as 40 tons apiece, were sometimes
dragged many miles from the nearest quarry; but much heavier ones
were also used (see Fig. 18). These blocks were not smoothed but left
rough as they came from the mountain side

a large scale. It required organization and successful management of men to raise the earth walls of such a town, to
drive the fifty thousand piles supporting the lake settlement at
Wangen (Switzerland), or to move the enormous blocks of stone
for building the chieftain's tomb (Figs. 17, 18, 20, and 21).
In such achievements we see the beginnings of government,

organized under a leader. Many little states, each consisting of a fortified town with its surrounding fields, and each under a chieftain, must have grown up in Late Stone Age Europe. Out of such beginnings nations were yet to grow.

**39. Festivals and athletic contests shown by the stone buildings of Late Stone Age Europe**

Furthermore, these stone buildings furnish us very interesting glimpses into the life of the Late Stone Age towns. Some of them suggest to us pictures of whole communities issuing from the towns on feast days and marching to such places as the

FIG. 18. FALLEN MEMORIAL STONE OF THE LATE STONE AGE IN NORTHERN FRANCE

This vast block once stood upright, having been erected by the men of the Late Stone Age as a tombstone. It is almost 65 feet long and weighs some 300 tons. The fall has broken it into three pieces

huge stone circles at Stonehenge (Fig. 20). Here they held memorial contests, chariot races, and athletic games in honor of the dead chief buried within the stone circles. The domestic horse had now reached western Europe, and the straight chariot course, nearly two miles long, still to be seen at Stonehenge, must have resounded with the shouts of the multitudes as the competing chariots thundered down the course.[1] The long processional avenues, marked out by mighty stones, in northwest France (Fig. 21) must have been alive with festival processions and happy multitudes every season for centuries. To-day, silent and solitary, they stretch for miles across the fields of

[1] One of the chariots later used on such a course may be seen in Fig. 133.

the French peasants, a kind of voiceless echo of forgotten human joys, of ancient customs and beliefs long revered by the vanished races of prehistoric Europe.

While such monuments show us the Late Stone Age communities at play, other remains reveal them at their work. Each town was largely a home manufacturer and produced what it needed for itself. Men were beginning to adopt trades; for

40. Rise of trades in the outgoing Late Stone Age; mining as a trade

example, some men were probably wood-workers, others were potters, and still others were already miners. These early miners burrowed far into the earth in order to reach the finest deposits of flint for their stone tools. In the underground tunnels of the ancient flint mines at Brandon, England, eighty worn picks of deerhorn were found in recent times. At one place the roof had caved in, cutting

FIG. 19. VERTEBRA OF A LATE STONE AGE MAN WITH A FLINT ARROWHEAD STICKING IN IT

The arrowhead (*A*) struck the victim full in the pit of the stomach. It must have been driven by a heavy bow, for it passed clear through to the vertebra, producing peritonitis and death. (Photograph furnished by the great French archæologist Déchelette, who himself fell in battle not long after sending this photograph to the author)

off an ancient gallery of the mine. In this gallery, behind the fallen rocks, modern archæologists found two more deerhorn picks. These picks bore a coat of chalk dust in which were still visible the marks of the workmen's fingers, left there as they last laid down the implements, many thousands of years ago. In Belgium even the skeleton of one of these ancient miners, who had been crushed by falling rocks, was found in the mine with his deerhorn pick still lying between his hands (Fig. 22).

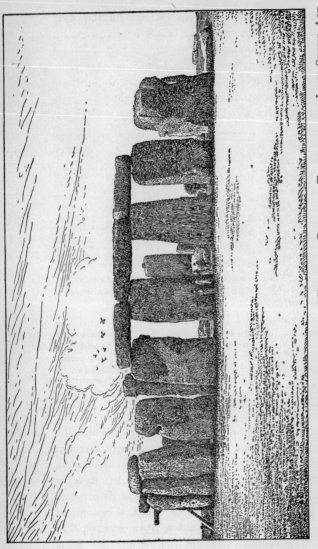

FIG. 20. GREAT STONE CIRCLE INCLOSING A TOMB, OR GROUP OF TOMBS, OF THE LATE STONE AGE CHIEFTAINS AT STONEHENGE, ENGLAND

The circle is about 100 feet across, and a long avenue connecting it with the neighboring Late Stone Age town is still traceable. Not far away is the Late Stone Age race course, nearly 2 miles long. Western Europe produced nothing more than this rude architecture in stone until the coming of the Romans (§ 1047)

Exchange and traffic between the communities already existed. This primitive commerce carried far and wide an especially fine variety of French flint, recognizable to-day by its color. The amber gathered on the shores of the Baltic was already passing from hand to hand and thus found its way southward. Stone implements found on the islands around Europe show that men of this age lived on such islands, and they must have had boats sufficiently strong to carry them thither. Several of the

*41. Commerce and intercourse in the Late Stone Age*

FIG. 21. AVENUES OF THE LATE STONE AGE IN NORTHERN FRANCE (CARNAC, BRITTANY)

The tall stones mark out avenues nearly 2½ miles long, containing nearly three thousand stones. These avenues were used for festival processions or for races, as on the course at Stonehenge (Fig. 20 and § 39), at the religious celebrations of the Late Stone Age communities

dugouts (Fig. 14) of the lake-dwellers have been found lying on the lake bottom among the piles, but vessels with *sails* had not yet been devised in Europe.

The business of such an age was of course very primitive. There were no metals and no money. Buying and selling were only exchange of one kind of wares for another kind. In all Europe there was no writing, nor did the continent of Europe *ever* devise a system of writing. If credit was given, the transaction might be recorded in a few strokes scratched in the mud plaster of the wattle house wall (Fig. 11) to aid the memory as to the number of fish or jars of grain to be paid for later.

*42. Primitive business methods of Late Stone Age Europe*

**43.** Wars of the Late Stone Age

But the intercourse between these prehistoric communities was not always peaceful. The earthen walls and wooden stockades with which such towns were protected (§ 38) show us that the chieftain's war-horn must often have summoned these people from feasts and athletic games, or from the fields and mines, to expel the invader. Grim evidence of these earliest wars of Europe still survives. A skull taken out of a tomb of this age in Sweden contains a flint arrowhead still sticking in

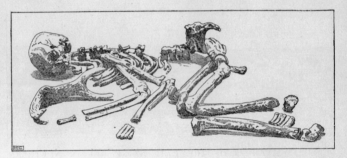

FIG. 22. SKELETON OF A MINER OF THE LATE STONE AGE

The skeleton of this ancient miner was found lying on the floor of a flint mine in Belgium, under the rocks which had caved in and crushed him. Before him, just as it dropped from his hands at the instant of the cave-in, lies the double-pointed pick of deerhorn (§ 40) with which he was loosening the lumps of flint from their chalk bed, when the rock ceiling fell upon him and he was killed

one eyehole, while in France more than one human vertebra has been found with a flint arrowhead driven deep into it (Fig. 19). A stone coffin found in a Scottish cairn contained the body of a man of huge size, with one arm almost severed from the shoulder by the stroke of a stone ax. A fragment of stone broken out of the ax blade still remained in the gashed arm bone.

**44.** Late Stone Age Europe and the Orient

After fifty thousand years of progress carried on by their own efforts, the men of Stone Age Europe seemed now (about 3000 B.C.) to have reached a point where they could advance no farther. They were still without *writing*, for making the records of business, government, and tradition; they were still without *metals* [1] with which to make tools and to develop industries and manufactures; and they had no *sailing ships* in which to carry on commerce. Without these things they could go no farther. All these and many other possessions of civilization came to early Europe from the nearer Orient,[2] the lands around the eastern end of the Mediterranean (see map, p. 102). In order to understand the further course of European history, we must therefore turn to the Orient, whence came these indispensable things which made it possible for our European ancestors to gain the civilization we have inherited.

As we go to the Orient let us remember that we have been following man's *prehistoric* progress as it went on for some fifty thousand years after he began making stone implements. In the Orient, during the thousand years from 4000 to 3000 B.C. (see diagram, Fig. 38), men slowly built up a high civilization, forming the beginning of the *Historic Epoch*.[3] Civilization thus began in the Orient, and it is between five and six thousand years old. There it long flourished and produced great and

45. Historical summary

---

[1] Metal was introduced in *southeastern* Europe about 3000 B.C. and passed like a slow wave, moving gradually westward and northward across Europe. It probably did not reach Britain until about 2000 B.C. Hence we have included the great stone monuments of western Europe (like Stonehenge) in our survey of Stone Age Europe. They were erected long after *southeastern* Europe had received metal, but before metal came into common use in *western* Europe.

[2] The word "Orient" is used to-day to include Japan, China, and India. These lands make up a *farther* Orient. There is also a *nearer* Orient, consisting of the lands around the eastern end of the Mediterranean, that is, Egypt and Western Asia, including Asia Minor. We shall use the word "Orient" in this book to designate the *nearer* Orient.

[3] We may best describe the Historic Epoch by saying that it is the epoch beginning when written documents were first produced by man — documents which tell us in written words something of man's life and career. All that we know of man in the age previous to the appearance of writing has to be learned from weapons, tools, implements, buildings, and other things (bearing no writing) which he has left behind. These are the things from which we have been learning something of the story of prehistoric Europe in Chapter I. The transition from the Prehistoric to the Historic Epoch was everywhere a slow and gradual one. In the Orient this transition took place in the thousand years between 4000 and 3000 B.C.

powerful nations, while the men of Late Stone Age Europe continued to live without metals or writing. As they gradually acquired these things, civilized leadership both in peace and war shifted slowly from the Orient to Europe. As we turn to watch civilization emerging in the East, with metals, government, writing, great ships, and many other creations of civilization, let us realize that its later movement will steadily carry us from east to west as we follow it from the Orient to Europe.

## QUESTIONS

SECTION 1. What progress in invention have you noticed in your own lifetime? Has every device or convenience man now possesses had to be invented in the same way? Was there a time when man possessed none of these things? Did he have anyone to teach him? Describe the life of the Tasmanians in recent times. Describe prehistoric Europe and the life of the earliest men there. What three ages ensued?

SECTION 2. Give examples of the discovery of man's great age on the earth. Describe the earliest stone weapon. About when did the Early Stone Age begin? (See map, p. 8, and read description.) What age did it introduce? Describe the life of the Early Stone Age hunter. What great change ended this age? Describe it.

SECTION 3. Where did the Middle Stone Age hunters take refuge? What improvement did they make in their stone tools (Fig. 5)? What new materials came in? What new inventions? Describe the results. Discuss Middle Stone Age art. Draw cross section of a cave with contents and describe (Fig. 9). What great change ended the Middle Stone Age, and when?

SECTION 4. Where were the earliest settlements of the Late Stone Age known to us? Describe them and their remains. What new inventions came in? Discuss carpentry with *ground* stone tools. Describe the lake-villages and life in them. Describe the domestication of grain and its social results. Describe the domestication of animals and the two resulting methods of life. Discuss stone structures and the life they reveal — industries, traffic, and war. What important things did the Late Stone Age in Europe still lack? Is civilization possible without these things? Where did these things first appear?

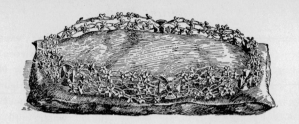

# PART II. THE ORIENT

## CHAPTER II

### THE STORY OF EGYPT: THE EARLIEST NILE-DWELLERS AND THE PYRAMID AGE

SECTION 5. EGYPT AND ITS EARLIEST INHABITANTS

We are to begin our study of the early Orient in Egypt. The traveler who visits Egypt at the present day lands in a very modern-looking harbor at Alexandria (see map, p. 36). He is presently seated in a comfortable railway car in which we may accompany him as he is carried rapidly across a low, flat country stretching far away to the sunlit horizon. The wide expanse is dotted with little villages of dark mud-brick huts, and here and there rise groves of graceful date palms. The landscape is carpeted with stretches of bright and vivid green as far as the eye can see, and wandering through this verdure is a network of irrigation canals (Fig. 23). Brown-skinned men of slender build, with dark hair, are seen at intervals along the banks of these canals, swaying up and down as they rhythmically lift an irrigation bucket attached to a simple

46. Egypt of to-day

NOTE. The tiara, or diadem, at the top of this page was found resting on the head of an Egyptian princess of the Feudal Age as she lay in her coffin. The diadem had been placed there nearly four thousand years ago. It is in the form of a chaplet, or wreath, of star flowers wrought of gold and set with bright-colored precious stones, and is one of the best examples of the work of the Egyptian goldsmiths and jewelers (Fig. 47 and § 82). It is shown here lying on a cushion.

FIG. 23. AN EGYPTIAN *SHADOOF*, THE
OLDEST OF WELL SWEEPS, IRRIGAT-
ING THE FIELDS

The man below stands in the water, holding his leather bucket (*A*). The pole (*B*)
of the sweep is above him, with large ball
of dried Nile mud on its lower end (*C*)
as a lifting weight, or counterpoise, seen
just behind the supporting post (*D*). This
man lifts the water into a mud basin (*E*).
A second man (in the middle) lifts it
from this first basin (*E*) to a second
basin (*F*) into which he is just empty-
ing his bucket; while a third man (*G*)
lifts the water from the middle basin (*F*)
to the uppermost basin (*H*) on the top of
the bank, where it runs off to the left into
trenches spreading over the fields. The
low water makes necessary three successive lifts (to *E*, to *F*, to *H*) without ceas-
ing night and day for one hundred days

**47.** Its soil, shape, and area

device (Fig. 23) exactly
like the well sweep of
our grandfathers in New
England. The irrigation
trenches are thus kept
full of water until the
grain ripens. This shows
us that Egypt enjoys
no rain.

The black soil we see
from the train is unex-
celled in fertility, and it
is enriched each year by
the overflow of the river,
whose turbid waters rise
above its banks every
summer, spread far over
the flats (Fig. 24), and
stand there long enough
to deposit a very thin
layer of rich earthy
sediment. This sedi-
ment has built up the
Nile Delta which we
are now crossing. The
Delta and the valley
above, as far as the
First Cataract, contain
together over ten thou-
sand square miles of
cultivable soil, or some-
what more than the
state of Vermont.

As our train ap-
proaches the southern

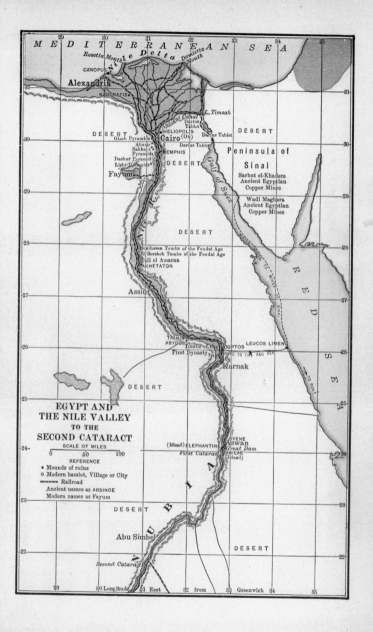

MEDITERRANEAN SEA

Rosetta Mouth *Nile Delta* Damietta Mouth

CANOPUS

Alexandria

NAUCRATIS

L. Timsah

Ancient Canal
Darius
Tablet
HELIOPOLIS Darius Tablet
Cairo (On)

DESERT

DESERT

Gizeh Pyramids
Abusir
Sakkara Darius Tablet
Pyramids
Dashur Pyramid MEMPHIS
Lisht Pyramids

DESERT

Fayum

Peninsula of
Sinai

Sarbut el-Khadem
Ancient Egyptian
Copper Mines

Wadi Maghara
Ancient Egyptian
Copper Mines

Gulf of Suez

DESERT

Benihasan Tombs of the Feudal Age
Bersheh Tombs of the Feudal Age
Tell el Amarna
AKHETATON

Assiut

THINIS
ABYDOS
Tombs of the
First Dynasty

COPTOS LEUCOS LIMEN

Karnak

ROAD TO THE RED SEA

RED SEA

ROAD TO MT. SINAI

TO PUNT

DESERT

**EGYPT AND
THE NILE VALLEY
TO THE
SECOND CATARACT**

SCALE OF MILES

0        50        100

REFERENCE

• Mounds of ruins
o Modern hamlet, Village or City
▬▬▬ Railroad
Ancient names as ARSINOE
Modern names as Fayum

(Island) ELEPHANTINE
First Cataract

SYENE
ASWAN
Great Dam
PHILAE
(Island)

DESERT

N U B I A

Abu Simbel

DESERT

Second Cataract

29    30 Longitude 31 East    32 from    33 Greenwich 34    35

point of the Delta we begin to see the heights on either side of the valley into which the narrow end of the Delta merges. These heights (Figs. 24 and 69) are the plateau of the Sahara Desert, through which the Nile has cut a vast, deep trench as it winds its way northward from inner Africa. This trench, or valley, is seldom more than thirty miles wide, while the strip of soil on each

FIG. 24.  THE INUNDATION SEEN FROM THE ROAD TO THE PYRAMIDS OF GIZEH

On the right is the road leading to the pyramids; at the left the waters of the inundation cover the level floor of the Nile valley. In the distance is the desert plateau on which the pyramids stand. The trees and the small modern village just in front of the pyramids occupy part of the ground where once the royal city of the pyramid-builders stood (§ 75)

side of the river rarely exceeds ten miles in width. On either edge of the soil strip one steps out of the green fields into the sand of the desert, which has drifted down into the trench; or if one climbs the cliffs, forming the walls of the trench, he stands looking out over a vast waste of rocky hills and stretches of sand trembling in the heat of the blazing sunshine.

**49. The
Stone Age
Egyptians**

As we journey on let us realize that this valley can tell us an unbroken story of human progress such as we can find nowhere else. We look out upon the sandy margin of the desert, where there are thousands of low, undulating mounds covering

Fig. 25. Looking down into the Grave of a Late Stone Age Egyptian

An oval pit 4 or 5 feet deep (cf. Fig. 38, *1*). The body is surrounded by pottery jars once containing food and drink. A few small objects of copper have been found even in the earliest of such Egyptian graves, which therefore belong to the end of the Late Stone Age

the graves of the earliest ancestors of the brown men we see in the Delta fields. When we have dug out such a grave to the bottom, we find lying there the ancient Nile peasant, surrounded by pottery jars and stone implements (Fig. 25). There he has been lying for over six thousand years, and these *stone* tools, which he used so long ago, tell us of generations of Nile-dwellers who, like the Late Stone Age men of Europe, lived without the use of metal. Barley and split wheat[1] are sometimes found in the jars around the body (Fig. 25), for the dead were supplied with food by those who buried them. These and fragments of linen found in such graves show us from what country the first grain and flax came into Europe. These ancient Nile peasants were therefore watering their fields of flax and grain over six thousand years ago, just as the brown men whom the traveler sees from the car windows to-day are still doing.

[1] This split wheat is a variety which differs from our common wheat. The kernel is split into halves. When threshed, the two halves are still held together by the hull, and a second threshing or hard rubbing is necessary to break off this hull and get out the two half kernels. Split wheat is still raised in parts of Europe, especially for use in making starch, and is often called starch wheat. This was the earliest variety of wheat cultivated by man. It has recently been rediscovered growing in a wild state in Palestine. Barley and split wheat were the two leading grains used by early man in the oriental world.

The villages of low, mud-brick huts which flash by the car windows furnish us also with an exact picture of those vanished prehistoric villages, the homes of the early Nile-dwellers who are still lying in yonder cemeteries on the desert margin. In each such village, six to seven thousand years ago, lived a local chieftain who controlled the irrigation trenches of the district. To him the peasants were obliged to carry every season a share of the grain and flax which they gathered from their fields; otherwise the supply of water for their crops would be stopped, and they would receive an unpleasant visit from the chieftain, demanding instant payment. These were the earliest taxes.

**50. Earliest government and taxes**

FIG. 26. PICTORIAL MESSAGE SCRATCHED ON WOOD BY ALASKAN INDIANS

Such transactions led to scratching a rude picture of the basket grain-measure and a number of strokes on the mud wall of the peasant's hut, indicating the number of measures of grain he had paid (cf. § 42). The use of these purely pictorial signs formed the earliest stage in the process of learning to write.

**51. Pictorial records**

A figure with empty hands hanging down helplessly, palms down, as an Indian gesture for uncertainty, ignorance, emptiness, or nothing, means "no." A figure with one hand on its mouth means "eating" or "food." It points toward the tent, and this means "in the tent." The whole is a message stating, "(There is) no food in the tent" (§ 51)

Such pictorial writing is still in use among the uncivilized peoples in our *own* land. Thus, the Alaskan natives send messages in pictorial form, scratched on a piece of wood (Fig. 26). The *exact words* of the message are not represented. Fig. 26 might be read by one man, "No food in the tent," while another might read, "Lack of meat in the wigwam." Such pictorial signs thus conveyed ideas without expressing the exact words. Among our own Indians the desire of a brave to record his personal exploits also led to pictorial records of them (Fig. 27). It should be noticed again that the *exact words* are not indicated by this record

(Fig. 27), but the exploit is merely so suggested that it might be put into words in a number of different ways. The early Egyptian kings of six thousand years ago prepared strikingly similar picture records (Fig. 28).

**52.** First step leading from the pictorial to the phonetic stage

FIG. 27. PICTORIAL RECORD OF THE VICTORY OF A DAKOTA CHIEF NAMED RUNNING ANTELOPE

This Dakota Indian prepared his autobiography in a series of eleven drawings, of which Fig. 27 is but one. It records how he slew five hostile braves in a single day. The hero, Running Antelope, with rifle in hand, is mounted upon a horse. His shield bears a falcon, the animal emblem of his family, while beneath the horse is a running antelope, which is of course intended to inform you of the hero's name. We see the trail of his horse as he swept round the copse at the left, in which were concealed the five hostile braves whom he slew. Of these, one figure bearing a rifle represents all five, while four other rifles in the act of being discharged indicate the number of braves in the copse

But this pictorial stage, beyond which native American records never passed, was not real writing. Two steps had to be taken before the picture records could become phonetic writing. *First*, each object drawn had to gain a fixed form, always the same and always recognized as the sign for a *particular word* denoting that object. Thus, it would become a habit that the drawing of a loaf should always be read "loaf," not "bread" or "food"; the sign for a leaf would always be read "leaf," not "foliage."[1]

The *second* step then naturally followed; that

**53.** Second step leading from the pictorial to the phonetic stage

is, the leaf , for example, became the sign for the *syllable* "leaf" wherever it might occur. By the same process

[1] The author is of course obliged to use *English* words and syllables here, and consequently also signs not existing in Egyptian but devised for this demonstration.

might become the sign for the syllable "bee" wherever found. Having thus a means of writing the syllables "bee" and "leaf," the next step was to put them together, thus, 🐝🍃, and they would then represent the word "belief." Notice, however, that in the word "belief" the sign 🐝 has ceased to suggest the idea of an insect. It now represents only the *syllable* "be." That is to say, 🐝 has become a *phonetic* sign.

If the writing of the Egyptian had remained merely a series of pictures, such words as "belief," "hate," "love," "beauty," and the like could never have been written.[1] But when a large number of his pictures had become phonetic signs, each representing a syllable, it was possible for the Egyptian to write any word he knew, whether the word meant a thing of which he could draw a picture or not. This possession of *phonetic* signs was what made real writing for the first time. It arose among these Nile-dwellers earlier than anywhere else in the ancient world.

Egyptian writing contained at last over six hundred signs, many of them representing whole syllables, like 🍃. The Egyptian scribe gradually learned many groups of such syllable signs. Each group, like 🐝🍃, represented a *word*. Writing thus became to him a large number of sign-groups, each group being a word; and a series of such groups formed a sentence.

FIG. 28. EXAMPLE OF EGYPTIAN WRITING IN THE PICTORIAL STAGE

**54.** Advantage of phonetic signs

Interpretation: Above is the falcon, symbol of a king (cf. the falcon on the shield of Running Antelope in Fig. 27), leading a human head by a cord; behind the head are six lotus leaves (each the sign for 1000) growing out of the ground to which the head is attached; below is a single-barbed harpoon head and a little rectangle (the sign of a lake). The whole tells the picture story that the falcon king led captive six thousand men of the land of the Harpoon Lake (§ 51)

**55.** Syllable signs and sign-groups

[1] See the word "beauty," the last three signs in the inscription over the ship (Fig. 41).

Nevertheless, the Egyptian went still farther, for he finally possessed a series of signs, each representing only a *letter*; that is, *alphabetic* signs, or, as we say, real letters. There were twenty-four letters in this alphabet, which was known in Egypt

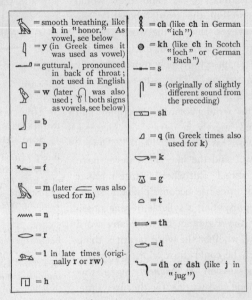

FIG. 29. THE EGYPTIAN ALPHABET

Each of these letters represents a consonant. The Egyptians of course *pronounced* their words with vowels as we do, but they did not *write* the vowels. This will be clear by a study of Fig. 30. Just as the consonants *w* and *y* are sometimes used as vowels in English, so three of the Egyptian consonants came to be employed as vowels in Greek times. The first letter (smooth breathing) was thus used as *a* or *e*; the second letter (*y*) as *i*; and the fourth (*w*) as *u* or *o* (cf. Fig. 76)

long before 3000 B.C. It was thus the earliest alphabet known. The Egyptian might then have written his language with twenty-four alphabetic letters (Fig. 29) if the *sign*-group habit had not been too strong for the scribe, just as the *letter*-group habit is strong enough with us to-day to prevent the introduction of a simplified phonetic system of spelling English. If we smile at the Egyptian's cumbrous sign-groups, future generations may as justly smile at our often absurd letter-groups.

The Egyptian soon devised a convenient equipment for writing. He found out that he could make an excellent paint or ink by thickening water with a little vegetable gum and then

**57.** Invention of writing materials: ink and pen

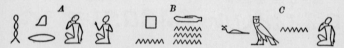

FIG. 30. AN EGYPTIAN WORD (*A*) AND TWO ENGLISH
WORDS (*B*) AND (*C*) WRITTEN IN HIEROGLYPHIC

The first three signs in word *A* are *ch–q–r* (see Fig. 29); we do not know the vowels. The word means "pauper" (literally, "hungry"); as it denotes a person, the Egyptian adds a little kneeling man at the end. Before him is another man with hand on mouth, an indication of hunger, thirst, or speech. These two are old pictorial signs surviving from the pictorial stage. Such pictorial signs at the end of a word have no phonetic value and are called *determinatives*. *B* is an English word spelled for illustration in hieroglyphic. The first three signs indicate the letters *p–n–d* (see Fig. 29), while the three wavy lines form the determinative for "water"; hence *p–n–d* spells "pond." *C* is another English word in hieroglyphic. The first three signs indicate the letters *f–m–n* (see Fig. 29), and the last sign is the determinative for "hunger" (see Fig. 30, *A*); hence *f–m–n* spells "famine." With the alphabet (Fig. 29) and the above determinatives the student can put a number of English words into hieroglyphic; for example, "man" (*m–n* and determinative of kneeling man, Fig. 30, *A*), "drink" (*d–r–n–k* and determinative of kneeling man with hand on mouth, Fig. 30, *C*), "speak" (*s–p–k* and same determinative), or "brook" (*b–r–k* and determinative for "water," as in "pond," Fig. 30, *B*)

mixing in soot from the blackened pots over his fire. Dipping a pointed reed into this mixture, he found he could write very well.

He also learned that he could split a kind of river reed, called *papyrus*, into thin strips, and that he could write on them much better than on bits of pottery, bone, and wood. Desiring a larger sheet, he hit upon the idea of pasting his

**58.** Invention of writing materials: paper

papyrus strips together with overlapping edges. This gave him a very thin sheet, but by pasting two such sheets together, back to back with the grain crossing at right angles, he produced a smooth, tough, pale-yellow paper (Fig. 58). The Egyptian had thus made the discovery that a thin vegetable membrane offers the most practical surface on which to write, and the world has

FIG. 31. AN EXAMPLE OF EGYPTIAN HIEROGLYPHIC (UPPER LINE) AND ITS EQUIVALENT IN THE RAPID RUNNING HAND (LOWER LINE) WRITTEN WITH PEN AND INK ON PAPYRUS AND CALLED HIERATIC, THE WRITING OF ALL ORDINARY BUSINESS

The daily business of an Egyptian community of course required much writing and thousands of records. Such writing, after it began to be done with pen and ink on papyrus (Fig. 40), soon became very rapid. In course of time therefore there arose a rapid or running hand in which each hieroglyphic sign was much abbreviated. This running hand is called *hieratic*. It corresponds to our handwriting, while hieroglyphic corresponds to our print. In the above example the signs in the lower row show clearly that they are the result of an effort to make quickly the signs in the hieroglyphic row above (compare sign for sign). We must notice also that the Egyptian wrote from right to left, for this line begins at the right and reads to the left. Vertical lines, that is, downward reading, was also employed (Fig. 58). A third still more rapid and abbreviated hand, corresponding in some ways to our shorthand, arose still later (eighth century B.C.). It was called *demotic*, and one of the versions on the Rosetta Stone (Fig. 207) is written in demotic

since discovered nothing better. In this way arose pen, ink, and paper (see Fig. 40). All three of these devices have descended to us from the Egyptians, and paper still bears its ancient name, "papyros,"[1] but slightly changed.

---

[1] The change from "papyros" to "paper" is really a very slight one. For *os* is merely the Greek grammatical ending, which must be omitted in English. This leaves us *papyr* as the ancestor of our word "paper," from which it differs by only one letter. On the other Greek word for "papyrus," from which came our word "Bible," see § 405. On the rapid or running handwriting which resulted from using a pen on paper, see Fig. 31.

The invention of writing and of a convenient system of records on paper has had a greater influence in uplifting the human race than any other intellectual achievement in the career of man. It was more important than all the battles ever fought and all the constitutions ever devised.

59. Un-equaled importance of introduction of writing

The Egyptians early found it necessary to measure time. Like all other early peoples, they used the time from new moon to new moon as a very convenient rough measure. If a man had agreed to pay back some borrowed grain at the end of nine moons, and eight of them had passed, he knew that he had one more moon in which to make the payment. But the moon-month varies in length from twenty-nine to thirty days, and it does not evenly divide the year. The Egyptian soon showed himself much more practical in removing this inconvenience than his neighbors in other lands.

60. Beginnings of a calendar

He decided to use the moon no longer for dividing his year. He would have twelve months, and he would make his months all of the same length, that is, thirty days each; then he would celebrate five feast days, a kind of holiday week five days long, at the end of the year. This gave him a year of three hundred and sixty-five days. He was not yet enough of an astronomer to know that every four years he ought to have a leap year of three hundred and sixty-six days, although he discovered this fact later (§ 741). This convenient Egyptian calendar was devised in 4241 B.C., and its introduction is the *earliest dated event in history*. Furthermore, this calendar is the very one which has descended to us, after more than six thousand years — unfortunately with awkward alterations in the lengths of the months, but for these alterations the Egyptians were not responsible (see § 968).

61. Egyptian invention of our calendar, 4241 B.C., earliest fixed date in history

At the same time, as documents dated by this convenient calendar accumulated through many years, it was found that a document like a lease or a note, signed in a certain *month*, was not sufficiently dated, unless the *year* was also included. The system of numbering years from some great event, like

62. Lack of a means of identifying any past year; invention of year-names

our method of numbering them from the birth of Christ, was still unknown. In order to have some means of identifying a year when it was long past, each year was given a name after some prominent event which had happened in it. This method is still in use among our own North American Indians (Fig. 32),

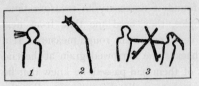

FIG. 32. PART OF A DAKOTA CHIEF'S LIST OF SEVENTY-ONE NAMED YEARS

and even among ourselves, as people in Chicago say "the year of the great fire." We find the earliest written monuments of Egypt dated by means of named years (Fig. 33).

**63.** Lists of year-names, the earliest chronicles; and lists of kings with numbered years

Lone Dog, a Dakota chief, had a buffalo robe with seventy-one named years recorded on it, beginning in 1800, when he was a child of four. A year when whooping cough was very bad was called the "Whooping-cough Year"; its sign shows a human head violently coughing! (*1*) Another year, very plentiful in meteors, was called the Meteor Year, and its sign was a rude drawing of a falling meteor (*2*). A third year saw the arrangement of peace between the Dakotas and the Crows; its sign was therefore two Indians, with differing style of hair, indicating the two different tribes, exchanging pipes of peace (*3*). Thus, instead of saying, as we do, that a thing happened in the year 1813, the Indian said it happened in the Whooping-cough Year, and by examining his table of years he could tell how far back that year was

Lists of year-names then began to be kept. As each year-name usually mentioned some great event (cf. Fig. 33), such lists of year-names were thus lists of great events, like historic chronicles. The earliest such year-list in human history now surviving, called the Palermo Stone (because it is preserved in the museum at Palermo, Sicily), begins about

3400 B.C., and contained when complete the names of some seven hundred years, ending about 2700 B.C. Later the Egyptians found it more convenient to number the years of each king's reign, and then to date events in the first year of King So-and-so or the tenth year of King So-and-so. They finally had lists of past kings, covering many centuries.

Meantime the Egyptians were making great progress in other matters. It was probably in the peninsula of Sinai (see map, p. 36) that some Egyptian, wandering thither, once happened to bank his camp fire with pieces of copper ore lying on the ground about the camp. The charcoal of his wood fire mingled with the hot fragments of ore piled around to shield the fire, and thus the ore was " reduced," as the miner says ; that is, the copper in metallic form was released from the lumps of ore. Next morning, as the Egyptian stirred the embers, he discovered a few glittering globules, now hardened into beads of metal. He drew them forth and turned them admiringly as they glittered in the morning sunshine. Before long, as the experience was repeated, he discovered whence these strange shining beads had come. He produced more of them, at first only to be worn as ornaments by the women. Then he learned to cast the metal into a blade, to replace the flint knife which he carried in his girdle.

Without knowing it this man stood at the dawning of a new

**64.** Discovery of metal (at least 4000 B.C.)

FIG. 33. EARLY EGYPTIAN DATE BY THE NAME OF THE YEAR

This large alabaster jar, now in the Philadelphia Museum, was presented by a primitive king of Egypt to a Sun-temple and bears the date of the presentation in the words, " Year of Fighting and Smiting the Northland," which is the name of the year, given to it because of the victory over the Northland (the Delta) gained in that year. A long series of such year-names furnishes us a valuable record of great events, by which the years were named (§ 63)

era, the Age of Metal ; and the little bead of shining copper which he drew from the ashes, if this Egyptian wanderer could have seen it, might have reflected to him a vision of steel

**65.** The dawning of the Age of Metal

buildings, Brooklyn bridges, huge factories roaring with the noise of thousands of machines of metal, and vast stretches of steel roads along which thunder hosts of rushing locomotives. For these things of our modern world, and all they signify, would never have come to pass but for the little bead of metal which the wondering Egyptian held in his hand for the first time on that eventful day so long ago. Since the discovery of fire over fifty thousand years earlier (§ 8), man had made no conquest of the things of the earth which could compare in importance with this discovery of metal.

**66. The Nile a vast historical volume**   At this point we realize that we have followed early man out of the Stone Age (where we left him in Europe) into a civilization possessed of metal, writing, and government. We also begin to see that dry and rainless Egypt furnishes the conditions for the preservation of such plentiful remains of early man as to make this valley an enormous storehouse of his ancient works and records. These remains are the only link connecting prehistoric man with the historic age of written documents, which we are now to study as we make the voyage up the Nile. We shall read the monuments along the great river like a vast historical volume, whose pages will tell us, age after age, the fascinating story of ancient man and all that he achieved here so many thousands of years ago, after his discovery of metals and his invention of writing.

**67. The first glimpse of the pyramids**   Such are the thoughts which occupy the mind of the well-informed traveler as his train carries him southward across the Delta. Perhaps he is pondering on the possible results which the Egyptians were to achieve as he sees them in imagination throwing away their flint chisels and replacing them with those of copper. The train rounds a bend, and through an opening in the palms he is fairly blinded by a burst of blazing sunshine from the western desert, in the midst of which he discovers a group of noble pyramids rising above the glare of the sands. It is his first glimpse of the great pyramids of Gizeh (Fig. 24), and it tells him better than any printed page what the Egyptian builders with the copper chisel in their hands could do. A few minutes later his train is moving among the modern buildings of Cairo, and the very next day will surely find him taking the seven-mile drive from Cairo out to Gizeh.

## Section 6. The Pyramid Age (about 3000 to 2500 b.c.)

No traveler ever forgets the first drive from Cairo to the pyramids of Gizeh, as he sees their giant forms rising higher and higher above the crest of the western desert (Fig. 24). A thousand questions arise in the visitor's mind. He has read that these vast buildings he is approaching are tombs, in which

**68.** The pyramids as royal tombs

FIG. 34. WINGED SUN-DISK, A SYMBOL OF THE SUN-GOD

In this form the Sun-god was believed to be a falcon flying across the sky. We shall later see how the other nations of the Orient in Asia also adopted this Egyptian symbol (see Figs. 102, 117, and 129)

the kings of Egypt were buried. Such mighty buildings reveal many things about the men who built them. In the first place, these tombs show that the Egyptians believed in a life after death, and that to obtain such life it was necessary to preserve the body from destruction. They built these tombs to shelter and protect the body after death. From this belief came also the practice of embalmment, by which the body was preserved as a mummy (Fig. 72). It was then placed in the great tomb, in a small room deep under the pyramid masonry. Other tombs of masonry, much smaller in size, cluster about the pyramids in great numbers (Figs. 39 and 42). Here were buried the relatives of the king, and the great men of his court, who assisted him in the government of the land.

**69.** The gods of Egypt: Re and Osiris

The Egyptians had many gods, but there were two whom they worshiped above all others. The sun, which shines so gloriously in the cloudless Egyptian sky, was their greatest god, and their most splendid temples were erected for his worship. Indeed, the pyramid is a symbol sacred to the Sun-god. (See another symbol in Fig. 34.) They called him Re (pronounced *ray*). The other great power which they revered was the shining Nile. The great river and the fertile soil he refreshes, and the green life which he brings forth — all these the Egyptian thought of together as a single god, Osiris, the imperishable life of the

FIG. 35. THE DEAD OSIRIS
EMBALMED

From the body of the god stalks of grain have sprouted, a symbol suggesting the imperishable life of the god, by means of which he survived death (§ 69)

earth, which revives and fades every year with the changes of the seasons (see Fig. 35). It was a beautiful thought to the Egyptian that this same life-giving power which furnished him his food in *this* world would care for him also in the *next*, when his body lay out yonder in the great cemetery of Gizeh, which we are approaching.[1]

**70.** The progress of the Egyptians before they built stone masonry

But this vast cemetery of Gizeh tells us of many other things besides the religion of the Egyptians. As we look up at the colossal pyramids behind the Sphinx (Fig. 54) we can hardly grasp the fact of the enormous forward stride taken by the Egyptians since the days when they used to be buried with their flint knives in a pit scooped out on the margin of the desert (Fig. 25). It was the use of metal which since then had carried them so far. That Egyptian in Sinai who noticed the first bit of metal (§ 65) lived over a thousand years before

[1] There were many other Egyptian gods whose earthly symbols were *animals*, but the animal worship usually attributed to Egypt was a degeneration belonging to the latest age. The animals were not gods in this early time, but only *symbols* of the divine beings, just as the winged sun-disk was a symbol of the Sun-god (Fig. 34).

these pyramids were built. He was buried in a pit like that of the earliest Egyptian peasant (Figs. 25 and 38, *1*).

It was a long time before the possession of metal resulted in copper tools which made possible great architecture in stone. Not more than a hundred and fifty years before the Great

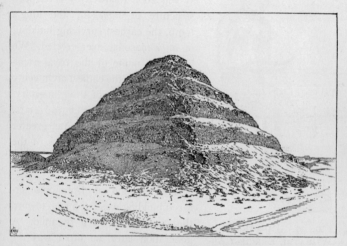

FIG. 36. THE OLDEST SURVIVING BUILDING OF STONE
MASONRY (NOT LONG AFTER 3000 B.C.)

This terraced building, often called the step-pyramid, was the tomb of King Zoser (early thirtieth century B.C.). It is about 200 feet high, and is composed of a series of buildings like those in Fig. 42, placed one on top of the other. It thus formed a tapering building (Fig. 38, *5*), out of which developed the pyramid form at the close of the thirtieth century (on the architect see Fig. 37 and § 71)

Pyramid of Gizeh, the Egyptians were still building the tombs of their kings out of sun-baked brick. Such a royal tomb was at first merely a chamber in the ground, roofed with wood and covered with a mound of sand and gravel (Fig. 38, *2*).

Then some skillful workman among them found out that he could use his copper tools to cut square blocks of limestone and line the chamber with these blocks in place of the soft bricks. So far as we know, this was the first piece of *stone* masonry ever put together (Fig. 38, *3*). It can hardly be called a building, for, like a cellar wall, it was all below ground. The next step, a real building above-ground, was still of brick (Fig. 38, *4*). It was soon followed by a terraced structure of *stone* for the king's tomb, the earliest surviving building of *stone* masonry ever erected. We know the name of the royal architect, Imhotep, the earliest architect to put up a building of stone masonry. He flourished just after 3000 B.C., and his name deserves far greater fame and respect than those of the early kings or conquerors themselves (Fig. 37).

The erection of Imhotep's terraced building was but a step toward the construction of a pyramid. A generation later, so rapid was the progress, the king's architects were building the Great Pyramid of Gizeh (2900 B.C.). From the earliest piece of stone masonry (Fig. 38, *3*) to the construction of the Great Pyramid (Fig. 38, *7*), less than a century and a half elapsed. Most of this advance was made during the thirtieth century B.C., that is, between 3000 and 2900 B.C. (Fig. 38). Such rapid progress in control of mechanical power can be found in no other period of the world's history until the nineteenth century.

FIG. 37. IMHOTEP THE WISE, THE EARLIEST AR-CHITECT OF STONE BUILD-INGS (NEARLY 3000 B.C.)

This architect of the earliest surviving building of stone (Fig. 36) was grand vizier at the court of King Zoser. He was also a great physician and wise man, and later on he was thought to be a god, until he was finally regarded as Asclepius (Æsculapius), the god of medicine among the Greeks and Romans. This little portrait of him is a bronze statuette, now in the Berlin Museum, and shows him reading from a papyrus roll

It helps us to realize this progress when we know that the Great Pyramid covers thirteen acres. It is a solid mass of masonry containing 2,300,000 blocks of limestone, each weighing on an average two and a half tons ; that is, each block is as heavy as a large wagonload of coal. The sides of the pyramid at the base are 755 feet long,[1] that is, about a block and three quarters (counting twelve city blocks to a mile), and the building was nearly 500 feet high. An ancient story tells us that a hundred thousand men were working on this royal tomb for twenty years, and we can well believe it (Fig. 39).

**73. The vast size of the Great Pyramid**

We perceive at once that it must have required a very skillful ruler and a great body of officials to manage and to feed a hundred thousand workmen around this great building. The king who controlled such vast undertakings was no longer a local chieftain (§ 50), but he now ruled a united Egypt, the earliest great unified nation, comprising several millions of people. The king was so reverenced that the people did not mention him by name, but instead they spoke of the palace in which he lived, that is, the "Great House," or, in Egyptian, "Pharaoh." He had his *local* officials collecting taxes all over Egypt (Fig. 40). It was also their business to try the law cases which arose, and every judge had before him the *written* law,[2] which bade him judge justly.

**74. Government in the Pyramid Age**

The king's huge *central* offices, occupying low, sun-baked-brick buildings, sheltered an army of clerks with their reed pens and their rolls of papyrus (Fig. 40), keeping the king's records and accounts. The taxes received from the people here were not in money, for coined money did not yet exist. Payments were made in produce — grain, live stock, wine, honey, linen, and the like. With the exception of the cattle, these had to be stored in granaries and storehouses, a vast group of which formed the treasury of the king.

---

[1] It should be remembered that the pyramid is *solid*. Compare the length of the Colosseum (about 600 feet), which is built around a *hollow* inclosure.

[2] This Egyptian code of laws has unfortunately been lost.

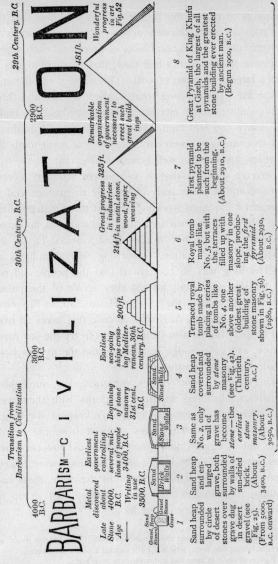

BARBARISM—CIVILIZATION

Transition from
Barbarism to Civilization

| 4000 B.C. | | 3000 B.C. | 30th Century, B.C. | 2900 B.C. | 29th Century, B.C. |
|---|---|---|---|---|---|

Late Stone Age →

Metal discovered about 4000, B.C. Writing in use 3500, B.C.

Earliest government controlling several millions of people 3400, B.C.

Beginning of stone masonry 31st cent. B.C.

Earliest sea-going ships crossing Mediterranean 30th century, B.C.

Great progress in industries: in metal, stone, wood, paper, weaving

Remarkable organization of government necessary to erect such great buildings

Wonderful progress in art Fig. 52

200 ft.  214 ft.  325 ft.  481 ft.

1

Sand heap surrounded by circle of desert stones over grave dug in desert gravel (see Fig. 25). (From 5000, B.C. onward)

2

Sand heap and enlarged grave, both surrounded by walls of sun-dried brick. (About 3400, B.C.)

3

Same as No. 2, only wall of grave has become stone — the earliest stone masonry. (About 3050, B.C.)

4

Sand heap covered and surrounded by stone masonry (see Fig. 42). (Thirtieth century, B.C.)

5

Terraced royal tomb made by placing a series of tombs like No. 4, one above another (oldest great building of stone masonry shown in Fig. 36). (2980, B.C.)

6

Royal tomb made like No. 5, but with the terraces filled up with masonry in one slope, producing the first pyramid. (About 2930, B.C.)

7

First pyramid planned to be such from the beginning. (About 2910, B.C.)

8

Great Pyramid of King Khufu at Gizeh, the largest of all pyramids and the greatest stone building ever erected by ancient man. (Begun 2900, B.C.)

At most 150 years
(from earliest stone masonry to the Great Pyramid)

54

The body of the Egyptian peasant in Fig. 25 lay at the bottom of a grave above which was a low heap of sand surrounded by a circle of rough desert stones to keep the sand in place. No. *1*, above, shows this grave, cut down through the middle to expose the inside with the sand heap above it. In Nos. *2*, *3*, and *4* we see the later tombs, also cut down through to expose the inside. They show how the circle of stones around the sand heap was slowly improved till it became real walls, first of brick (No. *2*) and then of stone masonry (No. *3*), enveloping the whole tomb, with the old sand heap still in the inside. Tombs like No. *4* were then placed one above the other, producing a tapering terraced building (No. *5*), which was soon improved until it became a pyramid (No. *6*). Thus the sand heap and its circle of stones were the germ out of which the mighty pyramids grew in the course of fifteen or twenty centuries. Notice how this wonderful growth in the art of building began with the sand heap in the barbarism of the Late Stone Age and thus carries us over from barbarism to civilization in the thousand years from 4000 to 3000 B.C. This great art of building was itself one of the things which marked the entrance upon civilization, and architecture passed from the earliest example of stone masonry to the Great Pyramid in only one hundred and fifty years. But incoming civilization was not marked only by progress in the art of building. The remarks inserted above, over the tombs and pyramids, suggest to us some of the other important achievements which helped to bring in and develop civilization, like the discovery of metal and the invention of writing, followed by the earliest government of a large population, the earliest seagoing ships, great progress in industries, and a remarkable development in art. We now see how the pyramids and their predecessors stand like milestones marking the long road by which man passed from barbarism to a highly developed civilization. We learn also what were the *visible* things which we must understand as making up civilization in the beginning. But there were some necessary things which also reached a high development at the same time and which are *not visible*. These were the belief in right living, in kindness to others, and that a good life here was the only thing which could bring happiness in the next world

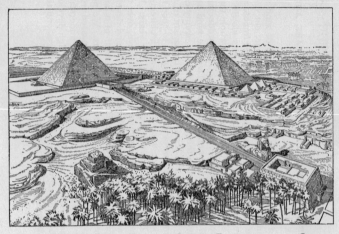

FIG. 39. RESTORATION OF THE GREAT PYRAMIDS AND OTHER TOMB-MONUMENTS IN THE ANCIENT CEMETERY OF GIZEH, EGYPT. (AFTER HOELSCHER)

These royal tombs (pyramids) belonged to the leading kings of the Fourth Dynasty, the early part (2900–2750 B.C.) of the Pyramid Age (about 3000 to 2500 B.C.). The Great Pyramid, the tomb of King Khufu (Greek, *Cheops*), is on the right (see § 73). Next in size is that of King Khafre (Greek, *Chephren*) (Fig. 54), on the left. On the east side (front) of each pyramid is a temple (see also Fig. 56), where the food, drink, and clothing were placed for the use of the dead king. These temples, like the pyramids, were built on the desert plateau above, while the royal town was in the valley below (on the right) (see § 75 and Fig. 24). For convenience, therefore, the temple was connected with the town below by a covered gallery, or corridor, of stone, seen here descending in a straight line from the temple of King Khafre and terminating below, just beside the Sphinx, in a large oblong building of stone, called a valley-temple. It was a splendid structure of granite (Fig. 55), serving not only as a temple but also as the entrance to the great corridor from the royal city. The pyramids are surrounded by the tombs of the queens and the great lords of the age (see Fig. 42). At the lower left-hand corner is an unfinished pyramid, showing the inclined ascents up which the stone blocks were dragged. These ascents (called ramps) were built of sun-baked brick and were removed after the pyramid was finished. (This scene will be found in color in *Outlines of European History*, Part I, Plate I)

56

The villas and gardens of the officials who assisted the king **75.** The royal city in all this business of government formed a large part of the royal city (Fig. 51). The chief quarter of the city, however, was occupied by the palace of the king and the luxurious parks and gardens which surrounded it. Thus the palace and its grounds, the official villas, and offices of the government made up the capital of Egypt, the royal city which extended along the foot of

the pyramid cemetery and stretched far away over the low plain, of which there is a fine view from the summit of the pyramid. But the city was all built of sun-baked brick and wood, and it has therefore vanished. It extended far southward from Gizeh and was later called Memphis.

The city of the dead, — the pyramids and the tombs clustering around

FIG. 40. COLLECTION OF TAXES BY LOCAL TREASURY OFFICIALS IN THE PYRAMID AGE

The clerks and scribes are in two rows at the right. All squat, and write on the raised right knee, except the two who have desks. The left hand holds a sheet of papyrus; the right, the pen. The taxpayers are delinquent village officers brought in (at the left) by deputies with staves under their arms. The inscription above reads, " Seizing the town rulers for a reckoning." The clerks had records of the taxpayers' names and how much they owed; and they issued receipts when the taxes were paid, just as at the present day. Such arrangements did not arise in Europe until far down in the Roman Empire (§§ 1026–1027)

**76.** Length and date of the Pyramid Age

them (Figs. 39 and 42), — being built of stone, has fortunately proved more durable. Hence it is that from the summit of the Great Pyramid there is a grand view southward, down a straggling but imposing line of pyramids rising dimly as far as one can see on the southern horizon. Each pyramid was a royal tomb, and for us each such tomb means that a king lived, ruled, and died. The line is over sixty miles long, and its oldest pyramids represent the first great age of Egyptian

civilization after the land was united under one king.[1] We may
call it the Pyramid Age, and it lasted about five hundred years,
from 3000 to 2500 B.C.

**77. Northern commerce and earliest seagoing ships**    In the Pyramid Age the Pharaoh was already powerful
enough to begin seeking wealth beyond the boundaries of
Egypt. We even possess painted reliefs (Fig. 41) showing

FIG. 41.  EARLIEST REPRESENTATION OF A SEAGOING SHIP
(TWENTY-EIGHTH CENTURY B.C.)

The scene is carved on the wall of a temple (Fig. 56). The people are
all bowing to the king whose figure (now lost) stood on shore (at the
left), and they salute him with the words written in a line of hieroglyphs
above, meaning: "Hail to thee! O Sahure [the king's name], thou god
of the living! We behold thy beauty." Some of these men are bearded
Phœnician prisoners brought by this Egyptian ship which with seven
others, making a fleet of eight vessels, had therefore crossed the east
end of the Mediterranean and returned. The big double mast is un-
shipped and lies on supports rising by the three steering oars in the
stern. The model and ornaments of these earliest-known ships spread
in later times to ships found in all waters from Italy to India

us the ships which he dared to send beyond the shelter of
the Nile mouths far across the end of the Mediterranean to
the coast of Phœnicia (see map, p. 102). This was in the

---

1 For a long time before this there had been little kingdoms scattered up and
down the valley. These finally merged into two leading kingdoms — one including the Delta, and the other the valley south of it. They long fought together
(see Fig. 33), until they were finally united into one kingdom, under a single
king. The first king to establish this union permanently was Menes, who united
Egypt under his rule about 3400 B.C. But it was not until four centuries or more
after Menes that the united kingdom became powerful and wealthy enough to
build these royal pyramid-tombs, marking for us the first great age of Egyptian
civilization.

middle of the twenty-eighth century B.C., and this relief
(Fig. 41) contains the oldest known representation of a seagoing ship. Yet at that time the Pharaoh had already been
carrying on such over-sea commerce for centuries.

Besides maintaining his copper mines in Sinai, the king was
also already sending caravans of donkeys far up the Nile into
the Sudan to traffic with the blacks of the south, and to bring
back ebony, ivory, ostrich feathers, and fragrant gums. The

78. Southern
commerce
and earliest
navigation on
the Red Sea

FIG. 42. RESTORATION OF A GROUP OF TOMBS OF THE NOBLES
IN THE PYRAMID AGE

These tombs are grouped about the royal pyramids, as seen in Fig. 39.
They are sometimes of vast size. The square openings in the top are
shafts leading down to the burial chambers in the native rock far below
the tomb structures. These structures are of stone, surrounding a heap
of sand and gravel inside (Fig. 38, *4*). The chapel room is in the east
side, of which the door can be seen in the front of each tomb. The
reliefs shown in Figs. 43–48 adorn the inside walls of these chapels

officials who conducted these caravans were the earliest explorers of inner Africa, and in their tombs at the First Cataract
they have left interesting records of their exciting adventures
among the wild tribes of the south — adventures in which some
of them lost their lives.[1] The Pharaoh was also sending his
ships on expeditions to a land called Punt, at the south end of
the Red Sea (see map, p. 36), to procure the same products and
to bring them back by water.

[1] The teacher will find it of interest to read these records to the class. See
the author's *Ancient Records of Egypt*, Vol. I, pp. 325–336, 350–374.

79. The
tomb-chapels
of the Pyra-
mid Age ; the
life they
reveal

A stroll among the tombs clustering so thickly around the pyramids of Gizeh (Fig. 42) is almost like a walk among the busy communities which flourished in this populous valley in the days of the pyramid-builders. We find the door of every tomb standing open (Fig. 42), and there is nothing to prevent

FIG. 43. RELIEF SCENE FROM THE CHAPEL OF A NOBLE'S
TOMB (FIG. 42) IN THE PYRAMID AGE

The tall figure of the noble stands at the right. He is inspecting three lines of cattle and a line of fowl brought before him. Note the two scribes who head the two middle rows. Each is writing with pen on a sheet of papyrus, and one carries two pens behind his ear. Such reliefs after being carved were colored in bright hues by the painter (see § 93)

our entrance. We stand in an oblong room with walls of stone masonry. This is a chapel chamber, to which the Egyptian believed the dead man buried beneath the tomb might return every day. Here he would find food and drink left for him daily by his relatives. He would also find the stone walls of this room covered from floor to ceiling with carved scenes, beautifully painted, picturing the daily life on a great estate (Figs. 40, 43–48, and 50). The place is now silent and deserted, or if we hear the voices of the donkey boys talking outside, they are speaking Arabic, for the ancient Egyptian language of the men who built these tombs so many thousand years ago is no longer spoken. But everywhere, in bright and charming colors, we see pictures of the life — the days of toil and pleasure — which these men of nearly five thousand years ago actually lived.

FIG. 44. PLOWING AND SOWING IN THE PYRAMID AGE

There are two plowmen, one driving the oxen and one holding the plow. This wooden plow was derived from such a wooden hoe as we see in use in front of the oxen. The handle of the hoe, here grasped by the user, was lengthened so that oxen might be yoked to it. The hoe handle thus became the beam of a plow. Two short handles were then attached by which the plowman behind could guide it (§ 33). The man with the hoe breaks up the clods left by the plow, and in front of him is the sower, scattering the seed from the curious sack he carries before him. At the left is a scribe of the estate. The hieroglyphs at the top in all such scenes explain what is going on. Scene from the chapel of a noble's tomb (Fig. 42)

Dominating all these scenes on the walls is the tall form of the noble (Fig. 43), the lord of the estate, who was buried in this tomb. He stands looking out over his fields and inspecting the work going on there. These fields (Fig. 44) are the oldest scene of agriculture known to us. Here, too, are the herds, long lines of sleek, fat cattle grazing in the pasture, while the milch cows are led up and tied to be milked (Figs. 43 and 45). These cattle are also beasts of burden; we notice the oxen drawing the plow. But we find no horses in these tombs of the

80. Agriculture and cattle raising; beasts of burden

Pyramid Age, for the horse was still unknown to the Egyptian. The donkey, however, is everywhere, and it would be impossible to harvest the grain without him (Fig. 46).

FIG. 45. PEASANT MILKING IN THE PYRAMID AGE

The cow is restive and the ancient cowherd has tied her hind legs. Behind her another man is holding her calf, which rears and plunges in the effort to reach the milk. Scene from the chapel of a noble's tomb (Fig. 42)

On the next wall we find again the tall figure of the noble overseeing the booths and yards where the craftsmen of his estate are working. Yonder is the smith. He has never heard of his ancestor who picked up the first bead of copper, over a thousand years earlier (§ 65). Much progress has been made since that day. This man could make excellent copper tools of all sorts; but the tool which demanded the greatest skill was the long, flat ripsaw, which the smith knew how to hammer into shape out of a broad strip of copper five or six feet long. Such a saw may be seen in use in Fig. 50. Besides this he knew how to make one that would saw great blocks of stone for the pyramids. Moreover, this coppersmith was already able to deliver orders of considerable size. We know that he could furnish thirteen hundred feet

FIG. 46. DONKEY CARRYING A LOAD OF GRAIN SHEAVES IN THE PYRAMID AGE

The foal accompanies its mother while at work. Scene from the chapel of a noble's tomb (Fig. 42)

(about a quarter of a mile) of copper drain piping for a pyramid temple (Fig. 56), where recent excavation has found it — the earliest plumbing known to us.

On the same wall we see the lapidary holding up for the noble's admiration splendid stone bowls cut from diorite. Although this kind of stone is as hard as steel, the bowl is ground to such thinness that the sunlight glows through its dark gray sides (Fig. 134). Other workmen are cutting and grinding tiny pieces of beautiful blue turquoise. These pieces they inlay with remarkable accuracy into recesses in the surface of a magnificent golden vase just made ready by the goldsmith (Plate I).

**82. The lapidary, goldsmith, and jeweler**

The booth of the goldsmith is filled with workmen and apprentices (Fig. 47). They hammer and cast, solder and fit together richly wrought jewelry which is hardly surpassed by the work of the best goldsmiths and jewelers of to-day.

FIG. 47. GOLDSMITH'S WORKSHOP IN THE PYRAMID AGE

UPPER ROW. At left the chief goldsmith weighs precious stones and a scribe records them; next, six men with blowpipes blow the fire in a small clay furnace; next, a workman pours out molten metal or paste; at the right end four men are beating gold leaf. MIDDLE ROW. Pieces of finished jewelry and a jewel-box in the middle. LOWER ROW. Workmen seated at low benches are putting together and engraving pieces of jewelry. Several of these men are dwarfs. (See the finished work on Plate I, and headpiece, p. 35)

In the next space on this wall we find the potter no longer building up his jars

**83. The potter's wheel and furnace; the earliest glass**

and bowls with his fingers alone, as in the Stone Age. He now sits before a small horizontal *wheel* (Fig. 48), upon which he deftly shapes the whirling vessel. When the soft clay vessels are ready, they are no longer unevenly burned in an *open* fire, as among the Late Stone Age potters in the Swiss lake-villages (Fig. 16); but here in the Egyptian potter's yard are long rows of *closed* furnaces of clay as tall as a man. When the pottery is packed in these furnaces it is burned evenly, because it is protected from the wind (Fig. 48). On the tomb wall we also see the craftsman making glass. This art the Egyptians had discovered centuries earlier. The glass was spread on tiles in gorgeous glazes for adorning house and palace walls (Plate II), and later it was wrought into exquisite many-colored glass bottles and vases, which were widely exported (Fig. 49).

**84. The weavers and tapestry-makers**

Yonder the weaving women draw forth from the loom a gossamer fabric of linen. The picture would naturally give us no idea of its fineness, but fortunately pieces of it have survived, wrapped around the mummy of a king of this age.

FIG. 48. POTTER'S WHEEL AND FURNACES

The potter crouches before his horizontal wheel, which is like a flat round plate, on which rests the jar being shaped. The potter keeps the wheel whirling with one hand, and with the other he shapes the soft clay jar as it whirls on the wheel. This wheel is the ancestor of our lathe. Two men (at the right end) are just filling a tall furnace with bowls and jars, and another furnace (at the left) is already very hot, for the man stirring the fire is holding up his hand to shield his face from the heat

These specimens of royal linen are so fine that it requires a magnifying glass to distinguish them from silk, and the best work of the modern *machine* loom is coarse in comparison with this fabric of the ancient Egyptian *hand* loom. At one loom a lovely tapestry is being made, for these weavers of Egypt furnished the earliest-known specimens of such work, to be hung on the walls of the Pharaoh's palace or stretched out to shade the roof garden of the noble's villa (Fig. 51).

**85. Paper-makers**

In the next space on the wall we find huge bundles of papyrus reeds, which barelegged men are gathering along the edge of the Nile marsh. These reeds furnish piles of pale yellow paper in long narrow sheets (§ 58). The ships which we have followed on the Mediterranean (Fig. 41) will in course of time add bales of this Nile paper to their cargoes, and carry it to the European world.

We seem almost to hear the hubbub of hammers and mauls as we approach the next section of wall, where we find the ship-builders and cabinetmakers. Here is a long line of curving hulls, with workmen swarming over them like ants, fitting together the earliest seagoing ships (Fig. 41). Beside them are the busy cabinetmakers (Fig. 50), fashioning luxurious furniture for the noble's villa.

86. Ship-builders, carpenters, and cabinetmakers

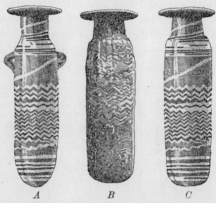

FIG. 49. EGYPTIAN GLASS BOTTLES AND THEIR DISTRIBUTION FROM BABYLONIA TO ANCIENT ITALY

*A*, as found in ancient Egypt; *B*, as found in ancient Babylonia; *C*, as found in ancient Italy. The shape is in imitation of Egyptian perfume bottles cut out of alabaster. This shape became the common form for perfume and toilet bottles among the Mediterranean peoples in later times (see Fig. 170)

The finished chairs and couches for the king or the rich are overlaid with gold and silver, inlaid with ebony and ivory, and upholstered with soft leathern cushions (Fig. 73).

As we look back over these painted chapel walls we see that the tombs of Gizeh have told us a very vivid story of how these early men learned to make for themselves the things they needed. We should notice how many more such things these men of the Nile could now make than the Stone Age men, who

87. Industrial progress of Egypt revealed by the tomb-chapels

were still living in the lake-villages and other towns of Europe (Fig. 14) at the very time these tomb-chapels were built.

**88.** River commerce ; the market place ; traffic in goods ; circulation of precious metal

It is easy to picture the bright, sunny river in those ancient days, alive with boats and barges (often depicted on these walls) moving hither and thither, bearing the products of all these industries, to be carried to the treasury of the Pharaoh as taxes or to the market of the town to be bartered for other goods. Here on the wall is the market place itself. We can watch the cobbler offering the baker a pair of sandals as

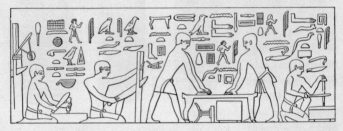

FIG. 50. CABINETMAKERS IN THE PYRAMID AGE

At the left a man is cutting with a chisel which he taps with a mallet; next, a man "rips" a board with a copper saw; next, two men are finishing off a couch, and at the right a man is drilling a hole with a bow-drill. Scene from the chapel of a noble's tomb (Fig 42). Compare a finished chair belonging to a wealthy noble of the Empire which was placed in his tomb and thus preserved (Fig. 73)

payment for a cake, or the carpenter's wife giving the fisherman a little wooden box to pay for a fish ; while the potter's wife proffers the apothecary two bowls fresh from the potter's furnace in exchange for a jar of fragrant ointment. We see, therefore, that the people have *no coined money* to use, and that in the market place trade is actual exchange of goods. Such is the business of the common people. If we could see the large transactions in the palace, we would find there heavy rings of gold of a standard weight, which circulated like money. Rings of copper also served the same purpose. Such rings were the forerunners of coin (§ 458).

These people in the gayly painted picture of the market place on the chapel wall were the common folk of Egypt in the Pyramid Age. Some of them were free men, following their own business or industry. Others were slaves, working the fields on the great estates. Neither of these humble classes owned any land. Over them were the landowners, the Pharaoh and his great lords and officials, like the owner of this tomb (Fig. 42). We know many more of them by name, and a walk through this cemetery would enable us to make a directory of the wealthy quarter of the royal city under the kings who were buried in these pyramids of Gizeh. We know the grand viziers and the chief treasurers, the chief judges and the architects, the chamberlains and marshals of the palace, and so on. We can even visit the tomb of the architect who built the Great Pyramid of Gizeh for Khufu.

89. Three classes of society in the Pyramid Age

We can observe with what pleasure these nobles and officials presided over this busy industrial and social life of the Nile valley in the Pyramid Age. Here on this chapel wall again we see its owner seated at ease in his palanquin, a luxurious wheel-less carriage borne upon the shoulders of slaves, as he returns from the inspection of his estate where we have been following him. His bearers carry him into the shady garden before his house (Fig. 51), where they set down the palanquin and cease their song.[1] His wife advances at once to greet him. Her place is always at his side; she is his sole wife, held in all honor, and enjoys every right which belongs to her husband. This garden is the noble's paradise. Here he may recline for an hour of leisure with his family and friends, playing at draughts, listening to the music of harp, pipe, and lute, watching his women in the slow and stately dances of the time, while his children are sporting about among the arbors, splashing in the pool as they chase the fish, playing with ball, doll, and jumping jack, or teasing the tame monkey which takes refuge under their father's ivory-legged stool.

90. The noble of the Pyramid Age in his home

[1] Recorded, with other songs, on the tomb-chapel walls.

## SECTION 7. ART AND ARCHITECTURE IN THE PYRAMID AGE

**91. The noble's house**

The noble drops one hand idly upon the head of his favorite hound, and with the other beckons to the chief gardener and gives directions regarding the new pomegranates which he wishes to try for dinner. The house (Fig. 51) where this dinner awaits him is large and commodious, built of sun-dried brick and wood. Light and airy, as suits the climate, we find that it has many latticed windows on all sides. The walls of the living rooms are scarcely more than a frame to support gayly colored hangings (§ 84) which can be let down as a protection against winds and sand storms when necessary. These give the house a very bright and cheerful aspect. The house is a work of art, and we discern in it how naturally the Egyptian demanded beauty in his surroundings. This he secured by making all his *useful* things *beautiful*.

**92. The art of its furniture and decoration**

Beauty surrounds us on every hand as we follow him in to his dinner. The lotus blossoms on the handle of his carved spoon, and his wine sparkles in the deep blue calyx of the same flower, which forms the bowl of his wineglass. The muscular limbs of the lion or the ox, beautifully carved in ivory, support the chair in which he sits or the couch where he reclines. The painted ceiling over his head is a blue and starry heaven resting upon palm-trunk columns (Fig. 56), each crowned with its graceful tuft of drooping foliage carved in wood and colored in the dark green of the living tree; or columns in the form of lotus stalks rise from the floor as if to support the azure ceiling upon their swaying blossoms. Doves and butterflies, exquisitely painted, flit across this indoor sky. Beneath our feet we find the pavement of the dining hall carpeted in paintings picturing everywhere the deep green of disheveled marsh grasses, with gleaming water between and fish gliding among the swaying reeds. Around the margin, leaping among the rushes, we see the wild ox

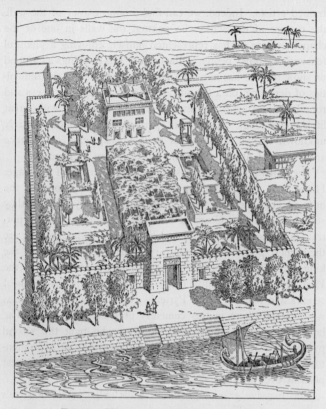

FIG. 51. VILLA OF AN EGYPTIAN NOBLE

The garden is inclosed with a high wall. There are pools on either
side as one enters, and a long arbor extends down the middle. The
house at the rear, embowered in trees, is crowned by a roof garden
shaded with awnings of tapestry (see § 84)

tossing his head at the birds twittering on the nodding rush
tops, as they vainly strive to frighten away the stealthy weasel
creeping up to plunder their nests.

The Egyptians could not have left us the beautifully painted
reliefs in the tomb-chapels we visited unless they had possessed

**93. Painting and relief in tombs and temples**

trained artists. Indeed, we can find, in one corner of the wall, the picture of the artist who painted the walls in one of the chapels, where he has represented himself enjoying a plentiful feast among other people of the estate. His drawings all around us show that he has not been able to overcome all the difficulties of depicting, on a flat surface, objects having thickness and roundness. Animal figures are drawn, however, with great lifelikeness (Figs. 43–46), but perspective is almost entirely unknown to him, and objects in the background or distance are drawn of almost the same size as those in front.

**94. Portrait sculpture**

The portrait sculptor was the greatest artist of this age. His statues were carved in stone or wood, and colored in the hues of life; the eyes were inlaid with rock crystal, and they still shine with the gleam of life (Fig. 53). More lifelike portraits have never been produced by any age, although they are the earliest portraits in the history of art. Such statues of the kings are often superb (Fig. 52). They were set up in the Pharaoh's pyramid temple (Figs. 55 and 56). In size the most remarkable statue of the Pyramid Age is the Great Sphinx, which stands here in this cemetery of Gizeh (Fig. 54). The head is a portrait of Khafre, the king who built the second pyramid of Gizeh (Fig. 54), and was carved from a promontory of rock which overlooked the royal city. It is the largest portrait ever wrought.

**95. Architecture: the earliest clerestory**

The massive granite piers and walls (Fig. 55) of Khafre's valley temple (Fig. 39) beside the Sphinx reveal to us the impressive architecture in stone which the men of the early part of the Pyramid Age were designing. This splendid hall (Fig. 55) was lighted by a series of oblique slits, which are really low roof windows. They occupied the difference in level between a higher roof over the middle aisle of the hall and a lower roof on each side of the middle (Fig. 271, *1*). Such an arrangement of roof windows, called a clerestory (*clearstory*), later passed over to Greece and Rome, and finally suggested the nave of the Christian basilica church or cathedral

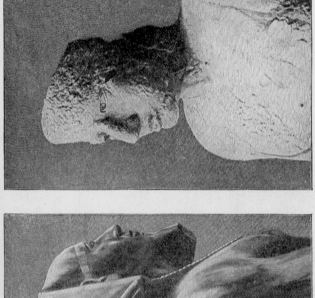

FIG. 53. HEAD OF A ROYAL STATUE OF BRONZE IN THE PYRAMID AGE

It represents King Pepi I (nearly 2600 B.C.). It was hammered into shape over a wooden form. The metal is encrusted with rust, but owing to the eyes, of inlaid rock crystal, the portrait is very lifelike (cf. Fig. 220)

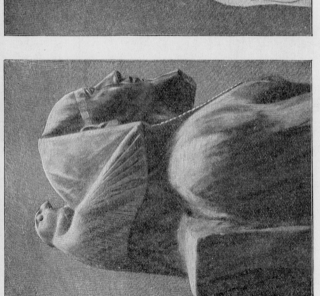

FIG. 52. PORTRAIT OF KING KHAFRE, BUILDER OF THE SECOND PYRAMID OF GIZEH

Found in his valley-temple (Fig. 39). It is carved in excessively hard stone, called diorite. The falcon with protecting wings outstretched is a symbol of the great god Horus (twenty-ninth century B.C.)

From an etching by George T. Plowman

FIG. 54. THE GREAT SPHINX OF GIZEH AND THE PYRAMID OF KHAFRE

A sphinx was the portrait head of a king attached to the body of a lion. This famous sphinx was a portrait of King Khafre (Fig. 52 and § 94), before whose pyramid it lies as a sentinel guarding the mighty cemetery of Gizeh. The body is 187 feet long, and the head is 66 feet high

(Fig. 271). And so this granite hall of Khafre in the Pyramid Age was the ancestor of the leading form of Christian architecture as it developed in Europe three thousand five hundred years later.

But before a century had passed, such massive grandeur as we find in this great hall of Khafre (Fig. 55) was being transformed by the Egyptian's growing sense of grace and beauty. Instead of ponderous *square* piers or pillars the architects now began to erect light and graceful *round* columns with beautiful capitals; these were ranged in long rows, the earliest colonnades (Fig. 56), dating from the twenty-eighth century B.C. They were peculiar to Egypt, for when our study

**96.** Earliest colonnades

FIG. 55. RESTORATION OF THE CLERESTORY HALL IN THE VALLEY-TEMPLE OF KHAFRE (CF. FIG. 39). (AFTER HOELSCHER)

The roof of this hall was supported on two rows of huge stone piers (see Fig. 271, *1*), each a single block of polished granite weighing 22 tons. This view shows only one row of the piers, the other being out of range at the right. At the left above, the light streams in obliquely from the very low clerestory windows (§ 95). Compare the cross section (Fig. 271, *1*). The statues shown here had been thrown by unknown enemies into a well in a connected hall, where they were found sixty years ago (see head of the finest in Fig. 52)

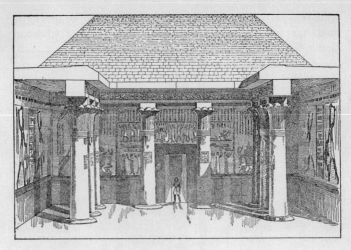

FIG. 56. COLONNADES IN THE COURT OF A PYRAMID-TEMPLE
(TWENTY-EIGHTH CENTURY B.C.). (AFTER BORCHARDT)

Notice the pyramid rising behind the temple (just as in Fig. 39 also).
The door in the middle leads to the holy place built against the
side of the pyramid, where a false door in the pyramid masonry
served as the portal through which the king came forth from the world
of the dead into this beautiful temple to enjoy the food and drink
placed here for him in magnificent vessels (Plate I) and to share in the
splendid feasts celebrated here. The center of the court is open to the
sky; the roof of the porch all around is supported on round columns,
the earliest known in the history of architecture. Contrast the square
piers without any capital which the architects of Khafre put into his
temple-hall (Fig. 55) over a century earlier than these columns. Each
column reproduces a palm tree, the capital being the crown of foliage.
The whole place was colored in the bright hues of nature, including
the painting on the walls behind the columns. Among these paintings
was the ship in Fig. 41. Thirteen hundred feet of copper piping, the
earliest-known plumbing, was installed in this building (§ 81)

carries us to earliest Asia, we shall find that the colonnade
was long unknown there (§ 195).

**97.** Decline
of the Pyra-
mid Age

The Pyramid cemeteries have shown us the grandeur of the
civilization gained by the Egyptians of the Pyramid Age. If
time permitted, we might find other records here, showing how

the nobles of the age (just such nobles as the one whose estate and home we have in imagination visited) gained more and more power until the Pharaohs could no longer control them. Then in struggles among themselves they destroyed the Pharaoh's government, and the last king of the Pyramid Age fell soon after 2500 B.C. It had lasted some five hundred years. Thus ended the first great civilized age of human history — the age which carried men for the first time out of barbarism into civilization (see Fig. 38). But the Pyramid Age was not the end of civilization on the Nile; other great periods were to follow. The monuments which these later ages left lie farther up the river, and we must make the voyage up the Nile in order to visit them and to recover the wonderful story which they still tell us.

## QUESTIONS

SECTION 5. Tell something of the life of the earliest Nile men and how we know about them. Trace the steps by which phonetic writing arose. Where did the first alphabet arise? Write three words in hieroglyphic (Fig. 30). Discuss the importance of the invention of writing. Describe early methods of measuring time. Describe the probable manner of the discovery of metal. Which metal was it?

SECTION 6. What do the tombs of Egypt tell us of religion? Describe the effect of the use of metal on architecture. Discuss the first architect in stone. Describe the government of the Pyramid Age. Study Fig. 38 and tell how the Egyptian tombs reveal the transition from barbarism to civilization. Describe the earliest sea-going ships. Make a list of the industries revealed in the tomb-chapel pictures. Discuss trade and commerce.

SECTION 7. Describe the house and garden of a noble in the Pyramid Age. Discuss painting and portrait sculpture. Make a sketch of the earliest piers or supports (Fig. 55). Were they beautiful? Draw a later pier (column) a hundred years after the Great Pyramid (Fig. 56). Was it beautiful? Describe the roof windows called clerestory windows (Figs. 55 and 271, *1*) and what they finally came to be. Give the date of the Pyramid Age, and tell why it was important.

# CHAPTER III

## THE STORY OF EGYPT: THE FEUDAL AGE AND THE EMPIRE

### SECTION 8. THE NILE VOYAGE AND THE FEUDAL AGE

**98. The Nile voyage begins**

As we begin our voyage up the Nile and our steamer moves away from the Cairo dock, we see, stretching far along the western horizon, the long line of pyramids, reminding us again of the splendor and progress of the Pyramid Age which we are now leaving behind. At length they drop down and disappear behind the fringe of palm groves. Other great monuments are before us. Along the palm-fringed shores far away to the south we shall find the buildings, tombs, and monuments

NOTE. At the left we see entering, in white robes, the deceased, a man named Ani, and his wife. Before them are the balances of judgment for weighing the human heart, to determine whether it is just or not. A Jackal-headed god adjusts the scales, while an Ibis-headed god stands behind him, pen in hand, ready to record the verdict of the balances. Behind him is a monster ready to devour the unjust soul, as his heart (symbolized by a tiny jar), in the left-hand scalepan, is weighed over against right and truth (symbolized by a feather) in the right-hand scalepan. The scene is painted in water colors on papyrus. Such a roll is sometimes as much as 90 feet long and filled from beginning to end with magical charms for the use of the dead in the next world. Hence the modern name for the whole roll, the "Book of the Dead."

74

FIG. 57. CLIFF-TOMB OF AN EGYPTIAN NOBLE OF THE
FEUDAL AGE

This tomb is not a masonry structure like the tomb of the Pyramid
Age (Fig. 42), but it is cut into the face of the cliff. The chapel
entered through this door contains painted reliefs like those of the
Pyramid Age (Figs. 43–47) and also many written records. In this
chapel the noble tells of his kind treatment of his people; he says:
"There was no citizen's daughter whom I misused; there was no
widow whom I oppressed; there was no peasant whom I evicted; there
was no shepherd whom I expelled; . . . there was none wretched
in my community, there was none hungry in my time. When years
of famine came I plowed all the fields of the Oryx barony [his estate]
. . . preserving its people alive and furnishing its food so that there
was none hungry therein. I gave to the widow as to her who had a
husband; I did not exalt the great above the humble in anything that
I gave " (§ 100). All this we can read inscribed in this tomb

which will tell us of two more great ages on the Nile — the
Feudal Age and the Empire. We steam steadily southward,
and soon the river begins to wind from side to side of the
deep valley, carrying the steamer at times close under the
scarred and weatherworn cliffs (Fig. 69). As we scan the rocks

we look up to many a tomb-door cut in the face of the cliff, and leading to a tomb-chapel excavated in the rock (Fig. 57).

**99. The tombs of the Feudal Age**

These cliff-tombs looking down upon the river belonged to the Feudal Age of Egyptian history. The men buried in these cliff-tombs looked back across five centuries to their ancestors of the Pyramid Age, as we look back upon our European ancestors before the discovery of America. But the nobles who made these cliff-tombs succeeded in gaining greater power than their ancestors. They were granted lands by the king, under arrangements which in later Europe we call feudal. They were thus powerful barons, living like little kings on their broad estates, made up of the fertile fields upon which these tomb-doors now look down. This Feudal Age lasted for several centuries and was flourishing by 2000 B.C. Fragments from the libraries of these feudal barons — the oldest libraries in the world — have fortunately been discovered in their tombs. These oldest of all surviving books are in the form of rolls of papyrus, which once were packed in jars, neatly labeled, and ranged in rows on the noble's library shelves. Here are the most ancient storybooks in the world: tales of wanderings and adventures in Asia; tales of shipwreck at the gate of the unknown ocean beyond the Red Sea — the earliest " Sindbad the Sailor " (Fig. 58); and tales of wonders wrought by ancient wise men and magicians.

**100. Books on kindness and justice**

Some of these stories set forth the sufferings of the poor and the humble, and seek to stir the rulers to be just and kind in their treatment of the weaker classes. Some describe the wickedness of men and the hopelessness of the future. Others tell of a righteous ruler who is yet to come, a " good shepherd " they call him, meaning a good king, who shall bring in justice and happiness for all. We notice here a contrast with the Pyramid Age. With the in-coming of the Pyramid builders we saw a tremendous growth in power, in building, and in art; but the Feudal Age reveals progress also in a higher realm, that of conduct and character (see description under Fig. 57).

Probably a number of rolls were required to contain the drama of Osiris—a great play in which the life, death, burial, and resurrection of Osiris (§ 69) were pictured at an annual feast in which all the people loved to join. It is our earliest

FIG. 58. A PAGE FROM THE STORY OF THE SHIPWRECKED SAILOR, THE EARLIEST SINDBAD, AS READ BY THE BOYS AND GIRLS OF EGYPT FOUR THOUSAND YEARS AGO (ONE THIRD OF SIZE OF ORIGINAL)

This page reads: "Those who were on board perished, and not one of them escaped. Then I was cast upon an island by a wave of the great sea. I passed three days alone, with (only) my heart as my companion, sleeping in the midst of a shelter of trees, till daylight enveloped me. Then I crept out for aught to fill my mouth. I found figs and grapes there and all fine vegetables etc. . . ." The tale then tells of his seizure by an enormous serpent with a long beard, who proves to be the king of this distant island in the Red Sea, at the entrance of the Indian Ocean. He keeps the sailor three months, treats him kindly, and returns him with much treasure to Egypt. In form such a book was a single strip of papyrus paper, 5 or 6 to 10 or 12 inches wide, and often 15 to 30 or 40 feet long. When not in use this strip was kept rolled up, and thus the earliest books were rolls, looking, when small, like a diploma or, when large, like a roll of wall paper

known drama—a kind of Passion Play; but the rolls containing it have perished. There were also rolls containing songs and poems, like the beautiful morning hymn sung by the nobles of the Pharaoh's court in greeting to the sovereign with the

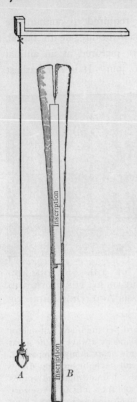

**FIG. 59. ANCIENT EGYP-
TIAN ASTRONOMICAL IN-
STRUMENT**

The oldest surviving astronomical device. It is now in the Berlin Museum.

**102. Books of science**

return of each new day. Another song in praise of the Pharaoh was arranged to be sung responsively by two groups at the great court festivals. It was constructed in parallel verses or lines, like the parallel lines of the Hebrew Psalms. It is the oldest surviving example of this form of poetry.

Very few rolls were needed to deal with the science of this time. The largest and the most valuable of all contained what they had learned about medicine and the organs of the human body. This oldest medical book, when unrolled, is to-day about sixty-six feet long and has recipes for all sorts of ailments. Some of them are still good and call for remedies which, like castor oil, are still in common use; others represent the ailment as due to demons, which were long believed to be the cause of disease. There are also rolls containing the simpler rules of arithmetic, based on the decimal system which we still use; others treat the beginnings of geometry and elementary algebra. Even observations

One part (*A*) is simply a plumb line with a handle attached at the top. It enabled the observer to hold the other part (*B*) directly over a given point on the ground while he sighted through the slot at the top toward some star like the North Star. By sighting over a rod between the observer and the North Star until the rod was exactly in line with the North Star, the astronomer could determine his meridian, observe each star that crossed it, measure time, and secure celestial data of value

of the heavenly bodies, with simple instruments, were made (Fig. 59); but these records, like those in geography, have been lost.

Along with this higher progress, the Pharaohs of the Feudal Age much improved the government. Every few years they made census lists to be used in taxation, and a few of these earliest census sheets in the world have survived. They erected huge earthen dikes and made vast basins, to store up the Nile waters for irrigation, thus greatly increasing the yield of the feudal lands and estates. They measured the height of the river from year to year, and their marks of the Nile levels are still to be found cut on the rocks at the Second Cataract. Thus nearly four thousand years ago they were already doing on a large scale what our government has only recently begun to do by its irrigation projects among our own arid lands.

103. Administration, and irrigation projects in the Feudal Age

At the same time these rulers of the Feudal Age reached out by sea for the wealth of other lands. Their fleets sailed over among the Ægean islands and probably controlled the large island of Crete (§§ 335–345). They dug a canal from the north end of the Red Sea westward to the nearest branch of the Nile in the eastern Delta, where the river divides into a number of mouths (see map, p. 36). The Pharaoh's Mediterranean ships could sail up the easternmost mouth of the Nile, then enter the canal and, passing eastward through it, reach the Red Sea. Thus the Mediterranean Sea and the Red Sea were first connected by this predecessor of the Suez Canal four thousand years ago. Such a connection was as important to the Egyptians as the Panama Canal is to us. Nile ships could likewise now sail from the eastern Delta directly to the land of Punt (§ 78) and to the straits leading to the Indian Ocean. These waters seemed to the sailors of the Feudal Age the end of the world, and their wondrous adventures there delighted many a circle of villagers on the feudal estates (Fig. 58).

104. Pharaoh's commerce by sea; a predecessor of the Suez Canal four thousand years ago

In this age the Pharaoh had organized a small standing army. He could now make his power felt both in north and south, in

105. Military expansion north and south, and the end of the Feudal Age

Palestine and in Nubia. He conquered the territory of Nubia as far south as the Second Cataract (see map, p. 36), and thus added two hundred miles of river to the kingdom of Egypt. Here he erected strong frontier fortresses against the Nubian tribes, and these fortresses still stand. The enlightened rule of the Pharaohs of the Feudal Age did much to prepare the way for Egyptian leadership in the early world. Three of these kings bore the name "Sesostris," which became one of the great and illustrious names in Egyptian history. But not long after 1800 B.C. the power of the Pharaohs of the Feudal Age suddenly declined and their line disappeared.

## SECTION 9. THE FOUNDING OF THE EMPIRE

106. The Nile voyage — arrival at Thebes

The monuments along the river banks have thus far told us the story of two of the three periods [1] into which the career of this great Nile people falls. After we have left the tombs of the Feudal Age and have continued our journey over four hundred miles southward from Cairo, all at once we catch glimpses of vast masses of stone masonry and lines of tall columns rising among the palms on the east side of the river. They are the ruins of the once great city of Thebes, which will tell us the story of the third period, the Empire.

107. Karnak — arrival of the horse in Egypt

Here we shall find not only a vast cemetery, but also great temples (see plan, p. 81). A walk around the Temple of Karnak at Thebes (Fig. 64) is as instructive to us in studying the Empire as we have found the Gizeh cemetery to be in studying the Pyramid Age. We find the walls of this immense temple covered with enormous sculptures in relief, depicting the wars of the Egyptians in Asia. We see the giant figure of the Pharaoh as he stands in his war chariot, scattering the enemy before his plunging horses (Fig. 60). The Pharaohs of the Pyramid Age had never seen a horse (§ 80), and this is the first time we

[1] These three ages are (1) the Pyramid Age, about 3000 to 2500 B.C. (Sections 6-7); (2) the Feudal Age, flourishing 2000 B.C. (Section 8); (3) the Empire, about 1580 to 1150 B.C. (Sections 9-11).

have met the horse on the ancient monuments. After the close
of the Feudal Age the animal began to be imported from Asia;
the chariot (Fig. 133) came with him, and Egypt, having learned
warfare on a scale unknown before, became a military empire.

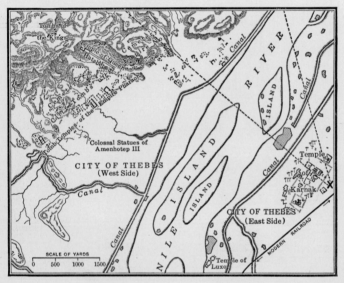

MAP OF EGYPTIAN THEBES

This map may be compared with the aëroplane view of Karnak (Fig. 64),
taken over point marked ×, and with the view of the western plain
toward the colossal statues of Amenhotep III and the western cliffs
(Fig. 69), in and along which lie the tombs of the vast cemetery. Before
it, and parallel with the cliffs, stretched a long line of temples facing
the great temples of Luxor and Karnak on the east side of the river.
The houses of the ancient city have passed away

The Pharaohs were now great generals with a well-organized
standing army made up chiefly of archers and heavy masses of
chariots. With these forces the Pharaoh conquered an empire
which extended from the Euphrates in Asia to the Fourth Cataract of the Nile in Africa (see map I, p. 184). By an empire we

108. Egypt
a military
empire

mean a group of nations subdued and ruled over by the most powerful among them. Government began with tiny city-states (§ 38), which gradually merged together into nations (§ 74); but the organization of men had now reached the point where

FIG. 60. A PHARAOH OF THE EMPIRE FIGHTING IN HIS CHARIOT

The tiny figures of the enemy are scattered beneath the Pharaoh's horses. This is one of an enormous series of such scenes, 170 feet long, carved in relief on the outside of the Great Hall of Karnak (Fig. 68). Such sculpture was brightly colored and served to enhance the architectural effect and to impress the people with the heroism of the Pharaoh. The color has now entirely disappeared, and the sculpture is much battered and weatherworn. This is the cause of the indistinctness in the above sketch

*many nations* were combined into an empire including a large part of the early oriental world. This world power of the Pharaohs lasted from the early sixteenth century to the twelfth century B.C. — something over four hundred years.

The Karnak Temple (Fig. 64), which stood in the once vast city of Thebes, is like a great historical volume telling us much of the story of the Egyptian Empire. Behind the great hall (Figs. 66 and 68) towers a huge obelisk, a shaft of granite in a single piece nearly a hundred feet high (Fig. 65). It was

109. The reign of Queen Hatshepsut, the first great woman in history

FIG. 61. TRANSPORTATION OF QUEEN HATSHEPSUT'S 350-TON OBELISKS DOWN THE NILE (FIFTEENTH CENTURY B.C.)

The two obelisks are lying base to base on a large Nile barge some 300 feet long. The obelisks are each 97½ feet long and weigh about 350 tons each, the two making a burden of some 700 tons in the barge. It is being towed by thirty tugboats in three rows of ten each. Each tugboat has thirty-two oarsmen, making nine hundred and sixty oarsmen in all. Under the guidance of the engineers in the other small boats these men towed the obelisks downstream from the granite quarries of the First Cataract to Thebes — a distance of about 150 miles. Under each obelisk we can see the sledge on which it was dragged on shore to the place where they were both set up in the Karnak Temple (Fig. 64). The scene is restored from a relief on the wall of the queen's temple at Thebes

erected early in the Empire by the first great woman in history, Queen Hatshepsut. There were once two of these enormous monuments (see Fig. 65), and it was no small task to cut out two such blocks as these from the granite quarries at the First Cataract, transport them on a huge boat down the river (Fig. 61), and erect them in this temple. But the queen did not stop with this achievement. She even dispatched an expedition of five ships (Fig. 62) through the Red Sea to Punt (§ 78), to bring back the luxuries of tropical Africa for another beautiful terraced temple which she was erecting against the western cliffs at Thebes (Plan, p. 81). Such achievements show what an efficient and successful ruler this first great woman was.

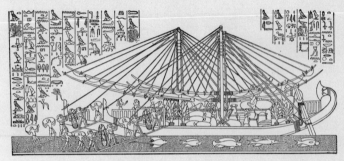

FIG. 62. PART OF THE FLEET OF QUEEN HATSHEPSUT LOADING IN THE LAND OF PUNT

Only two of Hatshepsut's fleet of five ships are shown. The sails on the long spars are furled and the vessels are moored. The sailors are carrying the cargo up the gangplanks, and one of them is teasing an ape on the roof of the cabin. The inscriptions above the ships read: "The loading of the ships very heavily with marvels of the country of Punt; all goodly fragrant woods of God's-Land [the East], heaps of myrrh-resin, with fresh myrrh trees, with ebony and pure ivory, with green gold of Emu, with cinnamon wood, khesyt wood, with two kinds of incense, eye-cosmetic, with apes, monkeys, dogs, and with skins of the southern panther, with natives and their children. Never was brought the like of this for any king who has been since the beginning." The scene is carved on the wall of the queen's temple at Thebes, in the garden of which she planted the myrrh trees

**110. The end of Hatshepsut and the triumph of Thutmose III**

As we examine the obelisk of Hatshepsut we find around the base the remains of stone masonry with which it was once walled in almost up to the top. This was done by the queen's half-brother and husband, Thutmose III, in order to cover up the records which proclaimed to the world the hated rule of a woman. Thus Thutmose III had the names of the queen and the men who aided her all cut out and obliterated, including that of the skillful architect and engineer who erected this obelisk and its companion. But the masonry covering the obelisk has fallen down, and it still proclaims the fame of Hatshepsut.

Thutmose III (Fig. 63) was the first great general in history, the Napoleon of Egypt, the greatest of the Egyptian conquerors.

111. The campaigns of Thutmose III (1501– 1447 B.C.)

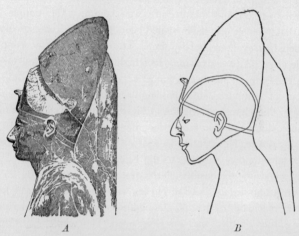

*A*          *B*

FIG. 63. PORTRAIT OF THUTMOSE III, THE NAPOLEON OF ANCIENT EGYPT (*A*), COMPARED WITH HIS MUMMY (*B*)

This portrait (*A*), carved in granite, can be compared with the actual face of the great conqueror as we have it in his mummy. Such a comparison is shown in *B*, where the profile of this granite portrait (outside lines) is placed over the profile of Thutmose III's mummy (inside lines). The correspondence is very close, showing great accuracy in the portrait art of this age

He ruled for over fifty years, beginning about 1500 B.C. On the temple walls at Karnak we can read the story of nearly twenty years of warfare, during which Thutmose crushed the cities and kingdoms of Western Asia and welded them into an enduring empire. At the same time his war fleet carried his power even to the Ægean, and one of his generals became governor of the Ægean islands (Fig. 143; see map I, p. 184).

## SECTION 10. THE HIGHER LIFE OF THE EMPIRE

**112. Temple architecture**

The wealth which the Pharaohs captured in Asia and Nubia during the Empire brought them power and magnificence unknown to the world before, especially as shown in their vast and splendid buildings. A new and impressive chapter in the history of art and architecture was begun. The temple of Karnak, which we have visited, contains the greatest colonnaded hall ever erected by man. The columns of the central aisle (Fig. 68) are sixty-nine feet high. The vast capital forming the summit of *each* column is large enough to contain a group of a hundred men standing crowded upon it at the same time. The clerestory windows (Fig. 68) on each side of these giant columns are no longer low, depressed openings, as in the Pyramid Age (Fig. 55 and Fig. 271, *1*), but they have now become fine, tall windows, showing us the Egyptian clerestory hall on its way to become the basilica church of much later times (Fig. 271).

**113. The surroundings of the Empire temples at Thebes**

Such temples as these at Thebes were seen through the deep green of clustering palms, among towering obelisks and colossal statues of the Pharaohs (Fig. 69). The whole was bright with color, flashing at many a point with gold and silver. Mirrored in the unruffled surface of the temple lake (Fig. 64), it made a picture of such splendor as the ancient world had never seen before. As the visitor entered he found himself

---

* This point of view is behind (east of) the great Karnak Temple at point marked × in plan (p. 81). We look northwestward across the Temple and the river to the western cliffs (cf. plan, p. 81). From the rear gate below us (lower right-hand corner of view) to the tall front wall nearest the river, the Temple is nearly a quarter of a mile long, and was nearly two thousand years in course of construction. The oldest portions were built by the kings of the Feudal Age, and the latest, the front wall, by the Greek kings (the Ptolemies, Section 66). The standing obelisk of Queen Hatshepsut (Fig. 65) can be seen rising in the middle of the Temple. Beyond it is the vast colonnaded Hall of Karnak (Figs. 66 and 68), on the outside wall of which are the great war reliefs (Fig. 60). Hidden by the huge front wall is the Avenue of Sphinxes (Fig. 67). On the left we see the pool — all that is left of the sacred lake (§ 113).

FIG. 64. THE GREAT TEMPLE OF KARNAK AND THE NILE
VALLEY AT THEBES SEEN FROM AN AËROPLANE *

The area included in this view will be found bounded by two diverging dotted lines on the map of Thebes (p. 81). It will be seen that
our view includes only a portion of the ancient city, which extended
up and down both sides of the river. For description of Karnak, see
note on opposite page

From an etching by George T. Plowman

FIG. 65. THE OBELISKS OF QUEEN HATSHEPSUT AND HER FATHER
THUTMOSE I AT KARNAK

The further obelisk is that of the queen. It was one of a pair transported
from the First Cataract (Fig. 61), but its mate has fallen and broken into
pieces. The shaft is 8½ feet thick at the base, and the human figure by
contrast conveys some idea of the vast size of the monument. Its position in the temple can be seen from the aëroplane view (Fig. 64)

From a pen etching by Sears Gallagher

FIG. 66. THE COLOSSAL COLUMNS OF THE NAVE IN THE GREAT
HALL OF KARNAK

These are the columns of the middle two rows in Fig. 68. On the top
of the capital of each one of these columns a hundred men can stand **at
once.** These great columns may be seen in the aëroplane view (Fig. 64)
just at the left of the two obelisks

From an etching by George T. Plowman

FIG. 67. AVENUE OF RAMS LEADING FROM THE KARNAK TEMPLE TO THE NILE

The temple is just behind us as we look toward the river, here too low to be seen. Beyond rise the heights of the western desert, where the kings and nobles of the Empire were buried. The low buildings on the right are part of a modern village, seen between the temple and the river in the aeroplane view (Fig. 64)

in a spacious and sunlit court, surrounded by splendid colon-naded porches. Beyond, all was mystery, as he looked into the somber forest of vast columns in the hall behind the court (Figs. 66 and 68). These temples were connected by imposing

FIG. 68. RESTORATION OF THE GREAT HALL OF KARNAK, AN-CIENT THEBES — LARGEST BUILDING OF THE EGYPTIAN EMPIRE

With the wealth taken in Asia the Egyptian conquerors of the Empire enabled their architects to build the greatest colonnaded hall ever erected by man. It is 338 feet wide and 170 feet deep, furnishing a floor area about equal to that of the cathedral of Notre Dame in Paris, although this is only a single room of the Temple. There are one hundred and thirty-six columns in sixteen rows. The nave (three central aisles) is 79 feet high and contains twelve columns in two rows, which the architects have made much higher than the rest, in order to insert lofty clerestory windows on each side. Compare the very low windows of the earliest clerestory (Fig. 55 and Fig. 271, *1* and *2*). In this higher form the clerestory passed over to Europe (Fig. 271)

avenues of sphinxes (Fig. 67), and thus grew up at Thebes the first great "monumental city" ever built by man — a city which as a whole was itself a vast and imposing monument.[1]

Much of the grandeur of Egyptian architecture was due to the sculptor and the painter. The colonnades, with flower capi-tals, were colored to suggest the plants they represented. The

114. Painting and sculpture in the temples

[1] City plans which treat a whole city as a symmetrical and harmonious unit are now beginning to be made in America.

Fig. 69. GIGANTIC PORTRAIT STATUES OF AMENHOTEP III AT THEBES (1400 B.C.)

They are 70 feet high; the right-hand figure bears many inscriptions of eminent Greek and Roman visitors
In the cliffs behind is the vast cemetery of Thebes (§§ 115–117, and plan, p. 81)

FIG. 70. COLOSSAL PORTRAIT FIGURE OF RAMSES II AT ABU-
SIMBEL IN EGYPTIAN NUBIA

Four such statues, 75 feet high, adorn the front of this temple, which, like
the statues, is hewn from the sandstone cliffs. The faces are better preserved than that of the Great Sphinx (Fig. 54) or the portrait statues of
Amenhotep III (Fig. 69), and we can here see that such vast figures were
portraits. The face of Ramses II here closely resembles that of his
mummy (Fig. 123). (From a photograph taken from the top of the crown
of one of the statues by The University of Chicago Expedition)

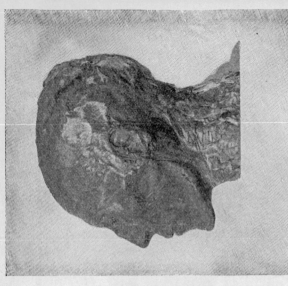

FIG. 71. REMARKABLE LIMESTONE PORTRAIT HEAD OF IKHNATON, THE EARLIEST MONOTHEIST

Recently discovered by Borchardt at Amarna (§ 119). It is carved in limestone and conveys a wonderful impression of the dreamy beauty of this extraordinary young king (§§ 118–120)

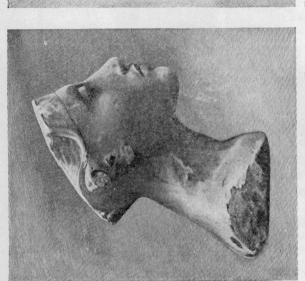

FIG. 72. HEAD OF THE MUMMY OF SETI I, FATHER OF RAMSES II, NOW IN THE CAIRO MUSEUM

One of the royal bodies discovered at Thebes (§ 125). The head of Seti is the best preserved of the entire group, but the royal mummies are all beginning to shor evidences of decay

vast battle scenes, carved on the temple wall (Fig. 60), were painted in bright colors. The portrait statues of the Pharaohs, set up before these temples, were often so large that they rose above the towers of the temple front itself, — the tallest part of the building, — and they could be seen for miles around (Figs. 69 and 70). The sculptors could cut these colossal figures from a single block, although they were sometimes eighty or ninety feet high and weighed as much as a thousand tons. This is a burden equal to the load drawn by a modern freight train, but unlike the trainload it was not cut up into small units of light weight, convenient for handling and loading. Nevertheless, the engineers of the Empire moved many such vast figures for hundreds of miles, using the same methods employed in moving obelisks. It is in works of this massive, monumental character that the art of Egypt excelled (Fig. 70).

Two enormous portraits of Amenhotep III, the most luxurious and splendid of the Egyptian emperors, still stand on the western plain of Thebes (Fig. 69), across the river from Karnak. As we approach them we see rising behind them the majestic western cliffs in which are cut hundreds of tomb-chapels belonging to the great men of the Empire. Here were buried the able generals who marched with the Pharaohs on their campaigns in Asia and in Nubia. Here lay the gifted artists and architects who built the vast monuments we have just visited, and made Thebes the first great "monumental city" of the ancient world. Here in these tomb-chapels we may read their names and often long accounts of their lives. Here is the story of the general who saved Thutmose III's life, in a great elephant hunt in Asia, by rushing in and cutting off the trunk of an enraged elephant which was pursuing the king. Here is the tomb of the general who captured the city of Joppa in Palestine by concealing his men in panniers loaded on the backs of donkeys, and thus bringing them into the city as merchandise — an adventure which afterward furnished part of the story of "Ali Baba and the Forty Thieves."

115. Tombs of the great men of the Empire

The very furniture which these great men used in their houses was put into their tombs. In a neighboring valley was recently found the tomb of the parents of Amenhotep III's queen. Their beautiful villa among the Theban gardens was filled with gorgeous furniture which their royal son-in-law, Amenhotep III, had given to them. When this worthy old couple died, the king had them wonderfully embalmed, and much of the furniture which he had given to them (Fig. 73) was carried to the cemetery and deposited in their tomb, including even the gold-covered chariot in which the old couple were accustomed to take their daily airing thirty-three hundred years ago. Here we find chairs covered with gold and silver and fitted with soft leathern cushions, a bed of sumptuous workmanship, jewel boxes, and perfume caskets. They are works of art — real triumphs of the skill of the Empire craftsmen — and almost as well preserved, leather cushion and all, as when first made. Even the shadow clock, which belonged to the furniture of a well-equipped household, still survives (Fig. 74).

FIG. 73. ARMCHAIR FROM THE HOUSE OF AN EGYPTIAN NOBLE OF THE EMPIRE

This chair with other furniture from his house was placed in his tomb at Thebes in the early part of the fourteenth century B.C. There it remained for nearly thirty-three hundred years, till it was discovered in 1905 and removed to the National Museum at Cairo (§ 116)

These tombs show us also how much farther the Egyptian has advanced in religion since the days of the pyramids of Gizeh. Each of these great men buried in the Theban cemetery looked forward to a judgment in the next world, where Osiris (§ 69) was the great judge and king. Every good man might rise from the dead as Osiris had done, but in the presence of Osiris he would be obliged to see his soul weighed in the

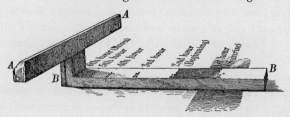

Fig. 74. The Oldest Clock in the World — an Egyptian Shadow Clock

In sunny Egypt a shadow clock was a very practical instrument. In the morning the crosspiece (*AA*) was turned toward the east, and its shadow fell on the long arm (*BB*), where we see it at the first hour. As the sun rose higher the shadow shortened and its place on the scale showed the hour, which could be read in figures for six hours until noon. At noon the head (*AA*) was turned around to the west and the *lengthening* afternoon shadow on the long arm (*BB*) was measured in the same way. It was from the introduction of such Egyptian clocks that the twelve-hour day reached Europe. This clock bears the name of Thutmose III and is therefore about thirty-four hundred years old. Nearly a thousand years later such clocks were adopted by the Greeks. It is now in the Berlin Museum. The headpiece (*AA*) is restored after Borchardt

balances over against the symbol of truth and justice (headpiece, p. 74). The dead man's friends put into his coffin a roll of papyrus containing prayers and magic charms which would aid him in the hereafter, and among these was a picture of the judgment. We now call this roll the " Book of the Dead " (headpiece, p. 74).

When the Empire was about two hundred years old, Amenhotep III's youthful son, Amenhotep IV, became Pharaoh in his father's place. He believed in only one god, the Sun-god,

**118. The religious revolution of Amenhotep IV (Ikhnaton)**

and he began a new and remarkable chapter in the religious history of Egypt by the attempt to destroy the old gods of Egypt and to induce the people to adopt the exclusive worship of the Sun-god. He commanded that throughout the great Empire, including its people in both Africa and Asia, only the Sun-god, whom he called *Aton*, should be worshiped. In order that the people might forget the old gods, he closed all the temples and cast out their priests. Everywhere he also had the names of the gods erased and cut out, especially on all temple walls. He particularly hated Amon, or Amen, the great Theban god of the Empire whose temple we visited at Karnak. His own royal name, Amen-hotep (meaning " Amen rests "), contained this god *Amen's* name, and he therefore changed his name Amenhotep to Ikhnaton, which means " Aton (the Sun-god) is satisfied."

**119. Ikhnaton's new capital, now called Amarna**

Ikhnaton, as we must now call him, finally forsook magnificent Thebes, where there were so many temples of the old gods, and built a new city farther down the river, which he named " Horizon of Aton." It is now called Amarna (see map, p. 36). The city was forsaken a few years after Ikhnaton's death, and beneath the rubbish of its ruins to-day we find the lower portions of the walls of the houses and palaces which once adorned it. Recently the ruins of the studio of a sculptor were uncovered there and found to contain many beautiful works, which have greatly increased our knowledge of the wonderful sculpture of the age (Fig. 71). The cliffs behind the city still contain the cliff-tombs of the followers whom the young king was able to convert to the new faith, and in them we find engraved on the walls beautifully sculptured scenes picturing the life of the now forgotten city.

**120. Ikhnaton's hymns to Aton, the sole God**

In these Amarna tomb-chapels we may still read on the walls the hymns of praise to the Sun-god, which Ikhnaton himself wrote. They show us the simplicity and beauty of the young king's faith in the sole God. He had gained the belief that one God created not only all the lower creatures but also all races of men, both Egyptians and foreigners. Moreover, the king saw in his God a kindly Father, who maintained all his creatures by his goodness, so that even the birds in the marshes were aware of his kindness, and uplifted their wings like arms to praise him, as a beautiful line in one of the hymns tells us. In all the progress of men which we have followed through thousands of years, no one had ever before caught such a vision of the great Father of all. Such a belief in one god is called monotheism, which literally means one-god-ism.

## Section 11. The Decline and Fall of the Egyptian Empire

A new faith like this could not be understood by the common people of the fourteenth century B.C. The country was full of the discontented priests of the old gods, and equally dissatisfied soldiers of the neglected army. The priests secretly plotted with the troops against the king, and they found willing ears among the idle soldiery. Confusion and disturbance arose in Egypt, and the conquered countries in Asia were preparing to revolt.

121. Ikhnaton's troubles at home

The consequences in Asia have been revealed to us by a remarkable group of over three hundred letters, part of the royal records stored in one of Ikhnaton's government offices at Amarna. Here they had lain for over three thousand years, when they were found some years ago by native diggers. They are written on clay tablets (§ 147), in Babylonian writing (§ 148). Most of these letters proved to be from the kings of Western Asia to the Pharaoh, and they form the oldest international correspondence in the world (Fig. 126). They show us how these kings were gradually shaking off the rule of the Pharaoh, so that the Egyptian Empire in Asia was rapidly falling to pieces. The Pharaoh's *northern* territory in Syria (see map I, p. 184) was being taken by the Hittites, who came in from Asia Minor (§ 359), while his *southern* territory in

122. Ikhnaton's troubles abroad; the Amarna letters

Palestine was being invaded by the Hebrews, who were drifting in from the desert (§ 293).

**123.** Death of Ikhnaton; partial restoration of the Egyptian Empire, last great power of Age of Bronze; coming of iron

In the midst of these troubles at home and abroad the young Ikhnaton died, leaving no son behind him. Although a visionary and an idealist, he was the most remarkable genius of the early oriental world before the Hebrews; but the faith in one god which he attempted to introduce perished with him. A new line of kings, the greatest of whom were Seti I (Fig. 72) and his son Ramses II (Fig. 123), after desperate efforts were able to restore to some extent the Egyptian Empire. But they were unable to drive the Hittites out of Syria, for these Hittite invaders from Asia Minor possessed iron (§ 360), which they could use for weapons, while the declining Egyptian Empire was the last great power of the Age of Bronze.

**124.** Foreign mercenaries in the Egyptian army; invasion of the Northerners; fall of the Empire

At Thebes the symptoms of the coming fall may be seen even at the present day. If we examine the great war pictures on the Theban temples which we have been visiting, we find in the battle scenes of the later Empire great numbers of foreigners serving in the Egyptian army. This shows that the Egyptians had finally lost their temporary interest in war and were calling in foreigners to fight their battles. Among these strangers are the peoples of the northern Mediterranean whom we left there in the Late Stone Age (§ 44). Here on the Egyptian monuments we find them after they have got from eastern peoples the art of using metal. With huge bronze swords in their hands we see them serving as hired soldiers in the Egyptian army (tailpiece, p. 519). They and other Mediterranean foreigners (§ 378) finally invaded Egypt in such numbers that the weakened Egyptian Empire fell, in the middle of the twelfth century B.C.

**125.** The bodies of the Egyptian emperors

The great Pharaohs, who maintained themselves for over four hundred years as emperors, were buried here at Thebes. On the other side of the cliffs behind the huge statues of Amenhotep III (Fig. 69) is a wild and desolate valley formed by a deep depression in the western desert (Fig. 75). Here, in over forty vast rock-hewn galleries reaching hundreds of feet into the mountain, the bodies of the Egyptian emperors were laid to rest, only to suffer pillage and robbery after the fall of the Empire. Their weak successors as kings at Thebes hurried the royal bodies from one hiding place to another, and finally concealed them in a secret chamber hewn for this purpose in the western cliffs. Here they lay undisturbed for nearly three thousand years, until, in 1881, they were discovered and removed to the National Museum at Cairo, where they still rest (cf. Fig. 72). Thus we are still able to look into the very faces of these lords of Egypt and Western Asia who lived and ruled from thirty-one hundred to thirty-five hundred years ago.

Fig. 75. Valley at Thebes where the Pharaohs of the Empire were buried

In the Empire (after 1600 B.C.) the Pharaohs had ceased to erect pyramids. They excavated their tombs in the cliff walls of this valley (see plan, p. 81), penetrating in long galleries hundreds of feet into the rock. Taken from here and concealed near by, the bodies of many of the Pharaohs, although long ago stripped of their valuables by tomb robbers, have survived and now lie in the National Museum of Egypt at Cairo (Fig. 72)

Thus ends the story of the Empire at Thebes. The pyramids, tombs, and temples along the Nile have told us the history of early Egypt in three epochs: the Pyramids of Gizeh and the neighboring cemeteries of Memphis have told us about the Pyramid Age; the cliff-tombs, which we found on the Nile voyage, have revealed the history of the Feudal Age; and the temples and cliff-tombs of Thebes have given us the story of the Empire. The Nile has become for us a great volume of history. Let us remember, however,

**126.** Final significance of the Nile voyage

that, preceding these three great chapters of civilization on the Nile, we also found here the earlier story of how man passed from Stone Age barbarism to a civilization possessed of metal, writing, and government (§ 66). On the other hand, as we

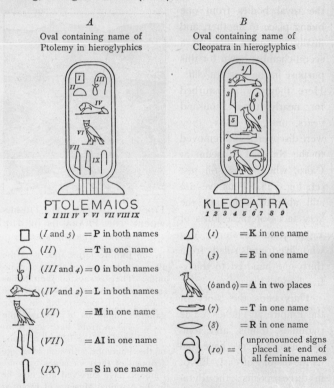

| A | B |
|---|---|
| Oval containing name of Ptolemy in hieroglyphics | Oval containing name of Cleopatra in hieroglyphics |

PTOLEMAIOS
I II III IV V VI VII VIII IX

KLEOPATRA
1 2 3 4 5 6 7 8 9

(*I* and *5*) = **P** in both names
(*II*) = **T** in one name
(*III* and *4*) = **O** in both names
(*IV* and *2*) = **L** in both names
(*VI*) = **M** in one name
(*VII*) = **AI** in one name
(*IX*) = **S** in one name

(*1*) = **K** in one name
(*3*) = **E** in one name
(*6* and *9*) = **A** in two places
(*7*) = **T** in one name
(*8*) = **R** in one name
(*10*) = { unpronounced signs placed at end of all feminine names

FIG. 76. DIAGRAM SHOWING THE FIRST STEPS IN CHAMPOLLION'S DECIPHERMENT OF EGYPTIAN HIEROGLYPHICS *

look forward, we should remember also that the three great chapters did not end the story; for Egyptian institutions and civilization continued far down into the Christian Age and greatly influenced later history in Europe (§§ 657, 981, and 1063).

## Section 12. The Decipherment of Egyptian Writing by Champollion

Finally, our Nile voyage has also shown us how we gain knowledge of ancient men and their deeds from the monuments and records which they have left behind. We have also noticed how greatly the use of the earliest *written* documents aids us in putting together the story. If we had made our journey up

127. In modern times no one able to read Egyptian writing before 1822

\* Champollion found an obelisk bearing on its *base* a Greek inscription, showing that the obelisk belonged to a king Ptolemy and his queen Cleopatra. The obelisk *shaft* bore an inscription in hieroglyphics which he therefore thought must somewhere contain the names Ptolemy and Cleopatra. Other scholars had shown that the ovals, or "cartouches" (see opposite page), so common on Egyptian monuments, contained royal names. Examination showed *two* such ovals on the shaft of the obelisk. He concluded that the hieroglyphs in these two ovals spelled the names Ptolemy and Cleopatra. He then proceeded to compare them with the Greek spelling of Ptolemy (*Ptolemaios*) and Cleopatra. These Greek spellings (in *our* letters) will be found in Fig. 76, each paired with its corresponding hieroglyphic form. All signs and letters in the left pair are numbered with Roman numerals, and in the right pair with Arabic numerals. The first sign (I) in oval *A* is an oblong rectangle, and if it really is the first letter in Ptolemy's name, it must be the letter P. Now the fifth letter in Cleopatra's name is also a P, and so the fifth sign in the oval *B* ought also to be an oblong rectangle. To Champollion's delight oval *B* did not disappoint him, and sign 5 proved to be an oblong rectangle. He was at first troubled by the fact that in his next comparison, II and 7 in the two ovals did not prove to be alike as the sign for T, but he concluded that 7 must be a second form for T, and he was right. The next two signs in oval *A* (III and IV) corresponded exactly with 4 and 2 in oval *B*, and showed him that he was certainly on the right road. Although the vowels (e.g. VII and 3) caused him some trouble, he soon saw that Egyptian was inaccurate in writing the vowels, or even omitted them (see Fig. 29). From these two names he had proved that the Egyptians possessed an alphabet and not merely signs for whole syllables or whole words. He had also learned the sounds of twelve of the letters (see table of signs below the names) and laid the foundation for completing the decipherment, by the aid of the Rosetta Stone (Fig. 207), which he then for the first time understood how to use, after scholars had been working on it in vain for over twenty years. This was in 1822, and Champollion then announced his discovery to the French Academy in Paris.

the Nile a hundred years ago, however, we would have had no one to tell us what these Egyptian records meant. For the last man who could read Egyptian hieroglyphs died over a thousand years ago. A hundred years ago, therefore, no one understood the curious writing which travelers found covering the great monuments along the Nile.

**128. Champollion's first efforts at decipherment**

For a long time scholars puzzled over the strange Nile records, but made little progress in reading them. Then a young Frenchman named Champollion took up the problem, and after years of discouraging failure he began to make progress. He discovered the names of Ptolemy and Cleopatra written in hieroglyphics. He was thus able to determine the sounds of twelve hieroglyphic signs which he proved to be alphabetic (see explanation of Fig. 76). Champollion was then able to read several other royal names, and in 1822, in a famous letter to the French Academy, he announced his discovery and explained the steps he had taken.

**129. Champollion's successful decipherment**

It was not until this point was reached that he was able to make use of the well-known Rosetta Stone, which was therefore not the first key employed by Champollion. But the Rosetta Stone (Fig. 207) then enabled him rapidly to increase his list of known hieroglyphic signs and to learn the meanings of words and the construction of sentences. When he died, in 1832, he had written a little grammar and prepared a small dictionary of hieroglyphic. There remains even now much to learn about the Egyptian language and writing, but Champollion's marvelous achievement laid the foundations of a new science now called Egyptology, which has restored to the world a lost chapter of human history nearly three thousand years in length. Thus the monuments of the Nile have gained a voice and have told us their wonderful story of how man gained civilization.

**130. Transition to Asia**

In a similar way the monuments discovered along the Tigris and Euphrates rivers in Asia have been deciphered and made to tell their story. They show us that, following the Egyptians, the peoples of Asia emerged from barbarism, gained industries, learned the use of metals, devised a system of writing, and finally rose to the leading position of power in the ancient world. We must therefore turn, in the next chapter, to the story of the early Orient in Asia.

## QUESTIONS

SECTION 8. What ages do the monuments up the Nile reveal to us? Describe the rule of a Feudal Age baron. Describe his library. What kind of progress had been made since the Pyramid Age? Describe the science of the time. What great commercial link between two seas was created?

SECTION 9. Write a description of what you see from an aëroplane over the east end of the Temple of Karnak. How did the Pharaohs who built Karnak differ from those who built the pyramids? Who was the first great woman in history? Tell something of her reign. Tell about the reign of the greatest Egyptian general. What is an empire? What was the extent of the Egyptian Empire?

SECTION 10. What did the Egyptian emperors do with the wealth gained from subject peoples? Describe an empire temple and its surroundings. Describe the great Karnak hall, and tell how the clerestory was improved. Give an account of the Theban cemetery and what it contains. Who tried to introduce the earliest belief in one god? Describe the attempt.

SECTION 11. What were the consequences of Ikhnaton's movement? Tell about the Amarna letters. What Northerners held Syria, and what new weapons did they have? What do the war pictures at Thebes show us about the Egyptian army? What foreigners invaded Egypt and aided in destroying the Empire? What happened to the bodies of the emperors? Summarize the ages we have learned along the Nile from the pyramids to Thebes.

SECTION 12. Why were our great-grandfathers unable to read hieroglyphic? Who deciphered it, and when? What Egyptian sign represents the first letter in Ptolemy's name? What Egyptian sign represents the fifth sign in Cleopatra's name? Compare the fourth Egyptian sign in Ptolemy's name with the second sign in Cleopatra's name. Would you call this an accident or proof that the lion equals *L*? What monument did Champollion next use? Describe it (Fig. 207).

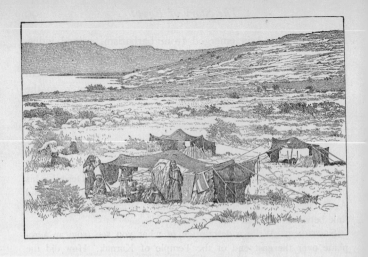

# CHAPTER IV

## WESTERN ASIA: BABYLONIA

### Section 13. The Lands and Races of Western Asia

**131. Water boundaries of Western Asia; mountainous north, desert south**

The westernmost extension of Asia is an irregular region roughly included within the circuit of waters marked out by the Caspian and Black seas on the north, by the Mediterranean and Red seas on the west, and by the Indian Ocean and the Persian Gulf on the south and east. It is a region consisting chiefly of mountains in the north and desert in the south. The earliest home of men in this great arena of Western Asia is a borderland between the desert and the mountains, a kind of cultivable fringe of the desert, a fertile crescent having the mountains on one side and the desert on the other.

NOTE. The above scene shows us the Semitic nomads on the Fertile Crescent along the Sea of Galilee. In spring the region is richly overgrown, but the vegetation soon fades. The dark camel's-hair tents of these wandering shepherds are easily carried from place to place as they seek new pasturage (§ 134). They live on the milk and flesh of the flocks.

This fertile crescent is approximately a semicircle, with the open side toward the south, having the west end at the south-east corner of the Mediterranean, the center directly north of Arabia, and the east end at the north end of the Persian Gulf (see map, p. 102). It lies like an army facing south, with one wing stretching along the eastern shore of the Mediterranean and the other reaching out to the Persian Gulf, while the center has its back against the northern mountains. The end of the western wing is Palestine; Assyria makes up a large part of the center; while the end of the eastern wing is Babylonia.

This great semicircle, for lack of a name, may be called the Fertile Crescent.[1] It may also be likened to the shores of a desert-bay, upon which the mountains behind look down — a bay not of water but of sandy waste, some five hundred miles across, forming a northern extension of the Arabian desert and sweeping as far north as the latitude of the northeast corner of the Mediterranean. This desert-bay is a limestone plateau of some height — too high indeed to be watered by the Tigris and Euphrates, which have cut cañons obliquely across it. Nevertheless, after the meager winter rains, wide tracts of the northern desert-bay are clothed with scanty grass, and spring thus turns the region for a short time into grass-lands. The history of Western Asia may be described as an age-long struggle between the mountain peoples of the north and the desert wanderers of these grasslands — a struggle which is still going on — for the possession of the Fertile Crescent, the shores of the desert-bay.

Arabia is totally lacking in rivers and enjoys but a few weeks of rain in midwinter; hence it is a desert very little of which is habitable. Its people are and have been from the remotest ages a great white race called Semites. The Semites have always been divided into many tribes and groups, just as

[1] There is no name, either geographical or political, which includes all of this great semicircle (see map, p. 102). Hence we are obliged to coin a term and call it the Fertile Crescent.

were the American Indians, whom we call Sioux, or Seminoles, or Iroquois. So we shall find many tribal or group names among the Semites. With two of these we are familiar — the Arabs, and the Hebrews whose descendants dwell among us. They all spoke and still speak dialects of the same tongue, of which Hebrew was one. For ages they have moved up and down the habitable portions of the Arabian world, seeking pasturage for their flocks and herds (headpiece, p. 100). Such wandering shepherds are called nomads, and we remember how their manner of life arose after the domestication of sheep and goats (see §§ 35–36).

**135. Ceaseless shift of the nomad from the desert to the Fertile Crescent** From the earliest times, when the spring grass of the northern wilderness is gone, they have been constantly drifting in from the sandy sea upon the shores of the northern desert-bay. If they can secure a footing there, they slowly make the transition from the *wandering* life of the desert nomad to the *settled* life of the agricultural peasant (see § 36). This slow shift at times swells into a great tidal wave of migration, when the wild hordes of the wilderness roll in upon the fertile shores of the desert-bay — a human tide from the desert to the towns which they overwhelm. We can see this process going on for thousands of years. Among such movements we are familiar with the passage of the Hebrews from the desert into Palestine, as described in the Bible, and some readers will recall the invasions of the Arab hosts which, when converted to Mohammedanism, even reached Europe and threatened to girdle the Mediterranean (§ 1155). After they had adopted a settled town life, the colonies of the Semites stretched far westward through the Mediterranean, especially in northern Africa, even to southern Spain and the Atlantic (see diagram, Fig. 112, and map, p. 288). But it took many centuries for the long line of their settlements to creep slowly westward until it reached the Atlantic, and we must begin with the Semites in the desert.

Out on the wide reaches of the desert there are no boundaries; the pasturage is free as air to the first comer. No man

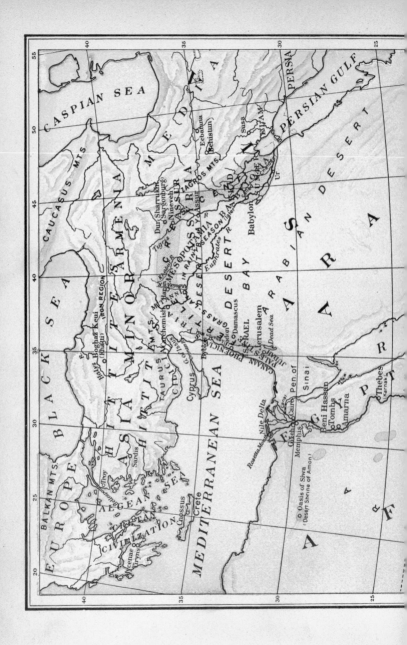

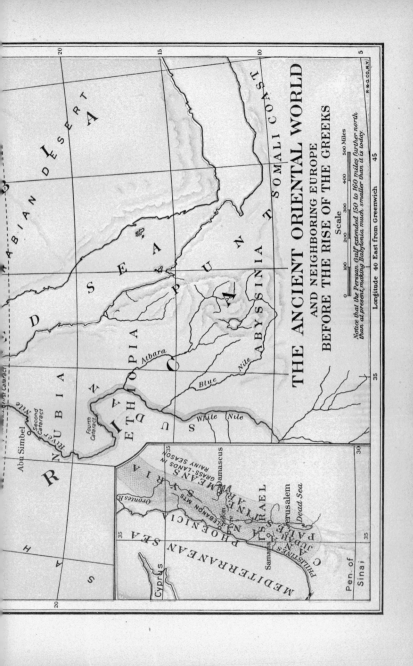

THE ANCIENT ORIENTAL WORLD AND NEIGHBORING EUROPE BEFORE THE RISE OF THE GREEKS

of the tribe owns land; there are no landholding rich and no landless poor. The men of the desert know no law. The keen-eyed desert marauder looks with envy across the hills dotted with the flocks of the neighboring tribe, which may be his when he has slain the solitary shepherd at the well. But if he does so, he knows that his *own* family will suffer death or heavy damages, not at the hands of the State, but at the hands of the slain shepherd's family. This custom, known as "blood revenge," has a restraining influence like that of law. Under such conditions there is no State. Writing and records are unknown, industries are practically nonexistent, and the desert tribesmen lead a life of complete freedom. The Turkish government owning Arabia to-day is as powerless to control the wandering Arabs of the wilderness as were formerly our own authorities in suppressing the lawlessness of our own herdsmen whom we called cowboys.

**136.** Lack of institutions and industries among the Semitic nomads of Arabia

The tribesmen drift with their flocks along the margin of the Fertile Crescent till they discern a town among the palm groves. Objects of picturesque interest to the curious eyes of the townsmen, they appear in the market place to traffic for the weapons, utensils, and raiment with which the nomad cannot dispense (headpiece, p. 197). They soon learn to carry goods from place to place and thus become not only the common carriers of the settled communities but also traders on their own account, fearlessly leading their caravans across the wastes of the desert-bay, lying like a sea between Syria-Palestine and Babylonia. They became the greatest merchants of the ancient world, as their Hebrew descendants among us still are at the present day.

**137.** Traffic and the caravan

The wilderness is the nomad's home. Its vast solitudes have tinged his soul with solemnity. His imagination peoples the far reaches of the desert with invisible and uncanny creatures, who inhabit every rock and tree, hilltop and spring. These creatures are his gods, whom he believes he can control by the utterance of magic charms — the earliest prayers. He believes

**138.** Religion of the nomad

that such charms render these uncanny gods powerless to do him injury and compel them to grant him aid.

**139.** The tribal god of the nomad

The nomad pictures each one of these beings as controlling only a little corner of the great world, perhaps only a well and its surrounding pastures. At the next well, only a day's march away, there is another god, belonging to the next tribe. For each tribe have a favorite or tribal god, who, as they believe, journeys with them from pasture to pasture, sharing their food and their feasts and receiving as his due from the tribesmen the firstborn of their flocks and herds.

**140.** The nomad's thoughts about his tribal god; his ideas of right

The thoughts of the desert wanderer about the character of such a god are crude and barbarous, and his religious customs are often savage, even leading him to sacrifice his children to appease the angry god. On the other hand, the nomad has a dawning sense of justice and of right, and he feels some obligations of kindness to his fellows which he believes are the compelling voice of his god. Such feelings at last became lofty moral vision, which made the Semites the religious teachers of the civilized world.

**141.** The western Semites on the west end of the Fertile Crescent

As early as 3000 B.C. they were drifting in from the desert and settling in Palestine, on the *western* end of the Fertile Crescent, where we find them in possession of walled towns by 2500 B.C. (Fig. 124). These predecessors of the Hebrews in Palestine were a tribe called Canaanites (§§ 293-294); farther north settled a powerful tribe known as Amorites (§ 175); while along the shores of north Syria (Fig. 159) some of these one-time desert wanderers had taken to the sea, and had become the Phœnicians (§ 396). By 2000 B.C. all these settled communities of the western Semites had developed no mean degree of civilization, drawn for the most part from Egypt and Babylonia. Their home along the east end of the Mediterranean was on the highway between these two countries, and they were in constant contact with both (map, p. 102). The Phœnicians, however, belonged to the Mediterranean, and we shall take up their story in discussing the history of the eastern Mediterranean (Sections 39 and 40).

At the same time we can watch similar movements of the nomads at the *eastern* end of the Fertile Crescent, along the lower course of the Tigris and Euphrates (Fig. 77), which we shall henceforth speak of as the "Two Rivers." They rise in the northern mountains (see map, p. 102), whence they issue to cross the Fertile Crescent and to cut obliquely southeastward through the northern bay of the desert. Here

FIG. 77. THE EUPHRATES AT BABYLON IN WINTER

The winter rainfall (§ 144) is so slight that the river shrinks to a very low level and its bed is exposed and dry almost to the middle. In summer the rains and melting snows in the northern mountains swell the river till it overflows its banks and inundates the Babylonian plain. The house on the right was the dwelling of the archæological expedition which until 1917 was engaged in excavating Babylon (Fig. 111)

on these two great rivers of Western Asia developed the earliest civilization known in Asia. Just as on the Nile, so here on the Two Rivers we shall find three great chapters in the story.

As on the Nile, so also the earliest of the three chapters of Tigris-Euphrates history will be found in the lower valley near the rivers' mouths. This earliest chapter is the story of Babylonia.[1] As the Two Rivers approach most closely to each other, about one hundred and sixty or seventy miles from the Persian

---

[1] The other two chapters of Tigris-Euphrates history are Assyria and the Chaldean Empire (Chapter V).

**142.** The east end of the Fertile Crescent; the Two Rivers and the three great chapters in their history

**143.** The Plain of Shinar (or Babylonia), the scene of the earliest chapter of Tigris-Euphrates history

Gulf,[1] they emerge from the desert and enter a low plain of
fertile soil, formerly brought down by the rivers. This plain
is Babylonia, the eastern end of the Fertile Crescent. But
during the first thousand years of the known history of this
plain the later city of Babylon had not yet arisen, or was a
mere village playing little or no part in the history of the

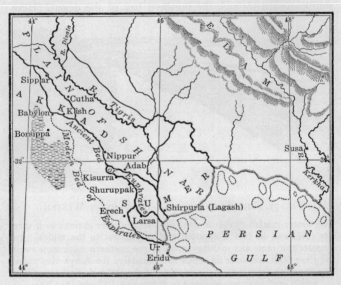

SKETCH MAP OF SUMER AND AKKAD

region. The plain was then called Shinar, and Babylonia is
a name that properly should not be applied to it until after
2100 B.C. (see § 176).

**144.** Area of
the Plain of
Shinar; its
fertility

Rarely more than forty miles wide, the Plain of Shinar contained probably less than eight thousand square miles of
cultivable soil — roughly equal to the state of New Jersey or the

[1] This distance applies only to ancient Babylonian and Assyrian days. The
rivers have since then filled up the Persian Gulf for one hundred and fifty to
one hundred and sixty miles, and the gulf is that much shorter at the present
day (see note under scale on map, p. 102).

area of Wales.[1] It lies in the Mediterranean belt of rainy winter and dry summer, but the rainfall is so scanty (less than three inches a year) that irrigation of the fields is required in order to ripen the grain. When properly irrigated the Plain of Shinar is prodigiously fertile, and the chief source of wealth in ancient Shinar was agriculture. This plain was the scene of the most important and long-continued of those frequent struggles between the mountaineer and the nomad, of which we have spoken (§ 133). We are now to follow the story of the first series of those struggles, lasting something like a thousand years, and ending about 2100 B.C.

## SECTION 14. RISE OF SUMERIAN CIVILIZATION AND EARLY STRUGGLE OF SUMERIAN AND SEMITE

The mountaineers were not Semitic and show no relationship to the Semitic nomads of the Arabian desert.[2] We are indeed unable to connect the earliest of these mountain peoples with any of the great racial groups known to us. We find them shown on monuments of stone as having shaven heads and wearing shaggy woolen kilts (Fig. 90). While they were still using stone implements, some of these mountaineers, now known as Sumerians, pushed through the passes of the eastern mountains at a very early date. Long before 3000 B.C. they had reclaimed the marshes around the mouths of the Two Rivers.

145. Unknown race of the early mountaineers

---

[1] The current impressions of the cultivable area of Babylonia take no account of the fact that the Babylonian plain was once much shorter than it is now (p. 106, note), nor of the further fact that on the north of it Mesopotamia is a desert which, moreover, does not belong to Babylonia. Only northern Mesopotamia is cultivable (especially the upper valleys of the Balikh and the Khabur rivers). The modern maps do not show this fact; for example, the *Century Atlas* confines the desert to the right bank of the Euphrates and does not admit it to Mesopotamia! The usually accepted ideas of the cultivable area of Babylonia are therefore enormously in excess of the actual area reached by irrigation.

[2] On the other hand, although they were certainly white races, the mountaineers exhibited no relationship to the Indo-European group of peoples who were already spreading through the country north and east of the Caspian at a very early date. The Indo-European peoples, from whom we ourselves have descended, are discussed in Section 21.

They gradually took possession of the southern section of the Plain of Shinar, and the region they held at length came to be called Sumer (see map, p. 106).

Their settlements of low mud-brick huts crept gradually north-ward along the Euphrates (see map, p. 106); for the banks of the Tigris were too high for convenient irrigation. They learned to control the spring freshets with dikes, to distribute the waters

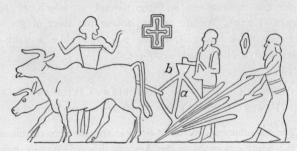

Fig. 78. Ancient Babylonian Seeder, or Machine Planter
(After Clay)

The seeder is drawn by a yoke of oxen, with their driver beside them. Behind the seeder follows a man holding it by two handles. It is very pointed and evidently makes a shallow trench in the soil as it moves. Rising from the frame of the seeder is a vertical tube (*a*) on the top of which is a funnel (*b*). A third man walking beside the seeder is shown dropping the grain into this funnel with one hand; with the other he holds what is probably a sack of seed grain suspended from his shoulders. The grain drops down through the tube and falls into the trench made by the seeder. The scene is carved on a small stone seal

in irrigation trenches, and to reap large harvests of grain (Fig. 78). They had already received barley and split wheat (p. 38, note), which were their two chief grains as in Egypt; and they called the split wheat by its Egyptian name. They also already possessed cattle, sheep, and goats. Oxen drew the plow, and donkeys pulled *wheeled* carts and chariots; the wheel as a burden-bearing device appeared here for the first time.[1] But

[1] Probably earlier than the wheel in the Swiss lake-villages or on the chariot race courses of the Late Stone Age (§ 39) in the West.

the horse was still unknown. Traffic with the upper river had also brought in metal, probably from the Nile valley, and the smith learned to fashion utensils of copper. But he had not

FIG. 79. EARLY SUMERIAN CLAY TABLET WITH CUNEIFORM WRITING (TWENTY-EIGHTH CENTURY B.C.)

This tablet was written toward the close of the early period of the city-kings (§ 162), a generation before the accession of Sargon I (§ 166). It contains business accounts; the numbers can be recognized as circles and other curved signs made with the circular *upper* end of the scribe's stylus. The picture signs have at this time long since become groups of wedges as shown in Fig. 80. (By permission of Dr. Hussey)

yet learned to harden the copper into bronze by admixture of tin (§ 336).

Trade and government taught these people to make records scratched in rude pictures (cf. Fig. 26) with the tip of a reed on a flat oval or disk of soft clay. When dried in the sun

147. Rise of Sumerian pictorial writing on clay

such a clay record became very hard; and if well baked in an oven, it became an almost imperishable pottery tablet (Fig. 79).

148. Transformation of Sumerian picture signs into cuneiform signs, and resulting loss of the pictures

|   |   | 1 | 2 | 3 |
|---|---|---|---|---|
| I | Foot turned around in 2 | | | |
| II | Donkey | | | |
| III | Bird; turned over with feet to the right | | | |
| IV | Fish | | | |
| V | Star | | | |
| VI | Ox; turned over in 2 | | | |
| VII | Sun or Day | | | |
| VIII | Grain; top of stalk turned over | | | |

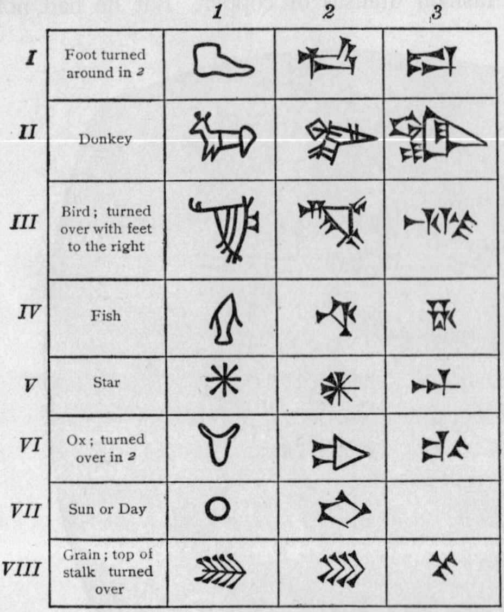

Fig. 80. Early Babylonian Signs showing their Pictorial Origin. (Chiefly from Barton)

This list of eight signs shows clearly the pictures from which the signs came. The oldest form is in column *1*; column *2* shows the departure from the picture and the appearance of the signs as the lines began to become wedges. In column *3* are the later forms, consisting only of wedges and showing no resemblance to the original picture. The original forms of signs *V*, *VI*, and *VII*, in column *1*, have not yet been actually found, but they are assumed from the existent forms shown in column *2*

On the earliest surviving specimens of such tablets we can still recognize the original pictures (Fig. 80) which made up the writing, just as in Egypt.

The reed with which the pictures were made usually had a blunt, square-tipped end. The tablet was held at an oblique angle as the stylus held straight up was applied to the clay. We may see a writer so using it in Fig. 101. The writer did not scratch the lines of his picture; but in making a single line he impressed one corner of the square tip of the reed into the soft clay, and then raised it again to impress another line in the same way. Owing to the oblique tilt of the tablet, each line thus made was wider at one end than at the other, and hence appeared triangular or wedge-shaped, thus ▸━ or ⟨. Every picture or sign thus came to be made up of a group of wedge-shaped lines like ▸━⊤, which was once a star, or ⛭, once a foot (Fig. 80, *V, 3*, and *I, 3*). We therefore call the system *cuneiform* (Latin, *cuneus*, meaning "wedge"), or wedge-form writing. Pictures made up of these wedge lines became more and more difficult to recognize, especially as speed in writing increased. All resemblance to the earlier pictures finally disappeared.

The transition from the picture stage to the phonetic stage (§ 53) was early made. Sumerian writing finally possessed over three hundred and fifty signs, but each such sign represented a syllable[1] or a word, that is, a group of sounds; the Sumerian system never developed an alphabet of the letters which made up the syllables. That is, there were signs for syllables like *kar* or *ban*, but no signs for the letters *k* or *r*, *b* or *n*, which made up such syllables. Hence we cannot insert here an alphabet, as we did in discussing Egypt. **149.** Rise of phonetic cuneiform signs; no alphabetic cuneiform signs

These clay records show us that in measuring time the Sumerian scribe began a new month with every new moon, and he made his year of twelve of these moon-months. We remember (see § 60) that twelve such months fell far short of making up a year. The scribe therefore slipped in an extra month whenever he found that he had reached the end of his calendar year a month or so ahead of the seasons. This inconvenient and inaccurate calendar was inherited by the Jews and Persians, and is still used by the oriental Jews and the Mohammedans. As in Egypt (Fig. 33), the years themselves were not numbered, but each year was named after some important event occurring in the course of the year. **150.** The Sumerian moon-calendar; year-names

---

[1] The only exceptions were later the vowels and some surviving pictorial signs which served as graphic hints, like the Egyptian determinatives (Fig. 30). On the story of how this writing was deciphered, see Section 25.

**151.** Sumerian numerals and weights

The Sumerian system of numerals was not based on tens, but had the unit sixty as a basis. A large number was given as so many sixties, just as we employ a score (fourscore, five-score). From this unit of sixty has descended our division of the circle (six sixties) and of the hour and minute. The leading unit of weight which they used was a *mina*, divided into sixty shekels. The mina had the weight of our pound, and traffic with the East at last brought this measure of weight to us, though under another name.

**152.** Nippur as a religious center; its temple-mount or tower, the ancestor of our church steeple

Almost in the center of the Plain of Shinar (see map, p. 106) rose a great tower (Fig. 104). It was of baked brick, for there was no stone in all Babylonia. This tower was the sacred mount of Enlil, the great Sumerian god of the air, at the ancient town of Nippur (Fig. 84), a holy place greatly revered among all the Sumerian communities. This temple-mount was in shape a building tapering upward somewhat like a pyramid. Around the outside of the square towerlike building was a broad steep footway, which rose as it turned, till it reached the top (see tailpiece, p. 170). The Sumerians erected this building at Nippur, probably in the effort to give their god a home on a mountain top such as he had once occupied, before they left their mountain home to dwell on the Babylonian plain (see § 145). Other towns also adopted the idea, and the temple tower at Babylon in later ages gave rise to the tale of the Tower of Babel (or Babylon), as preserved by the Hebrews. This Babylonian temple tower is the ancestor of our church steeple (Fig. 272).

**153.** The low temple building beside the temple tower

But the tower was not itself the temple of the god, although he had a shrine at the top. Alongside the tower there was a small, low temple building serving as the temple proper. Such sanctuaries have all perished in Babylonia, but enough remains to show the simple character of this lower building (Fig. 206). Approaching from the outside the visitor saw only bare walls of sun-dried brick. These inclosed a court, behind which was the sacred chamber. Indeed, it is clear that this lower dwelling of the god was simply a dwelling house like those of the townsmen (Fig. 82).

Around the temple and its mount were grouped the store-houses and business offices of the temple, while a massive wall forming an inclosure surrounded and protected the whole (Fig. 84). Here ruled a wealthy priesthood. Assisted by a group of scribes (Fig. 101), they rented and cared for the temple lands and property. The king or ruler of the town at their head was really also a priest, called a "patesi" (pronounced pa-tay'see). His temple duties kept him about as busy as did the task of ruling the community outside of the temple walls.

154. The temple in-closure; the priesthood and their ruler

At this sanctuary under the shadow of the temple-mount the peasant brought in his offering, a goat and a jar of water containing a few green palm branches intended to symbolize the vegetable life of the land, which the god maintained by the annual rise of the river. The jar with the green palm branches in it later became "the tree of life," a symbol often depicted on the monuments of the land (Fig. 102). These gifts the worshiper laid before the gods of earth, of air, of sky, or sea, praying that there might be plentiful waters and gener-ous harvests, but praying also for deliverance from the de-stroying flood which the god had once sent to overwhelm the land. Of this catastrophe the peasant's fathers had told him, and the tradition of this flood finally passed over to the Hebrews.

155. Sume-rian religion and worship

In one important matter of religion the Sumerians were very different from the Egyptians. The dead were buried in the town, under the court of a house or the floor of a room (Fig. 81), often without any tomb or coffin or much equip-ment for the life beyond the grave. Of the next world they had only vague and somber impressions, as a forbidding place of darkness and dust beneath the earth, to which all men, both good and bad, descended. Great cemeteries and elaborate tomb equipment, such as those which told us so much of early Egypt, do not help us here in Babylonia.

156. Sume-rian burials and beliefs about the hereafter

**157. Sume-rian house and town**   Around the temple inclosure extended the houses of the citi-zens — bare rectangular structures of sun-dried brick (Fig. 82), each with a court on the north side, and on the south side of the court a main chamber from which the other rooms were

FIG. 81. An Ancient Babylonian Burial. (After Scheil)

Two large pottery jars laid with their open ends together served as a coffin. Sometimes the body lay on the bottom of a rectangular grave lined with sun-dried brick, forming a rough vault. The usual burial was not in a cemetery but was in the house under the floor of the court or some room. Only one small cemetery, containing some thirty burials, has as yet been found in Babylonia. Little, if any, equipment for the hereafter was placed with the body, although some burials were sup-plied with a few jars of pottery or copper and ornaments of silver, gold, copper, or mother-of-pearl, with an occasional weapon or tool

entered. At first only a few hundred feet across, the town slowly spread out, although it always remained of very limited extent.[1] Such a town usually stood upon an artificial mound (Fig. 83), which it is important for us to examine.

---

[1] There were no really large cities in Babylonia until the Chaldean Empire (606–538 B.C., Section 20).

The ordinary building material of the entire ancient world was sun-baked brick. The houses of the common people in the Orient even at the present day are still built of such brick. The walls of such houses in course of time are slowly eaten away by the rains, till after a heavy rain an old house sometimes falls down. When this happens at the present day the rubbish is leveled off and the house is rebuilt on top of it. This modern practice has been going on for thousands of years. It was this kind of a house whose fall Jesus had in mind in his parable (Matt. vii, 27). As this process went on for many centuries it produced a high mound of rubbish, on which the town stood.

**158.** The formation of ancient city mounds

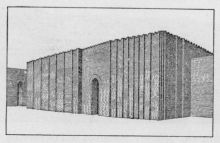

FIG. 82. RESTORATION OF AN EARLY BABYLONIAN HOUSE. (AFTER KOLDEWEY)

The towns of the early Babylonians were small and were chiefly made up of such sun-baked-brick houses as these. Their simple adornment consisted only of vertical panels and a stepped (crenelated) edge at the top of the wall. The doors were crowned by arches in contrast with those of the Egyptians, who knew the arch but preferred a horizontal line above all doorways

Many a surviving oriental town still stands on such an ancient mound. These mounds are to be found in all the ancient lands, like the mound of Troy (Fig. 149), that of Jericho in Palestine (Fig. 124), or Elephantine in Egypt (Fig. 211). Babylonia is to-day full of such great mounds long since forsaken and deserted, and Fig. 83 shows us how they look at the present day.

**159.** Distribution of such early mounds to-day

The clay tablets (Fig. 79) containing the household records, letters, bills, receipts, notes, accounts, etc., which were in the houses when they fell, were often covered by the falling walls, and they still lie in the mound. In the temples and public

**160.** Contents preserved in such ancient mounds

buildings the documents covered up were often important government records; while in the dwelling or offices of the ruler they were often narratives of wars and conquests. Sometimes the ruler placed accounts of his buildings, his victories, and other great deeds deep in the foundations of his buildings in order that later rulers might find them. Besides

FIG. 83. MOUND COVERING A PORTION OF THE ANCIENT BABYLONIAN CITY OF NIPPUR

The bare ground in front of us now showing a scanty growth of desert shrubs once formed a court, or open square, for public business, unloading caravans, etc. The great mound beyond contains the chief temple buildings of Nippur, occupying the south corner of the temple inclosure. Its highest portion covers the temple mount (§ 152), of which only the lower parts still survive under the mound. In the buildings covered by these mounds lived the scribes (clerks) and officials who carried on the temple and government business of this town nearly five thousand years ago (§ 154). See also Fig. 84 for a view from the top of the temple-mount. (By courtesy of the University Museum, Philadelphia)

all these written records, many articles of household use or sculptured works of art still lie hidden in such mounds. Here too lie the gaunt and somber remains of the early Babylonian buildings themselves (Fig. 84). But these town buildings have fallen into such ruin that we cannot make them tell us a story such as we found in Egypt. Nevertheless, a city mound is a rich storehouse of ancient Babylonian civilization, the story of which we are now to follow.

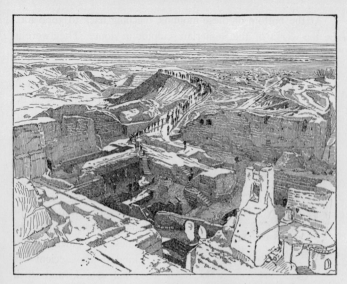

FIG. 84. EXCAVATION OF THE RUINS OF ANCIENT NIPPUR

These ruins were excavated by the University of Pennsylvania Expedition in three campaigns between 1889 and 1900. This view shows the work of excavation going on. The earth (once sun-dried brick) is taken out in baskets and carried away by a long line of native laborers, who empty their baskets at the far end of an ever-growing bank of excavated earth. The ruinous buildings, once entirely covered (Fig. 83), are slowly exposed, and among them, often clay tablets or objects of pottery, stone, or metal. Thus are recovered the records and antiquities of ancient Babylonia (§ 161). They lie at different levels, the oldest things nearer the bottom and the later ones higher up. This is a view seen from the top of the highest mound in Fig. 83. Beyond the laborers the view to the horizon gives a good idea of the flat Babylonian plain. Only two generations ago the monuments and records of Babylonia and Assyria preserved in Europe could all be contained in a show case only a few feet square. Since 1840, however, archæological excavation, as we call such digging, has recovered great quantities of antiquities and records. Such work is now slowly recovering for us the story of the ancient world. (Drawn from a photograph furnished by courtesy of the University Museum, Philadelphia)

**161.** Early Sumerian art: sculpture, seal-cutting, metal work

At the bottom of these mounds, reaching back to 3000 B.C., lie the works of the Sumerian sculptor in stone. They were in the beginning very rough and crude. The demand for personal seals cut in stone (Fig. 86) soon developed a beautiful art of engraving tiny figures on a hard stone surface (Fig. 106, *A*). We call a craftsman who could do such work a lapidary. The early Sumerian lapidaries soon became the finest craftsmen of the kind in the ancient oriental world, and their work has had an influence on our own decorative art which has not yet disappeared (see description, Fig. 85). The Sumerian craftsmen also did skillful work in metal, sometimes beautifully decorated (Fig. 85).

FIG. 85. SILVER VASE OF A SUMERIAN CITY-KING

This vase, the finest piece of metal work from early Babylonia, is adorned with two broad bands of engraving extending entirely around it. They furnish an excellent example of early Sumerian decorative art. In the broader band we see a lion-headed eagle clutching the backs of two lions, which in their turn are biting two ibexes. This balanced arrangement of animal figures in violent action was a discovery of Sumerian art about 3000 B.C. The eagle and the lions here form the symbol, or arms, of the Sumerian city-kingdom of Lagash. Such symbols made up of balanced pairs of animal figures passed over to Europe, where they are still used in decorative art and in the heraldic symbols, or arms, of the kings and nations. The eagle still appears in the arms of Russia, Austria, Prussia, and other European nations, and finally reached us as our "American" eagle, really the eagle of Lagash, five thousand years ago

In all these monuments and the writings on clay tablets we find revealed to us the life which once filled the streets of the ancient Babylonian towns now sleeping under the silent mounds. We see a class of free landholding citizens in the town, working their lands with numerous slaves and trading with caravans and small boats up and down the river. Over these free, middle-class folk were the officials and priests, the aristocrats of the town. Such a community, owning the lands for a few miles round about the town, formed the political unit, or state, which we call a city-kingdom. We may therefore call the first three centuries after about 3050 B.C. the Age of the Sumerian City-Kingdoms.

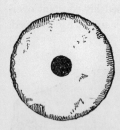

FIG. 86. AN EARLY SUMERIAN CYLINDER SEAL

Instead of signing his *name* to a clay-tablet

**162.** Early Sumerian society and state; the Age of the City-Kingdoms (about 3050–2750 B.C.)

The leading Sumerian city-kingdoms formed a group in the South, occupying the land of Sumer (see map, p. 106). These towns are still marked for us by a straggling line of mounds distributed along the Euphrates. In spite of oppressive and dishonest taxation, such a community owed much to its ruler, or patesi (§ 154). He was useful in a number of matters, but chiefly in two ways : in war and in irrigation. The irrigation canals

**163.** The Sumerian city-kingdoms and their patesis

document, the early Sumerian rolled over the soft clay a little stone roller, or cylinder, engraved with beautiful pictures (Figs. 90, 91, and 106, *A*) and sometimes also bearing the owner's name (Fig. 91). The impression left by the roller in the soft clay served as a signature. They have been found in great numbers in the ruins of Babylonia. By a study of these works the growth and decline of Babylonian art may be traced for twenty-five hundred years, from about 3000 B.C. to about 500 B.C. The picture shows end view and side view

and dikes required constant repairs. The planting and harvesting of the fields would have stopped and the whole community would have starved if the ruler had ceased his constant oversight of the dikes and canals and the water supply had stopped.

FIG. 87. A SUMERIAN CITY-KING LEADING A PHALANX OF HIS TROOPS (ABOUT 2900 B.C.)

The king himself, whose face is broken off from the stone, marches at the right, heading his troops, who follow in a compact group. This is the earliest example of grouping men together in a mass, forming a single fighting unit, called a phalanx. This must have required a long drill and discipline, after many centuries of loose, irregular, scattered fighting (Fig. 88). This was the first chapter in the long history of the art of war, and it took place in Asia. Such discipline was unknown at this time in Egypt. These Sumerian troops have their spears set for the charge, but they carry no bows. Tall shields cover their entire bodies, and they wear close-fitting helmets, probably of leather. They are marching over dead bodies (symbolical of the overthrow of the enemy). The scene is carved in stone and is a good example of the rude Sumerian sculpture in Babylonia in the days of the Great Pyramid and the remarkable portrait sculpture of Egypt (contrast with Figs. 52 and 53)

**164. The wars among the Sumerian city-kingdoms**
As to war, we can watch more than one of these city rulers marching out at the head of troops heavily armed with shield and spear (but without the bow) and marshaled in massive phalanx (Fig. 87). We found on the Nile the earliest highly

developed arts of peace; we find here among the Sumerians the earliest highly developed art of war in the history of man. When the townspeople heard that a neighboring city-kingdom was trying to take possession of a strip of their land, they were glad to follow the patesi's leadership in order to drive out the invaders. As such occurrences were common, the

FIG. 88. SEMITIC BOWMEN OF EARLY BABYLONIA FIGHTING IN OPEN ORDER

The nomads had no organization and no discipline; each man leaped about in the fray as he pleased, and the fight was a loose group of single combats between two antagonists. This loose rough-and-tumble fighting was the earliest method of warfare, before men learned to train and drill themselves to fight in groups or masses. The Sumerians were the earliest men who took this step (Fig. 87). The disciplined Sumerian townsmen were therefore long superior to these disorganized nomads of the desert along the Fertile Crescent

early history of Sumer for some three centuries (about 3050 to 2750 B.C.) was largely made up of the ever-changing fortunes of these city-kingdoms in war.

But while the city-kingdoms of Sumer were thus often fighting among themselves, they were also called upon to meet an enemy from the outside. The Semitic nomads of the desert (§ 135) early began to settle north of Sumer. This region called Akkad (see map, p. 106), where the Two Rivers are

**165. Earliest wars of Sumerians and Semites**

closest together, was on the main road from the Two Rivers to the eastern mountains, and the leading Semitic tribe there bore the name Akkadians. These desert wanderers had never learned discipline and drill in war like the Sumerians. They depended on their skill as archers, and they gave battle therefore at a distance. Or if they came to close quarters, they fought single-handed, in open order (Fig. 88). Their thin and open line was evidently at first no match for the heavy phalanx of the Sumerians. Thus two hostile races faced each other on the Plain of Shinar: in the North the half-settled Semitic nomads of Akkad, and in the South the one-time mountaineers of Sumer. The long struggle between them was only one of the many struggles between nomad and mountaineer along the Fertile Crescent (§ 133).

## SECTION 15. THE FIRST SEMITIC TRIUMPH: THE AGE OF SARGON

**166.** The first Semitic triumph; Sargon of Akkad and his line (2750–2550 B.C.)

About 2750, that is, about the middle of the twenty-eighth century B.C., there arose in Akkad a Semitic chieftain named Sargon. So skillful in war was he, that he succeeded in scattering the compact Sumerian spearmen, and making himself lord of all the Plain of Shinar. The old Sumerian city-kings were defeated and the Sumerian towns down to the mouths of the Two Rivers submitted to him. He led his swift Akkadian archers from the eastern mountains of Elam westward up the Euphrates to the shores of the Mediterranean. There, as we remember, the Pharaoh's galleys (Fig. 41) were already moored in the harbors of the Phœnician cities. Some day chance may disclose to us the messages, written on clay tablets, which now probably passed between the lord of the Euphrates and the lord of the Nile living in the splendors of his pyramid-city at Gizeh. Sargon was the first great leader in the history of the Semitic race, and he was the first ruler to build up a great nation in Western Asia, reaching from Elam (Fig. 89, and map, p. 102) to the Mediterranean and far up the Two Rivers northward. His splendid conquests made an impression upon the Tigris-Euphrates world which never faded, and he left them to his descendants, one of whom, his great-grandson Naram-Sin, even extended them.

Sargon's conquests forced his nomad tribesmen (the Akkadians) to make a complete change in their manner of life. The once wandering shepherds were obliged to drop their unsettled life and to take up fixed abodes. We may best picture the change if we say that they forsook their tents (headpiece, p. 100) and built houses of sun-dried brick (Fig. 82), which could not be picked up every morning and set up somewhere else at night. At first they did not even know how to write, and they had no industries (§ 136). Some of them now learned to write their Semitic tongue by using the Sumerian wedge-form signs for the purpose. Then it was, therefore, that a Semitic language began to be written for the first time. These former nomads had never before attempted to manage the affairs of settled communities, — such business as we call government administration. All this too they were now obliged to learn from the Sumerians. The Semitic Akkadians therefore adopted the Sumerian calendar, weights and measures, system of numerals and business methods. With the arts of peace the Akkadians also gained those of war. They learned to make helmets of leather and copper weighing over two pounds. These are the earliest-known examples of the use of metal as a protection in war. From such beginnings as these were to come the steel-clad battleships and gun turrets of modern times.

**167.** The Semitic Akkadians adopt Sumerian civilization

Among other things the Akkadians learned also the art of sculpture, but they soon far surpassed their Sumerian teachers. The relief of Naram-Sin (Fig. 89) belongs among the real triumphs of art in the early world — especially interesting as the first great work of art produced by the Semitic race. The beautiful Sumerian art of seal-cutting, the Akkadians now carried to a wonderful degree of perfection (Figs. 90, 91, and 106, *A*).

**168.** The great Semitic art of the Age of Sargon

Fig. 89. A King of Akkad storming a Fortress — the Earliest Great Semitic Work of Art (about 2700 b.c.)

King Naram-Sin of Akkad (great-grandson of Sargon I, § 166) has pursued the enemy into a mountain stronghold in Elam. His heroic figure towers above his pygmy enemies, each one of whom has fixed his eyes on the conqueror, awaiting his signal of mercy. The sculptor, with fine insight, has depicted the dramatic instant when the king lowers his weapon as the sign that he grants the conquered their lives. Compare the superiority of this *Semitic* sculpture of Akkad over the *Sumerian* art of two centuries earlier (Fig. 87)

Thus the life of the desert Semite mingled with that of the non-Semitic mountaineer on the Babylonian plain, much as Norman and English mingled in England. On the streets and in the market places of the Euphrates towns, where once the bare feet, clean-shaven heads, and beardless faces of the Sumerian townsmen were the only ones to be seen, there was now a

FIG. 90. A SEMITIC PRINCE AND HIS SUMERIAN SECRETARY (TWENTY-SEVENTH CENTURY B.C.)

The third figure (wearing a cap) is that of the prince, Ubil-Ishtar, who is brother of the king. He is a Semite, as his beard shows. Three of his four attendants are also Semites, with beards and long hair; but one of them (just behind the prince) is beardless and shaven-headed (§ 169). He is the noble's secretary, for being a Sumerian he is skilled in writing. His name "Kalki" we learn from the inscription in the corner, which reads, "Ubil-Ishtar, brother of the king; Kalki, the scribe, thy servant." This inscription is in the Semitic (Akkadian) tongue of the time and illustrates how the Semites have learned the Sumerian signs for writing (§ 167). The scene is engraved on Kalki's personal seal (Fig. 86), and the above drawing shows the impression on the soft clay when the seal was rolled over it. It is a fine example of the Babylonian art of seal-cutting in hard stone (§ 168). The original is in the British Museum

plentiful sprinkling of sandaled feet, of dark beards, and heavy black locks hanging down over the shoulders of the swarthy Semites of Akkad (Fig. 90). The shaven Sumerian served in the army with shield and lance (Fig. 87) along with his bearded Semitic lord carrying only the bow (Fig. 88). The Semitic noble could not do without the deft Sumerian clerk, for we see the king's brother with his Semitic attendants, followed also by his shaven-headed Sumerian secretary (Fig. 90).

## Section 16. Union of Sumerians and Semites: the Kings of Sumer and Akkad

**170. The Kings of Sumer and Akkad (from the twenty-fifth to the twenty-third century B.C.)**

When at last the Semites of Akkad were enfeebled by the town life which they had adopted, the line of Sargon declined. As a result the Sumerian cities of the South were able to recover control of the country not long after 2500 B.C. Headed by the ancient city of Ur, three of the old Sumerian cities gained the leadership one after another. But the Semites of Akkad were henceforth recognized as part of the unified nation on the ancient Plain of Shinar, which now for the first time gained a national name. It was called " Sumer and Akkad." The kings of this age, who called themselves "Kings of Sumer and Akkad," were both Sumerians and Semites. They have left us no great buildings or imposing monuments, but the new United States of Sumer and Akkad prospered greatly and survived for over three centuries. For the first time literature flourished.

**171. Thought and myth under the Kings of Sumer and Akkad: the source of life; the Etana story**

In simple stories these men of the Tigris-Euphrates world now began to answer those natural questions regarding life and death, which always rose in the minds of early men. They finally told of the wonderful adventures of the shepherd Etana, when his flocks were stricken with unfruitfulness, and no more lambs were born. Etana then mounted on the back of an eagle (Fig. 91) and rose to the skies in search of the herb in which was the source of life. But as he neared his goal he was hurled to the earth again. This is the earliest tale of flying by man.

**172. Death and eternal life: the Adapa story**

The strange mystery of death led to the story of the fisher-man Adapa. When the South-wind goddess overturned his boat, Adapa flew into a rage and broke her wing. Thereupon he was summoned to the throne of the Sky-god, whose wrath was at length appeased so that he offered to Adapa the bread and water of life. This would have made him immortal and destroyed death. But suspicious and forewarned of danger, the unhappy Adapa refused the food and thus lost both for himself and for mankind the treasure of immortal life.

In the same way they told how the gigantic hero Gilgamesh, after many mighty deeds and strange adventures (Fig. 106, *A*), failed to gain immortal life. Among all these heroes, indeed, there was but one who was granted endless life. Of him there was a strange tale, telling how, together with his wife, he survived

FIG. 91. THE FLIGHT OF ETANA TO THE SKIES

At the right Etana sits on the back of the flying eagle (§ 171), with his arm around the bird's neck. Above him is the moon, while below, two dogs look up after him, barking. At the left approaches a goatherd driving three goats; before them walks a man with an object shaped like an umbrella. All, including the goats, are looking up in amazement at the flight of Etana. Over the goatherd a potter is making jars, and at the right of his jars a squatting baker is making round loaves. The scene is carved on a cylinder seal (Fig. 86), and our drawing shows the impression on the soft clay when the seal is rolled over it. It is a fine specimen of the Babylonian lapidary's skill

the great deluge (§ 155) in a large ship. Then the gods carried them both away to blessedness. But not even the *kings* of Sumer and Akkad were supposed to enter a blessed hereafter, much less the common people. Many of these stories of creation and flood were afterward known to the Hebrews.

Mingled with touches from the life of both Sumerian and Semite, these tales now circulated in both the Semitic and

**174.** Decline of the Sumerian language; its survival as a sacred tongue

Sumerian languages. It was the old Sumerian tongue, however, which was regarded as the more sacred. It later continued in use as a kind of sacred language, like Latin in the Roman Catholic Church. The old Sumerian towns were now rapidly declining (twenty-third century B.C.), but religious stories were written in Sumerian, centuries after it was no longer spoken.

## SECTION 17. THE SECOND SEMITIC TRIUMPH: THE AGE OF HAMMURAPI AND AFTER

**175.** Return of Semitic supremacy; rise of Babylon

As the "Kings of Sumer and Akkad" slowly weakened, a new tribe of Semites began descending the Euphrates, just as the men of Akkad had done under Sargon (§ 166). These newcomers were the Semitic Amorites of Syria by the Mediterranean (§ 141). About a generation before 2200 B.C. this new tribe of western Semites seized the little town of Babylon, which was at that time still an obscure village on the Euphrates. The Amorite kings of Babylon at once began to fight their way toward the leadership of Sumer and Akkad.

**176.** Rise of Hammurapi and supremacy of Babylon

After a century of such warfare there came to the throne as the sixth in the Amorite line of kings at Babylon one Hammurapi, who was flourishing by 2100 B.C. In the now feeble old Sumerian cities of the South, Hammurapi found the warlike Elamites who had come in from Elam in the eastern mountains. They fought him for over thirty years before he succeeded in driving them out and capturing the Sumerian towns. Victorious at last, Hammurapi then made his city of Babylon for the first time supreme throughout the land. It was therefore not until after 2100 B.C. that Babylon finally gained such a position of power and influence that we may call the land "Babylonia."

**177.** Hammurapi, the organizer

Hammurapi survived his triumph twelve years, and in those years of peace, as he had done in war, he proved himself the ablest of his line. He was the second great Semitic ruler, as Sargon had been the first. Only a few generations earlier his ancestors, like those of Sargon, had been drifting about the desert, without any organization. He still betrayed in his shaven upper lip, a desert custom, the evidence of his desert ancestry (Fig. 93). But he now put forth his powerful hand upon the teeming life of the Babylonian towns, and with a touch he brought in order and system such as Babylonia had never seen before. Two chief sources of information have survived over four thousand years to reveal to us the deeds and the character of this great king: these are a group of fifty-five of his letters, and the splendid monument bearing his laws.

Hammurapi's letters afford us for the first time in history a glimpse into the busy life of a powerful oriental ruler in Asia. They disclose him to us sitting in the executive office of his palace at Babylon with his secretary at his side. In short, clear sentences the king begins dictating his brief letters, conveying his commands to the local governors of the old Sumerian cities which he now rules. The secretary draws a reed stylus (Fig. 101) from a leathern holder at his girdle, and quickly covers the small clay tablet (Fig. 92) with its lines of wedge groups. The writer then sprinkles over the soft wet tablet a handful of dry powdered clay. This is to prevent the clay envelope, which he now deftly wraps about the letter, from adhering to the written surface. On this soft clay envelope he writes the address and sends the letter out to be put into the furnace and baked.

**178.** Hammurapi's letters: their dictation and preparation

Messengers constantly hand him similarly closed letters. This secretary of Hammurapi is a trusted confidential clerk. He therefore breaks to pieces the hard clay envelopes in the king's presence and reads aloud to him letters from his officials all over the kingdom. The king quickly dictates his replies. The flood has obstructed the Euphrates between Ur and Larsa, and of course a long string of boats have been tied up and are waiting. The king's reply orders the governor of Larsa to clear the channel at the earliest moment and make it navigable again.

**179.** Hammurapi's letters: navigation

**180. Hammurapi's letters: feasts and the calendar**

The king is much interested in his vast flocks of sheep, as if the nomad instinct had not altogether vanished from the blood of his line. He orders the officials to appear in Babylon to celebrate the spring sheep-shearing as if it were a great feast. The calendar has slipped forward a whole month in advance of the proper season (§ 150), and the king sends out a circular letter to all the governors, saying, "Since the year hath a deficiency, let the month which is now beginning be registered as a second (month of) Elul."

**181. Hammurapi's letters: delinquents**

But he warns the governor that all taxes otherwise falling due within the next month are not to be deferred by this insertion. Delinquent tax gatherers are firmly reminded of their obligations and called upon to settle without delay. Prompt punishment of an official guilty of bribery is authorized, and we can see the king's face darken as he dictates the order for the arrest of three officials of the palace gate who have fallen under his displeasure. More than once the governor of Larsa is sharply reminded of the king's orders and bidden to see that they are carried out at once.

**182. Hammurapi's letters: justice and religion**

Many a petitioner who has not been able to secure justice before the board of judges in his home city is led in before the king, confident of just treatment; and he is not disappointed (Fig. 92). The chief of the temple bakers finds that royal orders to look after a religious feast at Ur will call him away from the capital city just at the time when he has an important lawsuit coming on. He easily obtains an order from the king postponing the lawsuit. The king's interest in the religious feast is here as much concerned as his sense of justice, for many of the letters which he dictates have to do with temple property and temple administration, in which he constantly shows his interest.

**183. The code of Hammurapi**

With his eye thus upon every corner of the land, alert, vigorous, and full of decision, the great king finally saw how necessary it was to bring into uniformity all the various and sometimes conflicting laws and business customs of the land.

He therefore collected all the older written laws and usages of business and social life, and arranged them systematically.

He improved them or added new laws where his own judgment deemed wise, and he then combined them into a great code or body of laws. It was written, not in Sumerian, as some of the old laws were, but in the Semitic speech of the Akkadians and Amorites. He then had it engraved upon a splendid shaft of stone. At the top was a sculptured scene in which the king was shown receiving the law from the Sun-god (Fig. 93). The new code was then set up in the temple of the great god Marduk in Babylon. This shaft has survived to our day, the oldest preserved code of ancient law. Fragments of other copies on clay tablets, the copies used by the local courts, have also been found.

Hammurapi's code insists on justice to the widow, the orphan, and the poor; but it also allows many of the old and naïve ideas of justice to stand. Especially prominent is the principle that the punishment for an injury should

FIG. 92. A LETTER WRITTEN BY HAMMURAPI, KING OF BABYLONIA (ABOUT 2100 B.C.)

One of the numerous clay-tablet letters of this king (§ 178) which have survived four thousand years. The writing, done while the clay was still soft, shows clear signs of the speed with which the writer, Hammurapi's secretary, took down the king's dictation (§ 178). The tablet has been baked. It was also inclosed in a baked-clay envelope bearing the address, but this has been broken off and thrown away (§ 179). This letter orders a local governor to hear the appeal of an official who thinks himself unjustly defeated in law (§ 182)

184. Spirit of Hammurapi's code; position of woman

require the infliction of the same injury on the culprit — the principle of " an eye for an eye, a tooth for a tooth." Injustice often resulted. For example, when a house fell (§ 158) and killed the son of the householder, the guilty builder must also suffer the loss of *his* son, and the innocent son was therefore condemned to die. Marriage was already a relation requiring legal agreements between the man and his wife, and these are carefully regulated in Hammurapi's code. Indeed the position of women in this early Babylonian world, as in Egypt, was a high one. Women engaged in business on their own account, and even became

FIG. 93. THE LAWS OF HAMMURAPI, THE OLDEST SURVIVING CODE OF LAWS (2100 B.C.)*

* A shaft of stone (diorite) nearly 8 feet high, on which the laws are engraved, extending entirely around the shaft and occupying over thirty-six hundred lines. Above is a fine relief showing King Hammurapi standing at the left, receiving the laws from the Sun-god seated at the right. Hammurapi's shaven upper lip proclaiming him a man of the Syrian desert (§ 177) is here in the shadow and cannot be seen. The flames rising from the god's shoulders indicate who he is. The flames on the left shoulder are commonly shown in the current textbooks as part of a staff in the god's left hand. This is an error. This scene is an impressive work of Semitic art, six hundred years later than Fig. 89.

professional scribes. They must have attended such a school as that described below (Fig. 95).

Thus regulated, the busy Babylonian communities prospered as never before. Their products were chiefly agricultural, especially grain and dates; but they had also flocks and herds, leather and wool. The weaving of wool was a great industry, for woolen clothing was commonly worn in Western Asia. Copper had been displaced by bronze (§ 146), and one document refers to iron, but this metal was still much too rare to play any part in industry. Iron for common use was still a thousand years in the future in Hammurapi's time (§§ 360, 392).

**185.** Industries of Hammurapi's time

A standing army kept the frontiers safe and quiet, and the slow donkey caravans of the Babylonian merchants, plodding from town to town, were able to penetrate far into the surrounding communities. They were so common on the upper Euphrates (map, p. 102) that a town there was called Haran (or Kharan) from the Babylonian word *kharanu*, meaning "journey." Many a courtyard was piled high with bales, each bearing a clay seal with the impression of the merchant's name (cf. Fig. 91). These clay seals, broken away as the bales were opened, to-day lie in the rubbish of the Babylonian towns, where the modern excavator picks them up, still displaying on one side the merchant's name and on the other the impression of the cord which bound the bale.

**186.** Babylonian commerce in Hammurapi's time

Such seals and the clay-tablet bills which accompanied the bales had to be read by many a local merchant in the towns of Syria and beyond the passes of the northern mountains. Thus Babylonian cuneiform writing slowly made its way through Western Asia, and the merchants of Syria began to write bills and letters of their own on clay tablets (see § 291 and Fig. 126). Hammurapi's commercial influence was widely felt in the West. The memory of his name had not wholly died out in Syria-Palestine in Hebrew days over a thousand years after his death.

**187.** Spread of cuneiform writing through Western Asia

**188.** The temples the center of business

While the Babylonian merchants were a powerful class and were even called the "rulers" in some communities, it was the temples with their large possessions which were the center of business life. They loaned money like banks, dealt in merchandise, and controlled extensive lands.

**189.** Money and loans

There was as yet no coined money, but lumps of silver of a given weight circulated so commonly that values were given in *weight* of silver. Thus a man could say that an ox was worth so many ounces of silver, only he would use "shekels" in place of ounces. Loans were common, though the rate of interest was high: twenty per cent a year, payable in monthly installments. Gold was also in sparing use, for it was fifteen times as valuable as silver.

**190.** Babylonian religion in the Age of Hammurapi

These commercial interests were the leading influences in Babylonian life, even in religion. The temples, as we have said, had a large place in business life; and religion never proclaimed the rights of the poor and the humble, nor championed their cause against the rich and powerful. To be sure, the ritual of the temple contained some prayers which indicated a sense of sin and unworthiness. But the advantages of religion consisted in being able to obtain substantial benefits from the gods and to avoid their displeasure.

**191.** Marduk and Ishtar

The people still worshiped the old Sumerian gods, but the political leadership of Babylon had enabled the men of that city to put their Semitic god Marduk at the head of all the gods, and in the old mythical stories (§§ 171–173) they inserted the name Marduk where once the ancient Sumerian god Enlil had played the leading part. At the same time the great Asiatic goddess of love, Ishtar, rose to be the leading goddess of Babylon. She was later to pass over to the Mediterranean to become the Aphrodite of the Greeks (§ 420).

**192.** Babylonian methods of reading the future, or divination

Among the benefits granted by the gods was the ability to foretell the future. This art we call divination, and the priest who practiced it was a diviner. The skilled diviner could interpret the mysterious signs on the liver of the sheep (Fig. 94)

slain in sacrifice, and his anxious inquirers believed that he could thus reveal the unknown future. He could note the positions of the stars and the planets, and he could thus discern the decrees of the gods for the future. These practices later spread westward. We shall find the reading of the liver a common practice in Rome (Fig. 234), and star-reading later developed, under the Chaldeans (§ 238), into the science of astrology, the mother of astronomy. It was taken up by the Greeks and has even survived into our own day.

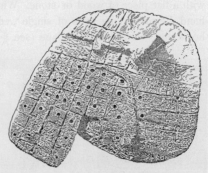

FIG. 94. ANCIENT BABYLONIAN DIVI-
NER'S BAKED-CLAY MODEL OF SHEEP'S
LIVER (ABOUT 2100 B.C.)

To train such men and to furnish clerks for business and government, schools were necessary. These were usually in or connected with the temple. A schoolhouse of the time of Hammurapi has ac-tually been uncovered

The surface of the model is marked with lines and holes, indicating the places where the diviner must look for the mysterious signs which disclosed the future. These signs were of course the highly varied natural shapes and markings to be observed in *any* sheep's liver. But the Babylonian believed that these things were signs placed on the liver by the god to whom the sheep had been given, when it was slain as a sac-rifice. The meaning of each part of the liver is here written in cuneiform in the proper place. The whole forms a kind of map 'of the surface and shape of the liver with written explanations. Absurd as all this seems to us, the art of reading the future in this way was believed in by millions of people, and finally reached Europe (§ 793 and Fig. 234)

193. Edu-
cation: a
Babylonian
schoolhouse

(Fig. 95), with the clay-tablet exercises of the boys and girls of four thousand years ago still lying on the floor. They show how the child began his long and difficult task of learning to understand and to write three or four hundred different signs.

The pupil's slate was a soft clay tablet, on which he could rub out his exercises at any time by smoothing off the surface with a flat piece of wood or stone. With his reed stylus in his hand, he made long rows of single wedges in three positions, horizontal, vertical, and oblique (see § 148). When he could

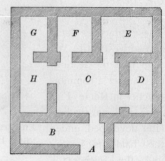

FIG. 95. AN ANCIENT BABYLONIAN SCHOOLHOUSE IN THE DAYS OF HAMMURAPI (ABOUT 2100 B.C.). (AFTER SCHEIL)

On the right is the ground plan of the schoolhouse, which was about 55 feet square. The children went in at the door (*A*), across the end of the long room (*B*) where the doorkeeper sat and perhaps kept a clay-tablet tardy-list of the pupils who came late. Then the children entered a court (*C*) which was open to the sky, and we may suppose that they separated here, the big boys and girls going into their own rooms, while the little ones went into others. Somewhere in the schoolhouse, and probably in the court (*C*), was a pile or box of soft clay, where a boy who had already filled his clay-tablet slate with wedge-marks (§ 194) could quickly make himself a new slate by flattening a ball of soft clay. On the left we look through one of the doors of this oldest schoolhouse in the world, as it appeared on the day when it was uncovered by the French in 1894. The native Arab workmen who uncovered it stand in the doorway. The walls of sun-dried brick are still 8 or 9 feet high

make the single wedges neatly enough, the master set him at work on the wedge-groups forming the signs themselves. Lastly, he was able to undertake words and simple phrases, leading up to sentences and quotations from old documents. One of the tablets found in the schoolhouse contains a proverb which shows how highly the Babylonians valued the art of writing. It reads: " He who shall excel in tablet-writing shall shine like the sun." Doubtless many a Babylonian lad was encouraged in the long and wearisome task of learning to write, by copying this enthusiastic sentiment.

Of the higher life of Babylon in this age as expressed in great works of art and architecture, very little has survived on the spot. Indeed, the city of Hammurapi has perished utterly. Not a single building erected by him now stands. Enough remains in other old Babylonian mounds to show us that Western Asia was still without the colonnades already so common on the Nile (Fig. 56). In these Babylonian buildings the arch for the first time assumed a prominent place on the front of a structure. As a result of its early prominence here, the arch traveled slowly westward into Europe (§ 787 and Fig. 248). The chief architectural creation of early Babylonia was the temple tower, which we have already seen (Fig. 104); but of the temples themselves no surviving example has been excavated.[1]

195. Scanty remains of art from Hammurapi's time; architecture

There seems to have been no painting in Hammurapi's time. The sculptured scene in which Hammurapi receives the law from the Sun-god (Fig. 93) is a work displaying a certain fine dignity and impressiveness. But this scene shows us how Babylonian custom now muffled the human form in heavy woolen garments, so that the sculptor had little opportunity to depict the beauty of the human figure (contrast Fig. 89). Portraiture was scarcely able to distinguish one individual from another. The beautiful art of seal-cutting, the greatest art of the Babylonians, had noticeably declined since the wonderful works of Sargon's age (Fig. 106, *A*). Although it was *commercially* so successful, yet in art the great age of Hammurapi was already declining.

196. Sculpture in Hammurapi's time

[1] The common restorations to be found in our current histories of art and architecture, showing us complete early Babylonian temples, rest entirely on imagination, and are pure guesswork. The temples of late Babylonia (Chaldean Empire, Section 20) have been excavated and restored by the German Expedition (Fig. 206).

**197.** Earliest
appearance of
the domestic
horse in
history
(2100 B.C.);
fall of
Hammurapi's
line

The decline in art was perhaps a prophecy of what was to
come, for the Babylonian nation which Hammurapi had so
splendidly organized and started on its way did not survive
his death. The mountaineers, whom Hammurapi had driven
out of the Sumerian cities (§ 176), again descended upon the
Babylonian plain, as the Sumerians had done so long before.
They probably brought with them a newcomer even more
important than themselves; for, as they began to appear more
and more often on the streets of the Babylonian towns, they
seem to have led with them a strange animal, for which the
Babylonians had no name. They called it the " animal of the
mountains." Thus about four thousand years ago the tamed
horse appeared for the first time in a civilized community,
and began to play that important part in war and industry
which he has played ever since.[1] In this continuation of the
age-long struggle between nomad and mountaineer on the
Babylonian plain, even the line of Hammurapi was swept
away, and the horse-breeders of the highlands triumphed
(twentieth century B.C.). Their rule was rude and almost
barbaric, and their triumph marked the end of old Babylonian
progress in civilization. Until its revival under the Chaldeans
(Section 20) Babylonia relapsed into stagnation so complete
that it was rarely interrupted.

**198.** Summary and
retrospect

As we look back over this first chapter of early human
progress along the Two Rivers, we see that it lasted about a
thousand years, beginning a generation or two before 3000 B.C.
The Sumerian mountaineers laid the foundations of civilization
in Shinar and began a thousand-year struggle with the Semites
of the desert. In spite of the mingling and union of the two

---

[1] These mountaineers (called by the Babylonians Kassites) who probably
brought the horse into Babylonia did not domesticate him themselves. They
received him in trade from the North or from Asia Minor, from tribes of the
Indo-Europeans (§ 247), who had long before tamed or domesticated the animal.
The chariot courses which show his presence in prehistoric western Europe
(§ 39) were probably a little later than this. We recall the appearance of the
horse in Egypt about 1700 B.C. (§ 107), some four hundred years later than in
Babylonia.

races, the Semites triumphed twice under two great leaders, Sargon (2750 B.C.) and Hammurapi (2100 B.C.). The Sumerians then disappeared, and the language of Babylonia became Semitic. The reign of Hammurapi, in spite of some weakening in art, marks the highest point and the end of the thousand-year development — the conclusion of the first great chapter of history along the Two Rivers. The scene of the second chapter will carry us up the river valley, just as it did in our study of the Nile.

### QUESTIONS

SECTION 13. Describe the Fertile Crescent. How can we summarize its history? Discuss its relation to the desert. Who were the inhabitants of the desert? Describe their life. Into what lands did they shift at the west end of the Fertile Crescent? at the east end? What rivers cross the east half of the Crescent? Describe the plain they have made.

SECTION 14. Who were the early dwellers in the Plain of Shinar? Describe their life. Describe their writing materials and their writing. Summarize their civilization. Describe their buildings and towns. What are such towns like to-day? What do we find in them? Were the Sumerians all united in one nation? What progress had they made in war?

SECTION 15. What outsiders defeated the Sumerians? Who was the first great Semitic king? What did the Akkadians learn from the Sumerians? What did the Akkadians accomplish in art? Describe the mingling of Akkadians and Sumerians.

SECTION 16. What nation resulted from the mingling of Sumerians and Akkadians? How long did it last? Describe its literature. What became of the Sumerian language?

SECTION 17. Who were the Amorites, and what city in the Plain of Shinar did they seize? Who was their greatest king? Describe his administration as seen in his letters. Tell about his achievements in adjusting the laws of Babylonia. Discuss Babylonian commerce. What did it carry to the peoples along the west of the Fertile Crescent? Describe Babylonian divination, education, architecture. What happened at Hammurapi's death? How long had the first chapter of civilization on the Two Rivers lasted?

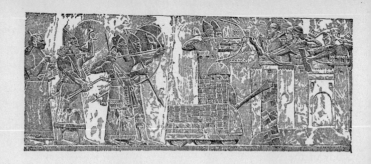

# CHAPTER V

## THE ASSYRIANS AND CHALDEANS

### SECTION 18. EARLY ASSYRIA AND HER RIVALS

**199. The situation of Assur, the earliest capital of Assyria**

The second chapter of history along the Two Rivers carries us up-river from Babylonia to the northeast corner of the desert-bay. Here, overlooking the Tigris on the east and the desert on the west and south, was an easily defended elevation (Fig. 96), possessing a natural strength unknown to the towns in the flat Plain of Shinar. The place was known as Assur (see map, p. 102), and it later gave its name to the land of Assyria.

NOTE. The headpiece shows an Assyrian king attacking a fortified city (ninth century B.C.). A century before the Empire the Assyrians had already developed powerful appliances for destroying a city wall. The city at the right is protected by walls of sun-dried brick like those of Samal (Fig. 97). The defending archers on the wall are trying to drive away a huge Assyrian battering-ram, mounted on six wheels, which has been rolled up to the wall from the left. It is an ancient "tank" with its front protected by metal armor plate. It carries a tower as high as the city wall, and Assyrian sharpshooters (archers) in the top of the tower are picking off the defenders of the wall. Within the tank unseen men work the heavy beam of the ram. It is capped with metal and is shown smashing a hole in the city wall, from which the bricks fall out. An observation tower with a metal-covered dome, and holes for peeping out, shields the officer in command as he directs the operation of the machine. In the rear (at the left) is the Assyrian king shooting arrows into the hostile city. He uses a powerful bow, invented in Egypt, which will shoot an arrow with great force from 1000 to 1400 feet, and hence he can stand at a safe distance. This scene, carved on a slab of alabaster, is among the earliest Assyrian palace reliefs which have survived (§ 209), and hence the artist's childish representation of men as tall as city walls.

The region about Assur was a highland, enjoying a climate much more invigorating than the hot Babylonian plain. It had many fertile valleys winding up into the eastern and northern mountains, where rival cities were already in existence. Here an occasional promontory of rock furnished quarries of limestone, alabaster, and likewise harder stone. Herein Assyria differed greatly from Babylonia, which was without building stone, and had therefore developed only architecture in brick. These eastern valleys were green with rolling pastures and billowing fields of barley and wheat. Herds of oxen and flocks of sheep and goats dotted the hillside pastures. Donkeys served as the chief draft animals, and the horse was unknown in the beginning, just as it was originally unknown in Babylonia (§ 146). Here flourished an

**200. Climate, soil, and products of Assyria**

FIG. 96. THE TIGRIS AND THE PROMONTORY OF ASSUR AFTER A SNOWSTORM

The river is at the left, and the fertile plain beyond it soon breaks into hills, leading up to the eastern mountains. The ruins of the ancient city occupy the promontory on the right (§ 199). The buildings in the foreground are those of the archæological expedition which excavated the ruins

agricultural population, little given to other industries or to trade. In this last particular Assyria was again in sharp contrast with Babylonia.

By 3000 B.C. a Semitic tribe of nomads from the desert-bay had settled at Assur, as their kindred of Akkad were doing at the same time in the Plain of Shinar. As Semites they spoke a Semitic dialect like that of the Semites of Babylonia, with

**201. Founding of Assur (3000 B.C.) under Sumerian influence**

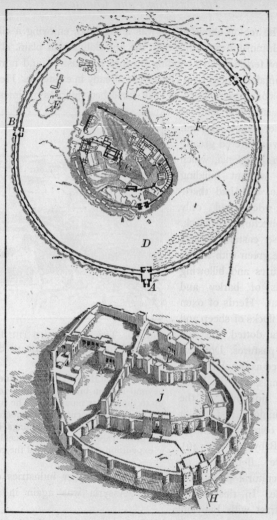

FIG. 97. THE ARAMEAN CITY OF SAMAL, ONE OF THE WESTERN
RIVALS OF ASSYRIA. (AFTER VON LUSCHAN)*

differences no greater than we find between the dialects of different parts of Germany. The men of Assur at first formed a tiny city-kingdom like those of their Sumerian neighbors in the South (§ 162). It is evident that they were in close contact with the Sumerian towns, whose sculpture and writing (Fig. 79) they adopted. They likewise received the Sumerian calendar (§ 150) and most of the conveniences of Sumerian civilization. There may even have been some Sumerians among the early population of the town.

While the early civilization of Assur thus came from the south, the little city-kingdom was equally exposed to influences from the north and west. There in Asia Minor were the hostile Hittite communities, some of which were venturing eastward to the Two Rivers. More than once Assur was ruled by Hittite lords, only to fall back again under the control of Sargon, Hammurapi, or some other ruler of Babylonia. Thus obliged for nearly fifteen hundred years after Sargon's reign to defend their uncertain frontiers against their neighbors on both north and south, the Assyrians were toughened by the strain of unceasing war. Meantime, too, they introduced the horse (§ 197) and added chariots to their army. Then the Assyrian kings

202. Assur the vassal of Babylonia and the Hittites alternately; earliest expansion of Assur north and south

* PLAN (above). The city was nearly half a mile across. It was defended by a double wall of sun-dried brick on a heavy stone foundation (*ABC*). The wall was strengthened with towers every 50 feet, entirely round the city, making one hundred towers in all. The castle of the kings of Samal occupied a hill in the middle (*G*), and the houses of the townsmen filled the space between the city walls and the castle (*D, E, F*). These houses built of sun-dried brick have disappeared, but the castle can be restored. RESTORATION OF THE CASTLE (*H, I, J, K, L,* below). This is the castle, or citadel, marked *G* in the city plan (above). The walls of sun-dried brick rest on heavy stone foundations widening at the base. Samal in north Syria, midway between the Mediterranean and the Euphrates (map, p. 102). received influences both from the Hittites in Asia Minor (§ 353) and from Egypt. The columned porches (*K* and *L*) in front of the palaces were built on a Hittite plan with columns suggested by Egyptian architecture. Hittite art in relief (Fig. 148) adorned this porch. The Assyrians adopted these Western innovations (Fig. 105).

began pushing westward, and by 1300 B.C. they crossed the Euphrates and swept back the Hittites from the great river. At the same time they began to descend the Tigris with such power that they even captured and ruled for a time their old conqueror, Babylon, still under the rule of the half-barbaric eastern Kassites, who had brought in the horse (§ 197).

FIG. 98. GENERAL VIEW OF MODERN DAMASCUS

Damascus is still the largest city of Syria, having probably three hundred thousand inhabitants. When it became the most powerful Aramean city-kingdom (§ 203) it must have been surrounded by a wall like that of Samal (Fig. 97), with a splendid royal castle. The ruins of all these ancient Aramean buildings must now lie under those of the modern city, and hence ancient Damascus will never be excavated

**203. The Western rivals of Assyria: Phœnicians, Hebrews, and Arameans**

Assur was still an inland power, much like modern Russia, and could not hope to rule Western Asia without access to the Mediterranean. Along the Mediterranean coast new rivals arose to dispute her progress in the West. Here the harbor towns of former Semitic nomads (§ 141) had become a fringe of wealthy Phœnician city-kingdoms carrying on a flourishing commerce by sea (§ 396). These Phœnician cities proved obstinate enemies of the Assyrian kings. Meantime a new wave of Semitic nomads had rolled in from the desert-bay (§ 135). By 1400 B.C. they were endeavoring to occupy its western shores, that is, Palestine and Syria, just as the Assyrians had done at Assur. These Western nomads were the Hebrews in Palestine, and north of them the Arameans,[1] or Syrians, occupying Syria. They soon held the entire west end of the Fertile Crescent and cut off Assyria from the sea. After 1200 B.C. the Arameans established a group of flourishing kingdoms in the West. Here, under the influence of Hittite civilization on one

side and Egyptian on the other, these Aramean kingdoms of Syria built royal cities (Fig. 97), and luxurious palaces for their kings (Fig. 97, *H–L*), filled with sumptuous furniture (Fig. 100). Among these Aramean kingdoms of Syria the most powerful was Damascus (Fig. 98).

FIG. 99. ARAMEAN WEIGHT FOUND IN ASSYRIA

The weight is of bronze, cast in the shape of a lion and equipped with a handle. The inscription on the edge of the base is in Aramaic. Fifteen of these Aramean lion weights were found at one place, showing the common presence of Aramean merchants in the Assyrian markets (§ 204)

**204. Widespread Aramean commerce**

The energetic Aramean merchants extended their business far beyond their own kingdoms. They pushed their caravans all along the shores of the desert-bay, even as far north as the sources of the Tigris, and they finally held the commerce of Western Asia. Their bronze weights found in the ruins of Nineveh (Fig. 99) show us how common were the Aramean merchants in the Assyrian market places. Like their kinsmen the Jews in modern civilized states, although they were not organized as a single nation, they were the great commercial leaders of the age.

---

[1] The Arameans are often called Syrians, and the region north of Palestine (see map, p. 102) is commonly called Syria. These two names, Syria and Syrians, are not to be confused with Assyria and Assyrians.

205. The
Aramean
merchants
spread the
first alphabet
in Asia

The Arameans were a highly civilized race. By 1000 B.C. they were using *alphabetic* writing, which they had borrowed from the Phœnicians (Section 40). It was the earliest system of writing known which employed exclusively alphabetic signs (Fig. 160). Along with the alphabet the Arameans also received the Egyptian pen and ink, conveniences indispensable in the use of the new alphabet (Fig. 100). As the Babylonian caravans had in earlier times carried cuneiform tablets throughout Western Asia (§ 187), so the Aramean caravans, with their bills and receipts, began to carry through the same region the alphabet which was to displace cuneiform signs. Thus spread throughout Western Asia the Phœnician Aramean alphabet. It passed down the Euphrates, to Persia and the inner Asiatic lands, and even to the frontiers of India, to furnish at length even the East Indian peoples with their alphabet.

FIG. 100. AN ARAMEAN KING OF SAMAL AND HIS SECRETARY HOLDING AN EGYPTIAN WRITING OUTFIT (EIGHTH CENTURY B.C.)

The king sits at the left on a richly carved throne of ebony, ivory, and gold, with a footstool of the same design. Before him stands his secretary, carrying under his left arm something which looks much like a book; but bound books were still unknown at this time. In his left hand he holds an Egyptian writing case containing pen and ink (cf. Fig. 101). The flat relief in which the entire scene is carved had its origin on the Nile. From Syria, in such cities as Samal, it passed to Assyria, where it was immensely improved (Fig. 107). (From a photograph by von Luschan)

The Aramean merchants of course carried their language (called Aramaic) with them, and Aramaic gradually became very common all around the desert-bay. Indeed, in the old Assyrian

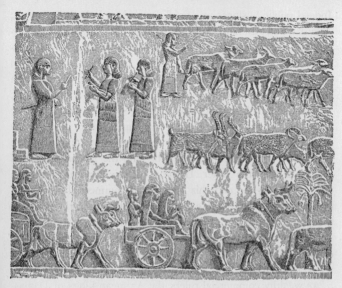

FIG. 101. AN ASSYRIAN AND AN ARAMEAN SCRIBE RECORDING
THE PLUNDER TAKEN FROM A CAPTURED ASIATIC CITY (EIGHTH
CENTURY B.C.)

The captive women and children ride by in oxcarts on their way to
slavery in Assyria, and a shepherd drives off the captured flocks. At the
left an Assyrian officer reads from a tablet his notes of the spoil taken
in the city. Two scribes write as he reads. The first (in front) holds in
his left hand a thick clay *tablet*, from which he has just lifted the stylus
grasped in his right hand, as he pauses in his writing. The other scribe
holds spread out on his left hand a *roll* of papyrus, on which he is
busily writing with a pen held in his right hand. He is an Aramean (§ 205),
writing Aramaic with pen and ink. We see here, then, the two different
methods of writing practiced at this time in Western Asia — the outgoing
Asiatic clay tablet and the incoming Egyptian paper, pen, and ink

communities the people who spoke Aramaic finally outnumbered
the citizens of Assyrian speech. When an Aramean received a
cuneiform tablet recording business matters in the Assyrian
language, he sometimes took his pen and marked it with memoranda in Aramaic. Assyrian tablets bearing such notes in
Aramaic have been found in the ruins of Assyrian buildings.

206. Assyrian
and Aramaic
side by side in
business and
government

Indeed public business was finally carried on in both languages, Assyrian and Aramaic. Aramean clerks were appointed to government offices, and it was a very common thing for an Aramean official of the Assyrian Empire to keep his records on papyrus, writing with pen and ink on a roll, while his Assyrian companion in office wrote with a stylus on a clay tablet (Fig. 101).

**207.** Complete triumph of the Aramaic language along the whole Fertile Crescent

Aramaic finally became the language of the entire Fertile Crescent. It even displaced its very similar sister tongue, the Hebrew of Palestine, and thus this merchant tongue of the Arameans, many centuries later, became the language spoken by Jesus and the other Hebrews of his time in Palestine (Fig. 131). In the end this widespread commercial civilization of the Arameans left more lasting influences behind than even the powerful military state of the Assyrians, as we shall see. Unfortunately the Aramean city mounds of Syria, with one exception (Fig. 97), still remain unexcavated; hence we have recovered but few monuments to tell us of their career.

**208.** Aramean Damascus and her Semitic allies along the west end of the Fertile Crescent halt westward expansion of Assyria

As wealthy commercial rulers, the Aramean kings of Damascus were long able to make their city so strong as to block further Assyrian advance toward the Mediterranean. One of the best illustrations of the effect of their power is the fact that Damascus long sheltered the feeble little Hebrew kingdoms from Assyrian attack (see map, p. 102). The Assyrian army marched westward and looked out upon the Mediterranean by 1100 B.C., but for more than three centuries after this the kings of Assur were unable to conquer and hold this western region against the strong group of Aramean, Phœnician, and Hebrew kingdoms. They held the Assyrian armies at bay until the eighth century B.C.

**209.** Growth of Assyrian civilization before the Empire, under influences from Babylonia and the Hittites

As Assyrian power thus seemed to pause at the threshold of the Empire, let us look back for a moment over the long two thousand years of development and see what progress Assur had made in civilization since it had received from the Sumerians such things as cuneiform writing (§ 201), etc. Assur was near enough to the North and West to feel influences from there also, especially from the Hittites (§ 356), who contributed much both in art and in religion. All these inherited things Assur

had also cultivated and developed. She had added some two hundred cuneiform signs to the list received from Babylonia. Under influences from the Hittite art of north Syria (Fig. 100) the sculptors of Assur were learning to tell the story of the king's valiant exploits in elaborate stone pictures cut in flat relief on great slabs of alabaster (Figs. 101 and 105). These were set up in long rows along the palace walls. This architectural sculpture was an art not practiced in Babylonia. As in sculpture, so also in architecture, the possession of stone enabled the Assyrians to do what had been impossible in stoneless Babylonia. The Assyrian builder could erect heavy foundations of stone under his buildings, as the Hittite and Syrian had long been doing. Above the foundation the Assyrian building itself, however, continued to be made of sun-dried brick, as in Babylonia.

FIG. 102. SYMBOL OF THE GOD ASSUR SURMOUNTING AN ASSYRIAN REPRESENTATION OF THE OLD BABYLONIAN TREE OF LIFE

Above is the winged sun-disk of Egypt, the borrowed symbol of the Assyrian Sun-god Assur (§ 210), whom we see shooting his deadly arrows. Below is the beautiful symbol of the tree of life, which originated in old Babylonia (see § 155). The early Babylonian worshiper's palm branch in a jar of water (§ 155) had been developed by artists into a decorative palm tree seen here rising like a post in the middle, with its spreading crown of leaves at the top and festooned with tufts of palm leaves like those on the top of the tree. In this form it was later much used by the Greeks

**210.** Religion of Assur

The sacred stories and symbols of the gods which had grown up among the Babylonian communities (§§ 171–173) were taken over by the men of Assur, who copied and studied

Fig. 103. Stone Coffin of a King of Assyria a Century before the Empire

In this limestone sarcophagus (coffin) lay the body of an Assyrian king buried here twenty-eight hundred years ago, in the ninth century B.C. Above this sun-dried-brick vault in which he was buried rose the palace of Assur. The German excavators found here five such vaults under the floor of the palace. The dead Assyrian king was thus buried under his dwelling like ordinary Assyrians or Babylonians (Fig. 81). These are the first royal tombs ever found in Assyria. They had been broken open and robbed, the bodies of the kings scattered, and the coffins mostly shattered to pieces, over two thousand years ago, by the Parthians (§ 1023), and they were found empty by the excavators

and revered them (Fig. 102). But the Assyrians clung to their old tribal god Assur, whose name was the same as that of their city and their tribe. He was a fierce god of war, whom they identified with the sun. He led the Assyrian kings on their victorious campaigns, and shot his deadly arrows far and wide among the foe (Fig. 102). As his symbol, the Assyrians borrowed the winged sun-disk from the Hittites of Syria, who had received it from Egypt (cf. Figs. 34 and 102). Their great goddess was Ishtar, the goddess of love, whom we have already met in Babylonia. Religion among the warlike Assyrians, as in Babylonia, had little effect upon the conduct of the worshiper. One reason for this was the fact that the Assyrians had much the same notions of the hereafter as the Babylonians, with no belief in a judgment to come. Their burials, as in Babylonia (Fig. 81), were placed under the floor or court of the dead man's house.

Recent excavations at Assur uncovered a series of brick vaults under the pavement of the royal palace. In these vaults were found fragments of massive stone coffins, two of which, however, had not been broken up (Fig. 103). These are the oldest royal burials known in Asia, and the first ever found in Assyria; for in these coffins once lay the bodies of the powerful kings of Assur, who lived and ruled and built there, toward the end of the long two-thousand-year development which led up to the Assyrian Empire.

**211. Discovery of the tombs of the kings of Assur**

## Section 19. The Assyrian Empire (about 750 to 612 b.c.)

By the middle of the eighth century b.c., Assyria was again pushing her plans of westward expansion. Damascus, combined with the other Western kingdoms, made a desperate resistance, only to be slowly crushed. When at last Damascus fell (732 b.c.), the countries of the West were all subdued and made subject kingdoms. Thus the once obscure little city of Assur gained the lordship over Western Asia as head of an empire, a great group of conquered and vassal nations (§ 108). The story of that Empire forms the second great chapter of history along the Two Rivers.

**212. Continued westward expansion of Assyria**

**213.** Sargon II of Assyria (722–705 B.C.)

In the midst of these great Western campaigns of Assyria, while he was besieging the unhappy Hebrew city of Samaria (§ 306), one of the leading Assyrian generals usurped the throne (722 B.C.), and as king he took the name of Sargon, the first great Semite of Babylonia, who had reigned two thousand years earlier (§ 166). The new Sargon raised Assyria to the height of her grandeur and power as a military empire. His descendants were the great emperors of Assyria.[1] On the northeast of Nineveh he built a new royal residence on a vaster scale and more magnificent than any Asia had ever seen before. He called it *Dur-Sharrukin* (Sargonburg). Its inclosure was a mile square, large enough to shelter a community of eighty thousand people, and the palace building itself (Fig. 104) covered twenty-five acres. Babylonia in her greatest days had never possessed a seat of power like this. In no uncertain terms it proclaimed Assyria mistress of Western Asia.

**214.** Sennacherib (705–681 B.C.)

The grandeur of Sargon II was even surpassed by his son Sennacherib, one of the great statesmen of the early Orient. Far up in Asia Minor the name of Sennacherib was known and feared, as he plundered Tarsus and the easternmost Ionian Greek strongholds (§ 438) just after 700 B.C. Thence his campaigns swept southward along the Mediterranean to the very borders of Egypt. To be sure, much of Sennacherib's army was destroyed by a pest which smote them from the Delta marshes (§ 309), and hence Sennacherib never crossed the Egyptian frontier. But against Babylon, his other ancient rival, he adopted the severest measures. Exasperated by one revolt after another, Sennacherib completely destroyed the venerable city of Hammurapi and even turned the waters of a canal over the desolate ruins.

[1] The leading kings of the dynasty of Sargon II are as follows:

Sargon II . . . . . . . . . . . . . . . 722–705 B.C.
Sennacherib . . . . . . . . . . . . . 705–681 B.C.
Esarhaddon . . . . . . . . . . . . . 681–668 B.C.
Assurbanipal (called Sardanapalus by the Greeks) . . 668–626 B.C.

Thus Babylon was annihilated; but the ancient power on the Nile remained a continual disturber of Assyrian control. A crushing burden of Assyrian tribute had been laid on all

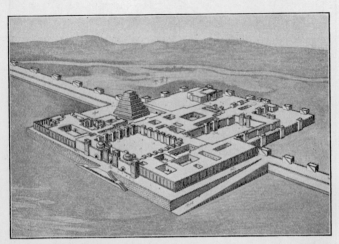

FIG. 104. RESTORATION OF THE PALACE AND A PORTION OF THE CITY OF SARGONBURG, THE ROYAL RESIDENCE OF SARGON II (722–705 B.C.). (AFTER PLACE)

The palace stands partly inside and partly outside of the city wall on a vast elevated platform of brick masonry containing about 25 acres. Inclined roadways and stairways rise from the *inside* of the city wall. The king could thus drive up in his chariot from the streets of the city below to the palace pavement above. The rooms and halls are clustered about a number of courts open to the sky. The main entrance (with stairs before it leading down to the city) is adorned with massive towers and arched doorways (§ 222) built of richly colored glazed brick (Plate II, p. 164) and embellished with huge human-headed bulls carved of alabaster. The temple tower behind the great court, inherited from Babylonia, was the ancestor of the Christian Church spire (Fig. 272). The streets and houses of the city filled the space below the palace within the city walls, which could accommodate some eighty thousand people (§ 213)

subject states, and hence Egypt was constantly able to stir revolt among the oppressed Western peoples, who longed to be freed from the payment of this tribute. Assyria perceived

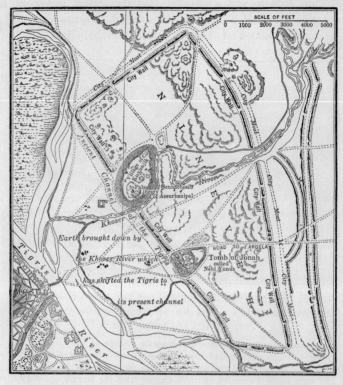

## SKETCH MAP OF NINEVEH

Notice the changes in the course of the Tigris, which formerly flowed along the west wall of the city. This change has been caused by the Khoser River, which has carried down soil and formed a plain between the wall of the city and the Tigris. In Fig. 203 we have a view from a housetop in Mosul, across the river from Nineveh, showing us this plain, with the mound of Kuyunjik just behind it. This mound covers the palaces of Sennacherib and Assurbanipal. A destructive overflow of the Khoser River, which flooded the city and broke down a section of the eastern wall, was one of the chief causes of the fall of Nineveh

154

that Egypt's interference must be stopped. Sennacherib's son, therefore, appeared before the gates of the eastern Delta forts by 674 B.C. Repulsed at first, he returned to the attack, and although he died before entering the Delta, Egypt at last fell a prey to the Assyrian armies, and Sennacherib's grandson was for a time lord of the lower Nile.

By 700 B.C. the Assyrian Empire included all of the Fertile Crescent. It thus extended entirely around the great desert-bay; but it furthermore included much of the northern mountain country far behind. The conquest of Egypt gave it also the lower Nile valley in the west, though this last was too distant and too detached to be kept long. Built up by irresistible and far-reaching military campaigns which went on for two generations after Sargon II, the Assyrian conquests finally formed the most extensive empire the world had yet seen.

**216.** Extent of the Assyrian Empire

Sennacherib was not satisfied merely to enlarge the old royal residences of his fathers at Assur or at Sargonburg. He devoted himself to the city of Nineveh, north of Assur, and it now became the far-famed capital of Assyria. Along the Tigris the vast palaces (Fig. 104) and imposing temple towers of the Assyrian emperors arose, reign after reign. The lofty and massive walls of Nineveh which Sennacherib built stretched two miles and a half along the banks of the Tigris. Here in his gorgeous palace he ruled the western Asiatic world with an iron hand, and collected tribute from all the subject peoples.

**217.** Nineveh becomes the Assyrian capital

The whole administration centered in the king's business office. He maintained a system of royal messengers, and in each of the more important places on the main roads he appointed an official to attend to the transmission of all royal business. In this manner all clay-tablet letters or produce and merchandise belonging to the royal house were sure of being forwarded. This organization formed the beginnings of a postal system [1] which continued for many centuries in the Orient (§ 273).

**218.** Means of communication and the organization of the Assyrian Empire

[1] There are indications that it was already in existence in Asia, under Egyptian rule, as far back as 2000 B.C.

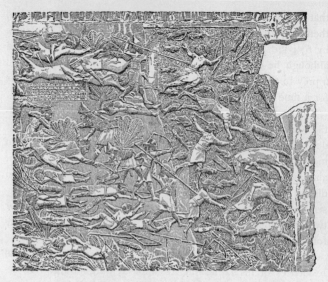

FIG. 105. ASSYRIAN SOLDIERS PURSUING THE FLEEING ENEMY
ACROSS A STREAM

The stream occupies the right half of the scene. As drawn by the
Assyrian artist, it may be recognized by the fish and the curling waves;
also by the bows and quivers full of arrows floating downstream, along
with the bodies of two dead horses, one on his back with feet up. Two
dead men, with arrows sticking in their bodies, are drifting in mid-
stream. Three of the living leap from the bank as their pursuers stab
them with spears or shoot them with drawn bow. The Assyrian spearmen carry tall shields, but the archer needs both hands for his bow and
carries no shield. The dead are strewn along the shore, occupying the
left half of the scene. At the top the vultures are plucking out their
eyes; in the middle an Assyrian is cutting off a head; beside him another plants his foot on a dead man's head and steals his weapons.
The vegetation along the river is shown among the bodies

In this way the emperor received the letters and reports of
some sixty governors over districts and provinces, besides
many subject kings who were sometimes allowed to continue
their rule under Assyrian control. We even have several clay-
tablet letters dispatched by Sennacherib himself while he was

*A*

*B*

FIG. 106. ANIMAL SCULPTURE OF THE BABYLONIANS AND ASSYRIANS

*A* shows us the wonderful work of the Babylonian seal-cutter in the time of Sargon (§ 168). At the extreme left the bearded hero Gilgamesh (§ 173), the ancestor of Hercules, is slaying a wild bull. He is aided by the hero Engidu, half man, half bull. Next, Gilgamesh alone is slaying a lion. In the right-hand seal, in balanced heraldic arrangement (Fig. 85), a lion is twice shown slaying a wild bull. In *B*, the lion hunt, we have one of the best examples of Assyrian relief sculpture of the reign of Assurbanipal (§ 223). It clearly shows the influence of the animal sculpture of the old Babylonian seals, over two thousand years older

FIG. 107. ASSYRIAN SOLDIERS OF THE EMPIRE. (FROM THE
PALACE RELIEFS OF ASSURBANIPAL)

It was the valor of these stalwart archers and spearmen which made
Assyria mistress of the East for about a century and a half (§§ 220–221)

crown prince, and addressed to his royal father, Sargon. To maintain the army was the chief work of the State. The State was a vast military machine, more terrible than any mankind had ever yet seen (Fig. 105). We shall understand this situation if we imagine that our war department were the central office in Washington, and that our government should devote itself chiefly to supporting it.

An important new fact aided in bringing about this result. Through contact with the Hittite west (§ 360) iron had been introduced among the Assyrians. The Assyrian forces were therefore *the first large armies equipped with weapons of iron.* A single arsenal room of Sargon's palace was found to contain two hundred tons of iron implements. To a certain extent the rise and power of the Assyrian Empire were among the results of the incoming of iron.

**219. The Assyrian Empire and the Iron Age**

The bulk of the Assyrian army was composed of archers, supported by heavy-armed spearmen and shield bearers (Fig. 107). Besides these, the famous horsemen and chariotry of Nineveh (Fig. 106, *B*) became the scourge of the East. For the first time too the Assyrians employed the battering-ram (headpiece, p. 140) and formidable siege machinery. The sun-dried-brick walls of the Asiatic cities could thus be battered down or pierced, and no fortified place could long repulse the assaults of the fierce Assyrian infantry.

**220. The arms of the Assyrians**

Besides their iron weapons and their war machines the Assyrian soldiers displayed a certain inborn ferocity which held all Western Asia in abject terror before the thundering squadrons of the Ninevites.[1] Wherever the terrible Assyrian armies swept through the land, they left a trail of ruin and desolation behind. Around smoking heaps which had once been towns, stretched lines of tall stakes, on which were stuck the bodies of rebellious rulers flayed alive; while all around rose mounds and piles of the slaughtered, heaped up to celebrate the great king's triumph and serve as a warning to all revolters.

**221. Terrors of the Assyrian army**

[1] See Nahum iii, 2–3.

Through clouds of dust rising along all the main roads of the Empire the men of the subject kingdoms beheld great herds of cattle, horses, and asses, flocks of goats and sheep, and long lines of camels loaded with gold and silver, the wealth of the conquered, converging upon the palace at Nineveh. Before them marched the chief men of the plundered kingdoms, with the severed heads of their former princes tied about their necks.

**222. Civilization of the Assyrian Empire: architecture**

While this plundered wealth was necessary for the support of the army, it also served higher purposes. As we have seen (Fig. 104), the Assyrian palaces were now imposing buildings, suggesting in architecture the far-reaching power of their builder. In the hands of the Assyrian architects the arch, inherited from Babylonia, for the first time became an imposing monumental feature of architecture. The impressive triple arches of the Assyrian palace entrance, faced with glazed brick in gorgeous colors (Plate II), were the ancestor of the Roman triumphal arches (Fig. 248). On either side were vast human-headed bulls wrought in alabaster, and above the whole towered lofty castellated walls of baked brick, visible far across the royal city (Fig. 104).

**223. Civilization of the Assyrian Empire: sculpture**

Within the palace, as a dado running along the lower portion of the walls, were hundreds of feet of relief pictures cut in alabaster (see Figs. 101, 105, 106, *B*, and 107). They show great improvement over the older work (headpiece, p. 140) a century before the Empire. They display especially the great deeds of the emperor in campaign and hunting field (Figs. 105 and 106, *B*). The human figures are monotonously alike, hard, cold, and unfeeling. Nowhere is there a human form which shows any trace of feeling, either joy or sorrow, pleasure or pain. The Assyrian sculptor's wild beasts, however, are sometimes magnificent in the abandon of animal ferocity which they display (Fig. 106, *B*). The tiger was in the blood of the Assyrian, and it came out in the work of his chisel. On the other hand, the pathetic expression of suffering exhibited by some of these wonderful animal forms (Fig. 106, *B*) was a triumph of art, which the

Assyrian sculptor owed to a study of the superb lions and bulls (Fig. 106, *A*) on the exquisite old Babylonian seals of the age of Sargon I, two thousand years earlier. The art of portraiture in statue form never got beyond very crude and unskillful efforts.

The emperors were obliged to depend much on foreign skill, both in art and industries. The art of glazing colored brick had been borrowed from Egypt (§ 83). All the patterns of Assyrian decorative art likewise came from Egypt, and their furniture made by Phœnician workmen, of ebony and ivory, often betrays Egyptian origin (Fig. 108). Phœnician craftsmen at Nineveh wrought splendidly engraved bronze platters (Fig. 158). Sennacherib tells us that he had in his palace " a portal made after the model of a Hittite palace," and his predecessors had long before built similar portals like those they had seen in the Hittite west (Fig. 97). It is in this ability to use foreign resources that we must recognize one of the greatest traits of the Assyrian emperors.

FIG. 108. IVORY FRAGMENT OF AN EGYPTIAN WINGED SPHINX FOUND IN AN ASSYRIAN PALACE

Such fragments of carved ivory were used in inlaying furniture like that in Fig. 100. They were the work of Phœnician craftsmen in the service of the Assyrian kings (§ 224). These workmen constantly employed Egyptian designs and symbols combined with those of Assyria. The winged animal, first found in Egyptian art, passed to the Phœnicians and Hittites in Syria and thence to Assyria, where it finally developed into the huge winged bull-figure adorning the front of the king's palace

In the fine gardens which Sennacherib laid out along the river above and below Nineveh he planted strange trees and

**225.** Intro-
duction of for-
eign plants,
including
earliest
cotton

plants from all quarters of his great empire. Among them
were cotton trees, of which he says, "The trees that bore wool
they clipped and they carded it for garments." These cotton
trees came from India. We thus see appearing for the first
time in the ancient world the cotton which now furnishes so
large a part of our own national wealth.[1]

**226.** Assur-
banipal's
library

Higher interests were also cultivated among the Assyrians,
and literature flourished. Assurbanipal, grandson of Sennacherib, and the last great Assyrian emperor, boasts that his
father instructed him not only in riding and shooting with bow
and arrow but also in writing on clay tablets and in all the
wisdom of his time. A great collection of twenty-two thousand clay tablets was discovered in Assurbanipal's fallen library
rooms at Nineveh, where they had been lying on the floor for
twenty-five hundred years. They are now in the British
Museum. In this library the religious, scientific, and literary
works of past ages had been systematically collected by the
emperor's orders (Fig. 109). They formed the earliest library
known in Asia. The Assyrians were far more advanced in
these matters than the Babylonians, and Assyrian civilization
was far from being a mere echo of Babylonian culture.

**227.** Internal
decay; eco-
nomic and
agricultural
decline

Like many another later ruler, however, the Assyrian emperors made a profound mistake in policy. For their wars of
conquest led to the destruction of the industrial and wealth-
producing population, first within their own territory and then
throughout the subject kingdoms. In spite of interest in introducing a new textile like cotton, the Assyrian rulers did not
or could not build up industries or commerce like those of
Babylonia. The people were chiefly agricultural, and in the
old days it had sufficed to call them from their farming for
short periods to defend the frontiers. With the expansion of
the Empire, however, such temporary bodies of troops were
insufficient, and the peasants were *permanently taken from the*

[1] This cotton tree was doubtless related to the lower-growing cotton plant of
our Southern states.

FIG. 109. PORTION OF OLD BABYLONIAN STORY OF THE FLOOD
FROM ASSURBANIPAL'S LIBRARY AT NINEVEH

This large flat tablet was part of an Assyrian cuneiform book consisting of a series of such tablets. This flood story (§ 155) tells how the
hero, Ut-napishtim, built a great ship and thus survived a terrible flood,
in which all his countrymen perished. Each of these clay-tablet books,
collected in fresh copies by Assurbanipal for his library (§ 226), bore
his "bookmark" just like a book in a modern library. To prevent anyone else from taking the book, or writing his name on it, the Assyrian
king's bookmark contained the following warning: "Whosoever shall
carry off this tablet, or shall inscribe his name upon it side by side with
mine own, may Assur and Belit overthrow him in wrath and anger, and
may they destroy his name and posterity in the land"

*fields* to fill the ranks of an ever-growing standing army. It is
not improbable that the ruling class were buying up the small
farms to form great estates. We learn of disused canals and

idle fields as we read of Sargon's efforts to restore the old farming communities. Nevertheless, so vast an expansion of the Empire exceeded the power of the standing army to defend it.

**228. Foreign levies in the army; Aramean merchants controlling trade**

As reports of new revolts came in, the harassed ruler at Nineveh forced the subjects of his foreign vassal kingdoms to enter the army. With an army made up to a dangerous extent of such foreigners, with no industries, with fields lying idle, with the commerce of the country in the hands of the Aramean traders (§ 204), and Aramean speech more common in the cities of the Empire, even in Nineveh, than that of the Assyrians themselves — under these conditions the Assyrian nation fast lost its inner strength.

**229. Assaults from without: the Chaldeans from the desert**

In addition to such weakness within, there were the most threatening dangers from without. These came, as of old, from both sides of the Fertile Crescent. Drifting in from the desert, the Aramean hordes were constantly occupying the territory of the Empire. Sennacherib in one campaign took over two hundred thousand captives out of Babylonia, mostly Arameans. At the same time another desert tribe called the " Kaldi," whom we know as the Chaldeans, had been for centuries creeping slowly around the head of the Persian Gulf and settling along its shores at the foot of the eastern mountains. They were Semitic nomads, repeating what the Akkadians had done in Akkad (§ 166), the Amorites in Babylon (§ 175), and the Assyrians at Assur (§ 201).

**230. Assaults from without: Indo-European peoples from the mountains**

On the other hand, in the northern mountains the advancing hordes of Indo-European peoples were in full view (see Section 21), led by the tribes of the Medes and Persians (§ 251). These movements shook the Assyrian State to its foundations. The Chaldeans mastered Babylonia, and then, in combination with the Median hosts from the northeastern mountains, they assailed the walls of Nineveh.

Weakened by a generation of decline within, and struggling vainly against this combined assault from without, the mighty city of the Assyrian emperors fell (612 B.C.). In the voice of the Hebrew prophet Nahum (ii, 8, 13, and iii entire), we hear an echo of the exulting shout which resounded from the Caspian to the Nile as the nations discovered that the terrible scourge of the East had at last been laid low. Its fall was forever, and when two centuries later Xenophon and his ten thousand Greeks marched past the place (§ 630), the Assyrian nation was but a vague tradition, and Nineveh, its great city, was a vast heap of rubbish as it is to-day (Fig. 203). Even Assyrian speech passed away, and Aramaic became the tongue of the region which had once been Assyria, just as it was also to become the language of Babylonia (§ 265). The second great chapter of history on the Two Rivers was ended, having lasted but a scant century and a half (about 750 to 612 B.C.).

**231. Fall of Assyria; destruction of Nineveh (612 B.C.)**

The fall of Assyria, while dramatically sudden and tragically complete, nevertheless left the nations of Western Asia in a very different situation from that in which the first Assyrian emperors had found them. The rule of a single sovereign had been enforced upon the whole great group of nations around the eastern end of the Mediterranean, and the methods of organizing such an empire had been much improved. It was really in continuance of this organization that the great Persian Empire was built up (§ 260), sixty-six years after the fall of Assyria. The Assyrian Empire, especially in its great military organization, marked a long step forward in that gradual growth of the idea of all-including world power, which culminated at last in the Roman Empire. In spite of its often ferocious harshness, the Assyrian rule had furthered civilization. The building of the magnificent palaces in and near Nineveh formed the first chapter in great architecture in Asia. At the same time Nineveh possessed the first libraries as yet known there. Finally, the Assyrian dominion, as we shall see (§ 307), created the international situation which enabled the Hebrews to gain the loftiest conceptions of their own God, as they matched him against the great war god of Assyria — conceptions which have profoundly influenced the entire later history of mankind.

**232. Progress effected by the Assyrian Empire**

## SECTION 20. THE CHALDEAN EMPIRE: THE LAST SEMITIC EMPIRE

**233.** Rise of the Chaldean Empire

The Kaldi, or Chaldeans, the new masters of Babylonia, now founded an empire whose brief career formed the third great chapter of history on the Two Rivers.[1] They were the last Semitic lords of Babylonia. The Chaldeans made their capital at Babylon, rebuilt after its destruction by Sennacherib (§ 214). They gave their name to the land, so that we now know it as Chaldea (from " Kaldi "). While they left the Medes in possession of the northern mountains, the empire of the Chaldeans included the entire Fertile Crescent.

**234.** Reign of Nebuchadnezzar (604–561 B.C.)

At Babylon, Nebuchadnezzar, the greatest of the Chaldean emperors, now (604 B.C.) began a reign of over forty years—a reign of such power and magnificence, especially as reflected to us in the Bible, that he has become one of the great figures of oriental history. Exasperated by the obstinate revolts encouraged by Egypt in the West, Nebuchadnezzar punished the Western nations, especially the little Hebrew kingdom of Judah. He finally carried away many Hebrews as captives to Babylonia and destroyed Jerusalem, their capital (586 B.C.).

**235.** Magnificent buildings of Chaldean Babylon

In spite of long and serious wars, the great king found time and wealth to devote to the enlargement and beautification of Babylon. Copying much from Assyria, Nebuchadnezzar was able to surpass his Assyrian predecessors in the splendor of the great buildings which he now erected. In the large temple quarter in the south of the city he rebuilt the temples of the long-revered Babylonian divinities (Fig. 206). Leading from

---

[1] The three great chapters of history on the Two Rivers are:

1. Early Babylonia (thirty-first century to twenty-first century B.C.; Sargon I about 2750 B.C., Hammurapi about 2100 B.C.). See Sections 14–17.

2. The Assyrian Empire (about 750 to 612 B.C.). See Section 19.

3. The Chaldean Empire (about 612 to 539 B.C.). See Section 20.

With the exception of parts of the first, these three epochs were periods of *Semitic* power. To these we might in later times add a *fourth* period of Semitic supremacy, the triumph of Islam in the seventh century A.D., after the death of Mohammed (§ 1154).

PLATE II. Glazed Brick Lion from the Wall of Nebuchadnezzar's Palace. (After Koldewey)

The Egyptian art of covering walls with decorative designs in glazed tile or brick passed over to Asia. It was employed with magnificent effect on the walls of the Assyrian palaces and at Babylon (Fig. 184, *B*) in the Chaldean Age. Nebuchadnezzar's festival avenue (§ 235) was inclosed on either side with walls adorned with lines of lions like this, leading up to the Gate of Ishtar (Fig. 110)

these to the palace, he laid out a festival avenue which passed
through an imposing gateway called the "Ishtar Gate" (Fig.
110), for it was dedicated to this goddess.   Behind it lay

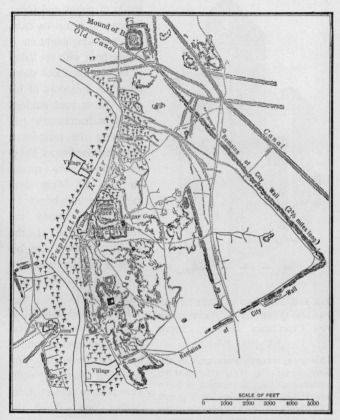

MAP OF BABYLON IN THE CHALDEAN AGE

the vast imperial palace and the offices of government, while
high over all towered the temple-mount which rose by the
Marduk temple as a veritable "Tower of Babel" (see § 152).
Masses of rich tropical verdure, rising in terrace upon terrace,

forming a lofty garden, crowned the roof of the imperial palace and, overlooking the Ishtar Gate, enhanced the brightness of its colors. Here in the cool shade of palms and ferns, inviting to luxurious ease, the great king might enjoy an idle hour with the ladies of his court and look down upon the splendors of his city. These roof gardens of Nebuchadnezzar's palace were the mysterious Hanging Gardens of Babylon, whose fame spread far into the West until they were numbered by the Greeks among the Seven Wonders of the World. Babylon thus became a monumental city like those of Assyria and Egypt (§ 113).

**236.** Extent and modern excavation of Chaldean Babylon

FIG. 110. THE ISHTAR GATE OF THE PALACE QUARTER OF BABYLON IN THE CHALDEAN EMPIRE (SIXTH CENTURY B.C.)

This gate, recently excavated by the Germans (cf. Fig. 111), is the most important building still standing in Babylon. It is not a restoration like Fig. 206. The towers rising on either side of the gate are adorned with the figures of animals in splendidly colored glazed tile, as used also in the Assyrian palaces (Plate II, p. 164). Behind this gate rose the sumptuous palace of Nebuchadnezzar, crowned by the beautiful roof gardens known as the Hanging Gardens of Babylon (§ 235)

For the first time Babylonia saw a very large city. It was immensely extended by Nebuchadnezzar, and enormous fortified walls were built to protect it, including one (above the city) that extended entirely across from river to river. It is this Babylon of Nebuchadnezzar whose marvels over a century later so impressed Herodotus (§ 567), as is shown in the description of the city which he has left us. This, too, is the Babylon which has become familiar to all Christian peoples as the great city of the Hebrew captivity (Section 31). Of all the glories which made it world renowned in its time, little now remains. The excavations in the city

FIG. 111. BEGINNING OF THE EXCAVATION OF ANCIENT BABYLON ON MARCH 26, 1899

The mounds shown are the rubbish covering the palace of Nebuchadnezzar (§ 235). The palms in the background fringe the Euphrates. The Arab workmen in the foreground have just uncovered part of the pavement of Nebuchadnezzar's splendid Festival Street, or processional avenue, which connected the palace and the Ishtar Gate (Fig. 110) with one of the great temples. Beneath all these works of *Chaldean* Babylon (Section 20) should lie the remains of old Babylon of Hammurapi's age (Section 17); but Sennacherib's destruction of the city (§ 214) swept away the older Babylon. Since the first day's work shown above, eighteen years of excavation at Babylon have uncovered almost nothing older than the city of Nebuchadnezzar

(Fig. 111), which continued from 1899 to 1917, slowly revealed one building after another, the scanty wreckage of the ages. These excavations revealed the Festival Street and the Ishtar Gate (Fig. 110), but the Ishtar Gate is almost the only building in all Babylonia of which any impressive remains survive. Elsewhere the broken fragments of dingy sun-baked-brick walls suggest little of the brilliant life which once ebbed and flowed through these streets and public places.

**237.** Civilization of Chaldean Babylon

The Chaldeans seem to have absorbed the civilization of Babylonia in much the same way as other earlier Semitic invaders of this ancient plain (§§ 167, 175). Commerce and business flourished, the arts and industries were highly developed, religion and literature were cultivated and their records were put into wedge-writing on clay tablets as of old.

**238.** Rise of astronomy and astrology

Science made notable progress in one important branch — astronomy. The Babylonians continued the ancient practice of trying to discover the future in the heavenly bodies (see § 192). This art, which we call "astrology," was now very systematically pursued and was really becoming astronomy. The equator was divided into 360 degrees, and for the first time the Chaldean astrologers laid out the twelve groups of stars which we call the "Twelve Signs of the Zodiac." Thus for the first time the sky and its worlds were being mapped out.

**239.** Origin of names of the planets

The five planets then known (Mercury, Venus, Mars, Jupiter, and Saturn) were especially regarded as the powers controlling the fortunes of men, and as such the five leading Babylonian divinities were identified with these five heavenly bodies. The names of these Babylonian divinities have descended to us as the names of the planets. But on their way to us through Europe, the ancient Babylonian divine names were translated into Roman forms. So the planet of Ishtar, the goddess of love, became Venus, while that of the great god Marduk became Jupiter, and so on. The celestial observations made by these Chaldean "astrologers," as we call them, slowly became sufficiently accurate, so that the observers could already foretell an eclipse. These observations when inherited by the Greeks formed the basis of the science of astronomy, which the Greeks carried so much further (§ 492). The practice of astrology has survived to our own day; we still unconsciously recall it in such phrases as "his lucky star" or an "ill-starred undertaking."

We can discern in the new architecture of Babylon how this Chaldean Age brought Babylonia up to the new and higher

level of civilization attained by Assyria. Nevertheless, the
Chaldeans themselves fancied that they were restoring the
civilization of the old Babylonia of Hammurapi. The scribes
loved to employ an ancient style of writing and out-of-date
forms of speech; the kings tunneled deep under the temple
foundations and searched for years that they might find the
old foundation records buried (like our corner-stone documents)
by kings of ancient days (§ 160).

240. The oriental revival of the past

This dependence upon the past meant decline. After the
death of Nebuchadnezzar (561 B.C.), whose reign was the high-
water mark of Chaldean civilization, the old civilized lands of
the Orient seemed to have lost most of their former power to
go forward and to make fresh discoveries and new conquests
in civilization, such as they had been making during three great
ages on the Nile and three similar ages on the Two Rivers.
Indeed the leadership of the Semitic peoples in the early world
was drawing near its close, and they were about to give way
before the advance of new peoples of the Indo-European race
(Section 21). The nomads of the southern desert were about
to yield to the hardy peoples of the northern and eastern mountains, and to these we must now turn.

241. Decline of the old oriental lands

## QUESTIONS

SECTION 18. Where does the second chapter of history on the
Two Rivers carry us? Describe the region about Assur. Who
founded Assur, and when? Whence did they gain the beginnings of
civilization? Was Assur also exposed to influences from the North?
What was the result? Who were the Western rivals of Assur? Tell
about the Arameans and what they accomplished. What important
thing did they carry throughout Western Asia? What prevented
Assyria from reaching the Mediterranean? What had Assyrian civilization achieved by this time? What has recent excavation discovered
under the palace of Assur?

SECTION 19. What city had chiefly prevented Assyria from conquering the West? When was Damascus captured by Assyria? What
was the result in the West? Who was the founder of the leading

line of Assyrian emperors? Describe his new city. What was the extent of the Assyrian Empire? How was its government carried on? What can you say about Assyrian warfare? about architecture and sculpture? Was all this of Assyrian origin? What can you say of the reign of Sennacherib in war, building, or any other important matters? What can you tell of Assurbanipal? What dangers within and without caused the fall of Assyria? What peoples destroyed Nineveh, and when? What became of the ruins of the city? What progress resulted from the rule of the Assyrian Empire?

SECTION 20. What empire formed the third chapter of history on the Two Rivers? Who founded it, and when? Whence did they come? Who was the greatest Chaldean king? What did he accomplish in war? What people did he carry away captive? Describe his buildings at Babylon. Had there been any large cities in Babylonia before his time? Whence did he borrow much in the architecture of his palace? What has become of his buildings? In what science did the Chaldeans make great progress? What astronomical names have descended to us from them? Could they predict an eclipse? To what race did the Chaldeans belong? What race was to follow them in oriental leadership?

NOTE. The following sketch shows us a temple of the Assyrians at Assur as restored by the excavators. Behind the temple court is the holy of holies, and on each side of it rises a temple tower with a winding ascent, after the old Babylonian manner (§ 152). It was from such towers that the tower architecture of the early world arose, eventually producing our own church spires, of which the Babylonian temple tower was the ancestor (see Fig. 272).

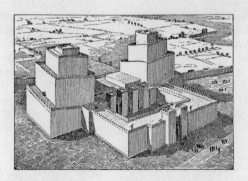

# CHAPTER VI

## THE MEDO-PERSIAN EMPIRE

### Section 21. The Indo-European Peoples and their Dispersion [1]

We have seen that the Arabian desert has been a great reservoir of unsettled population, which was continually leaving the grasslands on the margin of the desert and shifting over into the towns to begin a settled life (§ 135). Corresponding to these grasslands of the *South*, there are similar grasslands in the *North* (Fig. 112). These Northern grasslands stretch from the lower Danube eastward along the north side of the Black Sea through southern Russia and far into Asia north and east

242. The Northern grasslands

NOTE. The headpiece above shows ancient fire altars still surviving in Persia. Near by are the tombs of the great Persian kings (Fig. 118) not far from Persepolis (Fig. 116), the capital of Persia, and these kings doubtless often worshiped before the fires blazing on these altars.

[1] Section 21 should be carefully worked over by the teacher with the class before the class is permitted to study it alone. The diagram (Fig. 112) should be put on the blackboard and explained in detail by the teacher, and the class should then be prepared to put the diagram on the board from memory. This should be done again when the study of the Greeks is begun (§ 370), and a third time when Italy and the Romans are taken up.

of the Caspian (see map, p. 678). In ancient times they always had a wandering shepherd population, and time after time, for thousands of years, these Northern nomads have poured forth over Europe and Western Asia, just as the desert Semites of the South have done over the Fertile Crescent (§ 135).

**243. The two lines — Indo-European and Semitic**

These nomads of the North were from the earliest times a great white race, which we call *Indo-European*. We can perhaps best explain this term by saying that these Indo-Europeans were the ancestors of the present peoples of Europe. As our forefathers came from Europe, the Indo-European nomads were also our own ancestors. These nomads of the *Northern* grasslands, our ancestors, began to migrate in very ancient times, moving out along diverging routes. They at last extended in an imposing line from the frontiers of India on the east, westward across all Europe to the Atlantic, as they do to-day (Fig. 112). This great northern line was confronted on the south by a similar line of Semitic peoples, extending from Babylonia on the east, through Phœnicia and the Hebrews westward to Carthage and similar Semitic settlements of Phœnicia in the western Mediterranean (§ 135, and map, p. 288).

**244. The struggle between the two lines — Indo-European and Semitic**

The history of the ancient world, as we are now to follow it, was largely made up of the struggle between this *southern Semitic* line, which issued from the Southern grasslands, and the *northern Indo-European* line, which came forth from the Northern grasslands to confront the older civilizations represented in the southern line. Thus as we look at the diagram (Fig. 112) we see the two great races facing each other across the Mediterranean like two vast armies stretching from Western Asia westward to the Atlantic. The later wars between Rome and Carthage (Sections 78, 79) represent some of the operations on the Semitic left wing; while the triumph of Persia over Chaldea (Section 23) is a similar outcome on the Semitic right wing.

The result of the long conflict was the complete triumph of our ancestors, the Indo-European line, which conquered along the center and both wings and finally gained unchallenged

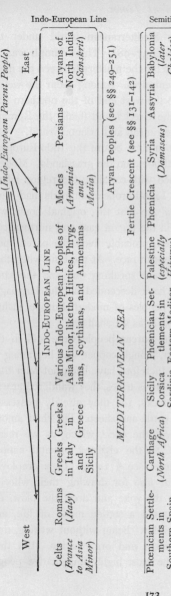

FIG. 112. DIAGRAM SUGGESTING THE TWO LINES OF SEMITIC AND INDO-EUROPEAN DISPERSION

The actual lines along which these peoples lie are of course not straight. The lines sometimes overlie each other, as in Sicily, mentioned in both lines. Egypt, which geographically belongs in the southern line, has been omitted because it is not purely Semitic, although closely related to the Semites. Notice also that in the West the two races face each other for the most part across the Mediterranean; in the East they confront each other along the Fertile Crescent (§ 132). The Hittites, included above among the Indo-European peoples, became so in language, though evidently not originally so in blood (§ 376)

**245. Triumph of the European end of the Indo-European line**

supremacy throughout the Mediterranean world under the Greeks and Romans (Sections 37–98). This triumph was accompanied by a long struggle for the mastery between the members of the northern line themselves. Among them the victory moved from the east end to the west end of the northern line, as first the Persians, then the Greeks, and finally the Romans, gained control of the Mediterranean and oriental world.

**246. The Indo-European parent people and their original home**

Let us now turn back to a time before the Indo-European people had left their original home on the grasslands. Modern study has not yet determined with certainty the region where the parent people of the Indo-European nomads had their home. The indications now are that this original home was on the great grassy steppe in the region east and northeast of the Caspian Sea. Here, then, probably lived the parent people of all the later Indo-European race. At the time when they were still one people, they were speaking one and the same tongue. From this tongue have descended all the languages later spoken by the civilized peoples of modern Europe, including, of course, our own English, as we shall see.

**247. Civilization of the Indo-European parent people**

Before they dispersed, the parent people were still in the Stone Age for the most part, though copper was beginning to come in, and the time must therefore have been not later than 2500 B.C. Divided into numerous tribes, they wandered at will, seeking pasture for their flocks, for they already possessed domestic animals, including cattle and sheep. But chief among their domesticated beasts was the *horse*, which, as we recall, was still entirely unknown to the civilized oriental nations until after Hammurapi's time (see § 197). They employed him not only for riding but also for drawing their wheeled carts. The ox already bore the yoke and drew the plow, for some of the tribes had adopted a settled mode of life, and cultivated grain, especially barley. Being without writing, they possessed but little government and organization. But they were the most gifted and the most highly imaginative people of the ancient world.

As their tribes wandered farther and farther apart they lost contact with each other. Local peculiarities in speech and customs became more and more marked, until wide differences resulted. While at first the different groups could doubtless understand one another when they met, these differences in speech gradually became so great that the widely scattered tribes, even if they happened to meet, could no longer make themselves understood, and finally they lost all knowledge of their original kinship. This kinship has only been rediscovered in very recent times. The final outcome, in so far as speech was concerned, was the languages of modern civilized Europe; so that, beginning with England in the West and going eastward, we can trace more than one common word from people to people entirely across Europe into northern India. Note the following:

**248.** The dispersion of the Indo-European parent people

| WEST | | | | | EAST |
|---|---|---|---|---|---|
| ENGLISH | GERMAN | LATIN | GREEK | OLD PERSIAN and AVESTAN | EAST INDIAN (Sanskrit) |
| brother | bruder | fräter | phrātēr | brātar | bhrātar |
| mother | mutter | māter | mētēr | mātar | mātar |
| father | vater | pater | patēr | pitar | pitar |

In the West these wanderers from the Northern grasslands had already crossed the Danube and were far down in the Balkan peninsula by 2000 B.C. Some of them had doubtless already entered Italy by this time (§ 775), illustrating what we learned in studying Stone Age Europe, about the shifting habits of shepherd or nomad peoples, as they drive their flocks from pasture to pasture (§ 35). These Western tribes were, of course, the ancestors of the Greeks and Romans. We shall later join them and follow them in their conquest of the Mediterranean (Sections 37–98). Before doing so, however, we have to watch the *eastern* wing of the vast Indo-European line as it swings southward and comes into collision with the right wing of the Semitic line.

## SECTION 22. THE ARYAN PEOPLES AND THE IRANIAN PROPHET ZOROASTER

**249.** The Aryans; the advance of the eastern wing of the Indo-European line

It is now an established fact that the easternmost tribes of the Indo-European line, having left the parent people, were pasturing their herds in the great steppe on the east of the Caspian by about 2000 B.C. Here they formed a people properly called the Aryans [1] (see Fig. 112), and here they made their home for some time. The Aryan people had no writing, and they have left no monuments. Nevertheless, the beliefs of their descendants show that the Aryan tribes already possessed a high form of religion, which summed up conduct as "good thoughts, good deeds." Fire occupied an important place in this faith, and they had a group of priests whom they called "fire-kindlers."

**250.** Sanskrit-speaking tribes in India

When the Aryans broke up, perhaps about 1800 B.C., they separated into two groups. The Eastern tribes wandered southeastward and eventually arrived in India. In their sacred books, which we call the Vedas, written in Sanskrit, there are echoes of the days of Aryan unity, and they furnish many a hint of the ancient Aryan home on the east of the Caspian.

**251.** Medes and Persians further west toward the Fertile Crescent

The other group, whose tribes kept the name "Aryan" in the form "Iran," [2] also left this home and pushed westward and southwestward into the mountains bordering our Fertile Crescent (§ 133). We call them Iranians, and among them were two

[1] The Indo-European parent people apparently had no common name for all their tribes as a great group. The term "Aryan" is often popularly applied to the parent people, but this custom is incorrect. "Aryan" (from which "Iran" and "Iranian" are later derivatives) designated a group of tribes, a fragment of the parent people, which detached itself and found a home for some centuries just east of the Caspian Sea. When we hear the term "Aryan" applied to the Indo-European peoples of Europe, or when it is said that we ourselves are descended from the Aryans, we must remember that this use of the word is historically incorrect, though very common. The Aryans, then, were *Eastern* descendants of the Indo-European parent people, as we are *Western* descendants of the parent people. The Aryans are our distant cousins but not our ancestors.

[2] They have given their name to the great Iranian plateau, which stretches from the Zagros Mountains eastward to the Indus River. This whole region was known in Greek and Roman days as Ariana, which (like "Iran") is, of course, derived from "Aryan" (see map, p. 434).

powerful tribes, the Medes and the Persians.[1] We recall how, in the days of Assyria's imperial power the Medes descended from the northern mountains against Nineveh (§ 230). This southern advance of the Indo-European eastern wing was thus overwhelming the Semitic right wing (Fig. 112) occupying the Fertile Crescent.

By 600 B.C., after the fall of Assyria (§ 231), the Medes had established a powerful Iranian empire in the mountains east of the Tigris. It extended from the Persian Gulf, where it included the Persians, northwestward in the general line of the mountains to the Black Sea region. The front of the Indo-European eastern wing was thus roughly parallel with the Tigris at this point, but its advance was not to stop here. Nebuchadnezzar (§ 234) and the Chaldean masters of Babylon looked with anxious eyes at this dangerous Median power. The Chaldeans on the Euphrates represented the leadership of men of Semitic blood from the *southern* pastures. Their leadership was now to be followed by that of men of Indo-European blood from the *northern* pastures (§ 242). As we see the Chaldeans giving way before the Medes and Persians (§ 261), let us bear in mind that we are watching a great racial change, and remember that these new Iranian masters of the East were our kindred; for both we and they have descended from the same wandering shepherd ancestors, the Indo-European parent people, who once dwelt in the far-off pastures of inner Asia, probably five thousand years ago.

All of these Iranians possessed a beautiful religion inherited from old Aryan days (see § 249). Somewhere in the eastern mountains, as far back as 1000 B.C., an Iranian named Zoroaster began to look out upon the life of men in an effort to find a new religion which would meet the needs of man's life. He watched the ceaseless struggle between good and evil

**252.** The Median (Indo-European) Empire threatens Chaldean (Semitic) Babylonia

**253.** The religion of the Iranians

---

[1] About 2100 B.C., in the age of Hammurapi, long before the Iranians reached the Fertile Crescent, their coming was announced in advance by the arrival of the horse in Babylonia (see § 197).

which seemed to meet him wherever he turned. To him it seemed to be a struggle between a group of good beings on the one hand and of evil powers on the other. The Good became to him a divine person, whom he called Mazda, or Ahuramazda, which means "Lord of Wisdom" and whom he regarded as God. Ahuramazda was surrounded by a group of helpers much like angels, of whom one of the greatest was the Light, called "Mithras." Opposed to Ahuramazda and his helpers it was finally believed there was an evil group led by a great Spirit of Evil named Ahriman. It was he who later was inherited by Jews and Christians as Satan.

**254.** Judgment hereafter

Thus the faith of Zoroaster grew up out of the struggle of life itself, and became a great power in life. It was one of the noblest religions ever founded. It called upon every man to stand on one side or the other; to fill his soul with the Good and the Light or to dwell in the Evil and the Darkness. Whatever course a man pursued, he must expect a judgment hereafter. This was the earliest appearance in Asia of belief in a last judgment. Zoroaster maintained the old Aryan veneration of fire (§ 249) as a visible symbol of the Good and the Light, and he preserved the ancient fire-kindling priests (headpiece, p. 171).

**255.** Zoroaster preaches his new religion

Zoroaster went about among the Iranian people, preaching his new religion, and probably for many years found but little response to his efforts. We can discern his hopes and fears alike in the little group of hymns he has left, probably the only words of the great prophet which have survived. It is characteristic of the horse-loving Iranians that Zoroaster is said to have finally converted one of their great kings by miraculously healing the king's crippled horse. The new faith had gained a firm footing before the prophet's death, however, and before 700 B.C. it was the leading religion among the Medes in the mountains along the Fertile Crescent. Thus Zoroaster became the first great founder of a religious faith.

As in the case of Mohammed, it is probable that Zoroaster could neither read nor write, for the Iranians possessed no system of writing in his day (see § 266). Besides the hymns mentioned above, fragments of his teaching have descended to us in writings put together in the early Christian centuries, over a thousand years after the prophet's death. They form a book known as the *Avesta*. This we may call the Bible of the Persians.

**256.** The *Avesta*, the Persian Bible

## Section 23. Rise of the Persian Empire: Cyrus

No people became more zealous followers of Zoroaster than the group of Iranian tribes known as the Persians. Through them a knowledge of him has descended to us. At the fall of Nineveh (612 B.C.) (§ 231) they were already long settled in the region at the southeastern end of the Zagros Mountains, just north of the Persian Gulf. Its shores are here little better than desert, but the valleys of the mountainous hinterland are rich and fertile. Here the Persians occupied a district some four hundred miles long. They were a rude mountain peasant folk, leading a settled agricultural life, with simple institutions, no art, no writing or literature, but with stirring memories of their past. As they tilled their fields and watched their flocks they told many a tale of their Aryan ancestors and of the ancient prophet whose faith they held.

**257.** The emergence of the Persians; their land and traditions

They acknowledged themselves vassals of their kinsmen the Medes, who ruled far to the north and northwest of them. One of their tribes dwelling in the mountains of Elam (see map, p. 102), a tribe known as Anshan, was organized as a little kingdom. About sixty years after the fall of Nineveh this little kingdom of Anshan was ruled over by a Persian named Cyrus. He succeeded in uniting the other tribes of his kindred Persians into a nation. Thereupon Cyrus at once rebelled against the rule of the Medes. He gathered his peasant soldiery, and within three years he defeated the Median king and made himself master of the Median territory. The extraordinary career of Cyrus was now a spectacle upon which all eyes in the West were fastened with wonder and alarm.

**258.** Cyrus of Anshan organizes the Persian tribes into a nation and conquers the Medes

**259.** The Persian army

The overflowing energies of the new conqueror and his peasant soldiery proved irresistible. The Persian peasants seem to have been remarkable archers. The mass of the Persian army was made up of bowmen (Fig. 113), whose storm of arrows at long range overwhelmed the enemy long before the hand-to-hand fighting began. Bodies of the skillful Persian horsemen, hovering on either wing, then rode in and completed the destruction of the foe. These arrangements were taken by the Persians from the Assyrians, the greatest soldiers the East had ever seen.

FIG. 113. PERSIAN SOLDIERS

Although carrying spears when doing duty as palace guards, these men were chiefly archers (§ 259), as is shown by the size of the large quivers on their backs. The bow hangs on the left shoulder. The royal bodyguard may also be seen wielding their spears around the Persian king at the battle of Issus (Fig. 202). Notice the splendid robes worn by these palace guards. The figures are done in brightly colored glazed brick — an art borrowed by the Persians (see Plate II, p. 164) and employed to beautify the palace walls. The restoration in Fig. 204 shows such a frieze of archers in position along the wall of the palace court

**260.** Cyrus conquers the West

The great states Babylonia (Chaldea) and Egypt, Lydia under King Crœsus in western Asia Minor (§ 497), and even Sparta in Greece (§ 426) formed a powerful combination against this sudden menace, which had risen like the flash of a meteor in the eastern sky. Without an instant's delay Cyrus struck at Crœsus of Lydia, the chief author of the hostile combination. One Persian victory followed after another. By 546 B.C. Sardis, the Lydian capital (Fig. 173), had fallen, and Crœsus, the Lydian king, was a prisoner in the hands of Cyrus. Cyrus at once gained also the southern coasts of Asia Minor. Within five years the power of the little Persian kingdom in the mountains of Elam had swept across Asia Minor to the Mediterranean and had become the leading state in the oriental world.

FIG. 114. BARREL-SHAPED CLAY RECORD OF THE CAPTURE OF BABYLON BY CYRUS (539 B.C.)

It tells how "without battle and without fighting Marduk [God of Babylon] made him [Cyrus] enter into his city of Babylon; he spared Babylon tribulation, and Nabonidus the [Chaldean] king who feared him not, he delivered into his hand." Nabonidus, the Chaldean king of Babylon, was not in favor with the priests, and they assisted in delivering the city to Cyrus

Turning eastward again, Cyrus had no trouble in defeating the Chaldean army led by the young crown prince Belshazzar, whose name in the Book of Daniel (see Dan. v) is a household word throughout the Christian world. In spite of the vast walls erected by Nebuchadnezzar to protect Babylon (§ 236), the Persians entered the great city in 539 B.C., seemingly without resistance (Fig. 114).

Thus only seventy-three years after the fall of Nineveh (§ 231) had opened the conflict between the former dwellers in the Northern and the Southern grasslands, the Semitic East

261. Cyrus conquers Babylonia (Chaldea)

262. Collapse
of the Semitic
East before
the Indo-
European
assault

completely collapsed before the advance of the Indo-European
power. Some ten years later Cyrus fell in battle (528 B.C.)
as he was fighting with the nomads in northeastern Iran. His
body was reverently laid away in a massive tomb of impressive
simplicity at Pasargadæ (Fig. 115), where Cyrus himself had
established the capital of Persia. Thus passed away the first
great conqueror of Indo-European blood.

263. Cam-
byses con-
quers Egypt;
Persia rules
whole civi-
lized East

All Western Asia was now subject to the Persian king; but
in 525 B.C., only three years after the death of Cyrus, his son
Cambyses conquered Egypt. This conquest of the only remaining ancient oriental power rounded out the Persian Empire to
include the whole civilized East from the Nile Delta, around
the entire eastern end of the Mediterranean to the Ægean,
and from this western boundary eastward almost to India.
The great task had consumed just twenty-five years since the
overthrow of the Medes by Cyrus. It was an achievement for
which the Assyrian Empire had prepared the way, and the
Persians were now to learn much from the great civilizations
which had preceded them.

## Section 24. The Civilization of the Persian Empire (about 530 to 330 B.C.)

264. Persian
kings at
Babylon
absorb civili-
zation of the
East they
rule

The Persians found Babylon a great and splendid city, with
the vast fortifications of Nebuchadnezzar stretching from river
to river and his sumptuous buildings visible far across the Babylonian plain (§§ 235–236). The city was the center of the
commerce of Western Asia and the greatest market in the early
oriental world. Along the Nile the Persian emperors now ruled
the splendid cities whose colossal monuments we have visited.
These things and the civilized life which the Persians found
along the Nile and the Euphrates soon influenced them greatly,
as we shall see.

Aramaic, the speech of the Aramean merchants who filled
the busy market places of Babylon, had by that time become

Fig. 115. The Tomb of Cyrus near Persepolis

The oldest important Persian building, probably built by Cyrus himself. It was surrounded by a colonnade, of which the remains are visible at the left. The body of Cyrus lay here for nearly two hundred years, when Alexander the Great (§ 699) found it lying on the floor of the tomb, plundered of its royal ornaments. He ordered the body restored to its place, and had the tomb chamber closed up. It is now empty

From an etching by George T. Plowman

FIG. 116. GREAT STAIRWAY AND GATE OF THE PERSIAN PALACES AT PERSEPOLIS *

The grand terrace of which this is the entrance is as high as an average two-story house in America. It was occupied by a group of magnificent palaces, of which the ruins are shown on page 196. Below the terrace lay the royal city, just as in Fig. 104

the language of the whole Fertile Crescent. Business documents were now written in Aramaic with pen and ink on papyrus, and clay tablets bearing cuneiform writing were slowly disappearing. The Persian officials were therefore obliged to carry on their government business, like the collection of taxes, in the Aramaic tongue throughout the western half of the Persian Empire. Even as far as the Nile and western Asia Minor, they sent out their government documents in Aramaic, this universal language of business (Fig. 131).

265. Aramaic becomes the language of Persian administration in the West

The government of the Persian kings, like that of the Assyrian Empire, was thus "bilingual" (§ 206), by which we mean that it employed two languages — Aramaic and the old Persian tongue. Even in writing Persian, the Persians often employed Aramaic letters, as we write English with Roman letters. At the same time, having probably gained from Aramaic writing the idea of an alphabet, the Persian scribes devised another alphabet, of thirty-nine *cuneiform* signs, which they employed for writing Persian on clay tablets. They also used it when they wished to make records on large monuments of stone (Fig. 117). Thus the Persians, who had been so long entirely without writing, began to make enduring written records after they entered the Fertile Crescent. These monuments are the earliest Persian documents which have descended to us.

266. Persians devise a cuneiform alphabet

\* This royal stairway, the finest surviving from the ancient world, was laid out by Darius and finished by Xerxes. A proud inscription of Darius cut in cuneiform on the wall of the stairway looks down upon the visitor. It reads: "Darius the king saith: 'This land of Persia, which Ahuramazda has entrusted to me, the land that is beautiful, that hath good people and fine horses,— by the will of Ahuramazda and my will, it fears no enemy.'" The terrace wall is from 30 to 50 feet high, but the steps of the grand stairway are so low that a horse may be easily ridden up the steps to the terrace. Leading from the stairway is the magnificent gate built by Xerxes, guarded on either hand by huge winged bulls, an art symbol borrowed by Persia from Assyria. Beyond the gate still rise two splendid columns of the imposing colonnade erected by Xerxes to adorn this entrance.

FIG. 117. TRIUMPHAL MONUMENT OF DARIUS THE GREAT, THE ROSETTA STONE OF ASIA, ON THE CLIFF OF BEHISTUN

This impressive monument is the most important historical document surviving in Asia. It is made up of four important parts: the relief sculptures (*A*) and the three inscriptions (*B, C, D*). *B* is a great inscription, in columns some 12 feet high, recording the triumph of Darius over all his enemies in the extensive revolts which followed his coronation. It is in the Persian language, written with the new cuneiform alphabet of thirty-nine letters which the Persians devised (§ 266). The other two inscriptions (*C* and *D*) are translations of the Persian (*B*). *C* therefore contains the same record as the Persian (*B*); but it is in the Babylonian language and is written in Babylonian cuneiform with its several hundred wedge-signs (§ 149). *D*, the third inscription, is also cuneiform, in the language of the region of Susa, and hence is called Susian. Thus the Great King published his triumph in the three most important languages of this eastern region and placed the record overlooking a main road at Behistun (see map, p. 434) where the men of the caravans passing between Babylon and the Iranian Plateau would look up 300 feet and see the splendid monument 25 feet high and 50 feet wide. To reach it requires a dangerous climb, and it was on this lofty cliff, at the risk of his life, that Sir Henry Rawlinson copied all three of these cuneiform inscriptions (1835–1847). By the use of these copies Rawlinson succeeded in deciphering the ancient Babylonian cuneiform (§§ 282–283); and this great monument of Darius therefore enabled modern historians to recover the lost language and history of Babylonia and Assyria. It did for Western Asia what the Rosetta Stone did for Egypt.

(Drawn from photographs of the British Museum Expedition)

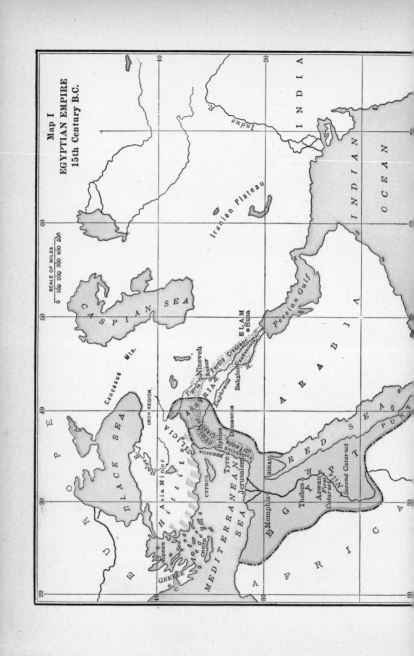

Map I
EGYPTIAN EMPIRE
15th Century B.C.

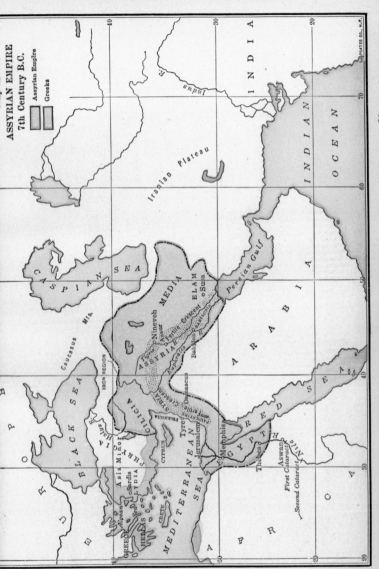

## ASSYRIAN EMPIRE
### 7th Century B.C.

▨ Assyrian Empire
▨ Greeks

SEQUENCE MAP SHOWING EXPANSION OF THE ORIENTAL EMPIRES FOR A THOUSAND YEARS (FROM ABOUT 1500 TO 500 B.C.). IN FOUR PARTS. (See Map III and Map IV following)

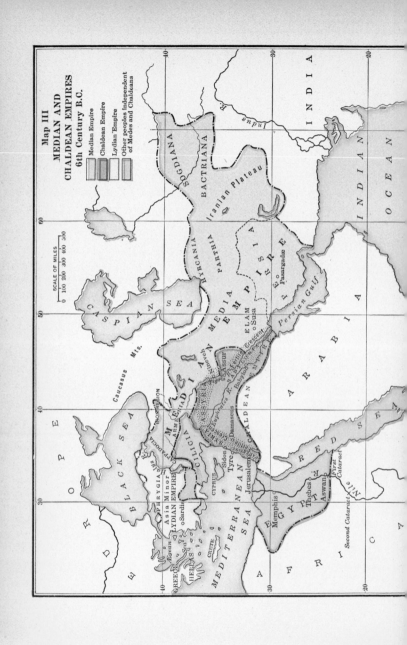

Map III
MEDIAN AND
CHALDEAN EMPIRES
6th Century B.C.

Median Empire
Chaldean Empire
Lydian Empire
Other peoples independent
of Medes and Chaldeans

SCALE OF MILES
0   100 200 300 400 500

INDIA

INDIAN
OCEAN

SOGDIANA

BACTRIANA

Iranian Plateau

Indus

HYRCANIA

PARTHIA

MEDIA
EMPIRE

CASPIAN SEA

ELAM
Susa

Pasargadae

Persian Gulf

Caucasus Mts.

ASSYRIA
Nineveh
Assur
Tigris R.
Euphrates R.
Fertile Crescent
Babylon
CHALDEAN

ARABIA

ARMENIA
MEDIAN

Mt. Ararat

CILICIA
Tarsus
Damascus

RED SEA

BLACK SEA

PHRYGIA
Asia Minor
LYDIAN EMPIRE
Sardis

CYPRUS
Sidon
Tyre
Jerusalem
Nile R.

EGYPT
Memphis
Thebes
Aswan
First Cataract
Second Cataract

EUROPE

GREECE
Athens
Aegean
CRETE

MEDITERRANEAN SEA

AFRICA

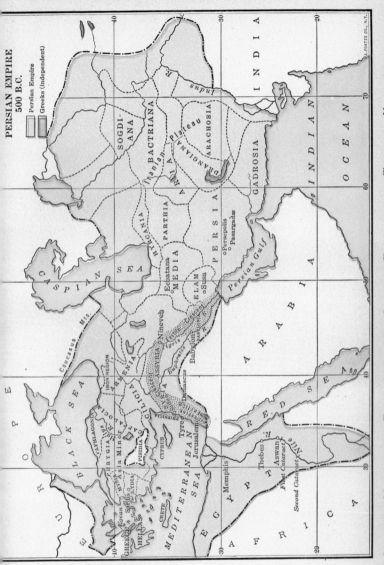

PERSIAN EMPIRE
500 B.C.

☐ Persian Empire
☐ Greeks (Independent)

SEQUENCE MAP SHOWING EXPANSION OF THE ORIENTAL EMPIRES FOR A THOUSAND YEARS (FROM ABOUT 1500 TO 500 B.C.). IN FOUR PARTS. (See Map I and Map II preceding)

to the Isthmus of Suez. Scylax was the first Western sailor known to have sailed along this south coast of Asia, so little known at that time (about 500 B.C.).

At Suez, Darius restored the ancient but long filled-up canal of the Egyptians connecting the Nile with the Red Sea (§ 104). Along the ancient route of this canal have been found fragments of great stone tablets erected by Darius (see map, p. 36). They bear an account of the restoration of the canal, in which we find the words of Darius: "I commanded to dig this canal, from the stream flowing in Egypt, called the Nile, to the sea [Red Sea] which stretches from Persia. Then this canal was dug as I commanded, and ships sailed from Egypt through this canal to Persia, according to my will." Darius evidently cherished what proved to be a vain hope, that the south coast of Persia might come to share in the now growing commerce between India and the Mediterranean world. As Persia was now lacking in small landowners, so also was she lacking in small and enterprising merchants, who might have become great promoters of commerce.

**271.** Darius links East and West by a Suez canal

Unlike the Assyrians, Darius treated the Phœnician cities with kindness, and succeeded in organizing a great Phœnician war fleet. We shall find that Darius' son Xerxes could depend upon many hundreds of ships for warfare and transportation in the eastern Mediterranean (§§ 501, 510). Thus the more enlightened Persian kings accomplished what the Assyrian emperors never achieved, and Persia became the first great sea power in Asia.

**272.** Persia becomes the earliest great sea power in Asia

The Persian emperors maintained communication by excellent roads from end to end of the vast Empire. On a smaller scale these roads must have done for the Persian Empire what railroads do for us. Royal messengers maintained a much more complete postal system than had already been introduced under the Assyrian Empire (§ 218). These messengers were surprisingly swift, although merchandise required about as much time to go from Susa to the Ægean Sea as we now need for going

**273.** System of roads and communication

around the world. A good example of the effect of these roads was the incoming of the domestic fowl, which we commonly call the chicken. Its home was in India and it was unknown

FIG. 118. TOMBS OF THE EARLIER KINGS OF PERSIA A FEW MILES FROM THE RUINS OF PERSEPOLIS

After Cyrus and his son Cambyses had passed away, the Persian kings, beginning with Darius, excavated their tombs in the face of this cliff, about six miles from their palaces at Persepolis (Fig. 118). Here then are the tombs of Darius I (the Great) (third from the left), Xerxes (at the far end), Darius II and Artaxerxes I (first and second from the left). Of the first six great kings of Persia we thus have the tombs of five (tomb of Cyrus, Fig. 115), leaving out Cambyses the conqueror of Egypt, whose tomb has never been found. The remaining three royal tombs belonging to the last three kings of the Achæmenian line (the line of Darius) (Artaxerxes II, Artaxerxes III, and Darius III) are cut in the cliff behind the palaces of Persepolis (Fig. 116). The square above the colonnade in each tomb front shows a sculptured picture of the king worshiping Ahuramazda before a fire altar. All of these tombs were broken open and robbed in ancient times, like the tomb of Cyrus (Fig. 115). Inside, in niches, are the massive stone coffins in which Darius, Xerxes, and the other kings and their families were buried

in the Mediterranean until Persian communications brought it from India to the Ægean Sea. Thus the Persians brought to Europe the barnyard fowl so familiar to us.

The ancient Elamite city of Susa, in the Zagros Mountains (see map, p. 102), was the chief residence and capital (Fig. 204). The mild air of the Babylonian plain, however, attracted the sovereign during the colder months, when he went to dwell in the palaces of the vanished Chaldean Empire at Babylon. In spite of its remoteness the earlier kings had made an effort to live in their old Persian home. Cyrus built a splendid palace near the battlefield where he had defeated the Medes at Pasargadæ (see map, p. 434), and Darius also established a magnificent residence at Persepolis (Fig. 116), some forty miles south of the palace of Cyrus. Near the ruins of these buildings the tombs of Cyrus, Darius, Xerxes, and the other Persian emperors still stand in their native Persia (Fig. 118).

*274. Capital and royal residences*

The Persian architects had to learn architecture from the old oriental peoples now subject to Persia. The enormous terraces (Fig. 116) on which the Persian palaces stood were imitated from Babylonia. The winged bulls at the palace gates (Fig. 116) were copied from those of Assyria and the West. The vast colonnades (Fig. 116) stretching along the front and filling the enormous halls — the earliest colonnades of Asia — had grown up over two thousand years earlier on the Nile (Fig. 56). Likewise the gorgeously colored palace walls of enameled brick (Figs. 113, 204, and Plate II, p. 164) reached Persia from the Nile by the way of Assyria and the West.[1] Thus the great civilizations which made up the Empire were merged together in the life of the Persian Empire.

*275. Architecture*

## SECTION 25. PERSIAN DOCUMENTS AND THE DECIPHERMENT OF CUNEIFORM

The adoption by the Persians of the mixed oriental civilization which they found on the Fertile Crescent has been of the greatest scientific importance. It was the documents

*276. The value and place of Persian documents in the decipherment of cuneiform*

[1] It is very noticeable that the Persian architects did not adopt the arch from Babylonia. On the contrary, each door in the palace of Darius (Fig. 204) is topped with a horizontal block of stone, copied from Egyptian doors.

produced by the Persians when they learned to write cuneiform there, which first enabled us to read the cuneiform inscriptions of Western Asia (§ 160). Without the documents left us by the Persians, modern scholars would still be unable to read the thousands of clay tablets which we discussed in our study of Babylonia and Assyria (Figs. 79, 92, 109, and 126).

**277.** Cuneiform writing ceases; Babylonia and Assyria are forgotten

When Aramaic had displaced the Babylonian and Assyrian languages (§ 265), there came a time when no one wrote any more clay tablets or other records in the ancient wedge-writing.[1] Nearly two thousand years ago the last man who could read a cuneiform tablet had passed away. The history of Babylonia and Assyria was consequently lost under the city mounds (§§ 158–161) along the Tigris and Euphrates.

**278.** Grotefend recovers the sounds of the first Persian signs (1802)

Before 1800 A.D. travelers in Persia had brought back to Europe a number of copies of cuneiform inscriptions which they had found engraved on the ruined walls of the Persian palaces (Fig. 116). These inscriptions were observed to contain a very limited number of cuneiform signs, and hence there seemed to be some possibility of learning their meaning. In 1802 a German schoolmaster at Göttingen named Grotefend identified and read the names of Darius and Xerxes and some other words and names in these Persian inscriptions. He was finally able to read two short Persian inscriptions in cuneiform (Fig. 119). These were the first Persian inscriptions to be read in modern times, but they were so short that they were far from including all the cuneiform signs in the Persian alphabet, and Persian cuneiform writing was still by no means deciphered.

**279.** Rawlinson's decipherment of Old Persian cuneiform (1847)

A number of other interested European scholars were able to discover the sounds of nearly all the other signs in the Persian cuneiform alphabet. Meantime a gifted British officer, Sir Henry Rawlinson, while he was stationed in Persia, had succeeded in collecting far more Persian inscriptions than were available in Europe. Among them was the great Behistun inscription

---

[1] The latest cuneiform document known is dated 68 B. C.

E

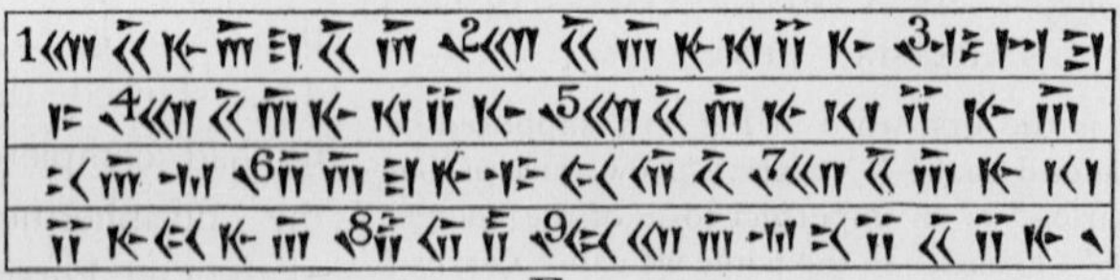

F

FIG. 119. THE TWO OLD PERSIAN INSCRIPTIONS WHICH WERE
FIRST DECIPHERED AND READ (§ 278)

The Persian scribes separated the words in their inscriptions by insert-
ing an oblique wedge between all words. The above Arabic numbers
are here added in order to be able to refer to the different words. It will
be seen that these numbers (except *1*) always stand where the oblique
wedge shows a new word begins. Grotefend (§ 278) noticed that the
same word is repeated a number of times in each of these inscriptions.
In *E* compare Nos. *2, 4, 5,* and *6*, and they will be recognized as the
same word. In *F* it occurs also four times (Nos. *2, 4, 5,* and *7*). As these
inscriptions were found above the figures of Persian kings, Grotefend
therefore suspected that this frequent word must be the Persian word
for "king." Moreover, as it occurs in both inscriptions as No. *2*, the
preceding word (No. *1*) would probably be the *name* of the king, the
two words being arranged thus: "Darius [the] king." Grotefend then
found that the words for the titles of the kings of Persia were known
in later Persian documents. Guided by the known titles, he attempted
the following guess as to the arrangement and meaning of the words:

| 1 | 2 | 3 | 4 |
|---|---|---|---|
| unknown name of a Persian king | [the] king | [the] great | king |

| 5 | 6 | 7 | 8 |
|---|---|---|---|
| of kings, | of king | unknown name of a Persian king | the son |

etc. (6, 7, and 8 meaning "the son of King So-and-so"). He next ex-
perimented with the known names of the kings of Persia, and judg-
ing from their length, he found that the probable name for No. *1*
in *E* was "Darius," and for No. *1* in *F* was "Xerxes." The result
may be seen in Fig. 120

of Darius (Fig. 117). In 1847 Rawlinson published a complete alphabet of the Old Persian cuneiform, containing thirty-nine phonetic signs. Along with this alphabet he published also a complete translation of the Persian portion of the long Behistun inscription (*B* in Fig. 117).

Kh - sha - y - a - r - sha - a

FIG. 120. THE NAME OF XERXES IN OLD PERSIAN CUNEIFORM

This is the first word in Fig. 119, supposed by Grotefend to be "Xerxes." Now, just as our "Charles" is an imperfect form of the ancient name "Carolus," so the name we call "Xerxes" was pronounced by the old Persians *Khshayarsha*. The above seven signs therefore should be read: Kh-sha-y-a-r-sha-a. Grotefend in this way learned the sounds for which these signs stood. Now some of these signs appear in the word Grotefend thought was "king" in Persian. Hence it was now possible for Grotefend to see if he could find out how to pronounce the ancient Persian word for "king." And the reader can do the same. Let him copy on a slip of paper the first three signs in the word supposedly meaning "king"; for example, use word *2* in Fig. 119. Now take these three signs and compare them with the signs in "Xerxes" (Fig. 120). The student will find that the three signs he has copied are the same as the first, second, and seventh signs in the word "Xerxes" (Fig. 120). Let us write down in a row the sounds of these three signs (first, second, and seventh), and we find we have *Kh-sha-a*. The ancient Persian word for "king" must have begun with the sounds *Kh-sha-a*. When we compare this with "shah," the title of the present king of Persia, it is evident that Grotefend was on the right road to decipher Old Persian cuneiform

This showed that he had completed the decipherment of the Old Persian cuneiform — a feat all the more remarkable on the part of Rawlinson because he worked in the Orient, almost entirely in ignorance of parallel work by scholars in Europe.

Scholars were now able for the first time to read Old Persian inscriptions, and much valuable information was gained, especially from a study of the great Behistun monument (Fig. 117). But the number of Persian inscriptions surviving is very small. The chief value of the ability to read ancient Persian cuneiform records lay in the fact that this

**280.** Value of Persian cuneiform in deciphering Babylonian cuneiform

Persian writing might form a bridge leading over to an under-standing of ancient *Babylonian* cuneiform.

281. Discovery that one of the Behistun inscriptions was in the same language and writing as those of Babylonia and Assyria

Scholars had early discovered that the inscription *C* on the Behistun monument was written with the same cuneiform signs which were also observable on many of the older clay tablets (Figs. 80 and 92) and stone monuments found in Babylonia. Meantime the museums of London and Paris were receiving great sculptured slabs of alabaster (Figs. 101, 105, and 106) from Nineveh and the palace of Sargon (Fig. 104), bearing many inscriptions, all in the language and writing of inscription *C* on the Behistun monument (Fig. 117). Scholars therefore perceived that if they could decipher inscription *C* at Behistun, they would be able to read all the ancient documents of Babylonia and Assyria, reaching back to a far greater age than the few surviving Persian inscriptions.

282. Behistun monument, the Rosetta Stone of Western Asia

Every indication led to the conclusion that inscription *C* at Behistun was a Babylonian translation of the Persian portion, already translated by Rawlinson. The Behistun monument might therefore become the Rosetta Stone of Western Asia, and enable scholars to read the ancient Babylonian language, as the Rosetta Stone had enabled them to read the ancient Egyptian language. We can diagram this situation thus:

| ROSETTA STONE | BEHISTUN MONUMENT |
|---|---|
| Containing: | Containing: |
| 1. Egyptian inscription deciphered by scholars by comparison with | 1. Babylonian cuneiform inscription to be deciphered by scholars by comparison with |
| 2. The Greek translation understood by scholars | 2. The Persian translation understood by scholars (since Rawlinson's translation, § 279) |

283. Rawlinson's decipherment of Babylonian (1850)

Many scholars attacked the problem, but they found it far more difficult than the decipherment of the Persian had been; for the Persian cuneiform had contained only forty signs, while the Babylonian was found to use over five hundred (see § 209).

It was again Rawlinson, however, who accomplished the task. In 1850 he published his results. They were followed the next year by a full translation of the *Babylonian* portion of the Behistun inscription.

**284. The modern science of Assyriology**

The city-mounds of Babylonia and Assyria at once began to speak and to tell us, piece by piece, the three great chapters of history along the Two Rivers (Sections 14–20) — something over twenty-five hundred years of the story of man in Western Asia, of which the world before had been entirely ignorant. A group of scholars arose who devoted themselves to the study of the vast body of cuneiform documents on clay and stone which was then coming and still continues to come from the ruined cities of Assyria and Babylonia (Fig. 84). We call such scholars Assyriologists. Thus it happened that we owe to documents left us by the Persian kings the creation of a new and wonderful branch of knowledge and the recovery of the ancient history of Western Asia.

## Section 26. The Results of Persian Rule and its Religious Influence

**285. Decline of Persia**

For the oriental world as a whole, Persian rule meant about two hundred years of peaceful prosperity (ending about 333 B.C.). The Persian kings, however, as time went on, were no longer as strong and skillful as Cyrus and Darius. They loved luxury and ease and left much of the task of ruling to their governors and officials. This meant corrupt and ineffective government; the result was weakness and decline.

**286. Character of the Persian kings and their rule**

The later world, especially the Greeks, often represented the Persian rulers as cruel and barbarous oriental tyrants. This unfavorable opinion is not wholly justified. The Persian emperors felt a deep sense of obligation to give just government to the nations of the earth. Darius the Great in the Behistun Inscription (Fig. 117) says: "On this account Ahuramazda brought me help, . . . because I was not wicked, nor was I a liar, nor was I a tyrant, neither I nor any of my line. I have ruled according to righteousness." There can be no doubt that the Persian Empire, the largest the ancient world had thus far seen, enjoyed a government far more just and humane than any that had preceded it in the East.

Many such statements as that of Darius just quoted show that the Persian rulers were devoted followers of Zoroaster's teaching. Their power carried this noble faith throughout Western Asia and especially into Asia Minor. Here Mithras, regarded by Zoroaster as a helper of Ahuramazda (§ 253), appeared as a hero of light, and finally as a Sun-god, who gradually outshone Ahuramazda himself. From Asia Minor Mithras passed into Europe, and, as we shall see, the faith in the mighty Persian god spread far and wide through the Roman Empire, to become a dangerous competitor of Christianity (§ 1064).

**287.** Spread of Persian religion

In matters of religion, as in many other things, the Persian Empire completed the breakdown of national boundaries and the beginning of a long period when the leading religions of the East were called upon to compete in a great contest for the mastery among all the nations. The most important of the religions which thus found themselves thrown into a world struggle for chief place under the dominion of Persia was the religion of the Hebrews. While we leave the imperial family of Persia to suffer that slow decline which always besets a long royal line in the Orient, we may glance briefly at the little Hebrew kingdom among the Persian vassals in the West, which was destined to influence the history of man more profoundly than any of the great empires of the early world.

**288.** Far-reaching competition among oriental religions

## QUESTIONS

SECTION 21. What great race inhabited the northern grasslands? How did their migrations finally distribute them? What rival line confronted them on the south? Describe the life and dispersion of the Indo-European parent people. Where are their descendants now?

SECTION 22. From whom did the Aryan people come forth? What became of them when they left their first home? What great tribes of the Aryans came toward the Fertile Crescent? Who was their great prophet, and what did he teach? When did he probably live?

SECTION 23. What can you say of the rise and conquests of Cyrus? What race did he subdue on the Fertile Crescent? What race thus became the leaders? What was the extent of the Persian Empire? How long had it taken to conquer it? Give dates.

SECTION 24. Did the Persians possess a civilization like those which they found in Babylonia and Egypt? Describe the organization of the Empire by Darius, and his rule. What was the land system like? What can you say about his plans for commerce by sea and land? Where was the capital? How did Persian architecture arise? Give examples.

SECTION 25. Can you write the three signs with which the *ancient* Persians began their word for " king "? What is the *modern* Persian word for " king "? What monument became the Rosetta Stone of Western Asia? Can you explain how? What was the result?

SECTION 26. How long did the Persian Empire last? Give dates. What can you say about the character of the Persian kings? What was happening among the religions of the East? What great religion was involved in this struggle?

NOTE. The sketch below shows the ruins of Persepolis (cf. Fig. 116).

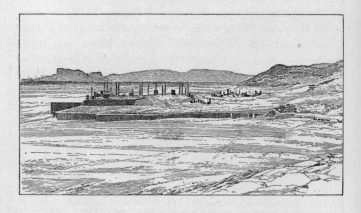

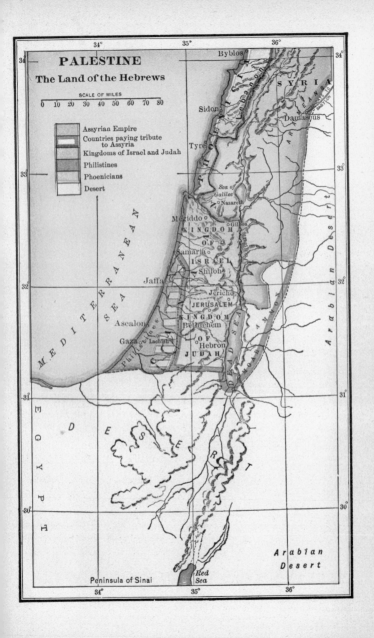

# PALESTINE
## The Land of the Hebrews

SCALE OF MILES

0  10  20  30  40  50  60  70  80

Assyrian Empire
Countries paying tribute
to Assyria
Kingdoms of Israel and Judah
Philistines
Phoenicians
Desert

Byblos

SYRIA

Sidon

Damascus

Tyre

PHOENICIA

Lebanon

ARMENIA

Sea of
Galilee
Nazareth

MEDITERRANEAN SEA

Megiddo
Gibeon

KINGDOM

OF

Samaria
ISRAEL
Shiloh

Jaffa

Jericho

JERUSALEM

KINGDOM

Ascalon
Bethlehem

OF

Gaza
Hebron
Lachish

JUDAH

Philistines

Arabian Desert

EGYPT

DESERT

Peninsula of Sinai

Red
Sea

Arabian
Desert

# CHAPTER VII

## THE HEBREWS AND THE DECLINE OF THE ORIENT

SECTION 27. PALESTINE AND THE PREDECESSORS OF THE HEBREWS THERE

The home of the Hebrews was on the west end of the Fertile Crescent (§ 132), in a land now called Palestine.[1] It is the region lying along the southeast corner of the Mediterranean — a narrow strip between desert and sea; for while the sea limits it on the west, the wastes of the desert-bay (§ 133) sweep northward, forming the eastern boundary of Palestine (see map, p. 102). It was about one hundred and fifty miles long, and less than ten thousand square miles are included within these limits; that is, Palestine was somewhat larger than the state of Vermont.

289. Situation and extent of Palestine, the home of the Hebrews

Much of this area is unproductive, for the desert intrudes upon southern Palestine and rolls northward in gaunt and arid limestone hills, even surrounding Jerusalem (Fig. 127). The valleys of northern Palestine, however, are rich and

290. Character of Palestine

NOTE. The above headpiece shows us a caravan of Canaanites trading in Egypt about 1900 B.C. as they appeared on the estate of a feudal baron in Egypt (§ 99). The Egyptian noble had this picture of them painted with others in his tomb (Fig. 57), where it still is. Observe the shoes, sandals, and gay woolen clothing, the costume of the Palestinian towns, worn by these Canaanites; observe also the metal weapons which they carry. The manufacture of these things created industries which had begun to flourish among the towns in Syria and Palestine by this time. Notice also the type of face, with the prominent nose, which shows that Hittite blood was already mixed with the Semitic blood of these early dwellers in Palestine (Fig. 146).

[1] On the origin of the name see § 379.

productive. The entire land is without summer rains and is dependent upon a rainy season (the winter) for moisture. There is no opportunity for irrigation, and the harvest is therefore scantier than in lands enjoying summer rains. Only

FIG. 121. ANCIENT EGYPTIAN PAINTING OF A BRICKYARD WITH ASIATIC CAPTIVES ENGAGED IN BRICKMAKING (FIFTEENTH CENTURY B.C.)

The Hebrew slaves working in the Egyptian brickyards (see Exod. i, 14 and v, 6–19) must have looked like this when Moses led them forth into Asia (§ 293). At the left below, the soft clay is being mixed in two piles; one laborer helps load a basket of clay on the shoulder of another, who carries it to the brick-molder, at the right above. Here a laborer empties the clay from his basket, while the molder before him fills with clay an oblong box, which is the mold. He has already finished three bricks. At the left above, a molder spreads out the soft bricks with spaces between for the circulation of air to make them dry quickly in the sun. The overseer, staff in hand, sits in the upper right-hand corner, and below him we see a workman carrying away the dried bricks, hanging from a yoke on his shoulders. Thus were made the bricks used for thousands of years for the buildings forming so large a part of the cities of the ancient world, from the Orient to Athens and Rome (§ 548)

the northern end of the Palestinian coast has any harbors (Fig. 159), but these were early seized by the Phœnicians (Sections 39–40). Palestine thus remained cut off from the sea. In natural resources it was too poor (Fig. 129) ever to develop prosperity or political power like its great civilized neighbors on the Nile and Euphrates or in Syria and Phœnicia.

Here at the *west* end of the Fertile Crescent, as at the east end, the Semitic nomads from the desert-bay (reread Section 13) mingled with the dwellers in the northern mountains. The Northerners, chiefly Hittites from Asia Minor (§§ 351–360), left their mark on the Semites of Palestine. The prominent aquiline nose, still considered to be the mark of the Semite, especially of the Jew, was really a feature belonging to the (non-Semitic) Hittites, who intermarried with the people of Palestine and gave them this Hittite type of face (see Fig. 146). Strange faces from many a foreign clime therefore crowded the market places of Palestine, amid a babel of various dialects. Here the rich jewelry, bronze dishes, and ivory furniture of the Nile craftsmen (Fig. 73) mingled with the pottery of the Ægean Islands (Fig. 136), the red earthenware of the Hittites, or the gay woolens of Babylonia. The donkeys (headpiece, p. 197), which lifted their complaining voices above the hubbub of the market, had grazed along the shores of both Nile and Euphrates, and their masters had trafficked beneath the Babylonian temple towers (Fig. 104) as well as under the shadow of the Theban obelisks (Fig. 65). We recall how traffic with Babylonia had taught these Western Semites to write the cuneiform hand (§ 187). Palestine was the entrance to the bridge between Asia and Africa — a middle ground where the civilizations of Egypt and Babylonia, of Phœnicia, the Ægean, and Asia Minor, all represented by their wares, met and commingled as they did nowhere else in the early Orient.

**291.** Mixture of races and civilization in Palestine before the Hebrews possessed it: Babylonian writing

Just as the merchandise of the surrounding nations met in peaceful competition in the markets of Palestine, so the armies of these nations also met there in battle. The situation of Palestine, between its powerful neighbors on the Nile and on the Euphrates, made it the battleground where these great nations fought for many centuries (§ 213). Over and over again unhappy Palestine went through the experience of little Belgium in the conflict between Germany and France in 1914. Egypt held Palestine for many centuries (§ 108). Later we recall

**292.** Palestine, the great battle-ground of the early Orient

how Assyria conquered it (§§ 212–214). Chaldea also held it (§ 234), and we finally found it in the power of Persia (§ 263). When, therefore, the Hebrews originally took possession of the land, there was little prospect that they would ever long enjoy freedom from foreign oppression.

## Section 28. The Settlement of the Hebrews in Palestine and the United Hebrew Kingdom

**293.** The Hebrew invasion of Palestine (about 1400–1200 B.C.)

The Hebrews were all originally men of the Arabian desert, wandering with their flocks and herds and slowly drifting over into their final home in Palestine (read §§ 133–141). For two centuries (about 1400 to 1200 B.C.) their movement from the desert into Palestine continued. Another group of their tribes had been slaves in Egypt, where they had suffered much hardship (Figs. 121 and 122) under a cruel Pharaoh (Fig. 123).

Fig. 122. Brick Storehouse Rooms thought to have been built by Hebrew Slaves in Egypt (Thirteenth Century B.C.)

This storehouse is in the city of Pithom on the east of the Nile Delta. It was built by Ramses II, whose face we see in Fig. 123. The making of the brick for such buildings may be seen in Fig. 121

They were successfully led out of Egypt by their heroic leader Moses, a great national hero whose achievements they never forgot. On entering Palestine the Hebrews found the Canaanites (§ 141) already dwelling there in flourishing towns protected by massive walls (Figs. 124 and 125). The Hebrews were able to capture only the weaker Canaanite towns (Fig. 126). As the rough Hebrew shepherds looked across the highlands of north Palestine they beheld their kindred scattered over far-stretching hilltops, with the frowning walls of many a Canaanite stronghold (Fig. 127) rising between them. Even Jerusalem in the Judean highlands (Fig. 127) for centuries defied the assaults of the Hebrew invaders (Fig. 126).

Let us remember that these uncon-quered Canaanite towns now possessed a civilization fifteen hundred years old, with comfortable houses, government, industries, trade, writing, and religion — a civilization which the rude Hebrew shepherds were soon adopting; for they could not avoid inter-course with the un-subdued Canaanite

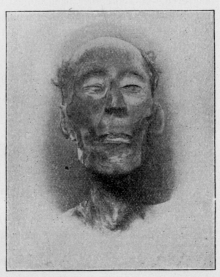

294. The Hebrews adopt Canaanite civilization and acquire Hittite type of face

FIG. 123. MUMMY OF RAMSES II, COMMONLY THOUGHT TO BE THE PHARAOH WHO EN-SLAVED THE HEBREWS

See § 125 for account of the preservation of the bodies of the kings of Egypt. Ramses II died about 1225 B.C., that is, over thirty-one hun-dred years ago. He was about ninety years old. It was probably he who treated the Hebrews so cruelly, as told in Exodus v, 6-19 (§ 293)

towns, as trade and business threw them together. This min-gling with the Canaanites produced the most profound changes in the life of the Hebrews. Most of them left their tents (head-piece, p. 100) and began to build houses like those of the Ca-naanites (Fig. 125); they put off the rough sheepskin they had

worn in the desert, and they put on fine Canaanite raiment of
gayly colored woven wool (headpiece, p. 197). After a time, in
appearance, occupation, and manner of life the Hebrews were
not to be distinguished from the Canaanites among whom they
now lived. In short, they had adopted Canaanite civilization,
just as newly arrived immigrants among *us* soon adopt our
clothing and our ways. Indeed, as the Hebrews intermarried
with the Canaanites, they received enough Hittite blood to
acquire the Hittite type of face (Fig. 146).

**295. Differences in life and customs among the Hebrews; antagonism between North and South**

These changes did not proceed everywhere at the same rate.
The Hebrews in the less fertile South were more attached to
the old desert life, so that many would not give up the tent

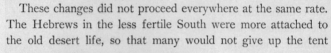

FIG. 124. THE LONG MOUND OF THE ANCIENT CITY OF JERICHO

The walls of the city and the ruins of the houses (Fig. 125) are buried
under the rubbish which makes up this mound. Many of the ancient
cities of Palestine, as old as 2500 B.C., are now such mounds as this

and the old freedom of the desert. The wandering life of the
nomad shepherd on the Judean hills could still be seen from
the walls of Jerusalem. Here, then, were two differing modes
of life among the Hebrews: in the fertile North of Palestine
we find the settled life of the town and its outlying fields; in
the South, on the other hand, the wandering life of the nomad
still went on. For centuries this difference formed an important
cause of discord among the Hebrews.

**296. Foundation of the Hebrew nation; Saul, the first king**

Fortunately for the Hebrews, Egypt was now in a state of
decline (1100 B.C.) (§ 124) and Assyria had not yet conquered
the West (§ 208). But a Mediterranean people called Philistines
(headpiece, p. 252, and § 379) had at this time migrated from
the island of Crete to the sea plain at the southwest corner of

Palestine (see map, p. 196). By 1100 B.C. these Philistines formed a highly civilized and warlike nation, or group of city-kingdoms. Hard pressed by the Philistines, the Hebrew local leaders, or judges, as they were called, found it hard to unite their people into a nation. About a generation before the year 1000 B.C.,

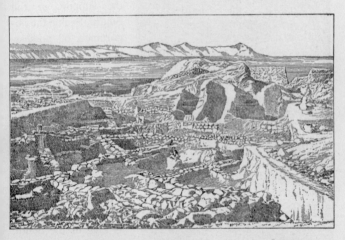

FIG. 125. RUINS OF THE HOUSES OF ANCIENT JERICHO

Only the stone foundations of these houses are preserved. The walls were of sun-baked brick, and the rains of over three thousand years have washed them away; for these houses date from about 1500 B.C., and in them lived the Canaanites, whom the Hebrews found in Palestine (§ 293). Here we find the pottery jars, glass, and dishes of the household; also things carved of stone, like seals, amulets, and ornaments of metal. The *industries* of these people were clearly learned from Egypt (§ 291). Cuneiform tablets of clay found in these ruins show the influence of Babylonian business (§§ 187, and 291)

however, a popular leader named Saul succeeded in gaining for himself the office of king. The new king was a Southerner who still loved the old nomad customs; he had no fixed abode and dwelt in a tent. In the fierce struggle to thrust back the Philistines, Saul was disastrously defeated, and, seeing the rout of his army, he fell upon his own sword and so died (about 1000 B.C.).

**297. David
(about 1000–
960 B.C.)**

FIG. 126. LETTER OF THE EGYPTIAN
GOVERNOR OF JERUSALEM TELLING OF
THE INVASION OF PALESTINE BY THE
HEBREWS (FOURTEENTH CENTURY B.C.)

The letter is a clay tablet written in Babylonian cuneiform by the terrified Egyptian

In a few years the
ability of David, one
of Saul's daring men
at arms whom he had
unjustly outlawed, won
the support of the
South. Seeing the im-
portance of possess-
ing a strong castle,
the sagacious David
selected the ancient
fortress on the steep
hill of Jerusalem (Fig.
127), hitherto held by
the Canaanites. He
therefore gained pos-
session of it and made
it his residence. Here
he ruled for a time
as king of the South,
till his valor as a sol-
dier and his victories
on all sides won him
also the support of
the more prosperous
North. The Philis-
tines were now beaten

governor, who begs the Pharaoh for help, saying: "The Khabiru
[Hebrews] are taking the cities of the king. No ruler remains to the
king, my lord; all are lost." The king of Egypt to whom he wrote
thus was Ikhnaton, at a time when the Egyptian Empire in Asia was
falling to pieces (§ 122). This letter is one of a group of three hundred such cuneiform letters found in one of the rooms of Ikhnaton's
palace at Tell el-Amarna (or Amarna), and called the Amarna Letters,
the oldest body of international correspondence in the world. We find
in them the earliest mention of the Hebrews (cf. Fig. 92 and see § 187)

off, and David ruled over an extensive Hebrew kingdom. He enjoyed a long and prosperous reign, and his people never forgot his heroic deeds as a warrior nor his skill as a poet and singer.

FIG. 127. GLIMPSE OF THE WALLS OF JERUSALEM FROM THE LOW VALLEY BELOW THE OLD CANAANITE FORTRESS

The houses on the right of this valley belong to the modern village of Siloam; but on the left we see the high walls of Jerusalem where they pass around the ancient place of the temple. Here above us at the left, looking down several hundred feet into this valley, was the Canaanite fortress captured by David (§ 297), but it long ago fell into ruin and disappeared. The wall we see here is of a much later date. The Canaanite fortress must have looked very much like the castle of David's northern neighbor, the king of Samal (Fig. 97). (Drawn from photograph by Underwood & Underwood)

David's son, Solomon, became, like Hammurapi, one of the leading merchants of the East. He trafficked in horses and launched a trading fleet in partnership with Hiram, the Phœnician

298. Solo-
mon and the
division of
his kingdom
(about
930 B.C.)

king of Tyre. His wealth enabled him to marry a daughter
of the king of Egypt, and he delighted in oriental luxury and
display. He removed the portable tent which the Hebrews had
thus far used as a temple, and with the aid of his friend Hiram,
who loaned him skilled Phœnician workmen, he built a rich
temple of stone in Jerusalem (Fig. 127). Such splendor demanded a great income, and to secure it he weighed down
the Hebrews with heavy taxes. The resulting discontent of his
subjects was so great that, under Solomon's son, the Northern
tribes withdrew from the nation and set up a king of their
own. Thus the Hebrew nation was divided into two kingdoms
before it was a century old.

## SECTION 29. THE TWO HEBREW KINGDOMS

There was much hard feeling between the two Hebrew kingdoms, and sometimes fighting. Israel, as we call the Northern
kingdom, was rich and prosperous; its market places were filled
with industry and commerce; its fertile fields produced plentiful crops. Israel displayed the wealth and success of town
life. On the other hand, Judah, the Southern kingdom, was
poor; her land was meager (Fig. 128); besides Jerusalem she
had no large towns; many of the people still wandered with
their flocks.

These two methods of life came into conflict in many ways,
but especially in religion. Every old Canaanite town had for
centuries its local town god, called its "baal," or "lord." The
Hebrew townsmen found it very natural to worship the gods
of their neighbors, the Canaanite townsmen. They were thus
unfaithful to their old Hebrew God Yahveh (or Jehovah).[1] To
some devout Hebrews, therefore, and especially to those in the
South, the Canaanite gods seemed to be the protectors of the
wealthy class in the towns, with their luxury and injustice to

[1] The Hebrews pronounced the name of their God "Yahveh." The pronunciation "Jehovah" began less than six hundred years ago and was due to a
misunderstanding of the pronunciation of the word "Yahveh."

the poor, while Yahveh appeared as the guardian of the simpler shepherd life of the desert, and therefore the protector of the poor and needy.

There was growing reason for such beliefs. Less than a century after the separation of the two kingdoms, Ahab, a king of the North, had had Naboth, one of his subjects, killed in order to seize a vineyard belonging to Naboth, and thus to enlarge

**301.** Elijah and the violence of the older ideas of Yahveh

FIG. 128. THE STONY AND UNPRODUCTIVE FIELDS OF JUDAH

Judah is largely made up of sterile ridges like this in the background. Note the scantiness of the growing grain in the foreground

his palace gardens. Reports of such wrongs stirred the anger of Elijah, a Hebrew of old nomad habits, who lived in the desert east of the Jordan. Still wearing his desert sheepskin, he suddenly appeared before Ahab in the ill-gotten vineyard and denounced the king for his seizure of it. Thus this uncouth figure from the desert proclaimed war between Yahveh and the injustice of town life. Elijah's followers finally slew not only the entire Northern royal family, but also the priests of the Canaanite gods (or baals). Such violent methods, however, could not accomplish lasting good. They were the methods of Hebrews who thought of Yahveh only as a war god.

**302. The earliest historical writing among the Hebrews**

Besides such violent leaders as these, there were also among the Hebrews more peaceable men, who likewise chafed under the injustice of town life. These men turned fondly back to the grand old days of their shepherd wanderings, out on the broad reaches of the desert, where no man " ground the faces of the poor." This point of view is picturesquely set forth in a simple narrative history of the Hebrew forefathers — a glorified picture of their shepherd life, as we find it in the immortal tales of the Hebrew patriarchs, of Abraham and Isaac, of Jacob and Joseph. These tales belong among the noblest literature which has survived to us from the past (see Gen. xxiv, xxvii, xxviii, xxxvii, xxxix–xlvii, 12). We should notice also that they are the earliest example of historical writing in prose which we have inherited from any people.

**303. Amos, and the peaceful methods of reformer and prophet (750 B.C.)**

Another century passed, and about 750 B. C. another dingy figure in sheepskin appeared in the streets of Bethel, where the Northern kingdom had an important temple. It was Amos, a shepherd from the hills of Judah in the south. In the solitudes of his shepherd life Amos had learned to see in Yahveh far more than a war god of the desert. To him Yahveh seemed to be a God of fatherly kindness, not demanding bloody butchery like that practiced by Elijah's followers (§ 301), but nevertheless a God who rebuked the selfish and oppressive wealthy class of the towns. The simple shepherd could not resist the inner impulse to journey to the Northern kingdom and proclaim to the luxurious townsmen there the evils of their manner of life.

**304. Amos denounces the corrupt living of the Northern kingdom**

We can imagine the surprise of the prosperous Northern Hebrews as they suddenly met this rude shepherd figure clad in sheepskin, standing at a street corner addressing a crowd of townsmen. He was denouncing their showy clothes, fine houses, beautiful furniture (Fig. 100), and, above all, their corrupt lives and hard-heartedness toward the poor, whose lands they seized for debt and whose labor they gained by enslaving their fellow Hebrews. These things had been unknown in the desert. By such addresses as these Amos, of course, endangered his life, but he thus became the first social reformer in Asia. We apply the term " prophet " to such great Hebrew leaders who pointed out the way toward unselfish living, brotherly kindness, and a higher type of religion. The same kind of effort to lead men to show justice and kindness toward all, especially toward the poor, had long been known in Egypt (§ 100), and it is possible that Amos had heard of such Egyptian teachings. Fearing that his teachings might be lost if they remained merely spoken words, Amos finally sat down and put his sermons into writing, and thus they have survived to us (§§ 316–317).

For while all this had been going on, the Hebrews had been learning to write, as so many of their nomad predecessors on the Fertile Crescent had done before them (§§ 167 and 201). They were now abandoning the clay tablet (Fig. 126), and they wrote on papyrus with the Egyptian pen and ink (Fig. 101). They borrowed their alphabet from the Phœnician and Aramæan merchants (§ 205). There is no doubt that our earliest Hebrew historian's admiration for the *nomad* life (§ 302) — although the nomads were without writing — did not prevent him from making use of this new and great convenience of *town* life; that is, writing. The rolls containing the beautiful tales of the patriarchs, or bearing the teachings of such men as Amos, were the first books which the Hebrews produced — their first literature. Such rolls of papyrus were exactly like those which had been in use in Egypt for over two thousand years. The discovery of the household papers of a Hebrew community in Egypt has shown us just how such a page of Hebrew or Aramaic writing looked (Fig. 131). But literature remained the only art the Hebrews possessed. They had no painting, sculpture, or architecture, and if they needed these things they borrowed from their great neighbors — Egypt, Phœnicia (§ 398), Damascus, or Assyria.

**305.** The Hebrews learn to write

## Section 30. The Destruction of the Hebrew Kingdoms by Assyria and Chaldea

**306.** Destruction of the Northern kingdom by Assyria (722 B.C.)

While the Hebrews had been deeply stirred by their own conflicts *at home*, such men as Amos had also perceived and proclaimed the dangers coming from *abroad*, from beyond the borders of Palestine, especially Assyria. Amos indeed announced the coming destruction of the Northern kingdom by Assyria, because of the evil lives of the people. As Amos had foreseen, Assyria first swept away Damascus (§§ 208 and 212). The kingdom of Israel, thus left exposed, was the next victim, and Samaria, its capital, was captured by the Assyrians in 722 B.C. (§ 213). Many of the unhappy Northern Hebrews were carried away as captives, and the Northern nation, called Israel, was destroyed after having existed for a little over two centuries.

**307.** Yahveh, the God of Palestine, in conflict with Assur, god of Assyria

The national hopes of the Hebrews were now centered in the helpless little kingdom of Judah, which struggled on for over a century and a quarter more, in the midst of a great world conflict, in which Assyria was the unchallenged champion. Thus far thoughtful Hebrews had been accustomed to think of their God as dwelling and ruling in Palestine only. Did he have power also over the vast world arena where all the great nations were fighting? But if so, was not Assur (Fig. 102), the great god of victorious Assyria, stronger than Yahveh, the God of the Hebrews? And many a despairing Hebrew, as he looked out over the hills of Palestine, wasted by the armies of Assyria (Fig. 129), felt in his heart that Assur, the god of the Assyrians, must indeed be stronger than Yahveh, God of the Hebrews.

**308.** Isaiah and the siege of Jerusalem by Sennacherib

It was in the midst of somber doubts like these, in the years before 700 B.C., that the princely prophet Isaiah, in one great oration after another, addressed the multitudes which filled the streets of Jerusalem. The hosts of Sennacherib were at the gates (Fig. 130), and the terrified throngs in the city were expecting at any moment to hear the thunder of the great

Assyrian war engines (headpiece, p. 140) battering down the crumbling walls of their city, as they had crushed the walls of Damascus and Samaria. Then the bold words of the dauntless Isaiah lifted them from despair like the triumphant call of a trumpet. He told them that Yahveh ruled a kingdom far larger

FIG. 129. HEBREWS PAYING TRIBUTE TO THE KING OF ASSYRIA

The Assyrian king, Shalmaneser III, stands at the left, followed by two attendants. Before him hovers the winged sun-disk (§ 210 and Fig. 102). His appearance in the middle of the ninth century B.C., campaigning in the West against Damascus (§ 208), so frightened the Hebrews of the Northern kingdom that their king (Jehu) sent gifts to the Assyrian king by an envoy whom we see here bowing down at the king's feet. Behind the Hebrew envoy are two Assyrian officers who are leading up a line of thirteen Hebrews (not included here) bearing gifts of silver, gold, etc. Although it was over a century before the Assyrian kings succeeded in capturing Damascus (§§ 208, 212, and 213), this incident showed the Hebrews what they might expect. The scene is carved on a black stone shaft set up by the Assyrian king in his palace on the Tigris, where the modern excavators found it. It is now in the British Museum

than Palestine — that He controlled the great world arena, where *He*, and not Assur, was the triumphant champion. If the Assyrians had wasted and plundered Palestine, it was because they were but the lash in the hands of Yahveh, who was using them as a scourge to punish Judah for its wrongdoing. Isaiah made this all clear to the people by vivid oriental illustrations, calling Assyria the " rod " of Yahveh's anger, scourging the Hebrews (Isa. x, 5–15).

FIG. 130. SENNACHERIB, KING OF ASSYRIA, RECEIVING CAPTIVE HEBREWS

The artist, endeavoring to sketch the stony hills of southern Palestine, has made the surface of the ground look like scales. We see the Assyrian king seated on a throne, while advancing up the hill is a group of Assyrian soldiers headed by the grand vizier, who stands before the king, announcing the coming of the Hebrew captives. At the left, behind the soldiers, appear three of the captives kneeling on the ground and lifting up their hands to appeal for mercy. The inscription over the vizier's head reads, "Sennacherib, king of the world, king of Assyria, seated himself upon a throne, while the captives of Lachish passed before him." Lachish was a small town of southern Palestine. Sennacherib captured many such Hebrew towns and carried off over two hundred thousand captives; but even his own records make no claim that he captured Jerusalem (cf. § 309). The scene is engraved on a large slab of alabaster, which with many others adorned the palace of Sennacherib at Nineveh

Thus while the people were momentarily expecting the destruction of Jerusalem, Isaiah undauntedly proclaimed a great and glorious future for the Hebrews and speedy disaster for the Assyrians. When at length a pestilence from the marshes of the eastern Nile Delta swept away the army of Sennacherib and saved Jerusalem, it seemed to the Hebrews the destroying angel of Yahveh who had smitten the Assyrian host (see 2 Kings xix, 32–37). Some of the Hebrews then began to see that they must think of Yahveh as ruling a larger world than Palestine.

Nearly a century after the deliverance from Sennacherib they beheld and rejoiced over the destruction of Nineveh (612 B.C., § 231), and they fondly hoped that the fall of Assyria meant final deliverance from foreign oppression. But they had only exchanged one foreign lord for another, and Chaldea followed Assyria in control of Palestine (§ 233). Then their unwillingness to submit brought upon the Hebrews of Judah the same fate which their kindred of Israel had suffered (§ 306). In 586 B.C. Nebuchadnezzar, the Chaldean king, destroyed Jerusalem and carried away the people to exile in Babylonia. The Hebrew nation both North and South was thus wiped out, after having existed about four and a half centuries since the crowning of Saul.

## SECTION 31. THE HEBREWS IN EXILE AND THEIR DELIVERANCE BY THE PERSIANS

Some of the fugitives fled to Egypt. Among them was the melancholy prophet Jeremiah, who had foreseen the coming destruction of Jerusalem with its temple of Yahveh. He strove to teach his people that each must regard his own heart as a temple of Yahveh, which would endure long after His temple in Jerusalem had crashed into ruin. Recent excavation has restored to us the actual papers of a colony of Hebrews in Egypt at Elephantine (see map, p. 36, and Fig. 211). These papers (Fig. 131) show that the exiled Hebrews in Egypt had not yet reached Jeremiah's ideal of a temple of Yahveh in every human heart; for they had built a temple of their own, in which they carried on the worship of Yahveh.

**311.** Jeremiah and a temple of the Hebrews in Egypt

Similarly, the Hebrew exiles in Babylonia were not yet convinced of the truth of the teaching they had heard from their great leaders the prophets. There were at first only grief and unanswered questionings, of which the echo still reaches us:

**312.** Doubts of the exiled Hebrews in Babylonia and the great prophet of the exile

> By the rivers of Babylon,
> There we sat down, yea we wept,
> When we remembered Zion [Jerusalem].
> Upon the willows in the midst thereof

We hanged up our harps.

.    .    .    .    .    .    .

How shall we sing Yahveh's song
In a strange land? (Psalms 137, 1–4)

Had they not left Yahveh behind in Palestine? And then
arose a wonderful teacher [1] among the Hebrew exiles, and out
of centuries of affliction gave them the answer. In a series of
triumphant speeches this greatest of the Hebrews declared
Yahveh to be the creator and sole God of the universe. He
explained to his fellow exiles that suffering and affliction were
the best possible training and discipline to prepare a people
for service. He announced therefore that by afflicting them
Yahveh was only preparing His suffering people for service to
the world and that He would yet restore them and enable them
to fulfil a great mission to all men. He greeted the sudden rise
of Cyrus the Persian (§ 258) with joy. All kings, he taught,
were but instruments in the hands of Yahveh, who through
the Persians would overthrow the Chaldeans and return the
Hebrews to their land.

**313. Mono-
theism
reached by
the Hebrews
in exile**
Thus had the Hebrew vision of Yahveh slowly grown from
the days of their nomad life, when they had seen him only as a
fierce tribal war god, having no power beyond the corner of the
desert where they lived, until now when they had come to see
that He was a kindly father and a righteous ruler of all the earth.
This was monotheism (§ 120), a belief which made Yahveh the
sole God. They had reached it only through a long development,
which brought them suffering and disaster—a discipline lasting
many centuries. Just as the individual to-day, especially a young
person, learns from his mistakes, and develops character as he
suffers for his own errors, so the suffering Hebrews had out-
grown many imperfect ideas. They thus illustrated the words
of the greatest of Hebrew teachers, " First the blade, then the

[1] A great poet-preacher, a prophet of the exile, whose addresses to his fellow
exiles are preserved in sixteen chapters imbedded in the Old Testament book of
Isaiah (chaps. xl–lv, inclusive).

FIG. 131. ARAMAIC LETTER WRITTEN BY A HEBREW COMMUNITY IN EGYPT TO THE PERSIAN GOVERNOR OF PALESTINE IN THE FIFTH CENTURY B.C.

This remarkable letter was discovered in 1907, with many other similar papers, lying in the ruins of the town of Elephantine (Fig. 211) in Upper Egypt. Here lived a community of some six or seven hundred Hebrews, some of whom had probably migrated to Egypt before Nebuchadnezzar destroyed Jerusalem (§ 310). They had built a temple to Yahveh (Jehovah) on the banks of the Nile. This letter tells how the jealous Egyptian priests formed a mob, burned the Hebrew temple, and plundered it of its gold and silver vessels. Thereupon the whole Hebrew community sat down in mourning, and for three years they tried in vain to secure permission to rebuild. Then in 407 B.C. their leaders wrote this letter to Bagoas, the Persian governor of Palestine, begging him to use his influence with the Persian governor of Egypt, to permit them to rebuild their ruined temple. They refer by name to persons in Palestine who are also mentioned in the Old Testament. The letter is written with pen and ink on papyrus, in the Aramaic language (§ 205 and Fig. 101), which was now rapidly displacing Hebrew (§ 207). This writing used the Phœnician letters long before adopted throughout Western Asia (§ 205). This beautifully written sheet of papyrus, about 10 by 13 inches, bearing the same letters which the Hebrews used (§ 305), shows us exactly how a page of their ancient writings in the Old Testament looked. They read the stories of Abraham, Isaac, Jacob, and Joseph (§ 305) from pages like this

ear, then the full grain in the ear." [1]  By this rich and wonderful experience of the Hebrews in religious progress the whole
world was yet to profit.

**314.** Restoration of the exiled Hebrews by the Persian kings

When the victorious Cyrus entered Babylon (§ 261) the
Hebrew exiles there greeted him as their deliverer.  His
triumph gave the Hebrews a Persian ruler.  With great
humanity the Persian kings allowed the exiles to return to
their native land.  Some had prospered in Babylonia and did
not care to return.  But at different times enough of them went
back to Jerusalem to rebuild the city on a very modest scale
and to restore the temple.

**315.** Jewish law and Judaism; the restored Jewish state a church

The authority given by the Persian government to the
returned Hebrew leaders enabled them to establish and publish
the religious laws which have ever since been revered by the
Jews.  The religion thus organized by the returned Hebrew
leaders we now call Judaism, the religion of the Jews.  Under
it the old Hebrew kingship was not revived.  In its place a
High Priest at Jerusalem became the ruler of the Jews.  The
Jewish state was thus a *religious* organization, a church with a
priest at its head.

**316.** Editing of Hebrew writings: the Prophets and the Psalms

The leaders of this church devoted themselves to the study of
the ancient writings of their race still surviving in their hands.
A number of the old writings, some of them mentioned in the
Old Testament, had been lost.  They arranged and copied the
orations and addresses of the prophets, and all the old Hebrew
writings they possessed.  As time went on, and the service of
the restored temple developed, they arranged a remarkable
book of a hundred and fifty religious songs — the hymn book of
the second temple, known to us as the Book of Psalms.
For a long time, indeed for centuries, these various Hebrew
books, such as the Law, the Prophets, the Psalms, and others,
circulated in separate rolls, and it did not occur to anyone to
put them together to form one book.

---

[1] The words of Jesus; see Mark iv, 28.

It was not until Christian times that the Jewish leaders put all these old writings of their fathers together to form one book. Printed in Hebrew, as they were originally written, they form the Bible of the Jews at the present day. These Hebrew writings have also become a sacred book of the Christian nations. When translated into English, it is called the Old Testament. It forms to-day the most precious legacy which we have inherited from the older Orient before the coming of Christ (§ 1067). It tells the story of how a rude shepherd folk issued from the wilds of the Arabian desert, to live in Palestine and to go through experiences there which made them the religious teachers of the civilized world. And we should further remember, that, crowning all their history, there came forth from them in due time the founder of the Christian religion (§ 1067). One of the most important things that we owe to the Persians, therefore, was their restoration of the Hebrews to Palestine. The Persians thus saved and aided in transmitting to us the great legacy from Hebrew life which we have in the Old Testament, and in the life of the Founder of Christianity.

317. The Old Testament and our legacy in Hebrew religion

## Section 32. Decline of Oriental Leadership; Estimate of Oriental Civilization

Persia was the last of the great oriental powers and, as its decline continued after 400 B.C., it gave way to the Greeks, another Indo-European people who arose not in Asia but in Europe, to which we must now go. Before we do so, however, let us look back over oriental civilization for a moment and review what it accomplished in over thirty-five hundred years. We recall how it passed from the discovery of metal and the invention of writing, through three great chapters of history on the Nile (about 3000 to 1150 B.C.), and three more on the Two Rivers (thirty-first century to 539 B.C.). When the six great chapters were ended, the East finally fell under the

318. Decline of the Orient and end of its leadership of the ancient world (fifth to fourth centuries B.C.)

rule of the incoming Indo-Europeans, led by the Persians (from 539 B.C. on).

**319. The achievements of the Orient: inventions**

What did the Ancient Orient really accomplish for the human race in the course of this long career? It gave the world the first highly developed practical arts, like metal work, weaving, glassmaking, paper-making, and many other similar industries. To distribute the products of these industries among other peoples and carry on commerce, it built the earliest seagoing ships. It first was able to move great weights and undertake large building enterprises — large even for us of to-day. The early Orient therefore brought forth a great group of inventions surpassed in importance only by those of the modern world.

**320. The achievements of the Orient: earliest architecture, sculpture, alphabet, literature, calendar, science, government**

The Orient also gave us the earliest architecture in stone masonry, the colonnade, the arch, and the tower or spire. It produced the earliest refined sculpture, from the wonderful portrait figures and colossal statues of Egypt to the exquisite seals of early Babylonia. It gave us writing and the earliest alphabet. In literature it brought forth the earliest known tales in narrative prose, poems, historical works, social discussions, and even a drama. It gave us the calendar we still use. It made a beginning in mathematics, astronomy, and medicine. It first produced government on a large scale, whether of a single great nation or of an empire made up of a group of nations.

**321. The achievements of the Orient: religion**

Finally, in religion the East developed the earliest belief in a sole God and his fatherly care for all men, and it laid the foundations of a religious life from which came forth the founder of the leading religion of the civilized world to-day. For these things, accomplished—most of them—while Europe was still undeveloped, our debt to the Orient is enormous.

Let us see, however, if there were not some important things which the East had not yet gained. The East had always accepted as a matter of course the rule of a king, and believed that his rule should be kindly and just. It had never occurred to anyone there, that the *people* should have a voice in the government, and something to say about how they should be governed. No one had ever gained the idea of a free citizen, a man feeling what we call patriotism, and under obligations to vote and to share in the government. Liberty as we understand it was unknown, and the rule of the people, which we call "democracy," was never dreamed of in the Orient. Hence the life of the individual man lacked the stimulating responsibilities which come with citizenship. Such responsibilities, — like that of thinking about public questions and then voting, or of serving as a soldier to defend the nation, — these duties quicken the mind and force men to action, and they were among the strongest influences in producing great men in Greece and Rome.

322. Lack of political freedom, democratic government, and citizenship in the Ancient Orient

Just as the Orientals accepted the rule of *kings* without question, so they accepted the rule of the *gods*. It was a tradition which they and their fathers had always accepted. This limited their ideas of the world about them. They thought that every storm was due to the interference of some god, and that every eclipse must be the angry act of a god or demon. Hence the Orientals made little inquiry into the *natural* causes of such things. In general, then, they suffered from a lack of freedom of the mind — a kind of intellectual bondage to religion and to old ideas.[1] Under these circumstances natural science could not go very far, and religion was much darkened by superstition, while art and literature lacked some of their greatest sources of stimulus and inspiration.

323. Lack of freedom of mind from religious tradition in the Ancient Orient

There were, therefore, still boundless things for mankind to do in government, in thought about the natural world, in gaining deeper views of the wonders and beauties of nature, as well as in art, in literature, and in many other lines. This future progress was to be made in Europe — that Europe

324. Limitations caused by lack of political and intellectual freedom; transition to Europe

[1] Intellectual freedom from tradition was earliest shown by the great Egyptian king Ikhnaton (§§ 118-120) and by the Hebrew prophets (§ 304). Perhaps we could also include Zoroaster; but complete intellectual freedom was first attained by the Greeks.

which we left at the end of our first chapter in the Late Stone Age. To Europe, therefore, we must now turn, to follow across the eastern Mediterranean the course of rising civilization, as it passed from the Orient to our forefathers in early Europe four to five thousand years ago.

## QUESTIONS

SECTION 27. Describe the situation and character of the land of the Hebrews. What can you say about the character of its civilization? Was it likely to offer a tranquil home? Why?

SECTION 28. Where was the *original* home of the Hebrews? Where did some of them suffer bondage? What was the result of their living among the Canaanites? Did all the Hebrews adopt the settled life? When did they gain their first king and who was he? Who was their leading enemy? Describe the reign of David; of Solomon. What happened to the kingdom after Solomon?

SECTION 29. What were the relations between the two Hebrew kingdoms? Contrast the two kingdoms. How did this contrast affect religion? What work did Elijah do? Were there more peaceful men of similar opinions? What can you say of the tales of the patriarchs? Tell the story of Amos. What was the work of a prophet? Whence did the Hebrews learn to write and what were their first books?

SECTION 30. What danger threatened the Hebrews from abroad? What happened to the Northern kingdom? Did the Hebrews believe Yahveh to be stronger than Assur? What can you say of the work of Isaiah? Tell about Sennacherib's campaign against Jerusalem. Describe the destruction of the Southern kingdom.

SECTION 31. What became of the Hebrews of Judah? What did they think about Yahveh? Who taught them better and what was his teaching? Did the Hebrews reach their highest ideas about Yahveh all at once or were such ideas a gradual growth? What did the returned Hebrews accomplish and by what authority?

SECTION 32. What were the most important things which the Orient contributed to human life? Did the people there ever have any voice in government? Were there any citizens? What was the attitude of the Orientals toward the gods? What was the effect upon science? To what region do we now follow the story of early man?

# PART III. THE GREEKS

## CHAPTER VIII

### THE DAWN OF EUROPEAN CIVILIZATION AND THE RISE OF THE EASTERN MEDITERRANEAN WORLD

#### SECTION 33. THE DAWN OF CIVILIZATION IN EUROPE

We have already studied the life of earliest man in Europe, where we followed his progress step by step through some fifty thousand years (Sections 1–4). At that point we were obliged to leave him and to pass over from Europe to the Orient, to watch there the birth and growth of civilization, while all Europe remained in the barbarism of the Late Stone Age. Meantime

**325.** Late Stone Age Europe and its future

NOTE. The above drawing shows us the upper part of a stone vase carved by a Cretan sculptor. The lower part is lost. The scene depicts a procession of Cretan peasants with wooden pitchforks over their shoulders. Among them is a chorus of youths with wide-open mouths, lustily singing a harvest song, doubtless in honor of the great Earth Mother (§ 357), to whom the peasants believed they owed the fertility of the earth. The music is led by a priest with head shaven after the Egyptian manner, and he carries upraised before his face a sistrum, a musical rattle which came from Egypt. The work is so wonderfully carved that we seem to feel the forward motion of the procession.

the towns and villages of the Late Stone Age men had stretched far across Europe. The smoke of their settlements rose through the forests and high over the lakes and valleys of Switzerland. Their roofs dotted the plains and nestled in the inlets of the sea, whence they were thickly strewn far up the winding valleys of the rivers into inner Europe. In southeastern Europe these men had finally reached the dawn of the Age of Metal, about three thousand years before Christ.[1]

**326. The wares distributed in Late Stone Age Europe by traders from the Mediterranean**

The occasional visits of the traders from the coast settlements along the Mediterranean were welcome events. Such a trader's wares were eagerly inspected. Some bargained with him for a few decorated jars of pottery, while others preferred glittering blue-glaze beads. Great was the interest, too, when the trader exhibited a few shining beads or neck rings of a strange, heavy, gleaming, reddish substance, so beautiful that the villagers trafficked eagerly for them. Most desired of all, however, was the dagger (Fig. 132) or ax head made of the same unknown substance. Such ax heads, though they were much thinner, did not break like stone axes, and they could be ground to a better edge than the ground stone ax ever gained.

**327. The oriental source of the European trader's wares**

To the communities of inner Europe, the trader brought also vague rumors of the lands from which his wares had come, of great peoples who dwelt beyond the wide waters of the Mediterranean Sea. Whereupon some of the Late Stone Age villagers of Europe perhaps recalled a dim tradition of their fathers that grain and flax, and even cattle and sheep, first came to them from the same wonderlands of the Far East.

**328. Europe hears of the earliest ships in the far-away Nile**

With rapt attention and awe-struck faces they listened to the trader's tales, telling of huge ships (Fig. 41) which made the rude European dugouts (Fig. 14) look like tiny chips. They

---

[1] As we shall see, the Stone Age was only very gradually succeeded by the Copper or Bronze Age. Metal reached southeastern Europe not long after 3000 B.C., but in western and northern Europe it was almost 2000 B.C. before the beginning of the Copper Age, which soon became the Bronze Age.

had many oarsmen on each side, and mighty fir trunks were mounted upright in the craft, carrying huge sheets of linen to catch the favoring wind, which thus drove them swiftly from land to land. They came out of the many mouths of the vast river of Egypt, greater than any river in the world, said the trader, and they bore heavy cargoes across the Mediterranean

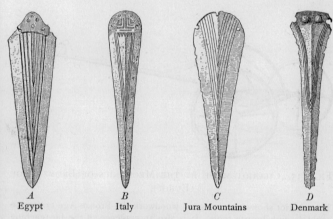

| *A* | *B* | *C* | *D* |
| Egypt | Italy | Jura Mountains | Denmark |

FIG. 132. SERIES OF FOUR DAGGER BLADES OF COPPER AND BRONZE, SHOWING INFLUENCE FROM EGYPT TO DENMARK

The lost handles were of wood, bone, or ivory, and the rivet holes for fastening them can still be seen. We see in this series how the early Egyptian form (*A*) passed from Egypt across Europe to the Scandinavian countries. The later swords of western Europe were simply the old Egyptian dagger elongated

to the islands and coasts of southeastern Europe or neighboring Asia. Thus at the dawn of history, barbarian Europe looked across the Mediterranean to the great civilization of the Nile, as our own North American Indians fixed their wondering eyes on the first Europeans who landed in America, and listened to like strange tales of great and distant peoples.

Slowly Europe learned the use of metal (Fig. 133 and p. 222, footnote). In spite of much progress in craftsmanship and a more civilized life in general, the possession of metal did not enable the peoples of Europe to advance to a high type of civilization. They still remained without writing, without architecture in hewn-stone masonry, and without large sailing ships for commerce.[1] The failure to make progress in architecture beyond such rough stone structures as Stonehenge (Fig. 20)

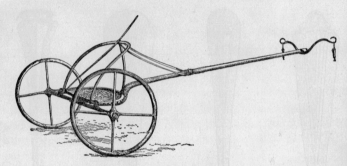

FIG. 133. CHARIOT MADE BY THE MECHANICS OF BRONZE AGE EUROPE

This chariot shows us what good woodwork the Bronze Age craftsmen could do with bronze tools. It is also an evidence of the far-reaching commerce of the Bronze Age; for it was transported across the Mediterranean to Egypt, where it was placed in a cliff-tomb, to be used by some wealthy Egyptian after death. There it has survived in perfect condition to our day. It is built of elm and ash, with bindings of birch fiber. The birch does not grow south of the Mediterranean, and hence the chariot must have been made on the north of the Mediterranean (§ 329)

is an illustration of this backwardness of western and northern Europe. It clearly proves the failure of Bronze Age Europe to bring forth a high civilization, such as we have found in the Orient. It was naturally in that portion of Europe nearest Egypt that civilization developed most rapidly; namely, around the Ægean Sea.

---

[1] In this matter the Norsemen were the leaders in northern Europe, and seem to have developed considerable skill in navigation by 1500 B.C.

## Section 34. The Ægean World : the Islands

The Ægean Sea is like a large lake, almost completely encircled by the surrounding lands (see map, p. 252). Around its west and north sides stretches the mainland of Europe, on the east is Asia Minor, while the long Island of Crete on the south lies like a breakwater, shutting off the Mediterranean from the Ægean Sea. From north to south this sea is at no point more than four hundred miles in length, while its width varies greatly. It is a good deal longer than Lake Michigan, and in places over twice as wide. Its coast is deeply indented with many bays and harbors, and it is so thickly sprinkled with hundreds of islands that it is often possible to sail from one island to another in an hour or two. Indeed it is almost impossible to cross the Ægean without seeing land all the way, and in a number of directions at the same time. Just as Chicago, Milwaukee, and other towns around Lake Michigan are linked together by modern steamboats, so we shall see incoming civilization connecting the shores of the Ægean by sailing ships. This sea, therefore, with its islands and the fringe of shores around it, formed a region by itself, which we may call the Ægean world.

330. The Ægean Sea and the Ægean world

It enjoys a mild and sunny climate; for this region of the Mediterranean lies in the belt of rainy winters and dry summers. Here and there, along the bold and broken, but picturesque and beautiful, shores (Plate III, p. 278), river valleys and small plains descend to the water's edge. Here wheat and barley, grapes and olives, may be cultivated without irrigation. Hence bread, wine, and oil were the chief food, as among most Mediterranean peoples to this day. Wine is their tea and coffee, and oil is their butter. So in the Homeric poems (§§ 408–411) bread and wine are spoken of as the food of all, even of the children. The wet season clothes the uplands with rich green pastures, where the shepherds may feed the flocks which dot the hillsides far and near. Few regions of the world are

331. Climate and products of the Ægean world

better suited to be the home of happy and prosperous communities, grateful to the gods for all their plentiful gifts by land and sea.

**332.** The Ægean world and its nearness to the Orient

A map of the Mediterranean (p. 678) shows us that the Ægean world is the region where Europe thrusts forward its southernmost and easternmost peninsula (Greece), with its island outposts, especially Crete, reaching far out into the oriental waters so early crossed and recrossed by Egyptian ships (§ 77). The map thus shows us why the earliest high civilization on the north side of the Mediterranean appeared on the Island of Crete. At the same time we should notice that the Ægean world is touched by Asia, which here throws out its westernmost heights (Asia Minor), so that Asia and Europe face each other across the waters of the Ægean. Asia Minor with its trade routes was a link which connected the Ægean world with the Fertile Crescent.

**333.** The Ægean Islands outposts of the Orient; progress of these islands and backwardness of the mainland

We see here, then, that the older oriental civilizations converged upon the Ægean by two routes: first and earliest by ship across the Mediterranean from Egypt; second by land through Asia Minor from the Euphrates world. Thus the Ægean islands became a bridge connecting the Orient and Europe. Already in the Late Stone Age the Ægean islands had unavoidably become outposts of the great oriental civilizations which we have found so early on the Nile and the Euphrates. It was on the Ægean *islands* and not on the *mainland* of Europe that the earliest high civilization on the north side of the Mediterranean grew up.

**334.** The people of the Ægean world

We call the earliest inhabitants of the Ægean world Ægeans. They were inhabiting this region when civilization dawned there (about 3000 B.C.), and they continued to live there for many centuries before the race known to us as the Greeks entered the region. These Ægeans, the predecessors of the Greeks in the northern Mediterranean, belonged to a great and gifted white race having no connection with the Greeks. They were, and their descendants still are, widely extended along the northern shores of the Mediterranean.[1] We call them the Mediterranean race, but their origin and their relationships with other peoples are as yet little understood. At a time far earlier than any of our written records, they had occupied not only the mainland of Greece and the islands of the Ægean, but they had also settled on the neighboring shores of Asia Minor.

From the beginning the leader in this island civilization of the Ægeans was Crete. This large island lies so far out in the Mediterranean that one is almost in doubt whether it belongs to Europe or to Africa (see map, p. 252). At the dawn of civilization " Crete was as much a part of the East . . . as Constantinople is to-day." [2] Even in ancient ships the mariners issuing from the mouths of the Nile and steering northwestward would sight the Cretan mountains in a few days. Thus Crete was the link between Egypt on the south and the Ægean Sea on the north (see map, p. 252).

**335. Crete the link between the Ægean and the Nile**

The little sun-dried-brick villages, forming the Late Stone Age settlements of Crete, received copper from the ships of the Nile by 3000 B.C., as we have seen (§ 326). Somewhat later the Cretan metal workers received, probably from mines in the northern Mediterranean, supplies of copper mixed with tin, giving them the hard mixture we call bronze, which is much harder than copper. Thus began the Bronze Age in Crete after 3000 B.C. For a thousand years afterward their progress was slow, but it gained for them some very important things. While the great pyramids of Egypt were being built, the Cretan craftsmen learned from their Egyptian neighbors the use of the potter's wheel and the closed oven (Fig. 48). They could then shape and bake much finer clay jars and vases. By copying Egyptian stone vessels they learned also to hollow out hard varieties of stone and to make beautifully wrought stone vases, bowls, and jars (Fig. 134). For some time the Cretans had been

**336. Rise of Cretan civilization under Egyptian influence (3000–2000 B.C.)**

---

[1] It has been thought that this race had its home in North Africa and that they spread entirely around the Mediterranean. The Egyptians and Semites may be branches of it. [2] Burrows, *The Discoveries in Crete.*

employing rude picture records like Figs. 26 and 32. Under the influence of Egypt these picture signs now gradually developed into real phonetic writing (Figs. 135 and 137), the earliest writing in the Ægean world (about 2000 B.C.).

**337.** Rise of the sea-kings of Crete (2000 B.C.)

By 2000 B.C. the Cretans had become a highly civilized people. Near the coast, for convenient access to ships, were

Egypt                                    Crete

FIG. 134. EARLY STONE VASES OF CRETE AND THE EGYPTIAN ORIGINALS FROM WHICH THEY WERE COPIED

The earlier vases from Egypt (on the left) compared with those of Crete (on the right) show that the Cretan craftsmen copied the Egyptian forms (§ 336) in the latter part of the Pyramid Age (about 2700–2600 B.C.)

the manufacturing towns, with thriving industries in pottery and metal work, enabling them to trade with other peoples. Farther inland the green valleys of the island must have been filled with prosperous villages cultivating their fields of grain and pasturing their flocks. At Cnossus, not far from the middle of the northern coast (see map, p. 252), there grew up a kingdom which may finally have included a large part of the island. The

Late Stone Age town at Cnossus had long since fallen to ruin and been forgotten. Over a deep layer of its rubbish a line of splendid Cretan kings now built a fine palace arranged in the Egyptian manner, with a large cluster of rooms around a central court. Farther inland toward the south shore arose another palace at Phæstus, perhaps another residence of the same royal family, or the capital of a second kingdom.

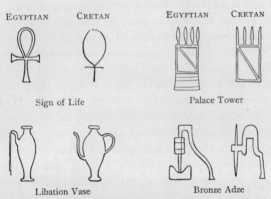

FIG. 135. CRETAN HIEROGLYPHS AND THE EGYPTIAN SIGNS FROM WHICH THEY WERE TAKEN. (AFTER SIR ARTHUR EVANS)

These examples show us in the first column the Egyptian originals from which the Cretan hieroglyphic signs shown in the second column were taken (see § 336)

**338. Power of the sea-kings of Crete** These palaces were not fortified castles, for neither they nor the towns connected with them possessed any protecting walls. But the Cretan kings were not without means of defense. They already had their palace armories, where brazen armor and weapons were stored. Hundreds of bronze arrowheads, with the charred shafts of the arrows, along with written lists of weapons and armor and chariots, have been found still lying in the ruins of the armory rooms in the palace at Cnossus (§ 340). The troops who used these weapons were of course not lacking. Moreover, the Cretan kings were also learning to use ships in warfare, and it has become a modern habit to call them the " sea-kings of Crete." [1]

**339. Expansion of Cretan commerce and industry**

Cretan industries henceforth flourished as never before. The potters of Cnossus began to produce exquisite cups as thin and delicate as modern porcelain teacups. These and their pottery jars and vases they painted in bright colors with decorative designs, which made them the most beautiful ware to be had in the East (Fig. 136, *A*). Such ware was in demand in the houses of the rich as far away as the Nile, just as fine French table porcelain is widely sold outside of France at the present day. The new many-colored Cretan vases were so highly prized by the Egyptian nobles of the Feudal Age that they even placed them in their tombs for use in the next world. In these Egyptian tombs modern excavators have recovered them, to tell us the story of the wide popularity of Cretan industrial art in the nineteenth and twentieth centuries B.C. Egyptian ships, common in the eastern Mediterranean since the thirtieth century B.C., must have been frequent visitors in the Cretan harbors. At the same time the prevailing north wind of summer easily carried the galleys which the Cretans had learned to build, across to the mouths of the Nile. There were many things in Egypt which the Cretans needed. Hence commerce between Crete and the Nile was constant (see map, p. 252).

**340. Development of Cretan linear writing and records**

Cretan business now required much greater speed and convenience in writing than was possible in using the old picture signs (Fig. 135). These pictures were therefore much abbreviated and reduced to simpler forms, each picture consisting of only a few lines. This more rapid hand, called *linear* writing (Fig. 137), was scratched on clay tablets. The chests of arms and weapons in the palace armory had each a clay-tablet label hanging in front of it. Great numbers of clay tablets stored in

---

[1] The sea power of the Cretans has been much exaggerated by recent writers. One of the old Cretan sea kings, according to later tradition, was named Minos. For this reason early Cretan civilization has been called Minoan, and this is now the most common term applied to it. We use the term " Ægean "; for the term " Mycenæan," see § 347.

A                                    B

FIG. 136. TWO CRETAN VASES SHOWING PROGRESS IN THE ART
OF DECORATION

The first vase (*A*) is an example of the earlier pottery, painted on a
dark background with rich designs in "white, orange, crimson, red and
yellow." The potters who made such vases were, together with the
seal-cutters, the first really gifted decorative artists to arise in Crete.
They flourished from 2000 B.C. onward, in the days of the first palace
of Cnossus (§ 337). We should notice that their designs do not picture
carefully anything in nature, like flowers or animals (even though a
hint of a lotus flower appears in the angle of the spiral); but the figures are almost purely *imaginative* and drawn from Egyptian art. The
second vase (*B*), however (some five hundred years later than the first),
shows how the artists of the Grand Age had learned from Egyptian
decorative art to take their decorative figures from the *natural* world,
for we see that the design consists chiefly of Egyptian lotus flowers
(§ 341). Such designs were no longer in many colors; on this jar,
indeed, they are molded in relief. This jar (*B*) is nearly 4 feet high
and much larger then the first example (*A*). Stone and metal vases
of the Grand Age were sometimes superbly decorated with carved
bands of human figures in action. See the fine examples of this style
in Fig 140, and the headpiece, p. 221

chests seem to have contained the records, invoices, and book-keeping lists necessary in conducting the affairs of a large royal household. Masses of these have been found covered by the rubbish and ruins of the fallen palace. In spite of much study, scholars are not yet able to read these precious records, the earliest-known writing on the borders of the European world.

**341.** The Grand Age in Crete and its art (1600–1500 B.C.)

FIG. 137. CLAY TABLET BEARING A RECORD IN THE RAPID CRETAN HAND-WRITING OFTEN CALLED LINEAR

This writing is a later stage of the hiero-glyphs in Fig. 135 (see also § 340)

The Cretan kings, how-ever, did not erect large stone monuments engraved with written records of their build-ings, their victories, and their great deeds, like those we have found in the Orient.

A few centuries of such development as this carried Cretan civ-ilization to its highest level, and the Cretans entered upon what we may call their Grand Age (1600–1500 B.C.). As the older palace of Cnossus gave way to a larger and more splen-did building (Fig. 138), the life of Crete began to unfold in all directions. The new palace itself, with its colon-naded hall, its fine stairways (Fig. 138), and its impressive open areas, represented the first real architecture in the northern Mediterranean. The palace walls were painted with fresh and beautiful scenes from daily life, all aquiver with movement and action; or by learning the Egyptian art of glassmaking the Cre-tans adorned them with glazed figures attached to the surface of the wall. The pottery painters had by this time given up the use of many colors. They now employed one dark tone on a light background, or they modeled the design in relief. Noble vases (Fig. 136, *B*) were painted in grand designs drawn from plant life or often from the life of the sea, where the Cretans were now more and more at home. This wonderful pottery shows the most powerful, vigorous, and impressive decorative art of the early oriental world. Indeed, it belongs among the finest works of decorative art ever produced by any people.

The method of use and the execution of the work everywhere show that this art was developing under suggestion from Egypt; for example, walls covered with colored glazed tiles were in use

FIG. 138. COLONNADED HALL AND STAIR-CASE IN THE CRETAN PALACE OF THE GRAND AGE AT CNOSSUS

The columns and roof of the hall are modern restorations. This hall is in the lower portion of the palace, and the stairway, concealed by the balustrade at the back of the hall, led up by five flights of fifty-two massive steps to the main floor of the palace. On the painted interior decoration of this palace consult § 341 and see Fig. 139

**342.** Independence and power of Cretan artists in spite of Egyptian influence

in Egypt nearly two thousand years earlier than in Crete. But in spite of this fact the Cretan artist did not follow slavishly the Egyptian model. A growing plant painted on an Egyptian wall seems sometimes so rigid and stiff that it looks as if done with a stencil. The Cretan artist drew the same plant with such free and splendidly curving lines (Fig. 136, *B*) that we seem to hear the wind swaying the stems and giving us

" The soft eye-music of slow-moving boughs " (Wordsworth).
The Cretan sculptor in ivory, too, as well as the goldsmith and
worker in bronze wrought masterpieces which remain to-day
among the world's greatest works of art (Figs. 140 and 141).

**343.** The
life of the
Cretans in
the Grand
Age: the
common folk

The palace of Cnossus looked out upon a town of plain,
sun-dried-brick houses.  Here must have lived the merchants and
traders, the potters, metal workers, painters, and other craftsmen, though many of these also lived and worked in the palace

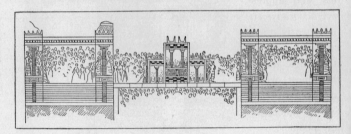

FIG. 139. CRETAN LORDS AND LADIES OF THE GRAND AGE ON
THE TERRACES OF THE PALACE AT CNOSSUS. (AFTER DURM)

This scene was painted on the walls of the palace as part of the interior
wall decoration.  It has been somewhat restored, as shown above, but it
forms a remarkable example of the Cretan artist's ability to produce
the impression of an animated multitude of people seen from a distance
and blending into a somewhat confused whole (see also § 341)

itself ; while on the outskirts, or up the valley, dwelt the peasants who cultivated the fields.  On one occasion we see the
peasants marching in joyous procession, probably celebrating a
harvest festival (headpiece, p. 221).

**344.** The
nobles about
the king

Upon such celebrations of the people there looked down
from the palace a company of lords and ladies, who lived an
astonishingly free and modern life.  The ladies, wearing costumes (Fig. 141) which might tastefully appear in the streets of
modern New York or Chicago, crowded the palace terraces and
watched their champions struggling in fierce boxing matches, in
which the contestants wore heavy metal helmets (Fig. 139).

FIG. 140. WILD BULLS PICTURED BY A CRETAN GOLDSMITH
AROUND TWO GOLDEN CUPS

These cups were found at Vaphio, near Sparta, whither they were imported from Crete. The goldsmith beat out these marvelous designs with a hammer and punch over a mold, and then cut in finer details with a graving tool. His work must be ranked among the greatest works of art produced by any people

FIG. 141. IVORY AND GOLD STATUETTE OF A CRETAN LADY
OF THE GRAND AGE. (BOSTON MUSEUM OF FINE ARTS)

The proud little figure stands with shoulders thrown far back and arms
extended, each hand grasping a golden serpent, which coils about her
arms to the elbow. She wears a high tiara perched daintily on her
elaborately curled hair. Her dress consists of a flounced skirt and a
tight bodice tapering to her slender waist. The whole forms a costume
so surprisingly modern that this little Cretan lady would hardly create
any comment if she appeared so dressed on one of our crowded city
streets of to-day. The figure is carved in ivory, while the flounces are
edged with bands of gold and the belt about the waist is of the same
metal. She represents either the great Cretan mother goddess or possibly only a graceful snake-charmer of the court. In any case the
sculptor has given her the appearance of one of the noble ladies of his
time. Even the Greek sculptor never surpassed the vitality and the
winsome charm which passed from the fingers of the ancient Cretan
artist into this tiny figure

Or the assembled court (Fig. 139) cheered the plucky bull-fighters tossed on the horns of huge wild bulls (Fig. 140), — the same huge creatures which were hunted by the Late Stone Age men of Europe a thousand years before (Fig. 12). These people lived in comfortable quarters in the palace, where they even had bathrooms and sanitary drainage (Fig. 142).

From the palace of Cnossus the Cretan king could issue at the North Gate and, mounting his chariot, ride in half an hour to the harbor, three and a half miles away. At the harbor he looked out northward where the nearest islands of the Ægean could be clearly seen breaking the northern horizon (see map, p. 252). Here the trading galleys of the Cretan kings were spreading Cretan art and industries far and wide through the Mediterranean. These Cretan fleets formed the earliest naval power which grew up in the northern Mediterranean, and the student should contrast the dugouts of the Late Stone Age (Fig. 14). Nevertheless, the kings of Crete were now vassals of the Pharaoh. An Egyptian general of Thutmose III (§ 111) in the fifteenth century B.C. bore

**345.** Political and commercial position of Crete in and after the Grand Age

FIG. 142. TILE DRAINPIPES FROM THE CRETAN PALACE OF CNOSSUS

These joints of pottery drainpipe (2½ feet long and 4 to 6 inches across) are part of an elaborate system of drainage in the palace, the oldest drainage system in the European world. The oldest-known system of drainpipe (copper) is in the pyramid-temple of Abusir, Egypt (see Fig. 56), about a thousand years earlier than this system at Cnossus

the title of " governor of the islands in the midst of the sea,"
as the Egyptians called the islands of the Ægean (Fig. 143).

**346.** Crete to be regarded as the home of the third great civilization in the ancient world

Here, then, in the island of Crete, there had arisen a new
world. The culture of the gifted Cretans, stimulated by the
magic touch of riper Egyptian culture, shook off the Late Stone
Age lethargy of early Europe
and sprang into a vigorous life
all its own. Beside the two
older centers of civilization on
the Nile and the two rivers in
this age, there thus grew up
here in the eastern Mediterranean, as a *third* great civilization, this splendid world of
Crete and the Ægean Sea.
It is this *third* great civilization which forms the link between the civilization of the
Orient and the later progress
of man in Greece and western
Europe.

FIG. 143. GOLDEN DISH OF
THE EGYPTIAN GOVERNOR OF
THE ÆGEAN ISLANDS IN THE
GRAND AGE

This golden dish was given by the
Pharaoh Thutmose III (§ 111) to
one of his favorite generals, whom
he had made governor of the
Ægean islands. The dish bears an
inscription which calls him "governor of the islands in the midst
of the sea," by which the Egyptians meant the Ægean islands
and coasts of Asia Minor

## SECTION 35. THE ÆGEAN WORLD : THE MAINLAND

As yet, the mainland, both
in Europe and in Asia Minor,
had continued to lag behind

**347.** Cretan civilization reaches the mainland of Greece; the Mycenæan Age

the advanced civilization of the islands. Nevertheless, the fleets
of Egypt and of Crete maintained commerce with the mainland of Greece. They naturally entered the southern bays,
and especially the Gulf of Argos, which looks southward directly toward Crete (see map, p. 252). In the plain of Argos
(Plate III), behind the sheltered inlet, massive strongholds,
with heavy stone masonry foundations and walls, arose at

Tiryns (Fig. 144) and Mycenæ (Fig. 145). The Ægean princes who built such strongholds a little after 1500 B.C. imported works of Cretan and Egyptian art in pottery and metal (Fig. 140). These triumphs of Cretan art, with fragments of Egyptian glaze and wall decorations, still surviving in the ruins of palaces and tombs, are to-day the earliest tokens of a life of higher refinement on the continent of Europe. This period (about 1500 to 1200 B.C.) is commonly known as the Mycenæan Age, after Mycenæ, where such civilization was first discovered (Section 36).

But the mainland still lagged behind the islands, for Cretan writing seems not to have

FIG. 144. RESTORATION OF THE CASTLE AND PALACE OF TIRYNS. (AFTER LUCKENBACH)

Unlike the Cretan palaces, this dwelling of an Ægean prince is massively fortified. A rising road (*A*) leads up to the main gate (*B*), where the great walls are double. An assaulting party bearing their shields on the *left* arm must here (*C, D*) march with the exposed *right* side toward the city. By the gate (*E*) the visitor arrives in the large court (*F*) on which the palace faces. The main entrance of the palace (*G*) leads to its forecourt (*H*), where the excavators found the place of the household altar of the king (§ 423). Behind the forecourt (*H*) is the main hall of the palace (*I*). This was the earliest castle in Europe with outer walls of stone. The villages of the common people clustered about the foot of the castle hill. The whole formed the nucleus of a city-state (§ 390) in the plain of Argos (see Plate III, p. 278)

348. Continued backwardness of the European mainland

followed Cretan commerce, and there was as yet no writing prevalent on the continent of Europe. Regions of northern Greece, such as Thessaly, were covered with scattered settlements which had advanced but little beyond Late Stone Age civilization. Metal, although known, was not common in Thessaly until about 1500 B.C., and the cultured Cretans had little influence here in the north.

**349.** Asiatic mainland: foundation of Troy (about 3000 B.C.)

FIG. 145. THE MAIN ENTRANCE OF THE CASTLE OF MYCENÆ, CALLED THE LION GATE

This shows us a good example of the heavy stone masonry with which were built the great gates of the two cities of the Ægean Grand Age, Tiryns and Mycenæ, on the plain of Argos (§ 347). Above the gate is a large triangular block of stone, carved to represent two lions grouped on either side of a central column. The whole doubtless formed the emblem of the city, or the arms of its kings. It is of course a descendant of the two Babylonian lions of Lagash, showing a similar balanced arrangement with one on each side of the center (Fig. 85)

Along the Asiatic side of the Ægean Sea we find much earlier progress than on the European side, although this was but slightly due to the commerce from Crete, which seems to have had little effect along the shores of Asia Minor. In the days when Crete was first receiving metal (after 3000 B.C.), there arose at the northwest corner of Asia Minor a shabby little Late Stone Age village known as Troy. It was probably built by traders attracted by the profitable traffic which was already crossing back and forth between Asia and Europe at this point (see map, p. **252**).

By 2500 B.C., some centuries after the first metal had been introduced, the rulers of Troy were wealthy commercial kings, and their castle was the earliest fortress in the Ægean world, for it was a thousand years older than the fortresses at Mycenæ and Tiryns. During this thousand years (2500 to 1500 B.C.) Troy was rebuilt several times (Fig. 150), but it continued to flourish, and it finally must have controlled a kingdom of considerable extent in northwestern Asia Minor. Thus about 1500 B.C. the splendid and cultivated city of Troy was a power-ful stronghold (Sixth City), which had grown up as a northern rival of that sumptuous Cnossus we have seen in the south. The two rival cities faced each other from opposite ends of the Ægean, but we infer that Cnossus was superior in civiliza-tion, for it is still uncertain whether the Trojans of this age could write.

350. Growth of Troy (2500–1500 B.C.)

Inland from Troy and the Ægean world, across the far-stretching hills and mountains of Asia Minor, were the settle-ments of a great group of white peoples who were kindred of the Ægeans in civilization, though not in blood. We call them Hittites. Although the larger part of their land lay outside of the Ægean world, nevertheless, one end of it formed the eastern shores of the Ægean Sea. Asia Minor, their land, is a vast penin-sula from six hundred and fifty to seven hundred miles long and from three to four hundred miles wide, being about as large as the state of Texas. The interior is a lofty table-land, little better than a desert in its central region. Around most of this table-land rise mountain ridges, fringing both the table-land and the sea. On both sides of the mountain fringe are fertile valleys and plains, producing plentiful crops. The seaward slopes of the mountains, especially along the Black Sea, are clad with flourishing forests. The northern shores of Asia Minor, east of the Halys River, rise into ridges containing rich deposits of iron. The Hittites thus became the earliest distributors of iron when it began to displace bronze in the Mediterranean world and the East (§ 219).

351. Asia Minor, the land of the Hittites

**352. The Hittites a link between the Fertile Crescent and the Ægean**

In discussing oriental influences in the Ægean, we have already seen (§ 332) how Asia Minor formed a link between the Ægean and the world of the Two Rivers. The people who made it such a link were these Hittites. For at the eastern end of their land they passed easily down the upper Euphrates to the Fertile Crescent, where they merged with the peoples

FIG. 146. AN ANCIENT HITTITE AND HIS MODERN ARMENIAN DESCENDANT

At the left is the head of an ancient Hittite as carved by an Egyptian sculptor on the wall of a temple at Thebes, Egypt, over three thousand years ago. It strikingly resembles the profile of the Armenians still living in the Hittite country, as shown in the modern portrait on the right. The strongly aquiline and prominent nose (§ 146) of the Hittites was also acquired by the neighboring Semites along the eastern end of the Mediterranean, including the Canaanites (see headpiece, p. 197)

there whose history we have already studied. We recall, for example, how they held early Assur, in competition with Babylon (§ 202). We find also that the Hittites early borrowed the old Babylonian coat of arms, a lion-headed, or sometimes a double-headed, eagle. They handed it on across the Ægean to later Europe, from which it passed to us in the United States as the "American" eagle (Fig. 85).

**353. The Hittites influence their neighbors both in east and west**

Both in the Ægean and in the Fertile Crescent, that is, at *both* ends of their land, the Hittites left their mark upon their neighbors. We recall the prominent aquiline nose of the Hittite people (Fig. 146). The same feature among the Hebrews shows how the Hittites drifted down the west end of the Fertile Crescent, until they reached Palestine (§ 291) in sufficient numbers to affect the Hebrew type of face. On the west in the same way, Hittite life greatly influenced the cities along the Ægean coast of Asia Minor, where we shall find that even the later Greeks still bore marks of Hittite influence, especially in important matters of business, like coinage (§ 458), but also in religion and architecture.

It was from their contact with the Fertile Crescent that the Hittites received the first influences leading to a higher civilization. The most important of these was writing. The Babylonian caravans, passing up the Euphrates in the days of Hammurapi (§ 187) and earlier, brought into Asia Minor business and traffic, with bills and other commercial documents in cuneiform writing on clay tablets (Fig. 79). In this way, like other peoples in the West, the

354. Rise of Hittite civilization : Babylonian writing

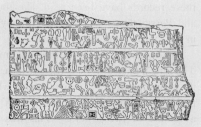

FIG. 147. AN INSCRIPTION IN HITTITE HIEROGLYPHS

This example shows us the hieroglyphic writing devised by the Hittites in imitation of the Egyptian (§ 335). It was found at Carchemish on the Euphrates. The same writing may also be seen accompanying the scene in Fig. 148

Hittites learned cuneiform by 2000 B.C. or earlier. Excavation in Asia Minor has even recovered fragments of the clay-tablet dictionaries used by the Hittites in learning to write and spell words in cuneiform. It was probably through the Hittites that the use of the clay tablet passed over to Crete (Fig. 137).

The Hittites profited by the Egyptian civilization also, as they received it through the cities of northern Syria, like Samal (Fig. 97). Here, under the influence of Egyptian hieroglyphic writing, they devised a system of picture signs with phonetic values (Fig. 147). With these hieroglyphic signs they engraved great stone records like those of Egypt. These records (Fig. 147), cut into the face of rocky cliffs or masonry walls,

355. Hittite hieroglyphic writing

still look down upon the passing traveler throughout a great part of Asia Minor from the Ægean to the Euphrates, and new ones are constantly being found by excavation. The Hittites thus used two methods of writing — cuneiform and hieroglyphic. Unfortunately, the Hittite records written in *hieroglyphs* carved on stone are not yet deciphered. Just as this book goes to press the decipherment of the Hittite *cuneiform* records has been accomplished by Hrozny, an Austrian scholar. When all these records have been read, like those of Egypt, Babylonia, and Persia, they will reveal to us many new and wonderful facts in the story of the ancient world.

**356. Hittite art and architecture**

At the same time the Hittites had made progress in building. The king's palace front consisted of a porch in the middle, with its roof supported on two columns, while on either side of the porch was a square tower (Fig. 97, *K*). It was therefore called a "house of two towers." This was the porch adopted from the Hittites by the great Assyrian emperors (§ 224). It finally reached even the Persians. It was adorned with great sentinel lions carved in stone on either side of the entrance, an idea suggested by the Egyptian sphinx. From the Hittite palaces this idea of protecting beasts on either side of the palace entrance passed also to Assyria. The Hittite palace porch was furthermore adorned with a dado, consisting of large flat slabs of stone carved with relief pictures (Fig. 148), probably suggested by similar Egyptian arrangements (Fig. 60). This idea, too, finally passed by way of the Hittites to Assyria, where we recall the long rows of stone pictures adorning the Assyrian palaces (Figs. 105 and 106, *B*). The Hittite sculptors, however, had little skill with the chisel. The Assyrians far surpassed them, and under Assyrian influence the Hittites improved somewhat.

**357. Hittite religion**

In these scenes we find also evidences of religious influences from both Egypt and Babylonia, as we note among them the Babylonian eagle already mentioned and the winged sun-disk from the Nile. We should notice furthermore the devotion of the Hittites to the great Earth-Mother as their chief goddess, whom we have also found in Crete (headpiece, p. 221), and who later was revered by the Greeks (§ 416).

In the great days of the Egyptian Empire, while Cnossus was still in the Grand Age and Troy her northern rival was building the splendid Sixth City, that is, about 1500 B.C., one of the Hittite kingdoms on the east of the Halys River (see map, p. 102) was gaining great power. It had established

358. Rise of the Hittite Empire (fifteenth century B.C.)

FIG. 148. A HITTITE PRINCE HUNTING DEER

The prince accompanied by his driver stands in the moving chariot, shooting with bow and arrow at the fleeing stag. A hound runs beside the horses. Over the scene is an inscription in Hittite hieroglyphs (§ 355). The whole is sculptured in stone, and forms a good example of the rather crude Hittite art

a strong fortified capital at a city called Khatti (map, p. 102). This name is simply an ancient form of the modern name " Hittite." The kings of Khatti erected imposing palaces and temples, and built a great wall about the city (Fig. 152). They succeeded in gaining control of the other Hittite kingdoms and combining them into an empire which included a large part of Asia Minor.

This Hittite Empire lasted for some two centuries and a half (about 1450 to 1200 B.C.). The Hittites had received the horse,

**359. The Hittite Empire (about 1450–1200 B.C.)**

perhaps even earlier than the Babylonians (§ 197), and the kings of Khatti were able to muster large and powerful bodies of chari.teers. They thus played a vigorous part in the great group of nations around the eastern end of the Mediterranean after Egypt established the first empire there (Section 9). They had much to do with breaking down the Egyptian Empire (§ 122), and they survived to fight fierce battles with the Assyrians.

**360. The Hittites contribute the first iron to the ancient world**

One of the most important things we should remember about the Hittites is the fact that they began working the iron mines along the Black Sea (§ 351). A clay-tablet letter written by one of the Hittite kings tells us that he was about to send a shipment of " pure iron " to Ramses II, who had asked for it, and that meantime a sword of iron was being sent to the Egyptian king as a gift (thirteenth century B.C.). We shall soon see the Iron Age beginning in the Ægean (§ 392), and it was from the Hittite iron mines that the metal first became common in the eastern Mediterranean. While the Hittite civilization was inferior to that of Egypt and Babylonia, it played a very important part in the group of civilizations forming the oriental neighbors of the Ægeans.

## SECTION 36. MODERN DISCOVERY IN THE NORTHERN MEDITERRANEAN AND THE RISE OF AN EASTERN MEDITERRANEAN WORLD

**361. Modern ignorance of Ægean civilization**

We have been putting together the story of the rise and early history of civilization along the north side of the eastern end of the Mediterranean (see map, p. **252**), extending from the Ægean world at one end, through the Hittite country to the Two Rivers at the other. Only a few years ago this story was entirely unknown. Less than fifty years ago no one supposed that civilized people had lived in the Ægean world before the Greeks arrived there. Much less did anyone dream that we would ever be able to find the actual handiwork of the predecessors of the

Greeks in the Ægean world. The discoverer of the Ægean civilization which we have been studying was Heinrich Schliemann.

Schliemann was an American citizen of German birth. In his youth before coming to America he had a romantic business career. After being shipwrecked on the coast of Holland, he began his business experience there while a mere lad, as a

362. Life of Heinrich Schliemann

FIG. 149. THE MOUND CONTAINING THE NINE CITIES OF ANCIENT TROY (ILIUM)

The process by which such artificial mounds grow up is explained in § 158. When Schliemann first visited this mound (see map, p. 254) in 1868, it was about 125 feet high, and the Turks were cultivating grain on its summit. In 1870 he excavated a pit like a crater in the top of the hill, passing downward in the course of four years through nine successive cities built each on the ruins of its predecessors. At the bottom of his pit (about 50 feet deep) Schliemann found the original once bare hilltop about 75 feet high, on which the men of the Late Stone Age (§ 349) had established a small settlement of sun-baked brick houses about 3000 B.C. (see Fig. 150). Above the scanty ruins of this Late Stone Age settlement rose, in layer after layer, the ruins of the later cities, with the Roman buildings at the top. The entire depth of 50 feet of ruins represented a period of about thirty-five hundred years from the First City (Late Stone Age) to the Ninth City (Roman) at the top. The Second City (§ 350) contained the earliest copper found in the series; the Sixth City was that of the Trojan War and the Homeric songs (§ 410). Its masonry walls may be seen in Fig. 151

clerk in a little grocer's shop. In the brief intervals of leisure between dealing out smoked herring and rolls of butter, he taught himself Greek and began to read Homer (§ 410). In the infatuated ears of this enthusiastic boy the shouts of the Greek heroes on the plain of Troy mingled with the jingle of small change and the rustle of wrapping paper in the dingy little Dutch grocery. He had not lost this fascinating vision of the early world, when years afterward he retired from business, after having won a large fortune in Russian petroleum.

**363. Schliemann's excavation and discovery of Troy**

It was therefore as the fulfillment of a dream of his youth that Schliemann led a body of Turkish laborers to begin excavations in the great mound of Troy in 1870 (see map, p. 252, and Fig. 149). In less than four years he uncovered the central

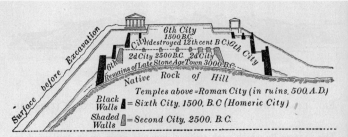

FIG. 150. DIAGRAM OF THE MOUND OF ANCIENT TROY SHOWING THE WALLS OF THE SECOND AND SIXTH CITIES AND THE ROMAN TEMPLE AT THE TOP (NINTH CITY)

This diagram is much too high for its width, as you will see by comparing the width and height of the mound in Fig. 149. It has been pushed together at the sides and narrowed to include it within the available space. Below is the native rock of the hill on which the Late Stone Age settlement was built. Then come the sloping walls of the Second City (shaded). Outside of these and rising much higher are the walls of the Sixth City (black), which may be seen as they are to-day in Fig. 151. The other cities of the nine are less important and have been left out for the sake of clearness. Schliemann never saw the walls of the Sixth City, the real Homeric city, because as he dug down in the middle of the mound inside the ancient walls, he covered the walls of the Sixth City with the rubbish he dug out

portions of nine successive cities, each built upon the ruins of the next city beneath, which had preceded it (Fig. 150). A towered gateway in the Second City contained a splendid treasure of golden jewelry, and Schliemann believed that he had here discovered the Troy of Homer's Greek heroes (§ 408). But we now know that this Second City was built a thousand years before Homer's Troy (the Sixth City (Fig. 150)).

The sensation aroused by these discoveries among the scholars of Europe and America was mild compared with that which followed when Schliemann, crossing to the mainland of Greece, began excavating the prehistoric fortress or castle of

FIG. 151. THE WALLS OF HOMERIC TROY (BUILT ABOUT 1500 B.C.)

A section of the outer walls of the Sixth City in the mound of Troy (Fig. 150). The sloping outer surface of the walls faces toward the right; the inside of the city is on the left. These are the walls built in the days when Mycenæ was flourishing — walls which protected the inhabitants of the place from the assaults of the Greeks in a remote war which laid it in ruins after 1200 B.C., a war of which vague traditions and heroic tales have survived in the Homeric poems (§ 408). These are the walls, scaled by the Greek heroes, which Schliemann never saw (compare description, Fig. 150). The walls of the houses of the Seventh City are visible here resting on those of the Sixth

Mycenæ (Fig. 145). Beneath the pavement of the market place he found a group of stone tomb chambers containing a magnificent series of vessels and ornaments in gold, including an elaborate golden crown, indicating the royalty of one of the dead. Again Schliemann thought that these things belonged to the Greek heroes of the Trojan wars (§ 408), but in reality they were older. At the neighboring prehistoric castle of Tiryns (Fig. 144 and § 347) Schliemann made similar discoveries. Thus within a few years an unskilled and untrained excavator disclosed to us a new and entirely unknown world of civilization in the Ægean, which had flourished for centuries before the Greeks appeared there.

**365.** Excavations in Crete since 1900

The question of the original home of this early Ægean civilization, however, was not settled by Schliemann's work. Since 1900 the excavations in Crete have shown this island to have been the place where Ægean civilization made its start, and the center from which it passed to the other islands and to the mainland of Greece at Tiryns and Mycenæ (§ 347). In these discoveries American explorers have had an honorable share ; but they have been due chiefly to the remarkable excavations of Sir Arthur Evans, the English archæologist, at the city of Cnossus. Here Evans has uncovered the splendid Cretan palaces (Fig. 138), clearing out layer after layer of rubbish containing works of Cretan art and industry, which carry us back age after age to the rubbish of the Late Stone Age settlement deep down at the bottom of the mound, over which the first palace was built (§ 337).

**366.** Excavation and discovery in Asia Minor, the land of the Hittites

At the same time exploration in Asia Minor has revealed increasing numbers of Hittite monuments. Of these discoveries the most important were those of the German expedition at Khatti (Fig. 152), beginning in the winter of 1906–1907. Lying just under the surface of the soil, where it was quite possible to kick them out with the heel of one's boot, the explorers found the clay tablets which once filled the state record chambers in the palace of the Hittite kings at Khatti during the great days of their empire three thousand years ago. Here were letters to and from the kings of Egypt, Babylon, Assyria and all the great powers of the oriental world which we have studied. Among them was the letter already mentioned, containing the Hittite king's notice of the coming shipment of iron. Besides recovering the lost records, the German expedition gradually

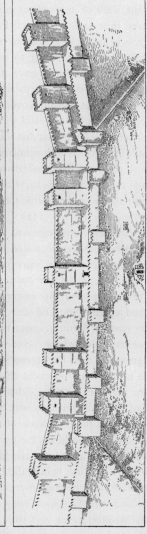

Fig. 152. The Ancient Capital of the Hittites in Central Asia Minor (recently excavated)

The view at the top shows the ruins of the great walled city which covered a group of hills like those of Rome. A modern village close by, called Boghaz-Köi, has given the place its modern name; but the Hittites called the city Khatti. The view below shows a portion of the masonry walls of the city as they once were, when the Hittite kings lived here in the thirteenth century B.C. (After Puchstein)

excavated the walls of the ancient city and its chief buildings, and recovered their architecture (cf. Fig. 152).

**367.** Modern recovery of early civilization entirely around the eastern end of the Mediterranean

Although we are still unable to read the records of the Cretans and are only beginning to read those of the Hittites, the discoveries in their lands have revealed to us the earliest chapter of civilization on the north side of the eastern Mediterranean. If we connect these discoveries along the north side of the Mediterranean at its east end with the earlier story of discovery in the oriental lands east and south of the Mediterranean, the student will perceive how scholars and explorers have carried the work of excavation and discovery entirely around the east end of the Mediterranean, from the lower Nile valley, through the nations of the Fertile Crescent, to Asia Minor and the Ægean Sea (see map, p. 102).

**368.** Rise of an eastern Mediterranean world (3000–1500 B.C.)

These discoveries have begun to show us how the civilized peoples all around the eastern end of the Mediterranean, by their industries and commerce, were gradually creating a civilized world of which the Ægean Sea was merely a northern bay. We recall our first glimpse of this eastern Mediterranean world as we journeyed up the Nile and saw the Egyptian ships which crossed the eastern Mediterranean nearly 3000 B.C. (Fig. 41). But now we have studied the peoples on the east and north of the Mediterranean and have seen how, at the close of the Grand Age in Crete, the splendid Ægean civilization had been mingling for centuries with the older oriental civilizations, especially that of the Nile, but also with that of Hittite Asia Minor and through it with the civilization of the Fertile Crescent.

**369.** Northern intruders

Into this civilized world of the eastern Mediterranean, with its arts, its industries, and its far-reaching commerce, the uncivilized peoples of the North behind the Balkan mountains and the Black Sea were now beginning to intrude. These uncivilized northerners were the Greeks. They were soon to overwhelm the eastern Mediterranean, and with these Northern intruders we must begin a new chapter in the history of the eastern Mediterranean world.

## QUESTIONS

Section 33. At what point in their progress did we leave the Europeans when we first passed over to the Orient? What products of the eastern Mediterranean reached the Late Stone Age Europeans? How did these things reach Europe? Did the possession of metal raise the Europeans to a high civilization?

Section 34. Was there any part of Europe nearer the Orient than the Ægean world? By what two ways was it connected with the Orient? What island of the Ægean is nearest to Egypt? Describe the rise of civilization there. Can you mention some evidences of Egyptian influence there? Where did the Cretan sea-kings arise? What survives to tell us of their power? What industries flourished? Can you mention some evidence of Cretan commerce? What now happened to Cretan writing? Tell something of Cretan decorative art in the Grand Age; of the work of sculptor and goldsmith. Tell something of the life of the palace and of the peasants. Under what foreign power were the Cretans at this time? What three great civilizations now existed?

Section 35. Had the European mainland advanced as fast as Crete in civilization? Where do we find evidences of the first civilization on the continent of Europe, and what are they? Date them. Was there yet any writing common in Europe? Where and when did civilization arise on the east side of the Ægean? What led men to this point? What can you say about the history and civilization of Troy? What people occupied most of Asia Minor? Mention some things which they passed on to the West from the East. Recall some evidences of their influence in the East. What influences reached the Hittites from the Fertile Crescent and from Egypt? When did the Hittite Empire arise, and what can you say about its influence? What was the most important thing which the Hittites contributed to other peoples?

Section 36. Who first discovered remains of people who had occupied the Ægean world before the Greeks? Tell something of his life. What did he find at Troy? in Greece? What has excavation in Crete since shown? What has excavation in Asia Minor revealed? With reference to the eastern end of the Mediterranean how far have excavation and discovery been carried? What kind of a world has discovery revealed in the eastern Mediterranean? What uncivilized Northerners were now intruding into this eastern Mediterranean world?

# CHAPTER IX

### THE GREEK CONQUEST OF THE ÆGEAN WORLD

#### SECTION 37. THE COMING OF THE GREEKS

**370.** South-ward advance of the Indo-European line in Europe

The people whom we call the Greeks were a large group of tribes of Indo-European race. We have already followed the Indo-European parent people until their diverging migrations finally ranged them in a line from the Atlantic Ocean to northern India (§ 243 and Fig. 112). While their eastern kindred

NOTE. The above headpiece shows a line of captive warriors with their hands shackled before them or pinioned over their heads. They wear a tall feathered headdress, which shows them to be Philistines (§ 296), a tribe of Cretan warriors driven out of Crete by the Greeks (§ 379). Some of them, invading Egypt in their flight, were taken captive by Ramses III, the last of the Egyptian emperors, not long after 1200 B.C. He therefore placed this picture of them on the walls of his temple at Thebes, Egypt. Other pictures of them may be seen in Fig. 154, recognizable by their headdress.

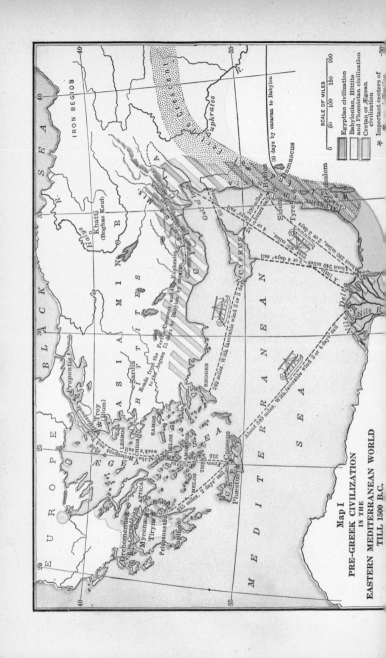

Map I

PRE-GREEK CIVILIZATION
IN THE
EASTERN MEDITERRANEAN WORLD
TILL 1500 B.C.

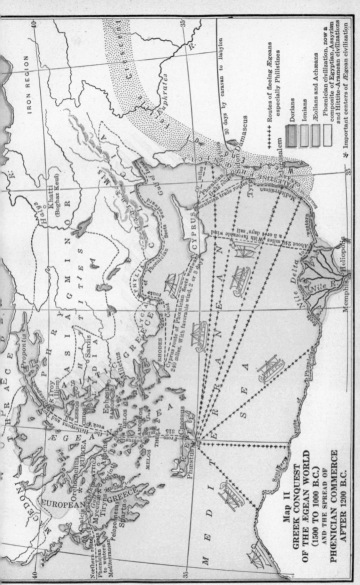

Map II
GREEK CONQUEST
OF THE ÆGEAN WORLD
(1500 TO 1000 B.C.)
AND THE SPREAD OF
PHOENICIAN COMMERCE
AFTER 1200 B.C.

IRON REGION

+++++ Routes of fleeing Ægeans
especially Philistines

Dorians

Ionians

Æolians and Achaeans

Phoenician civilization, now a
composite of Egyptian, Assyrian
and Hittite-Aramean civilizations

☆ Important centers of Ægean civilization

SEQUENCE MAP OF THE EASTERN MEDITERRANEAN WORLD FROM THE GRAND AGE OF CRETAN
CIVILIZATION (ABOUT 1500 B.C.) TO THE CONQUEST OF THE ÆGEAN BY THE GREEKS

were drifting southward on the east side of the Caspian, the Greeks on the west side of the Black Sea were likewise moving southward from their broad pastures along the Danube (see map II, p. 252).

Driving their herds before them, with their families in rough carts drawn by horses, the rude Greek tribesmen must have looked out upon the fair pastures of Thessaly, the snowy summit of Mount Olympus (Fig. 153), and the blue waters of the Ægean not long after 2000 B.C. The Greek peninsula which they had entered contains about twenty-five thousand square miles.[1] It is everywhere cut up by mountains and inlets of the sea into small plains and peninsulas, separated from each other either by the sea or the mountain ridges.

371. The Greeks enter the Greek peninsula

FIG. 153.  MOUNT OLYMPUS — THE HOME OF THE GODS

Although Mount Olympus is on the northern borders of Greece, it can be seen from Attica and the south end of Eubœa. It approaches 10,000 feet in height, and looks down upon Macedonia on one side and Thessaly on the other (see map, p. 262). As we look at it here from the south, we have a portion of the plain of Thessaly in the foreground, where the first Greeks entered Hellas (§ 371), and where later the earliest Homeric songs of the Greek heroes were composed (§ 408)

No less than five hundred islands are scattered along its deeply indented eastern shores (map, p. 262 and Plate III). On its climate and products see § 331.

[1] About one sixth smaller than South Carolina — so small that Mount Olympus on the northern boundary of Greece is visible over much of the peninsula. From the mountains of Sparta one can see from Crete to the mountains north of the Corinthian Gulf (see Fig. 163), a distance of two hundred and twenty-five miles.

**372.** The barbarian Greek nomads and the settled Ægean civilization

The wandering shepherds whom we have seen so often invading the Fertile Crescent (§§ 135, 167, and 294) to find a settled and civilized town life there, furnish us the best possible illustration of the situation of the Greeks as they invaded the Ægean towns and settlements like Tiryns and Mycenæ (§ 347). As the newcomers looked out across the waters they could dimly discern the islands, where flourishing towns were carrying on busy industries, especially in pottery and metal, which a thriving commerce was distributing (§§ 339 and 345).

**373.** The barbarian Greek nomads on the margin of the great oriental world

We can imagine the wonder with which these barbarian Greeks must have looked out upon the white sails that flecked the blue surface of the Ægean Sea. It was to be long, however, before these inland shepherds would themselves venture timidly out upon the great waters which they were viewing for the first time. Had the gaze of the Greek nomads been able to penetrate beyond the Ægean isles, they would have seen a vast panorama of great and flourishing oriental states. Here on the borders of the great oriental world and under its influences the Greeks were now to go forward toward the development of a civilization higher than any the Orient had yet produced, the highest indeed which ancient man ever attained.

**374.** Achæan Greeks followed by Dorian Greeks in Peloponnesus by 1500 B.C.

Gradually their vanguard (called the Achæans) pushed southward into the Peloponnesus, and doubtless some of them mingled with the Ægean dwellers in the villages which were grouped under the walls of Tiryns and Mycenæ (Figs. 144, 145, and Plate III), just as the Hebrew nomads mingled with the Canaanite townsmen (§ 294). Some of the Greek leaders may have captured these Ægean fortresses, just as David took Jerusalem (§ 297). But our knowledge of the situation in Greece is very meager because the peoples settled here could not yet write, and therefore have left no written documents to tell the story. It is evident, however, that a second wave of Greek nomads (called the Dorians) reached the Peloponnesus by 1500 B.C. and subdued their earlier kinsmen (the Achæans) as well as the Ægean townsmen, the original inhabitants of the region.

The Dorians did not stop at the southern limits of Greece, but, learning a little navigation from their Ægean predecessors, they passed over to Crete, where they must have arrived by 1400 B.C. Cnossus, unfortified as it was, and without any walled castle (§ 338), must have fallen an easy prey to the invading Dorians, who took possession of the island, and likewise seized the other southern islands of the Ægean. Between 1300 and 1000 B.C. the Greek tribes took possession of the remaining islands, as well as the coast of Asia Minor — the Dorians in the south, the Ionians in the middle, and the Æolians in the north. Here a memorable Greek expedition in the twelfth century B.C., after a long siege, captured and burned the prosperous city of Troy (§ 350), a feat which the Greeks never after forgot (§ 408). During the thousand years between 2000 and 1000 B.C. the Greeks thus took possession not only of the whole Greek peninsula but likewise of the entire Ægean world.

375. The Greeks take possession of the Ægean world; Dorians in Crete and southern Ægean

The *interior* of Asia Minor suffered likewise. Other Indo-Europeans, kindred of the Greeks, were pushing southward behind them. Some of these rearward Indo-European tribes found it easier to cross the Hellespont and invade Asia Minor than to push on into Greece. Probably before 1500 B.C. some of these invaders of Asia Minor had become so numerous among the Hittites, who were not originally Indo-Europeans, that the Hittite communities began to lose their own tongue and to speak the Indo-European language of the newcomers. Thus the Hittite cuneiform tablets (§ 354) are in a language which contains Indo-European words and grammatical forms akin to those in Greek, as the new decipherment (§ 355) has recently shown. By 1200 B.C. a second wave of Indo-Europeans, especially the Phrygians and the Armenians, were invading the Hittite country in Asia Minor.

376. Phrygians and Armenians invade Asia Minor

The northern Mediterranean all along its eastern end was thus being absorbed by Indo-European peoples. The result was that both the Ægeans and their Hittite neighbors in Asia Minor were overwhelmed by the advancing Indo-European

377. Flight of the well-to-do Ægeans

line   The Hittite Empire (§ 359) completely collapsed.   The splendid Ægean civilization which we saw rising so prosperously was unable to repel the invaders.   Probably few of the common people of the Ægean towns were able to flee.   On the other hand, the noble and well-to-do Ægean families, the class to which our elegantly dressed little Cretan lady of the statuette (Fig. 141) belonged, — forming, all told, considerable numbers, — must have taken to the sea and fled.   They looked back upon burning towns and villas, and they must have seen the splendid palace of Cnossus, with all its beautiful treasures of Cretan art, going up in smoke and flame.

**378.** Egyptian repulse of the fugitive Ægeans

By 1200 B.C. the movement of the Greek or Indo-European invasion from the north had thus set in motion before it a wave of fleeing Ægeans, which crossed the sea and broke upon the shores of the southeastern Mediterranean from the Nile Delta to the harbors of Phœnicia.   It was this wave of Ægean fugitives which aided in overturning the tottering Egyptian Empire.   An Egyptian relief scene shows us the earliest-known picture of a naval battle (Fig. 154) — a sea fight off the coast of Syria, in which the last of the Egyptian emperors beat off an Ægean fleet (§ 124).

**379.** Cretan Philistines find a home in Southern Palestine

The only region where the fleeing Ægeans were numerous enough to settle and to form a nation was in Southern Palestine.   Here a tribe of Cretans called Philistines (headpiece, p. 252), although they had been beaten in the sea fight just mentioned, were able to establish themselves and build up a group of prosperous cities, in the twelfth century B.C.   We recall how they nearly succeeded in crushing the young Hebrew nation just then emerging (§ 296).   Curiously enough, it was these fugitives from the Ægean world who gave to Palestine its present name, for " Palestine " is simply a later form of the name " Philistine."

**380.** Fall of Ægean civilization

The Indo-European invasion of the Ægean world thus broke up the prosperous and highly civilized communities which we have seen there, especially in Crete.   By 1200 B.C. the splendid

Ægean civilization had been almost submerged by northern barbarism, little better than the Late Stone Age life which we have already seen in Europe. Some important things in Ægean civilization perished entirely — among them Cretan

FIG. 154. BATTLE BETWEEN A FLEET OF FLEEING ÆGEANS AND AN EGYPTIAN FLEET

This scene, sculptured on the walls of an Egyptian temple at Thebes (§ 124), is the earliest surviving picture of a naval battle. It shows us the Mediterranean peoples defeated by the last Egyptian emperor, Ramses III, not long after 1200 B.C., somewhere along the Syrian coast (§ 378). Of the nine ships engaged four are Egyptian (lion's head on the prow) — three at the left and one in the lower right-hand corner. The remaining five are Ægean ships (goose-head on the prow). One Ægean ship (middle, below) has been overturned. The Ægeans are Philistines with feathered headdress (see headpiece, p. 252), and we see here how they passed from Crete to Palestine (§ 379). The Ægeans are armed only with round shields and spears or two-edged swords (§ 776), whereas the Egyptians are chiefly archers, who overwhelm the enemy with archery volleys at long range and then close in, taking Philistine prisoners who may be seen standing bound in the Egyptian ships

writing, which disappeared after the Greek invasion. Enough of Ægean industries survived, however, to form an essential part of the foundation upon which the barbarian Greeks were yet to build up the highest civilization of the ancient world.

Such of the Ægean population as had not fled before the incoming Greeks mingled with their Greek conquerors, just as

**381. Min-gling of Ægeans and Greeks**

we have seen the civilized Canaanites of Palestine mingling with the invading Hebrew nomads (§ 294). This commingling of Ægeans and Greeks produced a mixed race, the people known to us as the Greeks of history. How much Ægean blood may have flowed in their veins we are unable to determine. But the supreme genius of the classical Greeks may well have been due, in some measure, to this admixture of the blood of the gifted Cretans, with their open-mindedness toward influences from abroad and their fine artistic instincts.

**382. Tri-umph of Greek speech**

The mingling of Greek and Ægean blood did not result in a similar mixture of speech, as English is made up of French and Anglo-Saxon. Greek, the language of the victorious invaders, gradually became the language of the Ægean world. At the same time Greek did not blot out every trace of the older *Ægean* language of the region. People continued to call the towns, rivers, and mountains, like Mount Parnassus, by the old Ægean names they found in use, just as we found *Indian* geographical names in America and continue to call our greatest river by its old *Indian* name, Mississippi ("Father of Waters"). Such names in Greece are to-day surviving remnants of the lost Ægean language, now no longer anywhere spoken.[1] It is interesting also to notice that a few Ægean words for civilized conveniences, such as the Greek invaders did not possess, likewise survived. So the word "bathtub" in Greek is really an old Ægean word. For of course a race of wandering shepherds such as the Greeks had been, had no such luxuries; whereas we have recovered the actual bathtubs of the refined Ægeans (§ 344), from whom the Greeks learned the name. Nevertheless, the Greek language was already developing as the richest and most beautiful instrument of speech man has ever possessed.

---

[1] We do not know to what group of languages the old Ægean speech, now lost, belonged. The still undeciphered Cretan writings (§ 340) may yet reveal this secret. The claim made in America that one variety of Cretan hieroglyphic has been deciphered, and found to be Greek, is without foundation. The recent decipherment of Hittite cuneiform (§§ 355 and 376) should aid in solving the problem.

## SECTION 38. THE NOMAD GREEKS MAKE THE
## TRANSITION TO THE SETTLED LIFE

In tranquil summer days one can pass from island to island and cross the entire Ægean Sea from Greece to Asia Minor in a rowboat. This is why a group of shepherd tribes like the Greeks had been able to cross and take possession of the islands of the Ægean and the coast of neighboring Asia Minor. But we must not conclude that at this early stage of their history they had already taken to the sea and become a people of sailors. Centuries later we find the Greek peasant-poet Hesiod (700 B.C.) looking with shrinking eye upon the sea. Long after they had taken possession of the Ægean world the Greeks remained a barbarous people of flocks and herds, without any commerce by sea.

383. Early Greeks not a maritime people

If we would understand the situation of the Greeks after their conquest of the civilized Ægean world, we must again recall nomad life as we have seen it along the Fertile Crescent in Asia (§ 136). We remember that the nomads possessed no organized government, for there was no public business which demanded it. Even to-day among such people no taxes are collected, for no one owns any land which can be taxed. There are no public officials, there are no cases at law, no legal business, and men are controlled by a few customs like the " blood revenge " (§ 136). Such was exactly the condition of the nomad Greeks when they began a settled life in the Ægean world.

384. Earliest social institutions of the Greeks

From their old wandering life on the grasslands they carried with them the loose groups of families known as tribes, and within each tribe an indefinite number of smaller groups of more intimate families called " brotherhoods." A " council " of the old men (" elders ") occasionally decided matters in dispute, or questions of tribal importance, and probably once a year, or at some important feast, an " assembly " of all the weapon-bearing men of the tribe might be held, to express its

385. Tribes, " council," and " assembly "

opinion of a proposed war or migration. These are the germs of later European political institutions and even of our own in the United States to-day.[1]

**386. Rise of Greek kings**

It was perhaps after they had found kings over such Ægean cities as Mycenæ (§ 347) that the Greeks (like the Hebrews, § 296) began to want kings themselves. Thus the old-time nomad leaders whom they had once followed in war, religion, and the settlement of disputes became rude shepherd kings of the tribes.

**387. Greeks begin agriculture**

Meantime the Greek shepherds slowly began the cultivation of land. This forced them to give up a wandering life to build houses and live in permanent homes. Nomad instincts and nomad customs were not easily rooted out however. War and the care of flocks continued to be the occupation of the *men*, as it had been for centuries on the Northern grasslands; while the cultivation of the fields was at first left to the *women*. Furthermore, flocks and herds continued to make up the chief wealth of the Greeks for centuries after they had taken up agriculture.

**388. Rise of land ownership and its consequences in government and society**

As each Greek tribe settled down and became a group of villages, the surrounding land was divided among the families by lot, though the tribe as a whole long continued to be the only real owner of the land. Nevertheless, private ownership of land by families gradually resulted. As a consequence there arose disputes about boundaries, about inheritances in land (§ 452), and much other legal business, which as it increased required more and more attention by those in authority. The settlement of such business tended to create a government. During the four centuries from 1000 to 600 B.C. we see the Greeks struggling with the problem of learning how to transact the business of settled landholding communities, and how to

---

[1] Compare the House of Lords ( = the above "council") and the House of Commons ( = the above "assembly") in England, or the Senate (derived from the Latin word meaning "old man") and the House of Representatives in the United States.

adjust the ever-growing friction and strife between the rich and the poor, the social classes created by the holding of land and the settled life (cf. § 31).

We have seen the Semitic nomads struggling with the same problems on the Fertile Crescent (§ 167). But for them the situation was in one important particular much easier. They found among their settled predecessors a system of writing which they quickly learned (§ 167). But the old Cretan writing (§ 340), once used by the Ægean predecessors of the Greeks, had perished. No one had ever yet written a word of the Greek language in this age when the Greeks were adopting the settled agricultural life. This lack of writing greatly increased the difficulties to be met as a government arose and its transactions began. There arose in some communities a "rememberer," whose duty it was to notice carefully the terms of a contract, the amount of a loan, or the conditions of a treaty with a neighboring people, that he might remember these and innumerable other things, which in a more civilized society are recorded in writing.

**389. Lack of writing among the early Greeks**

In course of time the group of villages forming the nucleus of a tribe grew together and merged at last into a city. This was the most important process in Greek political development; for the organized city became the only nation which the Greeks ever knew. Each city-state was a sovereign power; each had its own laws, its own army and gods, and each citizen felt a patriotic duty toward his own city and no other. Overlooking the city from the heights in its midst was the king's castle (Fig. 144), which we call the "citadel," or "acropolis." Eventually, the houses and the market below were protected by a wall. The king had now become a revered and powerful ruler of the city, and guardian of the worship of the city gods. King and Council sat all day in the market and adjusted the business and the disputes between the people. Though crude, corrupt, and often unjust, these continuous sessions for the first time created a state and an uninterrupted government.

**390. Rise of the city-state**

391. Rise of
Greek civili-
zation in the
Age of the
Kings (1000
750 B.C.)

There were hundreds of such city-states throughout the mainland of Greece and the coasts and islands of the Ægean. Indeed the Ægean world was made up of such tiny nations after the Greeks had made the transition to the settled life there. It was while the Greeks were thus living in these little city-kingdoms under kings that Greek civilization arose. While there were Greek kings long before 1000 B.C., it is especially after that date, during the last two and a half centuries of the rule of the kings (1000–750 B.C.), that we are able to follow the rise of Greek civilization.

## QUESTIONS

SECTION 37. To what race did the Greeks belong? Had they always lived in Greece? Whence did they come? Were they accustomed to settled town life? What kind of surroundings as to civilization did they now enter? Describe their settlement and spread in the Ægean world; in Asia Minor. What was the effect upon the predecessors of the Greeks in the Ægean? in Asia Minor? Mention evidence of the flight of the Ægeans. Who were the Philistines and where did they settle? What happened to Ægean civilization? to architecture? to industries? to writing? What became of the Ægeans who remained behind? Describe the results as to language.

SECTION 38. Did the Greeks at once take to the sea? Did they take up town life at once? What other nomad peoples have we found in the same situation? What social institutions did the Greeks bring with them? What can you say of the social effects of agriculture and landownership? How did the Greeks get along without writing? What became of the villages around each Greek town? Did the Greek towns all unite into one great nation including all the Greeks? What was each Greek nation? Toward what did the Greek feel patriotism? Describe a Greek city-state. Were there many of them? Was there a nation including all the Ægean world? Who was at the head of each city-state? What was the form of government when Greek civilization arose? Date the period when we are able to trace the rise of Greek civilization.

# GREECE
## IN THE FIFTH CENTURY B.C.

SCALE OF MILES

0  10  20    40    60    80

Longitude    East    from    Greenwich

# CHAPTER X

## GREEK CIVILIZATION IN THE AGE OF THE KINGS

SECTION 39. THE ÆGEAN INHERITANCE AND THE
SPREAD OF PHŒNICIAN COMMERCE

In one very important matter the Greek invaders were more
fortunate than their Ægean predecessors. The iron which we
have seen spreading in the Orient from the Hittite country
(§ 360) had at the same time (thirteenth century B.C.) also
begun to reach the Greeks. It was of course a matter of
some centuries before iron tools and weapons entirely displaced
those of bronze, just as the automobile will be a long time
in entirely banishing the horse from among us. Indeed, after
iron had been in common use among the Greeks for over five
hundred years, the Greek poet Æschylus (§ 578) called it the
" stranger from across the sea," or " the Chalybean stranger,"
the Chalybean region being the iron district of Asia Minor (see

392. Begin-
ning of the
Iron Age
(about
1000 B.C.)

NOTE. The above headpiece is a Greek vase-painting showing a battle scene
from the Trojan War. In the middle is the fallen Achilles, for the possession of
whose body a desperate combat is going on (§ 407). Here we see the armor of
the early Greek warriors — a round shield on the left arm, a long spear in the
right hand. A heavy two-edged sword was also carried, but the bow was not
common. Only one warrior here uses it. The face is protected by a heavy helmet
crowned by a tall plume of horsehair, and the body is covered by a bronze corselet, a jacket of metal reaching from the neck to the waist. Below the knees the
legs are protected by bronze fronts called greaves. At the extreme left a comrade binds up a wounded warrior, on whose shield is the bird of his family arms
(cf. Fig. 27). Behind him the goddess Athena watches the combat. The painting is done in the older style of black figures on a red ground (contrast Fig. 170).
The artist has inserted the names of the warriors, some written from left to right
and some in the other direction (cf. headpiece, p. 282).

map, p. 102). By 1000 B.C. iron was common in Greece. The Bronze Age had therefore lasted about two thousand years, that is, about as long as the career of the Ægean civilization. We may say indeed that the period of Ægean civilization coincided with the Bronze Age (3000–1000 B.C.), while the civilization of the Greeks arose at the incoming of the Iron Age (about 1000 B.C.).

**393. Memories of Ægean civilization, and the dawn of Greek civilization**

Long after 1000 B.C. the life of the Greeks continued to be rude and even barbarous. Memories of the old Ægean splendor lingered in the plain of Argos. Above the Greek village at Mycenæ still towered the massive stone walls (Fig. 145) of the ancient Ægean princes, who had long before passed away. To these huge walls the Greeks looked up with awe-struck faces and thought that they had been built by vanished giants called Cyclops. Or with wondering admiration they fingered some surviving piece of rich metal work wrought by the skill of the ancient Ægean craftsmen (Fig. 140). The tradition that Crete was the earliest home of their civilization never died out among the Greeks. Without any skill in craftsmanship, the Greek shepherds and peasants were slow to take up building, industries, and manufacturing on their own account. Their slowness is also evident in the matter of writing, which the Greeks, as we have seen (§ 389), failed to learn from their Ægean predecessors. For a long time even the dwellings of the Greek kings were usually but simple farmhouses of sun-dried brick, where the swine wandered unhindered into the court or slumbered in the sunshine beside the royal doorway. They made a beginning at pottery, and the rude paintings with which they decorated this rough ware (Fig. 155) show that the same methods employed by the Ægean potters in producing their fine ware in Crete a thousand years earlier (Fig. 136) were still lingering on in a decadent state.

**394. Oriental influences: clothing**

When we remember the experience of the Ægean peoples (§§ 332–333), we perceive that the Greeks were now exposed to the same oriental influences which had so strongly affected early

FIG. 155. PRIMITIVE GREEK ART AS SHOWN IN A PAINTED VASE OF THE AGE OF THE KINGS

This very fine specimen, over $3\frac{1}{2}$ feet high, one of the few well-preserved primitive Greek vases, was recently acquired by the Metropolitan Museum of New York. It represents Greek art in its beginnings in the eighth century B.C. We see that the beautiful flowers, sea plants, and other *natural* objects employed by the Ægeans in their decorative art were abandoned by the early Greek vase-painters, in favor of bands of geometrical designs. The two rows of scenes show a funeral above, with the body lying on a high bier. Below is a procession of warriors with dumb-bell-shaped shields, and four-wheeled chariots each with three horses very rudely drawn. Compare the fine horses painted by the Greeks only a century and a half later (Fig. 164) and the magnificent steeds painted four and a half centuries later (Fig. 202). The practical working method employed in this work by the primitive Greek potter and vase-painter was wholly borrowed from his Ægean predecessors (§ 393)

Ægean civilization. The Greek townsmen had now put off the shaggy sheepskin of their former nomad life in favor of a shirt-like garment of woven wool. They had no name for it in Greek, but they heard the foreign merchants of whom they bought it calling it in their language a *kitōn* (ke tōn') (Fig. 156).

**395. The wares of the Phœnician merchants**

To purchase articles like this, which they did not themselves make, the townsmen often went down to the seashore, where they and their women gathered about a ship drawn up with stern on the beach. Black-bearded traders, who overlooked the crowd from the high stern of the ship, tempted the Greeks with glass or alabaster perfume bottles from Egypt (Fig. 49) and rich blue porcelain dishes. If the women did not bid for these, they were quite unable to resist certain handsome ivory combs carved with lions in open-work (Fig. 157), and polished till they shone in the sun.

Wealthy Greeks were attracted by furniture elaborately inlaid with ivory carvings (Fig. 108), and especially by magnificent large round platters of bronze or even of silver, richly engraved (Fig. 158). Splendid purple robes hanging over the stern of the ship enriched the display of golden jewelry with flashes of brilliant color. Here too were the *kitōns*, as we would have heard these swarthy strangers from the sea calling them. They were Phœnicians, and the word for the new garment adopted by the Greeks was a Phœnician word (see map II, p. 252).

**396. Expansion of Phœnician commerce**

FIG. 156. PHŒNICIAN GARMENT ADOPTED BY THE GREEKS

The Greeks called this garment a *kitōn* (early pronounced ke tōn′; later, chi tōn′) (see §§ 394–395). The garments of women may be seen in Fig. 170

We see then that with the fall of the Egyptian Empire (after 1200 B.C.) the ships of Egypt in the eastern Mediterranean had disappeared. The same fate had at the same time overtaken the fleets of the Ægeans. Thus the eastern Mediterranean was left unoccupied by merchant fleets, and by 1000 B.C. the Phœnician cities (Fig. 159) were taking advantage of this opportunity. Once dwellers in the desert like the Hebrews, we remember that the Phœnicians had early occupied the towns along the Syrian coast (§ 141), where they became clever navigators. The Greek craftsmen were as yet quite unable to produce such wares as the Phœnician merchant offered, and hence these oriental traders did a thriving business wherever they landed.

Nor did the Phœnicians stop with the Ægean world. They sought markets also in the West, and they were the discoverers of the western Mediterranean. They finally planted settlements even as far away as the Atlantic coast of Spain (Fig. 157). Their colony of Carthage (map, p. 288) became the most important commercial state in the western Mediterranean and the most dangerous rival of Rome, as we shall see (Sections 77 f.). For some three centuries after 1000 B.C. they were the greatest merchants in the Mediterranean, and their far-reaching traffic was beginning the slow creation of a great mercantile Mediterranean world. They had no armies, however, and little political organization. The only Phœnician colony that ever became a strong state was Carthage.

The Phœnicians learned the methods of manufacturing their goods, in almost all cases, from Egypt. There they learned to make glass and porcelain, to weave linen and dye it, to cast and hammer and engrave metal. On the other hand, we find that the *designs* employed in their art

**397.** The Phœnicians the earliest explorers of the western Mediterranean

FIG. 157. ANCIENT PHŒNICIAN COMB OF CARVED IVORY

Such wares, manufactured at Sidon and Tyre, were distributed by the Phœnician merchants through the Mediterranean (§ 395) as far west as Spain, where combs like this have been found in ancient graves. The lion adorning this comb is the form that developed in Syria (cf. Plate II). Phœnician craftsmen doing such work were also kept by the Assyrian emperors at Nineveh, and pieces of their work have been found there (Fig. 108) bearing Phœnican signs

**398.** Growth of Phœnician art and industries: their composite international character

were international. Their metal platters (Fig. 158) they engraved with designs which they found in both Egypt and Asia. The art of Phœnicia was thus a kind of oriental composite or combination, drawn chiefly from the Nile and the Two Rivers.

We remember that it was Phœnician workmen whom the Assyrian kings employed to make furniture and metal work for the royal palace (Fig. 108). King Solomon likewise employed Phœnician workmen to build for him the Hebrew temple at Jerusalem (1 Kings, v). After 1000 B.C. the Phœnicians were thus the artistic manufacturers of a great world extending from Nineveh on the east to Greece on the west.

FIG. 158. ANCIENT PHŒNICIAN PLATTER OF ENGRAVED AND BEATEN WORK

**399. Oriental decorative art reaches Europe**

This silver platter, now in the Berlin Museum, is of beautiful workmanship. A circular stream of water surrounds a rosette in the middle. On the water are four Nile boats (one of them in the form of a swan), outside of which is a circular border of papyrus flowers. The Phœnicians were very skillful in such metal work, which they thus adorned with Egyptian and Assyrian designs. Pieces of it have been found as far west as Spain and as far east as Nineveh, whither they were carried by the Phœnician merchants

On the metal platters and the furniture of carved ivory landed from the Phœnician ships (§ 395), the Greek craftsmen found decorations made up of palm trees, lotus flowers, hunting scenes along the Nile, the Assyrian tree of life (Fig. 102), and many other picturesque things, but especially those strange winged creatures of oriental fancy, the sphinx, the gryphon, the winged horse. The Greeks soon began to imitate these things in their own work. Thus the whole range of oriental decorative art entered Greek life, to fill forever after a large place in the decorative art of all civilized peoples of the West, including our own to-day. At the same time it is highly probable that in the Phœnician workshops in the Ægean islands the Greeks could work side by side with the Phœnician craftsmen and learn how

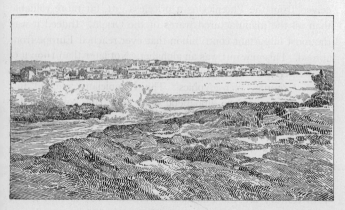

FIG. 159. THE ANCIENT PHŒNICIAN HARBOR OF SIDON AS IT NOW APPEARS

It was from this harbor that the Phœnician colonists sailed forth to establish new cities in the western Mediterranean, especially Carthage (§ 397). In the Homeric poems the Phœnicians are often called Sidonians. The town seen across the harbor is entirely modern, for the ancient city was again and again destroyed and rebuilt. Here the Phœnician ships were loaded with the goods manufactured in the city (Figs. 157 and 158), to be carried to the Greeks and other Mediterranean peoples ; and here an alphabet first came into common use (§ 400)

to make hollow bronze casts, an art invented in Egypt, and to manufacture many other things which were bringing such commercial success to the Phœnician merchants. Nevertheless, so little of the refined Ægean art of the Grand Age had survived that there are products of the Greeks in this period that are hardly as good as the work of the **Middle Stone Age** (compare the horses in Figs. 155 and 10, 6).

## SECTION 40. THE PHŒNICIANS BRING THE FIRST ALPHABET TO EUROPE

**400.** The Semites devise an alphabet (before 1600 B.C.)

But styles of dress, decorative art, and the practical methods of the craftsman were not the only things which the Phœnician merchants were bringing into Greece. For the Greeks now received from the Phœnicians a priceless gift, far more valuable than all the manufactured wares of the Orient. Indeed it was the most important contribution that ever reached Europe from abroad. This new gift was an alphabet. Not later than 1600 B.C. the western Semites near Egypt had devised an alphabet drawn from Egyptian hieroglyphics. The Phœnicians adopted this system of twenty-two alphabetic signs (Fig. 160, column I) for writing their own language. It contained no signs for syllables, but each sign represented a single consonant. There were no signs for the vowels, which remained unwritten. The western Semites were thus the first to devise a system of writing containing nothing but alphabetic signs, that is, true letters. In the 12th century B.C. the Phœnicians were therefore already giving up the inconvenient clay tablet of Babylonia (Fig. 79) and were importing great quantities of papyrus paper from Egypt.

**401.** The Phœnicians arrange their new letters in a fixed order and give them names

The Phœnicians arranged their new letters in a convenient order, so that the whole twenty-two might form a fixed list (Fig. 160, column I), easily learned. Such a list could not be learned without giving to each letter a name. They called the first letter of the alphabet *ox*, because the Phœnician word for ox, that is, *aleph*, began with the first letter. The second letter of the alphabet they called *house*, because *beth*, the Phœnician word for house, began with the second letter, and so on. This was not unlike our old primers, where our parents learned to say: "*A* is for 'Axe'; *B* is for 'Bed,'" etc. When the children of the Phœnician merchants learned their letters, and were called upon to repeat the alphabet, they therefore began: "*Aleph, beth*," etc., as if our children were to say: "Axe, Bed," etc., instead of "A, B," etc.

The Phœnicians seem to have had little literature, but their merchants kept all their business records in this new and convenient writing on papyrus. Just as the Arameans carried the Phœnician alphabet from the Mediterranean eastward through Asia to India (§ 205), so now the Phœnicians themselves carried it through the Mediterranean westward to Europe. The Greeks whom we have seen crowding around the Phœnician ships often found the Phœnicians handling bits of pale-yellow paper, on which were written bills and lists of merchandise in strange black signs. These the Greeks at first viewed with misgivings, as mysterious and dangerous symbols. One of their ancient songs of this age speaks of them as " baneful signs." Here and there a Greek merchant, thumbing the Phœnician tradesman's papyrus bills, finally learned the alphabet in which they were written, and slowly began to note down *Greek* words spelled with Phœnician letters.

402. Phœnician alphabet first seen by Greeks

Here the Greeks early displayed the mental superiority which, as we shall soon discover, they possessed. They noticed that there were no Phœnician letters standing for vowels. They also noticed in the Phœnician alphabet a few letters representing consonants which did not exist in Greek speech. These letters they began to use for the Greek vowels (Fig. 160; cf. columns I and II). They thus took the final step in the process of devising a complete system of alphabetic writing. It slowly spread among the Greek states, beginning in Ionia. For a long time it remained only a convenience in business and administration. For centuries the nobles, unable to read or write, continued to regard writing with misgivings. But even the painters of pottery jars had learned to use it by 700 B.C., when we find it on their decorated vases (see headpiece, p. 282). Shortly after this it was common among all classes. Literature nevertheless long remained an oral matter and was much slower than business to resort to writing.

403. Greeks adopt and perfect Phœnician alphabet by adding vowels (about 900 B.C.)

The Greek children, in learning to read, used for the letters the same names which had been employed in Phœnicia. The

**404.** Phœnician origin of the alphabets of the civilized world

Greeks, not knowing what these strange names meant, altered them somewhat; but the Greek children began to pronounce the foreign names of the letters in the fixed order already settled in Phœnicia, saying "Alpha, beta," etc. (instead of "Aleph, beth," etc.) (§ 401). As a child of to-day is said to be learning his A B C's, so the Greek child learned his Alpha Beta's, and thus arose our word "alphabet." The word "alphabet," therefore, should remind us of the great debt we owe to the Orient, and especially to the Phœnicians, for the priceless gift of alphabetic writing. For the Phœnician alphabet spread from Greece to Italy and at last throughout Europe. Indeed, every alphabet of the civilized world has descended from the Phœnician alphabet.

| I<br>PHOENICIAN | II<br>EARLY GREEK<br>read from right to left | III<br>LATER GREEK<br>read from left to right | IV<br>LATIN | V<br>ENGLISH |
|---|---|---|---|---|
| 𐤀 | A | A | A | A |
| 𐤁 | S 𐤁 | B | B | B |
| 𐤂 | 𐤂 | Γ | C G | C. G |
| 𐤃 | Δ | Δ | D | D |
| 𐤄 | 𐤄 | 𐤄 | E | E |
| 𐤅 | 𐤅 | Γ | F V | F. V. U |
| 𐤆 | I | I | ... | Z |
| 𐤇 | B | B | H | E. H |
| 𐤈 | ⊗ | ⊗ | ... | TH. PH |
| 𐤉 | ? | S | I | I |
| 𐤊 | ⅄ | K | ... | K. KH |
| 𐤋 | √ 𐤋 | L Λ | L | L |
| 𐤌 | ⋔ | ⋔ | M | M |
| 𐤍 | ⋎ | N | N | N |
| 𐤎 | ⊞ | ⊞ | X | X |
| 𐤏 | ○ | ○ | O | O |
| 𐤐 | ? | Γ | P | P |
| 𐤑 | ⋎ | M | ... | S |
| 𐤒 | Φ | 𐤒 | Q | Q |
| 𐤓 | ? | P | R | R |
| 𐤔 | 𐤔 | 𐤔 | S | S |
| X | T | T | T | T |

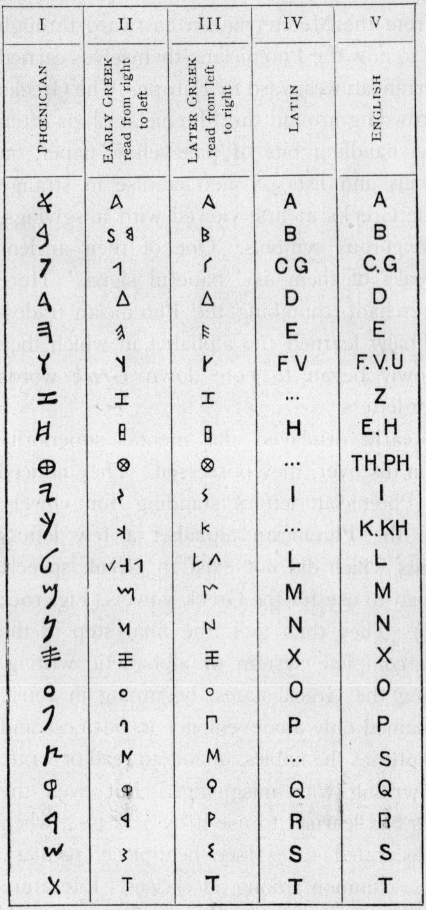

FIG. 160. TABLE SHOWING HOW THE PHŒNICIAN LETTERS PASSED THROUGH GREEK AND LATIN FORMS TO REACH THEIR PRESENT ENGLISH FORMS *

Along with the alphabet, the equipment for using it — that is, pen, ink, and paper — for the first time came into Europe. Paper also brought in with it its oriental names. For the Greeks received from abroad the word *papyros*, designating the Egyptian paper on which they wrote, and we remember that this word has in its English form become "paper" (see § 58). Much of the papyrus used by the Greeks was delivered to them by Phœnician merchants from Byblos, a famous Phœnician city. Just as we apply the word "china" to a kind of table ware which first came to us from China, so the Greeks often called papyrus *byblos* after the Phœnician city from which it came. Thus when they began to write books on rolls of such paper (Fig. 191) they called them *biblia*. It is from this term that we received our word "Bible" (literally "book" or "books"). Hence the English word "Bible," once the name of a Phœnician city, is another living evidence of the origin of books and the paper of which they are made in the ancient Orient, from which the Greeks received so much.

**405.** Oriental origin of the words "paper" and "Bible"

## Section 41. Greek Warriors and the Hero Songs

The Greek nobles of this age loved war and were devoted to fighting and plundering. It was a frequent sight to see the Greek warrior waving farewell to his family before the pillared porch of his home, as he mounted the waiting chariot and rode forth to battle. The vase-painters have often left us pictures

**406.** The equipment of the Greek warrior in the Age of the Kings

---

\* Column I contains the Phœnician alphabet made up exclusively of consonants (§ 400). The Phœnicians wrote from right to left, and hence the Greeks at first wrote in the same direction. The names of the warriors in the vase-painting (headpiece, p. 263) are several of them written in this way; hence column II shows letters like *B* "backward," as we say. The Greeks then gradually changed and wrote from left to right, and the next column (III) shows the letters facing as they do in our present alphabet (see *B* in column III). The transition from these later forms of the Greek letters (column III) to the Latin forms (column IV) was very easy, and the Latin forms hardly differed from those which we still use (column V).

of such warriors (headpiece, p. 263). While their protective armor was of bronze, their weapons were at this time commonly of iron, although bronze weapons still lingered on, and in their tales of the great wars of the past the Greeks still told how the heroes of older days fought with bronze weapons.

**407.** Battle and the customs of war in the Age of the Kings

It was only men of some wealth who possessed a fighting outfit like this. They were the leading warriors. The ordinary troops, lacking armor, were of little consequence in battle, which consisted of a series of single combats, each between two heroes. Their individual skill, experience, and daring won the battle, rather than the discipline of drilled masses. The victor seized his fallen adversary's armor and weapons; and having fastened the naked body of the vanquished to his chariot, he dragged it triumphantly across the field, only to expose it to be devoured by birds of prey and wild animals. There was thus many a savage struggle to rescue the body of a fallen hero (headpiece, p. 263). When a Greek town was captured, its unhappy people were slaughtered or carried away as slaves, and its houses plundered and burned. There was savage joy in such treatment of the vanquished, and such deeds were thought to increase the fame and glory of the victors.

**408.** Rise of the hero songs

Men delighted to sing of valiant achievements on the field of battle and to tell of the stirring deeds of mighty heroes. In the pastures of Thessaly, where the singer looked up at the cloud-veiled summit of Mount Olympus (Fig. 153), the home of the gods, there early grew up a group of such songs telling many a story of the feats of gods and heroes, the earliest literature of the Greeks. Into these songs were woven also vague memories of remote wars which had actually occurred, especially the war in which the Greeks had captured and destroyed the splendid city of Troy (§ 375 and Fig. 151). Probably by 1000 B.C. some of these songs had crossed to the coasts and islands of Ionia on the Asiatic side of the Ægean Sea.

Here arose a class of professional bards who graced the feasts of king and noble with songs of battle and adventure recited to the music of the harp. Framed in exalted and ancient forms of speech, and rolling on in stately measures,[1] these heroic songs resounded through many a royal hall — the oldest literature born in Europe. After the separate songs had greatly increased in number, they were finally woven together by the bards into a con-

**409.** The Ionian singers

nected whole — a great epic cycle especially clustering about the traditions of the Greek expedition against Troy. They were not the work of one man, but a growth of several centuries by generations of singers, some of whom were still living even after 700 B.C. It was then that they were first written down.

**410.** Homer

Among these ancient singers there seems to have been one of great fame whose name was Homer (Fig. 161). His reputation was such that the composition of the whole cycle of songs, then much larger than the remnant which has come down to us, was attributed to him. Then as the Greeks themselves later discerned the impossibility of Homer's author-

FIG. 161. AN IDEAL PORTRAIT OF HOMER

This head, from the Boston Museum of Fine Arts, is a noble example of the later Greek sculptor's ability to create an ideal portrait of a poet whom he had never seen. Such work was unknown in the archaic days of Greece; it was produced in the Hellenistic Age

ship of them *all*, they credited him only with the Iliad,[2] the story of the Greek expedition against Troy; and the Odyssey,

---

[1] These were in hexameter; that is, six feet to a line. This Greek verse is the oldest literary form in Europe.

[2] So named after Ilium, the Greek name of Troy.

or the tale of the wanderings of the hero Odysseus on his return from Troy. These are the only two series of songs that have entirely survived, and even the ancient world had its doubts about the Homeric authorship of the Odyssey.

**411. The Homeric songs our earliest literary record of the Greeks**

These ancient bards not only gave the world its greatest epic in the Iliad, but they were, moreover, the earliest Greeks to put into permanent literary form their thoughts regarding the world of gods and men. At that time the Greeks had no other sacred books, and the Homeric songs became the veritable Bible of Greece. They gave to the disunited Greeks a common literature and the inspiring belief that they had once all taken part in a common war against Asia.

## Section 42. The Beginnings and Early Development of Greek Religion

**412. The Homeric songs and Greek religion**

Just as devout Hebrews were taught much about their God by the beautiful tales of Him in the historical narratives of their forefathers (§ 302), so the wonderful Homeric songs brought vividly before the Greeks the life of the gods. Homer became the religious teacher of the Greeks. To us too he reveals a great chapter in the story of Greek religion. For like that of the Hebrews, the religion of the Greeks was a slow growth, passing gradually from a low stage to ever higher and nobler beliefs. There was, therefore, a chapter of Greek religion earlier than the Homeric songs. Let us look for a moment at the religion of Greece *before* the Homeric songs.

**413. Primitive Greek religion before the Homeric songs**

Every Greek, like all primitive men, once thought that the trees and springs, the stones and hilltops, the birds and beasts, were creatures possessed of strange and uncanny powers. He thought there was such a spirit in the dark recesses of the earth which made the grain sprout and the trees flourish; in the gloomy depths of the waters also, he believed there dwelt a like spirit which swayed the great sea; while still another ruled the far sweep of the overhanging sky. As the Greek peasant, terrified by the jagged lightning and the rolling thunder, or grateful for the gently falling rain, looked up into the misty cloudland of the sky, he often saw the solitary eagle soaring across the vast and lonely expanse. To him the lofty, mysterious bird seemed to be the mighty spirit of the sky, who dwelt there and in his wrath smote the great trees with fire, or in kinder moods sent down the refreshing rain. Thus to *some* Greeks the sky spirit seemed to be an eagle.

Each such spirit, friendly or hostile, dwelt in a limited region, and it was believed possible to gain his favor or avoid his anger by simple gifts, especially food. The earth spirit might be reached by slaying a sheep and letting the blood flow into the earth; while the sky spirit would be won by burning a thigh of the sheep so that its odor might rise to the sky with the soaring smoke. Thus these spirits of the world around the early Greeks became gods and goddesses, and thus arose worship with its sacred customs and usages. There were no temples or houses of worship, and all the simple usages of religion went on out of doors in a grove or in the open air in the court of the house.

**414.** The rise of worship and its customs

We remember that the Hebrews never lost their belief in their great God Yahveh, whom they brought with them into the land of Palestine; and so the Greeks likewise brought into Greece various ideas of the great Sky-god whom they had already worshiped in the old days on the grasslands. He had different names; in one valley they called him "Rain-giver," in another "Thunderbolt" (§ 413). But he was finally known to all as Zeus, which was simply the Greek form of an old word for "sky" in the language of the Indo-European parent people. He became the highest god among all the numerous gods and goddesses revered by the Greeks.

**415.** The Greeks bring Zeus the Sky-god into the Ægean world

But Greek religion continued to grow after the Greeks had reached the Ægean world. Here they found the Ægeans worshiping the great earth spirit, the Earth-Mother, or the Great Mother, who made the earth bring forth her grain and fruit

**416.** Divinities of the Ægean world accepted by the Greeks

as the food of man (headpiece, p. 221). From the Ægeans the Greeks learned to revere her also, so that she became one of the great goddesses of Greek religion. The Greeks thus accepted the gods and goddesses whom they found in the Ægean world, just as many of the Hebrews accepted the Canaanite Baals which they found already in Palestine (§ 300).

**417.** The gods gain human form; surviving traces of old animal forms

The Homeric songs, as we have said, reveal to us a second chapter in Greek religion, when the Greeks were gaining higher ideas about their gods. To be sure, even Homer has here and there an ancient reference which betrays their earlier animal forms, as when he speaks of a goddess as " owl-faced " or even " cow-faced." Likewise the Satyrs, merry spirits of the forest, always had goat's hoofs and horns; while the Centaurs were men with the bodies of horses. But those nature spirits, which gained a high place as gods and goddesses, appeared in the Homeric songs as entirely human in form and in qualities. Of course they possessed more power than mortals, and at the same time they enjoyed the gift of immortality.

**418.** Zeus and the dwelling of the gods on Mount Olympus; Apollo

In the Homeric songs and in the primitive tales about the gods, which we call myths, the Greeks heard how the gods dwelt in veiled splendor among the clouds on the summit of Mount Olympus. There, in his cloud palace, Zeus the Sky-god, with the lightning in his hand, ruled the gods like an earthly king. Each of the gods controlled as his own a realm of nature or of the affairs of men. Apollo, the Sun-god, whose beams were golden arrows, was the deadly archer of the gods. But he also shielded the flocks of the shepherds and the fields of the plowman, and he was a wondrous musician. Above all he knew the future ordained by Zeus and could, when properly consulted, tell anxious inquirers what the future had in store for them. These qualities gave him a larger place in the hearts of all Greeks than Zeus himself, and in actual worship he became the most beloved god of the Greek world.

Athena, the greatest goddess of the Greeks, seems in the beginning to have ruled the air, and swayed the destroying

PLATE III. THE PLAIN OF ARGOS AND THE SEA VIEWED FROM THE CASTLE OF TIRYNS

A typical Greek landscape with plain and mountain and sea (§ 371). Before us is one of the harbors of Argos, which looked southward directly upon Crete, whence came the first civilization that reached the mainland of Europe (§ 347) and created the cities of Tiryns (Fig. 144) and Mycenae (Fig. 145)

tempests that swept the Greek lands. Such power made her a warrior goddess, and the Greeks loved to think of her with shining weapons, protecting the Greek cities. But she held out her protecting hand over them also in times of peace, as the potters shaped their jars, the smiths wrought their metal, or the women wove their wool. Athena too had brought them the olive tree, as they believed, and thus she became the wise and gracious protectress of the peaceful life of industry and art. Of all her divine companions she was the wisest in counsel, and an ancient tale told how she had been born in the very brain of her father Zeus, from whose head she sprang forth full-armed. As the divine foster mother of all that was best in Greek life, she was the loveliest of the protecting powers which the quick and sensitive imagination of the Greeks felt everywhere watching over the life and work of men. These three then, Zeus, Apollo, and Athena, became the leading divinities of the Greek world.

**419.** Athena, protectress of Greek cities

At the same time a further group of ancient nature spirits had risen to be great gods, each controlling some special realm. In a brazen palace deep under the waters, Poseidon ruled the sea. The ancient Earth-Mother, whom they called Demeter, still brought forth the produce of the soil. At the same time they looked also to another earth god, Dionysus, for the fruit of the grapevine, and they rejoiced in the wine which he gave them. An old moon spirit had now become Hermes the messenger of the gods, with winged feet, doing the bidding of the gods, but he was also the patron of the intercourse of men, and hence the god of trade and commerce. Some of the Greeks, however, in the old days, seeing the moon above the forest margin, had believed it to be a goddess, a divine huntress riding through the forests at night. They called her Artemis. Others, however, had fancied the moon to belong in the sky as the wife of Zeus, whom they called Hera, and she became the protectress of marriage. The Semitic goddess of love, whom we have met on the Fertile Crescent as Ishtar (§ 191), had

**420.** Poseidon, Demeter, Dionysus, Hermes, Artemis, Hera, and Aphrodite now passed over from the Syrian cities by way of Cyprus, to become likewise the Greek goddess of love, whom the Greeks called Aphrodite.

421. The Greek gods at first show human defects of character

All these divinities and some others less important, the Greeks now pictured in human form. It was but natural, too, that they should be thought of as possessing human traits. Homer pictures to us the family quarrels between the august Zeus and his wife Hera, just as such things must have occurred in the household life of the Greeks, and certainly in a manner absurdly undignified for such exalted divinities. The Greeks thought of the gods therefore as showing decidedly human defects of character. They practiced all sorts of deceit and displayed many other human frailties. Such gods were not likely to require anything better in the character of men. Religion was therefore not yet an influence leading to good conduct and right character. In this particular, then, the Greeks were passing through an early stage of an uncompleted development, just such as we have found in the civilizations of the Orient.

422. Greek beliefs about the dead

One reason why the Greeks did not yet think that the gods required right conduct of men was their notion of life after death. They believed that all men passed at death into a gloomy kingdom beneath the earth (Hades), where the fate of good men did not differ from that of the wicked. Here ruled Pluto as king, and his wife, the goddess Persephone. As a special favor of the gods, the heroes, men of mighty and godlike deeds, were endowed with immortality and permitted to enjoy a life of endless bliss in the beautiful Elysian Fields, or the Islands of the Blest, somewhere in the Far West, toward the unexplored ocean. The Greeks seem to have brought with them from their earlier wanderings the custom of burning their dead. They continued this custom on reaching Greece, but they adopted also the Ægean usage of preserving the body as in Egypt and burying it. The primitive notion that the dead must be furnished with food and drink still survived. The tombs of the ancestors thus became sacred places where gifts of food and drink were regularly brought and offered to the dead.

Every household in the little Greek towns felt that the safety of the house was in the hands of Hestia, the goddess of the hearth. But in the Age of the Kings the symbols of the great gods were set up in every house, while in the dwelling of the king there was a special room which served as a kind of shrine for them. There was also an altar in the forecourt where sacrifices could be offered under the open sky (Fig. 144). In so far as the gods had any dwellings at all, we see that they were in the houses of men, and there probably were no temples as yet. Here and there in some communities men were to be found who were thought to possess rare knowledge of the desires of the gods. As these men were more and more often consulted by those who felt ignorant of the proper ceremonies of sacrifice and worship, such men gradually became *priests*.

**423.** Lack of temples: rise of priests

### QUESTIONS

Section 39. What important metal came in at the rise of Greek civilization? What had happened to the arts and crafts of the Ægeans? Did the Greeks possess any craftsmen? What do you think of the horses on the Greek vase of the Age of the Kings? Compare it with Middle Stone Age carving? From whom did the Greeks chiefly buy manufactured products? What can you tell about this commerce? What did it teach the Greeks?

Section 40. What else did the Phœnicians bring in besides manufactured goods? Tell about the Phœnician alphabet. How did it reach Greece? What is the origin of the word "alphabet"? How far has the Phœnician alphabet spread?

Section 41. Describe early Greek arms and warfare. What was the relation of valiant deeds and song? Around what event did such songs cluster? Tell of Homer and the poems attributed to him.

Section 42. How did the Homeric songs affect religion? What can you say of Greek religion before the Homeric songs arose? Did the Greeks bring in some gods when they entered Greece? Name the leading Greek divinities, and tell something of each. Discuss Greek beliefs about the dead; customs and places of worship.

# CHAPTER XI

## THE AGE OF THE NOBLES AND GREEK EXPANSION IN THE MEDITERRANEAN

### SECTION 43. THE DISAPPEARANCE OF THE KINGS AND THE LEADERSHIP OF THE NOBLES

**424.** Geographical influences against a union of all Greeks in one nation

We have seen Greek civilization beginning under oriental influences. In its *political* development, however, the Greek world showed striking differences from what we have seen in the Orient. There we watched the early city-states finally

NOTE. The headpiece above is of an early Greek sea fight in the days of the kings. This Greek vase-painting shows us the Greek nobles in the days when they were taking to the water as pirates (§ 431). The warriors are armed as on land (see headpiece, p. 263). As to the model of the ships, see Fig. 162. Aristonothos, the artist who made this vase-painting, has inserted his name over the standard at the right, in the lower row, where the letters run to the right and drop down. It reads "Aristonothos made it." This is not only the earliest-signed vase, but is likewise the earliest-signed work of art, crude though it may be, in Europe. It shows us that the Greek artist was gaining increasing pride in his work, and it is one of the earliest signs of individuality in Greek history about 700 B.C.

uniting into two large and powerful nations, one on the Nile and another on the Two Rivers. In Greece, however, there were influences which tended to prevent such a union of the Greeks into one nation. In the first place the country was cut up by mountain ridges and deep bays, so that the different communities were quite separated. The cities of Greece were likewise separated from their kindred in the islands and in Asia Minor.

Furthermore, no recollection of their former unity on the grasslands survived, even in their oldest traditions. They had now lived so long in separated communities that they had developed permanent local habits and local dialects, as different as those of North and South Germany or even more different than those between our own Louisiana and New England. The various Greek communities thus displayed such intense devotion to their own town and their own local gods that a union of all the Greek city-states into one nation, such as we have seen in the Orient, failed to take place. As a result of these separative influences we find in Greece after 1000 B.C. scores of little city-states such as we have already described (§ 390). Not only did the islands and the Greek city-states of Asia Minor fail to unite, but on the island of Crete alone there were more than fifty such small city-states. **425.** Other influences operating against political unity

Four regions on the mainland of Greece, each forming a pretty clearly outlined geographical whole, like the peninsula of Laconia or that of Attica (see map, p. 262), permitted the union of city-states into a larger nation. The oldest of these four nations seems to have been Argos (map, p. 262). In this plain the town of Argos subdued the ancient strongholds of Mycenæ and Tiryns (Figs. 144 and 145) and others in the vicinity, forming the nation of Argos and giving its name to the plain (Plate III, p. 278). In the same way the kings of Sparta conquered the two peninsulas on the south of them and finally also the land of the Messenians on the west. The two kingdoms of Argos and Sparta thus held a large part of the Peloponnese. **426.** The four unions Argos and Sparta

**427. Athens and Thebes**

In the Attic peninsula, likewise, the little city-kingdoms were slowly absorbed by Athens, which at last gained control of the entire peninsula. On the northern borders of Attica the region of Bœotia fell under the leadership of Thebes, but the other Bœotian cities were too strong to be wholly subdued. Bœotia, therefore, did not form a nation but a group of city-states in alliance, with Thebes at the head of the alliance. Elsewhere no large and permanent unions were formed. Sparta and Athens, therefore, led the most important two unions among all the Greeks. Let it be borne in mind that such a nation remained a city-state in spite of its increased territory. The nation occupying the Attic peninsula was called Athens, and every peasant in Attica was called an Athenian. The city government of Athens covered the whole Attic peninsula.

**428. Internal development of the Greek state contrasted with the Orient**

In the matter of governing such a little city-state the Greeks about 750 B.C. entered upon a new stage of their development, which was again very different from that which we have found in the Orient. However discontented the common people of an oriental state might become, their discontent never accomplished more than the overthrow of one king and the enthronement of another. The *office* of king was never abolished, nor did any other form of government than that of monarchy ever arise in the ancient East (§ 322).

**429. The Greek state and the struggle toward democracy**

Among the Greeks, too, the common people struggled for centuries to better their lot. As we shall see, this long and bitter struggle finally resulted in giving the people in some Greek states so large a share in governing that the form of the government might be called democracy. This is a word of Greek origin, meaning "the rule of the people," and the Greeks were the first people of the ancient world to gain it.

**430. Rise of a noble class, the eupatrids**

The cause of this struggle was not only the corrupt rule of the kings but also the oppression of the *nobles*. We have watched these men of wealth buying the luxuries of the Phœnician merchants. They now stood in the way, opposing the rights of the peasants. By fraud, unjust seizure of lands, union of families in marriage, and many other influences, the strong men of ability and cleverness were able to enlarge their lands. Thus there had arisen a class of hereditary nobles — large landholders and men of wealth, called eupatrids.

Their fields stretched for some miles around the city and its neighboring villages. In order to be near the king or secure membership in the Council (§ 385) and control the government, these men often left their lands and lived in the city. Such was the power of the eupatrids that the Council finally consisted only of men of this class. Wealthy enough to buy costly weapons, with leisure for continual exercise in the use of arms, these nobles had also become the chief protection of the State in time of war (§ 407). They were also continual marauders on their own account. As they grew more and more accustomed to the sea (headpiece, p. 282), they coasted from harbor to harbor, plundering and burning, and returned home laden with rich spoil. Piracy at last became the common calling of the nobles, and a great source of wealth.

> 431. Political and military power of the eupatrids

Thus grew up a sharp distinction between the city community and the peasants living in the country. The country peasant was obliged to divide the family lands with his brothers. His fields were therefore small, and he was poor. He went about clad in a goatskin, and his labors never ceased. Hence he had no leisure to learn the use of arms, nor any way to meet the expense of purchasing them. He and his neighbors were therefore of small account in war (§ 407). Indeed, he was fortunate if he could struggle on and maintain himself and family from his scanty fields. Many of his neighbors sank into debt, lost their lands to the noble class, and themselves became day laborers for more fortunate men, or, still worse, sold themselves to discharge their debts and thus became slaves. These day laborers and slaves had no political rights and were not permitted to vote in the Assembly.

> 432. Misery and weakness of the peasants

If the peasant desired to exert any influence in government, he was obliged to go up to the city and attend the Assembly

433. The weakness of the Assembly

of the people there. When he did so, he found but few of his fellows from the countryside gathered there — a dingy group, clad in their rough goatskins. The powerful Council in beautiful oriental raiment (§§ 394 and 395) was backed by the whole class of wealthy nobles, all trained in war and splendid in their glittering weapons. Intimidated by the powerful nobles, the meager Assembly, which had once been a muster of all the weapon-bearing men of the tribe, became a feeble gathering of a few peasants and lesser townsmen, who could gain no greater recognition of their old-time rights than the poor privilege of voting to concur in the actions already decided upon by the king and the Council. The peasant returned to his little farm and was less and less inclined to attend the Assembly at all.

434. The decline and disappearance of the kings (800-650 B.C.)

It was, however, not alone the people whose rights the nobles were disregarding; for they also began to consider themselves the equals of the king, whose chief support in war they were. The king could not carry on a war without them or control the state without their help. By 750 B.C. the office of the king was in some states nothing more than a name. While the king was in some cases violently overthrown, in most states the nobles established from among themselves certain elective officers to take charge of matters formerly controlled by the king. Thus in Athens they appointed a noble to be leader in war, while another noble was chosen as "archon," or ruler, to assist the king in attending to the increasing business of the State. Thus the Athenian king was gradually but peacefully deprived of his powers, until he became nothing more than the leader of the people in religious matters. In Sparta the power of the king was checked by the appointment of a second king, and on this plan Sparta continued to retain her kings. Elsewhere in the century, between 750 and 650 B.C., the kingship quite generally disappeared, although it lingered on in some states until long after this time. The result of the political and social struggle was thus the triumph of the nobles, who were henceforth in control in many states.

With the disappearance of the king, the royal castle (Fig. 144) was of course vacated. As it fell into decay, the shrines and holy places which it contained (§ 423) were still protected and revered as religious buildings, and, as we shall see in discussing architecture, they became temples. In this way the castle of the ancient Attic kings on the citadel mount, called the Acropolis of Athens (Figs. 182 and 183), was followed by the famous temples there.

435. Survival of the shrines in the old palaces

## SECTION 44. GREEK EXPANSION IN THE AGE OF THE NOBLES

The Age of the Nobles witnessed another great change in Greek life. Sea-roving and piracy, as we have seen (§ 431), were common among the nobles. At length, as the Greek merchants gradually took up sea trade, the demand for ships led the Greek mechanics to undertake shipbuilding. They built their new craft on Phœnician models (see Fig. 162, *A* and *B*), the only ones with which they were acquainted. When the Phœnician merchants entered the Ægean harbors they now found them more and more occupied by Greek ships. Especially important was the traffic between the Greek cities of the Asiatic coast on the east and Attica and Eubœa on the European side. Among the Asiatic Greeks it was the Ionian cities which led in this commerce. The Ægean waters gradually grew familiar to the Greek communities, until the sea routes became far easier lines of communication than roads through the same number of miles of forest and mountains (§ 330).

436. Beginnings of commerce and shipbuilding among the Greeks

The oppressive rule of the nobles, and the resulting impoverishment of the peasants, was an important influence, leading the Greek farmers to seek new homes and new lands beyond the Ægean world. Greek merchants were not only trafficking with the northern Ægean, but their vessels had penetrated the great northern sea, which they called the "Pontus," known to us as the Black Sea (see map, p. 288). Their trading stations

437. Greek colonies in the Black Sea

among the descendants of the Stone Age peoples in these distant regions offered to the discontented farmers of Greece plenty of land with which to begin life over again. Before 600 B.C. they girdled the Black Sea with their towns and settlements, reaching the broad grainfields along the lower Danube, and the iron mines of the old Hittite country on the southeastern coast of the Black Sea (§ 360). But no such development of Greek genius took place in this harsher climate

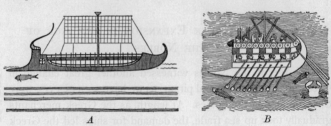

*A*        *B*

FIG. 162. AN EARLY GREEK SHIP AND THE PHŒNICIAN SHIP
AFTER WHICH IT WAS MODELED

The earliest ships in the Mediterranean, those of Egypt, were turned up at both ends (Fig. 41), and the early Ægean ships were copies of this Egyptian model (Fig. 154). The Phœnicians, however, introduced a change in the model, by giving their ships at the bow a sharp projecting beak below water. Such a Phœnician ship used by the Assyrian king Sennacherib is shown here in a drawing from one of his palace reliefs (*B*). The Greeks did not adopt the old Ægean form, turned up at both ends, but took up the Phœnician form with beaked prow, as shown in the vase-paintings, from which the above drawing of an eighth-century Greek ship (*A*) has been restored

of the North as we shall find in the Ægean. Not a single great artist or writer ever came from the North. Although the Pontus became the granary of Greece, it never contributed anything to the higher life of the Greeks.

**438.** Greek colonies in the East — southern Asia Minor and Cyprus      In the East, along the southern coasts of Asia Minor, Greek expansion was stopped by the Assyrian Sennacherib (§ 214) when he defeated a body of Greeks in Cilicia about 700 B.C., in the earliest collision between the Hellenes and a great power of the oriental world. The Greek colonies of Cyprus long remained

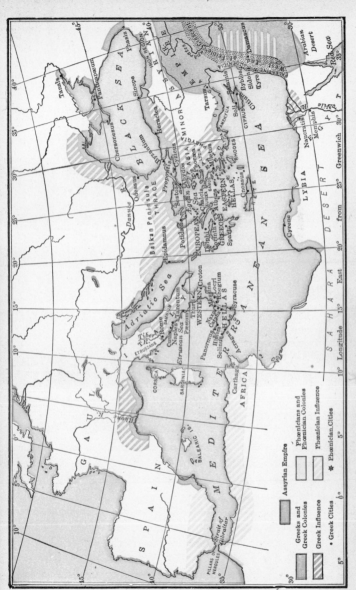

COLONIAL EXPANSION OF THE GREEKS AND PHŒNICIANS DOWN TO THE SIXTH CENTURY B.C.

the easternmost outposts of the Greek world. In the South they found a friendly reception in Egypt, and there in the Nile Delta they were permitted to establish a trading city at Naucratis (Mistress of Ships), the predecessor of Alexandria. West of the Delta also they eventually founded Cyrene (map, p. 288).

It was the unknown West, however, which became the America of the early Greek colonists. Many a Columbus pushed his ship into this strange region of mysterious dangers on the distant borders of the world, where the heroes were believed to live in the Islands of the Blest. Looking westward from the western coast of Greece the seamen could discover the shores of the heel of Italy, only fifty miles distant. When they had once crossed to it, they coasted around Sicily and far into the West. Here was a new world. Although the Phœnicians were already there (§ 397), its discovery was as momentous for the Greeks as that of America for later Europe (see map, p. 288).

**439. Discovery of the West**

By 750 B.C. their colonies appeared in this new Western world, and within a century they fringed southern Italy from the heel to a point well above the instep north of Naples, so that this region of southern Italy came to be known as " Great Greece " (see map, p. 484). Here the Greek colonists looked northward to the hills crowned by the rude settlements which were destined to become Rome. They little dreamed that this insignificant town would yet rule the world, making even the proud cities of their homeland its vassals. As the Greeks were superior in civilization to all the other dwellers in Italy, *the civilized history of that great peninsula begins with the advent of the Hellenes.* They first brought in such things as writing, literature, architecture, and art (Section 76, Fig. 219, and Plate VII, p. 558).

**440. Greek colonies in the West — southern Italy**

The Greek colonists crossed over also to Sicily (Plate VII), where they drove out the Phœnician trading posts except at the western end of the island, where the Phœnicians held their own. These Greek colonists in the West shared in the higher life of the homeland; and Syracuse, at the southeast corner of the Island of Sicily, became at one time the most cultivated,

**441. Sicily and the Far West**

as well as the most powerful, city of the Greek world. At Massilia (Marseilles), on the coast of later France, the Western Greeks founded a town which controlled the trade up the Rhone valley; and they reached over even to the Mediterranean coasts of Spain, attracted by the silver mines of Tartessus.

**442. Racial aspects of ancient colonization in the Mediterranean**

Thus, under the rule of the nobles, the Greeks expanded till they stretched from the Black Sea along the north shore of the Mediterranean almost to the Atlantic. In this imposing movement we recognize a part of the far outstretched western wing of the Indo-European line (see § 243); but at the same time we remember that in the Phœnician Empire of Carthage, the Semite has likewise flung out his western wing along the *southern* Mediterranean, facing the Indo-European peoples on the *north* (Fig. 112 and § 397; see map, p. 288).

**443. Tendency toward creation of a Mediterranean world; what civilization was to conquer it?**

This wide expansion of Greeks and Phœnicians (§ 397) tended at last to produce a great Mediterranean world. Was the leading civilization in that Mediterranean world to be Greek, springing from the Greeks and their colonies, or was it to be oriental, carried by the Phœnician galleys and spread by their far-reaching settlements? That was the great question, and its answer was to depend on how Greek civilization succeeded in its growth and development at home in the Ægean, to which we must now turn.

## SECTION 45. GREEK CIVILIZATION IN THE AGE OF THE NOBLES

**444. Influences leading toward unity: athletic games**

We have already noticed the tendencies which kept the Greek states apart and prevented their union as a single nation (§ 425). There were now, on the other hand, influences which tended toward unity. Among such influences were the contests in arms and the athletic games, which arose from the early custom of honoring the burial of a hero with such celebrations. In spite of the local rivalries at such contests, a sentiment of unity was greatly encouraged by the celebration and common management of these athletic games. They finally came to be practiced at stated seasons in honor of the gods. As early as 776 B.C. such contests were celebrated as public festivals at Olympia.[1] Repeated every four years, they finally aroused the interest and participation of all Greece.

Religion also became a strong influence toward unity, because there were some gods at whose temples all the Greeks worshiped. The different city-states therefore formed several religious councils, made up of representatives from the various Greek cities concerned. They came together at stated periods, and in this way each city had a voice in such joint management of the temples. These councils were among the nearest approaches to representative government ever devised in the ancient world. The most notable of them were the council for the control of the Olympic games, another for the famous sanctuary of Apollo at Delphi (Fig. 172), and also the council for the great annual feast of Apollo in the island of Delos.

**445.** Greek unity favored by religious councils (amphictyonies)

These representatives spoke various Greek dialects at their meetings. They could understand each other, however, just as in our own land a citizen from Maine understands another from Louisiana, though they may laugh at each other's oddities of speech. Their common language thus helped to bind together the people of the many different Greek cities. A sentiment of unity also arose under the influence of the Homeric songs (§ 410) with which every Greek was familiar — a common inheritance depicting all the Greeks united against the Asiatic city of Troy (Fig. 151).

**446.** Greek unity furthered by language

Thus bound together by ties of custom, religion, language, and common traditions, the Greeks gained a feeling of race unity, which set them apart from other races. They called all men not of Greek blood "barbarians," not originally a term of reproach for the non-Greeks. Then the Greek sense of unity found expression in the first all-inclusive term for *themselves*.

**447.** Barbarians and Hellenes

---

[1] Every schoolboy knows that these Olympic games have been revived in modern times as an international project.

They gradually came to call themselves "Hellenes," and found pleasure in the belief that they had all descended from a common ancestor called Hellen. But it should be clearly understood that this new designation did not represent a Greek *nation* or state, but only the group of Greek-speaking peoples or states, often at war with one another.

**448.** Greek unity and trade

The lack of political unity evident in such wars was also very noticeable in trade relations. No merchant of one city had any legal rights in another city where he was not a citizen. Even his life was not safe, for no city made any laws protecting the stranger. He could secure protection only by appealing to the old desert custom of "hospitality," after he had been received by a friendly citizen as a guest. For the reception of any stranger who might have no such friend to be his host, a city might appoint a citizen to act as its official host. These primitive arrangements are a revelation of the strong *local* prejudice of each Greek city. The most fatal defect in Greek character was the inability of the various states to forget their local differences and jealousies and to unite into a common federation or great nation including all Greeks.[1]

**449.** Architecture and sculpture

In spite of oriental luxuries, like gaudy clothing and wavy oriental wigs (§ 395), Greek life in the Age of the Nobles was still rude and simple. The Greek cities of which we have been talking were groups of dingy sun-dried-brick houses, with narrow wandering streets which we would call alleys. On the height where the palace or castle of the king had once stood was an oblong building of brick, like the houses of the town below. In front it had a porch with a row of wooden posts, and it was covered by a "peaked" roof with a triangular gable at each end. This rude building was the earliest Greek temple. As for sculpture in this age, the figure of a god consisted merely

---

[1] We may recall here how slow were the thirteen colonies of America to suppress local pride sufficiently to adopt a constitution uniting all thirteen into a nation. It was local differences similar to those among the Greeks which afterward caused our Civil War.

of a wooden post with a rough-hewn head at the top. When draped with a garment it could be made to serve its purpose.

While there were still very few who could read, there was here and there a man who owned and read a written copy of Homer. Men told their children quaint fables, representing animals acting like human creatures, and by means of these tales with a moral made it clear what a man ought or ought not to do. The Greeks were beginning to think about human conduct. The old Greek word for virtue no longer meant merely valor in war, but also kindly and unselfish conduct toward others. Duty towards a man's own country was now beginning to be felt in the sentiment we call patriotism. Right conduct, as it seemed to some, was even required by the gods, and it was finally no longer respectable for the nobles to practice piracy (§ 431).

**450.** Rise of *written* literature; moral progress; patriotism

Under these circumstances it was natural that a new literature should arise, as the Greeks began to discuss *themselves* and *their own* conduct. The old Homeric singers never referred to themselves; they never spoke of their *own* lives. They were absorbed in describing the valiant deeds of their heroes who had died long before. The heroic world of glorious achievement in which the vision of these early singers moved had passed away, and with it passed their art. Meanwhile the problems of the *present* began to press hard upon the minds of men; the peasant farmer's distressing struggle for existence (see § 432) made men conscious of very present needs. Their *own* lives became a great and living theme.

**451.** Transference of literary interest to the *present*

The voices that once chanted the hero songs therefore died away, and now men heard the first voice raised in Europe on behalf of the poor and the humble. Hesiod, an obscure farmer under the shadow of Mount Helicon in Bœotia, sang of the dreary and hopeless life of the peasant — of his *own* life as he struggled on under a burden too heavy for his shoulders. We even hear how his brother Persis seized the lands left by their father, and then bribed the judges to confirm him in their possession.

**452.** Hesiod and the earliest cry for social justice in Europe (750-700 B.C.)

This earliest European protest against the tyrannies of wealthy town life was raised at the very moment when across the corner of the Mediterranean the once nomad Hebrews were passing through the same experience (see §§ 303–304). The voice of Hesiod raising the cry for social justice in Greece sounds like an echo from Palestine. But we should notice that in Palestine the cry for social justice resulted finally in a *religion* of brotherly kindness, whereas in Greece it resulted in democratic *institutions*, the rule of the people who refused longer to submit to the oppressions of the few and powerful. In the next chapter we shall watch the progress of the struggle by which the rule of the people came about.

### QUESTIONS

SECTION 43. Were the geographical influences in Greece favorable to a political union of all Greeks? How many important unions arose? Name them and describe the leading two. How did the political development of the Orient differ from that of Greece? What is a democracy? Where did democracies first arise? What was the attitude of the nobles toward democracy? Describe their political power; their military power. What was the situation of the peasants? What happened to the Assembly? What happened to the kings? What became of the shrines in the palace?

SECTION 44. On what models did the Greeks build their first ships? Tell about Greek colonization in the North; in the East; in the South; in the West. What competing race had already colonized in the West? To what extent had the world of sea commerce thus expanded?

SECTION 45. Discuss athletic games as an influence toward unity. How did religion favor Greek unity? language? What names for Greeks and non-Greeks arose? What can you say about the attitude of Greek cities toward Greeks who were not citizens? Describe the earliest Greek temples. Were literature and reading now common? What thoughts about conduct were arising? As men began to think about themselves rather than the ancient heroes, what was the effect upon literature? Tell about Hesiod. To what struggle were the feelings of such men as Hesiod leading?

# CHAPTER XII

## THE INDUSTRIAL REVOLUTION AND THE AGE OF THE TYRANTS

### Section 46. The Industrial and Commercial Revolution

The remarkable colonial expansion of the Greeks, together with the growth of industries in the home cities, led to profound changes. The new colonies not only had needs of their own, but they also had dealings with the inland, which finally opened up extensive regions of Europe as a market for Greek wares. The home cities at once began to meet this demand for goods

**453.** Growth of Greek commerce and industry

NOTE. The above headpiece shows us the ruins of the temple of Hera at Olympia, the oldest temple in Greece. The remains of columns which surrounded the outside of the building (cf. Fig. 185) are of different sizes and proportions; for they were inserted at different times to replace the old wooden ones with which the temple was first built (§ 449). They are of the Doric style (Fig. 167). The walls were of sun-dried brick (§ 449), and have therefore disappeared. In their fall they covered up the magnificent statue of Hermes by Praxiteles (Fig. 187), which was thus preserved until modern excavators found it.

of all sorts. The Ionian cities led the way as formerly, but the islands also, and finally the Greek mainland, felt the new impulse. Corinth first (Fig. 163), and then Athens, began to share

FIG. 163. THE ISTHMUS OF CORINTH, THE LINK BETWEEN THE PELOPONNESUS AND NORTHERN GREECE

The observer stands on the hills south of ancient Corinth (out of range on the left) and looks northeastward along the isthmus, on both sides of which the sea is visible. On the left (west) we see the tip of the Gulf of Corinth (see map, p. 352), and on the right (east) the Saronic Gulf. The commerce across this isthmus from the Orient to the West made the Gulf of Corinth an important center of traffic westward, and Corinth early became a flourishing commercial city. Through this sole gateway of the Peloponnesus (see map, p. 262) passed back and forth for centuries the leading men of Greece, and especially the armies of Sparta, some 60 miles distant (behind the observer). The faint white line in the middle of the isthmus is the modern canal—a cut from sea to sea, about 4 miles long and nearly 200 feet deep at the crest of the watershed

in the increased Greek trade. Ere long the commercial fleets of the Hellenes were threading their way along all the coasts of the northern, western, and southeastern Mediterranean, bearing to distant communities Greek metal work, woven goods, and pottery. They brought back either raw materials and foodstuffs, such as grain, fish, and amber, or finished products like the magnificent utensils in bronze from the cities of the Etruscans in northern Italy (§ 787 and Fig. 231). At the yearly feast and market on the island of Delos the Greek householder found the Etruscan bronzes of the West side by side with the gay carpets of the Orient.

To satisfy the increasing demands of trade, and to meet Phœnician competition, the Greek craftsmen greatly improved their work. During the seventh century Greek industries were still unequal to those of the Orient, but after 600 B.C. the

FIG. 164. AN ATHENIAN PAINTED VASE OF THE EARLY SIXTH CENTURY B.C.

This magnificent work (over 30 inches high) was found in an Etruscan tomb in Italy (see map, p. 484), whither it had been exported by the Athenian makers in the days of Solon (§§ 468 ff.). It is signed by the potter Ergotimos, who gave the vase its beautiful shape, and also by the painter Clitias, whose skillful hand executed the sumptuous painted scenes extending in bands entirely around the vase. On the wide distribution of the works of these two artists see § 456. These decorations represent the final emancipation of the Greek painter from oriental influences and the triumph of his own imagination in depicting scenes from Greek stories of the gods and heroes. Before the end of this century (the sixth) the vase-painters had begun to blacken the whole vase and then to put on their paintings in red on the black background. This enabled them to add details in black within the figures, and greatly improved their work (see Fig. 170). The Greeks were now the best draftsmen in the world. Note the progress in two hundred years (compare above horses and those in Fig. 155)

**454.** Greek industry begins to shake off oriental influence

Greeks began to surpass their oriental teachers. In Samos they learned to make *hollow* bronze castings, like those of the Egyptians. They painted pottery with *their own* decorative scenes, taken from the lives of gods and men, and these more and more displaced the rows of oriental figures, half animal, half human (Fig. 164). Thus in industry Greece began to emancipate herself from the Orient.

**455.** Greeks introduce industrial slave labor

At the same time, growing trade obliged every Greek craftsman to enlarge his small shop — once, perhaps, only large enough to supply the wants of a single estate. Unable to find the necessary workmen, the proprietor who had the means bought slaves, trained them to the work, and thus enlarged his little stall into a factory with a score of hands. Henceforth industrial slave labor became an important part of Greek life.

**456.** Expansion of Athenian commerce

Athens entered the field of industry much later than the Ionian cities, but when she did so, she won victories not less decisive than her later triumphs in art, literature, philosophy, or war. The potters early required an extensive quarter of the town to accommodate their workshops (see plan, p. 352). The Athenian factories must have assumed a size quite unprecedented in the Greek world, for of the painted Greek vases — discovered by excavation — which are signed by the artist, about half are found to have come from only six factories at Athens. It is not a little impressive at the present day to see the modern excavator opening tombs far toward the interior of Asia Minor and taking out vases bearing the signature of the same Athenian vase-painter whose name you may also read on vases dug out of the Nile Delta in northern Africa, or taken from tombs in the cemeteries of the Etruscan cities of Italy (Fig. 164). We suddenly gain a picture of the Athenian manufacturer in touch with a vast commercial domain extending far across the ancient world.

**457.** Improvement and enlargement of ships

Soon the shipbuilder, responding to the growing commerce, began to build craft far larger than the old "fifty-oar" galleys. The new "merchantmen" were driven only by sails, an

Egyptian invention of ages before (Fig. 41). They were so large that they could no longer be drawn up on the strand as before. Hence sheltered harbors were necessary, and for the same reason the anchor was now invented. The protection of such merchant ships demanded more effective warships, and the distinction arose between a "man-o'-war," or battleship, and a "merchantman." Corinth boasted the production of the first decked warships, a great improvement, giving the warriors above more room and better footing, and protecting the oarsmen below. For warships must be independent of the wind, and hence they were still propelled by oars. The oarsmen were arranged in three rows, three men on the same bench, each man wielding an oar, and thus the power of an old "fifty-oar" could be multiplied by three without much increasing the size of the craft. These innovations were all in common use by 500 B.C. With their superior equipment on the sea, and the marked improvement of their industries, the Hellenes were soon beating the Phœnicians in the Mediterranean markets.

Meantime Greek business life had entered upon a new epoch due to the introduction of coined money. From the peoples of inner Asia Minor the Ionians had learned to use the precious metals by weight in making business payments after the oriental manner (§ 189). The basis of weight was the Babylonian "mina." Sixty such minas (pounds) made a talent, and a talent of silver was worth about $1125. Not long after 700 B.C., the kings of Lydia in Asia Minor (see map, p. 262) began to cut up silver into lumps of a fixed weight, small enough to be of convenient size and value. These they stamped with some symbol of the king or State to show that the State guaranteed their value, and such pieces formed the earliest-known coins (Fig. 165).

458. Precious metals and coinage in the Orient (700 B.C.)

The Ionian cities soon took over this great convenience, and it quickly passed thence to the islands and the European Greeks. The Athenians divided the mina of silver into a hundred parts. A lump of silver weighing the hundredth part of

459. Adoption of coinage by the Greeks (early seventh century B.C.)

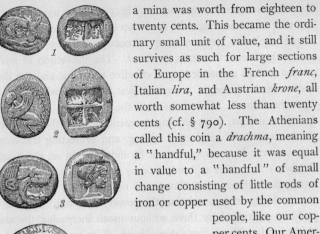

a mina was worth from eighteen to twenty cents. This became the ordinary small unit of value, and it still survives as such for large sections of Europe in the French *franc*, Italian *lira*, and Austrian *krone*, all worth somewhat less than twenty cents (cf. § 790). The Athenians called this coin a *drachma*, meaning a "handful," because it was equal in value to a "handful" of small change consisting of little rods of iron or copper used by the common people, like our copper cents. Our American dollar is simply five of these drachmas, and the Athenians themselves issued a four-drachma piece (Fig. 165, *4*) which served as their dollar. The purchasing power of a drachma was in ancient times very much greater than in our day. For example, a sheep cost one drachma, an ox five drachmas, and

FIG. 165. SPECIMENS ILLUSTRATING THE BEGINNING OF COINAGE

These are rough lumps of silver such as were long before used in the Orient (§ 189), flattened by the pressure of the stamp. Two of the examples (*1* and *2*) are marked by the bench tool which held the lump while the stamp was struck upon it. This defect was slowly overcome, and the coins became round as the stamp itself was made round instead of square. *1*, both sides of a Lydian coin (§ 458) (about 550 B.C.); *2*, both sides of a coin of the Greek island of Chios (500 B.C.), showing how the Greeks followed the Lydian model (*1*); *3*, both sides of a Carian coin of Cnidus (650–550 B.C.), an example of the square stamp; *4*, both sides of a four-drachma piece of Athens (sixth century B.C.), bearing head of goddess Athena and an owl with olive branch (square stamp). The inscription contains the first three letters of "Athens"

a landowner with an income of five hundred drachmas ($100) a year was considered a wealthy man.

Greek wealth had formerly consisted of lands and flocks, but now men began to accumulate capital in *money*. Loans were made and the use of interest came in from the Orient. The usual rate was 18 per cent yearly. Men who could never have hoped for wealth as farmers were now growing rich. For the growing industries and the commercial ventures on the seas rapidly created fortunes among a class before obscure. There arose thus a prosperous industrial and commercial *middle class* who demanded a voice in the government. They soon became a political power of much influence, and the noble class were obliged to consider them. At the beginning of the sixth century B.C. even a noble like Solon could say, "Money makes the man."

**460. Rise of a capitalistic class**

The prosperity we have sketched was still insufficient to produce large cities as we now have them. Athens and Corinth probably had about 25,000 inhabitants each. In spite of commercial prosperity the Greeks were still dependent on agriculture as their greatest source of income. But here again the farms and estates were from our point of view very small. The largest farms contained not over a hundred acres, while a man who had fifty acres was classed among the rich.

**461. Greek cities and estates**

## Section 47. Rise of the Democracy and the Age of the Tyrants

While the prosperous capitalistic class was thus arising, the condition of the peasant on his lands grew steadily worse. His fields were dotted with stones, each the sign of a mortgage, which the Greeks were accustomed to mark in this way. The wealthy creditors were foreclosing these mortgages and taking the lands, and the unhappy owners were being sold into foreign slavery or were fleeing abroad to escape such bonds. The nobles in control did nothing as a class to improve the situation; on the contrary, they did all in their

**462. Decline of the peasantry**

power to take advantage of the helplessness of the peasants and small farmers (see § 432).

**463. Power of the people increased by prosperity of the commercial class and by military changes**

But new enemies now opposed the noble class. In the first place, the new men of fortune (§ 460) were bitterly hostile to the nobles; in the second place, the improvement in Greek industries had so cheapened all work in metal that it was possible for the ordinary man to purchase weapons and a suit of armor. Moreover, the development of tactics under the leadership of the Spartans had produced close masses of spearmen, each mass (phalanx) standing like an unbroken wall throughout the battle (cf. Fig. 87). The war chariot of the individual hero of ancient times could not penetrate such a battle line. The chariot disappeared and was seen only in chariot races. These changes increased the importance of the ordinary citizen in the army and therefore greatly increased the power of the lower classes in the State.

**464. Disunion among nobles and rise of tyrants**

At the same time the nobles were far from united. Serious feuds between the various noble families often divided them into hostile factions. The leader of such a faction among the nobles often placed himself at the head of the dissatisfied people in real or feigned sympathy with their cause. Both the peasants and the new commercial class of citizens often rallied around such a noble leader. Thus supported, he was able to overcome and expel his rivals among the noble class and to gain undisputed control of the State. In this way he became the ruler of the State.

**465. The tyrant and public opinion of his office**

Such a ruler was in reality a king, but the new king differed from the kings of old in that he had no royal ancestors and had seized the control of the State by violence. The people did not reverence him as of ancient royal lineage, and while they may have felt gratitude to him, they felt no loyalty. The position of such a ruler always remained insecure. The Greeks called such a man a "tyrant," which was not at that time a term of reproach, as it is with us. The word "tyranny" was merely a term for the high office held by such a ruler.

Nevertheless, the instinctive feeling of the Greeks was that they were no longer free under such a prince, and the slayer of a tyrant was regarded as a hero and a savior of the people.

By 650 B.C. such rulers had begun to appear, but it was especially the sixth century (from 600 to 500 B.C.) which we may call the Age of the Tyrants. They arose chiefly in the Ionian cities of Asia Minor and the islands; also Eubœa, Athens, Corinth, and the colonies of Sicily — that is, in all the progressive Greek city-states where the people had gained power by commercial prosperity. Their rise was one of the direct consequences of the growing power of the people, and in spite of public opinion about them, they were the first champions of democracy. Such men as Periander of Corinth and Pisistratus of Athens looked after the rights of the people, curbed the nobles, gave great attention to public works like harbor improvements, state buildings, and temples, and cultivated art, music, and literature. **466.** Age of the Tyrants (sixth century B.C.)

Hitherto all law, so long ago reduced to writing in the Orient (Fig. 93), had been a matter of oral tradition in Greece. It was very easy for a judge to twist oral law to favor the man who gave him the largest present (§ 452). The people were now demanding that the inherited oral laws be put into writing (Fig. 166). After a long struggle the Athenians secured such a written code, arranged by a man named Draco, about 624 B.C. It was an exceedingly severe code — so severe, in fact, that the adjective " Draconic " has passed into our language as a synonym for " harsh." **467.** Earliest written Greek codes of law

Meantime the situation in Athens was much complicated by hostilities with neighboring powers. The merchants of Megara had seized the island of Salamis, overlooking the port of Athens (Fig. 177). The loss of Salamis and the failure of the nobles to recover it aroused intense indignation among the Athenians. Then a man of the old family to which the ancient kings of Athens had belonged, a noble named Solon, who had gained wealth by many a commercial venture on the seas, roused his **468.** Foreign complications of Athens countrymen by fiery verses, calling upon the Athenians not to endure the shame of such a loss. Salamis was recovered, and Solon gained great popularity with all classes of Athenians.

Fig. 166. Ruins of the Ancient Courthouse of Gortyna and the Early Greek Code of Laws engraved on its Walls

This hall at Gortyna in Crete, dating from the sixth century B.C., was a circular building about 140 feet across, which served as a courthouse. If any citizen thought himself unjustly treated, he could appeal to the great code engraved in twelve columns on the inside of the stone wall of the building. It covers the curved surface of the wall for about 30 feet, but extends only as high as would permit it to be read easily. It forms the longest Greek inscription now surviving. This code shows a growing sense of justice toward a debtor and forbids a creditor to seize a debtor's tools or furniture for debt; this illustrates the tendency among the Greeks in the age of Solon (§ 469)

**469.** Solon elected archon; his financial reforms

The result was Solon's election as archon (§ 434) in 594 B.C. He was given full power to improve the evil condition of the peasants. He declared void all mortgages on land and all claims of creditors which endangered the liberty of a citizen.

But Solon was a true statesman, and to the demands of the lower classes for a new apportionment of lands held by the nobles he would not yield. He did, however, set a limit to the amount of land which a noble might hold.

Solon also made a law that anyone who, like Hesiod (§ 452), had lost a lawsuit, could appeal the case to a jury of citizens over thirty years of age selected by lot. This change and some others greatly improved a citizen's chance of securing justice. Solon's laws were all written, and they formed the first Greek code of laws by which all free men were given equal rights in the courts. Some of these laws have descended to our own time and are still in force.

**470.** Solon's new code of laws

Furthermore, Solon proclaimed a new constitution which gave to all a voice in the control of the State. It made but few changes. It recognized four classes of citizens, graded according to the amount of their income. The wealthy nobles were the only ones who could hold the highest offices, and the peasants were permitted to hold only the lower offices. The government thus remained in the hands of the nobles, but the humblest free citizen could now be assured of the right to vote in the assembly of the people.

**471.** Solon's new constitution

Solon is the first great Greek statesman of whom we obtain an authentic picture, chiefly through his surviving poems. The leading trait of his character was moderation, combined with unfailing decision. When all expected that he would make himself "tyrant" he laid down his expiring archonship without a moment's hesitation and left Athens for several years, to give his constitution a fair chance to work.

**472.** Estimate of Solon

Solon saved Attica from a great social catastrophe, and it was largely due to his wise reforms that Athens achieved her industrial and commercial triumphs. But his constitution gave the prosperous commercial class no right to hold the leading offices of government. They continued the struggle for power. Hence Solon's work, though it deferred the humiliation, could not save the Athenian State from subjection to the tyrant.

**473.** Failure of Solon's work to prevent the rise of a tyrant in Attica

**474.** Pisistratus, tyrant of Athens (540–528 B.C.)

Returning from exile, backed by an army of hired soldiers, Pisistratus, a member of one of the powerful noble families, finally held control of the Athenian State. He ruled with great sagacity and success, and many of the Athenians gave him sincere support. Having built a war fleet of probably forty-eight ships, he seized the mouth of the Hellespont (Dardanelles). This control of the gateway to the Black Sea proved of enormous value to Athens in later days (§ 616). He carried out many public improvements at Athens, and transferred to the city the old peasant spring feast of Dionysus, from which were yet to come the theater and the great dramas of Athens (§ 484). Athenian manufactures and commerce flourished as never before, and when Pisistratus died (in the same year as Cyrus the Persian, 528 B.C.) he had laid a foundation to which much of the later greatness of Athens was due.

**475.** Fall of the sons of Pisistratus

In spite of their great ability, the sons of Pisistratus, Hipparchus and Hippias, were unable to overcome the prejudice of the people against a ruler on whom they had not conferred authority. One of the earliest exhibitions of Greek patriotism is the outburst of enthusiasm at Athens when two youths, Harmodius and Aristogiton (Fig. 169), at the sacrifice of their own lives, struck down one of the tyrants (Hipparchus). Hippias, the other one, was eventually obliged to flee. Thus, shortly before 500 B.C., Athens was freed from her tyrants.

**476.** The reforms of Clisthenes reduce the power of the nobles

The people were now able to gain new power against the nobles by the efforts of Clisthenes, a noble friendly to the lower classes. He broke up the old tribal divisions on the basis of blood relationship, and established purely *local* lines of division. He thus cut up the old noble clans and assigned the fragments to different local divisions, where they were in the minority. This prevented the nobles from acting together and broke their power.

**477.** Ostracism

In order to avoid the rise of a new tyrant, Clisthenes established a law that once a year the people might by vote declare any prominent citizen dangerous to the State and banish him for ten years. To cast his vote against a man, a citizen had only to pick up one of the pieces of broken pottery lying about the market place, write upon it the name of the citizen to be banished, and deposit it in the voting urn. As such a bit of pottery was called an "ostracon" (headpiece, p. 336), to "ostracize" a man (literally to "potsherd" him) meant to interrupt his political career by banishment. Although the nobles were still the only ones to whom the high offices of government were open, the possession of other forms of wealth besides land gave a citizen important political rights, and Athens had thus (about 500 B.C.) gained a form of government giving the people a high degree of power. The State was in large measure a democracy.

Meantime Sparta also had greatly increased in power. The Spartans had pushed their military successes until they held over a third of the Peloponnesian peninsula. The result was that long before 500 B.C. the Spartans had forced the neighboring states into a combination, the " Spartan league," which included nearly the whole of the Peloponnese. As the leader of this league, Sparta was the most powerful state in Greece. It had no industries, and it therefore did not possess the prosperous commercial class which had elsewhere done so much to overthrow the nobles and bring about the rise of the tyrants. For this and other reasons Sparta had escaped the rule of a tyrant. While it had divided the power of its king by appointing two kings to rule jointly, it was opposed to the rule of the people, and it looked with a jealous eye on the rising democracy of Athens.

**478.** Expansion of Sparta; foundation of the Spartan "league"

## Section 48. Civilization of the Age of the Tyrants

Although the nobles of Athens had been forced to yield much of their political power to the people, nevertheless, as we have seen, they still held the exclusive right to be elected to the important offices in the government. They continued also to

**479.** The nobles continue to be the social leaders; athletic games

be the leaders in all those matters which we call social. They created the social life of the time, and they were the prominent figures on all public occasions. The multitudes which thronged to the public games looked down at the best-born youths of Greece contesting for the prizes in the athletic matches (§ 444), and the wealthier nobles put the swiftest horses into the chariot races. To the laurel wreath which was granted the winner at the Olympian games Athens added a prize of five hundred drachmas when the winner was an Athenian. He was also entitled to take his meals at tables maintained by the State. Not seldom the greatest poets of the time, especially Pindar (§ 482), celebrated the victors in triumphant verses.

**480. Education**

In the matter of education, noble youths might be found spending the larger part of the day practicing in the public inclosure devoted to athletic exercises. To be sure, writing was now so common that a young man could not afford to be without it, and hence he submitted to some instruction in this art — a discipline which he was probably very reluctant to exchange for the applause of the idlers gathered around the gymnastic training ground. The women had no share in either the education or the social life of the men, and one of the greatest weaknesses of Greek civilization was the very limited part played by women in the life of the nation.

**481. Music, instrumental**

The education of the time was not complete without some instruction also in music. It was in the Age of the Tyrants that the music of Greece rose to the level of a real art. A system of writing musical notes, meaning for music what the alphabet meant for literature, now arose. The flute had been brought from Egypt to Crete in early times, and from the Cretans the Greeks had received it. Long a favorite instrument, it was now much more cultivated, and one musician even wrote a composition for the flute which was intended to tell the story of Apollo's fight with the dragon of Delphi. The lyre, which formerly had but four strings, was now made with eight, and compositions for the lyre alone were popular. Either of these instruments might be played as the accompaniment of song, or both together, with choruses of boys and girls. Here we have the beginnings of orchestral music as the accompaniment of choruses.

Music had a great influence on the literature of the age, for the poets now began to write verses to be sung with the music of the lyre, and hence such verses are called " lyric " poetry. From serious discussions like those of Solon (§ 468) the poets passed to songs of momentary moods, longings, dreams, hopes, and fiery storms of passion. Each in his way found a wondrous world within *himself*, which he thus pictured in short songs. Probably the greatest of these poets was Pindar of Thebes. Proud of his noble birth, the friend and intimate of tyrants and nobles, but also their fearless admonisher, Pindar gloried both in the pleasures and the responsibilities of wealth and rank. He sang in praise of pomp and splendor with a vividness which makes us see the chariots flashing down the course and hear the shouting of the multitude as the proud victor receives the laurel wreath of triumph. In exalted speech, often difficult to understand, Pindar delighted thus to glorify the life and rule of the nobles. At the same time his immortal word pictures of their life and their triumphs are always suffused with the beauty of unquestioning belief in the gods, especially Apollo, for whom Pindar seemed to speak almost as a prophet. He was the last great spokesman of a dying order of society, the rule of the nobles, which was to give way to the rule of the people. Another great lyric singer of the age was the poetess Sappho, the earliest woman to gain undying fame in literature. Indeed, she was perhaps the greatest poetess the world has ever seen.

A favorite form of song was the chorus, with which the country folk loved to celebrate their rustic feasts (headpiece; p. 221). The poet Stesichorus, who lived in Sicily, began to write choruses which told the stories of the gods as they were found in the old myths. The singers as they marched in rustic procession wore goatskins, and their faces were concealed by masks.

482. Lyric poetry: Pindar and Sappho

483. Festival choruses become drama

Some of the songs were sung responsively by the chorus and their leader. For the diversion of the listening peasants the leader would illustrate with gestures the story told in the song. He thus became to some extent an actor, the forerunner of the actors on our own stage. After Pisistratus introduced the spring feast of Dionysus at Athens (§ 474), this form of presentation made rapid progress. A second leader was introduced, and dialogue between the two was then possible, though the chorus continued to recite most of the narrative. Thus arose a form of musical play or drama, the action or narrative of which was carried on by the chorus and two actors. The Greeks called such a play a tragedy, which means "goat's play," probably because of the rustic disguise as goats which the chorus had always worn.

**484.** Origin of the theater

The grassy circle where the chorus danced and sang was usually on a slope in the hills, from which the spectators had a fine view of the country and the sea beyond. At Athens the people sat on the slope of the Acropolis, and as they watched the play they could look far across the sea to the heights of Argos. Here, under the southern brow of the Acropolis, where Pisistratus laid out the sacred precinct of Dionysus (see plan, p. 352), the theater began to take form and furnished the arrangements which have finally been inherited by us in our theaters (see Fig. 189).

**485.** Architecture

The tyrants were so devoted to building that architecture made very important advances. The Greek cities, including the buildings of the government, were still simply groups of sun-dried-brick buildings. Great stone buildings such as we have seen on the Nile had been unknown in Europe since the time of the Ægeans (Fig. 145), but now the rough Greek temples of sun-dried brick were rebuilt in limestone by the tyrants. Indeed, the front of the temple of Apollo at Delphi was even built of marble. At no other time before or since were so many temples erected as in the Greek world in the Age of the Tyrants. In Sicily and southern Italy a number of the noble temples of this age still stand to display to us the beauty and

simplicity of Greek architecture when it was still at an undeveloped stage (Fig. 219). Instead of the wooden posts of
the Age of the Nobles
(§ 449), these temples
were surrounded by lines
of plain *stone* columns
(colonnades) in a style
which we call Doric
(Fig. 167). Although the
architects of the tyrants
borrowed the idea and
the *form* of these colonnades from Egypt, they
improved them until they
made them the most
beautiful columns ever
designed by early archi-
tects. Like those on the
Nile, these Greek tem-
ples were painted in
bright colors (see p. 340).

Such temples were
adorned, in the triangu-
lar gable end, with sculptured relief figures of
the gods, grouped in
scenes representing in-
cidents in the myths.
Although at first very
much influenced by ori-
ental reliefs, the sculptor
soon produced works of
real beauty and inde-
pendence (Fig. 169). In
meeting the demand for

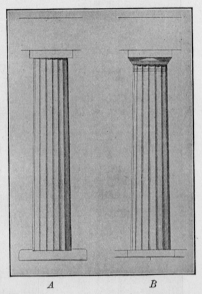

A                          B

FIG. 167. An Old Egyptian Column and the Doric Column derived from it

486. Sculp-
ture

The earliest form of column used by the
Greeks was a fluted shaft of stone (*B*)
closely resembling the simplest form (*A*)
which we found in Egypt, dating nearly
2000 B.C. (Fig. 57). Not only the whole
idea of a rhythmic row of piers but also
the form of each shaft was thus taken
by the Greeks from Egypt. The Greeks
gave this form completeness and increased beauty by adding a capital and
shaping it with great refinement of line
and contour. We should recall that colonnades were not in use in the Asiatic
Orient until the Persians introduced them
there (Fig. 116). See also diagram, p. 340

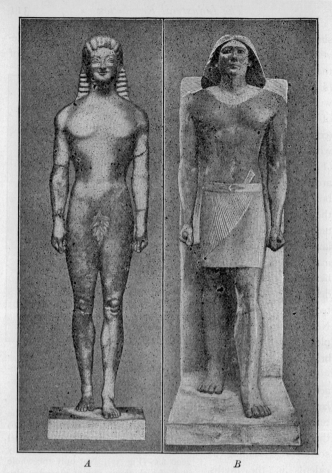

FIG. 168. EARLY GREEK STATUE AND EGYPTIAN PORTRAIT
STATUE BY WHICH IT WAS INFLUENCED

The Egyptian portrait (*B*) is over two thousand years older than the
Greek figure (*A*). The noble (*B*), one of those whose estate we visited
on the Nile (§ 80), stands in the customary posture of such figures in
Egyptian art, with the arms hanging down and the left foot thrust
forward. The Greek figure (*A*) stands in the same posture, with the
left foot thrust forward. Both look straight ahead, as was customary
in undeveloped art. The Greek figure shows clearly the influence
of Egyptian sculpture

statues of the victors at the games, the Greek sculptors were
also much influenced by the Egyptian figures they had seen.
Their earliest figures in stone were therefore still stiff and un-
graceful (Fig. 168). Moved by patriotic impulses, however,

FIG. 169. MONUMENT OF THE TYRANT SLAYERS OF ATHENS,
HARMODIUS AND ARISTOGITON, FROM TWO POINTS OF VIEW

On the slopes of the Areopagus (see plan, p. 352, and Fig. 182) overlooking the market place, the Athenians set up this group, depicting
at the moment of attack the two heroic youths who lost their lives in an
attempt to slay the two sons of Pisistratus and to free Athens from
the two tyrants (514 B.C.) (§ 475). The group was carried off by the
Persians after the battle of Salamis; the Athenians had another made
to replace the first one. It was afterward recovered in Persia by
Alexander or his successors and restored to its old place where both
groups stood side by side. Our illustration is an ancient copy in
marble, probably reproducing the later of the two groups

the Athenian sculptors went still farther and attempted a kind
of work which never had arisen in the Orient. They wrought
a noble memorial of the two youths who endeavored to free
Athens from the sons of Pisistratus. It was in the form of
a group depicting the two at the moment of their attack on
the tyrants, and although it still displayed some of the old
stiffness, it also showed remarkable progress toward free and

vigorous action of the human body (Fig. 169). These figures
were cast in bronze.

**487. Painting**    Similar progress was made by the painters of the age. Just
as the poets had begun to call upon their own imagination for
subject matter, so the vase-painters now began to depict not
only scenes from the myths of the gods and heroes, but also
pictures from the everyday life of the times (see the school,

FIG. 170. GREEK VASE-PAINTING, SHOWING THE HOME LIFE
OF WOMEN

A maidservant at the right presents to her mistress an Egyptian
alabaster perfume bottle (see the same shape in glass, Fig. 49). The
mistress sits arranging her hair before a hand mirror. Behind her
approaches another woman. At the left a lady is working at an em-
broidery frame, while a visitor in street costume watches her work.
Behind stands a lady with a basket. Notice the grace and beauty of the
figures, which at this time were in red (the natural color of the terra
cotta), showing through a shining black pigment laid on by the artist

Fig. 181). At the same time they improved their method greatly
(cf. Fig. 170). They made drawings of the human figure that
were more natural and true than early artists had ever before
been able to do. Their skill in depicting limbs shortened by
being seen from one end was surprising. These problems, called
foreshortening and perspective, were first solved by the Greek
painters. The vases of this age are a wonderful treasury of
beautiful scenes from Greek life (Fig. 170), reminding us of
our glimpses into the life of Egypt two thousand five hundred
years earlier, in the tomb-chapel scenes of the Nile.

Literature and painting show us that the Greeks of this age were intensely interested in the life of their own time. In the first place, they were thinking more deeply than ever before about conduct, and they were better able to distinguish between right and wrong. Men could no longer believe that the gods led the evil lives pictured in the Homeric songs. Stesichorus (§ 483) had so high an idea of womanly fidelity that he could not accept the tale of the beautiful Helen's faithlessness, and in his festival songs he told the ancient story in another way. Men now felt that even Zeus and his Olympian divinities must do the right. Mortals too must do the same, for men had now come to believe that in the world of the dead there was punishment for the evildoer. Hades became a place of torment for the wicked, guarded by Cerberus, a monstrous dog, one of those sentinel animals of the Orient of which the Sphinx of Gizeh (Fig. 54), also guarding the dead, is the oldest example.

**488.** Growing sense of right and wrong; punishment hereafter

Likewise it was believed that there must be a place of blessedness for the good in the next world. Accordingly, in the temple at Eleusis scenes from the mysterious earth life of Demeter and Dionysus, to whom men owed the fruits of the earth, were presented by the priests in dramatic form before the initiated, and he who viewed them mysteriously received immortal life and might be admitted into the Islands of the Blessed, where once none but the ancient heroes could be received. Even the poorest slave was permitted to enter this fellowship and be initiated into the "mysteries," as they were called.

**489.** Blessedness hereafter; "mysteries" of Eleusis

More than ever, also, men now turned to the gods for a knowledge of the future in this world. Everywhere it was believed that the oracle voice of Apollo revealed the outcome of every untried venture, and his shrine at Delphi (Figs. 171 and 172) became a national religious center, to which the whole Greek world resorted.

**490.** Oracles

Some thoughtful men, on the other hand, were rejecting the beliefs of older times, especially regarding the world and

**491.** Thales
and his pre-
diction of
an eclipse
(585 B.C.)

its control by the gods. The Ionian cities, long the commercial leaders of the Ægean, now likewise led the way in
thinking of these
new problems. In
constant contact
with Egypt and the
Phœnician cities,
they gained the
beginnings of math-
ematics and as-
tronomy as known
in the Orient, and
one of the Ionian
thinkers had in-
deed set up an
Egyptian shadow
clock (Fig. 74).
At Miletus, the
leader of these Io-
nian cities, there
was an able states-
man named Thales,
who had traveled
widely, and re-
ceived from Baby-
lonia a list of ob-
servations of the
heavenly bodies.
From such lists the
Babylonians had al-
ready learned that
eclipses of the sun

FIG. 171. VIEW OVER THE VALLEY AND
RUINS OF DELPHI TO THE SEA

This splendid gorge in the slopes of Mount Parnassus on the north side of the Corinthian Gulf
(see map, p. 352) was very early sacred to Apollo,
who was said to have slain the dragon Pytho
which lived here. The white line of road in the
foreground is the highway descending to the
distant arm of the Corinthian Gulf. On the left
of this road the cliff descends sheer 1000 feet,
and above the road (on its right) on the steep
slope are the ruins of the sacred buildings of
ancient Delphi, excavated by the French in recent years. We can see the zigzag road leading up the hill among the ruins just at the right
of the main road (cf. also Fig. 172)

occurred at periodic intervals (§ 239). With these lists in his
hands Thales could calculate when the next eclipse would
occur. He therefore told the people of Miletus that they might

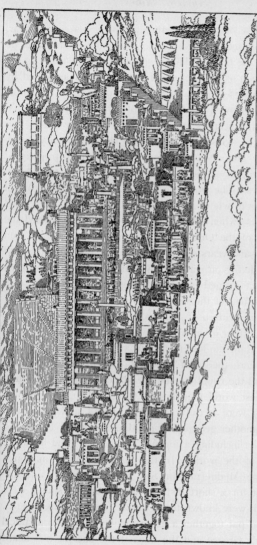

FIG. 172. THE BUILDINGS OF DELPHI RESTORED. (AFTER HOMOLLE-TOURNAIRE)

Beginning with the seventh century B.C. this place became a national sanctuary of the Greeks, where all Greece and many foreigners came to hear the oracles of the revered Apollo (§ 490). His temple, many times rebuilt, was a Doric structure which we see rising in the middle of the inclosure. A zigzag way (cf. Fig. 171) passed up from the lower right-hand corner of this inclosure, and on each side of this way were ranged the treasuries containing the votive offerings of the Greeks to the great god — the statues and victorious trophies, many of them of gold and silver, presented by states, kings, and individuals. The value of these things proved fatal. It was finally plundered by the Romans (§ 1043), but although the Roman emperor Nero (54–68 A.D.) removed five hundred statues, there were still three thousand left here when Pliny visited the place some years later. Part of a magnificent tripod taken away from here by the Romans to adorn Constantinople may be seen in Fig. 269

expect an eclipse of the sun before the end of a certain year. When the promised eclipse (585 B.C.) actually occurred as he had predicted, the fame of Thales spread far and wide.

**492. Natural law versus the gods; rise of science and philosophy among the Ionians**

The prediction of an eclipse, a feat already accomplished by the Babylonians (§ 239), was not so important as the *consequences* which followed in the mind of Thales. Hitherto men had believed that eclipses and all the other strange things that happened in the skies were caused by the momentary angry whim of some god. Now, however, Thales boldly proclaimed that the movements of the heavenly bodies were in accordance with fixed laws. The gods were thus banished from control of the sky-world where the eagle of Zeus had once ruled (§ 413). So also when a Greek traveler like Thales visited the vast buildings of the Orient, like the pyramids of Gizeh, then over two thousand years old, he at once saw that the gods had not been wandering on earth a few generations before his own time. This fact seemed to banish the gods from the past, and from the beginning of the world likewise.

**493. Ionian geography and history**

Hence another citizen of Miletus, perhaps a pupil of Thales, explained the origin of animals by assuming a development of higher forms from the lower ones, in a manner which reminds us of the modern theory of evolution. He studied the forms of the seas and the countries, and he made a map of the world. It is the earliest world map known to us, although maps of a limited region were already in use in Egypt and Babylonia. A little later another geographer of Miletus, named Hecatæus, traveled widely, including a journey up the Nile, and he wrote a geography of the world. In this book, as in the map just mentioned, the Mediterranean Sea was the center, and the lands about it for a short distance back from its shores were all those which were known to the author (see his map, p. 319). Hecatæus also put together a history made up of the mythical stories of early Greece and the tales of the past he had heard in the Orient. After the historian of the Hebrew patriarchs (§ 302), he was the first historical writer of the early world.

Another Ionian thinker, who migrated to southern Italy, was Pythagoras. He investigated mathematics and natural science. He or his pupils discovered that the square of the hypotenuse equals the sum of the squares of the other two sides of a right-angled triangle. They also found out that the length of a musical string is in exact mathematical relation to the height of its tone. They likewise discovered that the earth is a sphere which possesses its own motion. Another of these Ionians, in his account of the origin of the earth, called attention to the presence of petrified sea plants and fish in the rocks, to prove that the sea had at one time covered the land.

494. Ionian mathematics and natural science

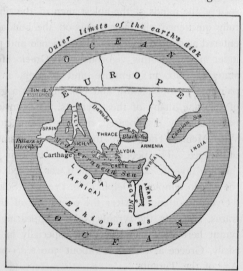

MAP OF THE WORLD BY HECATÆUS (517 B.C.)

Thus these Ionian thinkers, having gradually abandoned the old myths, took the natural world out of the hands of the gods. They therefore became the forerunners of natural scientists and philosophers, for they strove to discern what were the *natural* laws which in the beginning had brought the world into existence, and still continued to control it. At this point in their thinking they entered upon a new world of thought, which we call *science* and *philosophy* — a world which had never dawned upon the greatest minds of the early East. This step, taken by Thales and the great men of the Ionian cities, remains and

495. The great step taken by the Ionian thinkers

will forever remain the greatest achievement of the human in tellect — an achievement to call forth the reverence and admiration of all time.

**496.** Summary and end of the Age of the Tyrants

The Age of the Tyrants was therefore one of the great epochs of the world's history. Under the stimulus of the keen struggle for leadership in business, in government, and in society, the minds of the ablest men of the time were wonderfully quickened, till they threw off the bondage of habit and entered an entirely new world of science and philosophy. The inner power of this vigorous new Greek life flowed out in statesmanship, in literature and religion, in sculpture and painting, in architecture and building. As a group the leaders of this age, many of them tyrants, made an impression which never entirely disappeared, and they were called " the Seven Wise Men." They were the earliest statesmen and thinkers of Greece. The people loved to quote their sayings, such as " Know thyself," a proverb which was carved over the door of the Apollo temple at Delphi (Fig. 172); or Solon's wise maxim, " Overdo nothing." After the overthrow of the sons of Pisistratus, however, the tyrants were disappearing, and although a tyrant here and there survived, especially in Asia Minor and Sicily, Greece at this time (about 500 B.C.) passed out of the Age of the Tyrants.

### QUESTIONS

SECTION 46. How did the new colonies of the Greeks influence manufacturing at home? What can you tell of commerce and manufactures? What step toward freedom from foreign influences did Greek manufactures take? What evidence have we of the extent of Athenian commerce? Discuss the effect upon shipbuilding. What new business convenience came in from the East? How did coinage arise? What leading coins did Athens possess? How did coinage affect business and the accumulation of wealth? From our point of view did the Greeks have any large cities or farms?

SECTION 47. What was now happening to the Greek farmers in the matter of wealth? in the matter of military and political power?

Were the nobles all united? What attitude toward the common people did a leading noble often take? What was the result? How did the Greeks feel toward a tyrant? When may we date the period of the tyrants?

In what form had Greek laws thus far existed? What did the people now demand? What code of laws was made at Athens? Who now aroused Athens to meet her foreign difficulties? What did Solon accomplish after he was elected archon? What can you say of his character? Did his work save Athens from the rule of a tyrant?

What did Pisistratus accomplish? When did he die? What happened to his sons? How did Clisthenes aid the people? What was ostracism? What was meantime happening in Sparta? How did Sparta feel toward Athens?

SECTION 48. Describe the social position of the nobles in the Age of the Tyrants. What was their attitude toward the athletic games? What can you say of education in this age? Discuss instrumental music; vocal music. What was lyric poetry? Who was the leading lyric poet, and what can you say of his poetry? Of what class was he the spokesman? Who was the greatest poetess? How did festal choruses lead to drama? What was the origin of the theater?

Had the Greeks any fine buildings in this age? What was the building material? Had they never seen any stone buildings? In what style of architecture were the temples erected? Where did the form of the Doric column arise? Did the Greeks improve these columns? Did they color them? What other adornment of his temples did the Greek architect employ? Under what influences did Greek sculpture arise? What progress does the monument of the tyrant-slayers show?

Discuss Greek vase-painting in this age. What subjects did the vase-painters select? Compare the human figures in Fig. 170 and those in Fig. 155 and express your opinion of the progress made in two and a half centuries. How was the method of vase-painting improved? What progress was made in ideas of conduct? Discuss the ideas of the hereafter; oracles. What did Thales do? Was he the first to make such a calculation? What conclusions did he make about the gods and their control of the world? Tell about the first maps of the world. What new world had the Ionian thinkers entered upon? What can you say of the Age of the Tyrants as a whole?

# CHAPTER XIII

## THE REPULSE OF PERSIA

### Section 49. The Coming of the Persians

**497.** Rise of Lydia in Asia Minor

The leadership gained by the Ionian cities in the Age of the Tyrants was now seriously checked by their neighbors in Asia Minor. Here still lived the descendants of the Hittites (§ 351), mingled with later invaders (§ 376). The kings of Lydia, their leading kingdom, where we have already met Crœsus (§ 260), made their capital, Sardis, the strongest city of Asia Minor (Fig. 173). From them the practice of coinage had passed to the Greeks (§ 458). The Lydians had finally conquered all the Greek cities along the Ægean coast of Asia Minor except Miletus, which still resisted capture.

**498.** Fall of Lydia and advance of Persia to the Ægean

The Lydians had been strong enough to halt the Medes, but we remember that when Cyrus the Persian invaded Asia Minor, he defeated Crœsus and captured Sardis (§ 260). In the midst

NOTE. The above headpiece represents a scene sculptured in relief on a doorway in the palace of Xerxes at Persepolis (Fig. 116). It shows us Xerxes as he was accustomed to appear when enthroned before his nobles, with his attendants and fan-bearers. At Salamis he took his station on the heights of Ægaleos overlooking the bay (§ 513), and as he sat there viewing the battle below him, he must have been enthroned as we see him here.

of the most remarkable progress in civilization (§§ 491–496), the Ionian cities thus suddenly lost their liberty and became the subjects of Persia, a despotic oriental power. Moreover, the sudden advance of Persia to the Ægean made this power at one stroke a close neighbor of the Greek world now arising there.

FIG. 173. SARDIS, THE CITY OF CRŒSUS, IN COURSE OF EXCAVATION

The natural drainage from the mountain slope in the background has covered the ruins of the city with earth. The bank showing the edge of this earth and the limit of the excavations can be seen behind the columns of the temple rising in the middle. These excavations, which have produced very important results, are an American enterprise under the direction of Professor Howard Crosby Butler, to whose kindness the author owes this photograph

As we have already learned, the Persians represented a high civilization and an enlightened rule; but, on the other hand, the Orient lacked free citizenship, and in place of science the Orientals felt complete subjection of the mind to religious tradition. Persian supremacy in Greece would therefore have

**499.** The coming conflict and the revolt of the Ionians

checked the free development of Greek genius along its own
exalted lines. There seemed little prospect that the tiny Greek
states, even if they united, could successfully resist the vast
oriental empire, controlling as it did all the countries of the
ancient East, which we have been studying. Nevertheless the
Ionian cities revolted against their Persian lords.

**500. First Persian invasion of Europe**

During the struggle with Persia which followed this revolt,
the Athenians sent twenty ships to aid their Ionian kindred.
This act brought a Persian army of revenge, under Darius,
into Europe. The long march across the Hellespont and
through Thrace cost the invaders many men, and the fleet
which accompanied the Persian advance was wrecked in trying
to round the high promontory of Mount Athos (492 B.C.).
This advance into Greece was therefore abandoned for a plan
of invasion by water across the Ægean.

**501. Second Persian invasion**

In the early summer of 490 B.C. a considerable fleet of
transports and warships bearing the Persian host put out from
the Island of Samos, sailed straight across the Ægean, and
entered the straits between Eubœa and Attica (see map 1,
p. 344, and Fig. 174). The Persians began by burning the
little city of Eretria, which had also sent ships to aid the
Ionians. They then landed on the shores of Attica, in the Bay
of Marathon (see map, p. 352, and Fig. 174), intending to
march on Athens, the greater offender. They were guided by
the aged Hippias, son of Pisistratus, once tyrant of Athens,
who accompanied them with high hopes of regaining control
of his native city.

**502. Consternation in Athens and Greece**

All was excitement and confusion among the Greek states.
The defeat of the revolting Ionian cities, and especially the
Persian sack of Miletus, had made a deep impression throughout Greece. An Athenian dramatist had depicted in a play the
plunder of the unhappy city and so incensed the Athenians that
they passed weeping from the theater to prosecute and fine the
author. Now this Persian foe who had crushed the Ionian
cities was camping behind the hills only a few miles northeast

of Athens. After dispatching messengers in desperate haste to seek aid in Sparta, the Athenian citizens turned to contemplate the seemingly hopeless situation of their beloved city.

FIG. 174. THE PLAIN OF MARATHON

This view is taken from the hills at the south end of the plain, and we look northeastward across a corner of the Bay of Marathon to the mountains in the background, which are on the large island of Eubœa (see map, p. 352). The Persian camp was on the plain at the very shore line, where their ships were moored or drawn up. The Greeks held a position in the hills overlooking the plain (just out of range on the left) and commanding the road to Athens, which is 25 miles distant behind us. When the Persians began to move along the shore road toward the right, the Greeks crossed the plain and attacked. The memorial mound (Fig. 175) is too far away to be visible from this point

Thinking to find the Athenians unprepared, Darius had not sent a large army. The Persian forces probably numbered no more than twenty thousand men, but at the utmost the Athenians could not put more than half this number into the field. Fortunately for them there was among their generals a skilled and experienced commander named Miltiades, a man

503. The armies and Greek leadership

of resolution and firmness, who, moreover, had lived on the Hellespont and was familiar with Persian methods of fighting. To his judgment the commander-in-chief, Callimachus, yielded at all points. As the citizen-soldiers of Attica flocked to the city at the call to arms, Miltiades was able to induce the leaders not to await the assault of the Persians at Athens, but to march across the peninsula (see map, p. 352) and block the Persian advance among the hills overlooking the eastern coast and commanding the road to the city. This bold and resolute move roused courage and enthusiasm in the downcast ranks of the Greeks.

**504.** The Greek position

Nevertheless, when they issued between the hills and looked down upon the Persian host encamped upon the Plain of Marathon (Fig. 174), flanked by a fleet of hundreds of vessels, misgiving and despair chilled the hearts of the little Attic army made up as it was of citizen militia without experience in war, and pitted against a Persian army of professional soldiers of many battles. But Miltiades held the leaders firmly in hand, and the arrival of a thousand Greeks from Platæa revived the courage of the Athenians. The Greek position overlooked the main road to Athens, and the Persians could not advance without leaving their line of march exposed on one side to the Athenian attack.

**505.** The battle of Marathon (490 B.C.)

Unable to lure the Greeks from their advantageous position after several days' waiting, the Persians at length attempted to march along the road to Athens, at the same time endeavoring to cover their exposed line of march with a sufficient force thrown out in battle array. Miltiades was familiar with the Persian custom of massing troops in the center. He therefore massed his own troops on both wings, leaving his center weak. It was a battle between bow and spear. The Athenians undauntedly faced the storm of Persian arrows (§ 259 and Fig. 113), and then both wings pushed boldly forward to the line of shields behind which the Persian archers were kneeling. In the meantime the Persian center, finding the Greek center weak, had pushed it back, while the two Greek wings closed in on either side and thrust back the Persian wings in confusion. The Asiatic army crumbled into a broken multitude between the two advancing lines of Greeks. The Persian bow was useless, and the Greek spear everywhere spread death and terror. As the Persians fled to their ships they left over six thousand

FIG. 175. MOUND RAISED AS A MONUMENT TO THE FALLEN GREEKS ON THE PLAIN AT MARATHON

The mound is nearly 50 feet high. Excavations undertaken in 1890 disclosed beneath it the bodies of the one hundred and ninety-two Athenian citizens who fell in the battle. Some of their weapons and the funeral vases buried with them were also recovered

dead upon the field, while the Athenians lost less than two hundred men (Fig. 175). When the Persian commander, unwilling to acknowledge defeat, sailed around the Attic peninsula and appeared with his fleet before the port of Athens, he found it unwise to attempt a landing, for the victorious Athenian army was already encamped beside the city. The Persians therefore retired, and we can imagine with what feelings the Athenian citizens watched the Persian ships as they disappeared.

## SECTION 50. THE GREEK REPULSE OF PERSIANS AND PHŒNICIANS

**506.** Rise of Themistocles

Among the men who stood in the Athenian ranks at Marathon was Themistocles, the ablest statesman in Greece, a man who had already occupied the office of archon, the head of the Athenian state. He was convinced of the necessity of building up a strong navy — a course already encouraged by Pisistratus (§ 474). As archon, Themistocles had therefore striven to show the Athenians that the only way in which Athens could hope to meet the assault of Persia was by making herself undisputed mistress of the sea. He had failed in his effort. But now the Athenians had seen the Persians cross the Ægean with their fleet and land at Marathon. It was evident that a powerful Athenian navy might have stopped them. They began to listen to the counsels of Themistocles to make Athens the great sea power of the Mediterranean.

**507.** Xerxes inherits the Persian quarrel with the Greeks

Darius the Great, whose remarkable reign we have studied (§§ 267–273), died without having avenged the defeat of his army at Marathon. His son and successor Xerxes therefore took up the unfinished task. Xerxes planned a far-reaching assault on Greek civilization all along the line from Greece to Sicily. This he could do through his control of the Phœnician cities. The naval policy of his father Darius (§ 270) had given the Persians a huge Phœnician war fleet. In so far as the coming attack on Greece was by sea it was chiefly a Semitic assault. At the same time Xerxes induced Phœnician Carthage to attack the Greeks in Sicily. Thus the two wings of the great Semitic line represented by the Phœnicians in east and west (Carthage) were to attack the Indo-European line (Fig. 112) represented in east and west by the Greeks. Xerxes was induced by his general Mardonius to adopt the Hellespont route (map I, p. 346).

Meantime the Greeks were making ready to meet the coming Persian assault. They soon saw that Xerxes' commanders were cutting a canal behind the promontory of Athos, to secure a short cut and thus to avoid all risk of such a wreck as had over-taken their former fleet in rounding this dangerous point. When the news of this operation reached Athens, Themistocles was able to induce the Athenian Assembly to build a great fleet of probably a hundred and eighty triremes. The Greeks were then able for the first time to meet the Persian advance by both sea and land (see map I, p. 346).

508. The-mistocles induces the Athenians to build a fleet

Themistocles' masterly plan of campaign corresponded ex-actly to the plan of the Persian advance. The Asiatics were coming in combined land and sea array, with army and fleet moving together down the east coast of the Greek mainland. It was as if the Persian forces had two wings, a sea wing and a land wing, moving side by side. The design of Themistocles was to meet the Persian sea wing first with full force and fight a decisive naval battle as soon as possible. If victorious, the Greek fleet commanding the Ægean would then be able to sail up the eastern coast of Greece and threaten the communica-tions and supplies of the Persian army. There must be no at-tempt of the small Greek army to meet the vast land forces of the Persians, beyond delaying them as long as possible at the narrow northern passes, which could be defended with a few men. An attempt to unite all the Greek states was not success-ful, but Sparta and Athens combined their forces to meet the common danger. Themistocles was able to induce the Spartans to accept his plan only on condition that Sparta be given com-mand of the allied Greek fleets.

509. Third Persian in-vasion — The-mistocles' plan of campaign

In the summer of 480 B.C. the Asiatic army was approaching the pass of Thermopylæ (Fig. 176), just opposite the western-most point of the Island of Eubœa (see map, p. 352). Their fleet moved with them. The Asiatic host must have numbered over two hundred thousand men, with probably as many more camp followers, while the enormous fleet contained presumably about a thousand vessels, of which perhaps two thirds were warships. Of these ships, the Persians lost a hundred or two in a storm, leaving probably about five hundred warships

510. Persians enter Greece

available for action. The Spartan king Leonidas led some five
thousand men to check the Persians at the pass of Thermopylæ,
while the Greek fleet of less than three hundred triremes was
endeavoring to hold together and strike the Persian navy at

FIG. 176. THE PASS OF THERMOPYLÆ

In the time of the Persian invasion the mountains to the left dropped
steeply to the sea, with barely room between for a narrow road. Since
then the rains of twenty-four hundred years have washed down the
mountainside, and it is no longer as steep as formerly, while the neighboring river has filled in the shore and pushed back the sea several
miles. Otherwise we would see it here on the right. The Persians,
coming from beyond the mountains toward our point of view, could not
spread out in battle array, being hemmed in by the sea on one side and
the cliff on the other. It was only when a traitorous Greek led a Persian
force by night over the mountain on the left, and they appeared behind
the Greeks in the pass, that Leonidas and his Spartans were crushed by
the simultaneous attack in front and rear (§§ 510–511)

Artemisium, on the northern coast of Eubœa. Thus the land
and sea forces of both contestants were face to face.

After several days' delay the Persians advanced to attack on
both land and sea. The Greek fleet made a skillful and credit-
able defense against superior numbers, and all day the dauntless

Leonidas held the pass of Thermopylæ against the Persian host. Meantime the Persians were executing two flank movements by land and by sea — one over the mountains to strike Leonidas in the rear, and the other with two hundred ships around Eubœa to take the Greek fleet likewise from behind. A storm destroyed the flanking Persian ships, and a second combat between the two main fleets was indecisive. The flank movement by sea therefore failed; but the flanking of the pass was successful. Taken in front and rear, the heroic Leonidas died fighting at the head of his small force, which the Persian host completely annihilated. The death of Leonidas stirred all Greece. With the defeat of the Greek land forces and the advance of the Persian army, the Greek fleet, seriously damaged, was obliged to withdraw to the south. It took up its position in the Bay of Salamis (see map, p. 352, and Fig. 177), while the main army of the Spartans and their allies was drawn up on the Isthmus of Corinth (Fig. 163), the only point at which the Greek land forces could hope to make another defensive stand.

511. The battles of Thermopylæ and Artemisium

As the Persian army moved southward from Thermopylæ, the indomitable Themistocles gathered together the Athenian population and carried them in transports to the little islands of Salamis and Ægina and to the shores of Argolis (see map, p. 352, and Pl. III, p. 278). Meantime the Greek fleet had been repaired, and with reinforcements numbered over three hundred battleships. Nevertheless it shook the courage of many at Salamis as they looked northward, where the far-stretching Persian host darkened the coast road, while in the south they could see the Asiatic fleet drawn up off the old port of Athens at Phalerum (see map, p. 352). High over the Attic hills the flames of the burning Acropolis showed red against the sullen masses of smoke that obscured the eastern horizon and told them that the homes of the Athenians lay in ashes. With masterly skill Themistocles held together the irresolute Greek leaders, while he induced Xerxes to attack by the false message that the Greek fleet was about to slip out of the bay.

512. Persian advance into Attica and burning of Athens

**513.** Battle of Salamis (480 B.C.)

On the heights overlooking the Bay of Salamis the Persian king, seated on his throne (headpiece, p. 322) in the midst of his brilliant oriental court, took up his station to watch the battle.

FIG. 177. PIRÆUS, THE PORT OF ATHENS, AND THE STRAIT AND ISLAND OF SALAMIS

The view shows the very modern houses and buildings of this flourishing harbor town of Athens (see map, p. 352). The mountains in the background are the heights of the island of Salamis, which extends also far over to the right (north), opposite Eleusis (see map, p. 352). The four steamers at the right are lying at the place where the hottest fighting in the great naval battle here (§ 513) took place. The Persian fleet advanced from the left (south) and could not spread out in a long front to enfold the Greek fleet because of the little island just beyond the four steamers, which was called Psyttaleia. The Greek fleet lying behind Psyttaleia and a long point of Salamis came into action from the right (north), around Psyttaleia, and met the front of the Persian fleet about where the four steamers lie. A body of Persian troops stationed by Xerxes on Psyttaleia were all slain by the Greeks

The Greek position between the jutting headlands of Salamis and the Attic mainland (see map, p. 352, and Fig. 177) was too cramped for the maneuvers of a large fleet. Crowded and hampered by the narrow sea room, the huge Asiatic fleet soon fell into confusion before the Greek attack. There was no room for retreat. The combat lasted the entire day, and when darkness settled on the Bay of Salamis the Persian fleet had been almost annihilated. The Athenians were masters of the sea, and it was impossible for the army of Xerxes to operate with the same freedom as before. By the creation of its powerful fleet Athens had saved Greece, and Themistocles had shown himself the greatest of Greek statesmen.

Xerxes was now troubled lest he should be cut off from Asia by the victorious Greek fleet. Indeed, Themistocles made every effort to induce Sparta to join with Athens in doing this very thing; but the cautious Spartans could not be prevailed upon to undertake what seemed to them so dangerous an enterprise. Had Themistocles' plan of sending the Greek fleet immediately to the Hellespont been carried out, Greece would have been saved another year of anxious campaigning against the Persian army. With many losses from disease and insufficient supplies, Xerxes retreated to the Hellespont and withdrew into Asia, leaving his able general Mardonius with an army of perhaps fifty thousand men to winter in Thessaly. Meantime the news reached Greece that the army of Carthaginians which had crossed from Africa to Sicily had been completely defeated by the Greeks under the leadership of Gelon, tyrant of Syracuse. Thus the assault of the Asiatics upon the Hellenic world was beaten back in both east and west in the same year (480 B.C.). **514.** Retreat of Xerxes in the East; defeat of Carthage in the West

The brilliant statesmanship of Themistocles, so evident to us of to-day, was not so clear to the Athenians as the winter passed and they realized that the victory at Salamis had not relieved Greece of the presence of a Persian army, and that Mardonius would invade Attica with the coming of spring. Themistocles, whose proposed naval expedition to the Hellespont would have forced the Persian army out of Greece, was removed from command by the factions of his ungrateful city. Nevertheless the most tempting offers from Mardonius could not induce the Athenians to forsake the cause of Greek liberty and join hands with Persia. **515.** Reaction against Themistocles

**516.** Persians again in Attica

As Mardonius, at the end of the winter rains, led his army again into Attica, the unhappy Athenians were obliged to flee as before, this time chiefly to Salamis. Sparta, always reluctant and slow when the crisis demanded quick and vigorous action, was finally induced to put her army into the field. When Mardonius in Attica saw the Spartan king Pausanias advancing through the Corinthian Isthmus and threatening his rear, he withdrew northward, having for the second time laid waste Attica far and wide. With the united armies of Sparta, Athens, and other allies behind him, Pausanias was able to lead some thirty thousand heavy-armed Greeks of the phalanx, as he followed Mardonius into Bœotia.

**517.** Battle of Platæa; final defeat of Persia (479 B.C.)

In several days of preliminary movements which brought the two armies into contact at Platæa, the clever Persian showed his superiority, out-maneuvering Pausanias and even gaining possession of the southern passes behind the Greeks and capturing a train of their supply wagons. But when Mardonius led his archers forward at double-quick, and the Persians, kneeling behind their line of shields, rained deadly volleys of arrows into the compact Greek lines, the Hellenes never flinched, although their comrades were falling on every hand. With the gaps closed up, the massive Greek phalanx pushed through the line of Persian shields, and, as at Marathon, the spear proved invincible against the bow. In a heroic but hopeless effort to rally his broken lines, Mardonius himself fell. The Persian cavalry covered the rear of the flying Asiatic army and saved it from destruction.

**518.** Athenian fleet victorious in Ionia and the North

Not only European Greece, but Ionia too, was saved from Asiatic despotism; for the Greek triremes, having meantime crossed to the peninsula of Mycale on the north of Miletus, drove out or destroyed the remnants of the Persian fleet. The Athenians now also captured and occupied Sestus on the European side of the Hellespont, and thus held the crossing from Asia into Europe closed against further Persian invasion. Thus the grandsons of the men who had seen Persia advance to the Ægean had blocked her further progress in the West and thrust her back from Europe. Indeed, no Persian army ever set foot in European Greece again.

## QUESTIONS

SECTION 49. What was the leading kingdom of Asia Minor beyond the fringe of Greek coast cities? What had happened to these Greek cities in the middle of the sixth century B.C.? Who was the last king of Lydia? Who crushed the Lydian kingdom? When? What great oriental power thus advanced to the east side of the Ægean? What do you think of the prospects for Greek resistance?

What did the Ionian cities of Asia do? What part did Athens take in their revolt? How did the Persians respond? When? Who was their king? Where did they land in Greece? How far is Marathon from Athens? What did the Athenians do? Discuss the numbers of the two armies. Did the Athenians wait for the Persians at Athens? Who was their leader? What position did the Greeks take up, and what advantages were thus gained? Describe the battle of Marathon.

SECTION 50. What great Greek statesman had fought at Marathon? What was his policy for the future defense of Athens? Describe the plans of Xerxes for the subjection of Greece. What did the Athenians do? Describe Themistocles' plan of campaign. What first two battles took place? Describe them. What was the next move of the Persian army? Describe the battle of Salamis.

What did Xerxes do after the battle of Salamis? What move did Themistocles urge? What was the result of the Greek failure to accept Themistocles' advice? What victory did the Greeks win in Sicily at the same time? What racial conflict do these victories represent? What happened to Themistocles? What did the Persian commander now do? Who was he? Where did the final battle take place? Describe it. What final results were obtained by the Greeks at sea?

## CHAPTER XIV

### THE GROWING RIVALRY BETWEEN ATHENS AND SPARTA, AND THE RISE OF THE ATHENIAN EMPIRE

#### SECTION 51. THE BEGINNINGS OF THE RIVALRY BETWEEN ATHENS AND SPARTA

**519. Athenian feeling after Salamis**

As the Athenians returned to look out over the ashes of what was once Athens, amid which rose the smoke-blackened heights of the naked Acropolis (Fig. 182), they began to realize the greatness of their deliverance and the magnitude of their achievement. With the not too ready help of Sparta, they had met and crushed the hoary power of Asia. They felt themselves masters of the world. The past seemed narrow and limited. A new and greater Athens dawned upon their vision.

**520. Spartan soldier-citizens**

Of all this the Spartans, on the other hand, felt very little. The Spartan citizens were all soldiers and devoted themselves exclusively to military training. The State maintained public meals, where each soldier-citizen ate with a group of about fifteen friends, all men, at the same table every day. Each citizen contributed to the support of these meals, and as long as he paid this contribution he retained his citizenship. His lands

NOTE. The above headpiece represents a potsherd bearing the name of Themistocles, which is scratched in the surface of this fragment of a pottery jar (*ostracon*, § 477). It was written there by some citizen of the six thousand who desired and secured his ostracism in 472 B.C., or may have served a similar purpose in the earlier but unsuccessful attempt to ostracize him.

336

were cultivated for him by slaves, and his only occupation was military drill and exercise. The State thus became a military machine.

The number of such Spartan soldier-citizens was quite limited, sometimes being all together only a few thousand. As distinguished from the large non-voting population of the other towns in the Laconian peninsula, the citizens of Sparta formed a small superior class. Thus their rule of the larger surrounding population was the tyranny of a limited military class devoted to war and almost without commerce or any interest in the arts and industries. So old-fashioned were they, and so confident in their own military power, that they would not surround their city with a wall (Fig. 178). Sparta remained a group of straggling villages, not deserving the name of city and entirely without fine public buildings or great monuments of any kind. Like a large military club or camp, it lived off its own slave-worked lands and from the taxes it squeezed out of its subject towns without allowing them any vote. In case of war the two kings (§ 478) were still the military leaders.

**521. Spartan soldier-citizens as a ruling class**

We can now understand that the stolid Spartans, wearing the fetters of a rigid military organization, and gifted with no imagination, looked with misgivings upon the larger world which was opening to Greek life. Although they desired to lead Greece in military power, they shrank from assuming the responsibilities of expansion. They represented the past and the privileges of the few. Athens represented the future and the rights of the many. Thus Greece fell into two camps as it were: Sparta (Fig. 178), the bulwark of tradition and limited privileges; Athens (Fig. 182), the champion of progress and the sovereign people. Thus the sentiment of union born in the common struggle for liberty, which might have united the Hellenes into one Greek nation, was followed by an unquenchable rivalry between the two leading states of Hellas, which went on for another century and finally cost the Greeks the supremacy of the ancient world.

**522. Conservative Sparta and progressive Athens**

FIG. 178. THE PLAIN WHERE ONCE SPARTA STOOD

The olive groves now grow where the Spartans once had their houses.
The town was not walled until long after the days of Spartan and
Greek power were over. From the mountains (nearly 8000 feet high)
behind the plain the visitor can see northeastward far beyond Athens,
almost to Eubœa; 100 miles northward to the mountains on the north
of the Corinthian Gulf (see map, p. 262); and 125 miles southward to
the island of Crete. This view shows also how Greece is cut up by
such mountains

**523. Themistocles and the fortification of Athens**    Themistocles was now the soul of Athens and her policy of
progress and expansion. He determined that Athens should no
longer follow Sparta. He cleverly hoodwinked the Spartans and,
in spite of their objections, completed the erection of strong

walls around a new and larger Athens. At the same time he fortified the Piræus, the Athenian port (see map, p. 352, and Fig. 177). When the Spartans, after the repulse of Persia, relinquished the command of the combined Greek fleets, the powerful Athenian fleet, the creation of Themistocles, was master of the Ægean.

## Section 52. The Rise of the Athenian Empire and the Triumph of Democracy

As the Greek cities of Asia still feared the vengeance of the Persian king, it was easy for the Athenians to form a permanent defensive league with the cities of their Greek kindred in Asia and the Ægean islands. The wealthier of these cities contributed ships, while others paid a sum of money each year into the treasury of the league. Athens was to have command of the combined fleet and collect the money. She placed in charge of the important task of adjusting all contributions of the league and collecting the tribute money a patriotic citizen named Aristides, whose friends called him "the Just" because of his honesty. He had opposed the naval plans of Themistocles and when defeated had been ostracized, but he had later distinguished himself at Salamis and Platæa. In spite of his former opposition to Themistocles' plans, he now did important service in vigorously aiding to establish the new naval league. The treasure he collected was placed for protection in the temple of Apollo, on the little island of Delos. Hence the federation was known as the Delian League. It was completed within three years after Salamis. The transformation of such a league into an empire, made up of states subject to Athens, could be foreseen as a very easy step (see map II, p. 346). All this was therefore viewed with increasing jealousy and distrust by Sparta.

*524. Establishment of the Delian League (478-477 B.C.)*

Under the leadership of Cimon, the son of Miltiades the hero of Marathon, the fleet of the league now drove the Persians entirely out of the region of the Hellespont. Cimon did not

*525. Rise of Cimon*

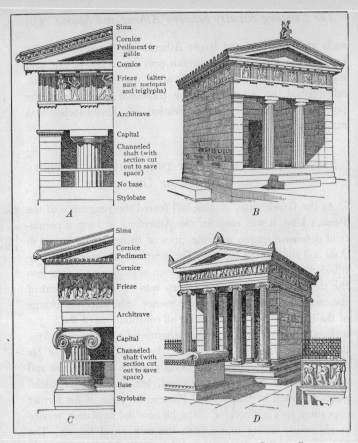

Sima
Cornice
Pediment or gable
Cornice
Frieze (alternate metopes and triglyphs)
Architrave
Capital
Channeled shaft (with section cut out to save space)
No base
Stylobate

*A*

*B*

Sima
Cornice
Pediment
Cornice
Frieze
Architrave
Capital
Channeled shaft (with section cut out to save space)
Base
Stylobate

*C*

*D*

COMPARATIVE DIAGRAM OF THE TWO LEADING GREEK STYLES OF
ARCHITECTURE, THE DORIC (*A* AND *B*) AND THE IONIC (*C* AND *D*)

The little Doric building (*B*) is the treasury of the Athenians at Delphi
(Fig. 172), containing their offerings of gratitude to Apollo. On the low
base at the left side of the building were placed the trophies from the
battle of Marathon. Over them on the walls are carved hymns to Apollo
with musical notes attached, the oldest musical notation surviving. The
beautiful Ionic building (*D*) is a restoration of the Temple of Victory on
the Athenian Acropolis (Fig. 183, *B*, and headpiece, p. 378). Contrast the
slender columns with the sturdier shafts of the Doric style, and it will be
seen that the Ionic order is a more delicate and graceful style. *A* and *C*
show details of both styles. (After Luckenbach)

340

understand the importance of Athenian supremacy in Greece, but favored a policy of friendship and alliance with Sparta. Hence political conflict arose at Athens over this question. Noble and wealthy and old-fashioned folk favored Cimon and friendship with Sparta, but progressive and modern Athenians followed Themistocles and his anti-Spartan plans.

Themistocles was unable to win the Assembly; he was ostracized (headpiece, p. 336), and at length, on false charges of treason, he was condemned and obliged to flee for his life. The greatest statesman in Athenian history spent the rest of his life in the service of the Persian king, and he never again saw the city he had saved from the Persians and made mistress of an empire.

**526.** Fall of Themistocles (472–471 B.C.)

In a final battle Cimon crushed the Persian navy in the west (468 B.C.), and returned to Athens covered with glory. In response to a request from the Spartans for help in quelling a revolt among their own subjects, Cimon urged the dispatch of troops to Sparta. Herein Cimon overestimated the good feeling of the Spartans toward Athens; for in spite of the continuance of the revolt, the Spartans after a time curtly demanded the withdrawal of the very Athenian troops they had asked for. Stung by this rebuff, to which Cimon's friendly policy toward Sparta had exposed them, the Athenians voted to ostracize Cimon (461 B.C.).

**527.** Fall of Cimon

The overthrow of Cimon was a victory of the people against the nobles. They followed it up by attacking the Council of Elders, once made up only of nobles (§ 431). It was called the Areopagus and used to meet on a hill of that name by the market place (Fig. 182, and plan, p. 352). The people now passed new laws restricting the power of the Areopagus to the trial of murder cases and the settlement of questions of state religion, thus completely depriving it of all political power. Meantime a more popular council of five hundred members had grown up and gained the power to conduct most of the government business. This it did by dividing itself into ten

**528.** Overthrow of the Council of the Areopagus; leadership of the popular council and the citizen-juries

groups of fifty each, each group serving a little over a month once a year. At the same time the citizen-juries introduced by Solon as a court of appeal (§ 470) were enlarged until they contained six thousand jurors divided into smaller juries, usually of five hundred and one each. Such a jury was really a group or court of temporary judges deciding cases brought before them. The poorest citizens could not afford to leave their work to serve on these juries, and so the people passed laws granting pay for jury service. These citizen-courts were at last so powerful that they formed the final lawmaking body in the State, and, in coöperation with the Assembly, they made the laws. The people were indeed in control.

**529.** Office of archon open to all except laboring class

Furthermore, the right to hold office was greatly extended. All citizens were permitted to hold the office of archon except members of the laboring class entirely without property. With one exception there was no longer any *election* of the higher officers, but they were now all *chosen by lot* from the whole body of eligible citizens. The result was that the men holding the once influential positions in the State were now mere chance "nobodies" and hence completely without influence. But at the same time the public services now rendered by so large a number of citizens were a means of education and of very profitable experience. Athens was gaining a more intelligent body of citizens than any other ancient state.

**530.** Political power still possible to the elective *strategus*

There was one kind of officer whom it was impossible to choose by lot, and that was the military commander (*strategus*). This important office remained elective and thus open to men of ability and influence, into whose hands the direction of affairs naturally fell. There were ten of these generals, one for each of the ten tribes established by Clisthenes (§ 476), and they not only led the army in war but they also managed the war department of the government, had large control of the government treasury and of the Empire, including foreign affairs. The leader, or president, of this body of generals was the most powerful man in the State, and his office was elective. It thus

FIG. 179. THE PNYX, THE ATHENIAN PLACE OF ASSEMBLY

The speakers' platform with its three steps is immediately in the fore-ground. The listening Athenian citizens of the Assembly sat on the ground now sloping away to the left, but at that time probably level. The ground they occupied was inclosed by a semicircular wall, begin-ning at the further end of the straight wall seen here on the right, extending then to the left, and returning to the straight wall again behind our present point of view (see semicircle on plan, p. 352). This was an open-air House of Commons, where, however, the citizen did not send a representative but came and voted himself as he was influenced from this platform by great Athenian leaders, like Themis-tocles, Pericles, or Demosthenes. Note the Acropolis and the Parthe-non, to which we look eastward from the Pnyx (see plan, p. 352). The Areopagus is just out of range on the left (see Fig. 182)

became more and more possible for a noble with military train-ing to make himself a strong and influential leader, and if he was a man of persuasive eloquence, to lay out a definite series of plans for the nation, and by his oratory to induce the Assembly of the Athenian citizens on the Pnyx (Fig. 179) to accept them.

**531. The leadership of Pericles**

After the fall of Cimon there came forward a handsome and brilliant young Athenian named Pericles, a descendant of one of the old noble families of the line of Clisthenes. He desired to build up the splendid Athenian Empire of which Themistocles had dreamed. He put himself at the head of the party of progress and of increased power of the people. He kept their confidence year after year, and thus secured his continued reëlection as strategus. The result was that he became the actual head of the State in power, or, as we might say, he was the undisputed political "boss" of Athens from about 460 B.C. until his untimely death over thirty years later.

## SECTION 53. COMMERCIAL DEVELOPMENT AND THE OPENING OF THE STRUGGLE BETWEEN ATHENS AND SPARTA

**532. Commercial supremacy of the Greeks after the Persian wars; rise of Piræus, the new port of Athens**

A period of commercial prosperity followed the Persian wars, which gave the Greeks a leadership in trade like that of the English before the Great War of 1914. Corinth and the little island of Ægina at the front door of Attica, and visible from Athens (Fig. 177), rapidly became the most flourishing trading cities in Greece. They were at once followed, however, by the little harbor town of Piræus (Fig. 177), built by the foresight of Themistocles as the port of Athens. Along its busy docks were moored Greek ships from all over the Mediterranean world, for the defeat of the Phœnicians in East and West had broken up their merchant fleets and thrown much of their trade into the hands of the Greeks. Here many a Greek ship from the Black Sea, laden with grain or fish, moored alongside the grain ships of Egypt and the mixed cargoes from Syracuse. For Attica was no longer producing food enough for her own need, and it was necessary to import it. The docks were piled high with goods from the Athenian factories, and long lines of perspiring porters were loading them into ships bound for all the harbors of the Mediterranean. Scores of battleships stretched far along the shores, and the busy shipyards and dry docks were filled with multitudes of workmen and noisy with the sound of many hammers.

In spite of much progress in navigation, we must not think of these ancient ships of Greece as very large. A merchant vessel carrying from two hundred and fifty to three hundred tons was considered large in fifth-century Greece (contrast Fig. 61). Moreover, the Greek ships still clung timidly to the shore, and they rarely ventured to sea in the stormy winter season. They had no compass or charts, there were no light-houses, and they were often plundered by pirates, so that commerce was still carried on at great risks. Moreover, ships did not last as long as with us, because the Greeks had no oil paint and the Egyptian invention of painting with hot wax was probably too expensive.

**533.** Limitations of navigation and shipbuilding

On the other hand, the profits gained from sea-borne commerce might be very large. A vessel which reached the north shores of the Black Sea or the pirate-infested Adriatic might sell out its cargo so profitably as to bring back to the owner double the first cost of the goods, after paying all expenses. Plenty of men were therefore willing to risk their capital in such ventures, and indeed many borrowed the money to do so. Interest was lower than in Solon's day, and money could be borrowed at 10 and 12 per cent. The returns from manufacturing industry were also high, even reaching 30 per cent.

**534.** Profits from commerce and industry

To measure this increased prosperity of Athens we must not apply the scale of modern business. A fortune of ten thousand dollars was looked upon as considerable, while double that amount was accounted great wealth. The day laborer's wages were from six to ten cents a day, while the skilled craftsman received as much as twenty cents a day. Greek soldiers were ready to furnish their own arms and enter the ranks of any foreign king at five dollars a month. Men of intellect, like an architect, received only from twenty to thirty cents a day, while the tuition for a course in rhetoric lasting several years cost the student from sixty to eighty dollars.

**535.** Wealth and wages

For nearly thirty years after the Persian wars it was easy to obtain Athenian citizenship. Some thirty thousand strangers therefore soon settled in Athens to share in its prosperity. Its population rose to above a hundred thousand in the days of Pericles (cf. § 461), while the inhabitants of Attica numbered over two hundred thousand. This included probably eighty thousand slaves, still the cheapest form of labor obtainable.

As a result of increased business the volume of money in Athens had also greatly increased. The silver tribute (§ 524) and the Attic silver mines furnished metal for additional coinage. In all the markets of the Mediterranean, Athenian silver money was the leading coin, and many Persian darics of gold (worth about five dollars) also came in. Just as with us, as money became more plentiful its value decreased, and a given sum would not buy as much as formerly. That is to say, prices went up. A measure of barley cost twice as much, and a sheep five times as much, as in Solon's day (§ 459). Nevertheless living would be called very cheap from our point of view. Even the well-to-do citizen did not spend over ten or twelve cents a day in food for his family, and a man of wealth was very extravagant if he owned furniture to the amount of two hundred dollars.

**538.** Cost of
government:
salaries,
temples,
and religious
services

Money had now become very necessary in carrying on the government. Formerly service to the State had been without pay. This was quite possible in a nation of peasants and shepherds; but with the incoming of coined money and steady employment in factories, it was no longer possible for a private citizen to give his time to the State for nothing. Many a citizen of Athens bought the bread his family needed for the day with the money he had earned the day before. The daily salaries to thousands of jurymen (§ 528) and to the members of the Council of Five Hundred, who were also paid, amounted to not less than a hundred thousand dollars a year. Large sums, even sums that would be large to-day, were also required for building the sumptuous marble temples now

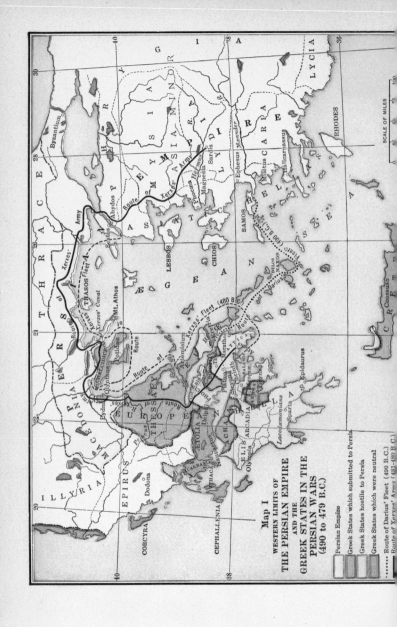

Map I

WESTERN LIMITS OF
THE PERSIAN EMPIRE
AND THE
GREEK STATES IN THE
PERSIAN WARS
(490 to 479 B.C.)

Persian Empire

Greek States which submitted to Persia

Greek States hostile to Persia

Greek States which were neutral

......... Route of Darius' Fleet (490 B.C.)
—·—·— Route of Xerxes' Army (481–480 B.C.)

SCALE OF MILES

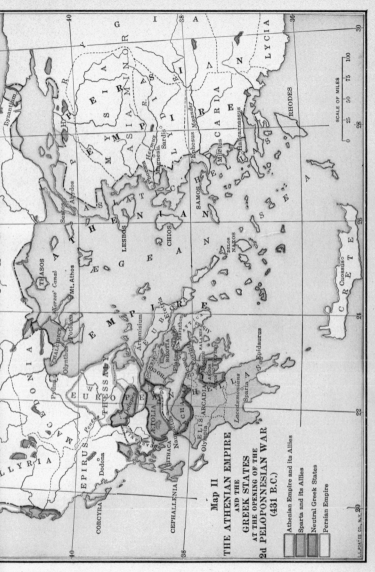

Map II
THE ATHENIAN EMPIRE
AND THE
GREEK STATES
AT THE OPENING OF THE
2d PELOPONNESIAN WAR
(431 B.C.)

Athenian Empire and its Allies
Sparta and its Allies
Neutral Greek States
Persian Empire

SCALE OF MILES
0  25  50  75  100

SEQUENCE MAP SHOWING WESTERN LIMITS OF THE PERSIAN EMPIRE AND THE GREEK STATES FROM THE PERSIAN WARS (BEGINNING 490 B.C.) TO THE BEGINNING OF THE SECOND PELOPONNESIAN WAR (431 B.C.)

frequently dedicated to the gods; while the offerings, feasts, and celebrations at these temples also consumed great sums.

Greater than all the other expenses of the State, however, was the cost of war. The cost of arming citizens who could not undertake this expense themselves and of feeding the army in the field, of course, fell upon the State. The war fleet was, however, the heaviest of all such expenses. Besides the first cost of building and equipping the battleships, there was always the further expense of maintaining them. A trireme, manned with about two hundred sailors and oarsmen, receiving daily half a drachma (nearly ten cents) per man, cost nearly six hundred dollars per month. A fleet of two hundred triremes therefore required nearly a hundred and twenty thousand dollars a month for wages.

539. Cost of government: war

The problem of securing the funds for maintaining and defending a nation had become a grave one. As for Athens, the Attic silver mines, however helpful, were far from furnishing enough to support the government. The bulk of the State funds had to be raised by taxation. The triumphant democracy disliked periodic taxes, and they assessed taxes only when the treasury was very low, especially in war time. Besides taxes the treasury received a good income from the customs duty on all goods imported or exported through Piræus. The Athenians kept these duties low, assessing only one per cent of the value of the goods until forced by war expenses to raise them. We have already mentioned the contributions (tribute) of the subject states of the empire (§ 524). The total income of the Athenian State hardly reached three quarters of a million dollars in the days of Pericles.

540. Income of the State: mines, taxes, customs duties

Small as this seems to us of modern times, no other Greek state could raise anything like such an annual income. Least of all could Sparta hope to rival such resources. Without the enterprise to enter the new world of commercial competition, Sparta clung to her old ways. She still issued only her ancient iron money and had no silver coins. To be sure, the standing

541. Sparta financially inferior to Athens

army of Sparta was always ready without expense to the government (§ 520); but when she led forth the combined armies of the Peloponnesian League, she could not bear the expense longer than a few weeks. The still greater expense of a large war fleet was quite impossible either for Sparta or her League. In so far as war was a matter of money, the commercial growth of Athens was giving her a constantly growing superiority over all other Greek states. We can understand then with what jealousy and fear Sparta viewed Athenian prosperity.

**542. New defenses of Athens; Long Walls**

Pericles had won favor with the people by favoring a policy of hostility to Sparta (§ 525). Foreseeing the coming struggle with Sparta, Pericles greatly strengthened the defenses of Athens by inducing the people to connect the fortifications of the city with those of the Piræus harbor by two Long Walls, thus forming a road completely walled in, connecting Athens and her harbor (plan, p. 352).

**543. First war between Athens and Sparta (459–446 B.C.)**

Not long after Pericles gained the leadership of the people, the inevitable war with Sparta broke out. It lasted nearly fifteen years, with varying fortunes on both sides. The Athenian merchants resented the keen commercial rivalry of Ægina, planted as the flourishing island was at the very front door of Attica (see map, p. 352). They finally captured the island after a long siege. Pericles likewise employed the Athenian navy in blockading for years the merchant fleets of the other great rival of Athens and friend of Sparta, Corinth (Fig. 163), and thus brought financial ruin on its merchants.

**544. War with Persia; the Egyptian expedition**

At the same time Athens dispatched a fleet of two hundred ships to assist Egypt, which had revolted against Persia. The Athenians were thus fighting both Sparta and Persia for years. The entire Athenian fleet in Egypt was lost. This loss so weakened the Athenian navy that the treasury of the Delian League was no longer safe in the little island of Delos, against a possible sea raid by the Persians. Pericles therefore shifted the treasury from Delos to Athens, an act which made the city more than ever the capital of an Athenian empire.

When peace was concluded (445 B.C.) all that Athens was able to retain was the island of Ægina, though at the same time she gained control of the large island of Eubœa. It was agreed that the peace should continue for thirty years. Thus ended what is often called the First Peloponnesian War with the complete exhaustion of Athens as well as of her enemies in the Peloponnesus. Pericles had not shown himself a great naval or military commander in this war. The Athenians had also arranged a peace with Persia, over forty years after Marathon. But the rivalry between Athens and Sparta for the leadership of the Greeks was still unsettled. The struggle was to be continued in another long and weary Peloponnesian War. Before we proceed with the story of this fatal struggle we must glance briefly at the new and glorious Athens now growing up under the leadership of Pericles.

**545. Peace with Sparta and Persia**

## QUESTIONS

SECTION 51. Describe the Spartan State. What can you say of the reasons for rivalry between Athens and Sparta? What did Themistocles now do?

SECTION 52. What combination did Athens now make with the eastern Greek cities? What part did Aristides play? To what might the Delian League easily lead? What policy did Cimon favor? What was Themistocles' attitude toward Cimon's policy? What then happened to Themistocles? to Cimon? What new victories did the people gain? What new council arose, and how did it govern? How could a statesman still hold the leadership? Who now became the leader of the people's party?

SECTION 53. What happened to Greek business after the Persian War? Discuss navigation; business profits. What can you say of the scale of values as compared with to-day? What happened to the population of Athens? How were prices affected? What were the chief expenses of the Athenian State? its chief sources of income? Could other states raise as much? Sketch the First Peloponnesian War.

## CHAPTER XV

### ATHENS IN THE AGE OF PERICLES

#### SECTION 54. SOCIETY, THE HOME, EDUCATION AND TRAINING OF YOUNG CITIZENS

**546. Athenian society: the wealthy classes**

As we have seen, the population of Attica was made up of citizens, foreigners, and slaves. In a mixed crowd there would usually be among every ten people about four slaves, one or two foreigners, and the rest free Athenians (see § 536). A large group of wealthy citizens lived at Athens upon the income from their lands. They continued to be the aristocracy of the nation, for land was still the most respectable form of wealth. The wealthy manufacturer hastened to buy land and join the landed aristocracy. The social position of his family might thus become an influential one, but it could not compare with that of a noble.

NOTE. The above headpiece gives us a glimpse into the house of a bride the day after the wedding. At the right, leaning against a couch, is the bride. Before her are two young friends, one sitting, the other standing, both playing with a tame bird. Another friend approaches carrying a tall and beautiful painted vase as a wedding gift. At the left a visitor arranges flowers in two painted vases, while another lady, adjusting her garment, is looking on. The walls are hung with festive wreaths. The furniture of such a house was usually of wood, but if the owner's wealth permitted, it was adorned with ivory, silver, and gold. It consisted chiefly of beds, like the couch above, chairs (see also Fig. 170), foot-stools (as at foot of couch above), small individual tables, and clothing chests which took the place of closets.

350

On the other hand, anyone who actually performed manual labor was looked down upon as without social station. Athens was a great beehive of skilled craftsmen and small shopkeepers. These classes were beginning to organize into guilds or unions of masons, carpenters, potters, jewelers, and many others — organizations somewhat like our labor unions. Below them was an army of unskilled laborers, free men, but little better than slaves, like the army of porters who swarmed along the docks at Piræus. All these classes contained many citizens. Nevertheless the majority of the Athenian citizens were still the farmers and peasants throughout Attica, although the Persian devastation (§§ 512, 516) had seriously reduced the amount of land still cultivated.

The hasty rebuilding of Athens after the Persians had burned it did not produce any noticeable changes in the houses, nor were there any of great size or splendor. Since the appearance of the first European houses (§ 26) many thousand years had passed, but there were still no beautiful houses anywhere in Europe, such as we found on the Nile (Fig. 51). The one-story front of even a wealthy man's house was simply a blank wall, usually of sun-dried brick, rarely of broken stone masonry. Often without any windows, it showed no other opening than the door, but a house of two stories might have a small window or two in the upper story. The door led into a court open to the sky and surrounded by a porch with columns. Here in the mild climate of Greece the family could spend much of their time as in a sitting room. In the middle stood an altar of the household Zeus, the protector of the family; while around the court opened a number of doors leading to a living room, sleeping rooms, dining room, storerooms, and also a tiny kitchen.

This Greek house lacked all conveniences. There was no chimney, and the smoke from the kitchen fire, though intended to drift up through a hole in the roof, choked the room or floated out the door. In winter gusty drafts filled the house, for many doorways were without doors, and glass in the form of flat panes for the windows was still unknown. In the mild Greek climate, however, a pan of burning charcoal, called a brazier, furnished enough heat to temper the chilly air of a room. Lacking windows, the ground-floor rooms depended entirely on the doors opening on the court for light. At night the dim light of an olive-oil lamp was all that was available. There was no plumbing or piping of any kind in the house, no drainage, and consequently no sanitary arrangements. The water supply was brought in jars by slaves from the nearest well or flowing spring.

**550. Decoration and equipment**

The floors were simply of dirt, with a surface of pebbles tramped and beaten hard. There was no oil paint, and a plain water-color wash, such as we call calcimine, might be used on the inside, but if used on the outside would soon wash off, exposing the mud brick. The simplicity and bareness of the house itself were in noticeable contrast with the beautiful furniture which the Greek craftsmen were now producing (headpiece, p. 350; see also the beautiful chairs in Fig. 170). There were many metal utensils, among which the ladies' hand mirrors of polished bronze were common; and most numerous of all were lovely painted jars, vases, and dishes, along with less pretentious pottery forming the household "crockery." For it will be remembered that Greek pottery was the most beautiful ever produced by ancient man (Fig. 164, and headpiece, p. 350).

**551. Streets of Athens**

The view from the Acropolis over the sea of low flat roofs disclosed not a single chimney, but revealed a much larger city than formerly. Though not laid out in blocks, the city was about ten modern city blocks wide and several more in length. The streets were merely lanes or alleys, narrow and crooked, winding between the bare mud-brick walls of the low houses standing wall to wall. There was no pavement, nor any sidewalk, and a stroll through the town after a rain meant wading through the mud. All household rubbish and garbage was thrown directly into the street, and there was no system of sewage. When one passed a two-story house he might hear a

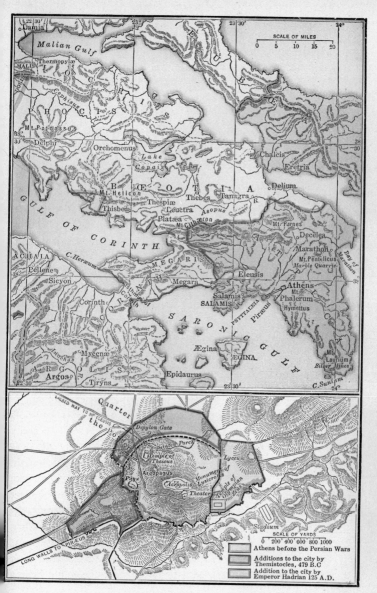

CENTRAL GREECE AND ATHENS

warning cry, and spring out of the way barely in time to escape being deluged with sweepings or filth thrown from a second-story window. The few wells and fountains fed by city water pipes did not furnish enough water to flush the streets, and there was no system of street cleaning. During the hot summers of the south, therefore, Athens was not a healthful place of residence.

All Athens lived out of doors. Athenian life was beautifully simple and unpretentious, especially since richly embroidered and colored oriental garments had passed away. Almost all citizens now appeared in the simple white garments which we of modern times have come to associate with the classical Greeks. Gorgeous costume thus disappeared in Greece, as it did among *us* in the days of our great great-grandfathers. Nevertheless, the man of elegant habits gained a practiced hand in draping his costume, and was proud of the gracefulness and the sweeping lines with which he could arrange its folds (Fig. 180).

The women were less inclined to give up the old finery, for unhappily they had little to think about but clothes and housekeeping (Fig. 170). For Greek citizens still kept their wives in the background, and

552. Costume of men

FIG. 180. STATUE OF THE TRAGIC POET SOPHOCLES

The great poet stands in thoughtful repose in an attitude of ease, which incidentally reveals the wonderful beauty of a well-draped Greek costume (§ 552). The figure is probably our most beautiful Greek portrait, and as a work of art illustrates the sculpture of the fourth century B.C., almost a century after Pericles

553. Women

they were more than ever mere housekeepers. They had no share in the intellectual life of the men, could not appear at their social meetings, where serious conversation was carried on; nor were they permitted to witness the athletic games at Olympia. Their position was even worse than in the Age of the Tyrants (§ 480), and a poetess like Sappho never appeared again among the later Greeks.

**554. Child-hood and school**

The usual house had no garden and the children therefore played in the court, running about with toy cart and dog or enjoying a swing at the hands of the nurse. There were no schools for the girls, but when the boy was old enough he was sent to school in charge of an old slave called a "pedagogue" (paidagogos), which really means "leader of a child." He carried the boy's books and outfit. There were no schools maintained by the state and no schoolhouses. School was conducted in his own house by some poor citizen, who had perhaps lost his means, or by some other poor person, perhaps an old soldier or even a foreigner. In any case the teacher was much looked down upon. He received his pay from the parents; but there was a board of state officials appointed to look after the schools and to see that nothing improper was taught.

**555. Subjects taught at school**

Without special education for his work, the teacher merely taught the old-time subjects he had learned in his own youth without change (§ 480). Proficiency in music was regarded very seriously by the Greeks, not merely for entertainment but also and chiefly as an influence toward good conduct. Besides learning to read and write as of old (§ 480 and Fig. 181), the pupil learned by heart many passages from the old poets, and here and there a boy with a good memory could repeat the entire Iliad and Odyssey. On the other hand, the boys still escaped all instruction in mathematics, geography, or natural science. This was doubtless a welcome exemption, for the masters were severe, and the Greek boy hated both school and schoolmaster.

When the Athenian lad reached the age of eighteen years and left school, he was received as a citizen, providing that both his parents were of Athenian citizenship. The oath which

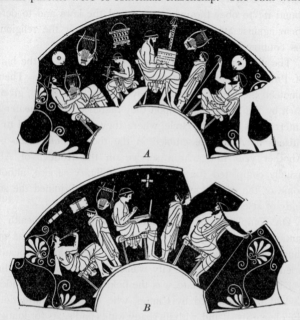

FIG. 181. AN ATHENIAN SCHOOL IN THE AGE OF PERICLES

These scenes are painted around the center of a shallow bowl, hence their peculiar shape. In *A* we see at the left a music teacher seated at his lyre, giving a lesson to the lad seated before him. In the middle sits a teacher of reading and literature, holding an open roll (Fig. 223) from which the boy standing before him is learning a poem. Behind the boy sits a slave (pedagogue) (§ 554) who brought him to school and carried his books. In *B* we have at the left a singing lesson, aided by the flute to fix the tones. In the middle the master sits correcting an exercise handed him by the boy standing before him, while behind the boy sits the slave (pedagogue) as before

he took was a solemn reminder of the obligations he now assumed. It had been composed by Solon, and it called upon the youth " never to disgrace his sacred arms; never to forsake his comrade in the ranks, but to fight for the sacred temples and the common welfare, whether alone or with others; to leave his country not in a worse, but in a better state than he found it; to obey the magistrates and the laws and to defend them against attack; finally to hold in honor the religion of his country."

**557. Incoming citizens' military service**

The youth then spent a year in garrison duty at the harbor of Piræus, where he was put through military drill. Then at nineteen the young recruits received spear and shield, given to each by the State. Thereupon they marched to the theater and entered the orchestra circle, where they were presented to the citizens of Athens assembled in the theater before the play. Another year of garrison service on the frontier of Attica usually completed the young man's military service, although some of the recruits, whose means permitted, joined the small body of select Athenian cavalry.

**558. Athletic grounds: Academy and Lyceum**

On completion of his military service, if the wealth and station of his family permitted, the Athenian youth was more than ever devoted to the new athletic fields in the beautiful open country outside the city walls. On the north of Athens, outside the Dipylon Gate, was the field known as the Academy. It had been adorned by Cimon, who gave great attention to the olive groves, and, with its shady walks and seats for loungers, it became a place where the Athenians loved to spend their idle hours. On the east of the city there was another similar athletic ground known as the Lyceum. The later custom of holding courses of instructive lectures in these places (§ 759) finally resulted in giving to the words "academy" and "lyceum" the associations which they now possess for us.

**559. The athletic events of the Greeks**

The chief events were boxing, wrestling, running, jumping, casting the javelin, and throwing the disk. Omitting the boxing, the remaining events formed a fivefold match called the *pentathlon*, which it was a great honor to win at Olympia. The earliest contest established at Olympia seems to have been a two-hundred-yard dash, which the Greeks called a *stadion*, that is, six hundred Greek feet. Many other contests were added to this, and in the age of Pericles, boxing, or boxing and wrestling combined, the pentathlon, chariot racing, and horseback races made up a program in which all Greek youths were anxious to gain distinction (§ 479). A generation later some of the philosophers severely criticized the Greeks for giving far too much of their time and attention to athletic pursuits.

But other pastimes less worthy were common. An hour or two of gossip with his friends in the market place often preceded the Greek youth's daily visit to the athletic grounds. The afternoon might be passed in dawdling about in the barber shop or dropping in at some drinking resort to shake dice or venture a few drachmas in other games of chance. As the shadows lengthened in the market place he frequently joined a company of young men at dinner at the house of a friend. Often followed by heavy drinking of wine and much singing with the lyre, such a dinner might break up in a drunken carouse leading to harum-scarum escapades upon the streets, that in our time would cause the arrest of the company for disorderly conduct.

**560. Social and other diversions**

## Section 55. Higher Education, Science, and the Training gained by State Service

On the other hand, there were serious-minded men, to whom such dinners meant delightful conversation with their companions on art, literature, music, or personal conduct. Such life among the Athenians had now been quickened by the appearance of more modern private teachers called Sophists, a class of new and clever-witted lecturers who wandered from city to city. Many a bright youth who had finished his music, reading, and writing at the old-fashioned private school (§ 554) annoyed his father by insisting that such schooling was not enough and by demanding money to pay for a course of lectures delivered by one of these new teachers.

**561. Coming of the Sophists**

**562. Higher education offered by the Sophists**

For the first time a higher education was thus open to young men who had hitherto thought of little more than a victory in the Olympic games or a fine appearance when parading with the crack cavalry of Athens. The appearance of these new teachers therefore marked a new age in the history of the Greeks, but especially in that of Athens. In the first place, the Sophists recognized the importance of effective public speaking in addressing the large citizen juries (§ 528) or in speaking before the Assembly of the people. The Sophists therefore taught rhetoric and oratory with great success, and many a father who had no gift of speech had the pleasure of seeing his son a practiced public speaker. It was through the teaching of the Sophists also that the first successful writing of Greek prose began. At the same time they really founded the study of language, which was yet to become grammar (§ 753). They also taught mathematics and astronomy, and the young men of Athens for the first time began to learn a little natural science. Thus the truths which Greek philosophers had begun to observe in the days of Thales (§§ 492–493) were, after a century and a half, beginning to spread among the people.

**563. The intellectual revolution; chasm between young and old**

In these new ideas the fathers were unable to follow their sons. When a father of that day found in the hands of his son a book by one of the great Sophists, which began with a statement doubting the existence of the gods, the new teachings seemed impious. The old-fashioned citizen could at least vote for the banishment of such impious teachers and the burning of their books, although he heard that they were read aloud in the houses of the greatest men of Athens. Indeed, some of the leading Sophists were friends of Pericles, who stepped in and tried to help them when they were prosecuted for their teachings. The revolution which had taken place in the mind of Thales (§ 495) was now taking place in the minds of ever-increasing numbers of Greeks, and the situation was yet to grow decidedly worse in the opinion of old-fashioned folk.

In spite of the spread of knowledge due to the Sophists, the average Athenian's acquaintance with science was still very limited. This gave him great trouble in the measurement of time. He still called the middle of the forenoon the "time of full market," and the Egyptian shadow clock in the market place had not yet led him to speak of an hour of the day by *number*, as the Egyptians had been doing for a thousand years. When it was necessary to limit the length of a citizen's speech before the law-court, it was done by allowing him to speak as long as it took a given measure of water to run out of a jar with a small hole in it. The Greeks still used the moon-months, and they were accustomed to insert an extra month every third, fifth, and eighth year (§ 150). To be sure, they had often seen on the Pnyx, where the Assembly met (Fig. 179), a strange-looking tablet bearing a new calendar, set up by a builder and engineer named Meton. This man had computed the length of the year with only half an hour's error. He had then devised his new calendar with a year still made up of moon-months, but so cleverly arranged that the last day of the last moon-month in every nineteenth year would also be the last day of the year as measured by the sun. But all this was quite beyond the average citizen's puzzled mind. The archons too shook their heads at it and would have nothing to do with it. The old inconvenient, inaccurate moon-month calendar, with three thirteen-month years in every eight years, was quite good enough for them and continued in use.

Individual scientists continued to make important discoveries. One of them now taught that the sun was a glowing mass of stone "larger than the Peloponnesus." He maintained also that the moon received its light from the sun, that it had mountains and valleys like the earth, and that it was inhabited by living creatures. Travel was difficult, for there were no passenger ships. Except rough carts or wagons, there were no conveyances by land. The roads were bad, and the traveler went on foot or rode a horse. Nevertheless, Greeks

**564.** Lack of general knowledge of science shown in time measurement

**565.** Progress of astronomy and geography

with means were now beginning to travel more frequently. This, however, was for information; travel for pleasure was still a century and a half in the future. From long journeys in Egypt, and other Eastern countries, Herodotus returned with much information regarding these lands. His map (p. 360) showed that the Red Sea connected with the Indian Ocean, a fact unknown to his predecessor Hecatæus (see map, p. 319).

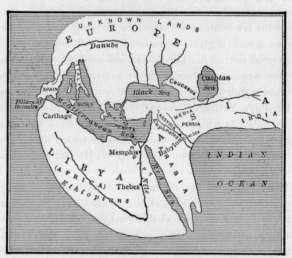

MAP OF THE WORLD ACCORDING TO HERODOTUS

The scientists were still much puzzled by the cold of the north and the warmth of the south, a curious difference which they could not yet explain.

**566. Progress in medicine**

Although without the microscope or the assistance of chemistry, medicine nevertheless made progress. In the first place, the Greek physicians rejected the older belief that disease was caused by evil demons, and endeavored to find the *natural causes* of the ailment. To do this they sought to understand the organs of the body. They had already discovered that the brain was the organ of thought, but the arterial system, the circulation of the blood, and the nervous system were still entirely unknown. Without a knowledge of the circulation of the blood, surgery was unable to attempt amputation, but otherwise it made much progress. The greatest physician of the time was Hippocrates, and he became the founder of scientific medicine. The fame of Greek medicine was such that the Persian king called a Greek physician to his court.

Just at the close of Pericles' life, in the midst of national calamities, the historian Herodotus, who had long been at work on his history, finally published his great work. It was a history of the world so told that the glorious leadership of Athens would be clear to all Greeks and would show them that to her the Hellenes owed their deliverance from Persia. Throughout Greece it created a deep impression, and so tremendous was its effect in Athens that, in spite of the financial drain of war, the Athenians voted Herodotus a reward of ten talents, some twelve thousand dollars. In this earliest history of the world which has come down to us, Herodotus traced the course of events as he believed them to be directed by the will of the gods, and as prophesied in their divine oracles. There was little or no effort to explain historical events as the result of natural processes.

567. Progress in history writing; Herodotus

Besides the instruction received from the Sophists by many young men, their constant share in public affairs was giving them an experience which greatly assisted in producing an intelligent body of citizens. In the Council of Five Hundred, citizens learned to carry on the daily business of the government. On some days also as many as six thousand citizens might be serving as jurors (§ 528). This service alone meant that one citizen in five was engaged in duties which sharpened his wits and gave him some training in legal and business affairs. At the same time such duties kept constantly in the citizen's mind his obligations toward the State and community.

568. Education and discipline gained from State service

This led many citizens to surprisingly generous contributions. It was not uncommon for a citizen to undertake the entire

**569. Voluntary contributions by citizens**

equipment of a warship except the hull and spars, though this service may have been compulsory. At national festivals a wealthy man would sometimes furnish a costly dinner for all the members of his "tribe." The choruses for public performances, especially at the theater, were organized by private citizens, who paid for their training and for their costumes at great expense (Fig. 190). We know of one citizen who spent in the voluntary support of feasts and choruses in nine years no less than fourteen thousand dollars, a considerable fortune in those days.

**570. State feasts**

Public festivals maintained by the State also played an important part in the lives of all Athenians. Every spring at the ancient Feast of Dionysus (§ 483) the greatest play-writers each submitted three tragedies and a comedy to be played in the theater for a prize given by the State. All Athens streamed to the theater to see them. Many other State festivals, celebrated with music and gayety, filled the year with holidays so numerous that they fell every six or seven days. The great State feast, called the *Panathenæa*, occurred every four years. A brilliant procession made up of the smart young Athenian cavalry, groups of dignified government officials, priests and sacrificial animals, marched with music and rejoicing across the market place, carrying a beautiful new robe embroidered by the women of Athens for the goddess Athena. The procession marched to the Acropolis, where the robe was delivered to the goddess amid splendid sacrifices and impressive ceremonies. Contests in music and in athletic games, war dances and a regatta in the channel off Salamis, served to furnish entertainment for the multitude which flocked to Athens for the great feast.

## SECTION 56. ART AND LITERATURE

**571. The higher life of imperial Athens; the glorified State**

Although the first fifteen years of the leadership of Pericles were burdened with the Spartan and Persian wars, the higher life of Athens continued to unfold. Under influences like those we have been discussing, a new vision of the glory of the State, discerned nowhere else in the world before this age, caught the imagination of poet and painter, of sculptor and architect; and not of these alone, but also of the humblest artisan and tradesman, as all classes alike took part in the common life of the community. Music, the drama, art, and architecture were profoundly inspired by this new and exalted vision of the State, and the citizen found great works of art so inspired thrust into the foreground of his life.

We can still follow the Athenian citizen and note a few of the noble monuments that met his eye as he went about the new Athens which Pericles was creating. When he wandered into the market place and stood chatting with his friends under the shade of the plane trees, he found at several points colonnaded porches looking out upon the market. One of these, which had been presented to the city by Cimon's family, was called the "Painted Porch"; for the wall behind the columns bore paintings by Polygnotus, an artist from one of the island possessions of Athens, a gift of the painter to the Athenians, depicting their glorious victory at Marathon. Here in splendid panorama was a vision of the heroic devotion of the fathers. In the thick of the fray the citizen might pick out the figure of Themistocles, of Miltiades, of Callimachus, who fell in the battle, of Æschylus the great tragic poet. He could see the host of the fleeing Persians and perhaps hear some old man tell how the brother of Æschylus seized and tried to stop one of the Persian boats drawn up on the beach, and how a desperate Persian raised his ax and slashed off the hand of the brave Greek. Perhaps among the group of eager listeners he noticed one questioning the veteran carefully and making full notes of all that he could learn from the graybeard. The questioner was Herodotus, collecting from survivors the tale of the Persian wars for his great history (§ 567).

Behind the citizen rose a low hill, known as "Market Hill," around which were grouped plain, bare government buildings. Here were the assembly rooms of the Areopagus (§ 528) and

**572. Painting**

**573. Lack of fine buildings for government offices**

FIG. 182. THE SO-CALLED TEMPLE OF THESEUS, THE AREOPAGUS, AND THE ACROPOLIS OF ATHENS *

**the** Council of Five Hundred. The Council's Committee of Fifty (§ 528), carrying on the current business of the government, also had its offices here. The citizen recalled how, as a member of this Council, he had lived here for over a month while serving on that committee and had taken his meals in the building before him, at the expense of the State, along with the Athenian victors in the Olympic games and other deserving citizens who were thus pensioned by the government. In spite of the growing sentiment for the glory of the State, these plain buildings, like the Athenian houses, were all built of sun-dried mud brick or, at most, of rough rubble. The idea of great and beautiful buildings for the offices of the government was still unknown in the Mediterranean world, and no such building yet existed in Europe.

The sentiment toward the State was so mingled with reverence for the gods who protected the State that patriotism was itself a deeply religious feeling. Hence the great public buildings of Greece were temples and not quarters for the offices of the government. As the citizen turned from the Painted Porch, therefore, he might observe crossing the market

574. The great State buildings are temples

* In this view we stand inside the wall of Themistocles, near the Dipylon Gate in the Potters' Quarter (see plan, p. 352). In the foreground is the temple of Theseus, the legendary unifier of Attica, whom all Athenians honored as a god and to whom this temple was long supposed (perhaps wrongly) to have been erected. It is built of Pentelic marble and was finished a few years after the death of Pericles; but now, after twenty-three hundred years or more, it is still the best preserved of all ancient Greek buildings. Above the houses, at the extreme right, may be seen one corner of the hill called the Areopagus (see plan, p. 352), often called Mars' Hill. It was probably here that the apostle Paul (§ 1068) preached in Athens (see Acts xvii). The buildings we see on the Acropolis are all ruins of the structures erected after the place had been laid waste by the Persians (§ 512). The Parthenon (§ 576), in the middle of the hill (see Fig. 183), shows the gaping hole caused by the explosion of a Turkish powder magazine ignited by a Venetian shell in 1687, when the entire central portion of the building was blown out. The space between the temple of Theseus, the Areopagus, and the Acropolis was largely occupied by the market place of Athens (§ 572, and plan, p. 352).

many a creaking wagon, heavily loaded with white blocks of marble for a new and still unfinished temple of Theseus (Fig. 182), the hero-god, who, as the Athenians thought, had once united Attica into a single nation.

**575. Plans of Pericles for the restoration of the Acropolis**

Above him towers the height of the Acropolis, about one thousand feet in length, two of our city blocks (Figs. 182 and 183). There, on its summit, had always been the dwelling place of Athena, whose arm was ever stretched out in protection over her beloved Athens. But for long years after the repulse of the Persians, the Acropolis rose smoke-blackened over the rebuilt houses of the city, and no temple of Athena appeared to replace the old building of Pisistratus, which the Persians had burned. Now at last Pericles has undertaken the restoration of the ancient shrines on a scale of magnificence and beauty before unknown anywhere in the Greek world. His sumptuous plans have demanded an expense of about two and a quarter millions of dollars, a sum far exceeding any such public outlay ever heard of among the Greeks. As he passes the Market Hill, where the Areopagus meets, the citizen remembers the discontented mutterings of the old men in this ancient Council as they heard of these vast expenses, and he smiles in satisfaction as he reflects that this unprogressive old body, once so powerful in Athenian affairs, has been deprived of all power to obstruct the will of the people. From here he also catches a glimpse of the Pnyx (Fig. 179), where he has heard Pericles make one eloquent speech after another in support of his new building plans before the assembly of the people, and he recalls with what enthusiasm the citizens voted to adopt them.

**576. The entrance to the Acropolis and the Parthenon**

As he looks up at the gleaming marble shafts, he feels that the architectural splendor now crowning the Acropolis is the work of the Athenian *people*, a world of new beauty in the creation of which every Athenian citizen has had a voice. Here before him rise the imposing marble colonnades of the magnificent monumental entrance to the Acropolis (Fig. 183).

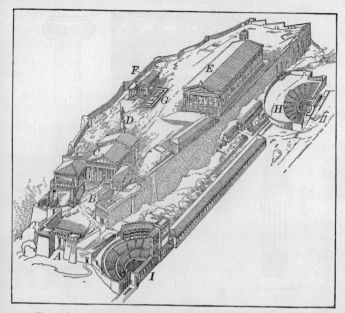

FIG. 183. RESTORATION OF THE ATHENIAN ACROPOLIS

The lower entrance (*A*) is of Roman date. Beyond it we have on the right the graceful little Temple of Victory (*B*, and see headpiece, p. 378), while before us rises the colonnaded entrance building (*C*) designed by Mnesicles (§ 576). As we pass through it we stand beside the colossal bronze statue of Athena (*D*) by Phidias (§ 577), beyond which at the left is the ancient sanctuary of the Erechtheum (*F* and § 644). To the right, along the south edge of the hill, is the wonderful temple of the Parthenon (*E*) (Fig. 185, and Plate IV, p. 380). Its farther corner looks down upon the theater (*H*) (Fig. 189). The other theater-like building (*I*) in the foreground is a concert hall, built by Herodes Atticus, a wealthy citizen, in Roman times (second century A.D.). *G* is the foundation of an ancient temple (now destroyed) older than the present Parthenon

It is still unfinished, and the architect Mnesicles, with a roll of plans under his arm, is perhaps at the moment directing a group of workmen to their task. He is beginning to employ a new style of column, called the Ionic (Fig. 184); it is lighter and more ornate than the stately Doric. The tinkle of many distant

FIG. 184. THE IONIC COLUMN AND ITS ORIENTAL PREDECESSORS
(AFTER PUCHSTEIN)

*A* is a column of wood as used in houses and shrines in Egypt (fifteenth century B.C.); notice at the top of *A* the lily with the ends of the petals rolled over in spirals called *volutes*. *B* is part of a wall with beautifully decorative designs in colored glazed brick from the throne room of Nebuchadnezzar at Babylon (Fig. 110); on this wall we see the same lily design appearing twice. *D* shows us a capital used in the beginnings of Greek architecture in Asia Minor, with the lily petals forming the volutes rolled further over but still showing its relationship with *A*. This process is carried so far in *F*, a capital dug up on the Acropolis of Athens, that we lose sight of the lily. *H* finally shows us the fully developed Ionic column, in which the volutes hardly resemble any longer the lily from which they came. This column (*H*) is taken from the colonnade of the Temple of Victory on the Acropolis of Athens (headpiece, p. 378). Examples of this style of column are now common in our own public buildings

hammers from the height above tells where the stonecutters are shaping the marble blocks for the still unfinished Parthenon, a noble temple dedicated to Athena (Figs. 183, 185, and Plate IV, p. 378); and there, too, the people often see Pericles intently inspecting the building, as Phidias the sculptor and Ictinus the architect of the building pace up and down the inclosure, explaining to him the progress of the work. In these wondrous Greek buildings architect and sculptor work hand in hand.

Phidias is the greatest of the sculptors at Athens. In a long band of carved marble extending entirely around the four sides of the Parthenon, at the top inside the colonnades (Plate IV, p. 378), Phidias and his pupils have portrayed, as in a glorified vision, the sovereign people of Athens moving in the stately procession (Fig. 186) of the Pan-Athenaic festival (§ 570). To be sure, these are not individual portraits of actual Athenian folk, but only types which lived in the exalted vision of the sculptor, and not on the streets of Athens. But such sculpture had never been seen before. How different is the supreme beauty of these perfect human forms from the cruder figures which adorned the temple burned by the Persians. The citizen has seen the shattered fragments of these older works cleared away and covered with rubbish when the architects leveled off the summit of the Acropolis.[1] Inside the new temple gleams the colossal figure of Athena, wrought by the cunning hand of Phidias in gold and ivory. Even from the city below the citizen can discern, touched with bright colors, the heroic figures of the gods with which Phidias has filled the triangular gable ends of the building (Fig. 185). Out in the open area behind the colonnaded entrance rises another great work of Phidias, a colossal bronze statue of Athena, seventy feet high as it stands on its tall base (Fig. 183, *D*). With shield and spear the goddess stands, the gracious protectress of Athens, and the glittering

577. Phidias and the sculptures of the Parthenon

---

[1] Till recently they lay buried under the rubbish on the slope (Fig. 182). The excavations of the Greek government have recovered them, and they are now in the Acropolis Museum at Athens.

point of her gilded spear can be seen shining like a beacon far across the land, even by the sailors as they round the southern tip of Attica (see map, p. 352) and sail homeward.

FIG. 185. RESTORATION OF THE PARTHENON, AS IT WAS IN THE FIFTH CENTURY B.C. (AFTER THIERSCH AND MICHAELIS)

This is the noble temple of Athena erected on the Acropolis of Athens (Fig. 183, *E*) by Pericles with the architect Ictinus and the sculptor Phidias (§ 576). The restoration shows us the wonderful beauty of the Doric colonnades as they were when they left the hands of the builders. In Plate IV, p. 378, we gain a glimpse of the same colonnades as they are to-day, after the explosion of the Turkish powder magazine, the effect of which can be seen in Fig. 182. The gable ends each contained a triangular group of sculpture depicting the birth of Athena and her struggle with Poseidon, god of the sea, for possession of Attica. The wonderful frieze of Phidias (Fig. 186 and § 577) extended around the building inside the colonnades at the top of the wall

**578. The drama; Æschylus**

In spite of the Sophists (§ 563), these are the gods to whom the faith of the Athenian people still reverently looks up. Have not Athena and these gods raised the power of Athens to the

FIG. 186. PART OF THE PARTHENON FRIEZE OF PHIDIAS (§ 577), SHOWING ATHENIAN YOUTHS RIDING IN THE PAN-ATHENAIC FESTIVAL (§ 570)

Notice the wonderful movement of the horses, and compare them with the horses of the barbarous Greek vase-painters three centuries earlier (Fig. 155). The reins and trappings were of metal and have disappeared

FIG. 187. PRAXITELES' FIGURE OF HERMES PLAYING WITH THE
CHILD DIONYSUS

This wonderful statue was discovered in the ruins of the Hera temple at
Olympia (headpiece, p. 295), and is one of the few original works of the
great Greek sculptors found in Greece. Nearly all such Greek originals
have perished, and we know them only in Roman copies (§ 1053). In his uplifted right hand (now broken off) the god probably held a bunch of grapes,
with which he was amusing the child (§ 648)

imperial position which she now occupies? Do not all the citizens recall Æschylus' drama "The Persians"? It told the story of the glorious victory of Salamis, and in it the memories of the great deliverance from Persian conquest were enshrined. How that tremendous day of Salamis was made to live again in the imposing picture which the poet's genius brought before them, disclosing the mighty purpose of the gods to save Hellas!

As he skirts the sheer precipice of the Acropolis the citizen reaches the theater (see plan, p. 352, and Fig. 183, *H*), where he finds the people are already entering, for the Feast of Dionysus (§ 570) has arrived. Only yesterday he and his neighbors received from the State treasury the money for their admission. It is natural that they should feel that the theater and all that is done there belong to the people, and not the less as the citizen looks down upon the orchestra circle and recognizes his friends and neighbors and their sons in the chorus for that day's performance. The seats are of wood, and they occupy the slope at the foot of the Acropolis. Hence they are not elevated on timbers, and there is no danger of their falling and killing the spectators as they once did when the theater was a temporary structure in the market place, in the days of the citizen's grandfather. All the citizens have turned out, including some less worthy and intelligent, who do not hesitate to indulge in cat-calls, or pelt the actors with food, if the play displeases them. The play would seem strange enough to us, for there is little or no scenery; and the actors, who are always men, wear grotesque masks, a survival of old days (§ 483). The narrative is largely carried on in song by the chorus (§ 483), but this is varied by the dialogue of the actors, and the whole is not unlike an opera.

**579. Theater and people**

A play of Sophocles (Fig. 180) is on, and the citizen's neighbor in the next seat leans over to tell him how as a lad many years ago he stood on the shore of Salamis, whither his family had fled (§ 512), and as they looked down upon the destruction

**580. Sophocles**

of the Persian fleet this same Sophocles, a boy of sixteen, was in the crowd looking on with the rest. How deeply must the events of that tragic day have sunk into the poet's soul! For does he not see the will of the gods in all that happens to men? Does he not celebrate the stern decree of Zeus everywhere hanging over human life, at the same time that he uplifts his

FIG. 188. PORTRAIT OF EURIPIDES

The name of the poet (§ 581) is engraved in Greek letters along the lower edge of the bust

audience to adore the splendor of Zeus, however dark the destiny he lays upon men? For Sophocles still believes in the gods, and is no friend of the Sophists. Hence the citizen feels that Sophocles is a veritable voice of the people, exalting the old gods in the new time. Moreover, in place of the former *two*, Sophocles has *three* actors in his plays, a change which makes them more interesting and full of action. Even old Æschylus yielded to this innovation once before he died. Yet too much innovation is also unwelcome to the citizen.

**581. Euripides**

The citizen feels this especially if it is one of the new sensational plays of Euripides which is presented. Euripides (Fig. 188) is the son of a farmer who lives over on the island of Salamis (Fig. 177). He has for some time been presenting plays at the spring competition (§ 570). He is a friend and companion of the Sophists, and in matters of religion his mind is shadowed with doubts. His new plays are all inwrought with problems and mental struggle regarding the gods, and they have raised a great many questions and doubts which the citizen has never been able to banish from his own mind since he heard them. The citizen determines that he will use all the influence he has to prevent the plays of Euripides from winning the prize. Indeed, Sophocles suits all the old-fashioned folk, and it is very rarely that Euripides has been able to carry off the prize, in spite of his great ability. The citizen feels some anxiety as he realizes that his own son and most of the other young men of his set are enthusiastic admirers of Euripides. They constantly read his plays and talk them over with the Sophists.

The great tragedies were given in the morning, and in the afternoon the people were ready for less serious entertainment, such as the comedy offered. Out of the old-time masques and burlesque frolics of the village communities at country feasts the comedy had developed into a stage performance, with all the uproarious antics of the unbridled comedian. The play-writer did not hesitate to introduce the greatest dignitaries of the State. Even Pericles was not spared, and great philosophers, or serious-minded writers like Euripides, were shown in absurd caricatures and made irresistibly ridiculous on the stage, while the multitudes of Athens vented their delight in roars of laughter mingled with shouts and cheers. Parodies on great passages of literature, too, were sure of a quick response, so keen was the wit of the Athenians and so widespread the acquaintance of the people with the literature which they had inherited. **582. Comedies**

When all was over they must wait until the next spring feast of Dionysus before they were privileged to see any more plays. But meantime they were greatly interested in the decision of the jury of citizens awarding prizes for tragedy, for comedy, and for the best chorus a bronze tripod to the citizen who had equipped and trained it (Fig. 190). Moreover, the interest in drama and the theater continued, for the next competition soon demanded that probably two thousand men and boys of Athens should put all their leisure time into learning their parts written out for them on sheets of papyrus and into **583. Continued and widespread interest in drama and literature**

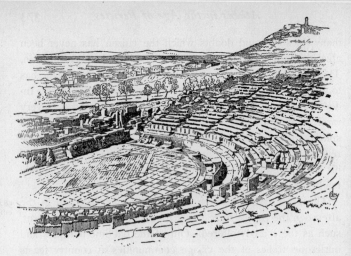

FIG. 189. THE THEATER OF ATHENS

This theater was the center of the growth and development of Greek drama, which began as a part of the celebration of the spring feast of Dionysus, god of the vine and the fruitfulness of the earth (§ 420). The temple of the god stood here, just at the left. Long before anyone knew of such a thing as a theater, the people gathered at this place to watch the celebration of the god's spring feast, where they formed a circle about the chorus, which narrated in song the stories of the gods (§ 483). This circle (called the orchestra) was finally marked out permanently, seats of wood for the spectators were erected in a semicircle on one side, but the singing and action all took place in the circle on the level of the ground. On the side opposite the public was a booth, or tent (Greek, *skēnē*, "scene"), for the actors, and out of this finally developed the stage. Here we see the circle, or orchestra, with the stage cutting off the back part of the circle. The seats are of stone and accommodated possibly seventeen thousand people. The fine marble seats in the front row were reserved for the leading men of Athens. The old wooden seats were still in use in the days when Æschylus, Sophocles, and Euripides presented their dramas here (§§ 578–582). From the seats the citizens had a grand view of the sea, with the island of Ægina, their old-time rival (§ 543); and even the heights of Argolis, 40 miles away, were visible; for orchestra and seats continued roofless, and a Greek theater was always open to the sky. In Roman times a colonnaded porch across the back of the stage was introduced, and such columns of Roman date may be seen in Plate VII, p. 558. For the best-preserved early Greek theater, see tailpiece, p. 393

374

training and rehearsals for the various choruses. Thousands of citizens too were reading the old plays that had already been presented.

For now at length books too had come to take an important place in the life of Athens. Rows of baskets of cylindrical shape held the books which filled the shelves in our Athenian citizen's library. Homer and the works of the old classic poets were now written on long rolls of papyrus, as much as a hundred and fifty or sixty feet in length. To one of these rolls the educated Greek sat down as the Egyptian had so long before been accustomed to do (Fig. 191). For lack of good artificial light, reading was necessarily done mostly by day, but studious Greeks also ventured to try their eyes in reading by the dim olive-oil lamp. Besides literary works, all sorts of books of instruction began to appear. The sculptors wrote of their art, and Ictinus produced a book on his design of the Parthenon (§ 576). There was a large group of books on medicine, bearing the name of Hippocrates. Textbooks on mathematics and rhetoric circulated, and the Athenian housekeeper could even find a cookbook at the bookshop.

**584. Books and reading**

In our voyage up the Nile (§ 115), we found that far back in the Egyptian Empire, a thousand years before the days of Pericles, there was a group of gifted men who created at Thebes a grand and imperial city of noble architecture. But that group of great Egyptians was not made up of *citizens*, nor had the multitudes of Thebes any share in government or in the creation of the magnificent city. It was very different in the Athens of Pericles. Here had grown up a whole community of intelligent men, who were the product of the most active interest in the life and government of the community, constantly sharing in its tasks and problems, in daily contact with the greatest works of art in literature, drama, painting, architecture, and sculpture — such a wonderful community indeed as the ancient world, Greek or oriental, had never seen before.

**585 Contrast between Athens and Egyptian Thebes**

**586.** The old Athens and the new

Not only was it totally different from any that we have found in the ancient Orient, but we see also how very different from the Athens of the old days before the Persian Wars was this imperial Athens of Pericles ! — throbbing with new life and astir with a thousand questions eagerly discussed at every corner. Keenly awake to the demands of the greater State and the sovereign people, the men of the new Athens were deeply pondering also the duties and privileges of the individual, who felt new and larger visions of himself conflicting with the exactions of the State and the old faith. Troubled by serious doubts, they were, nevertheless, clinging with wistful apprehension to the old gods and the old truths. Under Pericles Athens was becoming as he desired it should, the teacher of the Greek world. It now remained to be seen whether the *people*, in sovereign control of the State, could guide her wisely and maintain her new power. As we watch the citizens of Athens endeavoring to furnish her with wise and successful guidance, we shall find another and a sadly different side of the life of this wonderful community.

## QUESTIONS

SECTION 54. What can you say of the population of Attica as to social classes? Discuss the rich and the poor. Were there any beautiful houses in Europe in Pericles' time? Describe an Athenian house of this age; its conveniences; its equipment; its decoration. What were the streets of Athens like? Describe Greek costume in this age. What was now the position of women? Describe the usual school and its teacher. What subjects were taught? What did a boy do when he left school? What oath of citizenship did he take? Tell about his military service; his athletic training. What were the chief events in athletics?

SECTION 55. What new private teachers now began to appear? What did these men teach? Did a boy learn from them anything which his father had not been taught? What did the fathers think about the teaching of the Sophists? Was there any general knowledge of science? How was the time of day designated? How was time measured within the day? within the year? What were the difficulties? What discoveries were made in astronomy? in geography? What progress was made in medicine? in history-writing? How did government business train the citizens of Athens? Tell about voluntary contributions by the citizens. What can you say about official State feasts at Athens?

SECTION 56. How did warmth of patriotic feeling affect music, the drama, art, and architecture? Discuss the painting of Marathon in the Athenian market place. Do you see any connection between art and patriotism in such a work? Were there any fine government office buildings in Athens under Pericles? What was the material of such buildings? What were the beautiful public buildings of Greece at this time? How did the Athenian Acropolis look after the Persian Wars? What did Pericles do about it? Who opposed him? Was there a majority of Athenian citizens who wanted such great works as Pericles planned? How then did he put his plan through? Who assisted Pericles in carrying out the actual work on the Acropolis? What buildings did they erect? Describe the sculpture of Phidias.

What play did Æschylus write about the war with Persia? Do you see any connection between literature and patriotism in such a work? Describe the theater where such plays were presented at Athens. Did a citizen pay for his own ticket? Describe a play in such a theater. Who was Sophocles? What did he think about the gods and the Sophists? How many actors did he have?

What did Euripides think about the gods? To which of these two men did the Athenians vote the most prizes? What did an old-fashioned citizen think about having his son read the plays of Euripides? Tell about the comedies played at Athens. How did the Athenians take part in drama and music? What did a book look like in this age? What books could a citizen find at the bookshop? Contrast Athens and Egyptian Thebes. In what ways was the Athens of Pericles different from that of Solon?

NOTE. The sketch below shows us vase-paintings of Greek children at play.

# CHAPTER XVI

## THE STRUGGLE BETWEEN ATHENS AND SPARTA AND THE FALL OF THE ATHENIAN EMPIRE

### Section 57. The Tyranny of Athens and the Second Peloponnesian War

**587. States of the Athenian Empire become helpless subjects**

While Athens under the guiding hand of Pericles had thus made herself the chief center of refined and civilized life in the Greek world, her political situation was in a number of ways becoming a serious one both within and without her empire. When the danger from Persia had long passed and some of the island states of the Empire wished to withdraw, Athens

Note. The above headpiece shows us the lovely little Temple of Victory, still standing on the Acropolis (*B* in Fig. 183). It was demolished by the Turks, who built a battery out of its blocks. When the Turkish works were cleared away in 1835, the fragments of the temple were discovered and it was put together again. The roof, however, is still lacking (but see *D* in restoration, p. 340). It was probably built, or at least begun, in the latter part of the leadership of Pericles. The columns display the incoming Ionic form (Fig. 184) and are among the most beautiful examples of this style, or, as it is commonly called, " order."

PLATE IV. A CORNER OF THE PARTHENON

Looking through the Doric colonnades as they are to-day, at the southeast corner of the building, to the distant hills of Hymettus. On the left is the base of the wall of the interior, destroyed by the explosion (p. 365, footnote).

At the top of this wall was the frieze of Phidias (Fig. 186 and § 577)

would not permit them to do so. She sent out her war fleet, conquered the rebellious islands, and forced them to pay money tribute instead of contributing ships. Often many of their citizens were driven out and their lands were divided among the Athenian settlers. A section of the Athenian fleet was on constant duty to sail about in the Ægean and collect the tribute money by force (see map II, p. 346). These funds were used by Athens as she pleased, and the magnificent buildings of Pericles were paid for out of this tribute.

Moreover, the democracy of Athens was most undemocratic in its treatment of these outsiders in the other cities of the Empire. For, about the middle of the century the Athenians, led by Pericles, abolished the former liberal policy of granting citizenship to outsiders (§ 536) and passed a very strict law limiting Athenian citizenship to those whose parents were themselves citizens of Athens. This law kept the people of the Empire really foreigners and deprived Athens of the large body of loyal citizens which she might have gained from among the subject cities.

**588.** Change in the policy of Athens regarding citizenship

At the same time Athens forced the people of the Empire to come there to settle their legal differences before her citizen-juries. For this purpose the people of distant island states were often obliged to make the expensive and inconvenient journey to Athens. There was no feeling of unity within the Empire, for the Council of representatives from the states of the Empire, which once guided its affairs, no longer held any meetings. Athens was in complete control and governed them as she liked. They saw how much easier were the conditions under which the members of the Spartan League lived, and more than one of them sent secret messages to Sparta, with the purpose of throwing off Athenian control and going over to Sparta.

**589.** Tyranny of Athens and discontent in her Empire

While such was the state of affairs within the Athenian Empire, conditions outside were even more serious. The outward splendor of Athens, her commercial prosperity, the visible

**590.** Hostility of the rivals of Athens

growth of her power, her not very conciliatory attitude toward her rivals, and the example she offered of the seeming success of triumphant democracy — all these things were causes of jealousy to a backward and conservative military State like Sparta, where most of the citizens were still unable to read, iron money continued in use, and the town remained an open settlement without walls or defenses (Fig. 178). Moreover, this feeling of unfriendliness toward Athens was not confined to Sparta but was quite general throughout Greece. The merchants of Corinth (Fig. 163) found Athenian competition a continuous vexation, and when Athenian possessions in the north Ægean revolted and received support from Corinth and Sparta, the fact that hardly half of the thirty years' term of peace (§ 545) had expired did not prevent the outbreak of war.

**591. Opening of Second Peloponnesian War (431 B.C.) and Pericles' plan of campaign**

It seemed as if all European Greece not included in the Athenian Empire had united against Athens, for Sparta controlled the entire Peloponnesus except Argos, and north of Attica, Bœotia led by Thebes, as well as its neighbors on the west, were hostile to Athens. The support of Athens consisted of the Ægean cities which made up her empire and a few outlying allies of little power. She began the struggle with a large war treasury and a fleet which made her undisputed mistress of the sea. But she could not hope to cope with the land forces of the enemy, which, some thirty thousand strong, had planned to meet in the Isthmus in the spring of 431 B.C. Accordingly, Pericles' plan for the war was to throw all the resources of Athens into naval enterprises and make no effort to defend Attica by land. When the Peloponnesian army entered Attica the country communities were directed by Pericles to leave their homes and take refuge in the open markets and squares of Athens, the sanctuaries, and especially between the Long Walls leading to the Piræus. Here they were safe behind the strong defenses of Athens and her port. To offset the devastation of Attica by the Spartan army, all that Athens could do was to organize destructive sea raids and inflict as much damage as possible along the coasts of the Peloponnesus or blockade and destroy Corinthian commerce as of old (map II, p. 346).

The masses of people crowded within the walls of Athens under the unsanitary conditions we have already described (§ 551), exposed the city to disease; a plague, brought in from the Orient, raged with intermissions for several seasons. It carried off probably a third of the population, and from this unforeseen disaster Athens never recovered. Constantly under arms for the defense of the walls, deprived of any opportunity to strike the enemy, forced to sit still and see their land ravaged, the citizens at last broke out in discontent.

Even before the beginning of the war there had been signs that the power of Pericles was waning. He was a thoroughly modern man, associated openly with the Sophists, and very evidently held their views.

**592. The plague in Athens**

Fig. 190. Monument commemorating the Triumph of an Athenian Citizen in Music

An entire street of Athens was filled with such monuments (§ 583). We learn the name of the citizen, Lysicrates, who erected this beautiful monument, from the inscription it still bears, which reads: "Lysicrates . . . was choragus [leader of the chorus] when the boy-chorus of the tribe of Akamantis won the prize; Theon was a flute-player, Lysiades of Athens trained the choir. Euaenetus was archon." The archon's name dates the erection of the monument for us in 335 to 334 B.C. Beyond the monument we look westward to the back of the Acropolis (see plan, p. 352)

**593. Decline and fall of Pericles**

We can understand what this meant to the people, if we imagine one of our own political leaders of to-day declaring himself an infidel.[1] One of Pericles' particular friends among the Sophists had been prosecuted by the people for irreligious views (§ 563). He was legally condemned for his infidelity and, in spite of all that Pericles could do, was obliged to flee from Athens. At the same time a popular attack on the honesty of Pericles' friend Phidias, the great sculptor, resulted in his being thrown into prison, where he died. Finally, Pericles himself lost control, was tried for misappropriation of funds, and fined.

FIG. 191. GREEK YOUTH READING FROM A ROLL

It will be seen that the young man holds the roll so that he rolls up a portion of it with one hand as he unrolls another portion with the other. He soon has a roll in each hand, while he holds smoothly stretched out between the two rolls the exposed portion from which he reads a column of writing like that which we see photographed from the oldest-preserved Greek book (roll), in Fig. 223. Such a column formed for him a page, but when it was read, instead of turning a page as we do, he rolled it away to the left side, and brought into view a new column from the other roll on the right side

**594. Restoration, and death of Pericles (429 B.C.)**

The absence of his steadying hand and powerful leadership was at once felt by the people, for there was no one to take his place, although a swarm of small politicians were contending for control of the Assembly. Realizing their helplessness the people soon turned to Pericles again and elected him strategus.

---

[1] Those who remember Robert G. Ingersoll will recall that he sacrificed a political career because of his religious views.

But the great days of his leadership were over. His two sons died of the plague. Then he was himself stricken with it and died soon after his return to power (429 B.C.). Great statesman as he was, he had left Athens with a system of government which did not provide for the continuation of such leadership as he had furnished, and without such leadership the Athenian Empire was doomed.

Men of the prosperous manufacturing class now came to the fore. They possessed neither the high station in life, the ability as statesmen, nor the qualities of leadership to win the confidence and respect of the people. Moreover, these new leaders were not soldiers and could not command the fleet or the army as Pericles had done. The most notable exception was Alcibiades, a brilliant young man, a relative of Pericles and brought up in his house. The two legal sons of Pericles (there was another son by an illegal marriage, § 614) having died, Alcibiades, if he had enjoyed the guidance of his foster father a few years longer, might have become the savior of Athens and of Greece. As it happened, however, this young leader was more largely responsible than anyone else for the destruction of the Athenian Empire and the downfall of Greece.

595. Lack of leaders after death of Pericles

Lacking the steadying hand of a statesman whose well-formed plans and continuous policy might furnish a firm and guiding influence, the management of Athenian affairs fell into confusion. Wavering and changeableness were rarely interrupted by any display of stability, firmness, and wisdom; the leaders drifted from one policy to another, and usually from bad to worse. It seemed impossible to regain stable leadership. The youthful Aristophanes (§ 659) pictured the rudderless condition of the ship of State in one clever comedy after another, in which he ridiculed in irresistible satire the pretense to statesmanship of such "men of the people" as Cleon the tanner.

596. Unstable leadership of the Assembly

A typical example of the ill-considered actions of the Assembly was their treatment of the revolting citizens of Mitylene. When the men of Mitylene were finally subdued, the Assembly

597. Incident of Mitylene

on the Pnyx (Fig. 179) voted that they should all be put to death, and a ship departed with these orders. It was with great difficulty that a more moderate group in the Assembly secured a rehearing of the question and succeeded in inducing the people to modify their barbarous action to the condemnation and execution of the ringleaders only. A second ship then overtook the first barely in time to save from death the entire body of the citizens of Mitylene.

**598.** Cleon the tanner

In spite of such revolts Athenian naval supremacy continued; but as the war dragged on, the payment of army and fleet reduced Athenian funds to a very low state. Cleon the tanner was a man of much energy and a good deal of financial ability. He succeeded in having an income tax introduced, and later on the tribute of the Ægean cities was raised. But having always been a manufacturer, he lacked all military experience. For years the operations on both sides were in most cases utterly insignificant. This is best seen in Cleon's siege and capture of *four hundred* Spartans on one of the islands on the west coast of Greece — a disaster which made a great impression and, in view of some other reverses, led the Spartans to sue for peace! Later in an absurdly mismanaged expedition on the northern coast of the Ægean, Cleon lost his army of fifteen hundred men and his own life.

**599.** The first ten years of the war, and the Peace of Nicias (421 B.C.)

The attack of the allies on Athens did not succeed in breaking up her empire and overthrowing her leadership of the Ægean cities. It was the devastation wrought by the plague which had seriously affected her. Athens and the whole Greek world were demoralized and weakened. The contest had in it no longer the inspiration of a noble struggle such as the Greeks had maintained against Persia. Unprecedented brutality, like that at first adopted toward Mitylene, gave the struggle a savagery and a lack of respect for the enemy which completely obscured all finer issues, if there were any such involved in the war. With Cleon gone, Athenian leadership fell into the hands of a wealthy and noble citizen named Nicias, a man of no ability. When ten years of indecisive warfare had passed, Nicias arranged a peace to be kept for fifty years. Each contestant agreed to give up all new conquests and to retain only old possessions or subject cities (see map II, p. 346).

## SECTION 58. THIRD PELOPONNESIAN WAR AND DESTRUCTION OF THE ATHENIAN EMPIRE

Meantime serious difficulties arose in carrying out the conditions of the peace. One of the northern subject cities of Athens which had gone over to Sparta refused to return to Athenian allegiance. Athens took the questionable ground that Sparta should force the unwilling city to obey the terms of peace. It was at this juncture that Athens especially needed such guidance as a statesman like Pericles could have furnished. She was obliged to depend upon the feeble leadership of Nicias and the energetic but unprincipled Alcibiades.

**600. Difficulties in maintaining the new peace**

Nicias continued to urge a conciliatory attitude toward Sparta, but he failed of election as strategus. On the other hand, the gifted and reckless Alcibiades, seeing a great opportunity for a brilliant career, did all that he could to excite the war party in Athens. He was elected strategus, and, in spite of the fact that troubles at home had forced Sparta into a treaty of alliance with Athens, Alcibiades was able to carry the Assembly with him. He then involved Athens in an alliance with Argos against Sparta. In this way Attica, exhausted with plague and ten years of warfare, was enticed into a life-and-death struggle which was to prove final.

**601. Alcibiades brings on war again**

Several years of ill-planned military and naval operations followed the fruitless peace of Nicias. The Spartans did not at once respond with hostilities and sent no army into Attica. Alcibiades at length persuaded the Athenians to plan a great joint expedition of army and navy against Sicily, where the mighty city of Syracuse, founded as a colony of Corinth, was leading in the oppression of certain Western cities in alliance

**602. Third Peloponnesian War; Sicilian expedition**

with Athens. The Athenians placed Alcibiades and Nicias in command of the expedition.

**603.** Arrest of Alcibiades and his flight to Sparta

Just as the fleet was about to sail, certain sacred images in Athens were impiously mutilated, and the deed was attributed to Alcibiades. In spite of his demand for an immediate trial, the Athenians postponed the case until his return from Sicily.

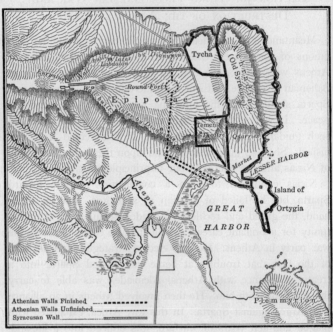

PLAN OF THE SIEGE OF SYRACUSE

When the fleet reached Italy, however, the Athenian people, with their usual inability to follow any consistent plan and also desiring to take Alcibiades at a great disadvantage, suddenly recalled him for trial. This procedure not only deprived the expedition of its only able leader but also gave Alcibiades an opportunity to desert to the Spartans, which he promptly did. His advice to the Spartans now proved fatal to the Athenians.

The appearance of the huge Athenian fleet off their coast struck dismay into the hearts of the Syracusans, but Nicias entirely failed to see the importance of immediate attack before the Syracusans could recover and make preparations for the defense of their city. He wasted the early days of the campaign in ill-planned maneuvers, only winning a barren victory over the Syracusan land forces. When Nicias was finally induced by the second general in command to begin the siege of the city, courage had returned to the Syracusans, and their defense was well organized.

604. Incompetence of Nicias

The Athenians now built a siege wall behind Syracuse nearly across the point of land on which the city was situated, in order to cut it entirely off from the outside world. The spirit of the Syracusans was much depressed, and surrender seemed not far off. Just at this point Gylippus, a Spartan leader and his troops, sent by the advice of Alcibiades, succeeded in passing the Athenian lines and gained entrance to the city. The courage of the Syracusans was at once restored. The Athenians were thrown upon the defensive. Meantime the Syracusans had also organized a fleet. The Athenian fleet had entered the harbor, and in these narrow quarters they were unable to maneuver or to take advantage of their superior seamanship. After some Athenian success at first, the fleet of Syracuse was victorious.

605. Athenian siege unsuccessful

There was now no prospect of the capture of the city, and Nicias would have withdrawn, but the leaders at home would not allow it. In spite of renewed Spartan invasion, the blinded democratic leaders sent out another fleet and more land forces to reinforce Nicias. No Greek state had ever mustered such power and sent it far across the waters. All Greece watched the spectacle with amazement. A night assault by the reinforced Athenians failed with large losses, and the position of the whole expedition at once became a dangerous one.

606. Reinforced Athenians repulsed

With disaster staring them in the face there was nothing for the Athenians to do but withdraw. But just at this point, an eclipse of the moon occurred, and the superstitious Nicias

607. Capture
of Athenian
fleet and
army before
Syracuse
(413 B.C.)

insisted on waiting for another more favorable moon. This
month's delay was fatal to the Athenians. The Syracusans
blockaded the channel to the sea and completely shut up the
Athenian fleet within the harbor, so that an attempt to break
through and escape disastrously failed. The desperate Athenian

Fig. 192. Stone Quarries of Syracuse in which the Athenians were Imprisoned

We look across the deep quarry and the Small Harbor to the ancient
island of Ortygia (see map, p. 386). It is now a cape, occupied by the
modern city of which we can see the buildings. The quarries are overgrown with ivy and masked with beautiful green foliage. Here the seven
thousand Athenians captured by the Syracusans (§ 607) were imprisoned
without sufficient water and provisions, and here most of them died

army, abandoning sick and wounded, too late endeavored to
escape into the interior, but was overtaken and forced to surrender. The Syracusans treated the captured Athenians with
savage barbarity. After executing the commanding generals,
they took the prisoners, seven thousand in number, and sold
them into slavery or threw them into the stone quarries of the
city (Fig. 192), where most of them miserably perished. Thus

the Athenian expedition was completely destroyed (413 B.C.). This disaster, together with the earlier ravages of the plague, brought Athens near the end of her resources.

Heretofore Sparta had stood more or less aloof, seemingly unwilling to break the peace of Nicias, and had not invaded Attica. But now seeing the unprotected condition of Athens, after the dispatch of the Sicilian expedition, Sparta again invaded Attica and, on the advice of Alcibiades, occupied the town of Decelea,[1] almost within sight of Athens. Here the Spartans established a permanent fort held by a strong garrison, and thus placed Athens in a state of perpetual siege. All agriculture ceased, and the Athenians lived on imported grain. The people now understood the folly of having sent away on a distant expedition the ships and the men that should have been kept at home to repel the attacks of a powerful and still uncrippled foe.

608. Spartan garrison in Attica

After these disasters the Athenian Empire began to show signs of breaking up. The failure of the democracy in the management of the war enabled the nobles to denounce popular rule as unsuccessful. The nobles regained power for a time; violence and bloodshed within were added to the dangerous assaults of the enemy from without. The finances were in a desperate condition. The tribute, already raised to the breaking point, was abolished and a customs duty of five per cent was levied on all goods exported or imported. The plan was a success and brought in a larger income than the tribute. But the measure did not unite nor quiet the discontented communities of which the Empire was made up. One after another they fell away. Spartan warships sailed about in the Ægean, aiding the rebels, who had of course dared to revolt only on promise of such assistance from Sparta.

609. Internal troubles of the Athenian Empire

To add to the Athenian distress, the powerful Persian satrap in western Asia Minor was supporting the Spartan fleet with money. Indeed, both Athens and Sparta had long been

610. Persia aids the Peloponnesians against Athens

[1] On this account the war with Sparta which now followed, lasting nine years (from 413 to 404 B.C.), is often called the "Decelean War" (see map, p. 352).

negotiating with Persia for aid, and Sparta had recognized Persian rule over the Greek cities of Asia. The Greek islands and the cities of Asia Minor which had once united in the Delian League with Athens to throw off Persian rule were now combining with Sparta and Persia against Athens. Thus the former union of the Greeks in a heroic struggle against the Asiatic enemy had given way to a disgraceful scramble for Persian support and favor.

**611. Alcibiades recovers command of the Athenian fleet (411 B.C.)**

Meantime Alcibiades, under the protection of the Persian satrap, had himself encouraged the revolters against Athens, hoping that her distress would finally oblige her to recall him and seek his aid. He was not disappointed. The small fleet which the Athenians were still able to put into the fight called upon Alcibiades for help, and finally put itself under his command, without any authorization from Athens. In several conflicts, chiefly through the skill of Alcibiades, the Peloponnesian fleet was finally completely destroyed, and Athens regained the command of the sea.

**612. Restoration of Alcibiades (407 B.C.)**

Sparta now made offers of peace, but Alcibiades skillfully used the war sentiment in the fleet against their acceptance, and the democratic leaders in power at Athens also refused to make peace. Alcibiades was then (407 B.C.) elected strategus and legally gained command of the fleet which he had already been leading for four years. At the head of a triumphant procession he entered Athens again for the first time since he had left it for Sicily eight years before. He was solemnly purified from the religious curse which rested upon him ; and his fortune, which had been confiscated, was returned to him.

**613. Fall and death of Alcibiades**

It now needed only the abilities of such a leader as Alcibiades to accomplish the union of the distracted Greek states, and the foundation of a great Greek nation. At this supreme moment, however, Alcibiades lacked the courage to seize the government, and the opportunity never returned again. When he put to sea again a slight defeat, inflicted on a part of his fleet when he was not present, cost him the favor of the fickle

Athenians. When they failed to reëlect him strategus he retired to a castle which he had kept in readiness on the Hellespont. He never saw his native land again and died in exile, the victim of a Persian dagger.

The Athenians had now lost their ablest leader again, but they continued the war on the sea as best they could. They won another important victory over a new Peloponnesian fleet on the coast of Asia Minor by the little islands of Arginusæ. As the battle ended a storm arose which prevented the commanders from saving the Athenian survivors clinging to the wreckage. For this accident the Athenian commanders were accused of criminal neglect before the Assembly and condemned to death. In spite of all that could be done, six of the eight naval commanders were executed, including the young Pericles, a son of the great statesman. The other two commanders had been wise enough to flee from such justice as they might expect at the hands of the Athenian democracy.

*614. Athenian victory of Arginusæ: execution of the commanders (406 B.C.)*

Athens now suffered worse than ever before for lack of competent commanders. The fleet numbering about one hundred and eighty triremes was placed in command of a group of officers, each of whom was to lead for a day at a time. The democratic leaders who had made this absurd arrangement watched the fleet sail out to continue a war which they themselves were prolonging by again refusing Spartan proffers of peace. For several days in succession the Athenians sailed out from their station near the river called Ægospotami on the Hellespont, and offered battle to the Peloponnesian fleet lying in a neighboring harbor. But the Peloponnesians refused battle. On their return from these maneuvers each day, the Athenians left their ships along the beach and themselves went ashore. Alcibiades from his neighboring castle, where he still was, came down and pointed out to the Athenian commanders the great danger they ran in leaving the fleet in this condition so near the enemy. His advice received no attention. The able Spartan, Lysander, the commander of the Peloponnesian

*615. Capture of the Athenian fleet at the battle of Ægospotami (405 B.C.)*

fleet, seeing this daily procedure, waited until the Athenians had gone ashore and left their ships as usual. Then, sailing over, he surprised and captured practically the whole Athenian fleet.

**616. Surrender of Athens and fall of the Athenian Empire (404 B.C.)**

At last, twenty-seven years after Pericles had provoked the war with Sparta, the resources of Athens were exhausted. Not a man slept on the night when the terrible news of final ruin reached Athens. It was soon confirmed by the appearance of Lysander's fleet blockading the Piræus. The grain ships from the Black Sea could no longer reach the port of Athens. The Spartan king pitched his camp in the grove of the Academy (§ 558) and called on the city to surrender. For some months the stubborn democratic leaders refused to accept terms of peace which meant the complete destruction of Athenian power. But the pinch of hunger finally convinced the Assembly, and the city surrendered. The Long Walls and the fortifications of the Piræus were torn down, the remnant of the fleet was handed over to Sparta, all foreign possessions were given up, and Athens was forced to enter the Spartan League. These hard conditions saved the city from the complete destruction demanded by Corinth. Thus the century which had begun so gloriously for Athens with the repulse of Persia, the century which under the leadership of such men as Themistocles and Pericles had seen her rise to supremacy in all that was best and noblest in Greek life, closed with the annihilation of the Athenian Empire (404 B.C.).

## QUESTIONS

SECTION 57. How did Athens treat the subject states of her Empire? What was now her policy regarding citizenship? regarding lawsuits in the subject states? How did these states now feel toward Athens? How did the states outside the Athenian Empire feel? What was the result? Who were the enemies of Athens in this war? What were her resources?

What was Pericles' plan of campaign? What disaster overtook Athens? How did this affect the fortunes of Pericles? By what associations had he displeased the people? What was the result? What young leader now came forward? What kind of leadership did the Assembly now furnish? Give an example. What business man now tried to lead the nation? How did he succeed? Were the military operations of the war on a large scale? What was the result of ten years' war? Who arranged the peace? When?

SECTION 58. Who was chiefly responsible for the reopening of the war? What great expedition did the Athenians plan? Who were the commanders? What prevented Alcibiades from going? Tell the story of the expedition and its end. What did Sparta now do? What was now the internal condition of the Athenian Empire? What part did Persia play in the war? What can you state of the restoration of Alcibiades to office? What was the result? How did the Athenians treat their naval commanders? What was the result? What was the situation of Athens after the loss of her fleet? What conditions did Sparta make? Contrast the beginning and the end of the fifth century in Athenian history.

NOTE. The tailpiece below shows us the theater of Epidaurus, which is unusually instructive because it is the best preserved of the Greek theaters. Although it was built late in the fourth century B.C., we see that the orchestra circle is still complete and has not been cut into by later stage arrangements behind it as at Athens (Fig. 189).

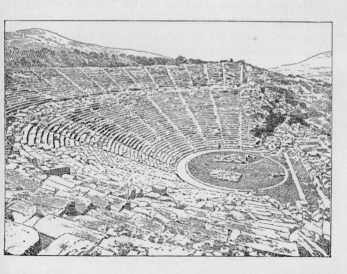

# CHAPTER XVII

## THE FINAL CONFLICTS AMONG THE GREEK STATES

### SECTION 59. SPARTAN LEADERSHIP AND THE DECLINE OF DEMOCRACY

**617. Unfitness of Sparta for leadership of the Greeks**

The long struggle of Athens for the political leadership of the Greek world had ignominiously failed. It now remained to be seen whether her victorious rival, Sparta, was any better suited to undertake such leadership. No nation which devotes itself exclusively to the development of military power, as Sparta had done, is fitted to control successfully the affairs of its neighbors. Military garrisons commanded by Spartan officers were now placed in many of the Greek cities, and Spartan

NOTE. The above headpiece shows us the lovely Porch of the Maidens built to adorn the temple on the Acropolis known as the Erechtheum (*F* in Fig. 183). This was a very ancient sanctuary of Athena, supposed to have gained its name because it was originally a shrine in the castle of the prehistoric king Erechtheus on the Acropolis. It was believed to stand on the spot where Athena overcame Poseidon in her battle with him for the possession of Attica, and here was the mark of the Sea-god's trident which he struck into the earth. Here also grew the original olive tree which Athena summoned from the earth as a gift to the Athenians (§ 654). The building was erected during the last Peloponnesian war, in spite of the financial distress of Athens at that time. It is one of the most beautiful architectural works left us by the Greeks.

control was maintained in a much more offensive form than was the old tyranny of Athens.

By such violent means Sparta was able to repress the democracies which had everywhere been hostile to her. In each city the Spartans established and supported by military force the rule of a small group of men from the noble or upper class. Such rule of a small group was called *oligarchy*, a Greek term meaning "rule of a few." The oligarchs were guilty of the worst excesses, murdering and banishing their political opponents and confiscating their fortunes. When the people regained power, they retaliated in the same way and drove the oligarchs from the city. As this kind of conflict went on, both parties banished so many that a large number of the leading Athenian citizens constantly lived in exile. From their foreign homes they plotted against their banishers and formed a constant danger from abroad.

**618. Struggle of oligarchy and democracy**

In spite of the failure of oligarchy, thoughtful men everywhere regarded popular rule also as an open failure. The splendid achievements of citizenship under Pericles (Chapter XV) must not blind us to the weaknesses of Athenian democracy. Some of these we have already seen in following the course of the Peloponnesian Wars; but the same weaknesses were evident in the people's control of the internal affairs of Athens. Let us examine some of the leading matters in which popular control had failed and continued to fail.

**619. Disrepute and weaknesses of democracy**

Nowhere were the mistakes of democracy more evident than in the Athenian law courts. The payment of the large citizen-juries (§ 538) often exhausted the treasury. When there was no money in the treasury with which to pay the juries, the jurymen, who preferred such service to hard work, found it very easy to fill the treasury again by fining any accused citizen brought before them, whether he was guilty or innocent. More than one lawyer of the time urged the court to confiscate the fortune of an accused citizen, in order that the jurymen to whom the lawyer was talking might thus receive their pay. It became

**620. Corruption and class prejudice of the Athenian citizen-juries**

a profitable trade to bring accusations and suits against wealthy men on all sorts of trumped-up charges. A man thus threatened usually preferred to buy off his accusers, in order to avoid going before five hundred poor and ignorant jurors.

**621. Evils of one-sided *class* rule**

In the days of Solon we remember that the rule of the *upper* classes over the lower was so oppressive that it almost resulted in the destruction of the State (§ 473). In the course of less than two hundred years the *lower* classes had gained complete control, and their rule, as we have just seen (§ 620), became so corruptly oppressive toward the upper classes that the final situation was again one-sided class rule, as bad as any that Athens had ever seen. To Athenian misfortunes in foreign wars were thus added the constant violence of weakening inner struggles between classes.

**622. Unwise financial policy of the democracy**

Another weakness of popular rule was its unwise financial policy, which continually exhausted the treasury of Athens. Her empty treasury was due to a number of causes, chiefly three. First, the payment of large numbers of citizens for services to the State, especially the thousands of citizen-jurors ; second, the payment to all citizens of " show-money " (§ 579), a heavy drain on the treasury ; and third, the long-continued expenses and losses of war (§ 539).

**623. Expensive means of collecting taxes**

To these we might add the expensive means of collecting taxes employed by both parties. Unlike the great oriental governments we have studied (Fig. 40), no Greek state possessed any officials to undertake the task of collecting taxes. It therefore sold its tax claims to the highest bidder, who then had the right to collect the taxes. In order to secure the large sums necessary for making such bids, a number of men of money would form themselves into a company. These companies by secretly combining gained a monopoly in the business of tax collecting. Their bid was always far less than the amount of the tax claims to be collected. Thus the people paid far more taxes than the State received from the collectors, into whose pockets the difference went. Consequently, the rate of taxation at Athens was now high, being at least from one to two per cent of a man's fortune and sometimes much higher.

The Athenians had early begun to use the treasure which had accumulated in the temple of Athena. The obligation to pay back this borrowed treasure was engraved upon a stone tablet set up on the Acropolis. To this day the surviving fragments of this broken stone bear witness to the unpaid debt to Athena and the bankruptcy of Athens. After the long struggle between Athens and Sparta was over, all the Greek states were practically bankrupt. An admiral or a general of this time often found himself facing the enemy without the money to pay his forces or to feed them. At the same time, if he failed in his campaign he would be punished for his failure by the democracy at home. There were times when the Athenian courts ceased to hold any sessions, for lack of funds to pay the citizen-juries, and a man with an important lawsuit on his hands could not get it tried.

**624.** Exhaustion of temple treasures; bankruptcy of the Greek states

Under these circumstances the Mediterranean states for the first time began to study the methods and theory of raising money for government expenses. A beginning was thus made in the science of national finances and political economy. Nevertheless, the method of collection of the taxes continued to be that of "farming" out the undertaking to the highest bidder. In this matter the Orient still remained far in advance of the northern Mediterranean states (§ 74). From now on the finances of a nation became more and more a matter of special training, and it became more difficult for the average citizen without experience to manage the financial offices of the government.

**625.** Beginnings of financial theory and political economy

Notwithstanding the great losses in property and in men during the long Peloponnesian Wars, Athens at length began to recover herself. The farms of Attica had been laid waste so often by the Spartan armies that agriculture never wholly recovered its former prosperity. There was a tendency among farmers to sell their land and to undertake some form of manufacturing in the city. This was a natural thing to do, for the

**626.** Beginning of the decline of farming, and appearance of large landowners

industries of Athens offered attractive opportunities to make a fortune. At the same time, men who had already gained wealth in manufactures bought one farm after another. This was a process which would finally concentrate the lands of Attica in the hands of a few large city landlords who were not farmers, but worked their great estates, each made up of many farms, with slaves under superintendents. The landowning farmers who worked their own lands and lived on them tended to disappear. In their place the great estates common in neighboring Asia Minor under the Persians (§ 269) were also appearing among the Greeks.

**627.** Growth of manufacturing and rise of banks

Athens was still the leading business center and the greatest city in the Mediterranean world. While manufacturing business was not often conducted by companies, groups of wealthy men, as we have seen, united to furnish the large sums necessary to bid for the contract to collect the taxes. Such combinations formed one of the evils of Athenian business life, as they have sometimes done in our own time. Other men combined their capital to form the first banks. The Greeks no longer left their accumulated money in a temple treasury, for safe-keeping, but gave it to such a bank that it might be loaned out, used in business, and earn interest. Athens thus became the financial center of the ancient world, as New York and London are to-day, and her bankers became the proverbially wealthy men of the time. The most successful among them was Pasion, a former slave, who had been able to purchase his liberty because of his great business ability.

**628.** Rise of prices; growing luxury

As the banking system resulted in keeping more money in circulation the old increase in prices (§ 537) went on, and the expenses for government were consequently higher; but the democracy continued to pay itself vast sums for jury service and show-money. There was a freer use of money in private life among the well-to-do classes. The houses of such people began to display rooms with painted wall decorations and adorned with rugs and hangings. An orator of the time condemns such luxurious houses, which he says were unknown in the days of Miltiades and the Persian War, just as some criticize our own modern fine houses and contrast them with the simplicity of George Washington and Revolutionary days.

Men were now becoming more and more interested in their own careers, and they were no longer so devoted to the State as formerly. This was especially true in the matter of military service. Except in Sparta, a Greek had heretofore left his occupation for a brief space to bear arms for a single short campaign, and then returned to his occupation. Such men made up a citizen militia, no more devoted to arms than our own modern militia. But the long Peloponnesian Wars had kept large numbers of Greeks so long under arms that many of them permanently adopted military life and became professional soldiers, serving for pay wherever they could find opportunity. Such soldiers serving a foreign state for pay are called " mercenaries." There were few unoccupied lands to which a young Greek could migrate as in the colonizing age ; and Persia blocked all such enterprises in the East. The Greek youths who could find no opportunities at home were therefore enlisting as soldiers in Egypt, in Asia Minor, and in Persia, and the best young blood of Greece was being spent to strengthen foreign states instead of building up the power of the Greeks.

**629.** Rise of the professional soldier as a result of the Peloponnesian Wars

During the Peloponnesian Wars military *leadership* had also become a profession. It was no longer possible for a citizen to leave private life and casually assume command of an army or a fleet. Athens produced a whole group of professional military leaders whose romantic exploits made them famous throughout the ancient world. The most talented among these was the Athenian, Xenophon. About 400 B.C. he took service in Asia Minor with Cyrus, a young Persian prince, who was planning to overthrow his brother, the Persian king. With ten thousand Greek mercenaries Cyrus marched entirely across Asia Minor to the Euphrates, and down the river almost to Babylon. Here the Greeks defeated the army of the Persian king ; but Cyrus

**630.** Rise of professional military leaders ; Xenophon and the Ten Thousand

was killed, and the Greeks were therefore obliged to retreat. Xenophon led them up the Tigris past the ruins of Nineveh (Fig. 203), and after months of fighting in dangerous mountain passes, suffering from cold and hunger, the survivors struggled on until they reached the Black Sea and finally gained Byzantium in safety.

**631. Rise of military science; "Anabasis" and other military treatises**

Of this extraordinary raid into the Persian Empire Xenophon has left a modest account called the "Anabasis" ("up-going"), one of the great books which have descended to us from ancient times. He explains the military operations involved, and the book thus became one of the treatises on military science which now began to appear. Such leaders were discussing the theory of operations in the field, methods of strategy, and the best kinds of weapons. Even Euripides, in his tragedy of *Hercules*, pictured the comparative effectiveness of bow and spear. Xenophon tells of an officer of Cyrus who divided his men into two parties and armed one party with clods and the other with clubs. After the two parties had fought it out, all agreed that the club in the hand at close quarters was more effective than missiles (that is, the clods) hurled from a distance. This was to demonstrate the effectiveness of the spear at close quarters over the arrows of distant archers.

**632. Greeks learn use of siege machinery and larger warships**

We recall that in Pericles' time the Spartans made no attempt to attack the walls of Athens, because the Greeks at that time knew nothing about methods of attacking fortifications. The Phœnician Carthaginians, however, had carried the Assyrian siege devices (p. 140) to the west, where the western Greeks had now learned to use them in Sicily. From Sicily the use of battering-rams, movable towers, and the like was carried to Greece itself, and against attack with such equipment Athens would no longer have been safe. The Mediterranean, which had so long ago received the arts of peace from the Orient, was now also learning to use war machinery from the same source. At the same time larger warships were constructed, some having as many as five banks of oars; and the old triremes with three banks could no longer stand against such powerful ships. All such equipment made war more expensive than before.

The remarkable feat of Xenophon's Ten Thousand (§ 630) finally stirred Spartan ambition to undertake conquest in Persian territory in Asia Minor. The Spartans, therefore, hired the surviving two thirds of the Ten Thousand, but the rule of Sparta had caused such dissatisfaction that her victories in Asia Minor were offset by revolts in Greece. In one of these Lysander was killed. The outcome of these rebellions was a league of Athens and Thebes against Sparta. Even Corinth, the old-time enemy of Athens, joined this league, and Argos also came in. Behind this combination was Persia, whose agents had brought it about in order to weaken Sparta. It was one of the ironies of the whole deplorable situation that a fleet of Athens made common cause with the Persians and helped to fasten Persian despotism on the Greek cities of Asia. The Greeks had learned nothing by their long and unhappy experience of fruitless fighting, and thus began an eight years' struggle, called the Corinthian War. The Athenians had been able to rebuild a fleet, with which they now destroyed the fleet of Sparta. They were then in a position to erect the Long Walls again.

**633.** War between Sparta and Persia; and the Corinthian War (395–387 B.C.)

At length the Persians began to fear lest Athens should again be strong enough to endanger Persian control in Asia Minor. The Spartans, therefore, found it easy to arrange a peace with Persia. The Greek states fighting Sparta were equally willing to come to terms, and when peace was at last established in Greece, it was under the humiliating terms of a treaty accepted by Hellas at the hands of the Persian king. It is known as the King's Peace (387 B.C.). It did not end the leadership of Sparta over the Greek states, and the Greek cities of Asia Minor were shamefully abandoned to Persia. The period following the King's Peace brought only added discontent with Sparta's illegal and tyrannical control, and no satisfactory solution of the problem of the relations of the Greek states among themselves.

**634.** King's Peace (387 B.C.)

## Section 60. The Fall of Sparta and the Leadership of Thebes

**635.** Thebes and a new Athenian league against Sparta (378 B.C.)

For twenty-five years since the last Peloponnesian war, the Spartans had been endeavoring to maintain control of the Greek world. Men like Lysander had been unable to transform the rigid Spartan system into a government which should sympathetically include and direct the activities of the whole Greek world. The Spartans were therefore more hated than Athens had ever been. A group of fearless and patriotic citizens at Thebes succeeded in slaying the oligarchs, the Spartan garrison surrendered and a democracy was set up, which gained the leadership of all Bœotia. At the same time Athens, which on the whole had been greatly strengthened by the terms of the King's Peace, was able to begin the formation of a second naval alliance like the original league from which the Athenian Empire had sprung. The combination included Thebes and so many of the other Greek cities that Sparta was greatly disturbed. The Spartans met disaster on land, and when this was followed by the defeat of their fleet by Athens, they were ready for peace.

**636.** Peace congress of the Greek states at Sparta

To arrange this peace all the Greek states met at Sparta, and such meetings gave them experience in the united management of their common affairs for the welfare of all Hellas. Spartan leadership might have held the Greek states together, and by giving them all a voice in the control of Hellas, Sparta might still have finally united the Greeks into a great nation. But this was not to be. When the conditions of peace were all agreed upon, the Spartans refused to allow Thebes to speak for the whole of Bœotia. The Thebans refused to enter the compact on any other terms, and the peace was concluded without them. This left Sparta and Thebes still in a state of war.

**637.** Spartan military tactics

All Greece now expected to see the Thebans crushed by the heavy Spartan phalanx, which had so long proved irresistible. The Spartan plan of battle hitherto followed by all commanders

consisted in making the phalanx of the right wing very heavy
and massive, by arraying it many warriors deep. The customary depth was eight men. The onset of a well-drilled phalanx
produced a pressure so terrible that the opposing lines gave
way and the unbroken phalanx pushed through. The effect
was that of a heavy mass play in American football, only we
must picture the phalanx as carrying out the operation on a
large scale. Having broken through at the first onset, the

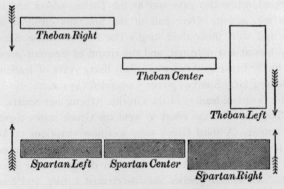

PLAN OF THE BATTLE OF LEUCTRA (371 B.C.)

victorious phalanx could then cut down singly the scattered
soldiers who had given way before them.

The Spartans had, as it were, but one " play " in their list;
but they were accustomed to see it automatically successful.
The Theban commander, a gifted and patriotic citizen named
Epaminondas, consequently knew in advance the only " play "
which the Spartans had ever used. He therefore devised an
altogether novel arrangement of his troops, such that it would
meet and more than offset the fearful pressure of the heavy
Spartan right. He drew up his line so that it was not parallel
with that of the Spartans, his right wing being much further
from the Spartan line than his left. At the same time he
massed his troops on his left wing, which he made fifty shields

**638. New
tactics of
Epaminon-
das, the
Theban**

deep. This great mass was to meet the shock of the heavy Spartan right wing (see plan, p. 403).

**639.** Battle of Leuctra and fall of Sparta (371 B.C.)

The battle took place at Leuctra, in southern Bœotia (see map, p. 352). As the lines moved into action the battle did not begin along the whole front at once; but the massive Theban left wing, being furthest advanced, met the Spartan line first and was at first engaged alone. Its onset proved so heavy that the Spartan right opposing it was soon crushed, and the rest of the Spartan line also gave way as the Theban center and right came into action. Over half of the Spartans engaged were slain and with them their king. The long-invincible Spartan army was at last defeated, and the charm of Spartan prestige was finally broken. After more than thirty years of leadership (since 404 B.C.) Spartan power was ended (371 B.C.)

**640.** Leadership and speedy collapse of Thebes

The two rival leaders of the Greeks, Athens and Sparta, had now both failed in the effort to weld the Greek states together as a nation. A third Greek state was now victorious on land, and it remained to be seen whether Thebes could accomplish what Athens and Sparta had failed in doing. Under Epaminondas' leadership Thebes likewise created a navy, and having greatly weakened Athens at sea, Thebes gained the leadership of Greece. But it was a supremacy based upon the genius of a single man, and when Epaminondas fell in a final battle with Sparta at Mantinea (362 B.C.), the power of Thebes by land and sea collapsed.

**641.** Final political prostration of the whole Greek world

Thus the only powerful Greek states, which might have developed a federation of the Hellenic world, having crushed each other, Hellas was ready to fall helplessly before a conqueror from the outside. The Greek world, whose civilization was everywhere supreme, was politically prostrate and helpless.

**642.** Progress of the Greeks in the higher life

It was less than two generations since the death of Pericles, and there were still old men living who had seen him in their childhood days. We have been following the *political* fortunes of Athens, Sparta, and Thebes during these two generations, but our narrative has been very far from telling the whole story. For in spite of their political decline during the two generations since Pericles, the Greeks, and especially the Athenians, had been achieving things in their higher life, in art, architecture, literature, and thought, which made this period perhaps the greatest in the history of man. To these achievements since the death of Pericles we must now turn back.

## QUESTIONS

SECTION 59. Why was Sparta unfitted to control the Greek states? What was her method of control? What is an oligarchy? How did it succeed? Had democracy succeeded any better? Describe the abuses practiced by the citizen-juries. Was class rule by the poor any better than class rule by the rich? What practices kept the Athenian treasury empty? What was the Athenian method of collecting taxes? Why was it unprofitable for the State? Describe the effects of lack of money on the work of government. What did the Greeks do in order to understand the national finances?

What was happening to small farm owners? Discuss business and finance at this time. How had the long Peloponnesian Wars affected the citizen soldiers of Greece? How was military leadership developing? Tell the story of Xenophon and the Ten Thousand. How has this story come down to us? What science was now arising? Where did the Greeks learn the use of siege machinery? What did the raid of the Ten Thousand lead Sparta to do? Sketch the Corinthian War. What was the result?

SECTION 60. What combination was formed to overthrow the leadership of Sparta? What did the Thebans do? What happened at the peace conference? In the resulting war between Sparta and Thebes what result was to be anticipated? Describe Spartan military tactics. How did Epaminondas plan to meet the Spartan tactics? Where and when did the armies meet? What was the result? How did Thebes succeed in leading the Greek states? In what condition politically was the whole Greek world?

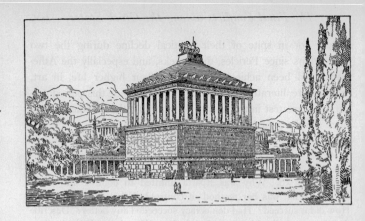

# CHAPTER XVIII

## THE HIGHER LIFE OF THE GREEKS FROM THE DEATH OF PERICLES TO THE FALL OF THE GREEK STATES

### SECTION 61. ARCHITECTURE, SCULPTURE, AND PAINTING

**643.** Decline of State support of art and architecture

The long wars and the demands of the democracy (§ 622) had swallowed up the wealth of Athens; the great and splendid works of the Age of Pericles were therefore no longer possible. At the same time Athens was obliged to rebuild her fortifications, erect war arsenals, and build sheds for her battleships. The old temporary wooden seats of the theater (§ 579) were replaced by a permanent structure of stone (Fig. 189). Here and there other Greek cities also were building durable stone theaters

NOTE. The above headpiece is a restoration by Adler of the famous tomb of King Mausolus of Caria, called after him the Mausoleum (§ 646). We now call any splendid tomb a mausoleum, thus preserving the old Hittite name of this king. It was when first built (in the middle of the fourth century B.C.) the most magnificent tomb on the north side of the Mediterranean, and it was because of its widespread fame that its name was preserved. Upon a high rectangular base a fine Ionic colonnade supported a step pyramid, upon which, crowning the whole monument, rose a splendid four-horse chariot bearing the king and queen. The work was designed and built by the architect and sculptor Pythius, and adorned with sculpture by Scopas and other Athenian sculptors whom the queen (§ 646) called to Caria for the purpose.

like that at Athens. Permanent stadiums for races were likewise erected by some communities (Fig. 212, *Q*). The maintenance of art and architecture in this age was, however, largely in the hands of individual artists, not supported by the State but producing works of art for private buyers.

Nevertheless, the Erechtheum (*F* in Fig. 183), one of the most beautiful buildings ever erected, a temple which had been begun before Pericles' death, was continued and, for the most part, completed during the unhappy days of the last Peloponnesian war. It was built in the Ionic style (p. 340), adorned with colonnades of wonderful refinement and beauty, and at one corner, over the grave of the legendary king Cecrops, the architects raised an exquisite porch, with its roof supported by lovely marble figures of Athenian maidens, watching over the burial place of the ancient king (headpiece, p. 394).

Egyptian architects, as we remember, had long before crowned their columns with a capital representing growing flowers or palm-tree tops (Fig. 56). The Greek architects now profited by this hint (see headpiece and note, p. 453). Perceiving the great beauty of their own acanthus plant, they now designed a capital adorned with a double row of acanthus leaves (Fig. 193). This new capital was richer and more

**644.** The Erechtheum on the Athenian Acropolis

FIG. 193. A CORINTHIAN CAPITAL

**645.** Rise of the Corinthian style of architecture

The shaft of this column has been cut out in the drawing between the base and the capital to save space. Like the capitals of Egypt (§ 92), this one represents a plant, the leaves of the acanthus, alternating in two rows around the capital and crowned by volutes rising to the four corners of a flat block upon which the supported stone above rests. The effect of this capital is peculiarly rich and ornate (§ 645)

sumptuous than the simpler Doric and Ionic forms (p. 340). Although our earliest example of such columns still survives at *Athens* (Fig. 190), they are now called Corinthian columns.

**646.** The Mausoleum in Asia Minor

While Athens no longer possessed the means to erect great state temples, other Greek states were not all so financially exhausted. In Asia Minor the widowed queen of the wealthy king of the Carians, Mausolus, so revered the memory of her royal husband that she devoted vast riches to the erection of a magnificent marble tomb for him, so splendid that it became one of the most famous monuments of the ancient world (headpiece, p. 406). While imposing as a monument of architecture, the Mausoleum (so named after Mausolus; see note, p. 406) was most impressive because of the rich and remarkable sculpture with which it was adorned. To do this work the widowed queen called in the greatest sculptors of the Greeks.

**647.** Contrast between sculpture of the Periclean Age and the later work

Sculpture had made great progress since the days of Pericles. Phidias and his pupils depicted the gods, whom they wrought in marble, as lofty, majestic, unapproachable beings, lifted high above human weaknesses and human feeling. We remember that even the *human* figures of Phidias were not the everyday men and women, youths and maidens whom we might have met on the streets of Athens (§ 577). When Phidias and his pupils had passed away, the sculptors who followed them began to put more of the feeling and the experience of daily human life into their work and thus brought their subjects nearer to us. Among them we must give a high place, perhaps the highest place, to the great Athenian sculptor Praxiteles.

**648.** The sculpture of Praxiteles and Scopas

His native city being without the money for great monumental works, Praxiteles wrought individual figures of life size, and most of these for foreign states. Unlike the majestic and exalted figures of Phidias, the gods of Praxiteles seem near to us. They at once appeal to us as being human like ourselves, interested in a life like ours, and doing things which we would like to do ourselves. As they stand at ease in attitudes of repose, the grace and balance of the flowing lines give them a splendor

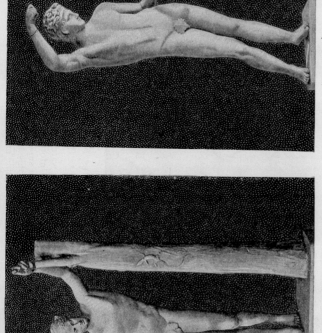

FIGS. 194 AND 195. TWO GREEK GODS AS SCULPTURED BY PRAXITELES

Notice the wonderful ease and grace with which these figures in repose are poised. In a country where lizards were darting along every sunny wall, a lad with stone poised to throw was a frequent sight. This common human action is the one which Praxiteles chose for his Apollo (Fig. 194), and another equally common, the pouring of wine, he has depicted in the figure of the satyr (Fig. 195). These very human gods are quite different from those of Phidias (§ 648)

Fig. 196. Battle Scene from the Sculptures of the Mausoleum (§ 646) in the Manner of Scopas (§ 648)

The superb vigor and violent action of these ancient warriors are in sharp contrast with the tranquillity and repose of Praxiteles' figures (Figs. 187, 194, and 195). Unfortunately, not a single one of the very numerous works of Scopas has survived. A number of fragments are supposed to be his work, and some of the frieze scenes surviving from the Mausoleum may be the work of his hands. The above scene is not ascribed to him, but shows his influence and is a fine example of the sculpture of violent action (§ 648) of beauty unattained by any earlier sculpture of the Greeks (Figs. 187, 194, and 195). In great contrast with the work of Praxiteles was that of Scopas, who did much of the sculpture of the Mausoleum. He loved to fashion figures not in tranquil moods, but in violent action, in moments of passionate excitement, like that of warriors in battle (Fig. 196). The *faces* sculptured by Praxiteles and Scopas were no longer expressionless, as in earlier sculpture (Figs. 168 and 169); but the artists began to put into them some of their own inner feeling. The artist's own individual life thus began to find expression in his work. In many ways the sculpture of this age was much influenced by the work of the painters, who really led the way.

The introduction of portable paintings on wooden tablets made it more easy for the painters to follow their own individual feelings, for they were thus freed from the necessity of painting large scenes on the walls of State buildings (§ 572). As we have already learned (§ 550), no oil colors were known in the ancient world, but the Greek painters now adopted the Egyptian method of mixing their colors in melted wax and then applying the fluid wax with a brush to a wooden tablet (Plate VIII, p. 654). The painter could then work in his own studio to please his own fancy, and could sell his paintings to any private purchaser who wished to buy. It thus became customary for people of wealth to set up paintings in their own houses, and in this way private support of art was much furthered, and painting made great progress. 649. Rise of paintings on wood

An Athenian painter named Apollodorus now began to notice that the light usually fell on an object from one side, leaving the unlighted side so dark that but little color showed on that side, while on the lighted side the colors came out very brightly. When he painted a woman's arm in this way, lo, it looked round and seemed to stand out from the surface of the painting (Fig. 197); whereas up in the Painted Porch all the human limbs in the old painting of Marathon (§ 572) looked perfectly flat. By representing figures in the background of his paintings, as 650. Discovery of how to paint light, shadow, and perspective

FIG. 197. A WALL-PAINTING AT POMPEII SHOWING THE SACRIFICE OF IPHIGENIA

The works of the great fourth-century artists (§ 651) have all perished, but it is supposed that the later house decorators and wall-painters of Italy copied the old masterpieces. Hence the scene here shown probably conveys some impression of old Greek painting. The scene shows us the maid Iphigenia as she is carried away to be slain as a sacrifice. The figure at the left, standing with veiled face, suggests, as often in modern art, the dreadfulness of a coming catastrophe, which human eyes are unwilling to behold. Note the skill with which human limbs are made to show thickness and roundness (§ 650)

smaller than those in front Apollodorus also introduced what we now call perspective. As a result, his paintings had an appearance of depth, and when he painted the interior of a house one seemed to be looking into the very room itself. He was called by the Athenians the "shadow painter," and the good old-fashioned folk shook their heads at his work, preferring the old style. Even the great philosopher Plato (§ 671) condemned this new method of painting as employing devices and creating illusions of depth which were really deception.

*A*      *B*

FIG. 198. GREEK BOY PULLING OUT A THORN (*A*) AND A LATER CARICATURE OF THE THORN PULLER (*B*)

The graceful figure of the slender boy so seriously striving to remove the thorn was probably wrought not long after the Persian Wars. It was very popular in antiquity, as it has also been in modern times. The comical caricature (*B*) in clay (terra cotta), though it has lost one foot, is a delightful example of Greek humor expressed in parody (§ 652)

Nevertheless, the new method triumphed, and the younger painters who adopted it produced work which was the talk of the town. People gossiped about it and told how a painter named Zeuxis, in order to outdo his rival Parrhasius, had painted grapes so naturally that the birds flew up to the painting and pecked at them. Thereupon Parrhasius invited Zeuxis over to his studio to inspect a painting of his. Zeuxis found it covered

651. Triumph of the new method of painting

with a curtain which he attempted to draw aside. But his hand fell on a painted surface and he discovered to his confusion that the curtain was no more real than his own painted grapes had been. Unfortunately, all such Greek paintings have perished, and we have only later copies (Fig. 197) at Pompeii.

The vase-painters of the time likewise often copied the famous works of the leading sculptors and painters. But after a wonderful revival in the last Peloponnesian war, the art of vase-painting passed into a melancholy decline from which it never recovered. At the same time, in order to meet the rising desire for objects of art among the people, small artists began to furnish delightful miniature copies of famous classic works, or again they made delicious caricatures of such well-known classics (Fig. 198, *B*). At the same time even stone-cutters wrought tomb-stones, bearing reliefs done with a soft and melancholy beauty, breathing the wistful uncertainty with which the Greeks of this age were beginning to look out into the shadow world (Fig. 199).

652. Vase-painters and other artist-craftsmen

FIG. 199. ATHENIAN GRAVESTONE SHOWING A DAUGHTER SAYING FARE-WELL TO HER PARENTS

This tombstone of a young girl shows us the fine feeling of which even a grave-yard stonecutter was capable. He has depicted the last farewell of the parents, as their daughter is carried away by death. The mother, seated at the left, grasps the young girl's hand, while the father stands with his fingers in his beard in somber and meditative reconciliation

## Section 62.  Religion, Literature, and Thought

Any young Athenian born at about the time of Pericles' death found himself in an age of conflict wherever he went: an age of conflict *abroad* on the field of battle as he stood with spear and shield in the Athenian ranks in the long years of warfare between Athens, Sparta, and Thebes; an age of conflict *at home* in Athens amid the excited shouting and applause of the turbulent Assembly or the tumult and even bloodshed of the streets and markets of the city as the common people, the democracy, struggled with the nobles for the leadership of the State; and finally in an age of conflict *in himself* as he felt his once confident faith in old things struggling to maintain itself against new views.

**653.** The age of conflict after the death of Pericles

He recalled the childhood tales of the gods, which he had heard at his nurse's knee. When he had asked her how Athena and the gods looked, she had pointed to a beautiful vase in his father's house, bearing graceful paintings of Athena presenting the olive tree to the Athenians, and of the angry Sea-god striking his trident into the ground and leaving a mark which the lad's nurse had shown him at the Erechtheum on the Acropolis (p. 394). There were the gods on the vase in human form, and so he had long thought of them as people like those of Athens. He had learned, too, that they were near by, for he had seen his father present gifts to them at household feasts. Later when he went to school and memorized long passages of the Homeric poems, he had learned more about their adventures on earth. Then he had stood on the edge of the crowd with his parents watching the magnificent State feasts, like the Panathenæa (§ 570), supported at great expense, in order to honor the gods and keep them favorable to Athens. Hence everyone seemed to him to believe that the gods had all power over Athens. On such occasions he vaguely felt the majesty and grandeur of the great gods, but when he looked upon figures of them, sculptured by such artists as Praxiteles

**654.** The Athenian citizen's religion and early life

(Fig. 194), the gods again appeared very much like earthly folk, as he had seen them on the vase in his childhood.

**655. Religion and conduct**

He never had any religious instruction, for there was nothing like a church, a clergy, or any religious teachers. There was no sacred book revered by all, like our Bible. He had not been taught that the gods had any interest in him or his conduct, or that they required him to be either good or bad. As long as he did not neglect any of the ceremonies desired by the gods, he knew he need have no fear of them. At the same time if he lived an evil life, he realized that he might be condemned to enter at death a dark and gruesome dwelling place beneath the earth (§ 488). On the other hand, a good life might bring him at last to the beautiful Elysian fields (§ 489).

**656. The religion of the multitude**

One of the ways of reaching this place of blessedness was by initiation into the mysteries at Eleusis (§ 489). Another way was to follow the teachings of the beggar-priests and sooth-sayers of Orpheus. These wandering teachers, like traveling revival preachers of to-day, went about in all Greece, followed by hordes of the poor and ignorant, who eagerly accepted their mysterious teachings, promising every blessing to those who listened and obeyed. The more mysterious it all was the better the multitude liked it. These teachings were recorded in the wonderful book of Orpheus, which finally gained wide circulation among the common people. It came nearer to being the sacred book of the Greeks than any that ever arose among them. All the lower classes believed in magic and were deeply impressed by the mysterious " stunts " of the magicians and soothsayers whom they constantly consulted on all the ordinary acts of life.

**657. The foreign gods from the Orient**

Down at Piræus, the harbor town, the Athenian citizen found the busy streets crowded with foreign merchants from Egypt, Phœnicia, and Asia Minor. They, too, had their assurances of divine help and blessedness, and they brought with them their strange gods : the Great Mother from Asia Minor, Isis from her lovely temple at the First Cataract of the Nile

(Plate V, p. 444), and Egyptian Amon from his mysterious shrine far away in the Sahara (Fig. 205), behind the Greek city of Cyrene (see map, p. 434). The famous Greek poet Pindar had written a poem in his honor, and erected a statue of the great Egyptian god. As a deliverer of oracles revealing the future, Amon had now become as great a favorite among the Greeks themselves as Apollo of Delphi (§ 490). There was an Athenian ship which regularly plied between the Piræus and Cyrene, carrying the Greeks to Amon's distant Sahara shrine. Egyptian symbols too were common on Greek tombstones.

Some of these foreign beliefs had once greatly impressed our citizen in his younger days. Then when he left his boyhood teacher behind, and went to hear the lectures of a noted Sophist (§ 561), he found that no one knew with any certainty whether the gods even existed; much less did anyone know what they were like. He now looked with some pity at the crowds of pilgrims who filled the sacred road leading to the hall of the mysteries at Eleusis. He had only contempt for the mob which filled the processions of the strange oriental gods, and almost every day marched with tumult and flute-playing through the streets of Athens. While he could not follow such superstitions of the ignorant poor, he found, nevertheless, that he was not yet quite ready to throw away the gods and reject them altogether, as some of his educated neighbors were doing.

**658. The Athenian citizen's later uncertainties**

He recalled the days of his youth, when he had detested these very doubts which he had now taken up. With great enjoyment he had once beheld the caricatures of Aristophanes, the greatest of the comedy writers (§ 582). Our citizen had shouted with delight at Aristophanes' mockery of the doubts and mental struggles of Euripides (§ 581), or the ridicule which the clever comedy heaped upon the Sophists. Since then, however, had come the new light which he had gained from the Sophists. Whatever the gods might be like, he was sure that

**659. The victory of doubt and the triumph of Euripides**

they were not such beings as he found pictured among his heroic forefathers in the Homeric poems. Now he had long since cast aside his Homer. In spite of Aristophanes, he and his educated friends were all reading the splendid tragedies of Euripides (§ 581), with their uncertainties, struggles, and doubts about life and the gods. Euripides, the victim of Aristophanes' ridicule, to whom the Athenians had rarely voted a victory during his lifetime (§ 581), had now triumphed, but his triumph meant the defeat of the old, the victory of doubt, the overthrow of the gods, and the incoming of a new age in thought and belief. But the old died hard, and the struggle was a tragic one.

The citizen remembered well another comedy of Aristophanes, which had likewise found a ready response from the Athenian audience. It had placed upon the stage the rude and comical figure of a poor Athenian named Socrates, whom Aristophanes had represented as a dangerous man, to be shunned or even chastised by good Athenians. He was the son of a stonecutter, or small

**660.** Aristophanes and Socrates

FIG. 200. PORTRAIT OF SOCRATES

This is not the best of the numerous surviving portraits of Socrates, but it is especially interesting because it bears under the philosopher's name nine inscribed lines containing a portion of his public defense as reported by Plato in his *Apology*

sculptor. The ill-clothed figure and ugly face (Fig. 200) of Socrates had become familiar in the streets to all the folk of Athens since the outbreak of the second war with Sparta. He was accustomed to stand about the market place all day long, engaging in conversation anyone he met, and asking a great many questions. Our citizen recalled that Socrates' questions left him in a very confused state of mind, for he seemed to call in question everything which the citizen had once regarded as settled.

Yet this familiar and homely figure of the stonecutter's son was the personification of the best and highest in Greek genius. Without desire for office or a political career, Socrates' supreme interest nevertheless was the State. He believed that the State, made up as it was of citizens, could be purified and saved only by the improvement of the individual citizen through the education of his mind to recognize virtue and right.

**661. The State the chief interest of Socrates**

Herein lies the supreme achievement of Socrates; namely, his unshakable conviction that the human mind is able to recognize and determine what are virtue and right, truth, beauty and honesty, and all the other great ideas which mean so much to human life. To him these ideas had *reality*. He taught that by keen questioning and *discussion* it is possible to reject error and discern these realities. Inspired by this impregnable belief, Socrates went about in Athens, engaging all his fellow citizens in such discussion, convinced that he might thus lead each citizen in turn to a knowledge of the leading and compelling virtues. Furthermore, he firmly believed that the citizen who had once recognized these virtues would shape every action and all his life by them. Socrates thus revealed the power of virtue and of similar ideas by argument and logic, but he made no appeal to religion as an influence toward good conduct. Nevertheless, he showed himself a deeply religious man, believing with devout heart in the gods, although they were not exactly those of the fathers, and even feeling, like the Hebrew prophets, that there was a divine voice within him, calling him to his high mission.

**662. His belief in man's power to discern the great truths as such and to shape his conduct by them**

The simple but powerful personality of this greatest of Greek teachers often opened to him the houses of the rich and noble. His fame spread far and wide, and when the

**663. Public opinion of Socrates**

Delphian oracle (§ 490) was asked who was the wisest of the living, it responded with the name of Socrates. A group of pupils gathered about him, among whom the most famous was Plato. But his aims and his noble efforts on behalf of the Athenian State were misunderstood. His keen questions seemed to throw doubt upon all the old beliefs. The Athenians had already vented their displeasure on more than one leading Sophist who had rejected the old faith and teaching (§ 593).

**664. The trial and death of Socrates (399 B.C.)** So the Athenians summoned Socrates to trial for corrupting the youth with all sorts of doubts and impious teachings. Such examples as Alcibiades, who had been his pupil, seemed convincing illustrations of the viciousness of his teaching; many had seen and still more had read with growing resentment the comedy of Aristophanes which held him up to contempt and execration. Socrates might easily have left Athens when the complaint was lodged against him. Nevertheless he appeared for trial, made a powerful and dignified defense, and, when the court voted the death penalty, passed his last days in tranquil conversation with his friends and pupils, in whose presence he then quietly drank the fatal hemlock (399 B.C.). Thus the Athenian democracy, which had so fatally mismanaged the affairs of the nation in war, brought upon itself much greater reproach in condemning to death, even though in accordance with law, the greatest and purest soul among its citizens (headpiece, p. 425).

**665. The influence of Socrates after his death** The undisturbed serenity of Socrates in his last hours, as pictured to us in Plato's idealized version of the scene, profoundly affected the whole Greek world and still forms one of the most precious possessions of humanity. He was the greatest Greek, and in him Greek civilization reached its highest level. But the glorified figure of Socrates, as he appears in the writings of his pupils, was to prove more powerful even than the living teacher.

Meantime there had been growing up a body of scientific knowledge about the visible world, which men had never possessed before. Moreover this new scientific knowledge was no longer confined to the few philosophers who were its discoverers, as formerly had been the case (§ 564). Our doubting citizen had at home a whole shelf of books on natural science. It included a treatise on mathematics, an astronomy in which the year was at last stated to contain $365\frac{1}{4}$ days, a zoölogy and a botany. There was also a mineralogy, a pamphlet on foretelling the weather, and a treatise on the calendar, besides several geographies with maps of the world then known. There were also practical books of guidance and instruction on drawing, war, farming, raising horses, or even cooking. **666.** Spread of scientific knowledge among the people

There was in our citizen's library also a remarkable history, treating the fortunes of nations in the same way in which natural science was treated. Its author was Thucydides, the first scientific writer of history. A generation earlier Herodotus' history (§ 567) had ascribed the fortunes of nations to the will of the gods, but Thucydides, with an insight like that of modern historians, traced historical events to their *earthly* causes in the world of men where they occur. There stood the two books, Herodotus and Thucydides, side by side in the citizen's library. There were only thirty years or so between them, but how different the beliefs of the two historians, the old and the new! Thucydides was one of the greatest writers of simple and beautiful prose that ever lived. His book which told the story of the long wars resulting in the fall of the Athenian Empire was received by the Greeks with enthusiastic approval. It has been one of the world's great classics ever since. **667.** Scientific writing of history

The success of Thucydides' work in prose shows that the interest of the Athenians was no longer in poetry but in the new and more youthful art of prose. Poetry, including play-writing, noticeably declined. A successful public speech was now written down beforehand, and the demand for such addresses in the Assembly, and especially before the citizen-juries, was a constant motive for the cultivation of skillful prose writing and public speaking. **668.** The decline of poetry and the triumph of prose

**669.** Athens the center of education; Isocrates

The teachers of rhetoric at Athens, the successors of the old Sophists (§ 562), became world renowned, and they made the city the center of education for the whole Greek world. The leader among them was Isocrates, the son of a well-to-do flute manufacturer. Having lost his father's fortune in the Peloponnesian Wars, he turned for a living to the teaching of rhetoric, in which he soon showed great ability. He chose as his theme the great political questions of his time. He was not a good speaker, and he therefore devoted himself especially to the *writing* of his speeches, which he then published as political essays. Throughout Greece these remarkable essays were read, and Isocrates finally became the political spokesman of Athens, if not of all Greece.

**670.** Rise of the science of government

Notwithstanding the new interest in natural science, the affairs of *men* rather than of *nature* were the burning questions at Athens. How should the governmental affairs of a community of men be conducted? — what should be the proper form of a free state? — these were the problems which Athenian experience and the efforts of Socrates toward an enlightened citizenship had thrust into the foreground. What should be the form of the ideal state? The Orient had already had its social idealism. In the Orient, however, it had never occurred to the social dreamers to discuss the *form of government* of the ideal state. They accepted as a matter of course the monarchy under which they lived as the obvious form for the State. But in Greece the question of the form of government, whether a kingdom, a republic, or an aristocracy, was now earnestly discussed. Thus there arose a new science, the *science of government*.

**671.** Plato

Plato, the most gifted pupil of Socrates, published much of his beloved master's teaching in the form of dialogues, supposedly reproducing the discussions of the great teacher himself. Then after extensive travels in Egypt and the west he returned to Athens, where he set up his school in the grove of the Academy (§ 558). Convinced of the hopelessness of democracy in Athens, he reluctantly gave up all thought of a career as a statesman, to which he had been strongly drawn, and settled down at Athens to devote himself to teaching.

Plato was both philosopher and poet. The *ideas* which Socrates maintained the human mind could discern, became for Plato eternal realities, having an existence independent of man and his mind. The human soul, he taught, had always existed, and in an earlier state had beheld the great ideas of goodness, beauty, evil, and the like, and had gained an intuitive vision of them which in this earthly life the soul now recalled and recognized again. The elect souls, gifted with such vision, were the ones to control the ideal state, for they would necessarily act in accordance with the ideas of virtue and justice which they had discerned. It was possible by education, thought Plato, to lead the souls of men to a clear vision of these ideas.

672. Plato's development of the Socratic ideas

In a noble essay entitled *The Republic* Plato presented a lofty vision of his ideal state. Here live the enlightened souls governing society in righteousness and justice. They do no work, but depend on craftsmen and slaves for all menial labor. And yet the comforts and leisure which they enjoy are the product of that very world of industry and commerce in a Greek city which Plato so thoroughly despises. The plan places far too much dependence on education and takes no account of the dignity and importance of labor in human society. Moreover, Plato's ideal state is the self-contained, self-controlling city-state as it had in times past supposedly existed in Greece. He failed to perceive that the vital question for Greece was now *the relation of these city-states to each other*. He did not discern that the life of a cultivated state unavoidably expands beyond its borders, and by its needs and its contributions affects the life of surrounding states. It cannot be confined within its *political* borders, for its *commercial* borders lie as far distant as its galleys can carry its produce.

673. Plato's ideal state

Thus boundary lines cannot separate nations; their life overlaps and interfuses with the life round about them. It was so within Greece, and it was so far beyond the borders of Greek

674. Growth of a Hellenized world

territory. There had grown up a *civilized world* which was reading Greek books, using Greek utensils, fitting up its houses with Greek furniture, decorating its house interiors with Greek paintings, building Greek theaters, learning Greek tactics in war — a great Mediterranean and oriental world bound together by lines of commerce, travel, and common economic interests. For this world, as a coming *political* unity, the lofty idealist Plato, in spite of his travels, had no eyes. To this world, once dominated by oriental culture, the Greeks had given the noblest and sanest ideas yet attained by the mind of civilized man, and to this world likewise the Greeks should have given political leadership.

**675. Motives toward unity: Isocrates and Xenophon**

Men in practical life, like Isocrates, clearly understood the situation at this time. Isocrates urged the Greeks to bury their petty differences and expand their purely *sectional* patriotism into loyalty toward a great nation which should unite the whole Greek world. He told his countrymen that, so united, they could easily overthrow the decaying Persian Empire and make themselves lords of the world, whereas now, while they continued to fight among themselves, the king of Persia could do as he pleased with them. In an inspiring address distributed to the Greeks at the Olympic games, he said: "Anyone coming from abroad and observing the present situation of Greece would regard us as great fools struggling among ourselves about trifles, and destroying our own land, when without danger we might conquer Asia." To all Greeks who had read Xenophon's story of the march of his Ten Thousand, the weakness of the Persian Empire was obvious. Every motive toward unity was present.

**676. Unalterable disunion the end of Greek political development**

Nevertheless, no Greek city was willing to submit to the leadership of another. *Local* patriotism, like the sectionalism which brought on our Civil War, prevailed, and unalterable disunion was the end of Greek political development. As a result the Greeks were now to be subjected by an outside power, which had never had any share in advancing Greek culture

(§ 678). Thus the fine theories of the ideal form of the state so warmly discussed at Athens were now to be met by the hard fact of irresistible power in the hands of a single ruler — the form of power which the Greek republics had in vain striven to destroy.

But in spite of this final and melancholy collapse of Greek political power, which even the wealth and splendor of the western Greek cities in Italy and Sicily, like Syracuse, had not been able to prevent, what an incomparably glorious age of Greek civilization was this which we have been sketching! The rivalries which proved so fatal to the political leadership of the Greeks had been a constant incentive spurring them all on, as each city strove to surpass its rivals in art and literature and all the finest things in civilization. Great as the age of Pericles had been, the age that followed was still greater. The tiny Athenian state, with a population not larger than that of our little state of Delaware in 1910, and having at best twenty-five or thirty thousand citizens, had furnished in this period a group of great names in all lines of human achievement, such as never in all the history of the world arose in an area and a population so limited. In a book like this we have been able to offer only a few hints of all that these men of Athens accomplished. Their names to-day are among the most illustrious in human history, and the achievements which we link with them form the greatest chapter in the higher life of man. Furthermore, Greek genius was to go on to many another future triumph, in spite of the loss of that political leadership which we are now to see passing into other hands.

**677.** Supremacy of Greek genius in spite of political collapse

## QUESTIONS

SECTION 61. Was Athens now able to support great works of art as in the days of Pericles? What was the effect upon art? What lovely building was nevertheless erected on the Acropolis? What new style of architecture was coming in? How did it differ from the older Doric and Ionic styles? Describe the Mausoleum. How did the sculpture of Praxiteles differ from that of Phidias? What kind of figures did Scopas love to carve? What new process of producing portable paintings came in? What new method of painting did Apollodorus introduce? What popular stories about the feats of the new shadow painters arose? Have any of these paintings survived? How do we know how they looked? What kind of small works did the lesser artists produce?

SECTION 62. In what respects was the age following Pericles one of conflict? What did an Athenian child of this time learn about the gods at home? at school? at public celebrations? from great works of art? Had he had any religious instruction? What did he believe about his own conduct and the relation of the gods to it? What did the common people believe? What teachers did they follow? Did they show intelligence or superstition in religious matters?

What foreign divinities were coming in? Tell about them. What did the educated citizen think about the beliefs of the common people? What had once been his feeling about religious doubt? Whose comedies had mocked such doubt? From whom did such a citizen himself learn to doubt? Whose tragedies were he and his friends reading? Did this mean the suppression or the triumph of doubt?

How did one of the comedies of Aristophanes represent Socrates? How did Socrates spend most of his time? What was his purpose in doing this? Can you sum up his teachings? Was he then an evil man? Was he irreligious? What was the general opinion about his wisdom? about his character? What did the Athenians finally do in order to silence Socrates? Tell about his trial and death. Did his influence cease at his death?

What was the condition of scientific knowledge at Athens? How did the history of Thucydides differ from that of Herodotus? How much time had elapsed between them? What can you say of prose and poetry in this age? Who was the leading teacher of rhetoric and prose writing at Athens? What can you say of his own writing? What new science was arising? What can you say of the life of Plato? What did he teach about government? What great question did he fail to perceive? What civilized world was growing up? Why had not the Greeks given this world of Greek culture also political unity? How did practical men like Isocrates feel about this problem? Did the Greeks follow his advice? What was to be the result?

# CHAPTER XIX

## ALEXANDER THE GREAT

### Section 63. The Rise of Macedonia

On the northern frontiers in the mountains of the Balkan Peninsula Greek civilization gradually faded and disappeared, merging into the barbarism which had descended from Stone Age
Europe. These backward Northerners, such as the Thracians,
spoke Indo-European tongues akin to Greek, but their Greek
kindred of the South could not understand them. A veneer

678. The un-
cultivated
states of the
Balkan Pen-
insula and
the North

NOTE. The above headpiece shows us one of the streets where it was the
custom of both the Greeks and Romans (Fig. 212, *H, K*) to bury their dead.
It was outside the Dipylon Gate (plan, p. 352), on the sacred way leading to
Eleusis, both sides of which were lined for some distance with marble tomb-
stones, of which Fig. 199 is an example. The Roman Sulla (§ 945), in his Eastern
war, while besieging Athens, piled up earth as a causeway leading to the top of
the wall of Athens (see plan, p. 352) at this point. The part of the cemetery which
he covered with earth was thus preserved, to be dug out in modern times — the
only surviving portion of such an ancient Greek street of tombs. In this cemetery the Athenians of Socrates' day were buried. The monument at the left shows
a brave Athenian youth on horseback, charging the fallen enemy. He was slain
in the Corinthian War (§ 633) and buried here a few years after the death of
Socrates (§ 664).

of Greek civilization began here and there to mask somewhat the rough and uncultivated life of the peasant population of Macedonia. The Macedonian kings began to cultivate Greek literature and art. The mother of Philip of Macedon was grateful that she had been able to learn to write in her old age.

**679.** Philip of Macedon and his policy of expansion

Philip himself had enjoyed a Greek education, and when he gained the power over Macedonia, in 360 B.C., he understood perfectly the situation of the disunited Greek world. He planned to make himself its master, and he began his task with the ability both of a skilled statesman and an able soldier. With clear recognition of the necessary means, he first created the indispensable military power. As a hostage at Thebes he had learned to lead an army under the eye of no less a master than Epaminondas himself, the conqueror of the Spartans. But Philip surpassed his teacher.

**680.** Philip creates Macedonian infantry

From the peasant population of his kingdom Philip drew off a number large enough to form a permanent or standing army of professional soldiers who never expected again to return to the flocks and fields. These men he armed as heavy infantry of the phalanx, as he had seen it in Greece; only he made the phalanx deeper and more massive and gave his men longer spears. They soon became famous as the " Macedonian phalanx."

**681.** Macedonian horsemen and Philip's combination of cavalry and infantry in unified operations

Heretofore horsemen had played but a small part in war in Europe. Horses were plentiful in Philip's kingdom, and the nobles forming a warrior class had always been accustomed to fight on horseback in a loose way, each for himself. Philip now drilled these riders to move about and to attack in a single mass. The charge of such a mass of horsemen was so terrible that it might of itself decide a battle. Philip then further improved the art of war by a final step, the most important of all. He so combined his heavy phalanx in the *center*, with the disciplined masses of horsemen on each *wing*, that the whole combined force, infantry and cavalry, moved and operated as one great unit, an irresistible machine in which every part worked together with all the others.

This new chapter in the art of warfare was possible only because a single mind was in unhampered control of the situation. The Greeks were now to witness the practical effectiveness of one-man control as exercised by a skillful leader for many years. With statesmanlike insight Philip first began his conquests in the region where he might expect the least resistance. He steadily extended the territory of his kingdom eastward and northward until it reached the Danube and the Hellespont.

His progress on the north of the Ægean soon brought him into conflict with the interests of the Greek states, which owned cities in this northern region. Philip's conquests were viewed with mixed feelings at Athens, toward which the Macedonian king himself felt very friendly, for he had the greatest admiration for the Greeks. Two parties therefore arose at Athens. One of them was quite willing to accept Philip's proffered friendship, and recognized in him the uniter and savior of the Greek

FIG. 201. PORTRAIT BUST OF DEMOSTHENES

world. The leader of this party was Isocrates (§ 675), now an aged man. The other party, on the contrary, denounced Philip as a barbarous tyrant who was endeavoring to enslave the free Greek cities.

The leader of this anti-Macedonian party was the great orator Demosthenes (Fig. 201). In one passionate appeal after another he addressed the Athenian people, as he strove to arouse them to the growing danger threatening the Greek states with every added triumph of Philip's powerful army. By the whirlwind of his marvelous eloquence he carried the Athenian Assembly with him. His " Philippics," as his denunciations of King Philip are called, are among the greatest specimens of Greek eloquence, and have become traditional among us as noble examples of oratorical power inspired by high and patriotic motives. But they were very immoderate in their abuse and denunciation of his opponents in Athens, nor can it be said that they display a statesmanlike understanding of the hopelessly disunited condition of the ever-warring Greek states.

**685. Philip gains the leadership of the Greeks (338 B.C.)**
The outcome of the struggle which unavoidably came on between Philip and the Greek states showed that the views of Isocrates, while less ideally attractive, were far more sagacious and statesmanlike than those of Demosthenes. After a long series of hostilities Philip defeated the Greek forces in a final battle at Chæronea (338 B.C.), and firmly established his position as head of a league of all the Greek states except Sparta, which still held out against him. He had begun operations in Asia Minor for the freedom of the Greek cities there, when two years after the battle of Chæronea he was stabbed by conspirators during the revelries at the wedding of his daughter (336 B.C.).

**686. The successors of Philip of Macedon**
The power passed into the hands of his son Alexander, a youth of only twenty years. Fortunately Philip also left behind him in the Macedonians of his court a group of remarkable men, of imperial abilities. They were devoted to the royal house, and Alexander's early successes were in no small measure due to them. But their very devotion and ability, as we shall see, later brought the young king into a personal conflict which contained all the elements of a tremendous tragedy (§ 709).

**687. Education and character of Alexander the Great**
When Alexander was thirteen years of age his father had summoned to the Macedonian court the great philosopher Aristotle (§ 760), a former pupil of Plato, to be the teacher of the young prince. Under his instruction the lad learned to know and love the masterpieces of Greek literature, especially the Homeric songs. The deeds of the ancient heroes touched

and kindled his youthful imagination and lent a heroic tinge to his whole character. As he grew older and his mind ripened, his whole personality was imbued with the splendor of Greek genius and Hellenic culture.

## SECTION 64. CAMPAIGNS OF ALEXANDER THE GREAT

The Greek states were still unwilling to submit to Macedonian leadership, and they fancied they could overthrow so youthful a ruler as Alexander. They were soon to learn how old a head there was on his young shoulders. When Thebes revolted against Macedonia for the second time after Philip's death, Alexander, knowing that he must take up the struggle with Persia, realized that it would not be safe for him to march into Asia without giving the Greek states a lesson which they would not soon forget. He therefore captured and completely destroyed the ancient city of Thebes, sparing only the house of the great poet Pindar. All Greece was thus taught to fear and respect his power, but learned at the same time to recognize his reverence for Greek genius. Feeling him to be their natural leader, therefore, the Greek states, with the exception of Sparta, formed a league and elected Alexander as its leader and general. As a result they all sent troops to increase his army.

**688. Alexander subjugates the Greek states and becomes head of a Greek league**

The Asiatic campaign which Alexander now planned was to vindicate his position as the champion of Hellas against Asia. He thought to lead the united Greeks against the Persian lord of Asia, as the Hellenes had once made common cause against Asiatic Troy (§ 411). Leading his army of Macedonians and allied Greeks into Asia Minor, he therefore stopped at Troy and camped upon the plain (Fig. 151, and map, p. 434) where the Greek heroes of the Homeric songs had once fought. Here he worshiped in the temple of Athena, and prayed for the success of his cause against Persia. He thus contrived to throw around himself the heroic atmosphere of the Trojan War, till all Hellas beheld the dauntless figure of the Macedonian

**689. Alexander, the champion of Hellas against Asia**

youth, as it were, against the background of that glorious age which in their belief had so long ago united Greek arms against Asia (§ 411).

**690. Battle of the Granicus (334 B.C.) and conquest of Asia Minor**

Meantime the Great King had hired thousands of Greek heavy-armed infantry, and they were now to do battle against their own Greek countrymen. At the river Granicus, in his first critical battle, Alexander had no difficulty in scattering the forces of the western Persian satraps. Following the Macedonian custom, the young king, then but twenty-two years of age, led his troops into the thick of the fray and exposed his royal person without hesitation. But for the timely support of Clitus, the brother of his childhood nurse, who bravely pushed in before him at a critical moment, the impetuous young king would have lost his life in the action on the Granicus. Marching southward, he took the Greek cities one by one and freed all western Asia Minor forever from the Persian yoke.

**691. Alexander's march through Asia Minor**

Meantime a huge Persian fleet was master of the Mediterranean. It was at this juncture that the young Macedonian, little more than a boy in years, began to display his mastery of a military situation which demanded the completest understanding of the art of war. He had left a strong force at home, and he believed that the lesson of his destruction of Thebes would prevent the Persian fleet in the Ægean from arousing Hellas to rebellion against him during his absence. He therefore pushed boldly eastward. Following the route of the Ten Thousand, Alexander led his army safely through the difficult pass, called the Cilician Gates (see map, p. 434), and rounded the northeast corner of the Mediterranean. Here, as he looked out upon the Fertile Crescent, there was spread out before him the vast Asiatic world of forty million souls, where the family of the Great King had been supreme for two hundred years. In this great arena he was to be the champion for the next ten years (333–323 B.C.).

At this important point, by the Gulf of Issus, Alexander met the main army of Persia, under the personal command of the

Great King, Darius III, the last of the Persian line. The tactics of his father Philip and Epaminondas, always to be the attacking party, were now adopted by Alexander, in spite of the enemy's strong defensive position behind a stream. His attack was on the old plan of the oblique battle line (§ 638), with the cavalry forming the right wing nearest the enemy. Heading this cavalry charge himself, Alexander led his Macedonian horsemen across the stream in such a fierce assault (Fig. 202) that the opposing Persian wing gave way. Along the center and the other wing, the battle was hotly fought and indecisive. But as Alexander's victorious horsemen of the right wing turned and attacked the exposed Persian center in the flank, the Macedonians swept the Asiatics from the field, and the disorderly retreat of Darius never stopped until it had crossed the Euphrates. The Great King then sent a letter to Alexander desiring terms of peace and offering to accept the Euphrates as a boundary between them, all Asia west of that river to be handed over to the Macedonians.

**692.** Defeat of Darius III at the battle of Issus (333 B.C.)

It was a dramatic picture, the figure of the young king, standing with this letter in his hand. As he pondered it he was surrounded by a group of the ablest Macedonian youth, who had grown up around him as his closest friends; but likewise by old and trusted counselors upon whom his father before him had leaned. The hazards of battle and of march, and the daily associations of camp and bivouac, had wrought the closest bonds of love and friendship and intimate influence between these loyal Macedonians and their ardent young king.

**693.** The situation after Issus, and Alexander's friends

As he considered the letter of Darius, therefore, his father's old general Parmenio, who had commanded the Macedonian left wing in the battle just won, proffered him serious counsel. We can almost see the old man leaning familiarly over the shoulder of this imperious boy of twenty-three and pointing out across the Mediterranean, as he bade Alexander remember the Persian fleet operating there in his rear and likely to stir up revolt against him in Greece. He said too that with Darius

**694.** The advice of Parmenio to accept Persian terms after Issus

Fig. 202. Alexander the Great charging the Bodyguard and Officers of the Persian King at the Battle of Issus *

behind the Euphrates, as proposed in the letter, Persia would be at a safe distance from Europe and the Greek world. The campaign against the Great King, he urged, had secured all that could reasonably be expected. Undoubtedly he added that Philip himself, the young king's father, had at the utmost no further plans against Persia than those already successfully carried out. There was nothing to do, said Parmenio, but to accept the terms offered by the Great King.

In this critical decision lay the parting of the ways. Before the kindling eyes of the young Alexander there rose a vision of world empire dominated by Greek civilization — a vision to which the duller eyes about him were entirely closed. He waved aside his father's old counselors and decided to advance to the conquest of the whole Persian Empire. In this far-reaching decision he disclosed at once the powerful personality which represented a new age. Thus arose the conflict which never ends — the conflict between the new age and the old,

**695. The decision after Issus, and Alexander's friction with his friends**

---

\* The artist who designed this great work has selected the supreme moment when the Persians (at the right) are endeavoring to rescue their king from the onset of the Macedonians (at the left). Alexander, the bareheaded figure on horseback at the left, charges furiously against the Persian king (Darius III), who stands in his chariot (at the right). The Macedonian attack is so impetuous that the Persian king's life is endangered. A Persian noble dismounts and offers his riderless horse, that the king may quickly mount and escape. Devoted Persian nobles heroically ride in between their king and the Macedonian onset, to give Darius an opportunity to mount. But Alexander's spear has passed entirely through the body of one of these Persian nobles, who has thus given his life for his king. Darius throws out his hand in grief and horror at the awful death of his noble friend. The driver of the royal chariot (behind the king) lashes his three horses, endeavoring to carry Darius from the field in flight (§ 692). This magnificent battle scene is put together from bits of colored glass (mosaic) forming a floor pavement, discovered in 1831 at the Roman town of Pompeii (Fig. 255). It has been injured in places, especially at the left, where parts of the figures of Alexander and his horse have disappeared. It was originally laid at Alexandria and suffered this damage in being moved to Italy. It is a copy of an older Hellenistic work, a painting done at Alexandria (§ 738). It is one of the greatest scenes of heroism in battle ever painted, and illustrates the splendor of Hellenistic art.

just as we have seen it at Athens (§ 653). Never has it been more dramatically staged than as we find it here in the daily growing friction between Alexander and that group of devoted, if less gifted, Macedonians who were now drawn by him into the labors of Heracles — the conquest of the world.

**696. Conquest of Phœnicia and Egypt; dispersion of the Persian fleet**

The danger from the Persian fleet was now carefully and deliberately met by a march southward along the eastern end of the Mediterranean. All the Phœnician seaports on the way were captured. Here Alexander's whole campaign would have collapsed but for the siege machinery, the use of which his father had learned from the western Greeks. Against the walls of Tyre, Alexander employed machines which had been devised in the Orient (headpiece, p. 140), and which he was now bringing back thither with Greek improvements. Feeble Egypt, so long a Persian province, then fell an easy prey to the Macedonian arms. The Persian fleet, thus deprived of all its home harbors and cut off from its home government, soon scattered and disappeared.

**697. Alexander's march to Persia: battle of Arbela (331 B.C.)**

Having thus cut off the enemy in his rear, Alexander returned from Egypt to Asia, and, marching along the Fertile Crescent, he crossed the Tigris close by the mounds which had long covered the ruins of Nineveh (Fig. 203). Here, near Arbela, the Great King had gathered his forces for a last stand. The Persians had not studied the progress in the art of war made by the Greeks and the Macedonians (§ 681), and they were as hopelessly behind the times as China was in her war with Japan. They had prepared one new device, a body of chariots with scythes fastened to the axles and projecting on each side. But the device failed to save the Persian army. Although greatly outnumbered, the Macedonians crushed the Asiatic army and forced the Great King into ignominious flight. In a few days Alexander was established in the winter palace of Persia in Babylon (§ 274).

As Darius fled into the eastern mountains he was stabbed by his own treacherous attendants (330 B.C.). Alexander rode

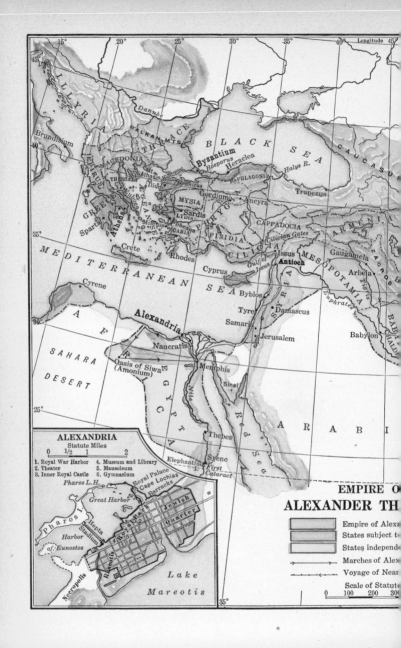

EMPIRE OF
ALEXANDER TH

Empire of Alexa
States subject to
States independe
Marches of Alex
Voyage of Near

Scale of Statute
0    100    200    300

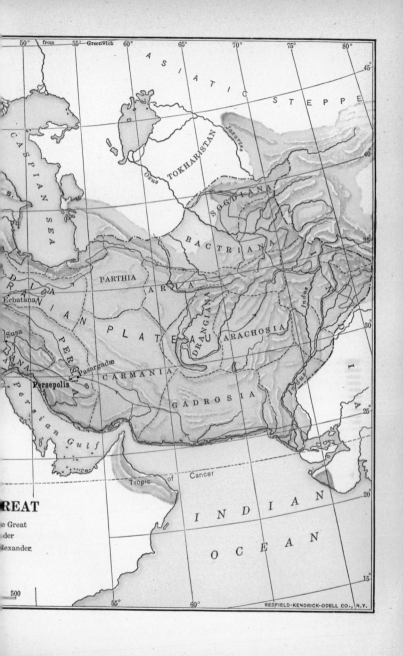

ASIATIC STEPPE

CASPIAN SEA

TOKHARISTAN

Oxus

Jaxartes

SOGDIANA

BACTRIANA

PARTHIA

ARIA

Ecbatana

DRANGIANA

Indus

PLATEAU

ARACHOSIA

Susa

PERSIS

Pasargadæ

CARMANIA

Persepolis

GADROSIA

Indus

Persian Gulf

Tropic of Cancer

INDIAN

OCEAN

REAT

e Great
der
lexander

500

REDFIELD-KENDRICK-ODELL CO., N.Y.

FIG. 203. VIEW ACROSS THE RUINS OF NINEVEH TO THE PLAIN
WHERE ALEXANDER THE GREAT OVERTHREW THE LAST ARMY
OF THE PERSIAN EMPIRE

We are supposed to be standing on the roof of a house in the modern
town of Mosul (see plan, p. 154) and looking eastward across the Tigris
to the ruins of Nineveh, with mound of Kuyunjik, containing the palaces
of Sennacherib and Assurbanipal, directly before us. Past this mound
(compare plan, p. 154) runs the road from Mosul to Arbela, about
30 miles east. These ruins must have been much like this when Alexander marched past them, less than three hundred years after the city
was destroyed. Somewhere in the plain toward Arbela, Alexander won
his last battle with the Persians (§ 697). Although no systematic clear-
ance of all the chief buildings, such as the French and Germans have
accomplished at Sargonburg (Khorsabad), Assur, and Babylon, has ever
been done here, a great many important monuments have been dug
out, like the library of Assurbanipal (§ 226)

up with a few of his officers in time to look upon the body of
the last of the Persian emperors, the lord of Asia, whose vast
realm had now passed into his hands. He punished the murderers and sent the body with all respect to the fallen ruler's

**698.** Death
of Darius III
(330 B.C.);
Alexander
lord of the
ancient East

FIG. 204. A CORNER OF THE COURT OF
THE PALACE OF DARIUS I AT SUSA, CAP-
TURED BY ALEXANDER THE GREAT (AS
RESTORED BY PILLET)

**699.** Alexander captures the Persian royal cities

The remarkable French excavations at Susa discovered the wonderful relief of Naram-Sin (Fig. 89), and the shaft bearing the code of Hammurapi (Fig. 93). At the same time the French uncovered the ruins of the palace built by Darius I in the days of Marathon and finished later under Xerxes at the time of Salamis, a hundred and fifty years before Alexander captured Susa. The French architect's restoration shows the Persian emperor and his attendants coming forth into a court of the palace. We see the gorgeous glazed-brick decorations along the base of the wall, showing lines of Persian soldiers, as in Fig. 113. It must have looked just as we see it here, when Alexander entered it for the first time, to take possession of the dead Persian emperor's magnificent residence

mother and sister, to whom he had extended protection and hospitality. Thus at last both the valley of the Nile and the Fertile Crescent, the homes of the earliest two civilizations, whose long and productive careers we have already sketched, were now in the hands of a European power and under the control of a newer and higher civilization. Less than five years had passed since the young Macedonian had entered Asia.

Although the Macedonians had nothing more to fear from the Persian arms, there still remained much for Alexander to do in order to establish his empire in Asia. On he marched through the original little kingdom of the Persian kings, whence Cyrus, the founder of the Persian Empire, had victoriously issued over two hundred years before (see § 258). He stopped at Susa (Fig. 204) and then passed on to visit the tomb of Cyrus (Fig. 115), near Persepolis. Here he gave a dramatic evidence of his supremacy in Asia by setting fire to the Persian palace (Fig. 116) with his own hand, as the Persians had once done to Miletus and to the temples on the Athenian Acropolis. It was but a symbolical act, and Alexander ordered the flames extinguished before serious damage was done.

After touching Ecbatana in the north, and leaving behind the trusted Parmenio in charge of the enormous treasure of gold and silver, accumulated for generations by the Persian kings, Alexander again moved eastward. In the course of the next five years, while the Greek world looked on in amazement, the young Macedonian seemed to disappear in the mists on the far-off fringes of the known world. He marched his army in one vast loop after another through the heart of the Iranian plateau (see map, p. 434), northward across the Oxus and the Jaxartes rivers, southward across the Indus and the frontiers of India, into the valley of the Ganges, where at last the murmurs of his intrepid army forced him to turn back.

*700. Alexander's campaigns in the Far East (330–324 B.C.)*

He descended the Indus, and even sailed the waters of the Indian Ocean. Then he began his westward march again along the shores of the Indian Ocean, accompanied by a fleet which he had built on the Indus. The return march through desert wastes cost many lives as the thirsty and ill-provisioned troops dropped by the way. Over seven years after he had left the great city of Babylon, Alexander entered it again. He had been less than twelve years in Asia, and he had carried Greek civilization into the very heart of the continent. At important points along his line of march he had founded Greek cities bearing his name and had set up kingdoms which were to be centers of Greek influence on the frontiers of India. From such centers Greek art entered India, to become the source of the art which still survives there; and the Greek works of art, especially coins, from Alexander's communities in these remote

*701. Alexander returns to Babylon (323 B.C.); some results of his Eastern campaigns*

regions of the East penetrated even to China, to contribute to the later art of China and Japan. Never before had East and West so interpenetrated as in these amazing marches and campaigns of Alexander.

## Section 65. International Policy of Alexander: its Personal Consequences

**702. Alexander's scientific enterprises**

During all these unparalleled achievements the mind of this young Hercules never ceased to busy itself with a thousand problems on every side. He dispatched an exploring expedition up the Nile to ascertain the causes of the annual overflow of the river, and another to the shores of the Caspian Sea to build a fleet and circumnavigate that sea, the northern end of which was still unknown. He brought a number of scientific men with him from Greece, and with their aid he sent hundreds of natural-history specimens home to Greece to his old teacher Aristotle, then teaching in Athens.

**703. His endeavor to merge European and Asiatic civilization**

Meantime he applied himself with diligence to the organization and administration of his vast conquests. Such problems must have kept him wearily bending over many a huge pile of state papers, or dictating his great plans to his secretaries and officers. He believed implicitly in the power and superiority of Greek culture. He was determined to Hellenize the world and to merge Asia with Europe by transplanting colonies of Greeks and Macedonians. In his army, Macedonians, Greeks, and Asiatics stood side by side. He also felt that he could not rule the world as a Macedonian, but must make concessions to the Persian world (Plate VI, p. 468). He married Roxana, an Asiatic princess, and at a gorgeous wedding festival he obliged his officers and friends also to marry the daughters of Asiatic nobles. Thousands of Macedonians in the army followed the example of their king and took Asiatic wives. He appointed Persians to high offices and set them over provinces as satraps. He even adopted Persian raiment in part.

Amid all this he carefully worked out a plan of campaign for the conquest of the western Mediterranean. It included instructions for the building of a fleet of a thousand battleships with which to subdue Italy, Sicily, and Carthage. It also planned the construction of a vast roadway along the northern coast of Africa, to be built at an appalling expense and to furnish a highway for his army from Egypt to Carthage and the Pillars of Hercules (Gibraltar). It is here that Alexander's statesmanship may be criticized. All this should have been done immediately after the destruction of Persia. But Alexander seems not to have perceived that he could convert the Mediterranean shores into a unified empire under a single ruler much more effectively than he could unite and control the scattered and far-reaching lands of the remote Orient.

704. Alexander makes plans for the conquest of the western Mediterranean

What was to be his own position in this colossal world-state of which he dreamed? In such a matter Alexander's imagination was without bounds. He had dreamed of having Mt. Athos carved into a vast statue of himself, with a town of ten thousand people in his right hand! And now he planned divinity for himself. The will of a god, in so far as a Greek might believe in him at all, was still a thing to which he bowed without question and with no feeling that he was being subjected to tyranny. Alexander found in this attitude of the Greek mind the solution of the question of his own position. Many a great Greek had come to be recognized as a god, and there was in Greek belief no sharp line dividing gods from men. He would have himself lifted to the realm of the gods, where he might impose his will upon the Greek cities without offense. This solution was the more easy because it had for ages been customary to regard the king as divine in Egypt, where he was a son of the Sun-god, and the idea was a common one in the Orient.

705. Deification of Alexander and its logical necessity

In Egypt therefore, seven years before, he had deliberately taken the time, while a still unconquered Persian army was awaiting him in Asia, to march with a small following far out into the Sahara Desert to the oasis shrine of Amon (§ 657 and

706. Alexander's visit to Siwa — the desert shrine of Amon

Fig. 205). Here in the vast solitude Alexander entered the
holy place alone. No one knew what took place there; but
when he issued again he was greeted by the high priest of the
temple as the son of Zeus-Amon. Alexander took good care
that all Greece should hear of this remarkable occurrence, but

FIG. 205. OASIS OF SIWA IN THE SAHARA

In this oasis was the famous temple of the Egyptian god Amon (or
Ammon) (§ 657). Alexander marched hither from the coast, a distance
of some 200 miles, and thence back to the Nile at Memphis, some 350
miles (see map, p. 434). A modern caravan requires twenty-one days to
go from the Nile to this oasis. Such an oasis is a deep depression in
the desert plateau; the level of the plateau is seen at the tops of the
cliffs on the right. Its fertility is due to many springs and flowing wells

the Hellenes had to wait some years before they learned what
it all meant.

**707.** Alexan-
der demands
his deification
by the Greek
cities of the
dissolved
league

Four years later the young king found that this divinity
which he claimed lacked outward and visible manifestations.
There must go with it some outward observances which would
vividly suggest his character as a god to the minds of the world
which he ruled. He adopted oriental usages, among which was
the requirement that all who approached him on official occasions should bow down to the earth and kiss his feet. He also

sent formal notification to all the Greek cities that the league of which he had been head was dissolved, that he was henceforth to be officially numbered among the gods of each city, and that as such he was to receive the State offerings which each city presented.

Thus were introduced into Europe absolute monarchy and the divine right of kings. Indeed, through Alexander there was transferred to Europe much of the spirit of that Orient which had been repulsed at Marathon and Salamis. But these measures of Alexander were not the efforts of a weak mind to gratify a vanity so drunk with power that it could be satisfied only with superhuman honors. They were carefully devised political measures dictated by State policy and systematically developed step by step for years.

**708. Absolute monarchy and divine right of kings**

This superhuman station of the world-king Alexander was gained at tragic cost to Alexander the Macedonian youth and to the group of friends and followers about him (§ 693). Beneath the Persian robes of the State-god Alexander beat the warm heart of a young Macedonian. He had lifted himself to an exalted and lonely eminence whither those devoted friends who had followed him to the ends of the earth could follow him no longer. Neither could they comprehend the necessity for measures which thus strained or snapped entirely those bonds of friendship which linked together comrades in arms. And then there were the Persian intruders treated like the equals of his personal friends (Plate VI, p. 468), or even placed over them! The tragic consequences of such a situation were inevitable.

**709. Personal consequences suffered by Alexander as a result of his deification and international policy**

Early in those tremendous marches eastward, after Darius's death, Philotas, son of Parmenio, had learned of a conspiracy against Alexander's life, but his bitterness and estrangement were such that he failed to report his guilty knowledge to the king. The conspirators were all given a fair and legal trial, and Alexander himself suffered the bitterness of seeing a whole group of his former friends and companions, including Philotas,

**710. Execution of Philotas, Parmenio, and their friends**

condemned and executed in the presence of the army. The
trusted Parmenio, father of Philotas, still guarding the Persian
treasure at Ecbatana, was also implicated, and a messenger
was sent back with orders for the old general's immediate execution. This was but the beginning of the ordeal through which

FIG. 206. TEMPLE BESIDE THE ROYAL PALACE AT BABYLON
WHERE ALEXANDER PRESENTED DAILY OFFERINGS

The German excavations at Babylon (Fig. 111) have found the ruins of
a temple at the door of the great palace (plan, p. 165), and the director
of the work, Professor Koldewey, has drawn the above restoration. The
ancient accounts tell us that Alexander was wont to sacrifice every day
at this temple on an altar, seen here before the door. He was restoring
the ruined buildings of Babylon, especially the fallen temple tower, when
he died. Koldewey found vast masses of earth which Alexander moved

the man Alexander was to pass, in order that the world-king
Alexander might mount the throne of a god.

**711. Alexan-
der slays his
friend Clitus**
Clitus also, who had saved his life at the Granicus, was filled
with grief and indignation at Alexander's political course. At
a royal feast, where these matters came up in conversation,
Clitus was guilty of unguarded criticisms of his lord and then,
entirely losing his self-mastery, he finally heaped such unbridled

reproaches upon the king that Alexander, rising in uncontrollable rage, seized a spear from a guard and thrust it through the bosom of the man to whom he owed his life. As we see the young king thereupon sitting for three days in his tent, speechless with grief and remorse, refusing all food, and prevented only by his officers from taking his own life, we gather some slight impression of the terrible personal cost of Alexander's state policy.

Similarly the demand that all should prostrate themselves and kiss his feet on entering his presence cost him the friendship of the historian Callisthenes. For, not long afterward, this friend was likewise found criminally guilty toward the king in connection with a conspiracy of the noble Macedonian pages who served Alexander, and he was put to death. He was a nephew of the king's old teacher, Aristotle, and thus the friendship between master and royal pupil was transformed into bitter enmity.

**712. Execution of Callisthenes**

On his return to Babylon (Fig. 206), Alexander was overcome with grief at the loss of his dearest friend Hephæstion, who had just died. He arranged for his dead friend one of the most magnificent funerals ever celebrated. Then, as he was preparing for a campaign to subjugate the Arabian peninsula and leave him free to carry out his great plans for the conquest of the western Mediterranean, Alexander himself fell sick, probably as the result of a drunken debauch, and after a few days he died (323 B.C.). He was thirty-three years of age and had reigned thirteen years.

**713. Death of Alexander (323 B.C.)**

## QUESTIONS

SECTION 63. What was the policy of Philip of Macedon? What new developments in the art of warfare did he introduce? What did the Athenians think about his plans? Who were the two party leaders? What can you say of Demosthenes? What was the outcome of Philip's struggle with the Greeks? Who succeeded Philip? How was Philip's successor educated?

SECTION 64. Discuss Alexander's relations with the Greeks. What was the outcome of their rebellion against him? As whose champion did he contrive to make himself appear? Describe his conquest of Asia Minor. Where and when did he meet the main Persian army? What was the result? What proposal did the Persian king make? What advice did Alexander receive? What did he do? What conflict arose? How did he dispose of the Phœnician fleet?

Where did Alexander go after conquering Egypt? Describe his next encounter with the Persians. What happened to Darius III? What had thus become of Egypt and Western Asia? To what great cities of the Persian Empire did Alexander then go? What happened there? Describe the remote marches which he now undertook. Can you trace them on the map? What was the result of these marches?

SECTION 65. What scientific enterprises did Alexander undertake? Discuss his plans for merging Greek and Asiatic civilization. What further great plans of conquest did he have? What was to be his own position in the new empire? How had he prepared for this position while he was in Egypt? How did he require his new position to be recognized? What effect had all this upon his friends? What happened to Parmenio? to Clitus? to Callisthenes? Where, when, and how did Alexander die?

NOTE. The sketch below shows us the lion erected by the Thebans on the battlefield of Chæronea in memory of their fallen citizens. Excavation has disclosed bodies and remains of the great funeral fire.

From a painting by C. Scott White

PLATE V.  THE TEMPLES AND PALMS OF PHILÆ AT THE HEAD OF THE FIRST CATARACT OF THE NILE

Much of the architecture on the island of Philæ was the work of the Ptolemies, and well illustrates the prosperity of Egypt under its Macedonian kings (§ 716).  Until a few years ago the palm-shaded temples made the island the most beautiful spot in Egypt and one of the most beautiful in the world.  Since the erection of a colossal irrigation dam below the island, the buildings have been covered with water a large part of each year

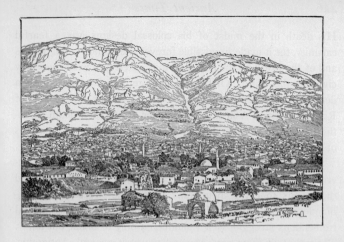

# PART IV. THE MEDITERRANEAN WORLD IN THE HELLENISTIC AGE AND THE ROMAN REPUBLIC

## CHAPTER XX

### THE HEIRS OF ALEXANDER

SECTION 66. THE HEIRS OF ALEXANDER'S EMPIRE

Alexander has been well termed "the Great." Few men of genius, and certainly none in so brief a career, have left so indelible a mark upon the course of human affairs. By his remarkable conquests, he gained for the Greeks that *political* supremacy, which their *civilization*, as we have seen, had long before attained.

**714. Consequences of Alexander's death**

NOTE. The headpiece above shows a view of modern Antioch in Syria. The great decisive battle among the generals of Alexander the Great at Ipsus in Phrygia in central Asia Minor (301 B.C.) made Seleucus lord of Asia (§ 718). He then founded this city of Antioch named after his father, Antiochus (§ 718). It finally became a great commercial center (§ 718), a magnificent city of several hundred thousand inhabitants. Many appalling earthquakes have destroyed the ancient city, and the modern town shown above has less than thirty thousand inhabitants.

His death in the midst of his colossal designs was a fearful calamity, for it made impossible forever the unification of Hellas and of the world by the power of that gifted race which was now civilizing the world. Of his line there remained in Macedonia a demented half brother and, erelong, Alexander II, the son of Roxana, born in Asia after Alexander the Great's death. Conflicts among the leaders at home swept away all these members of Alexander's family, even including his mother.

**715.** The successors of Alexander; their three realms in Europe, Asia, and Africa

His generals in Babylonia found the plans for his great Western campaign lying among his papers, but no man possessed the genius to carry them out. These able Macedonian commanders were soon involved among themselves in a long and tremendous struggle, which slumbered only to break out anew. The ablest of them was Alexander's great general, Antigonus, who determined to gain control of all the great Macedonian's vast empire. Then followed a generation of exhausting wars by land and sea, involving the greatest battles thus far fought by European armies. Antigonus was killed, and Alexander's empire fell into three main parts, in Europe, Asia, and Africa, with one of his generals or one of their successors at the head of each. In Europe, Macedonia was in the hands of Antigonus, grandson of Alexander's great commander of the same name. He endeavored to maintain control of Greece; in Asia most of the territory of the former Persian Empire was under the rule of Alexander's general, Seleucus; while in Africa, Egypt was held by Ptolemy, one of the cleverest of Alexander's Macedonian leaders (see map I, p. 450).

**716.** The Egyptian Empire of the Ptolemies

In Egypt, Ptolemy gradually made himself king, and became the founder of a dynasty or family of successive kings, whom we call the Ptolemies. Ptolemy at once saw that he would be constantly obliged to draw Greek mercenary troops from Greece. With statesmanlike judgment he therefore built up a fleet which gave him the mastery of the Mediterranean. He took up his residence at the great harbor city of Alexandria, the city which Alexander had founded in the western Nile Delta. As a result it became the greatest commercial port on the Mediterranean. Indeed, for nearly a century (roughly the third century B.C.) the eastern Mediterranean from Greece to Syria and from the Ægean to the Nile Delta was an Egyptian sea. As a barrier against their Asiatic rivals, the Ptolemies also took possession of Palestine and southern Syria. Thus arose an Egyptian empire in the eastern Mediterranean like that which we found nearly a thousand years earlier in our voyage up the Nile as we visited the great buildings of Thebes. Following the example of the Pharaohs (Fig. 62), the Ptolemies reached out also into the Red Sea with their fleets, and from the Indian Ocean to the Hellespont, from Sicily to Syria, the Egyptian fleets dotted the seas, bringing great wealth into the treasury of the ruler (map I, p. 450).

Although these new Hellenistic rulers of Egypt were Europeans, they did not set up a Greek or European form of state. They regarded themselves as the successors of the ancient Pharaohs, and like them they ruled over the kingdom of the Nile in absolute and unlimited power. To three Greek cities on the Nile, one of which was Alexandria, they granted the right to manage their own local affairs, like a city of Greece. Otherwise there were no voting *citizens* among the people of Egypt, and just as in ancient oriental days they had nothing whatever to say about the government or the acts of the ruler. The chief purpose of the ruler's government was to secure from the country as large receipts for his treasury as possible, in order that he might meet the expenses of his great war fleet and his army of Greek mercenaries. For thousands of years Egypt had been operating a great organization of local officials, trained to carry on the business of assessing and collecting taxes (Fig. 40). The Greek states possessed no such organization, but the Ptolemies found it too useful to be interfered with. The tiniest group of mud huts along the river was ruled and controlled by such officials. Thus the Macedonians ruling on the Nile were continuing an ancient oriental absolute monarchy. The example of this ancient form of state, thus preserved, was

717. The ancient oriental monarchy of the Ptolemies

of far-reaching influence throughout the Mediterranean world, and finally displaced the democracies of the Greeks and Romans.

**718.** The Asiatic empire of the Seleucids

Although they were not as powerful as the Ptolemies, the Seleucids, as we call Seleucus and his descendants, were the chief heirs of Alexander, for they held the larger part of his empire, extending from the Ægean to the frontiers of India. Its boundaries were not fixed, and its enormous extent made it very difficult to govern and maintain. The fleet of the Ptolemies hampered the commercial development and prosperity of the Seleucids, who therefore found it difficult to reach Greece for trade, troops, or colonists. They gave special attention to the region around the northeast corner of the Mediterranean reaching to the Euphrates, and here the Seleucids endeavored to develop another Macedonia. Their empire is often called *Syria*, after this region. Here on the lower Orontes, Seleucus founded the great city which he called Antioch (after his father, Antiochus). It finally enjoyed great prosperity and became the commercial rival of Alexandria and the greatest seat of commerce in the northern Mediterranean (headpiece, p. 445).

**719.** The government of the Seleucids: the free cities

In government the Seleucids adopted a very different plan from that of the Ptolemies. Seleucus was in hearty sympathy with Alexander's plan of transplanting Greeks to Asia and thus of mingling Greeks and Asiatics. He and his son Antiochus I founded scores of new Greek cities through Asia Minor, Syria, down the Two Rivers, in Persia, and far over on the borders of India. These cities were given self-government on the old Greek plan; that is, each city formed a little republic, with its local affairs controlled by its own citizens. The great Seleucid Empire was thickly dotted with these little free communities.

**720.** The government of the Seleucids: the kingship

To be sure they were under the king, and each such free city paid him tribute or taxes. The form which the royal authority took was the one, so ancient in the Orient, which Alexander had already adopted. The ruler was regarded as a god to whom each community owed divine reverence and hence obedience. This homage they paid without offense to their feelings as free citizens. Greek life, with all the noble and beautiful things we have learned it possessed, took root throughout Western Asia and was carried far into the heart of the great continent (see map I, p. 450).

Compared with her two great rivals in Egypt and Asia, Macedonia in Europe seemed small indeed. The tradition of independence still cherished by the Greek states made the Macedonian leadership of the Balkan-Greek peninsula a difficult undertaking. Fighting for their liberty after Alexander's death, they had proved too weak to maintain themselves against the Macedonian army; they were forced to submit, and the dauntless Demosthenes (§ 684), whose surrender along with other democratic leaders was demanded by the Macedonians, took his own life (see map I, p. 450).

721. The Macedonian Empire: revolt of the Greek states after Alexander's death

While the second Antigonus, grandson of Alexander's general, was struggling to establish himself as lord of Macedonia and the Greeks, he was suddenly confronted by a new danger from the far North and West. From France eastward to the lower Danube, Europe was now occupied by a vast group of Indo-European barbarians whom we call Celts, or Gauls. They had penetrated into Italy after 400 B.C. (§ 813), and a century later they were pushing far down into the Balkan Peninsula. By 280 B.C. they broke through the northern mountains, and having devastated Macedonia, they even invaded Greece and reached the sacred oracle of the Greeks at Delphi. The barbarian torrent overflowed also into Asia Minor, where a body of the invaders settled and gave their name to a region afterwards called Galatia. Antigonus II completely defeated the barbarians in Thrace and drove them out of Macedonia, of which he then became king (277 B.C.). This overwhelming flood of northern barbarians deeply impressed the Greeks, and left its mark even on the art of the age, as we shall see (§ 736).

722. Antigonus II stops the great Gallic invasion and becomes king of Macedonia (277 B.C.)

After the repulse of the Gauls, Antigonus II took up the problem of restoring his empire and establishing his power. The Egyptian fleet held complete command of the Ægean and

723. The
struggle for
control of
the eastern
Mediter-
ranean

thwarted him in every effort to control Greece. As Antiochus
in Asia was suffering from the Egyptian fleet in the same way
(§ 718), the two rulers, Antigonus and Antiochus, formed an
alliance against Egypt. The energetic Antigonus built a war
fleet at vast expense. In a long naval war with the Ptolemies,
which went on at intervals for fifteen years, Antigonus twice
defeated the Egyptian fleet. As the lax descendants of the
earlier Ptolemies did not rebuild the Egyptian fleet, both
Macedonia and Asia profited by this freedom of the eastern
Mediterranean. But not long after these Macedonian naval
victories, trouble arose in Greece, which involved Macedonia in
another long war with the Greek states.

## Section 67. The Decline of Greece

Greece was no longer commercial leader of the Mediterranean. The victories of Alexander the Great had opened the
vast Persian Empire to Greek commercial colonists, who poured
into all the favorable centers of trade. Not only did Greece
decline in population, but commercial prosperity and the leadership in trade passed eastward, especially to Alexandria and
Antioch, and also to the enterprising people of Rhodes and
the merchants of Ephesus. As the Greek cities lost their
wealth they could no longer support fleets or mercenary
armies, and they soon became too feeble to protect themselves.

They naturally began to combine in alliances or federations
for mutual protection. Not long after 300 B.C. two such
leagues were already in existence, one on each side of the
Corinthian Gulf. On the south side of the gulf was the
Achæan League and on the north side that of the Ætolians.
Such a league was in some ways a kind of tiny United States.
The league had its general, elected each year and commanding
the combined army of all the cities; it had also its other officials,
who attended to all matters of defense and to all relations with
foreign states outside the league. Each city, however, took care

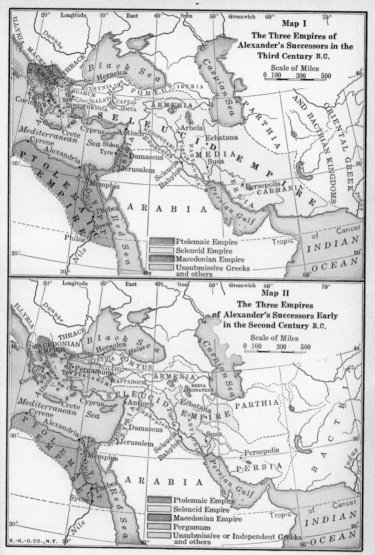

SEQUENCE MAP SHOWING THE THREE EMPIRES OF ALEXANDER'S SUC-
CESSORS FROM THE THIRD CENTURY B.C. TO THEIR DECLINE AT THE
COMING OF THE ROMANS AFTER 200 B.C.

of its own local affairs, like the levying and collecting of taxes. But the two leagues were mostly hostile to each other, and while they were successful for a time in throwing off Macedonian leadership, it was too late for a general federation of all the Greek states, and a United States of the Greeks never existed.

One reason for this was that Sparta and Athens refused to join these leagues. The Achæans endeavored to force Sparta into their league, but the gifted Spartan king Cleomenes defeated them in one battle after another. His victories and his reorganization of the State restored to Sparta some of her old-time vigor. The Achæans were obliged to call on Macedonia for help, and in this way Cleomenes was defeated and the Spartans were finally crushed. But the Achæan League was thereafter subject to Macedonia and never enjoyed liberty again. Henceforth the Macedonians were lords of all Greece except the Ætolian League. Meantime, while keeping out of the leagues, Athens preserved her self-government by securing recognition of her neutrality and liberty by the great powers, first by Egypt and later by Rome (§ 884). In spite of her political feebleness, Athens was still the home of those high and noble things in Greek civilization of which we have already learned something and to the further study of which we must now turn.

**726. Sparta and Athens**

## QUESTIONS

SECTION 66. What were the most important consequences of Alexander's death? What survivors of his line were there? What did his generals do? What was the result of a generation of fighting among them? Into what main divisions did Alexander's empire fall? Who ruled these divisions? What was the policy of the first Ptolemy? What was the result? What was at first the extent of Ptolemaic power? What kind of government did the Ptolemies establish in Egypt? Would you describe it as oriental or Greek? Was it financially better organized than the Greek states? In what respect?

What was the extent of the Seleucid Empire at first? How were the Seleucids hampered in the Mediterranean? To what region did they give special attention? What great city did they found there? What kind of a government did the Seleucids establish? What can you say of their Greek cities? Were such cities after all as free as Athens had once been? What form did the authority of the Seleucids take?

What was the first serious obstacle in the way of Macedonian leadership of the Balkan-Greek peninsula? What did Antigonus II accomplish by land? by sea? What was the extent of the Macedonian Empire (see map I, p. 450)?

SECTION 67. What were now the leading commercial cities of the Mediterranean? In what direction had commercial leadership shifted? What was the reason? What did the Greeks do? What happened to Greece commercially? politically? Did a federation of all the Greeks arise?

NOTE. The tailpiece below (on the right) is a pleasing example of the Alexandrian art of mosaic — the art of putting together brightly colored bits of glass or stone and forming figures or designs with them, as a child puts together a puzzle picture. It was an old Egyptian art, which was carried much further by the Greeks at Alexandria, where they seem to have learned it, and used it in making beautiful pavements (§ 738). They even copied many old Egyptian designs, such as this cat (seen below, at right), which was taken from an old Egyptian painting (seen below, at left) showing a cat with a bird in her mouth and also two more under her forepaws and hindpaws. The greatest example of mosaic is the copy of the painting of the battle of Issus (Fig. 202).

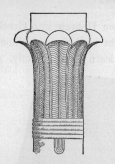

# CHAPTER XXI

## THE CIVILIZATION OF THE HELLENISTIC AGE

### SECTION 68. CITIES, ARCHITECTURE, AND ART

The three centuries following the death of Alexander we call the Hellenistic Age, meaning the period in which Greek civilization spread throughout the ancient world, especially the Orient, and was itself much modified by the culture of the Orient. Alexander's conquests placed Asia and Egypt in the hands of Macedonian rulers who were in civilization essentially Greek. Their language was the Greek spoken in Attica. The Orientals found the affairs of government carried on in the Greek language (Fig. 207); they transacted business with multitudes of Greek merchants; they found many Greek books, attracting them to read. Attic Greek became the tongue of which every man of education must be master. Thus the strong Jewish community living at Alexandria now found it necessary to translate

727. The Hellenistic Age—supremacy of the Greek language

NOTE. The above headpiece shows us the old palm-tree capital (on the left), with which we are familiar on the Nile (Fig. 56). The Egyptians were the first to take the patterns of their decorative art from the forms of plant life. Their example has influenced decorative art ever since. Thus this palm-tree column (on the right) was borrowed from Egypt by the Hellenistic architects of Pergamum. Such an example shows clearly that the idea of taking decorative architectural forms from the vegetable world was acquired by the Greeks from abroad, and the Corinthian column (Fig. 193) was doubtless suggested in the same way.

the books of the Old Testament from Hebrew into Greek, in order that their educated men might read them. While the country people of the East might learn it imperfectly, Attic

FIG. 207. THE ROSETTA STONE, BEARING THE SAME INSCRIPTION IN GREEK (*C*) AND EGYPTIAN (*A* AND *B*)*

Greek became, nevertheless, the daily language of the great cities and of an enormous world stretching from Sicily (Fig. 257) and southern Italy eastward on both sides of the Mediterranean and thence far into the Orient.

Civilized life in the cities was attended with more comfort and better equipped than ever before. The citizen's house, if he were in easy circumstances, might be built of stone masonry. The old central court was now often surrounded on all four sides by a pleasing colonnaded porch (Fig. 208). Most of the rooms were still small and bare, but the large living room, lighted from the court, might be floored with a bright mosaic pavement (tailpiece, p. 452), while the walls were plastered and adorned with decorative paintings, or even veneered with marble if the owner's wealth permitted. The furniture was more elaborate and artistic; there might be carpets and hangings; and the house now for the first time possessed its own water supply.

728. Improved houses and increased luxury

* This famous inscription is in two languages. It was written in Greek because the language of the government was Greek and also because there were so many Greek-speaking people in Egypt (§ 727). At the same time, as the stone was to be a public record, it was necessary that it should be read by Egyptians, who knew no Greek, just as in some New England factory towns notices are now put up in both English and Italian. The document was therefore first written out with pen and ink, just as we would do it, in ordinary Egyptian handwriting, called by the Egyptians demotic (see Fig. 31 for explanation). This demotic copy was then cut on the stone where it occupies the middle (*B*). The priests also wrote out the document in the ancient sacred hieroglyphics, and they put this hieroglyphic form in the place of honor at the top of the stone (*A*), where the two corners have since been broken off and lost. Both of these two forms, then, are Egyptian — the upper (*A*) corresponding to our print, the lower (*B*) corresponding to our handwriting. The Greek translation of the Egyptian we see at the bottom (*C*). The stone was intended as a public record of certain honors which the Egyptian priests were extending to the Greek king, one of the Ptolemies, in 195 B.C. After it fell down and was broken, the stone had been buried in rubbish for many centuries, when the soldiers of Napoleon accidentally found it while digging trenches near the Rosetta mouth of the Nile in 1799. Hence it is called the Rosetta Stone. It was afterward captured by the British and is now in the British Museum. After Champollion had learned the signs in the names of Cleopatra, Ptolemy, and some others (Fig. 76), he was finally able to read also the hieroglyphic form of this Rosetta document (*A*), because the Greek translation told him what the hieroglyphic form meant. It was in this way that the Rosetta Stone became the key by which Egyptian hieroglyphic was deciphered. The stone is a thick slab of black basalt, 2 feet 4½ inches wide and 3 feet 9 inches high.

The streets also were equipped with drainage channels or pipes, a thing unknown in the days of Pericles.

**729.** Household and business papers preserved in Egypt

The daily life of the time has been revealed to us, as it went on in Egypt, in a vast quantity of surviving household documents.

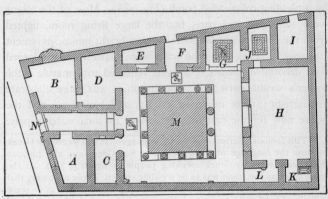

FIG. 208. PLAN OF A HOUSE OF A WEALTHY GREEK IN THE HELLENISTIC AGE

The rooms are arranged around a central court (*M*) which is open to the sky. A roofed porch with columns (called a peristyle) surrounds the court (cf. Fig. 56). The main entrance is at *N*, with the room of the door-keeper on the right (*A*). At the corner is a shop (*B*). *C*, *D*, and *E* are for storage and housekeeping. *F* is a back-door entry through which supplies were delivered; it contained a stairway to the second floor. *G* was used as a small living room. It had a built-in divan, and the entire side toward the peristyle was open. The finest room in the house was *H*, measuring about 16 by 26 feet, with a mosaic floor (tailpiece, p. 452), in seven colors, and richly decorated walls. It was lighted by a large door and two windows. *K* was a little sleeping room, with a large marble bath tub; otherwise the sleeping rooms were all on the second floor, which cannot now be reconstructed. *I* was a second tiny shop.

This house was excavated by the French on the island of Delos

Among the common people ordinary receipts and other business memoranda were scribbled with ink on bits of broken pottery (Fig. 209), which cost nothing. For more important documents, however, a piece of papyrus paper was used (Fig. 253). Such papers accumulated in the house, just as our old letters and papers do. In the rainless climate of Egypt they have survived in great numbers in the rubbish heaps now covering the remains of the houses of this age (§ 158 and Fig. 211). We can read a father's or a mother's invitation to the wedding of a daughter; the letter of a father to a worthy son absent at school; the repentant confessions of a wayward son who has run away from home; the assurances of sympathy from a friend when a family has lost a son, a father, a mother, or a brother. Indeed, these documents disclose to us the daily intercourse between friends and relatives, just as such matters are revealed by letters which pass between ourselves at the present day. Such word-pictures, thoughtlessly penned by long-vanished fingers, make the distant life of this far-off age seem surprisingly near and real (Figs. 210 and 253).

FIG. 209. POTSHERD DOCUMENT FROM THE RUINS OF AN EGYPTIAN TOWN

Thousands of personal documents of the Hellenistic Age have survived in Egypt, written with pen and ink on fragments of broken pottery, which cost nothing (§ 729). This specimen records a receipt for land rent and closes thus: " Eumelos, the son of Hermulos, being asked to do so, wrote for him, because he himself writes too slowly." The giver of the receipt probably could not write at all and, to avoid this humiliating confession, says that he wrote " too slowly " ! The hand which Eumelos wrote for him is the rapid-running business hand written by the Greeks of this age, very different from the capital letters which the Greek pottery painters made five centuries earlier (head-piece, p. 282). A modern college student, even though very familiar with printed Greek, would be unable to read it

The numerous new cities which this great Hellenistic Age brought forth were laid out on a very systematic plan, with the

**730. Equipment of Hellenistic cities; rise of secular public buildings**

streets at right angles and the buildings in rectangular blocks (Fig. 212). Recent excavation has uncovered as many as eleven metal water pipes side by side crossing a street under the pavement. But there never was any system of public-street lighting in the ancient world. In the public buildings also a great change had taken place. In Pericles' time the great state buildings were the temples (§ 573). But now the architects of the Hellenistic Age began to design large and splendid buildings to house the offices of the government.

**731. The public buildings of a Hellenistic city**

These fine public buildings occupied the center of the city where in early Greek and oriental cities the castle of the king

FIG. 210. A PAPYRUS LETTER ROLLED UP AND SEALED FOR DELIVERY

Large numbers of such letters have been found in the rubbish of the ancient towns of Egypt (Fig. 253). Their appearance when unrolled may be seen in Fig. 253, and the remarkable glimpses into ancient life which they afford are well illustrated by the same letter

had once stood. Near by was the spacious market square, surrounded by long colonnades; for the Greeks were now making large use of this airy and beautiful form of architecture contributed by Egypt. Here much private business of the citizens was transacted. There was, furthermore, a handsome building containing an audience room with seats arranged like a theater. The Assembly no longer met in the open air (Fig. 179), but held its sessions here, as did the Council also. The architects had also to provide gymnasiums and baths, a race track, and a theater. Even a small city of only four thousand people, like Priene in Asia Minor, possessed all these buildings (Fig. 212), besides several temples, one of which was erected by Alexander himself. It is very instructive to compare such a little Hellenistic city as Priene with a modern town of four thousand inhabitants in America. Our modern houses are much more roomy and comfortable, but our ordinary public buildings, like our court-houses and town halls, make but a poor showing as compared with those of little Priene over two thousand years ago.

FIG. 211. RUINS OF THE ANCIENT TOWN OF ELEPHANTINE ON AN ISLAND OF THE SAME NAME IN THE NILE

This island is at the foot of the First Cataract, 5 miles below Philæ (Plate V, p. 444). When the sun-dried-brick houses which we see here fell down (§ 158), they covered the owner's household papers, which in the rainless climate of Egypt have been remarkably well preserved (see especially Fig. 131). Some of these houses are as old as the twenty-seventh century B.C., and the oldest papyrus documents dug out here are therefore as old as the Pyramid Age (Fig. 40). Others are much later, like the Aramaic papers of the Hebrew colony (Fig. 131). Most of the documents found here, however, are from the Hellenistic Age or later, and are therefore in Greek, like the young soldier's letter (Fig. 253), which was found at another place like this one, or the certificate shown in Fig. 267. Near here was Eratosthenes' well (§ 745)

On one side of the market there opened a building called a basilica, lighted by roof windows, forming a clerestory (Fig. 271), which the Hellenistic architects had seen in Egypt (Fig. 68). At the same time they had become acquainted with the arch in Asia Minor, whither it had passed from the Fertile

732. The clerestory and the arch introduced from the Orient

FIG. 212. RESTORATION OF THE HELLENISTIC CITY OF PRIENE IN ASIA MINOR. (AFTER A DRAWING BY A. ZIPPELIUS)*

Crescent (Figs. 82 and 206). They began occasionally to introduce arches into their buildings (Fig. **224**), although we recall that Greek buildings had never before employed the arch. Thus the Orient, which had contributed the colonnade to Greek architecture (Fig. **167**), now furnished two more great forms, the clerestory and the arch, but the Greeks never made great use of the arch.

If a little provincial Greek city like Priene possessed such splendid public buildings, an imperial capital and vast commercial city like Alexandria was correspondingly more magnificent. In numbers, wealth, commerce, power, and in all the arts of civilization, it was now the greatest city of the whole ancient world. Along the harbors stretched extensive docks, where ships which had braved the Atlantic storms along the coasts of Spain and Africa moored beside oriental craft which had penetrated the

733. Alexandria: its commerce and great lighthouse

---

\* This little city when excavated proved to be almost a second Pompeii (Fig. 255), only older. Above *A*, on the top of the cliff, was the citadel with a path leading up to it (*B*). *C* shows the masonry flume which brought the mountain water down into the town. Entering the town one passed through the gate at *K*, and up a straight street to the little provision-market square (*L*). Just above the market was the temple of Athena (*I*), built by Alexander himself. Then one entered the spacious business market (*agora*) (*M*), surrounded by fine colonnades, with shops behind them, except on one side (under *N*) where there was a stately hall for business and festive occasions, like the basilica halls which were coming in at this time among the Greeks (Fig. 271, 3). Beyond (at *N*) were the offices of the city government, the hall in which the Council and Assembly met, and the theater (*E*). At *G* was the temple of Isis (§ 657), and in the foreground were the gymnasium (*P*) and the stadium (*Q*). The wash-room here still contains the marble basins and the lion-headed spouts from which the water flowed. An attached open hall was used for school instruction and lectures (Fig. 224). Above the seats of the stadium (*Q*) was a beautiful colonnade 600 feet long, for pleasure-strolling between the athletic events, to enjoy the grand view of the sea upon which the audience looked down. The houses fronting directly on the street were mostly like the one in Fig. 208; but the finer ones in the region of the theater (*E*) and the temple of Athena (*I*) were of well-joined stone masonry and had no shops in front. Around the whole city was a strong wall of masonry, with a gate at east (*H*) and west (*K*), while along the street outside these gates were the tombs of the ancestors as at Athens (headpiece, p. 425).

gates of the Indian Ocean (§ 104) and gathered the wares of the vast oriental world beyond. Side by side on these docks lay bars of tin from the British Isles with bolts of silk from

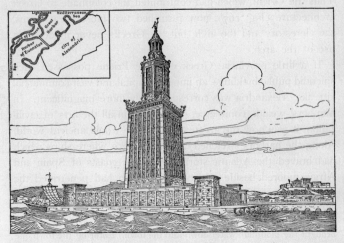

FIG. 213. THE LIGHTHOUSE OF THE HARBOR OF ALEXANDRIA IN THE HELLENISTIC AGE. (AFTER THIERSCH)

The harbor of Alexandria (see corner map, p. 434) was protected by an island called Pharos, which was connected with the city by a causeway of stone. On the island, and bearing its name (Pharos), was built (after 300 B.C.) a vast stone lighthouse, some 370 feet high (that is, over thirty stories, like those of a modern skyscraper). It shows how vast was the commerce and wealth of Alexandria only a generation after it was founded by Alexander the Great, when it became the New York or Liverpool of the ancient world, the greatest port on the Mediterranean (§ 733). The Pharos tower, the first of its kind, was influenced in design by oriental architecture, and in its turn it furnished the model for the earliest church spires, and also for the minarets of the Mohammedan mosques (Fig. 272). It stood for about sixteen hundred years, the greatest lighthouse in the world, and did not fall until 1326 A.D.

China and rolls of cotton goods from India. The growing commerce of the city even required the establishment of government banks. From far across the sea the mariners approaching at night could catch the gleaming of a lofty beacon shining from

a gigantic lighthouse tower (Fig. 213) which marked the
entrance of the harbor of Alexandria. This wonderful tower,
the tallest building ever erected by a Hellenistic engineer, was
a descendant of the old Babylonian temple tower (tailpiece,
p. 170), with which it was closely related (Fig. 272).

From the deck of a great merchant ship of over four thousand tons the incoming traveler might look cityward beyond
the lighthouse and behold the great war fleet of the Ptolemies
(§ 716) outlined against the green masses of the magnificent
royal gardens. Here, embowered in rich tropical verdure, rose
the marble residence of the Ptolemies, occupying a point of
land which extended out into the sea and formed the east side
of the harbor (see map, p. 434). From the royal parks of the
Persian kings and the villa gardens of the Egyptians (Fig. 51)
the Hellenistic rulers and their architects had learned to appreciate the beauty of parks and gardens artistically laid out and
adorned with tropical trees, lakes, fountains, and sculptured monuments. Thus the art of landscape gardening, combined with a
systematically planned city, — an art long familiar to the architects of the Orient, — was also being cultivated by Europeans.

734. Palace park of the Ptolemies; oriental origin of such parks

At the other end of the park from the palace were grouped
the marble buildings of the Royal Museum, with its great
library, lecture halls, exhibition rooms, courts and porticoes,
and living rooms for the philosophers and men of science who
resided in the institution. In the vicinity was the vast temple of
Serapis, the new State god (§ 764), and further in the city were
the magnificent public buildings, such as gymnasiums, baths, stadiums, assembly hall, concert hall, market places, and basilicas,
all surrounded by the residence quarters of the citizens. Unfortunately, not one of these splendid buildings still stands. Even
the scanty ruins which survive cannot be recovered, because in
most cases the modern city of Alexandria is built over them.

735. The public buildings of Alexandria

We are more fortunate in the case of Pergamum (map II,
p. 450), another splendid city of this age which grew up
under Athenian influences (Fig. 214). One of the kings of

736. Pergamum and its wonderful sculpture

Pergamum defeated and beat off the hordes of Gauls coming in from Europe (§ 722). This achievement greatly affected the art which Attic sculptors, supported by the kings of Pergamum, were creating there. They wrought heroic marble figures of

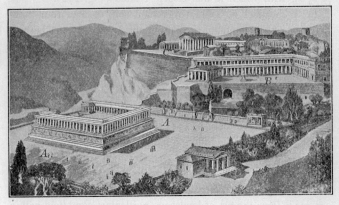

Fig. 214. Restoration of the Public Buildings of Pergamum, a Hellenistic City of Asia Minor. (After Thiersch)

Pergamum, on the west coast of Asia Minor (see map II, p. 450) became a flourishing city-kingdom in the third century B.C. under the successors of Alexander the Great (§ 736). The dwellings of the citizens were all lower down, in front of the group of buildings shown here. These public buildings stand on three terraces — lower, middle, and upper. The large *lower* terrace (*A*) was the main market place, adorned with a vast square marble altar of Zeus, having colonnades on three sides, beneath which was a long sculptured band (frieze) of warring gods and giants (Fig. 217). On the *middle* terrace (*B*), behind the colonnades, was the famous library of Pergamum, where the stone bases of library shelves still survive. The *upper* terrace (*C*) once contained the palace of the king; the temple now there was built by the Roman Emperor Trajan in the second century A.D.

the Northern barbarians in the tragic moment of death in battle with a dramatic impressiveness which has never been surpassed (Figs. 215 and 216). Reminiscences of this same struggle with the Gauls were also suggested by an enormous band of relief sculpture depicting the mythical battle between the gods and the

FIG. 215. A GALLIC CHIEFTAIN IN DEFEAT SLAYING HIS WIFE
AND HIMSELF

With one hand he supports his dying wife, and casting a terrible glance
at the pursuing enemy, he plunges his sword into his own breast. The
tremendous power of the barbarian's muscular figure is in startling contrast with the helpless limbs of the woman. The beholder feels both
terror at the wild impetuosity of the Northern barbarian, and at the
same time involuntary sympathy with his unconquerable courage, which
prefers death, for himself and his loved one, to shameful captivity
among the victors (§ 736)

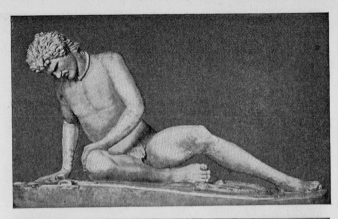

FIGS. 216 AND 217. SCULPTURES OF HELLENISTIC PERGAMUM

Above (Fig. 216) is a Gallic trumpeter, as he sinks in death with his
trumpet at his feet (§ 736). Below (Fig. 217) is a part of the frieze
around the great altar of Zeus at Pergamum (Fig. 214). It pictures the
mythical struggle between gods and giants. A giant at the left, whose
limbs end in serpents, raises over his head a great stone to hurl it at
the goddess on the right (§ 736)

FIG. 218. THE DEATH OF LAOCOÖN AND HIS TWO SONS

This famous group was wrought some time in the first century B.C. by
Agesander of Rhodes and two other sculptors, perhaps his sons. It shows
the priest Laocoön sinking down upon the altar, by which he had been
ministering, in a last agonizing struggle with the deadly serpents which
enfold him and his two sons. It is one of the most marvelous representa-
tions of human suffering (§ 737) ever created by art, but it does not move
us with such sympathy as the death of the Gallic chieftain (Fig. 215).
We should place with these works (Figs. 215–218) the sarcophagus reliefs
of Alexander (Plate VI, p. 468) and the mosaic picture of the battle of
Issus (Fig. 202) as the supreme creations of ancient art

From an etching by George T. Plowman

FIG. 219. GREEK TEMPLES AT PÆSTUM IN SOUTHERN ITALY

Pæstum (Greek, *Poseidonia*), one of the early Greek colonies in the vicinity of Naples, possesses to-day the ruins of three Greek temples. The temple of Neptune (Poseidon), the finest of the group, is the best-preserved Greek temple outside of Attica. Built toward the end of the sixth century, and perhaps as late as 500 B.C., it is one of the noblest examples of archaic Greek architecture (§§ 485, 782)

giants (Fig. 217). This vast work extended almost entirely around a colossal altar (Fig. 214) erected by the kings of Pergamum in honor of Zeus, to adorn the market place of the city.

It was the works of the Athenian sculptors which had inspired compositions of such tragic and overwhelming power, of such violent and thrilling action, at Pergamum. Some of these Athenian works have survived. They are best illustrated by the reliefs on a wonderful marble sarcophagus, showing Alexander the Great winning the battle of Issus, and again engaged in a lion hunt (Plate VI, p. 468). This sculpture of vigorous action in supremely tragic moments was also very beautifully followed out by a group of eminent sculptors on the island of Rhodes, which was a prosperous republic in the Hellenistic Age (§ 724). Most of their works have perished, but those which have survived are among

737. Athenian sculpture: the Alexander sarcophagus; Rhodian sculpture; Laocoön

FIG. 220. HELLENISTIC PORTRAIT HEAD IN BRONZE

This magnificent head of an unknown man, with wonderful representation of the hair, was recovered from the bottom of the sea. The eyes are inlaid as in the old Egyptian bronze head (Fig. 53). It is now in the Museum of Athens

the most famous works of sculpture from the ancient world. One of them depicts the Trojan priest Laocoön and his two sons as they are crushed to death in the folds of two deadly serpents (Fig. 218).

The great Greek painters of this age show the same tendencies as does the sculpture. They loved to depict dramatic and

738. Painting and mosaic

tragic incidents at the supreme moment. Their original works have all perished, but copies of some of them have survived, painted on the walls as interior decorations of fine houses or wrought in mosaic as floor pavement. It is the art of mosaic which has preserved to us the wonderful painting of Alexander charging on the Persian king at Issus, by an unknown Alexandrian painter of the Hellenistic Age (Fig. 202).

**739. Portraiture**

Both the sculptors and painters of this age made wonderful progress in portraiture, and their surviving works now begin to furnish us a continuous stream of portraits which show us how the great men of the age really looked (Fig. 220). Unfortunately these portraits are all works of the *sculptors* in stone or metal, either as statues and busts or as reliefs, especially on medallions and coins; the portraits executed by the *painter* in colors on wooden tablets have all perished. Alexander's favorite painter was Apelles. In one of his portraits of Alexander, the horse which the king was riding was said to have been painted with such lifelikeness that on one occasion a passing horse trotted up to it and whinnied. Later examples of this art of portrait painting have survived attached to mummies in Egypt (Plate VIII, p. 654).

## Section 69. Inventions and Science; Libraries and Literature

**740. Mechanical progress and practical inventions**

The keen and wide-awake intelligence of this wonderful age was everywhere evident, but especially in the application of science to the work and needs of daily life. It was an age of inventions, like our own. An up-to-date man would install an automatic door opener for the doorkeeper of his house, and a washing machine which delivered water and mineral soap as needed. On his estate olive oil was produced by a press operating with screw pressure. Outside the temples the priests set up automatic dispensers of holy water, while a water sprinkler operating by water pressure reduced the danger of fire. The application of levers, cranks, screws, and cogwheels to daily work brought forth cable roads for use in lowering stone from lofty quarries, or water wheels for drawing water on a large scale. A similar endless-chain apparatus was used for quickly raising heavy stone missiles to be discharged from huge missile-hurling war machines, some of which even operated by air pressure. As we go to see the "movies," so the people crowded to the market place to view the automatic theater, in which a clever mechanician presented an old Greek tragedy of the Trojan War in five scenes, displaying shipbuilding, the launch of the fleet, the voyage, with the dolphins playing in the water about the vessels, and finally a storm at sea, with thunder and lightning, amid which the Greek heroes promptly went to the bottom. Housekeepers told stories of the simpler days of their grandmothers, when there was no running water in the house and they actually had to go out and fetch it a long way from the nearest spring.

A public clock, either a shadow clock, such as the Egyptian had had in his house for over a thousand years (Fig. 74), or a water clock of Greek invention (Fig. 221), stood in the market place and furnished all the good townspeople with the hour of the day. The Ptolemies or the priests under them attempted to improve the calendar by the insertion every fourth year of a leap year with an additional day, but the people could not be roused out of the rut into which usage had fallen, and everywhere they continued to use the inconvenient moon month of the Greeks. There was no system for the numbering of the years anywhere except in Syria, where the Seleucids gave each year a number reckoned from the beginning of their sway. **741. Time and the calendar**

The most remarkable man of science of the time was probably Archimedes. He lived in Syracuse, and one of his famous feats was the arrangement of a series of pulleys and levers, which so multiplied power that the king was able by turning a light crank to move a large three-masted ship standing fully loaded on the dock, and to launch it into the water. After **742. Archimedes** witnessing such feats as this the people easily believed his proud boast, " Give me a place to stand on and I will move the earth." He devised such powerful and dangerous war machines that he greatly aided in defending his native city from capture by

FIG. 221. THE TOWN CLOCK OF ATHENS IN THE HELLENISTIC AGE

This tower, commonly called the " Tower of the Winds," now stands among modern houses, but once looked out on the Athenian market place (§ 564). The arches at the left support part of an ancient channel which supplied the water for the operation of a water clock in the tower. Such clocks were more or less like hourglasses, the flowing water filling a given measure in a given time, like the sand in the hourglass. This tower was built in the last century B.C., when Athens was under the control of Rome (§ 884)

the Romans (§ 868). But Archimedes was far more than an inventor of practical appliances. He was a scientific investigator of the first rank. He was able to prove to the king that one of the monarch's gold crowns was not of pure metal, because he had discovered the principle of determining the proportion of loss of weight when an object is immersed in water. He was thus the discoverer of what science now calls specific gravity. Besides his skill in physics he was also the greatest of ancient mathematicians (§ 744).

**743. The Alexandrian scientists**

Archimedes was in close correspondence with his friends in Alexandria, who formed the greatest body of scientists in the ancient world. They lived together at the Museum, where they were paid salaries and supported by the Ptolemies. They formed the first scientific institution founded and supported by

PLATE VI. GREEKS AND PERSIANS HUNTING LIONS WITH ALEXANDER THE GREAT

Alexander is out of range at the left. A Greek on horseback endeavors to pierce the wounded lion with his spear. A Persian on foot wields an ax. The scene is carved in relief on a marble sarcophagus, found at Sidon in 1881; the colors are exactly those of the original, now in the museum at Constantinople. It was made not long after Alexander's death, and is one of the greatest works of Hellenistic art (§ 737). (After Winter, *Alexandermosaik*)

a government. Without financial anxieties they could devote themselves to research, for which the halls, laboratories, and library of the institution were equipped. Thus the scientists of the Hellenistic Age, especially this remarkable group at Alexandria, became the founders of systematic scientific research, and their books formed the sum or body of scientific knowledge for nearly two thousand years, until the revival of science in modern times.

The very first generation of scientists at the Alexandrian Museum boasted a great name in mathematics which is still famous among us — that of Euclid. His complete system of geometry was so logically built up, that in modern England Euclid's geometry is still used as a schoolbook — the oldest schoolbook in use to-day. Archimedes then, for the first time, developed what is now called higher mathematics — certain difficult and advanced mathematical processes the knowledge of which having in the meantime been lost had to be rediscovered in modern times. Along with mathematics much progress was also made in astronomy. The Ptolemies built an astronomical observatory at Alexandria, and although it was, of course, without telescopes, important observations and discoveries were made. An astronomer of little fame named Aristarchus, who lived on the island of Samos, made the greatest of the discoveries of this age. He demonstrated that the earth and the planets revolve around the *sun*. Almost no one adopted his conclusion, however, and both the Hellenistic Greeks and all ancient scientists of later days wrongly believed that the *earth* was the center around which the sun and the planets revolved (§ 1059). One Hellenistic astronomer at the cost of immense labor, made a catalogue of eight or nine hundred fixed stars, to serve as a basis for determining any future changes that might take place in the skies.

**744.** Mathematics: Euclid and Archimedes. Astronomy: Aristarchus

Astronomy had now greatly aided in the progress of geography. Eratosthenes, a great mathematical astronomer of Alexandria, very cleverly computed the size of the earth by observing

**745.** Eratosthenes computes the size of the earth

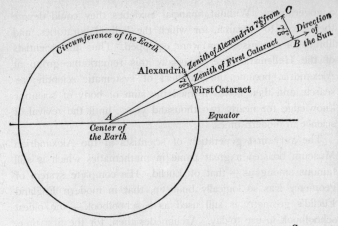

FIG. 222. DIAGRAM ROUGHLY INDICATING HOW THE SIZE OF THE EARTH WAS FIRST CALCULATED

The sun standing at noon directly over the First Cataract (line *AB*) was of course visible also at Alexandria. The result was just the same as if someone had stood at the First Cataract holding vertically upright a surveyor's pole tall enough to be seen from Alexandria. For Eratosthenes at Alexandria the sun was like the top of the pole. With his instruments set up at Alexandria, therefore, Eratosthenes found that the sun over the First Cataract (line *AB*) was 7⅕ degrees south of the zenith of his instrument at Alexandria (line *AC*). The lines *AB* and *AC* diverge 7⅕ degrees at all points, whether in the skies or on earth. Hence Eratosthenes knew that the First Cataract was 7⅕ degrees of the earth's circumference from Alexandria; that is, the distance between Alexandria and the First Cataract was 7⅕ degrees of the earth's circumference, or one fiftieth of its total circumference of 360 degrees. Now the actual distance between Alexandria and the First Cataract was supposed to be a little less than 500 miles. This distance (500 miles) then was one fiftieth of the earth's circumference, giving a few hundred less than 25,000 miles for the total circumference of the earth; and for its diameter about 7850 miles, which is within 50 miles of being correct

that when the summer sun, shifting steadily northward, reached its farthest north, it shone at noonday straight down to the bottom of a well at the First Cataract of the Nile (Fig. 211).

To this notion of the size of the earth, much information had been added regarding the extent and the character of the inhabited regions reached by navigation and exploration in this age. At home, in Greece, one geographer undertook to measure the heights of the mountains, though he was without a barometer. The campaigns of Alexander in the Far East had greatly extended the limits where the known world ended. Bold Alexandrian merchants had sailed to India and around its southern tip to Ceylon and the eastern coast of India, where they heard fabulous tales of the Chinese coast beyond.

746. Explorations eastward

In the Far West as early as 500 B.C. Phœnician navigators had passed Gibraltar, and turning southward had probably reached the coast of Guinea, whence they brought back marvelous stories of the hairy men whom the interpreters called "Gorillas"! A trained astronomer of Marseilles named Pytheas fitted out a ship at his own expense and coasted northward from Gibraltar. He discovered the triangular shape of the island of Britannia, and penetrating far into the North Sea he was the first civilized man to hear tales of the frozen sea beyond and the mysterious island of Thule (Iceland) on its margin. He discovered the influence of the full moon on the immense spring tides, and he brought back reports of such surprising things that he was generally regarded as a sensational fable monger.

747. Explorations westward and northward; Pytheas and the tides

With a greater mass of facts and reports than anyone before him had ever had, Eratosthenes was able to write a very full geography. His map of the known world (p. 472), including Europe, Asia, and Africa, not only showed the regions grouped about the Mediterranean with fair correctness, but he was the first geographer who was able to lay out on his map a cross-net of lines indicating latitude and longitude. He thus became the founder of scientific geography.

748. Eratosthenes, founder of scientific geography, makes first map with latitude and longitude

In the study of animal and vegetable life Aristotle and his pupils remained the leaders, and the ancient world never outgrew their observations. While their knowledge of botany, acquired without a microscope, was of course limited and contained errors, a large mass of new facts was observed and

749. Botany, zoölogy, anatomy, and medicine

arranged. For the study of anatomy there was a laboratory in Alexandria, at the Museum, which the Ptolemies furnished with condemned criminals on whom vivisection was practiced. In this way the nerves were discovered to be the lines along which messages of pain and pleasure pass to the brain. The brain was thus shown to be the center of the nervous system. Although such research came very near to discovering the circulation of the blood, the arteries were still misunderstood to be channels for the circulation of air from the lungs. Alexandria

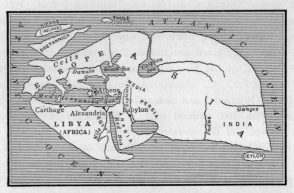

MAP OF THE WORLD ACCORDING TO ERATOSTHENES (200 B.C.)

became the greatest center of medical research in the ancient world, and here young men went through long studies to train themselves as physicians, just as they do at the present day.

**750.** Earliest state libraries of the Greeks; Alexandrian library

Notwithstanding the popularity of the natural sciences, there was now also much study of language and of the great mass of older literature. Although the ancient Orient had long before known royal libraries (§ 226), the first library founded and supported by a Greek government had been formed by the city of Heracleia, on the Black Sea, during the childhood of Alexander the Great (not long before 350 B.C.). Later the kings of Pergamum also founded a very notable library (Fig. 214). All these efforts were far surpassed by the Ptolemies at Alexandria.

Across the park from their palace they built a library for the Museum, where they had finally over half a million rolls.

**751.** Rise of library management and cataloguing

The art of cataloguing and managing such a great collection of books had to be taken up from the beginning. A gifted philosopher and poet named Callimachus was made a librarian by the first Ptolemy. Callimachus catalogued all the known books of value, both by titles and authors, and this first great book catalogue filled one hundred and twenty books or sections. As the founder of library management he introduced many improvements. One of his sayings was, "A big book is a big nuisance," by which he probably meant that a book in a single long and bulky roll was very inconvenient to handle (cf. Fig. 191). Hence he introduced the method of cutting up a work into a series of rolls, each roll called a "book," meaning a "part." Thus arose the division of the Homeric poems, the history of Herodotus, and other works into "books."

**752.** Great influence of the Alexandrian library on editing and publishing (in hand copies)

The immense amount of hand copying required to secure good and accurate editions of famous works for this library gradually created the new science of publishing correctly old and often badly copied works. The copies produced by the librarians and scholars of Alexandria became the standard editions on which other ancient libraries and copyists depended. The Hellenistic world was everywhere supplied with "Alexandrian editions," and from these are descended most of the manuscripts now preserved in the libraries of Europe, from which, in turn, have been copied our printed editions of Homer, Xenophon, and other great Greek authors. Unfortunately the library of Alexandria perished (§ 965), and the earliest example of a Greek book which has survived to us is a roll which was found in an Egyptian tomb by modern excavators only a few years ago (Fig. 223).

**753.** Language study; rise of dictionaries and grammars

The new art of editing and arranging the text of books naturally required much language study. Where two old copies differed, the question would often arise, which one was correct. Many strange and old words needed explanation, just as when we read Chaucer, and there were constant questions of spelling. The Alexandrian scholars therefore began to make dictionaries. At the same time grammatical questions demanded more

FIG. 223. A PAGE FROM THE EARLIEST SURVIVING GREEK BOOK

This book was found lying beside the body of a man buried in an Egyptian cemetery, and because of the rainless climate of Egypt it has been preserved, in spite of its being written on perishable papyrus paper (cf. Figs. 58, 131, 253, and 267). What we have called a *page* is really a *column* of writing, and the book consisted of a series of such columns side by side on the roll (see Fig. 191). This book contains a poem called *The Persians*, by the Greek poet Timotheos, who died 357 B.C. His name (Timotheos) may be seen in the third line from the bottom, at the beginning of the line. The poem tells the story of the battle of Salamis. This copy of the work was written in the lifetime of Alexander the Great. The column shown here is like those on the rolls which once filled the Alexandrian library, and shows us how the pages looked over which the great men of science there so industriously pored (§ 753)

and more attention. At last in 120 B.C. a scholar named Dionysius wrote the first Greek grammar. It contained the leading grammatical terms, like the names of the parts of speech, which we still use. As all these terms were explained and conveniently arranged in the grammar of Dionysius, his book was used for centuries and thus became the foundation of all later grammars of the languages of civilized peoples, including our own. Such a term as our " subjunctive mode " is simply a translation of the corresponding Greek term created by the Hellenistic scholars.

Literature was to a large extent in the hands of such learned men as those of Alexandria. The great librarian Callimachus was a famous poet of the age. These scholars no longer chose great and dramatic themes, like war, fate, and catastrophe, as the subjects of their writing. They loved to picture such scenes as the shepherd at the spring, listening to the music of over-hanging boughs, lazily watching his flocks, and dreaming the while of some winsome village maid who has scorned his devotion. Such pictures of country life set in the simplicity and beauty of peaceful hillsides, and wrought into melodious verse, delighted the cultivated circles of a great world-city like Alexandria more than even the revered classics of an older day. In such verse the greatest literary artist of the age was a Sicilian named Theocritus, whose idyls have taken a permanent place in the world's literature for two thousand years. At the same time the everyday life of the age was also pictured at the theater in a modern form of play, known as the "new comedy." With many amusing incidents the townsmen saw their faults and weaknesses of character here depicted on the stage, and Menander at Athens, the ablest of such play-writers, gained a great reputation for his keen knowledge of men and his ability to hit them off wittily in clever comedies.

754. Literature

## SECTION 70. EDUCATION, PHILOSOPHY, AND RELIGION

In such a cultivated world of fine cities, beautiful homes, sumptuous public buildings, noble works of art, state libraries and scientific research, it was natural that education should have made much progress. The elementary schools, once *private*,

755. Education: elementary schools and gymnasiums

were now often *supported by the State.* When the lad had finished at the elementary school, his father allowed him to attend lectures on rhetoric, science, philosophy, and mathematics in the lecture rooms of the gymnasium building. The wall of such a hall at Priene (Fig. 224) is still scribbled all over with the names of the boys of more than two thousand years ago, who thus recorded their permanent claims to certain seats near the wall.

The gymnasium thus became a place of helpful intellectual stimulus. When the fathers were no longer nimble enough for athletic games they often sat about in the colonnades watching the contests, or idling in groups, discussing the last lecture in science or the latest discovery in the laboratory of the Museum. Here many an argument in science or philosophy might be overheard by the young

**756.** Influence of gymnasium toward higher studies

FIG. 224. WALL OF A GYMNASIUM LECTURE HALL AT PRIENE, STILL COVERED WITH SCHOOLBOYS' NAMES

This lecture hall opened on the colonnades around the court of the gymnasium at Priene (Fig.212, *P*). The smooth blocks of marble are scratched with the names of hundreds of schoolboys, who heard lectures and classes here twenty-two hundred years ago. In order to set up a permanent claim to his seat, a boy would scratch into the wall the words, "Seat of Cleon, the son of Clearchos." When the wall was entirely filled with these names, the boys evidently mounted on the benches and then on the backs of comrades to find enough room to write their claims

fellows, fresh from the gymnasium baths, as they wandered out to greet their waiting fathers and wend their way homeward. Such an atmosphere was one to create great interest in science and philosophy, and often a youth besought his father to give him a few years' higher study at the Museum or at Athens.

Furthermore, in the pursuit of a profession, a special training had now become indispensable to a young man's success. Like the medical student, the architect now studied his profession and bent industriously over books that told him how to erect an arch that would be safe and secure, and what were the proper proportions for a column. Young fellows who wished to become engineers studied a host of things in mechanics, like bridge-building and devices for moving heavy bodies. It was an age of technical training. This specialization in the professions was also to be found among the scientists, who now specialized each in a particular branch, like astronomy, or mathematics, or geography. The youth who wished to study science turned to the great scientific specialists at the Alexandrian Museum.

757. Professional and scientific specialization

As he strolled for the first time through the beautiful gardens and into the Museum building, he found going on there lectures on astronomy, geography, physics, mathematics, botany, zoölogy, anatomy, medicine, or rhetoric, grammar, and literature. When he was sufficiently familiar with the *known* facts about these subjects, he could share in the endeavor to discover *new* facts about them. He might cross the court to the halls where the cries of suffering animals told him that vivisection was going on; he might climb the tower of the astronomical observatory, and sit there night after night at the elbow of some eminent astronomer, or assist Eratosthenes at noonday in taking an observation of the sun for his computation of the earth's size (§ 745). Or he might withdraw to the quiet library rooms and assist in making up the lists of famous old books, to be put together in Callimachus' great catalogue. If he showed ability enough, he might later be permitted to lecture to students himself, and finally become one of its group of famous scientific men.

758. The Alexandrian Museum as a university

On the other hand, Alexandria was not at first interested in philosophy, out of which science had grown (§ 494). Athens was still the leading home of philosophy. The youth who went there to take up philosophical studies found the successors of

759. The Academy and the Peripatetic school at Athens

Plato still continuing his teaching in the quiet grove of the Academy (§ 671), where his memory was greatly revered. Plato's pupil Aristotle, however, had not been able to accept his master's teachings. After the education of the young Alexander (§ 687), Aristotle had returned to Athens and established a school of his own at the Lyceum (§ 558), where he occupied a terrace called the "Walk" (Greek, *peripatos*). Here, he directed one group of advanced students after another in the arrangement and study of the different sciences, like anatomy, botany, zoölogy. All of these groups collected great masses of scientific observations, which were arranged under Aristotle's guidance. The result was a veritable encyclopedia of old and new facts. The work was never completed, and many of the essays and treatises which it included have been lost. When Aristotle died, soon after the death of Alexander, his school declined.

**760. Unrivaled authority of Aristotle's works**
Aristotle's works formed the greatest attempt ever made in ancient times to collect and to state in a clear way the whole mass of human knowledge. They never lost their importance and they justly gave him the reputation of having possessed the greatest mind produced by the ancient world. His works finally gained such unquestioned authority in later Europe that in medieval times men turned to Aristotle's books for the answer to every scientific question. Instead of endeavoring to discover new facts in nature for themselves, they turned to Aristotle for the solution of every scientific problem. The writings of no other man have ever enjoyed such widespread and unquestioned authority.[1]

**761. Two philosophies of practical living: Stoicism and Epicureanism**
But many Greeks found little satisfaction in the learned researches of Plato's Academy and of Aristotle's Peripatetic school (from *peripatos*, "walk"). They desired some teaching which would lead them to a happy and contented frame of mind in living, and enable one to live successfully. To meet this growing desire two more schools of philosophy arose at Athens.

[1] See Robinson, *Medieval and Modern Times*, pp. 252 ff.

The first was founded by an Oriental, a Semite named Zeno, born in Cyprus. He taught in the famous old "Painted Porch" in the market place of Athens (§ 572). Such a porch was called a *Stoa*, and Zeno's school was therefore called the Stoic school. Zeno taught that there was but one good and that was virtue, and but one evil and that was moral wrong. The great aim of life should be a tranquillity of soul, which comes from virtue, and is indifferent both to pleasure and to pain. His followers were famous for their fortitude, and hence our common use of the word "stoicism" to indicate indifference to suffering. The Stoic school was very popular and finally became the greatest of the schools of philosophy. The last school, founded by Epicurus in his own garden at Athens, taught that the highest good was pleasure, both of body and of mind, but always in accordance with virtue. Hence we still call a man devoted to pleasure, especially in eating, an "epicure." The school of Epicurus, too, flourished and attracted many disciples. Men later distorted his teachings into a justification for a life of sensual pleasure. The oriental proverb, "Eat, drink, and be merry, for to-morrow we die," has therefore been commonly applied to them.

These schools lived on the income of property left them by wealthy pupils and friends. The head of the school, with his assistants and followers, lived together in quarters with rooms for lectures, books, and study. The most successful of these organizations was that of Aristotle, at least as long as he lived. The Museum of Alexandria was modeled on these Athenian organizations, and they have also become the model of academies of science and of universities ever since. We may regard Hellenistic Athens then as possessing a university made up of four departments: the Academy, the Lyceum, the Stoa, and the Garden of Epicurus. Thus in the day when her political power had vanished, Athens had become even more than Pericles had hoped she might be. She was not only the teacher of all Greece, but she drew her pupils from all parts of the civilized world.

**762. The University of Athens and its historic influence**

**763. The fall of the old Greek gods**

For such highly educated men the beliefs of Stoicism or Epicureanism served as their religion. The gods had for such men usually ceased to exist, or were explained as merely glorified human beings. A romance writer of the day, a man named Euhemerus, wrote an attractive tale of an imaginary journey which he made to the Indian Ocean, where he found a group of mysterious islands. There, in a temple of Zeus, he found a golden tablet inscribed with a story telling how the great gods worshiped by the Greeks were once powerful kings who had done much for the civilization of mankind, and when they died they had been deified. This story of a novelist of the Hellenistic Age was widely believed, but these gods no longer attracted the reverence of religiously minded men. Moreover, there was now little pressure on any man to keep silence about his beliefs regarding the gods. There was great freedom of conscience — far more freedom than the Christian rulers of later Europe granted their subjects. The teachings of Socrates would no longer have caused his condemnation by his Athenian neighbors.

**764. Increased popularity of oriental gods**

The great multitude of the people had not the education to understand philosophy, nor the means to attend the philosophical schools. Yet gods in some form they must have. With the weakening of faith in the old gods, those of the Orient, which we have already seen invading Greek life (§ 657), became more and more popular. So the Ptolemies introduced as their great State god an oriental deity named Serapis, and they built for him a magnificent temple at Alexandria. From Babylonia the mysterious lore of the Chaldean astrologers (§§ 238, 239) was spreading widely through the Mediterranean. It was received and accepted in Egypt, and even Greek science did not escape its influence. Oriental beliefs and oriental symbols were everywhere. Men had long since grown accustomed to foreign gods, and they no longer looked askance at strange usages in religion. It was in such an age as this that Christianity, an oriental religion, passed easily from land to land (§ 1069).

## SECTION 71. FORMATION OF A HELLENISTIC WORLD OF HELLENIC-ORIENTAL CIVILIZATION; DECLINE OF CITIZENSHIP AND THE CITY-STATE

It is a great mistake to suppose that Marathon and Salamis once and for all banished the influence of the Orient from the Mediterranean, as an impenetrable dam keeps back a body of water. While Alexander's victories and conquests destroyed the military power of the Orient, the daily life and the civilization of the people of the Orient continued to be a permanent force exerting a steady pressure upon the life of the eastern Mediterranean world, in commerce, in form of government, in customs and usages, in art, industry, literature, and religion. When Christianity issued from Palestine, therefore, as we shall see (§ 1067), it found itself but one among many other influences from the Orient which were passing westward. Thus while Greek civilization, with its language, its art, its literature, its theaters and gymnasiums, was Hellenizing the Orient, the Orient in the same way was exercising a powerful influence on the West and was orientalizing the eastern Mediterranean world. In this way there was gradually formed an eastern Mediterranean world of Hellenic-oriental civilization.

765. Continued intrusion of oriental influences in the eastern Mediterranean

In this larger world the old Greek *city*-citizen, who had made Greek civilization what it was, played but a small part. He felt himself an *individual* belonging in an international world, a far larger world than the city in which he lived. But this larger world brought home no sense of citizenship in it. For in the great Hellenistic states there was no such thing as *national* citizenship. The city-citizen had no share in guiding the affairs of the great nation or empire of which his city-state was a part. It was as if a citizen of Chicago might vote at the election of a mayor of the city but had no right to vote at the election of a president of the United States. There was not even a name for the empire of the Seleucids, and their subjects, wherever

766. The Hellenistic world of the eastern Mediterranean and its lack of citizenship

they went, bore the names of their home cities or countries.[1] The conception of "native land" in the national sense was wanting, and patriotism did not exist.

**767.** The contributions of the city-state and the end of its usefulness

The centers of power and progress in Greek civilization had been the *city-states*, but the finest and most influential forces operating within the city-state had now disappeared. So, for example, the old city gods were gone. Likewise the citizen-soldier who defended his city had long ago given way, even in Greece, to the professional soldier who came from abroad and fought for hire. The Greek no longer stood weapon in hand ready to defend his home and his city-community against every assault. He found the holding of city offices becoming a profession, as that of the soldier had long been. Losing his interest in the State, he turned to his personal affairs, the cultivation of himself. The patriotic sense of responsibility for the welfare of the city-state which he loved, and the fine moral earnestness which this responsibility roused, no longer animated the Greek mind nor quickened it to the loftiest achievements in politics, in art, in architecture, in literature, and in original thought. The Greek city-states, *in competition among themselves*, had developed the highest type of civilization which the world had ever seen, but in this process the city-states themselves had politically perished. In many Greek cities only a discouraged remnant of the citizens was left after the emigration to Asia (§ 724). The cattle often browsed on the grass in the public square before the town hall in such cities of the Greeks. Not even their own Hellas was a unified nation.

**768.** Hellenistic world of the *eastern* Mediterranean under the power of the *western* Mediterranean

A larger world had engulfed the old Greek city-states. But this Hellenistic world of the *eastern* Mediterranean had by 200 B.C. reached a point in its own wars and rivalries when it was to feel the iron hand of a great new military power from the distant world of the *western* Mediterranean. At this point,

[1] It was as if the citizens of the United States were termed Bostonians, New Yorkers, Philadelphians, Chicagoans, etc.

therefore (200 B.C.), we shall be unable to understand the further story of the eastern Mediterranean, until we have turned back and taken up the career of the western Mediterranean world. There in the West for some three centuries the city of Rome had been developing a power which was to unite both the East and the West into a vast empire including the *whole Mediterranean*.

## QUESTIONS

SECTION 68. What was the prevalent language of the Hellenistic Age? How is the Rosetta Stone an example of this fact? Describe the improvements in houses. What written documents tell us of this age, and how have they been preserved? Describe the new Hellenistic cities, especially Priene. What new forms of architecture came in? Describe the commerce of Alexandria; its parks and public buildings. Describe the important examples of the sculpture of tragic and violent action. What can you say of such subjects in painting?

SECTION 69. What can you say of inventions in the Hellenistic Age? of improvements in time measurement? of the achievements of Archimedes? Tell about the life of the Alexandrian scientists. Which of them wrote a geometry that is still in use? What great truth did Aristarchus discover? How did Eratosthenes compute the size of the earth? Describe the growth of geographical knowledge; the world map of Eratosthenes; the study of animal life and medicine. What can you say of the rise of libraries? Who was the first great librarian, and what did he do? What effect had the libraries on publishing? on language study? Discuss the changes in literature.

SECTION 70. Discuss the gymnasium as a source of education. What professions could a boy study? How could he take up scientific study and research? Where did a youth study philosophy? What two philosophical schools first arose at Athens? What did Aristotle do? What can you say about his rank as a thinker? Name the two later schools of philosophy at Athens. What was their purpose? What had happened to the old gods?

SECTION 71. What kind of a world had now grown up in the eastern Mediterranean? What can you say of citizenship there? Under what form of state had Greek civilization chiefly developed? What had now become of the Greek city-state? What was now to become of the Hellenistic eastern Mediterranean world?

# CHAPTER XXII

## THE WESTERN MEDITERRANEAN WORLD AND THE ROMAN CONQUEST OF ITALY

### SECTION 72. THE WESTERN MEDITERRANEAN WORLD

**769. The Mediterranean and its shore lands form the main part of the ancient world**

While we have been following the history of the eastern Mediterranean and the peoples grouped about it, the story of its western shores has largely dropped out of sight. Before we turn to this Western world, however, let us endeavor to gain a picture of the Mediterranean world as a whole. This sea is a very large body of water, almost as long as Europe

NOTE. The above headpiece shows an ancient bronze wolf (sixth century B.C.), wrought by Greek artists in Italy (§ 831), and illustrates the influence of Greek civilization in Rome even before 500 B.C. The two infants nourished by the she-wolf are later additions put there in accordance with the tradition at Rome that the city was founded by these twin brothers named Romulus and Remus. Their ancestor, so said the tradition, was Æneas (§ 1003), one of the Trojan heroes, who had fled from Troy after its destruction (§ 375), and after many adventures had arrived in Italy. His son founded and became king of Alba Longa (§ 783). In the midst of a family feud among his descendants, these twin boys, the sons of the War-god, Mars, were born, and after they had been set adrift in the Tiber by the ruling king, they gently ran aground at the base of the Palatine Hill, where a she-wolf found and nourished them. When they grew up they returned home to Alba Longa, claimed their rights, and eventually founded Rome. Similar legends formed all that the Romans knew of their early history through the period of the kings (see p. 497, footnote) and far down into the Republic.

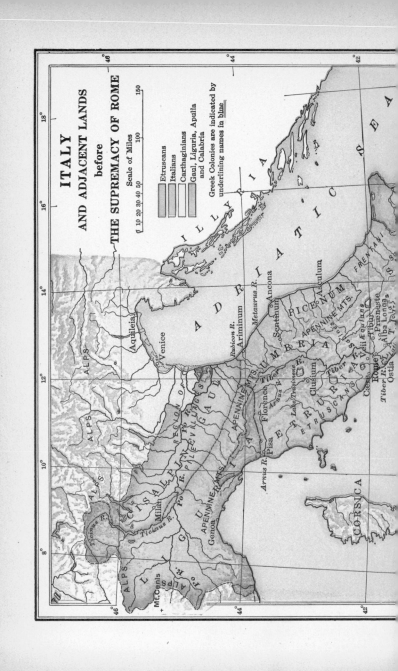

ITALY
AND ADJACENT LANDS
before
THE SUPREMACY OF ROME

Scale of Miles
0 10 20 30 40 50    100    150

Etruscans
Italians
Carthaginians
Gaul, Liguria, Apulia
and Calabria

Greek Colonies are indicated by
underlining names in blue

ALPS

MtCenis

Thoras R.

Ticinus R.

Po R.

Milan

CISALPINE

LIGURIA

Genoa

APENNINE MTS.

Pisa

Arnus R.

Florence

Arsa R.

Clusium

ETRURIA

ETRUSCANS

CORSICA

Lake Trasimene

Tiber

Veii

Caere

Tiber R.

Rome

Ostia

Tibur

Praeneste

Alba Longa

ALPS

ALPS

REGION OF THE CISALPINE GAULS

Aquileia

Venice

ILLYRIA

ADRIATIC SEA

Rubicon R.

Ariminum

Metaurus R.

Sentinum

Ancona

UMBRIA

APENNINE MTS.

PICENUM

Asculum

APENNINE MTS.

FRENTANI

T. Tota

Aequians

*(Map)*

Brundisium
CALABRIA
(PENINSULA)
Tarentum
GULF OF TARENTUM
Metapontum
Heraclea
Poseidonia or Pæstum
LUCANIA
CAMPANIA
Vesuvius
Mt. Vesuvius
Bay of Naples
Neapolis
Misenum
Baiæ
Cumæ
Croton
Lacinian Cape
Locri
Rhegium
Strait of Messina
Messina
Taormina
Mt. Ætna
Catana
Henna
SICILY
Syracuse
Segesta
Agrigentum
(Acragas)

ETRUSCAN OR TYRRHENIAN SEA

MEDITERRANEAN SEA

SARDINIA

AFRICA
Utica
Carthage
Hippo
Zama

38°
86°
16°
14°
12°
10°
8°
40°
38°
36°

Longitude    East    12°    from    Greenwich

THE M.·N. WORKS, BUFFALO

itself. Its length is about twenty-four hundred miles, and laid out across the United States, it would reach from New York over into California. It is important for us to bear in mind that the ancient world was largely made up of the lands surrounding the Mediterranean. To these shore lands we have chiefly to add the Black Sea and the oriental lands on the east. The stage of ancient history was then, to a large extent, the Mediterranean and its shores.

Now the Mediterranean is not a single compact body of water, like one of our Great Lakes. A land bridge made up of Italy and Sicily extends almost across this great sea and divides it into two parts, an eastern and a western basin. There are no accepted geographical names for these two basins, but we may call them, for convenience, the eastern and the western Mediterranean worlds. We have been following the story of civilized men in the eastern Mediterranean world; we must now turn back and take up the story of the western Mediterranean world also.

**770.** Division of the Mediterranean into an eastern and a western basin

The story of civilization in the *eastern* Mediterranean world began very early under the leadership of the Orient. On the other hand, the peoples of the *western* Mediterranean world were too far away to receive from the Orient such strong influences toward civilization. Hence the West had lagged far behind, and much of it had made little advance in civilization since the Stone Age life of the Swiss lake-villages. But a study of the map (p. 288) shows us that the western Mediterranean world is not wholly separated from the eastern, which, with its Greek and Hellenistic civilization, overlapped at its western end with the western Mediterranean world. Here then, in southern Italy and Sicily, we shall see the eastern Mediterranean civilizing the western.

**771.** Spread of civilization from the *eastern* Mediterranean world to the backward *western* Mediterranean

The most important land in the western Mediterranean world in early times was Italy. It slopes westward in the main; it thus faces and belongs to the western Mediterranean world. The Italian peninsula, thrusting far out into the sea (see map,

**772.** Italy: its geography and climate

p. **484**), is nearly six hundred miles long; that is, about half again as long as the peninsula of Florida. Italy [1] is not only four times as large as Greece, but, unlike Greece, it is not cut up by a tangle of mountains into tortuous valleys and tiny plains. The main chain of the Apennines, though crossing the peninsula obliquely in the north, is nearly parallel with the coasts, and many of its outlying ridges are quite so. There are larger plains for the cultivation of grain than we find anywhere in Greece; at the same time there is much more room for upland pasturage of flocks and herds. A considerably larger population can be supported in the plains of Italy than in Greece. At the same time the coast is not so cut up and indented as in Greece; there are fewer good harbors. Hence agriculture and live stock developed much earlier than trade.

**773.** Earliest migrations into Italy
The fertile plains and forest-clad slopes of Italy have always attracted the peoples of northern Europe to forsake their own bleak and wintry lands and migrate to this warm and sunny peninsula in the southern sea. By 2000 B.C. the lake-dwellers of Late Stone Age Switzerland (§§ 27–34) pushed southward through the Alpine passes and occupied the lakes of northern Italy. The remains of over a hundred of their pile-supported settlements (Fig. 225) have also been found under the soil of the Po valley, once a vast morass, which these people reclaimed by erecting their pile dwellings further and further out in it. The city of Venice, still standing on piles, although it is built mostly of stone, is a surviving example of the way the lake-dwellers once built their little wooden houses on piles in the same region. They had their influence on the later Romans, who afterward made their military camps on a plan exactly like that of the Po valley pile villages (Fig. 225).

**774.** Earliest metal in Italy and its oriental names
When these people reached the Po valley, they had already received metal, which is found in all their settlements. The oriental source of this metal is still evident in the names which

---

[1] The area of Italy is about 110,000 square miles, about twice as large a Illinois, and not quite four times the area of South Carolina.

copper and bronze brought with them from the East into Italy. Our word "copper" had the form *cuprum* in Italy, from the name of the island of *Cyprus* (ancient *Cuprus*) (see map, p. 288), whose rich mines supplied the Mediterranean lands with copper from very early times. Our word "bronze" is probably derived from the first part of the name of the city of Brondesium (later Brundisium, now called Brindisi) at the back of the heel of Italy, where it was so near the Ægean that it very early received bronze from there (§ 336).

While the pile villagers were settling in the Po valley, the tribes forming the western end of the Indo-European migration (Fig. 112) began to feel the attractiveness of the warm and verdant hills of Italy.

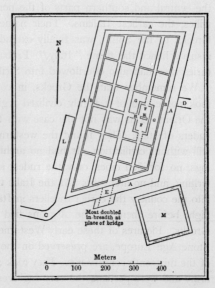

FIG. 225. GROUND PLAN OF A PREHISTORIC PILE VILLAGE IN NORTHERN ITALY

The settlement was surrounded by a moat (*A*) nearly 100 feet across, filled with water from a connected river (*C*). Inside the moat was an earth wall (*B*) about 50 feet thick at the base. The village thus inclosed was about 2000 feet long; that is, four city blocks. The whole village, being in the marshes of the Po valley, was supported on piles, like the lake-villages (Fig. 15). The plan and arrangement of streets are those of the Roman military camp later derived from it

**775. Western wing of the Indo-Europeans enters Italy**

Probably not long after the Greeks had pushed southward into the Greek peninsula (§ 371), the western tribes of Indo-European blood had entered the beautiful western Mediterranean world, into which the Italian peninsula extends. They came in successive migrations, but the most important group who settled in the central and southern parts of the peninsula were the Italic tribes, the earliest Italians. Their name, first applied by the Greeks to the South, was finally extended to the whole peninsula; hence the name "Italy." Probably within a few centuries they had also overflowed into Sicily.

**776. Uncivilized state of Italy and the West**

We remember that the Greeks, in conquering the Ægean, took possession of a highly civilized region on the borders of the Orient. This was not the case with the Indo-European invaders of Italy. They found the western Mediterranean world still without civilization. It had no architecture, no fine buildings, no fortified cities, only the rudest arts and industries, no writing, and no literature. As the Italic tribes fought their way into the country the earlier dwellers in Italy must have taken to flight before them, as the Ægeans fled before the on-coming Greeks. Pictures of these early Westerners, the descendants of Stone Age Europe, are preserved on the Egyptian monuments of the thirteenth century B.C. They took service in the Egyptian army and were perhaps the very fugitives who were driven out before the Italic invasion of the West. Their weapons were huge bronze swords, which were simply enlarged Egyptian daggers (see tailpiece, p. 519) such as they had long imported. Thus these prehistoric Westerners had enough skill in working metals to invent the sword,[1] which Europe still continues to use.

**777. The three Western rivals confronting the Italic tribes: first, the Etruscans**

Besides the Italic invaders there were in the western Mediterranean world three rival peoples, all of whom came from the eastern Mediterranean world. While fighting among themselves, the Italic peoples suddenly saw landing on the western coast of Italy a bold race of sea rovers whom we call the Etruscans. They were a people whose origin is still uncertain; they probably had an earlier home in western Asia Minor, and the

[1] A curved blade, of *one* edge only, was known in the Egyptian Empire and also in the Assyrian Empire, but it was little used and never became one of the recognized arms of an oriental army. The *two*-edged sword, the descendant of the dagger, as used by the Roman army, was of Western origin.

Egyptian monuments tell us of their sea raids on the coast of the Delta as far back as the thirteenth century B.C., at a time when they were perhaps leaving Asia Minor in search of a new home in Italy. In any case the Etruscans were settled in Italy by 1000 B.C. They thrust back the Indo-European tribes, and finally gained control of the west coast of Italy from the Bay of Naples almost to Genoa, inclu____ ____ch of

THE FOUR RIVAL PEOPLES OF THE WESTERN MEDITERRANEAN:
ETRUSCANS, ITALIC TRIBES, GREEKS, AND CARTHAGINIANS

the inland country as far back as the Apennines and even into the Po valley. They seemed destined to become the final lords of Italy, and they continued as an important people of the West far down into Roman history, as we shall see.

The Carthaginians were the *second* of the three rivals of the Italic tribes. During their great mercantile prosperity after 1000 B.C., the Phœnicians carried their commerce far into the western Mediterranean, as we have already stated (§ 397). On the African coast opposite Sicily they established

778. Seco
the Carth
ginians

a flourishing commercial city called Carthage, which was before
long the leading harbor in the western Mediterranean (Fig. 239).
The Carthaginians soon held the northern coast of Africa westward to the Atlantic. Besides gaining southern Spain, they
were also absorbing the islands of the western Mediterranean,
especially Sicily.

**779.** Third,
the Greeks

The Carthaginians were endeavoring to make the western
Mediterranean their own, when the Italic peoples saw their
*third* rivals invading the West. They were the Greeks. We
have already followed the expansion of the Greeks as they
founded their city-states along the coast of southern Italy and
in Sicily in the eighth century B.C. (§§ 437–443). The strife
among these city-states made the Greeks of the West as unable
to unite into a Greek nation as Greece itself had been. The
strongest of all the western Greek cities was Syracuse, which
took the lead more than once. We recall how the Athenians
tried to conquer the West by capturing Syracuse (§ 602).

**780.** The
Greeks re-
pulse the
Carthaginians
from Sicily
and the
Etruscans
from Great
Greece

Although we have spoken of these three peoples — Etruscans, Carthaginians, and Greeks — as the three rivals of the
Italic tribes in the West, these Italic tribes were at first so
insignificant that the rivalry was long a three-cornered one, with
the Greeks in Sicily and southern Italy maintaining themselves
on two fronts against both Carthaginians and Etruscans. We
remember how in the famous year of Salamis the Greeks of
Syracuse won a great battle against the Carthaginians (§ 514)
and saved Sicily from being conquered by them (480 B.C.).
Only a few years later it was also Syracuse which met the bold
Etruscan sea robbers as their fleets appeared in the South, and
totally defeated them (Fig. 226). The western Greeks therefore
played an important part in the political situation, first by long
preventing the Carthaginians from seizing Sicily and southern
Italy, and second by breaking the sea power of the Etruscans.

**781.** Empire
of Dionysius
of Syracuse
and its fall

By 400 B.C. Dionysius, the Greek tyrant of Syracuse, was
building up a powerful empire in Sicily and southern Italy,
which looked like a permanent union of the western Greeks

as a nation. But the successors of Dionysius were not as efficient as he. They called in the great philosopher Plato, and
they attempted to carry out some of his idealistic theories of
government (§ 673), but the result was a disastrous collapse of
the young Syracusan Empire (357–354 B.C.). Plato himself
expressed the fear that the Greek
language was then about to die
out in Sicily, and that the Carthaginians or one of the rising
Indo-European tribes of Italy
would triumph in Sicily.

Although the western Greeks,
like the homeland, failed to unite
in a strong and permanent state,
the influence of their civilization
in the West was all the more
important. Their civilization was
essentially the same as that which
we have already studied (Chapters
XI–XXI). At the very time when
Syracuse was victoriously beating back the Carthaginians and
Etruscans on two fronts, some of
the noblest monuments of Greek
architecture were rising in these
Western cities (Fig. 219, and Plate
VII, p. 558). In such wonderful
buildings as these, great architec-
ture made its first appearance in the western Mediterranean.
The same was true of many other contributions of Greek culture
with which we are now familiar. Thus fifteen hundred years
after the Italic tribes had first settled in Italy, there grew up
on the south of them a wonderful world of civilization, which
went on growing and developing to reach its highest in that
Hellenistic culture which brought forth an Archimedes at

**782.** Western
Greek cities
bring civili-
zation into
the western
Mediterra-
nean world

FIG. 226. ETRUSCAN HELMET
CAPTURED BY THE GREEKS
OF SYRACUSE IN THEIR VIC-
TORY OVER THE ETRUSCANS
AT CUMÆ IN 474 B.C.

Hiero, the Greek tyrant of Syracuse, dedicated this helmet at
Olympia as part of the spoil
which he took from the Etruscans in his great naval victory
of Cumæ (§ 780). It is now in
the British Museum, and it still
bears the dedicatory inscription
placed upon it by the Syracusan
tyrant nearly twenty-four hundred years ago

Syracuse (§ 742). Let us now turn back to follow the career of the barbarous Italic tribes of central Italy under the leadership of Rome, and watch them slowly gaining organization and power, and finally civilization, as they are dominated first by the Etruscan and then by the Greek culture which we have been recalling.

## SECTION 73. EARLIEST ROME

**783. The tribes of Latium, and Alba Longa the leading Latin town**

On the south or east bank of the Tiber, which flows into the sea in the middle of the west coast of Italy (see map, p. 484), there was a group of Italic tribes known as the Latins. In the

FIG. 227. A GLIMPSE ACROSS THE PLAIN OF LATIUM AND THE APPIAN WAY TO THE DISTANT ALBAN MOUNTAINS

In the foreground is a short stretch of the Appian Way, the earliest fine road built by the Romans. It extended from Rome southward to Capua, and was finally extended to Brundisium. The large round tower is a famous tomb, built for a noble Roman lady named Cecilia Metella

days when the Etruscan sea-raiders first landed on the shores north of the Tiber, these Latin tribes had occupied a plain (Fig. 227) less than thirty by forty miles,[1] that is, smaller than many an American county. They called it "Latium," whence

---

[1] Latium probably contained something over seven hundred square miles.

their own name, " Latins." Like their Italic neighbors they
lived, scattered in small communities, cultivating grain and pasturing flocks on the upland. Their land was not very fertile,
and the battle for existence developed hardy and tenacious children of the soil. Once a year they went up to the Alban Mount
(Fig. 227), where all the Latin tribes united in a feast of their

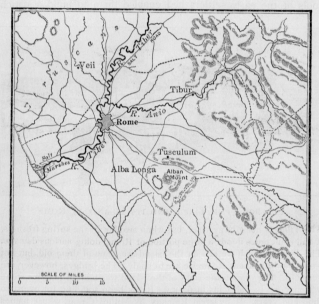

EARLY LATIUM

chief god, Jupiter, whose rude mud-brick sanctuary was on the
mount. Close by was a small town called Alba Longa, whose
leadership the Latin tribes followed when they were obliged, as
they very often were, to unite and repel the attacks of their
hostile neighbors on all sides. They watched very anxiously
the growth of the flourishing Etruscan towns on the other side
of the Tiber, and they did what they could to keep the Etruscans from crossing to the Latin side.

**784. The emergence of early Rome**

When these Latin peasants needed weapons or tools, they were obliged to carry up a little grain or an ox to a trading post on the south side of the Tiber, just above the coast marshes, which extended some ten or twelve miles inland from the river's mouth. Shallow water at this point, and an island (Fig. 228), made an easy crossing of the river, and the metal tools of the early settlers had enabled them to build a stanch

FIG. 228. THE TIBER AND ITS ISLAND AT ROME

The Tiber is not a large river, but when swollen by the spring freshets, it still sometimes floods a large portion of Rome, doing serious damage. The houses which we see on the island are some of them old, but not as old as the ancient Rome we are to study. The bridges, however, are very old. The one on the right of the island was built of massive stone masonry by L. Fabricius in 62 B.C. It has been standing for over two thousand years. Many great Romans, like Julius Cæsar, whose names are familiar to us, must have crossed this bridge often

bridge here. Overlooking the bridge was a bold hill called the Palatine, and a square stronghold crowning the hill guarded the river crossing. Several neighboring hills bore straggling villages, but the stronghold on the Palatine was their leader. Here, stopped by the shoals and the bridge, moored now and then an Etruscan ship which had sailed up the Tiber, the only navigable river in Italy. On the low marshy ground, encircled by the hills, was an open-air market, beside an old cemetery belonging to the villages (Fig. 229). Here in the Forum, as they called this valley market by the cemetery, our Latin peasant could meet the Etruscan traders and exchange his grain or his ox for the metal tools or weapons which he needed. These were now of iron, but he remembered the stories of his fathers, telling how all their tools and weapons were formerly of bronze. The population of the villages was very mixed — some Latin families who had taken to trading or owned fields near by, Etruscan traders and land-owners, and a few oversea strangers of various nationalities, with many outcasts and refugees from outlying communities. Such must have been the condition of the group of villages called Rome probably as early as 1000 B.C. (but cf. Fig. 229).

The fears of the Latin tribes regarding an invasion of the Etruscans were finally realized.

FIG. 229. GRAVE OF PREHISTORIC VIL-LAGER FOUND UNDER THE FORUM AT ROME

Excavations under the Forum (plan, p. 500) have disclosed a cemetery of graves like this. The skeleton which we see here is that of one of the prehistoric men who lived in the vil-lages on the summits of the neighboring hills, later united to form Rome (§ 785). The tools, weapons, and pottery found in these graves show that these people lived not many generations after 1000 B.C., in the days when bronze was giving way to iron (§ 784)

785. Rome seized by Etruscans (about 750 B.C.)

The Etruscan towns after 800 B.C. stretched far across north-ern Italy — a great group of allied city-kingdoms, each with its fortified city. Perhaps as early as 750 B.C. one of their princes crossed the Tiber, drove out the last of the line of Latin chieftains, and took possession of the stronghold on the Palatine. From this place as his castle and palace he gained control of the villages on the hills above the Tiber, which then gradually merged into the city of Rome. These Etruscan kings soon extended their power over the Latin tribes of the Plain of

FIG. 230. A STREET OF ETRUSCAN TOMBS AT ANCIENT CÆRE
NOT FAR NORTH OF ROME

The tomb-chamber, or sometimes several such chambers within, contained a sarcophagus in which the body was laid. It was often accompanied with jewelry of gold and silver, furniture, implements, and weapons (Fig. 231), besides beautiful vases (Fig. 164). The walls of the chambers were often painted with decorative scenes from the life of the Etruscans and from scenes of Greek mythology, learned by the Etruscans from their intercourse with the Greeks. The Etruscans buried here lived in a strong walled town of which the ruins lie near by. Their manufactures, especially in bronze, flourished, and they carried on profitable commerce through their harbor town, only a few miles below their city. In one of these tombs the name of the deceased is inscribed on the wall as "Tarkhnas," which can be nothing else than Tarquinius, the name preserved in Roman tradition as that of the latest kings of Rome

Latium, and the town of Alba Longa by the Alban Mount, which once led the Latins, disappeared. Thus Rome became a city-kingdom under an Etruscan king, like the other Etruscan cities which stretched from Capua far north to the harbor of Genoa. And such it remained for two centuries and a half. Although Rome was ruled by a line of Etruscan kings, it must be borne in mind that the population of Latium which the Etruscan kings governed contin- ued to be Latin and to speak the Latin tongue.[1]

Etruscan ships had known Greek

786. The Etruscans learn Greek writing

FIG. 231. ETRUSCAN CHARIOT OF BRONZE

This magnificent work is the finest surviving product of Etruscan skill in bronze (§ 787). It was found in an Etruscan tomb (Fig. 230) and is now in the possession of the Metropolitan Museum of New York. It probably dates from the sixth century B.C.

[1] The above pres- entation makes the line of early kings at Rome (about 750 to about 500 B.C.) exclu- sively Etruscan. The traditional founding of Rome not long before 750 B.C. would then correspond to its cap- ture and establishment as a strong kingdom by the Etruscans. We possess no written doc- uments of Rome for this early period. We are obliged to make our conclusions largely on the basis of a study of archæological re- mains surviving in Rome and Latium and vicinity. Had these remains, together with the important elements of Etruscan civilization adopted by the Romans, formed our only evidence, no one would ever have suggested any other theory than that the kings of Rome were Etrus- can. The later Romans themselves, however, with evident disinclination to be- lieve that their early kings had been outsiders, cherished a tradition that their kings were native Romans. This tradition, with many picturesque and pleasing incidents (headpiece, p. 484), has found a place in literature, and is still widely believed. It is possible that there may be some slight measure of truth in this tradition, but it is not very probable in view of all the known evidence.

waters since Mycenæan days, and the Etruscans were constantly trafficking in the Greek harbors. There they learned to write their language with Greek letters. Many tombs (Fig. 230) containing such inscriptions still survive in Italy. Although we know the letters and can pronounce the Etruscan words,

FIG. 232. A VIEW OF THE TIBER WITH THE AVENTINE HILL
AND THE ETRUSCAN DRAIN

As we look *down* the Tiber in this view, we stand not far from our former position looking *up* the river (Fig. 228) (cf. map, p. 500). The Aventine Hill is at the left. Along its foot, at the water's edge, extend the houses of modern Rome. At this end of this row of houses we see the arched opening of the ancient Etruscan sewer, or drain (§ 788), which served to drain the Forum under which it passed. The Romans called it the *Cloaca Maxima* (chief sewer). Although much altered in later times, its most ancient portions are probably the oldest surviving masonry at Rome

scholars are still unable to understand them; nor can the race of the Etruscans as yet be determined from them.

**787. Etruscans learn Greek industries, art, and architecture**

This intercourse with Greece brought in beautiful Greek pottery (Fig. 164), and the Etruscans quickly learned to make similar decorative paintings. Many such paintings still cover the walls of Etruscan tombs and show us how the Etruscans looked, the clothing they wore, and the weapons they carried.

Having learned to mine copper, they early produced such fine work in bronze (Fig. 231) that it even excelled the metal work of the Greeks for a time, and they developed a flourishing commerce in this industry. They likewise borrowed a great deal from Grecian architecture, but unlike the Greeks they made plentiful use of the arch, with which they had probably become acquainted in Asia Minor (Fig. 224). It was the Etruscans who introduced the arch into Italy. Their architecture was the earliest known in the city of Rome, and always had a great influence upon the architecture of the Romans.

The Etruscan kings introduced great improvements into Rome. The Forum, the low market valley, was often flooded in the rainy season, and they built a heavy masonry drain arched at the top, which carried off the water to the river and made the city much more healthful. This ancient sewer drain still survives (Fig. 232). On the hill called the Capitol, between the Forum and the Tiber, they built a temple to Jupiter, the State god, which survived for centuries. But the cruelty and tyranny of the Etruscan rulers finally caused a revolt, led probably by the Etruscan nobles themselves, and the kings of Rome were driven out. The fugitive king and his followers fled northward to their kinsmen, to Cære, where Etruscan tombs which probably belonged to them still survive (Fig. 230). Thus about 500 B.C. the career of Rome under kings came to an end; but the two and a half centuries of Etruscan rule left their mark on Rome, always afterward discernible in architecture, religion, tribal organization, and some other things.

788. Rule of the Etruscan kings of Rome and their expulsion (about 500 B.C.)

## Section 74. The Early Republic: its Progress and Government

During this Etruscan period, Greek influences were equally important in Latium. Down at the dock below the Tiber bridge, ships from the Greek cities of the south were becoming more and more common. Long before the Etruscan kings were

789. Greek alphabet adopted in Rome

driven out, the Roman trader had gradually learned to pick out the names of familiar objects of trade in the bills handed him by the Greek merchants. Erelong the Roman traders too were scribbling memoranda of their own with the same Greek

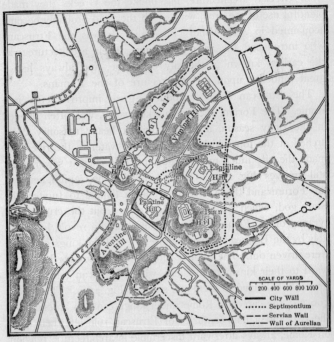

MAP OF EARLY ROME SHOWING THE SUCCESSIVE STAGES OF ITS GROWTH

letters, which thus became likewise the Roman alphabet, slightly changed to suit the Latin language. Thus the oriental alphabet was carried one step further in the long westward journey which finally made it the alphabet with which this book is printed. In the hands of the Carthaginians and Romans in the west, and the Arameans (§ 205) on the east, the

Phœnician alphabet and its descendent alphabets now stretched from India to the Atlantic (Fig. 160).

There had been no *Roman* ships at the Tiber docks at first, but as time passed a Roman mechanic here and there learned to build a ship like those of the Greeks alongside it. As Roman traffic thus grew, it was found very inconvenient to pay bills

**790.** Greek influence in shipbuilding, business, money, and measures in Rome

A            B

FIG. 233. SPECIMENS OF EARLY ROMAN COPPER MONEY

In the time of Alexander the Great (second half of the fourth century B.C.), the Romans found it too inconvenient to continue paying their debts in goods, especially in cattle (§ 784). They therefore cast copper in blocks, each block with the figure of an ox upon it (see *A*, above), to indicate its value. The Roman word for cattle (*pecus*) was the origin of their frequent word for property (*pecunia*) and has descended to us in our common word " pecuniary." These blocks were unwieldy, and influenced by the Greeks, the Romans then cast large disks of copper (*B*, above), which also were very ponderous, each weighing nearly a pound Troy. Hence this coin, called an *as*, was divided into twelve smaller coins, each called an ounce (Roman *uncia*), and there were copper coins of two, three, four, and six *uncias*. When two generations later (268 B.C.) the Romans began to coin silver (see Fig. 235), copper was no longer used for large payments and the *as* was reduced in size to one sixth its former weight

with grain and oxen while the Greek merchant at the dock paid his bills with copper and silver coins. For a long time instead of the oxen themselves, rough bars of copper were used, each bearing the figure of an ox (Fig. 233, *A*). It was not until over a hundred and fifty years after the Etruscan kings had been driven out that the Romans issued actual copper coins (Fig. 233, *B*). Later, as contact with the Greek cities increased, the Romans also began to issue silver coins, using as a basis the Attic drachma (§ 832). In the same way, too, the Romans gradually adopted the oriental measures of length and of bulk with which the Greeks measured out to them the things they bought.

**791. Traces of Greek speech in Rome and Latium**

Greek speech too began to leave its traces in the Latin speech of Rome. The Latin townsmen and peasants learned the Greek words for the clothing offered to them for sale, or for household utensils and pottery and other things brought in by the Greeks. So the Phœnician garment which the Greek merchants called *kitón* (§ 394), the Latin peasants pronounced *ktŭn* (ktoón), and in course of time they gave it a Latin ending *ic* and dropped the *k*, so that it became our familiar word " tunic."

**792. Greek influences — religion**

But the Greeks also brought in things which could not be weighed and measured like produce, from a realm of which the Roman was beginning to catch fleeting glimpses. For the peasant heard of strange gods of the Greeks, and he was told that they were the counterparts or the originals of his own gods. For him there was a god over each realm in nature and each field of human life : Jupiter was the great Sky-god and king of all the gods ; Mars, the patron of all warriors ; Venus, the queen of love ; Juno, an ancient Sky-goddess, was protectress of women, of birth and marriage, while Vesta, too, watched over the household life, with its hearth fire surviving from the nomad days of the fathers on the Asiatic steppe two thousand years before (§ 249) ; Ceres was the goddess who maintained the fruitfulness of the earth, and especially the grainfields (cf. English " cereal ") ; and Mercury was the messenger of the gods who protected intercourse and *merc*handising, as his name shows. The streets were full of Greek stories regarding the heroic adventures of these divinities when they were on earth. The Roman learned that Venus was the Greek Aphrodite, Mercury was Hermes, Ceres was Demeter, and so on.

**793. Oracles**

This process was aided by the influence of Greek oracles. The oracles delivered by the Greek Sibyl, the prophetess of

Apollo of Delphi (Fig. 172), were deeply reverenced in Italy. Gathered in the Sibylline Books, they were regarded by the Romans as mysterious revelations of the future. Another method of reading the future was brought in by the Etruscans, who were able to discover in the liver (Fig. 234) of a sheep killed for sacrifice signs which they believed revealed the future. This art had been received by the Etruscans from the

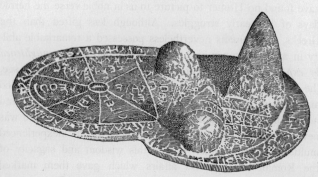

FIG. 234. BRONZE MODEL OF A LIVER USED BY THE ETRUSCANS FOR DIVINATION, AFTER THE OLD BABYLONIAN MANNER

The surface of the model is divided by lines into sections, forming a kind of guiding diagram like the model livers of baked clay employed by the Babylonians (Fig. 94). The Etruscans must have received the art in the East, presumably in Asia Minor, before they migrated to Italy

Babylonians (Fig. 94) by way of Asia Minor, whence the Etruscans brought it to Italy.

An art like this appealed to the rather coldly calculating mind of the Roman. As he looked toward his gods he felt no doubts or problems, like those which troubled the spirit of Euripides (§ 581). He lacked the warm and vivid imagination of the Greeks, which had created the beautiful Greek mythology. He was inclined to regard acts of worship as the mere fulfillment of a contract by which the gods must bestow favors if the worshiper was faithful in the performance of his duties. In religion, therefore, the Roman saw only a list of mechanical

**794.** Mechanical character of Roman religion and the Roman mind

duties, such as the presentation of offerings, the sacrifice of animals, and the like, and such duties were easily fulfilled. In accordance with this rather legal conception of religion, he was fitted for great achievements in political and legal organization, but not for new and original developments in religion, art, literature, or discoveries in science.

**795.** Practical sagacity of the Romans

Hence it is that in sketching the beginnings of Rome we have found no Homer to picture to us in noble verse the heroic days of her early struggles. Although less gifted than the Greeks, the Romans nevertheless possessed a remarkable ability in applying sober and practical common sense, *enlightened by experience*, to every problem they met. As we shall see, the Romans so contrived their government that it was led and guided by the combined experience of the ripest and most skilled leaders among them. Thus the Roman State was never exposed to the momentary whims of an inexperienced multitude as in Athens. It was this wisdom and sagacity of the Romans in practical affairs which gave them marked superiority over the Greeks in such matters. Let us now see how Roman political wisdom developed the invincible Roman State.

**796.** Elective consuls replace the kings; the Roman Republic is established

When the Etruscan kings were driven out of Rome, about 500 B.C., the nobles, called *patricians*, who had been chiefly instrumental in expelling them, were in control of the government. But none of their number was able to make himself king. Perhaps by compromise with the people, the patricians agreed that two of their number should be *elected* as heads of the State. These two magistrates, called *consuls*, were both to have the same powers, were to serve for a year only and then give way to two others. To choose them, annual elections were held in an assembly of the weapon-bearing men, largely under the control of the patricians. Nevertheless, we must call this new state a republic, of which the consuls were the presidents; for the people had a voice in electing them. But as only patricians could serve as consuls, their government was very oppressive. The people, called the plebs (compare our " plebeian "), especially among the Latin tribes, refused to submit to such oppression.

**797.** The tribunes defenders of the people

The patricians were unable to get on without the help of the peasants as soldiers in their frequent wars. They therefore agreed to give the people a larger share in the government, by allowing them in their own assembly to elect a group of new officials, called *tribunes*. The tribunes had the right to veto the action of any officer of the government — even that of the consuls themselves. When any citizen was treated unjustly by a consul he had only to appeal to the tribunes, and they could rescind the consul's unjust action and even save a citizen from sentence of death. The tribunes therefore gained great influence, because they could stop the enforcement of any law they thought unjust. Later, as government business increased, their number was also increased.

**798.** Inability of the consuls to attend to all the public business

In the beginning it would seem that almost all the business of government was in the hands of the consuls. They were the commanding generals of the army in war, they had charge of the public funds in the treasury, and they were the judges in all cases at law. It was difficult to combine all these duties. The consuls were often obliged to be absent from Rome for long periods while leading the army, and at such times they were of course unable to give any attention to cases at law, and two citizens having a lawsuit might be obliged to wait until the war was over. Much other ordinary business, like that of the treasury, demanded more time than the consuls could possibly give it. They found it difficult to carry on the volume of business which the government required.

**799.** Growing body of government officials

This situation made it necessary to create new officers for various kinds of business. To take care of the government funds, treasury officials called *quæstors* were appointed. Two public officers called *censors* were required to keep lists of the people, to assess the amount of taxes each citizen owed, to determine voting rights, and to look after the daily conduct of the people and see that nothing improper was permitted. Our own use of the word "censor" is derived from these Roman officials. For the decision of legal cases a judge called a *prætor* was appointed to assist the consul, and the number of such judges slowly increased. In times of great national danger it was customary to appoint some revered and trustworthy leader as the supreme ruler of the State. He was called the Dictator, and he could hold his power but a brief period.

**800. Public questions and the controlling power of the patricians**

But a government is called upon to do some other things of great importance besides attending to administrative, financial, and legal business. Important public questions arise which are not mere items of routine business. Examples of such questions are declaring war, restoring peace, and making new laws of all sorts. The consuls had great power and influence in all such matters, but they were much influenced by a council of patricians called the Senate (from Latin *senex*, meaning "old man"), which had existed even as far back as the Etruscan kings, who used to call upon the Senate for advice. Now the patricians enjoyed the exclusive right to serve as consuls, to sit in the Senate, and to hold almost all of the offices created to carry on the business of government (§ 799). The power which the patricians held, therefore, quite unfairly exceeded that of the plebeians.

**801. The struggle of the plebs and patricians**

The tribunes, as we have seen (§ 797), could protect the people from some injustices, and save their lives if they were illegally condemned to death. But they could not secure to the citizen all his rights. The tribunes could not recover for the cattle of the people the vanished grass in the public pastures, when they had been nipped clean by the great herds of the patricians. The tribunes could not secure for a citizen the right to be elected as consul, or to become a senator, or to marry a patrician's daughter. The struggle which had resulted in the appointment of the tribunes, therefore, went on — a struggle of the common people to win their rights from the wealthy and powerful. It was a struggle like that which we have followed in Athens and the other Greek states, but at Rome it reached a much wiser and more successful settlement. The citizens of Rome manfully stood forth for their rights, and without fighting, civil war, or bloodshed they secured them to a large extent in the course of the first two centuries after the founding of the Republic.

They insisted upon a record of the existing laws in writing, in order that they might know by what laws they were being judged. About fifty years after the establishment of the Republic, the earliest Roman laws were reduced to writing and engraved upon twelve tablets of bronze (450 B.C.). But at the same time the people demanded the right to share in the making of *new* laws, and to possess an assembly of the people, which might pass new laws.

802. The old laws reduced to writing and the question of new laws

Far back in the days of the kings the people had enjoyed the right to a limited share in the government. To express their opinion they gathered in an assembly called the *Comitia*. It was made up of groups of families or brotherhoods (like the Greek brotherhoods, § 385), each called a *curia*. Hence this assembly was called the *Comitia curiata*. Each such brotherhood assembled and voted by itself, and its decision then counted as one vote. A majority of the brotherhoods decided a question.

803. The earliest Roman assembly by brotherhoods (*Comitia curiata*)

In the early days of the Republic, when the frequent wars kept the people much together in camp, arrayed in their fighting hundreds, or " centuries," it easily became customary to call them together by centuries. Thus a new assembly by centuries arose, called for this reason the *Comitia centuriata*. Owing to the expense of arms and equipment, the men of wealth and influence in the centuries far outnumbered the poorer classes. The assembly by centuries was therefore controlled by the wealthy and noble classes ; they were soon electing the consuls, and erelong they had deprived the old assembly by brotherhoods of all its power.

804. The assembly by centuries (*Comitia centuriata*)

At the same time another assembly of the people arose, intended to give them an opportunity to transact their own

**805.** The tribal assembly (*Comitia tributa*)

plebeian public business concerning solely the common people. This third assembly came together by tribes, and it was therefore called the *Comitia tributa*, or tribal assembly. In this body every man's vote was as good as another's, and as it was presided over by the tribunes, elected to protect the people, the decisions of this assembly really expressed the will of the people.

**806.** Lawmaking power of the assemblies and resulting laws making for equality of plebs with patricians

Having shaken off the legal power of the Senate to control their action, these two assemblies, the centuriate and the tribal, became the lawmaking bodies of the Roman State. Eventually the people were also given voting rights in the centuriate assembly equal to those of the patricians and the wealthy. As a result the people were able to pass laws by which they, especially the last two assemblies, gained the right to make laws, and in this way the people gradually secured a fairer share of the public lands and further social rights. Finally, and most important of all, these new laws increased the rights of the people to hold office. In the end Roman citizens elected their plebeian neighbors as censors and quæstors, as judges and at last even as consuls, and they saw men of the people sitting in the Senate.

**807.** The new nobility of former magistrates

This progress of the people in power brought with it important new developments affecting both society and government. Roman citizens had a deep respect for government and for its officials. The Roman consul appeared in public attended by twelve men called *lictors*, bearing the symbols of State authority. Each man carried a bundle of rods, suggesting the consul's power to scourge the condemned; and from the midst of the rods rose an ax, symbolizing the consul's legal right to inflict the death penalty. The other officials of high rank were likewise attended by a smaller group of lictors. The consuls and all the higher officials wore white robes edged with purple, a costume which only these men had the right to wear. When a magistrate went out of office he might assume his official garment from time to time on feast days. There soon grew up a group of once plebeian families, thus distinguished by the public service of its members, to whom the Roman citizens looked up with great respect. When the voters were called upon to select their candidates, they preferred members of these eminent families, especially for the consulship. A new nobility was thus formed, made up of such illustrious families and the old patricians.

This situation directly affected the Senate, the members of which had formerly been appointed from among the patricians by the consuls. A new law, however, authorized the *censors* to make out the lists of senators, giving the preference to those who had been magistrates. Thus the new nobility of ex-magistrates, formerly plebeians, entered the Senate, bringing in fresh blood from the ranks of the people.

808. The new nobility gains control of the Senate

As a result of these changes the Senate was made up of the three hundred men of Rome who had gained the most experience in government and in public affairs. When the herald's trumpet echoed from the Forum, and the senators, responding to the call, crowded into the modest assembly hall beside the Forum and took their seats, the consul called them to order. He was president of the Senate, and he and his colleague, the other consul, were the heads of the State, with more power than any senator possessed. From his chair on the platform the consul looked down into the strong faces of wise and sagacious men, many of whom had already held his high office and knew far more about its duties than he did. Moreover, while he was in office for only a year, the men confronting him held their seats in the Senate for life, and most of them had been conducting public business there for years. The result was that their combined influence, operating steadily for many years, was too strong for the consul. Instead of telling the senators of his own plans and of the laws he desired, he found himself listening to the proposals of the Senate and carrying out the will of the senators. As a result the consul became a kind of senatorial minister, carrying on the government according to instructions from the Senate.

809. The Senate gains the leadership over the consul

**810. The Senate gains control of lawmaking**

In the matter of lawmaking a similar growth of the Senate's influence took place. Although the popular assemblies (§§ 803–805) had the right to make laws, it was not in their power to *propose* a new law. They could vote upon it only after it had been proposed by a *magistrate*, especially by one of the tribunes, who were the presiding officers of the tribal assembly. The influence of the Senate on the magistrates was such that the magistrates discussed with the senators every law to be brought before the assemblies for adoption. The tribunes could stop the operation of any law, and hence the Senate had become accustomed to consult with them before a law was passed. The result was that the tribunes were given membership and seats in the Senate, and so added to the power and influence of that already powerful body.

**811. The Roman Senate the supreme leader of the State**

By far the larger part of the Roman citizens lived too far away to come up to the city and vote. The small minority living in Rome, who could be present and vote at the meetings of the assemblies, were familiar with the faces of the senators and they well knew the wisdom, skill, and experience of these old statesmen. They also knew that there was a strong feeling of patriotism among the senators, and standing at the open doors of the Senate hall they had heard the voice of many a gray-haired ex-consul whom they revered, as it rang through the Forum, in eloquent support of some patriotic measure or in earnest summons to national defense. Feeling too their own ignorance of public affairs, the Roman citizens were not unwilling that important public questions should be settled by the Senate. Thus the Roman Senate became a large committee of experienced statesmen, guiding and controlling the Roman State. They formed the greatest council of rulers which ever grew up in the ancient world, or perhaps in any age. They were a body of aristocrats, and their control of Rome made it an aristocratic state, in spite of its republican form. We are now to watch the steady development and progress of Roman power (see map, p. 516) under the wise and stable leadership of the Senate. We should bear in mind, however, that the Senate's power was a slow growth, continuing during the wars and conquests which we are now to follow.

## Section 75. The Expansion of the Roman Republic and the Conquest of Italy

It was a tiny nation which began its uncertain career after the expulsion of the Etruscan kings. The territory of the Roman Republic was the mere city with the adjacent fields for a very few miles around. On the other side of the Tiber lived the dreaded Etruscans, and on the Roman side of the river, all around the little republic, lay the lands of the Latin tribes (§ 783), who had combined in what was called the Latin League (see map, p. 516). The league was independent and did not acknowledge itself subject to Rome. But in their own struggle with their enemies, the Latin tribes found the leadership of the city indispensable. The Latin League therefore made a perpetual treaty with Rome — a treaty uniting the league and the city in a combination for mutual defense under the leadership of Rome. But this arrangement produced only a loose union, not yet forming a unified nation. Nevertheless, the Roman Senate gave to the citizens of Latium privileges in Rome about equal to those of Roman citizens, and the Latins were therefore ready to fight for the defense of the city whose leadership they followed.

812. The Latin League and the treaty with Rome

For two generations the new republic struggled for the preservation of its mere existence. This struggle against threatening enemies on all its frontiers, especially the Etruscans, was the motive power which stirred the little nation to constant effort, to vigorous life, and to steady growth. Fortunately for the Romans, within a generation after the foundation of the Republic the fleet of Syracuse utterly destroyed the Etruscan fleet (474 B.C.) (Fig. 226). Later the Etruscans

813. Early struggles of the Republic: against Etruscans and Italic neighbors

were attacked in the rear by the Gauls (§ 722 and Fig. 215), who were at this time pouring over the Alpine passes into the valley of the Po and laying waste the Etruscan cities of the North. This weakening of the Etruscans at the hands of their enemies on both north and south probably saved Rome from destruction. It enabled the Romans to maintain a ten years' siege of Veii, a strong southern fortress of the Etruscans only eight miles from Rome, till they captured and destroyed it (396 B.C.). At the same time the Italic tribes surrounding Latium on the south, east, and north were constantly invading and plundering the fields and pastures of the Latin tribes and threatening the city. Rome beat off these marauders, and by establishing a group of colonies along the coast south of the Tiber, formed a buffer against such invasions from the South. By 400 B.C. or a little after, the Romans had conquered and taken possession of a fringe of new territory on all sides, which protected them from their enemies.

**814. Agricultural colonization and expansion the Roman policy**

In the new territory thus gained the Romans planted colonies of citizens, or they granted citizenship or other valuable privileges to the absorbed population. Roman peasants, obligated to bear Roman arms and having a voice in the government, thus pushed out into the expanding borders of Roman territory. This policy of *agricultural* expansion steadily and consistently followed by the Senate was irresistible, for it gave to Rome an ever-increasing body of brave and hardy citizen-soldiers, cultivating their own lands, and ready at all times to take up the sword in defense of the State which shielded them. The Roman policy was thus in striking contrast with the narrow methods of the Greek republics, which jealously prevented outsiders from gaining citizenship. It was the steady expansion of Rome under this policy which in a little over two centuries after the expulsion of the Etruscan kings made the little republic on the Tiber mistress of all Italy (see map, p. 516).

The second century of Roman expansion opened with a fearful catastrophe, which very nearly accomplished the complete destruction of the nation. In the first two decades after 400 B.C. the barbarian Gauls, who had been overrunning the territory of the Etruscans (§ 813), finally reached the lower Tiber, and the Roman army which went out to meet them was completely defeated. The city, still undefended by walls, was entirely at their mercy. They entered at once (382 B.C.), plundering and burning. Only the citadel on the Capitol hill held out against the barbarians. Long afterward Roman tradition told how even the citadel was being surprised at night by a party of Gauls who clambered up the heights, when the sacred geese, kept in a temple close by, aroused the garrison by their cackling, and the storming party was repulsed. Wearied by a long siege of the citadel the Gauls at length agreed to accept a ransom of gold and to return northward, where they settled in the valley of the Po. But they still remained a serious danger to the Romans.

815. Capture of Rome by the Gauls (382 B.C.)

As Rome recovered from this disaster, it was evident that the city needed fortifications, and for the first time masonry walls (plan, p. 500) were built around it. This gave the city a strength it had not before possessed. It gained the southern territory of the Etruscans, now much weakened by the inroads of the Gauls, and it also seized new possessions in the Campanian plain. The high-handed manner in which Rome was now taking new lands seems to have alarmed even the Latin tribes, and they endeavored to break away from the control of the powerful walled city. In the two years' war which resulted the city was completely victorious, and the Roman Senate forced the defeated Latin tribes to break up the Latin League (338 B.C.). The Roman Senate then proceeded to make separate treaties with each of the Latin tribes, and did not grant them as many privileges as formerly. Rome thus gained the undisputed leadership of the Latin tribes, which was at last to bring her the leadership of Italy.

816. Subjugation of the Latin tribes and collapse of the Latin League (338 B.C.)

The year 338 B.C., in which this important event took place, is a date to be well remembered, for it also witnessed

**817.** The leadership of Greeks and Latins decided in the same year (338 B.C.)

the defeat of the Greek cities at the hands of Philip of Macedon (§ 685). In the same year, therefore, both the Greeks and the Latins saw themselves conquered and falling under the leadership of a single state — the Greeks under that of Macedonia, the Latins under that of Rome. But in Greece that leadership was in the hands of one man who might and did perish; while in Italy the leadership of the Latins was in the hands of a whole body of wise leaders, the Roman Senate. In sixty-five years they were now to gain the leadership of all Italy (see maps II, III, and IV, p. 516).

**818.** The new Samnite enemy and the opening of hostilities

Meantime another formidable foe, a group of Italic tribes called the Samnites, had been gaining possession of the mountains which form the backbone of the Italian peninsula inland from Rome. They had gained some civilization from the Greek cities of the South, and they were able to muster a large army of hardy peasants, very dangerous in war. But they lacked the steadying and continuous leadership of a governing city like Rome. Some of them drifted down into the plains of Campania (see map, p. 484), where they captured Capua, one of the southern outposts of the Etruscans. Within forty years after the expulsion of the Gauls, the Samnites were in hostile collision with Rome. By 325 B.C. a fierce war broke out, which lasted with interruptions for a generation. The Romans lost several battles, and in one case were subjected by the Samnites to the ordeal of marching "under the yoke," a humiliation which the Romans never forgot.[1]

**819.** The Samnite Wars (325–290 B.C.) and the battle of Sentinum (295 B.C.)

But the resources of the Roman Senate were not confined to fighting. They gained lands and established Roman colonies on the east of the Apennines and in the plain of Campania. From these new possessions they were able to attack the Samnites from both sides of the mountains (see map II, p. 516). The Samnites attempted a combination of Rome's enemies against her. They succeeded in shifting their army northward and

[1] The defeated troops in token of their submission marched under a lance supported horizontally on two upright lances and called a "yoke."

joining forces with both the Etruscans and the Gauls. All central and much of northern Italy was now involved in the war. In the mountains midway between the upper Tiber and the eastern shores of Italy the Roman army met and crushed the combined forces of the allies in a terrible battle at Sentinum (295 B.C.). This battle decided the future of Italy for over two thousand years. It not only gave the Romans possession of central Italy, but it made them the leading power in the whole peninsula (see map III, p. 516).

Henceforth the Etruscans were unable to maintain themselves as a leading power. One by one their cities were taken by the Romans, or they entered into alliance with Rome. The Gallic barbarians were beaten off, and the stream of Gallic invasion which was thus forced back in northern Italy by Rome flowed over eastward and southward into the Balkan Peninsula, as we have seen (§ 722). The settled Gauls, however, continued to hold the Po valley, and the northern boundary of the Roman conquests was along the Arnus River, south of the Apennines. Southward the resistance of the Samnites was easily crushed within five years after the battle at Sentinum. They and the other leading peoples of southern Italy, with the exception of the Greeks there, were forced to enter the Roman alliance. The Romans were supreme from the Arnus to the Greek cities of southern Italy (see map III, p. 516).

**820. Rome the mistress of central and northern Italy to the Arnus River after Sentinum**

The great rivals in the Western world were now the Romans, the Greeks, and the Carthaginians. As for the home cities of the Greeks, they were under the successors of Alexander, fighting among themselves for possession of the fragments of his empire (Chap. XX), while Rome was gaining the leadership of Italy. As for the western Greek colonies (§§ 440–441) four centuries of conflict among themselves had left them still a disunited group of cities fringing southern Italy and Sicily. They had long been fighting with the Italic tribes and other peoples of southern Italy, and a number of the Greek cities of the region had fallen. The survivors, alarmed at the

**821. Endeavor of the western Greeks to unite against Rome**

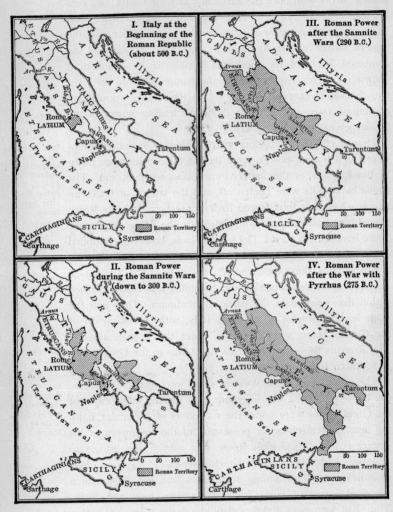

**I. Italy at the Beginning of the Roman Republic (about 500 B.C.)**

**II. Roman Power during the Samnite Wars (down to 300 B.C.)**

**III. Roman Power after the Samnite Wars (290 B.C.)**

**IV. Roman Power after the War with Pyrrhus (275 B.C.)**

EXPANSION OF ROMAN POWER IN ITALY

threatening expansion of Roman power, now made another endeavor to unite, and called in help from the outside.

The leading city of the Greeks in southern Italy was Tarentum. Unable to secure effective aid from the now declining home cities of Greece, the men of Tarentum sent an appeal to Pyrrhus, the vigorous and able king of Epirus, just across from the heel of Italy. Pyrrhus fully understood the highly developed art of war as it had grown up with Epaminondas (§ 638) and Philip of Macedon (§ 681). Besides Thessalian horsemen, the best cavalry in the world, he had secured from the Orient a formidable innovation in the form of fighting elephants. With an army of well-trained Greek infantry of the phalanx besides, and his well-known talent as a soldier, Pyrrhus was a highly dangerous foe. His purpose was to form a great nation of the western Greeks in Sicily and Italy. Such a nation would have proved a formidable rival of both Rome and Carthage.

On the arrival of Pyrrhus he completely defeated the Romans at Heraclea in 280 B.C., and in the following year they were routed again. Pyrrhus proceeded in triumph to Sicily, where he gained the whole island except the Carthaginian colony on the outermost western end (Lilybæum), which he could not capture for lack of a fleet. He seemed about to succeed in his effort to establish a powerful western Greek empire, when he met with serious difficulties. The Carthaginians, who saw a dangerous rival rising only a few hours' sail from their home harbor, sent a fleet to assist the Romans against Pyrrhus. When the ambassador of Pyrrhus arrived at Rome with proposals of peace, the Carthaginian fleet was at the mouth of the Tiber, and the Roman Senate resolutely refused to make peace while the army of Pyrrhus occupied Italian soil. At the same time the Greeks disagreed among themselves, as they always did at critical times. Pyrrhus then withdrew from Sicily, and finding himself unable to inflict a decisive defeat on the Romans, he returned to Epirus.

822. Pyrrhus of Epirus and his plan of forming an empire of the western Greeks

823. The war with Pyrrhus (280–275 B.C.); Roman defeats at Heraclea (280 B.C.) and Asculum (279 B.C.)

824. Rome
in possession
of the entire
Italian pen-
insula; result-
ing rivalry
between
Rome and
**Carthage**

One by one the helpless Greek cities now surrendered to the Roman army, and they had no choice but to accept alliance with the Romans (see map IV, p. 516). Thus ended all hope of a great Greek nation in the West. In two centuries and a quarter (500–275 B.C.) the tiny republic on the Tiber had gained the mastery of the entire Italian peninsula south of the Po valley (see map IV, p. 516). There were now but two rivals in the western Mediterranean world — Rome and Carthage. In following the inevitable struggle of these two for the mastery of the western Mediterranean world during the next two generations, we shall be watching the final conflict between the western wings of the two great racial lines, the Semitic and the Indo-European (Fig. 112). But before we take up this struggle we must learn more about the character and the civilization of the great Roman power which thus grew up in Italy. These men who won the supremacy of Italy for the little republic on the Tiber were the first generation of Romans about whom sufficient information has survived to make us well acquainted with them.

## QUESTIONS

SECTION 72. Into what divisions does the Mediterranean fall? In which did civilization arise? Why? Describe Italy. Tell about the earliest migrations into Italy and the incoming of metal. What Indo-European tribes came into Italy, and when? Did they find civilization there? What weapon had the western Mediterranean peoples devised? What three rivals of the Italic tribes came in? Tell about their coming. What did the Greeks accomplish against the Carthaginians and Etruscans? Did the western Greeks unite into a nation? What did they bring into Italy?

SECTION 73. Describe Latium. What tribes settled there? What town first led them? Where was the market of the Latins? Who traded there? Describe the place. What was it called? Who seized it in the eighth century B.C.? What line of kings arose? Describe their rule and civilization.

SECTION 74. Whence did the Romans gain their alphabet? What other Greek influences can you mention? What oriental mode of

divination did the Etruscans and the Romans practice? What can
you say of the religious ideas of the Romans? Who succeeded the
Etruscan kings as rulers of Rome? What magistrates did the people
elect for their own protection? What great council arose? Who
had the exclusive right to serve as consuls and to sit in the Senate?
Describe the assemblies of the people. Who had the power to make
laws? What new nobility arose? How did they gain control of the
Senate? How did the Senate gain the leadership of the State? What
can you say of this leadership?

SECTION 75. What was the relation between Rome and the Latin
tribes around it? What was happening to the Etruscans after
500 B.C.? Describe the colonial policy of the Roman Senate. Tell
about the coming of the Gauls. What happened to the Latin League
in 338 B.C.? What happened in Greece the same year? Who were
the Samnites? Tell the story of the Roman struggle with them.
What battle ended it? When? Were the western Greeks able to
unite against Rome? What did Tarentum do? Recount the war
with Pyrrhus. What happened to the Greeks of Italy after the retirement of Pyrrhus? How long had it taken Rome to gain the leadership of Italy?

NOTE. The tailpiece below shows us the prehistoric warriors of the western
Mediterranean in the thirteenth century B.C. Notice the heavy bronze swords
carried with point up. They are simply elongated Egyptian daggers (Fig. 132
and § 776). The scene is engraved on the walls of the temple of Abu Simbel in
Egypt (Fig. 70), built by Ramses II, in whose army these Westerners were
serving.

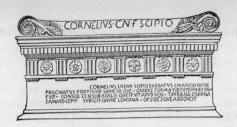

# CHAPTER XXIII

## THE SUPREMACY OF THE ROMAN REPUBLIC IN ITALY AND THE RIVALRY WITH CARTHAGE

### SECTION 76. ITALY UNDER THE EARLY ROMAN REPUBLIC

**825. The problem of making Italy a nation**

After the leadership of Italy had been gained by Rome, there were men still living who could remember the Latin war (ended 338 B.C.), when Rome had lost even the surrounding fields of little Latium. Now, sixty-five years later, the city on the Tiber was mistress of *all Italy*. The new power over a large group of cities and states, thus gained within a single lifetime, was exercised by the Roman Senate with the greatest skill and success. Had Rome *annexed* all the conquered lands, and endeavored to rule them from Rome, the population of Italy would have been dissatisfied, and constant revolts would have followed. How, then, was Italy to become a nation, controlled by Rome?

**826. Self-governing local communities made allies**

The Romans began by granting the defeated cities a kind of citizenship. It entitled them to all the protection of the Roman State in carrying on commerce and business, to all

NOTE. The above headpiece represents the beautiful stone sarcophagus of one of the early Scipios, found in the family tomb on the Appian Way (Fig. 227). It is adorned with details of Greek architecture, which clearly show that it was done by a Greek artist (§ 831). Verses in early Latin, on the side of the sarcophagus, contain praises of the departed Scipio.

the rights of every Roman citizen in the law courts, and, at the same time, to social privileges like that of intermarriage. But this citizenship did not entitle them to vote. In distant communities, however, no one felt the lack of this privilege, for in order to vote it was necessary to go to Rome. Cities and communities controlled by Rome in this way were called "allies." The protection of the powerful Roman State in carrying on business and commerce was of itself a very valuable advantage to the allies. They were therefore willing to place their troops entirely at the disposal of Rome, and also all their dealings with foreign peoples; for they still had full control of their own local internal affairs, except those of the army. In all this Rome wisely granted the different cities very different rights, and laid upon them highly varied restrictions. Thus no two cities were likely to feel the same grievances or make common cause against Roman rule of Italy.

Rome had, however, gradually annexed a good deal of territory to pay her war expenses and to supply her increasing numbers of citizens with land. Her own full citizens thus occupied about one sixth of the territory of Italy. It consisted chiefly of the region between the Apennine Mountains and the sea, from Cære on the north to Capua and Cumæ on the south (see map, p. 484). It likewise included some important areas in the Apennines and on the Adriatic coast. It was furthermore Rome's policy to sprinkle Roman colonies through the territory of the allies. All Italy was thus more or less dotted with communities of Roman citizens. By these wise measures Rome gained and kept control of Italy.

**827. Communities enjoying full Roman citizenship**

Rome thus brought into a kind of unity what we may *geographically* call Italy; but an examination of its population will readily show us how far Italy really was from being a *nation*, even though controlled by Rome. Besides the Gauls, whose territory in the Po valley had not yet been taken over by the Romans, were the conquered Etruscans, who occupied a large part of northern Italy. In the central region were the Latins

**828. Lack of national unity in Italy: diversity of language**

and the other Italic tribes. These tribes all spoke related dialects, which were, however, so different that no one tribe could understand any of the others. Finally, in the South were the Greek cities. There was therefore no common language in Italy, even among the Indo-Europeans, and this created a situation very different from that in Greece.

**829.** Lack of national unity in Italy: no common traditions

Neither did the peoples of Italy possess any common literary inheritance such as the Greeks had in the Homeric poems. Nothing in their history, like the Trojan War in that of the Greeks (§ 411), had ever given them common traditions. Roman organization had created a kind of United States of Italy, which might after a long time slowly merge into a nation. Meantime these peoples, of course, had no feeling of patriotism toward Rome. Speaking different languages, so that they did not understand one another when they met, they long remained quite distinct.

**830.** Italy to become Latin in speech, Greek in civilization

In language the future nation was to be Latin, the tongue of the ruling city; geographically it comprised Italy; politically it was Roman.[1] When we consider Rome from the point of view of *civilization*, however, we are obliged to add a fourth name. For as time went on, Italy was to become in civilization more and more Greek. The Greek cities extended as far north as the plains of Campania, where Rome had early taken Capua, in size the second city of Italy. In the days of the war with Pyrrhus and after, the Roman soldiers had beheld with wonder and admiration the beautiful Greek temples in such cities as Pæstum (Fig. 219) and Tarentum. Here for the first time they saw also fine theaters, and they must have attended Greek plays, of which they understood little or nothing. But the races and athletic games in the handsome stadium of such a Greek city required no interpretation in order to be understood by the sturdy Roman soldiers.

---

[1] Compare the similar application of three names to our own country. Politically we are the United States, geographically we are commonly called America, while our language is English.

In southern Italy the Romans had taken possession of the western fringe of the great Hellenistic world, whose wonderful civilization we have already studied (Chap. XXI). The Romans at once felt the superiority of this new world of cultivated life, which they had entered in southern Italy. When a highborn Roman family like that of the Scipios wished to have carved a beautiful sarcophagus (stone coffin) for their father, they employed a Greek sculptor from the South (headpiece, p. 520). At the same time the temples of Rome began to be laid out on an *oblong* ground plan, like those of the Greeks, and no longer on a *square* ground plan like those of the Etruscans. As Roman power expands we shall see this conquest of the Romans by Greek civilization making greater and greater progress.

831. Early evidences of Greek art and architecture in Rome

FIG. 235. A ROMAN DENARIUS OF SILVER

After the capture of the Greek cities of southern Italy, the Romans began the coinage of silver (268 B.C.) (see § 832). The large and inconvenient *as* (Fig. 233, *B*) was no longer necessary for large payments, and it was thereafter reduced in size to one sixth. Silver was then used for all large transactions. On the value of this coin see § 832

It was as yet chiefly in commerce and in business that Greek influences were evident. Greek merchants from the Southern cities now enjoyed Roman protection when they traded in Rome. Greek silver money appeared in greater quantities after the capture of the Greek cities. Copper coins were no longer sufficient for Roman business, and not long after the fall of Tarentum, in 268 B.C. (§ 824), Rome issued her first silver coin (Fig. 235). Just as Athens had once done (§ 460), so Rome now began to feel the influence of money, and a moneyed class, largely merchants, arose. They were not manufacturers, as at Athens, and Rome never became a great industrial center.

832. Greek influence on commerce and coinage of silver at Rome; rise of moneyed class

## Section 77. Rome and Carthage as Commercial Rivals

**833. Commercial expansion of Rome seaward**

The old policy of *agricultural* expansion (§ 814) had slowly brought Rome the leadership *within* Italy. A new policy of *commercial* expansion was to bring her into conflict with the Mediterranean world *outside of* Italy. The farmers had looked no farther than the shores of Italy, but the transactions of the Roman merchants reached out beyond those shores. Roman ships issuing from the Tiber entered a triangular inclosure of the Mediterranean, called the Etruscan Sea. The sides of the triangle were formed by Corsica and Sardinia on the west and Italy on the east, while on the south the bottom of the triangle was formed by Sicily and the Carthaginian coast of Africa. A glance at the map (I, p. 552) shows us how Rome and Carthage faced each other across this triangular sea, where both were now carrying on extensive business.

**834. Early mercantile successes of the Semites, and the foundation of Carthage**

It was indeed a dangerous rival which now confronted Rome across the Etruscan Sea. In the veins of the Carthaginians flowed the blood of those hardy desert mariners of Arabia, the Semitic caravaneers (§ 137) who had made the market places of Babylon the center of ancient Eastern trade two thousand years before Rome ever owned a ship. The fleets of their Phœnician ancestors had coursed the Mediterranean in the days when the Stone Age barbarians of Italy were eagerly looking for the merchant of the East and his metal implements (§ 328). While Rome was an obscure trading village on the Tiber, and before the Greeks ever entered these waters, the Phœnician merchants, the earliest explorers of the western Mediterranean, had perceived the advantageous position of the commanding projection where the African coast thrusts out toward Sicily. Here, on the northern edge of the region now called Tunis, they had planted the city which had become the commercial queen of the western Mediterranean and the most powerful rival of Rome (map I, p. 552).

This advantageous situation gave Carthage unrivaled commercial opportunities. Gradually, as her trade carried her in both directions, she had gained the coast on both sides — eastward to the frontiers of the Greek city of Cyrene, and westward to the Atlantic. Her merchants absorbed southern Spain, with its profitable silver mines, and they gained control of the import of British tin by way of the Strait of Gibraltar. Outside of this strait their settlements extended northward along the coast of Spain and southward along the Atlantic coast of Africa to the edge of the Sahara. In this direction Hanno, one of their fearless captains, explored the coast of Africa as far as Guinea (§ 747, and map I, p. 552).

**835. Carthaginian expansion in Africa and Spain**

It was only the incoming of the Greeks (§§ 440–441) which had prevented the Carthaginians from taking possession of the Mediterranean islands upon which their splendid harbor looked out. They usually held a large part of Sicily, the west end of which was almost visible from the housetops of Carthage. They planted their colonies in the islands of Sardinia and Corsica, and they had ports in the Balearic Islands, between Sardinia and Spain. They closed the Strait of Gibraltar and the ports of the islands *to ships from all other cities*. Foreign ships intruding in these waters were promptly rammed and sunk by Carthaginian warships.

**836. Carthaginian expansion in the western Mediterranean islands**

Unlike Rome, the military power of Carthage, supported by the profits from trade, was built up entirely on a basis of money, with which, as long as she prospered, she could support a large mercenary army. She had no farmers cultivating their own land, from whom she could draw an army of citizen-soldiers as did Rome. The rich and fertile region of Tunis just south of Carthage had indeed been taken by the Carthaginians from its native owners. Here the merchant princes of the city developed large and beautiful estates, worked by slaves; but such lands, supporting no small farmers, furnished no troops for the army.

**837. Lack of citizen-soldiers at Carthage; commercial prosperity and a mercenary army**

This was a serious weakness in the organization of the Carthaginian state. The rulers of the city never trusted the army,

**838. Carthaginian State**

made up as it was of foreigners, and they always felt some distrust even toward their own generals, although they were, of course, born Carthaginians. The fear lest the generals should endeavor to make themselves kings of Carthage caused much friction between the government and the Carthaginian commanders, and was frequently a cause of weakness to the nation. Although there were two elective magistrates called Judges at the head of the State, Carthage was really governed by a group of merchant nobles, a wealthy aristocracy whose members formed a Council in complete control. They were what the Greeks called an oligarchy (§ 618); but they were energetic and statesmanlike rulers. Centuries of shrewd guidance on their part made Carthage a great state, far exceeding in power any of the Greek states that ever arose, not excluding Athens.

**839. Carthaginian civilization**

But Carthage remained in civilization an oriental power. Wherever her works of art are dug up to-day, they show all the earlier limitations of oriental art, and seem to have been little influenced by the Greeks. Only in Sicily did Carthaginian merchants yield to Greek influence, take up coinage, and issue silver money. In Carthage herself they retained the old oriental commercial use of bars of precious metal (§ 189). As her business grew, however, her merchants found it necessary to have some convenient medium of exchange, and they issued leathern money, the earliest predecessor of paper money, stamped with the seal of the State, guaranteeing its value. In literature their great explorer Hanno (§ 835) wrote an account of his exploration of the Atlantic coast of Africa; and Mago, one of their statesmen, who organized and developed the great farming district of Tunis, wrote a treatise on agriculture, which the Roman Senate had translated into Latin. It became the standard book on agriculture in Italy.

**840. The city of Carthage**

In matters of household equipment and city building the Carthaginians were quite the equals of the Greeks. The city of Carthage itself was large and splendid (Fig. 239). It was in area three times as large as Rome. Behind wide docks and extensive piers of masonry, teeming with ships and merchandise, the city spread far inland, with spacious markets and busy manufacturing quarters humming with industry. Beyond the dwellings of the poorer craftsmen and artisans rose the stately houses of the wealthy merchants, with rich and sumptuous tropical gardens. Around the whole swept imposing walls and massive fortifications, inclosing the entire city and making its capture almost an impossibility. Behind the great city, outside the walls, stretched a wide expanse of waving palm groves and tropical plantations, dotted with the luxurious country houses of the splendid commercial lords of Carthage, who were to lead the coming struggle with Rome.

Back in the days of the Latin war (ended 338 B.C.), or a little before, when the Roman merchants were still doing a small business, they had been willing that the Senate should make a treaty with Carthage, drawing lines which the ships of neither side should cross. Indeed, about the middle of the Samnite Wars the Roman Senate had made a second treaty with Carthage (306 B.C.), in which it was agreed that no Roman ships would enter the harbors of Sicily and no Carthaginian ships should trade in the ports of Italy. The capture of the Greek cities of Italy by the Romans had left the Greeks of Sicily to face the power of Carthage entirely alone. In times past they had done this with great success (§ 780), but now, unable to unite against Carthage, they were slowly yielding, and the Carthaginians were steadily pushing eastward and absorbing Sicily. The merchants of Italy looked over at the busy harbors of Sicily, where so much profitable trade was going on, and it filled them with growing impatience that they were not permitted to do business there. With increasing vexation they realized that Rome had gained the supremacy of Italy and pushed her frontiers to the southernmost tip of the peninsula, only to look across and find that the merchant princes of Carthage had made the western Mediterranean a Carthaginian sea.

**841. Early commercial treaties and the growing friction between Carthage and Rome**

**842. Danger to Rome in the threatened loss of the Strait of Messina**

Indeed, Carthage was gaining a position which might cut off Rome from communication with even her own ports on the Adriatic side of Italy. To reach them, Roman ships must pass through the Strait of Messina between Italy and Sicily. The advance of Carthage in Sicily might enable her at any time to seize the Sicilian city of Messina and close this strait to Roman ships. We can understand the dread with which Italian merchants looked southward, thinking of the day when Carthaginian warships in the harbor at Messina would stop all traffic between the west coast of Italy and the Adriatic.

**843. War strength of the Romans**

The Roman Senate without doubt shared these apprehensions. Many a Roman senator must have asked himself the question, What would be Rome's chances of success in a struggle with the mighty North-African commercial empire? Rome had little or no navy. The Roman army had been barely able to maintain itself against a modern Hellenistic commander like Pyrrhus. The ancient regulation drawing the soldiers only from among the owners of land had formerly limited the size of the army, but it was greatly increased in size by the admission of the new class of men having property in money (§ 832). The introduction of pay for citizens in the army had also increased the possible length of military service among a people still chiefly made up of farmers obliged to return home to plow, sow, and reap. The Romans could thus put a citizen army of over three hundred thousand men into the field. Besides the troops made up of Roman citizens, the principle was adopted of having each army include also about an equal number of troops drawn from the allies. This plan, therefore, doubled the number of available troops. The Roman army consequently far exceeded in size any army ever organized in the Mediterranean world.

**844. Roman improvements in arms and tactics**

In arms and tactics the Romans had been able to make some improvements in the Hellenistic art of war (§ 681). The spear was now employed by the Romans only as the battle opened, when it was hurled into the ranks of the enemy at short range. After this the battle was fought by the Romans with short swords, which were much more easily handled at close quarters than long spears (Fig. 236). At the same time the Romans had likewise improved the phalanx, which we remember had thus far been a massive unit, possessing as a whole no flexibility (§ 637). It had no joints. The Romans gave it joints and flexibility by cutting it up in both directions; that is, lengthwise and crosswise.

They divided the phalanx lengthwise into three divisions, one forming the front, one the middle, and one the rear (Fig. 237). Each division was about six men deep, and there was only a narrow space between the divisions. The front division was made up of the young and vigorous troops, while the older men were placed in the other two divisions. If the steady old troops behind saw that a gap was being made in the front division, it was the business of the second division to advance at once and fill the gap. This made it necessary to cut up the divisions crosswise, into short sections, so that a section could advance without carrying the whole division forward. Such a section of a division had a front

845. The Romans cut up the phalanx into divisions and maniples

FIG. 236. A ROMAN SOLDIER OF THE LEGION

The figure of the soldier is carved upon a tombstone, erected in his memory by his brother. His offensive weapons are his spear (*pilum*), which he holds in his extended right hand with point upward, and his heavy short sword (*gladius*), which he wears girded high on his right side (see § 844). As defensive equipment he has a helmet, a leathern corselet stopping midway between the waist and knees, and a shield (*scutum*)

about twenty men long, and being, as we have said, six men deep, there were a hundred and twenty men in each section of a division. These sections were called *maniples*. Each maniple in advancing to fill a gap before it was like a football "back" when he springs forward to stop a gap in the line before him. But it is important to notice that thus far all three divisions of the phalanx were invariably kept together; they were *inseparable*. The middle and rear divisions

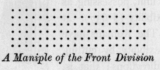

*A Maniple of the Front Division*

Rear

Rear Division
Middle Division
Front Division

Front

FIG. 237. PLAN OF A ROMAN THREEFOLD LINE OF BATTLE WITH DETAIL OF A SINGLE MANIPLE ABOVE IT

Here we see the once solid and indivisible phalanx of the Greeks broken up into three divisions lengthwise (lower diagram), — a front, middle, and rear division, — and likewise cut up crosswise into short sections (maniples). In the front and middle divisions these maniples were six men deep and twenty men long (see upper diagram) and half as long in the rear division. These sections (maniples) were so placed that the openings between them did not coincide, but the maniples of the middle division covered the openings, or joints, in the front division (§ 845)

were always only *supports of the front division immediately before them*. It had not yet occurred to the Romans to shift the middle or rear division, as football backs are shifted, to fight facing in another direction, or to post them in another part of the field, leaving the first division to fight unsupported (Fig. 237). When a great Roman, during the struggle with Carthage, discovered the possibility of thus shifting the middle and rear divisions (§ 874), a new chapter in the art of war began.

For purposes of mustering and feeding an army, the Romans divided it into larger bodies, called *legions*, each containing usually forty-five hundred men, of whom three hundred were cavalry, twelve hundred were light-armed troops, while the three thousand forming the body of the legion were the heavy-armed men making up the three divisions just described. Each maniple of one hundred and twenty men was divided into two centuries of sixty men each, for a "century" soon ceased always to contain a hundred men. Each century had a commander called a centurion. A centurion and his century roughly corresponded to our captain and his company.

**846.** Legions and centurions

Notwithstanding these improvements, the Romans did not at first see the importance of a commander in chief of long experience — a man who made warfare his calling and had become a professional military leader like the Hellenistic commanders (§ 630). Hence the Romans intrusted their armies without hesitation to the command of their consuls, who as presidents of the republic had often never had any experience in military leadership. Moreover, the consuls might be leading their troops just on the eve of battle, and find themselves deprived of command by the expiration of their term of office. In the Samnite Wars this difficulty had shown the Romans the necessity of extending a consul's military power under such circumstances. When this was done he was called a proconsul. But the Romans were still without professional generals like Xenophon (§ 630). At the same time the introduction of pay for officers and soldiers had made extended service possible, and an experienced body of lower officers such as the centurions had grown up.

**847.** Lack of experienced commanding generals

In military discipline the Romans surpassed all other peoples of ancient times; for even among the Greek troops there was great lack of discipline. We hear of a Roman father who ordered his son to be executed in the presence of the army, because the young man had, in disobedience of orders, accepted single combat with an enemy and slain him. Even an ex-consul, having won a victory after receiving orders from the Dictator not to give battle, was condemned to death by the Dictator as

**848.** Roman discipline and the fortified camp

the legal consequence of disobedience to a superior. It was only with the greatest difficulty that he was saved by his influential friends. In accordance with the strict system maintained in all their operations it was the invariable practice of a Roman army when it halted to construct a square fortified camp, surrounded by a ridge of earth bearing a stockade of wooden posts driven into the crest of the ridge. This camp was a descendant of the old prehistoric pile village of northern Italy (Fig. 225).

## QUESTIONS

SECTION 76. How much time elapsed from the final subjection of Latium to Roman leadership of all Italy? How did Rome govern the defeated cities of Italy? How much Italian territory was occupied by Roman citizens? Where was it? Where did Rome place her colonies? Was Italy a unified nation? Why not? Mention the races and languages of Italy. What was the future language to be? Mention some early influences of Greek art and architecture in Italy; of Greek business methods in Italy. What financial changes took place at Rome as a result?

SECTION 77. Had agriculture carried the Romans outside of Italy? Was commerce now to do so? Into what triangular sea does the Tiber flow? What great commercial rival of Rome lay on the same sea? Who were the ancestors of the Carthaginians? What had they achieved in business? What region did Carthage commercially control? How did she treat ships of other peoples in this region? Describe the military organization of Carthage. Had she any citizen-soldiers? What was the character of the Carthaginian State? of Carthaginian civilization? Describe the city and surroundings. What was happening to the Greeks of Sicily? In whose hands was the western Mediterranean commercially? Describe the danger at Messina.

Tell about the war strength of the Romans by land. Describe their improvement of the phalanx. What was the purpose of the legion? How large was it? What was a centurion? Had the Romans any commanding generals of long experience? Did they have any professional soldiers? What can you say about the discipline of a Roman army? What did the Romans do when they camped? Where had the plan of the Roman camp originated?

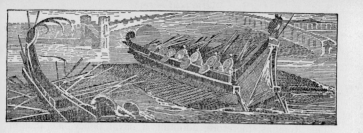

# CHAPTER XXIV

## THE ROMAN CONQUEST OF THE WESTERN MEDITERRANEAN WORLD

### SECTION 78. THE STRUGGLE WITH CARTHAGE: THE SICILIAN WAR, OR FIRST PUNIC WAR

Whatever might be the risks involved in a struggle with Carthage, the Romans were soon convinced that it could not be avoided. During a siege of Messina at the hands of the Syracusans, one party in the besieged place called in the aid of the Romans, while another party appealed to Carthage. The result was that a Carthaginian garrison quickly occupied the citadel of Messina, and the Carthaginians were then in command of the Strait of Messina. The Romans had long hesitated, but now they took the memorable step, and a Roman army, responding to the appeal of Messina, left the soil of

849. Opening of the Sicilian War (First Punic War) with Carthage at Messina (264 B.C.)

NOTE. The above fragment of a wall-painting at Pompeii shows us a Roman warship, seemingly in battle, for the wreck of another warship is visible at the left. Notice the two steering *oars* at each side of the stern — a device found on Nile ships three thousand years earlier (Fig. 41). The rudder had not yet developed from these steering oars. The Romans ascribed their success, in spite of inexperience, against the Carthaginians to a new boarding grappler, which they invented and called a "crow" (*corvus*). It consisted of a heavy upright timber, which was made to fall over with the end on the enemy's rail, where an iron hook attached to the end of the "crow" grappled and held the opposing craft until the Romans could climb over into it. In the hand-to-hand fighting which followed, the sturdy Romans more than made up for their inexperience in seamanship.

Italy and crossed the sea for the first time in Roman history. The struggle with Carthage had begun (264 B.C.).

**850. The Romans build a fleet**

An alliance with Syracuse soon gave the Romans possession of eastern Sicily, but they were long unable to make much progress into the central and western portion of the island. The chief reason for this was the lack of a strong war fleet. The Romans, therefore, adopting a naval policy like that of Themistocles (§ 506), determined to build a fleet. The Senate rapidly pushed the building of the new fleet, and in the fifth year of the war it put to sea for the first time. It numbered a hundred and twenty battleships, of which a full hundred were large, powerful vessels with five banks of oars.

**851. Roman victory and disaster at sea**

In spite of inexperience, the Roman fleet was victorious in two successive battles off the coast of Italy. It looked as if the war would be quickly over. The Senate, however, finding that the legions made little progress in Sicily, determined to invade Africa and strike Carthage at home. The invasion was at first very successful, but its progress was unwisely interfered with by the Senate, who recalled one of the consuls with many of the troops. The result was that the remaining consul, with his reduced army, was disastrously defeated. Then one Roman fleet after another was destroyed by heavy storms at sea, and one of them was badly defeated by the Carthaginians. The Romans thus lost their newly won command of the sea, and were long unable to make any progress in the war.

**852. Final naval victory of the Romans (241 B.C.)**

Year after year the struggle dragged on, while Hamilcar Barca, the Carthaginian commander, was plundering the coasts of Italy with his fleet. The treasury at Rome was empty, and the Romans were at the end of their resources; but by private contributions they succeeded in building another fleet, which put to sea in 242 B.C. with two hundred battleships of five banks of oars. The Carthaginian fleet was defeated and broken up (241 B.C.), and as a result the Carthaginians found themselves unable to send reënforcements across the sea to their army in Sicily.

They were therefore at last obliged to accept hard terms of peace at the hands of the Romans. The Carthaginians were to give up Sicily and the neighboring islands to Rome, and to pay the Romans as war damages the sum of thirty-two hundred talents, over three and a half million dollars, within ten years. Thus in 241 B.C., after more than twenty-three years of fighting, the first period of the struggle between Rome and Carthage ended with the victory of Rome.

853. Peace at the end of the Sicilian War (241 B.C.)

The struggle had been carried on till both contestants were completely exhausted. Both had learned much in the art of war, and Rome for the first time had become a sea power. At the same time she had taken a step which forever changed her future and altered her destiny; for the first time she held territory outside of Italy, and from this step she was never able to withdraw. It has been compared with the action of the United States in taking Porto Rico and the Philippines; for in gaining interests and responsibilities across the sea, a nation is at once thrown into conflict with other powers having similar interests, and this conflict of interests never reaches an end, but leads from one war to another.

854. Some results of the Sicilian War

## Section 79. The Hannibalic War (Second Punic War) and the Destruction of Carthage

Both the rivals now devoted themselves to increasing their strength, nor did Rome hesitate to do so at the expense of Carthage. Taking advantage of a revolt among the hired Carthaginian troops in Sardinia, the Romans accepted an invitation from these mercenaries to invade both Sardinia and Corsica; and in spite of protests from Carthage, only three years after the settlement of peace Rome took possession of these two islands. Rome now possessed three island outposts against Carthage. Some years later the Romans were involved in a serious war by an invasion of the Gauls from the Po valley. The Gauls were disastrously defeated, and their territory was

855. Roman seizure of Sardinia and Corsica and conquest of the Po valley

seized by the Romans without granting the Gauls any form of citizenship. Thus Roman power was extended northward to the foot of the Alps, and the entire peninsula from the Alps southward was held by Rome (map II, p. 552).

**856. New Carthaginian conquests in Spain and the rise of Hannibal**

To offset this increase of Roman power and to compensate for the loss of the three large islands, the Carthaginian leaders turned toward Spain. Here still dwelt the hardy descendants of the Late Stone Age Europeans of the West (§ 325). Hamilcar, the Carthaginian general, planned to secure the wealth of their silver mines, to enlist the natives in the army, and thus to build up a power able to meet that of Rome. He died before the completion of his plans, but they were taken up by his gifted son Hannibal, who extended Carthaginian rule in Spain as far north as the Ebro River (map II, p. 552). Although only twenty-four years of age, Hannibal was already forming colossal plans for a bold surprise of Rome in her own territory, which by its unexpectedness and audacity should crush Roman power in Italy.

**857. Hannibalic War is provoked by a frontier quarrel in Spain (219 B.C.)**

Rome, busily occupied in overthrowing the Gauls, had been unable to interfere with the Spanish enterprises of Carthage. She had, however, secured an agreement that Carthage should not advance northward beyond the Ebro River. To so bold and resolute a leader as Hannibal such a stipulation was only an opportunity for a frontier quarrel with Rome in Spain. In the tremendous struggle which followed he was the genius and the dominating spirit. It was a colossal contest between the *nation* Rome and the *man* Hannibal. We may therefore well call it the Hannibalic War.

**858. Opening of the Hannibalic War (218–202 B.C.); Hannibal's reasons for invading Italy by land from the north**

While the Roman Senate was demanding that the leaders at Carthage disavow his hostile acts, Hannibal, with a strong and well-drilled army of about forty thousand men, was already marching northward along the east coast of Spain (map, p. 538). Several reasons led him to this course. He knew that since the Sicilian war the defeated Carthaginian fleet would be unable to protect his army if he tried to cross by water from Carthage and to land in southern Italy. Moreover, his cavalry, over six thousand strong, was much too numerous to be transported by sea. In southern Italy, furthermore, he would have been met at once by a hostile population, whereas in northern Italy there were the newly conquered Gauls, burning for revenge on the Romans, their conquerors. Hannibal intended to offer them an opportunity for that revenge by enlistment in his ranks. Moreover, he had reports of dissatisfaction among the allies of Rome also, and he believed that by an early victory in northern Italy he could induce the allies to forsake Rome and join him in a war for independence which would destroy Roman leadership in Italy. For these reasons, while the Roman Senate was planning to invade Spain and Africa, they found their own land suddenly invaded by Hannibal from the north.

By clever maneuvering at the Rhone, Hannibal avoided the Roman army, which had arrived there on its way to Spain. The crossing of the Rhone, a wide, deep, and swift river, with elephants and cavalry and the long detour to avoid the Romans so delayed Hannibal that it was late autumn when he reached the Alps (218 B.C.). Overwhelmed by snowstorms; struggling over a steep and dangerous trail, sometimes so narrow that the rocks had to be cut away to make room for the elephants; looking down over dizzy precipices, or up to snow-covered heights where hostile natives rolled great stones down upon them, the discouraged army of Hannibal toiled on day after day, exhausted, cold, and hungry. At every point along the straggling line, where help was most needed, the young Carthaginian was always present, encouraging and guiding his men. But when they issued from the Alpine pass, perhaps Mt. Cenis, into the upper valley of the Po, they had suffered such losses that they were reduced to some thirty-four thousand men.

**859.** Hannibal evades the Romans at the Rhone and leads his army across the Alps (218 B.C.)

With this little army the dauntless Carthaginian youth had entered the territory of the strongest military power of the time — a nation which could now call to her defense over seven hundred thousand men, citizens and allies. From this vast number

**860.** Inferior size of Hannibal's army compared with Roman resources

Rome could recruit army after army; but Hannibal, on the other hand, as long as Carthage did not control the sea, could expect no reënforcements from home except through Spain. A military success was necessary at once in order to arouse the hopes of the Gauls and secure recruits from among them.

**861. Superiority of Hannibal's military knowledge over that of the Roman consuls**

Hannibal, who was in close contact with a number of Greeks, was thoroughly acquainted with the most highly developed

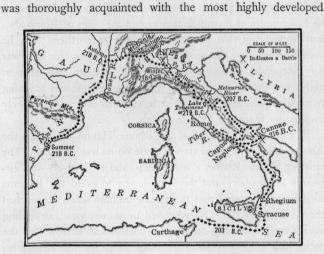

THE ROUTE AND MARCHES OF HANNIBAL FROM 218 TO 203 B.C.

The dates indicate the progress of the march. During Hannibal's long stay in southern Italy, he made many marches and local movements not indicated in the above sketch. Indeed, we know very little about many of his operations in this region

methods of warfare. The exploits of Alexander, who had died a little over a century before Hannibal's invasion of Italy, were familiar to him, and it is not impossible that the fascinating story of Alexander's campaigns was read to the young Carthaginian as he lay with his Greek companions around the camp fires in Italy. Furthermore, we recall that Roman consuls, commanding the Roman armies, were simply magistrates like our mayors or presidents, often without much more knowledge of handling an army than has a city mayor in our time. Gifted with little imagination, blunt and straightforward, brave and eager to meet the enemy at once, the Roman consuls were no match for the crafty young Carthaginian.

By skillful use of his cavalry, in which the Romans were weak, Hannibal at once won two engagements in the Po valley. The Gauls began to flock to his standards, but they were raw, undisciplined troops. He was still outside the barrier of Roman fortresses defending the Apennines, and this he must not fail to pierce without delay. By early spring, therefore (217 B.C.), amid fearful difficulties which would have broken the courage of most commanders, Hannibal successfully passed the belt of Roman strongholds blocking the roads through the Apennines. Even after he had crossed the Arnus, the Roman consul Flaminius had no notion of the Carthaginian advance, though he soon learned that the Carthaginians were between him and Rome. Nevertheless, on the shores of Lake Trasimene, Hannibal easily surprised the army of the unsuspecting consul on the march, ambushed the legions both in front and rear, and cut to pieces the entire Roman army, so that only a handful escaped and the consul himself fell. But a few days' march from Rome, Hannibal might now have advanced directly against the city; but he had no siege machinery (headpiece, p. 140), and his forces were not numerous enough for the siege of so strong a fortress. Moreover, his cavalry, in which he was superior to the Romans, would have been useless in a siege. He therefore desired another victory in the hope that the allies of Rome would revolt and join him in attacking the city.

**862. Hannibal's first three victories**

Hannibal therefore marched eastward to the Adriatic coast, where he secured numerous horses, much needed by his cavalry, and also found plentiful provisions, besides an opportunity to drill his Gallic recruits. At this dangerous crisis the Romans appointed a Dictator, a stable old citizen named Fabius, whose policy was to wear out Hannibal by refusing to give battle and by using every opportunity to harass the Carthaginians. This

**863. A year of delay and preparation (217–216 B.C.)**

policy of caution and delay did not meet with popular favor at
Rome. The people called Fabius the Laggard (*Cunctator*), a
name which ever afterward clung to him; and the new consuls
elected for 216 B.C. were urged to take action and destroy the
Carthaginian army without more delay. They therefore recruited an army of nearly seventy thousand men and pushed
southward toward the heel of the Italian peninsula to meet
Hannibal. The Carthaginian deftly outwitted them and, marching to Cannæ, captured the Roman supplies. The consuls
were then obliged to give battle or retire for more supplies.

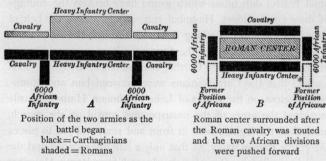

Position of the two armies as the
battle began
black = Carthaginians
shaded = Romans

Roman center surrounded after
the Roman cavalry was routed
and the two African divisions
were pushed forward

PLAN OF THE BATTLE OF CANNÆ (§§ 864–865)

**864. The
dispositions
at the battle
of Cannæ**

With their fifty-five thousand heavy-armed infantry the consuls
were almost twice as strong as Hannibal, who had but thirty-
two thousand such troops. On the other hand, Hannibal had
about ten thousand horse against six thousand of the Roman
cavalry, while both armies were about equally strong in light-
armed troops. Varro, the Roman consul, had been merely a
successful business man at Rome. He drew up his heavy-armed
troops in a deep mass in the center, with a short front. Had
he spread them out, so that their superior numbers might
form a longer front than that of Hannibal, they might have
enfolded and outflanked the Carthaginian army. Both armies
divided their cavalry, that it might form the two wings. Instead
of massing all his heavy-armed troops in the center to meet the

great mass of the Roman center, Hannibal took out some twelve thousand of his heavy-armed African infantry in two bodies of six thousand each and stationed them in a deep column behind each of his cavalry wings (plan *A*, p. 540).

Hannibal's stronger cavalry put to flight the Roman horse forming both wings. Then as his well-trained horsemen turned back to attack the heavy mass of the Roman center in the rear, he knew that it was too late for the Romans, perceiving their danger, to retreat and escape, for they were caught between the Carthaginian center before them and the Carthaginian cavalry behind them. Only the sides of the trap were open.

865. Hannibal annihilates the Roman army at the battle of Cannæ (216 B.C)

Then came a great moment in the young Carthaginian's life. With unerring judgment, just at the proper instant, he gave the orders which closed up the sides of the trap he had so cleverly prepared. The two bodies of Africans which he had posted behind the cavalry wings, on each side, pushed quietly forward till they occupied positions on each side of the fifty-five thousand brave Romans of the center, who were thus inclosed on

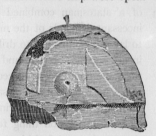

FIG. 238. CARTHAGINIAN HELMET PICKED UP ON THE BATTLEFIELD AT CANNÆ

all sides (plan *B*, p. 540). What ensued was simply a slaughter of the doomed Romans, lasting all the rest of the day. When night closed in the Roman army was annihilated. Ex-consuls, senators, nobles, thousands of the best citizens of Rome had fallen in this frightful battle. Every family in Rome was in mourning. Of the gold rings worn by Roman knights as an indication of their rank, Hannibal is reported to have sent a bushel to Carthage. Even in modern times pieces of armor have been picked up on the battlefield (Fig. 238).

Thus this masterful young Carthaginian, the greatest of Semite generals, within two years after his arrival in Italy and

**866.** Hannibal organizes the revolting Roman allies against Rome and calls in the Macedonians

before he was thirty years of age, had defeated his giant antagonist in four battles and destroyed three of the opposing armies. He might now count upon a revolt among the Roman allies. Within a few years southern Italy, including the Greek cities, and even Syracuse in Sicily forsook Rome and joined Hannibal. Only some of the southern Latin colonies held out against him. To make matters worse for Rome, immediately after Cannæ, Hannibal sent messengers to Macedonia, and one of the later Philips then reigning there agreed to send help to the Carthaginians in Italy.

**867.** Hannibal's statesmanship and the difficulties of his position

In all this Hannibal was displaying the judgment and insight of a statesman combined with amazing ability to meet the incessant demands of the military situation. This required him to lay out campaigns, to drill the inexperienced new recruits, to insure supplies of food and fresh horses for his army, while at the same time he was forced also to find the money with which to pay his turbulent and dissatisfied mercenaries. In carrying out all this work he was untiring, and his eye was everywhere. It was no uncommon thing for some private soldier to wake in the morning and find his young general sleeping on the ground by his side. There was a consuming fire of desire in his soul to save Carthage; and now his glorious victories were drawing together the foes of Rome in a great combination which he believed would bring about the destruction of his country's hated antagonist.

**868.** Roman diplomacy checkmates Macedonia and Roman determination recovers the revolting cities

But opposing the burning zeal of a single gifted soul were the dogged resolution, the ripe statesmanship, the unshaken organization, and the seemingly inexhaustible numbers of the Romans. It was a battle of giants for the mastery of the world; for the victor in this struggle would without any question be the greatest power in the Mediterranean. Had the successors of Alexander in the Hellenistic eastern Mediterranean discerned the nature of this gigantic struggle in Italy, and been able to combine against Rome, they might now have crushed her forever (see map I, p. 450). But the Roman Senate, with clever statesmanship, made an alliance with the Greeks, thus stirring up a revolt in Greece against the Macedonians and preventing them from furnishing help to Hannibal. In spite of Hannibal's victories, the steadiness and fine leadership of the Roman Senate held central Italy loyal to Rome. Although the Romans were finally compelled to place arms in the hands of slaves and mere boys, new armies were formed. With these forces the Romans proceeded to besiege and capture the revolting allied cities one after another. Even the clever devices of Archimedes during a desperate siege (§ 742) did not save Syracuse from being recaptured by the Romans (212 B.C.).

Capua likewise, the second city of Italy, which had gone over to his cause, was besieged by the Romans in spite of all Hannibal's efforts to drive them away. As a last hope he marched upon Rome itself, and with his bodyguard rode up to one of the gates of the great city, whose power seemed so unbroken. For a brief time the two antagonists faced each other, and many a Roman senator must have looked over the walls at the figure of the tremendous young Carthaginian who had shaken all Italy as with an earthquake. But they were not to be frightened into offers of peace in this way, nor did they send out any message to him. His army was not large enough to lay siege to the greatest city of Italy, nor had he been able to secure any siege machinery (§ 632), and he was obliged to retreat without accomplishing anything. Capua was thereupon captured by the Romans and punished without mercy.

**869.** Hannibal's fruitless advance to Rome and the recapture of Capua by the Romans (211 B.C.)

The hitherto dauntless spirit of the young Carthaginian at last began to feel the crushing weight of Roman confidence. When he had finally been ten years in Italy, he realized that unless powerful reënforcements could reach him, his cause was hopeless. His brother Hasdrubal in Spain had gathered an army and was now marching into Italy to aid him. At the Metaurus River, in the region of Sentinum, where the fate of Rome had once before been settled (§ 819), Hasdrubal was met by a Roman army. He was completely defeated and

**870.** Hannibal's reënforcements intercepted and destroyed (207 B.C.)

slain (207 B.C.). To the senators waiting in keenest anticipation at Rome the news of the victory meant the salvation of Italy and the final defeat of an enemy who had all but accomplished the destruction of Roman power. To Hannibal, anxiously awaiting tidings of his brother and of the needed reënforcements, the first announcement of the disaster and the crushing of his hopes was the head of Hasdrubal hurled into the Carthaginian camp by a Roman messenger.

**871.** The decline of Hannibal's power in Italy and the rise of Scipio

For a few years more Hannibal struggled on in the southern tip of Italy, the only territory remaining of all that he had captured. Meantime the Romans, taught by sad experience, had given the command of their forces in Spain to Scipio, one of the ablest of their younger leaders. He had routed the Carthaginians and driven them entirely out of Spain, thus cutting off their chief supply both of money and of troops. In Scipio the Romans had at last found a general, with the masterful qualities which make a great military leader. He demanded of the Senate that he be sent to Africa to invade the dominions of Carthage as Hannibal had invaded those of Rome.

**872.** Scipio and Hannibal meet at Zama (202 B.C.); the tactics of Hannibal

By 203 B.C. Scipio had twice defeated the Carthaginian forces in Africa, and Carthage was forced to call Hannibal home. He had spent fifteen years on the soil of Italy, and the great struggle between the almost exhausted rivals was now to be decided in Africa. At Zama, inland from Carthage, the final battle of the war took place. Hannibal, having insufficient cavalry, foresaw that his weak cavalry wings would be defeated by Scipio's opposing heavy bodies of horsemen. When, as he expected, the Roman cavalry wings disappeared in pursuit of his own fleeing horsemen, the wings of both armies were cleared away for one of those unexpected but carefully planned maneuvers by which the great Carthaginian had destroyed the Roman army at Cannæ. From behind his line Hannibal moved out two divisions in opposite directions, elongating his own line beyond the ends of the Roman line, which he intended to inclose on either side. In football language, Hannibal had ordered his backs to spread out and to execute a play around both the Roman ends at once. The fate of two empires was trembling in the balance as Hannibal's steel trap thus extended its jaws on either side to enfold the Roman army.

But behind the Roman army there was a mind like that of Hannibal. The keen eye of the Roman commander discovered the flash of moving steel behind the Carthaginian lines. He understood the movement and at once grasped the danger which threatened his army. As a result of Cannæ, Scipio had long before abandoned all Roman tradition, and had taught his front division to fight without the support of the rear divisions behind them (§ 845). In football language again, he too had learned to shift his backs and had taught the line to hold without them. The shrewd young Roman commander therefore gave his orders without hesitation. For the first time in history the rear divisions behind the front of a Roman center left the front division to fight alone. As quietly as on a parade march they parted to the left and right and, marching behind the fighting line in opposite directions, they took up their posts, extending the Roman front at either end where at first the cavalry wings had been. When Hannibal's spreading divisions pushed out beyond the Roman ends, where they were expected to carry out their "around-the-end" movements, they found facing them a Roman wall of steel, and the battle continued in two parallel lines longer than before. The great Carthaginian had been foiled at his own game by an equally great Roman. When the Roman cavalry returned from their pursuit and fell on the Carthaginian flank, Hannibal beheld his lines crumbling and giving way in final and complete defeat.

**873.** The counter-moves of Scipio bring Roman victory at Zama

In this great battle we see the conclusion of a long and remarkable development in the art of war, from the wild disorder of entirely undisciplined fighting (Fig. 88) to the formation of a heavy phalanx of disciplined men, the earliest trained-fighting team as it appeared in the Orient (Fig. 87). Then in Europe, after Philip and Alexander, the deep phalanx as

**874.** The new art of war; division tactics

used by the Greeks was no longer regarded by the Romans as a rigid, indivisible fighting unit, but it was broken up into a fighting line in front and a group of shifting backs behind. On the field of Zama, Scipio and Hannibal had advanced to a new stage in the art of warfare, and had created what is now known as " division tactics " — the art of manipulating an army on the field in *divisions* shifted behind the line of battle as a skillful football leader shifts his backs, trusting to the line to hold while he does so.

**875.** The treaty ending the Hannibalic War (201 B.C)　　The victory of Rome over Carthage made Rome the leading power in the whole ancient world. In the treaty which followed the battle of Zama, the Romans forced Carthage to pay ten thousand talents (over $11,000,000) in fifty years and to surrender all her warships but ten triremes. But what was worse she lost her independence as a nation, and according to the treaty she could not make war anywhere without the consent of the Romans. Although the Romans did not annex her territory in Africa, Carthage had become a vassal state.

**876.** The fate of Hannibal　　Hannibal had escaped after his lost battle at Zama. Although we learn of his deeds chiefly through his enemies, the story of his dauntless struggle to save his native country, begun when he was only twenty-four and continued for twenty years, reveals him as one of the greatest and most gifted leaders in all history — a lion-hearted man, so strong of purpose that only a great nation like Rome could have crushed him. Indeed, Rome now compelled the Carthaginians to expel Hannibal, and, a man of fifty, he went into exile in the East, where we shall find him stirring up the successors of Alexander to combine against Rome.

**877.** The destruction of Carthage (146 B.C.): Third Punic War　　Such was the commercial ability of the Carthaginians that they continued to prosper even while paying the heavy tribute with which Rome had burdened them. Meantime, the new mistress of the western Mediterranean kept an anxious eye on her old rival. Even the stalwart *Romans* remembered with uneasiness the invasion of Hannibal. Cato, a famous old-fashioned senator, was so convinced that Carthage was still a danger to Rome that he concluded all his speeches in the Senate with the words, "Carthage must be destroyed." For over fifty years more the merchants of Carthage were permitted to traffic in the western Mediterranean, and then the iron hand of Rome was laid upon the doomed city for the last time. To defend herself against the Numidians behind her, Carthage was finally obliged to begin war against them. This step, which

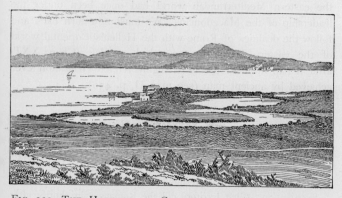

FIG. 239. THE HARBORS OF CARTHAGE AS THEY ARE TO-DAY

Of the city destroyed by the Romans almost nothing has survived. It was rebuilt under Julius Cæsar, but, as we see here, very little of this later city has survived. Thorough and systematic excavation would probably recover many valuable remains of ancient Carthaginian civilization, of which we know so little

the Romans had long been desiring, was a violation of the treaty with Rome. The Senate seized the opportunity at once and Carthage was called to account. In the three years' war (Third Punic War) which followed, the beautiful city was captured and completely destroyed (146 B.C.) (see Fig. 239). Its territory was taken by Rome and called the Province of Africa. A struggle of nearly one hundred and twenty years had resulted in the annihilation of Rome's only remaining rival in the West (see map III, p. 552).

**878.** Rome, supreme in the West, turns eastward

Thus the fourfold rivalry in the western Mediterranean, which had long included the Etruscans and Carthaginians, the Greeks and the Romans, had ended with the triumph of the once insignificant village above the prehistoric market on the Tiber (§ 784). Racially, the western wing of the Indo-European line had proved victorious over that of the Semite line (Fig. 112). The western Mediterranean world was now under the leadership of a single great nation, the Romans, as the eastern Mediterranean world had once been under the leadership of the Macedonians. We must now turn back and follow the dealings of Rome with the Hellenistic-oriental world of the eastern Mediterranean, which we left (Chap. XXI) after it had attained the most highly refined civilization ever achieved by ancient man (see map II, p. 450).

### QUESTIONS

SECTION 78. At what point did Rome and Carthage come into conflict? How? When? Had the Romans any sea power? How did they get it? Give a brief statement of the course of the Sicilian War. What were the main results?

SECTION 79. What territory did the Romans gain shortly after the Sicilian War? Whither did Carthage go for new resources? Who provoked the ensuing war? Describe Hannibal's plan of campaign in full. Recount his march into Italy. How did his numbers compare with those of Rome? What can you say of his military knowledge? Describe his first three encounters with the Romans. Where did he then go? What did the Romans do? Draw two plans, and tell the story of the battle of Cannæ. What political moves did Hannibal then make? How did the Romans meet them? What course did Rome follow toward her revolting allies? What happened at Capua? What did Hannibal's brother do?

What were the Romans meantime doing in Spain? Who was the Roman leader there? Recount the battle of Zama. What advance in the art of warfare was shown there? What were the main results of the Hannibalic War? What became of Hannibal? Recount the destruction of Carthage. How long had the struggle between Rome and Carthage lasted? Who was now leader of the West?

# CHAPTER XXV

## WORLD DOMINION AND DEGENERACY

SECTION 80. THE ROMAN CONQUEST OF THE EASTERN
MEDITERRANEAN WORLD

While the heirs of Alexander were carrying on their ceaseless feuds, plots, wars, and alliances in the eastern Mediterranean, as we have seen them doing down to about 200 B.C.
(Chap. XX), the vast power of Rome had been slowly rising
in the West. The serious consequences of Rome's growth, and,
especially of her expansion beyond the sea, were now evident.
The Roman Senate could not allow any state on the Mediterranean to develop such strength as to endanger Rome in the
way Carthage had done during the Hannibalic War. For this
and other reasons the western giant was now to overshadow
the whole Hellenistic world of the East, and finally to draw the

879. Coming
conflict be-
tween the
western and
the eastern
(Hellenistic)
Mediterra-
nean world

NOTE. The relief above, found in the Theater of Marcellus, built by Augustus
(§ 994), gives us a very vivacious glimpse of a battle between gladiators and wild
beasts, just as the Romans saw it. The gladiators in this combat wear only a
tunic and have no defensive armor except a helmet and a shield. Note the expression of pain on the face of the gladiator at the left, whose arm is being
lacerated by the lion.

three great states of Alexander's heirs into his grasp. Let us see what the reasons for the first collision were (see map II, p. 450).

**880. Causes of the Roman war with Macedon**

Hannibal had induced Macedonia to combine with him against Rome (§ 866). This hostile step could not be overlooked by the Romans after the Hannibalic War. Philip, the Macedonian king, was a gifted ruler and an able military commander like his great ancestor, the father of Alexander the Great, a hundred and fifty years earlier. The further plans of this later Philip filled the Senate with anxiety. For he had arranged a combination between himself and Antiochus the Great (the third of the name), the Seleucid king of Syria. By this alliance the two were to divide the dominions of Egypt between them. Because of what he had already done, and also because of what he would do if allowed to go on and gain greatly increased power, the Romans were now obliged to turn eastward and crush Philip of Macedon (map II, p. 450).

**881. Battle of Cynoscephalæ (197 B.C.); Macedon a vassal of Rome**

The Greek states had no reason to support the rule of Macedonia over them; Antiochus was too busy seizing the Asiatic territory of Egypt to send any help to Macedonia; and hence a year after the close of the Hannibalic War, Philip found himself without strong allies, face to face with a Roman army. By his unusual skill as a commander he evaded the Roman force for some time. But in the end the massive Macedonian phalanx, bristling with long spears, was obliged to meet the onset of the Roman legions, with their deadly short swords and the puzzling divisions behind the lines shifting into unexpected positions which the phalanx was not flexible enough to meet. On the field of Cynoscephalæ (dog's heads), in 197 B.C., the Macedonian army was disastrously routed, and the ancient realm of Alexander the Great became a vassal state under Rome. As allies of Rome, the Greek states were then granted their freedom by the Romans.

This war with Macedon brought the Romans into conflict with Antiochus the Great, the Seleucid king, who held a large part of the vast empire of Persia in Asia. For Antiochus now endeavored to profit by Philip's defeat and to seize some of Philip's former possessions which the Romans had declared free. A war with this powerful Asiatic empire was not a matter which the Romans could view without great anxiety. Moreover, Hannibal, expelled from Carthage (§ 876), was now in Greece with Antiochus, advising him. In spite of the warnings and urgent counsels of Hannibal, Antiochus threw away his opportunities in Greece until the Roman legions maneuvered him back into Asia Minor, whither the Romans followed him, and there the great power of the West for the first time confronted the motley forces of the ancient Orient as marshaled by the successor of Persia in Asia (see map II, p. 450).

882. Roman conflict with the Seleucid Empire, resulting from the conquest of Macedon

The conqueror of Hannibal at Zama was with the Roman army to counsel his brother, another Scipio, consul for the year, and therefore in command of the legions. There was no hope for the undisciplined troops of the Orient when confronted by a Roman army under such masters of the new tactics as these two Scipios. At Magnesia, the West led by Rome overthrew the East led by the dilatory Antiochus (190 B.C.), and the lands of Asia Minor eastward to the Halys River submitted to Roman control. Under the ensuing treaty Antiochus was not permitted to cross the Halys River westward or to send a warship west of the same longitude. Within twelve years (200 to 189 B.C.) Roman arms had reduced to the condition of vassal states two of the three great empires which succeeded Alexander in the East — Macedonia and Syria (see map III, p. 450). As for Egypt, the third, friendship had from the beginning existed between her and Rome. A little over thirty years after a Roman army had first appeared in the Hellenistic world, Egypt acknowledged herself a vassal of Rome (168 B.C.).

883. The overthrow of Antiochus at Magnesia (190 B.C.) and the voluntary vassalship of Egypt (168 B.C.)

Although defeated, the eastern Mediterranean world long continued to give the Romans much trouble. The quarrels of the eastern states among themselves were constantly carried to Rome for settlement. It became necessary to destroy Macedonia as a kingdom and to make her a Roman province. At

884. Annihilation of Macedon and the subjection of the Greeks

the same time Greek sympathy for Macedonia was made the
pretext for greater severity toward the Greeks. Many were
carried off to Italy as hostages, and among them no less than
a thousand noble and educated Achæans were brought to Rome.
When in spite of this the Achæan League (§ 725) rashly brought
on a war with Rome, the Romans applied the same methods
which they were using against Carthage. The same year
which saw the destruction of Carthage witnessed the burning of Corinth also (146 B.C.). Greek liberty was of course
ended, and while a city of such revered memories as Athens
might be given greater freedom (§ 726), those Greek states
whose careers of glorious achievement in civilization we have
followed, were reduced to the condition of Roman vassals.

**885.** The rapidity of the Roman conquests    It was little more than three generations since the Republic
on the Tiber took the fateful step of beginning the conflict with
Carthage for the leadership of the West. That struggle had led
her into a similar conflict for the leadership of the East. There
were old men still living who had talked with veterans of the
Sicilian War with Carthage, and the grandsons of the Romans
who had fought with Hannibal had burned Carthage and
Corinth at the end of the great wars. For nearly a century
and a quarter (beginning 264 B.C.) one great war had followed
another, and the Roman republic, beginning these struggles as
mistress of Italy only, had in this short space of time (from great-
grandfather to great-grandson) gained the political leadership of
the civilized world (cf. maps I, II, and III, p. 552).

**886.** Rome's great task of imperial organization    The Roman Senate had shown eminent ability in conducting the great wars, but now, having gained the supremacy
of the Mediterranean world, Rome was faced by the problem
of devising successful government for the vast dominions which
she had so quickly conquered. In extent they would have
reached entirely across the United States. To organize such
an empire was a task like that which had been so successfully
accomplished by Darius, the organizer of the Persian Empire
(§ 267). We shall find that the Roman Senate utterly failed

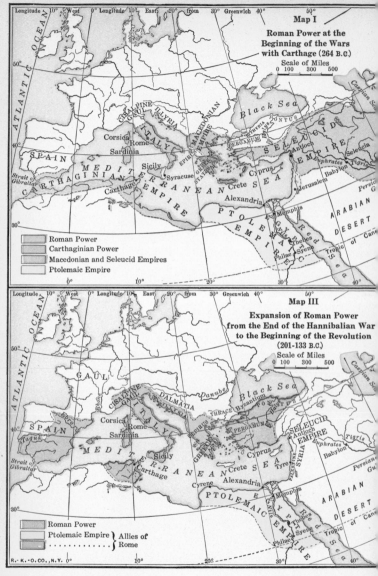

SEQUENCE MAP SHOWING THE EXPANSION OF THE ROMAN POW
TO THE DEATH

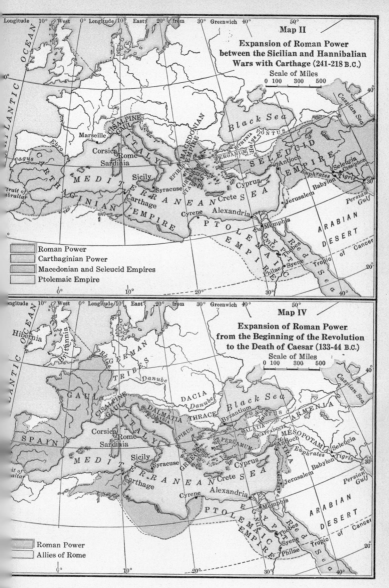

Map II

**Expansion of Roman Power between the Sicilian and Hannibalian Wars with Carthage (241-218 B.C.)**

Scale of Miles
0  100  300  500

Longitude 10° West  0° Longitude 10° East  20°  from  30° Greenwich 40°  50°

ATLANTIC OCEAN

Black Sea

Caspian Sea

Marseille  CISALPINE GAUL  ITALY  MACEDONIAN  BITHYNIA  PONTUS  SELEUCID EMPIRE

Corsica  Rome  EPIRUS  PERGAMUM  Antioch  Seleucia Ctesiphon

Sardinia  Euphrates  Tigris

Ebro  CARTHAGINIAN  MEDITERRANEAN  Sicily  Syracuse  Crete  SEA  Cyprus  Jerusalem  Babylon

Strait of Gibraltar  EMPIRE  Carthage  Cyrene  Alexandria

PTOLEMAIC  Memphis  ARABIAN DESERT  Persian Gulf

EGYPT  Thebes  Red Sea  Tropic of Cancer

EMPIRE  Syene  Philae

■ Roman Power
■ Carthaginian Power
■ Macedonian and Seleucid Empires
□ Ptolemaic Empire

0°  10°  20°  30°  40°

Map IV

**Expansion of Roman Power from the Beginning of the Revolution to the Death of Caesar (133-44 B.C.)**

Scale of Miles
0  100  300  500

Longitude 10° West  0° Longitude 10° East  20°  from  30° Greenwich 40°  50°

ATLANTIC OCEAN

Hibernia  Britannia

Caspian Sea

GERMAN TRIBES

Danube  DACIA  Danube  Black Sea  ARMENIA

GAUL  CISALPINE GAUL  ITALY  DALMATIA  THRACE  Byzantium  PONTUS

SPAIN  Corsica  Rome  EPIRUS  GREECE  PERGAMUM  GALATIA  CAPPADOCIA  MESOPOTAMIA  Seleucia

Sardinia  BITHYNIA  SYRIA  Antioch  Euphrates  Tigris

MEDITERRANEAN  Sicily  Syracuse  Crete  SEA  Cyprus  Jerusalem  Babylon

ait of altar  Carthage  Cyrene  Alexandria  Persian Gulf

PTOLEMAIC  Memphis  ARABIAN DESERT

EGYPT  Thebes  Tropic of Cancer

EMPIRE  Syene  Philae

■ Roman Power
□ Allies of Rome

0°  10°  20°  30°  40°

ROM THE BEGINNING OF THE WARS WITH CARTHAGE (264 B.C.)
ÆSAR (44 B.C.)

in the effort to organize the new dominions. The failure had a most disastrous influence on the Romans themselves and, together with the ruinous effects of the long wars on Italy, finally overthrew the Roman republic — an overthrow in which Rome as a nation almost perished. Let us now glance at the efforts of Rome to govern her new dominions and then observe the effect of the long wars and of world power on the Romans and their life.

## Section 81. Roman Government and Civilization in the Age of Conquest

The Romans had at first no experience in governing their conquered lands, as the United States had none when it took possession of the Philippines. Most of the conquered countries the Romans organized as provinces, somewhat after the manner of the provinces of the old Persian Empire. The people of a province were not permitted to maintain an army, but they were obliged to pay taxes and, lastly, to submit to the uncontrolled rule of a Roman magistrate who was *governor* of the province. It was chiefly the presence and power of this governor which made the condition of the provinces beyond the sea so different from that of the Roman possessions in Italy. The regulations for the rule of the provinces were made in each case by the Roman Senate, and on the whole they were not oppressive. But the Senate made no provisions for compelling the Roman governor to obey these regulations.

**887.** Establishment of Roman provinces

Such a governor, enjoying unlimited power like that of an oriental sovereign, found himself far from home with Roman troops at his elbow awaiting his slightest command. He had complete control of all the taxes of the province, and he could take what he needed from its people to support his troops and the expenses of his government. He usually held office for a single year and was generally without experience in provincial government. His eagerness to gain a fortune in his short term

**888.** The unlimited power and corruption of the Roman provincial governors

of office and his complete ignorance of the needs of his province frequently reduced his government to a mere system of looting and robbery. The Senate soon found it necessary to have laws passed for the punishment of such abuses; but these laws were found to be of little use in improving the situation.

**889.** The new wealth of Rome

The effects of this situation were soon apparent in Italy. In the first place, the income of the Roman government was so enormously increased that it was no longer necessary to collect direct taxes from Roman citizens. This new wealth was not confined to the State. The spoils from the wars were usually taken by the victorious commanders and their troops. At the same time the provinces were soon filled with Roman business men. There were contractors called publicans, who were allowed to collect the taxes for the State at a great profit (§ 623), or gained the right to work State lands. We remember the common references to these publicans in the New Testament, where they are regularly classified with " sinners." With them came Roman money-lenders, who enriched themselves by loaning money at high rates of interest to the numerous provincials who were obliged to borrow to pay the extortionate taxes claimed by the Roman governors. The publicans were themselves money-lenders, and all these men of money plundered the provinces worse than the greedy Roman governors themselves. As these people returned to Italy, there grew up a wealthy class such as had been unknown there before.

**890.** Growth of commerce and the rise of banking

Their ability to buy resulted in a vast import trade to supply the demand. From the Bay of Naples to the mouth of the Tiber the sea was white with Roman ships converging on the docks of Rome. The men who controlled all this traffic became wealthy merchants. To handle all the money in circulation, banks were required. During the Hannibalic War the first banks appeared at Rome occupying a line of booths on each side of the Forum. After 200 B.C. these booths gave way to a fine basilica (§ 732) like those which had appeared in the Hellenistic cities (Fig. 271, 3). Here the new wealthy class met to transact financial business, and here large companies were formed for the collection of taxes and for taking government contracts to build roads and bridges or to erect public buildings. Shares in such companies were daily sold, and a business like that of a modern stock exchange developed in the Forum.

Under these influences Rome greatly changed. With increasing wealth and growing population, there was a great increase in the demand for dwellings. Rents at once rose, and land in the city greatly increased in value. A good form of paying investment was apartments for rent, and as the value of property rose, a larger return in rents could be secured by increasing the number of floors. Hence owners began to erect tall buildings with

891. Rome becomes a profitable real-estate center

FIG. 240. AN OLD ROMAN ATRIUM-HOUSE

There was no attempt at beautiful architecture, and the bare front showed no adornment whatever. The opening in the roof, which lighted the atrium (§ 892), received the rainfall of a section of the roof sloping toward it, and this water collected in a pool built to receive it in the floor of the atrium below (Fig. 241, *B*). The tiny area, or garden, shown in the rear was not common. It was here that the later Romans added the Hellenistic peristyle (Fig. 242)

several stories, though these ancient "skyscrapers" were never as tall as ours. It became necessary to limit their height by law, as we do, and when badly built, as they sometimes were, they fell down, as they have been known to do in our own cities.

When a returned governor of Africa put up a showy new house, the citizen across the way who still lived in his father's old house began to be dissatisfied with it. It was built of sun-dried brick, and, like the old settler's cabin of early America, it had but one room. In this room all the household life centered. The stool and spinning outfit of the wife and the bed of the

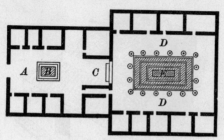

Fig. 241. Plan of a Roman House
with Peristyle

citizen were each assigned to a corner, while the kitchen was simply another corner where the family meals were cooked over an open fire. There was no chimney, and the smoke passed out of a square hole in the middle of the roof. The whole place was so begrimed by smoke that the room was called the *atrium*, a word perhaps connected with the Latin word for "black" (Fig. 240). Here, then, the family took their meals, here they slept, and here in full view of pots and kettles,

The earliest Roman house had consisted of a single room, the atrium (*A*), with the pool for the rain water (*B*). Then a small alcove, or lean-to, was erected at the rear (*C*), as a room for the master of the house. Later the bedrooms on each side of the atrium were added. Finally, under the influence of Greek life (§ 893), the garden court (*D* and Fig. 242) with its surrounding colonnaded porch (peristyle) (Fig. 208) and a fountain in the middle (*E*) was built at the rear. Then a dining room, sitting room, and bedrooms were added, which opened on this court, and being without windows, they were lighted from the court through the doors. In town houses it was quite easy to partition off a shop, or even a whole row of shops, along the front or side of the house, as in the Hellenistic house (Fig. 208). The houses of Pompeii (Fig. 255) were almost all built in this way

beds and tables, the master of the house received his friends and transacted his affairs with business or official callers.

The Roman citizen of the new age had walked the streets of the Hellenistic cities. Indeed, he had long before been familiar with the comfort, luxury, and beauty with which the Greek houses of Capua and Naples were filled (§§ 728 and 738). At first he added bedrooms on either side of his atrium and an additional small room at its rear, as the master's office and private room. Soon, however, even the enlarged atrium-house

FIG. 242. PERISTYLE OF A POMPEIAN HOUSE

We must imagine ourselves standing with our backs toward the atrium (having immediately behind us the room *C* in Fig. 241). We look out into the court, the garden of the house (Fig. 241, *D*). The marble tables and statues and the marble fountain basin in the middle (Fig. 241, *E*), just as we see them here in the drawing, were all found by the excavators in their places, as they were covered by volcanic ashes over eighteen hundred years ago (Fig. 255). Here centered the family life, and here the children played about the court, brightened with flowers and the tinkling music of the fountains

(Fig. 240) was not large enough, and behind it was added the Hellenistic court surrounded by its colonnaded porch (Figs. 241 and 242), from which opened bedrooms, a dining room, a library, rest rooms, and at the rear the kitchen. As luxury increased a second story might be added to receive the bedrooms and perhaps the dining room also. The atrium then became a large and stately reception hall where the master of the house could display his wealth in statues, paintings, and other works of art — the trophies of war from the East.

**894. The luxurious furnishings and adornment of the wealthy Roman's house**

The old Roman houses had been unadorned and had contained nothing but the bare necessities. Carthaginian ambassadors had been much amused to recognize at successive dinners in Rome the same silver dishes which had been loaned around from house to house. Not long before the Carthaginian wars an ex-consul had been fined for having more than ten pounds' weight of silverware in his house. A generation later a wealthy Roman was using in his household silverware which weighed some ten thousand pounds. One of the Roman conquerors of Macedonia entered Rome with two hundred and fifty wagonloads of Greek statues and paintings. The general who crushed the Ætolians carried off over five hundred bronze and marble statues, while the destroyer of Carthage filled all Rome with Greek sculptures. A wealthy citizen in even so small a city as Pompeii paved a dining alcove with a magnificent mosaic picture of Alexander in battle (Fig. 202), which had once formed a floor in a splendid Hellenistic house in Alexandria. In the same way the finest furniture, hangings, and carpets of the East now began to adorn the houses of the wealthy in Rome.

**895. The new conveniences and luxuries of the wealthy Roman household**

All those conveniences which we have found in the Hellenistic dwellings (§ 728) were likewise quickly introduced, such as pipes for running water, baths, and sanitary conveniences. The more elaborate houses were finally equipped with tile pipes conducting hot air for warming the important rooms, the earliest system of hot-air heating yet found. The kitchen was furnished with beautiful bronze utensils, far better than those commonly found in our own kitchens (Fig. 243). On social occasions the food on the table included imported delicacies and luxuries, purchased at enormous expense. A jar of salted fish from the Black Sea cost seventy-five or eighty dollars, and the old-fashioned senator Cato, in a speech in the Senate, protested against such

PLATE VII · THE GREEK THEATER AT TAORMINA, WITH ITS ROMAN ADDITIONS

The Greek colony (§ 441) of Tauromenium (modern Taormina) was on the east coast of Sicily (map, p. 484). We here look down from the seats of the theater, across the stage below (§ 898), where a gap in the Roman colonnade behind the stage reveals a long vista of the beautiful Sicilian shore; while in the distance towers the majestic volcano of Etna (nearly 11,000 feet high), often displaying a wisp of smoke above its crown of snow

luxury, stating that "Rome was the only city in the world where such a jar of fish cost more than a yoke of oxen."

Such luxury required a great body of household servants. There was a doorkeeper at the front door (he was called "janitor" from the Latin word *janua*, meaning "door"), and from

**896. Numerous household servants chiefly slaves**

FIG. 243. BRONZE KITCHEN UTENSILS EXCAVATED AT POMPEII

This kitchen ware used by the cooks of Pompeii was found still lying in the kitchens of the houses as they were uncovered by the excavators. The pieces have been lettered, and the student will find it interesting to make a list of them by name, identifying them by letter and indicating their use as far as possible

the front door inward there was a servant for every small duty in the house, even to the attendant who rubbed down the master of the house after his bath. Almost all these menials were slaves, but it was not always possible to secure a slave as cook, and a wealthy Roman would pay as much as five thousand dollars a year for a really good cook.

While the effect of all this luxury introduced from the East
was on the whole very bad, nevertheless the former plain,
matter-of-fact, prosaic life of the Roman citizen was stimulated
and refined both at home and in the Senate hall by the most
beautiful creations of Greek genius. Even while eating his
dinner, the commonplace citizen of Pompeii sat looking at the
heroic death of the Persian nobles of Darius (Fig. 202). But
there were never any *Roman* artists capable of producing such
works as these.

A Roman senator returning from Alexandria could not but
feel that Rome, in spite of some new and modern buildings,
was very plain and unattractive, with its simple temples and
old public buildings; and he realized that Alexandria was the
greatest and most splendid city in the world. Roman emula-
tion was aroused and forms of Hellenistic architecture, like the
basilica on the Forum (§ 890), were beginning to appear in
Rome. It was not long, too, before a Greek theater appeared,
improved by the Romans with awnings to keep out the hot
sunshine, a curtain in front of the stage, like ours, and seats
in the orchestra circle where once the Greek chorus had sung
(Plate VII, p. 558).

At the close of the Sicilian War (241 B.C.) a Greek slave
named Andronicus, who had been taken as a lad by the Romans
when they captured the Greek city of Tarentum (§ 824), was
given his freedom by his master at Rome. Seeing the interest
of the Romans in Greek literature, he translated the Odyssey
(§ 410) into Latin as a schoolbook for Roman children. For
their elders he likewise rendered into Latin the classic tragedies which we have seen in Athens (§ 579), and also a
number of Attic comedies (§ 582). This worthy Greek, Andronicus, was the first literary man in history to attempt
artistic translations possessing literary finish. He was, therefore, the founder of the art of literary translation. Through
his work the materials and the forms of Greek literature
began to enter Roman life.

The Romans had been accustomed to do very little in the way of educating their children. There were no schools at first, but the good old Roman custom had been for the father to instruct his own children. Even when schools arose, there was no literature for the Roman lads to learn, as Greek boys had learned Homer and the other poets (§ 555). The Roman father's respect for law and order led him to have his son taught the "Twelve Tables" of the law, and recite them to the schoolmaster, as English-speaking children are taught the Ten Commandments. Such schools had been very poorly equipped; some of them, indeed, were held in the open air in a side street or a corner of the Forum. At best they had met in a bare room belonging to a dwelling house, and there were no schoolhouses.

900. The old-fashioned Roman schools

Gradually parents began to send their children to the schools which the freed Greek slaves of Rome were beginning to open there. Moreover, there was here and there a household which possessed an educated Greek slave, like Andronicus, who might become the tutor of the children, giving regular instruction and teaching his pupils to read from the new primer of Andronicus, as we may call his Latin translation of Homer. Now and then Greek teachers of renown appeared and lectured in Rome. Young Roman nobles thus gained the opportunity of studying rhetoric and public speaking, which they knew to be of great practical use in the career of public office to which they all aspired. Indeed, it was not uncommon for a young Roman of station to complete his higher education in Athens itself (§ 762).

901. Greek influences in the new education in Rome

As Rome gained control of Greece, the mingling of Greek and Roman life was increasingly intimate. When a thousand of the leading Achæans were brought to Rome as hostages (§ 884), there was among them a Greek statesman of great refinement and literary culture named Polybius. He was taken into the family of the Scipios, traveled about with them on their great campaigns, and occupied a position of dignity and respect. He witnessed the destruction of both Carthage and

902. The influence of cultivated Greeks in Rome; Polybius

Corinth, and finally wrote an immortal history, in Greek, of
the great Roman wars. Such cultivated Greeks had a great
influence on the finer Romans like the Scipios. Polybius tells
how he stood with the younger Scipio and watched the burning of Carthage, while his young Roman lord burst into tears
and quoted Homer's noble lines regarding the destruction
of Troy.

**903.** Greek
foundations
of Latin
literature

Such familiarity with the only literature known to the Romans,
such daily and hourly intimacy with cultivated Greeks, aroused
the impulse toward literary expression among the Romans
themselves. To be sure, the Latins, like all peasant peoples,
had had their folk songs and their simple forms of verse, but
these natural products of the soil of Latium soon disappeared
as the men of Latin speech felt the influence of an already
highly finished literature. Latin literature, therefore, did not
develop along its own lines from native beginnings, as did
Greek literature, but it grew up on the basis of a great inheritance from abroad. Indeed, we now see, as the Roman poet
Horace said, that Rome, the conqueror, was herself conquered
by the civilization of the Greeks.

**904.** Rise
of Latin
literature

Poets and writers of history now arose in Italy, and educated
Romans could read of the great deeds of their ancestors in long
epic poems modeled on those of Homer. In such literature were
gradually recorded the picturesque legends of early Rome, like
the story of Romulus and Remus and similar tales (p. 484, note),
extending down through the early kings (p. 497, note). It is
from these sources, now no longer regarded as history, that the
early history of Rome used to be drawn. The Greek comedies
of Menander (§ 754) attracted the Romans greatly; imitating these, the new Latin play writers, especially Plautus (died
about 184 B.C.) and Terence (died about 159 B.C.), produced
very clever comedies caricaturing the society of Rome, to which
the Romans listened with uproarious delight. Their production
on the stage led to the highly developed theater buildings which
we have already mentioned (§ 898).

As the new Latin literature grew, papyrus rolls bearing Latin works were more and more common in Rome. Then publishers, in back rooms filled with slave copyists, began to appear in the city. One of the Roman conquerors of Macedon brought back the books of the Macedonian king, and founded the first private library in Rome. Wealthy Romans were now providing library rooms in their houses. A group of literary men arose, including the finest of the Roman leaders, and no man could claim to belong to this cultivated world without acquaintance with a well-stocked library of Greek and Latin books. Such Romans spoke Greek almost if not quite as well as Latin. These educated men were finally in sharp contrast with the uneducated mass of the Roman people, and there thus arose the two classes, educated and uneducated — a distinction unknown in the days of the early farmer republic.

905. Publishers, libraries, and the educated class

## Section 82. Degeneration in City and Country

The new life of Greek culture and luxury brought with it many evils. Even the younger Scipio, an ardent friend of Greek literature and art, expressed his pained surprise at finding Roman boys in a Greek dancing school, learning unwholesome dances, just as many worthy people among us disapprove of the new dances now widely cultivated in America. Cato, one of the hardiest of the old-fashioned Romans, denounced the new culture and the luxury which had come in with it (§ 895). As censor he had the power to stop many of the luxurious new practices, and he spread terror among the showy young dandies and ladies of fashion in Rome. He and other Romans like him succeeded in passing law after law against expensive habits of many kinds, like the growing love of showy jewelry among the women, or their use of carriages where they formerly went on foot. But such laws could not prevent the slow corruption of the people. The old simplicity, purity, and beauty of Roman family life was disappearing, and divorce was

906. Corrupting influences of the new luxury; laws against extravagance

becoming common. The greatest days of Roman character were past, and Roman power was to go on growing, without the restraining influence of old Roman virtue.

**907.** Inability of the masses to appreciate Greek literature

This was especially evident in the lives of the uneducated and poorer classes also. To them, as indeed to the vast majority of all classes, Greek civilization was chiefly attractive because of the numerous luxuries of Hellenistic life. The common people had no comprehension of Greek civilization. At the destruction of Corinth, Polybius saw Roman soldiers shaking dice on a wonderful old Greek painting which they had torn down from the wall and spread out on the ground like an old piece of awning. When a cultivated Roman thought to gain popular favor by arranging a program of Greek instrumental music at a public entertainment, the audience stopped the performance and shouted to the musicians to throw down their instruments and begin a boxing match! Contrast this with the Athenian public in the days of Pericles!

**908.** Gladiatorial combats as a political influence

It was to Roman citizens with tastes like these that the leaders of the new age were obliged to turn for votes and for support in order to gain office. To such tastes, therefore, the Roman nobles began to appeal. Early in the Sicilian War with Carthage there had been introduced the old Etruscan custom of single combats between condemned criminals or slaves, who slew each other to honor the funeral of some great Roman. These combatants came to be called gladiators, from a Latin word *gladius*, meaning " sword." The delight of the Roman people in these bloody displays was such that the officials in charge of the various public feasts, without waiting for a funeral, used to arrange a long program of such combats in the hope of pleasing the people, and thus gaining their votes and securing election to future higher offices.

**909.** Amphitheater for gladiatorial combats, and circuses for chariot races

These barbarous and bloody spectacles took place at first within a temporary circle of seats, which finally became a great stone structure especially built for the purpose. It was called an amphitheater, because it was formed by placing two (*amphi*)

theaters face to face (Fig. 262). Soon afterward combats between gladiators and wild beasts were introduced (headpiece,
p. 549). The athletic contests which had so interested the
Greeks were far too tame for the appetite of the Roman public.
The chariot race, however, did appeal to the Romans, and they
began to build enormous courses surrounded by seats for vast
numbers of spectators. These buildings they called circuses.

The common people of Rome were thus gradually debased
and taught to expect such public spectacles, sometimes lasting
for days, as their share of the plunder from the great conquests. At the same time, as their poverty increased, the free
food once furnished them by the wealthy classes far exceeded
what private donors were able to give. It was therefore taken
up by the State, which arranged regular distributions of grain
to the populace. Vicious as this custom was, it was far from
being so great an evil as the bribery which the candidates for
office now secretly practiced. Laws passed to prevent the
practice were of slight effect. The only Roman citizens who
could vote were those who attended the assemblies at Rome,
and henceforth we have only too often the spectacle of a
Roman candidate controlling the government that ruled the
world by bribing the little body of citizens who attended the
Roman assemblies.

910. Distri-
bution of
free grain
to the poor,
and bribery

All these practices enormously increased the expenses of a
political career. The young Roman, who formerly might have
demonstrated his ability and his worthy character in some minor
office as a claim upon the votes of the community, was now
obliged to borrow money to pay for a long program of gladiatorial games. In secret he might also spend a large sum in
bribing voters. If elected he received no salary, and in carrying on the business of his office he was again obliged to meet
heavy expenses. For the Roman government had never been
properly equipped with clerks, bookkeepers, and accountants;
that is, the staff of public servants whom we call the "civil
service." The newly elected official, therefore, had to supply

911. Ex-
penses of
a political
career; lack
of a civil
service

a staff of clerks at his own expense. Even a consul sat at home in a household room turned into an office and carried on government business with his own clerks and accountants, of whom one was usually a Greek.

**912. Growth of self-interest; the unrepublican character of returned provincial governors**

The Roman politician now sought office, in order that through it he might gain the influence which would bring him the governorship of a rich province. If he finally gained his object, he often reached his province burdened with debts incurred in winning elections in Rome. But the prize of a large province was worth all it cost. Indeed, the consulship itself was finally regarded as merely a stepping-stone to a provincial governorship. When a retired provincial governor returned to Rome, he was no longer the simple Roman of the good old days. He lived like a prince and, as we have seen, he surrounded himself with royal luxury. These men of self-interest, who had held the supreme power in a province, were a menace to the republic, for they had tasted the power of kings without the restraints of Roman law and Roman republican institutions to hamper them.

**913. Growth of great estates; decline of the small farms**

But the evils of the new wealth were not less evident in the *country*. It was not thought proper for a Roman senator or noble to undertake commercial enterprises or to engage in any business. The most respectable form of wealth was lands. Hence the successful Roman noble bought farm after farm, which he combined into a great estate or plantation. The capitalists who had plundered the provinces did the same. Looking northward from Rome, the old Etruscan country was now made up of extensive estates belonging to wealthy Romans of the city. Only here and there were still to be found the little farms of the good old Roman days. Large portions of Italy were in this condition. The small farm seemed in a fair way to disappear as it had done in Greece (§ 626).

**914. Captives of war as slaves**

It was impossible for a wealthy landowner to work these great estates with free, hired labor. Nor was he obliged to do so. From the close of the Hannibalic War onward the Roman conquests had brought to Italy great numbers of captives of war from Carthage, Spain, Gaul, Macedonia, Greece, and Asia Minor. These unhappy prisoners were sold as slaves. The coast of the Adriatic opposite Italy alone yielded one hundred and fifty thousand captives. An ordinary day laborer would bring about three hundred dollars at auction, a craftsman or a good clerk was much more valuable, and a young woman who could play the lyre would bring a thousand dollars. The sale of such captives was thus enormously profitable. We have already seen such slaves in the households at Rome. The estates of Italy were now filled with them.

Household slavery was usually not attended with much hardship, but the life of the slaves on the great plantations was little better than that of beasts. Worthy and free-born men from the eastern Mediterranean were branded with a hot iron like oxen, to identify them forever. They were herded at night in cellar barracks, and in the morning were driven like half-starved beasts of burden to work in the fields. The green fields of Italy, where sturdy farmers once watched the growing grain sown and cultivated by their own hands, were now worked by wretched and hopeless creatures who wished they had never been born. When the supply of captives from the wars failed, the Roman government winked at the practices of slave pirates, who carried on wholesale kidnaping in the Ægean and eastern Mediterranean for years. They sold the victims in the slave market at Delos, whence they were brought by Roman merchants to Italy. **915. Brutal treatment of plantation slaves**

Thus Italy and Sicily were fairly flooded with slaves. The brutal treatment which they received was so unbearable that at various places in Italy they finally rose against their masters. Even when they did not revolt, they were a grave danger to public safety. The lonelier roads of Italy were infested by slave herdsmen, lawless ancient cowboys who robbed and slew and in many districts made it unsafe to live in the country or travel the country roads. The conditions in Sicily were worse than in Italy. In central and southern Sicily the revolting **916. Slave revolts and disorders** slaves gathered some sixty thousand in number, slew their masters, captured towns, and set up a kingdom. It required a Roman consul at the head of an army and a war lasting several years to subdue them.

**917. Hostility between the rich and the poor, especially the small farmers** During the uprising of the slaves in Sicily the small farm owners, *free men*, went about burning the fine villas of the wealthy plantation proprietors. The slave rebellion therefore was a revelation of the hatred not only among the slaves but also among the poor farming class of *freemen* — the hatred toward the rich landowners felt by *all* the lower classes in the country, slave or free. The great conquests and the wealth they brought in had made the rich so much richer and the poor so much poorer that the two classes were completely thrust apart and they no longer had any common life. Italy was divided into two great social classes dangerously hostile to each other. The bulk of the population of Italy had formerly been small farmers, as we have seen. Let us examine the effect of the great wars on the small farmers.

**918. Destruction of farms and farm life in Italy by war** War seemed a great and glorious thing when we were following the brilliant victories of Hannibal and the splendid triumph of Scipio at Zama. But now we are to see the other side of the picture. Never has there been an age in which the terrible and desolating results of war have so tragically revealed the awful cost of such glory. The happy and industrious families cultivating the little farms which dotted the green hills and plains of Italy had now been helplessly scattered by the storms of war, as the wind drives the autumn leaves. The campaigns of Hannibal left southern Italy desolate far and wide, and much of central Italy was in little better condition. These devastated districts left lying waste were never again cultivated, and slowly became pasture lands. In regions untouched by invasion, fathers and elder sons had been absent from home for years holding their posts in the legion, fighting the battles which brought Rome her great position as mistress of the world. If the soldier returned he often found the monotonous round of farm duties much too tedious after his adventurous life of war abroad. Leaving the plow, therefore, he returned to his place in the legion to resume the exciting life of war and plunder under some great leader whom he loved. Home life and wholesome country influences were undermined and broken up. The mothers, left to bring up the younger children alone, saw the family scattered and drifting away from the little farm, till it was left forsaken.

Too often as the returning soldier approached the spot where he was born he no longer found the house that had sheltered his childhood. His family was gone and his little farm, sold for debt, had been bought up by some wealthy Roman of the city and absorbed into a great plantation like those which the Romans had found surrounding Carthage (§ 837). His neighbors, too, had disappeared and their farms had likewise gone to enlarge the rich man's great estate. Across the hills on a sunny eminence he saw the stately villa, the home of the Roman noble, who now owned the farms of all the surrounding country. He cursed the wealth which had done all this, and wandered up to the great city to look for free grain from the government, to enjoy the games and circuses, and to increase the poor class already there.

**919.** The small farms bought up by wealthy plantation owners

Or if he found his home and his little farm uninjured, and was willing to settle down to work its fields as of old, he was soon aware that the hordes of slaves now cultivating the great plantations around him were producing grain so cheaply, that when he had sold his harvest he had not received enough for it to enable him and his family to live. At the same time the markets of Italy were filled with cheap grain from Sicily, Africa, and Egypt. With this imported grain often given away by the government, he could not compete, and slowly he fell behind; he borrowed money, and his debts increased. Forced to sell the little farm at last, he too wandered into Rome, where he found thousands upon thousands of his kind, homeless, embittered, and dependent upon the State for food.

**920.** Inability of the farmer to compete with slave labor and cheap imported grain

**921. Degeneration and discontent in Italy**

The sturdy farmer-citizens who had made up the bulk of the citizenship of Rome, the yeomanry from whom she had drawn her splendid armies, — these men who had formed the very substance of the power upon which the Roman Senate had built up its world empire, were now perishing. After the Macedonian wars the census returns showed a steady decline in the number of citizens of the republic in Italy. At the same time there was serious discontent among the cities of the allies in Italy because they had never been given full citizenship. They saw the government of a world empire in the hands of a corrupt Senate and a small body of more and more brutalized citizens at Rome, and they demanded their share in the control of the great empire to whose armies they had contributed as many troops as the citizens of the Republic had done.

**922. Economic and agricultural decline in Greece**

The wealth and power which Roman world dominion had gained had thus brought Rome and Italy to the verge of destruction. Nor was the situation any better in the most civilized portions of the empire outside of Italy, and especially in Greece. Under the large plantation system, introduced from Asia Minor, where it had grown up under the Persians (§ 269), the Greek farmers had disappeared (§ 626), as those of Italy were now beginning to do. Add to this condition the robberies and extortions of the Roman taxgatherers and governors, the continuous slave raids of the Ægean pirates, whose pillaging and kidnaping the Roman Republic criminally failed to prevent, the shift of Greek commerce eastward (§ 724), and we have reasons enough for the destruction of business, of agriculture, and of prosperity in the Greek world.

**923. Decline of Hellenistic civilization**

But that wondrous development of higher civilization which we found in the Hellenistic world (Chap. XXI) was likewise showing signs of decline. The sumptuous buildings forming the great home of science in Alexandria (§ 743) now represented little more than the high aims once cherished and supported by the Macedonian kings of Egypt. For when such State support failed, with its salaries and pensions to scientists and philosophers, the line of scientists failed too. Hence we see how largely science in the Hellenistic Age was rooted in the treasuries of the Hellenistic kings, rather than in the minds of the Greek race as it had been of old, when for sheer love of knowledge the Greek philosopher carried on his studies without such support.

The Mediterranean was now the home of Greek civilization in the East and of Roman civilization in the West, but the failure of the Roman Senate to organize a successful government for the empire they had conquered, — a government even as good as that of Persia under Darius (§ 286), — this failure had brought the whole world of Mediterranean civilization perilously near destruction. In the European background beyond the Alpine frontiers, there were rumblings of vast movements among the northern barbarians, threatening to descend as of old and completely overwhelm the civilization which for over three thousand years had been slowly built up by Orientals and Greeks and Romans in the Mediterranean world. It now looked very much as if the Roman State was about to perish, and with it the civilization which had been growing for so many centuries. Was civilized man indeed to perish from the earth? Or would the Roman State be able to survive and to preserve civilization from destruction?

**924.** Failure of Roman government of the Mediterranean world; perilous situation of civilization

Rome was a city-state. The finest fruits of civilization in art, literature, science, and thought had been produced under the government of city-states, as we have seen (§ 767). But among the Greeks this very limited form of state had outlived its usefulness and had over and over again proved its inability to organize and control successfully a larger world, that is, an empire. The city-state of the Roman Republic had now also demonstrated that its limited machinery of government was quite unfitted to rule successfully the vast Mediterranean world which it was now endeavoring to control. Would it be able to transform itself into a great imperial State, with all the many offices necessary to give

**925.** The failure of the city-state in imperial government

successful government to the peoples and nations surrounding the Mediterranean? Would it then be able to do for the Mediterranean world what the oriental empires had once done for a world equally large in Western Asia and Egypt?

**926.** The responsibility of Rome to organize and defend the civilization of the Mediterranean world

We stand at the point where the civilization of the Hellenistic world began to decline, after the destruction of Carthage and Corinth (146 B.C.). We are now to watch the Roman people in the deadly internal struggle which we have seen impending between rich and poor. They had at the same time to continue their rule of the Mediterranean world as best they could, while the dangerous internal transformation was going on. In the midst of these grave responsibilities they had also to face the barbarian hordes of the North. In spite of all these threatening dangers, we shall see them gaining the needed imperial organization which enabled the Roman State to hurl back the Northern barbarians, to hold the northern frontiers for five hundred years, and thus to preserve the civilization which had cost mankind so many centuries of slow progress — the civilization which, because it was so preserved, has become our own inheritance to-day. This achievement of Rome we are now to follow in the final chapters of the story of the ancient world.

### QUESTIONS

SECTION 80. As mistress of the western Mediterranean world, what was to be Rome's attitude toward the other nations of the Mediterranean? Why was Rome bound to subdue Philip of Macedon? Describe the struggle between Rome and Macedon. By extending her power over Macedon, with what other eastern empire was Rome in contact? Describe the struggle between Rome and the Seleucid Empire. What then happened to Macedon? to the Greeks? What two splendid cities were destroyed in the same year by the Romans? What can you say of the rapidity of the Roman conquests? Describe the task of government now confronting Rome.

SECTION 81. Had the Romans any experience in governing provinces? Describe the rule of the usual Roman governor. What can you say of the increase of Roman wealth? What was the effect on business at Rome? What kind of a house had the Roman formerly lived in? What kind did he now build? How was it furnished, and whence did its luxuries often come? How did this compare with the situation before the Carthaginian wars? What can you say of the servants in a wealthy household? Describe the effect of Greek works of art in Rome. Were there any Roman artists equal to those in Greece? Tell how Greek literature became known in Rome. Describe the old Roman schools. How did educated Greeks affect teaching in Rome? Tell about Polybius. How did Latin literature arise? What can you say of libraries and the educated class?

SECTION 82. How was the new luxury affecting Roman life? What were the tastes of the ordinary Roman? Describe the rise of gladiatorial combats. What can you say about the expenses of a political career? What was happening to the small farms? Describe slavery on the large estates; slave revolts. Describe the effect of the wars on the small farmers; the effect of the large estates and cheap grain. Describe the situation of Italy as a whole; of Greece and the Ægean world. What was the situation of Hellenistic civilization as a whole? How then had Roman leadership of the Mediterranean world succeeded thus far? Did a city-state possess the organization fitted to rule a great empire? What three great tasks faced the Roman government: first in Italy, second in the whole Mediterranean world, and third on the northern and eastern frontiers?

NOTE. The sketch below shows us a corner of a Roman library. The books are all in the form of rolls (Fig. 191), arranged in large pigeonhole sections like rolls of wall paper, with the ends pointing outward and bearing tags containing the titles of the books. Thus the librarian was quickly able to find a given book or to return it to the shelves at the proper place, as he is engaged in doing in this relief.

# CHAPTER XXVI

## A CENTURY OF REVOLUTION AND THE END OF THE REPUBLIC

### SECTION 83. THE LAND SITUATION AND THE BEGINNING OF THE STRUGGLE BETWEEN SENATE AND PEOPLE

**927. The dangerous situation to be met by the Senate**

We must now recall the problems noticed at the close of the last chapter, demanding settlement by the Roman Senate. In Italy there was in the first place the perilous condition of the surviving farmers and the need of increasing in some way their numbers and their farms. Equally dangerous was the discontent of the Italian allies, who had never been given the vote or the right to hold office. The problems outside of Italy were not less pressing. They were, likewise, two in number. There were first the thoroughgoing reform of provincial government and the creation of a system of honest and successful administration of the vast Roman conquests. And second there were the settlement of the frontier boundaries and the repulse of the invading barbarians who were

NOTE. The above headpiece shows us the two sides of a coin issued by Brutus, one of the leading assassins of Julius Cæsar (§ 969). On one side the coin bears the head of Brutus, accompanied by his name and the title Imperator (abbreviated to IMP). On the other side are two daggers, intended to recall the assassination of Cæsar, and between them appears the cap of liberty, to suggest the liberty which the Romans supposedly gained by his murder. In order that the meaning of all this might be perfectly clear, there appears, below, the inscription EID MAR, which means the Ides of March (the Roman term for the fifteenth of March), the date of Cæsar's murder (§ 969).

threatening to crush the Mediterranean world and its civilization, as the prehistoric Greeks had crushed Ægean civilization (§ 380).

The Senate which was to meet this dangerous situation had been in practical control of the Roman government since the days of the Samnite War. The senators now formed an oligarchy of selfish aristocrats as in the Greek cities (§ 618). Yet there were no laws which had created the undisputed power of the Senate. It was merely by their great prestige and their combined influence as leading men and former magistrates (§ 811) that they maintained the control of the State. The *legal* power of the Roman State really rested in the hands of the Roman people, as they gathered in their assemblies (§ 806), and this power had never been surrendered to the Senate by any vote or any law.

928. Shortcomings of the Senate and lack of a legal basis for their power

The crying needs of the farming class in Italy failed to produce any effect upon the blinded and selfish aristocrats of the Senate as a whole. Even before the Hannibalic War the need of newly distributed farm lands was sorely felt. Led by the brave Flaminius, who afterward as consul fell at the head of his army in Hannibal's ambush at Trasimene (§ 862), the Assembly had passed a law in defiance of the Senate, providing for a distribution of public lands which the senators desired for themselves and their friends of the noble class. As a result Flaminius was always hated by the senatorial party, and ever after was regarded as the popular leader who opened the struggle between people and Senate, and having thus shown the people their power, had begun the dangerous policy of allowing the unstable populace to control the government. The conflict between Senate and people had subsided during the Hannibalic War, but when this great danger had passed, it would seem that a tribune named Licinius, who understood the needs of the people, had succeeded in having a law passed by the Assembly, which forbade any wealthy citizen from holding over five hundred acres of the public lands, or pasturing more than a hundred cattle or five hundred sheep on

929. The assignment of new farms to landless farmers and the opening of the struggle between Senate and people

these lands. Such was the power of the senatorial party, however, that these Licinian laws had become a dead letter.[1]

**930. The absorption of the public lands by the nobles**

In gaining control of Italy, Rome had finally annexed about half of the peninsula, and no more land could now be taken without seizing that of the Italian allies. About a decade before the destruction of Carthage and Corinth the last Roman colony had been founded. The only way to secure new farms for assignment to landless farmers was by making the Licinian laws effective, that is, by taking and assigning to farmers the public lands already belonging to the State — what we call "government lands" in the United States. But for generations these lands had been largely held under all sorts of arrangements by wealthy men, and it was sometimes difficult to decide whether a noble's estate was his legal property or merely public land which he was using. Under these circumstances we can easily imagine with what stubbornness and anger great landholders of the senatorial party would oppose any effort to redistribute the public lands on a basis fair to all.

**931. Tiberius Gracchus, tribune (133 B.C.)**

Flaminius had taught the people their power (§ 929). Since then they had lacked a skillful leader. The unselfish patriot who undertook to become the leader of the people and to save Italy from destruction by restoring the farmer class was a noble named Tiberius Gracchus. He was a grandson of the elder Scipio, the hero of Zama, and his sister had married the younger Scipio. Elected tribune (133 B.C.), he used to address the people with passionate eloquence and tell them of their wrongs: "The beasts that prowl about Italy have holes and lurking places, where they may make their beds. You who fight and die for Italy enjoy only the blessings of air and light. These alone are your heritage. Homeless, unsettled, you wander to and fro with your wives and children. . . . You fight and die to give wealth and luxury to others. You are called the masters of the world; yet there is no clod of earth that you can call your own."

---

[1] The usually accepted earlier date for the Licinian laws (376 B.C.) is quite impossible; nor is the date above suggested at all certain.

As tribune, Tiberius Gracchus submitted to the Assembly a law for the reassignment of public lands and the protection and support of the farming class. It was a statesmanlike and moderate law. It called for little, if anything, more than what was already demanded by the Licinian laws. It was an endeavor to do for Italy what Solon had done for Attica (§ 469), and was decidedly more moderate than the legislation of Solon. After a tragic struggle in which the new tribune resorted to methods not strictly legal, he succeeded in passing his law. In the effort to secure reëlection, that he might insure the *enforcement* of his law, Gracchus was slain by a mob of senators, who rushed out of the Senate house and attacked the tribune and his supporters. This was the first murderous deed introducing a century of revolution and civil war (133–31 B.C.), which terminated in the destruction of the Roman Republic.

932. Land laws of Tiberius Gracchus, and his death (132 B.C.)

Ten years after the tribunate of Tiberius Gracchus, his younger brother Gaius gained the same office (123 B.C.). He not only took up the struggle on behalf of the landless farmers, but he made it his definite object to attack and weaken the Senate. He endeavored to enlist on the side of the people every possible enemy of the Senate. He therefore organized the capitalists and men of large business affairs, who, of course, were not senators. Because of their wealth they had always furnished their own horses and served in the army as horsemen. They were therefore called knights; or, as a group, the equestrian order. Gaius Gracchus secured the support of these men by obtaining for them the right to collect the taxes in Asia, and he gave them great power by founding a court made up of knights for the trial of dishonest and extortionate Roman governors appointed by the Senate. At the same time he proposed to give to the Italian allies the long-desired full citizenship — a proposal which angered the people as much as it did the Senate. His efforts finally resulted in a riot in which Gaius Gracchus was killed, as his brother had been (121 B.C.).

933. Struggle of Gaius Gracchus with the Senate, and his death (123–121 B.C.)

## SECTION 84. THE RISE OF ONE-MAN POWER: MARIUS AND SULLA

**934.** Unreliability of popular support

The weakness in the reforms of the Gracchus brothers lay chiefly in their unavoidable reliance upon votes; that is, upon the unstable support of the people at the elections and at the meetings of the popular assembly. It was difficult to hold the interest of the people from election to election. In the Gracchan elections, when work on the farms was pressing, the country people around Rome would not take the time to go up to the city and vote, although they were the very ones to be benefited by the Gracchan laws. The work of Flaminius, and especially of the Gracchi, had taught the people to look up to a leader. This tendency was the beginning of one-man power. But the leader to whom the people now turned was not a magistrate, as the Gracchi had been, but a *military commander.*

**935.** The war with Jugurtha, and the appointment of the people's commander against the Senate

Meantime the blindness and corruption of the Senate offered the people more than one opportunity for gaining power. The misrule of the Senate abroad was now so scandalous that the people seized this opportunity. In a war between Rome and Jugurtha, ruler of the great kingdom of Numidia beside Carthage in North Africa, the African king, knowing the weakness of the Romans of this age, succeeded in bribing the consul, and thus inflicted a crushing defeat on the Roman army. The war then dragged disgracefully on. These events so incensed the people of Rome, that in spite of the fact that the Senate's commander. an able and honest consul named Metellus, had finally met and defeated Jugurtha, the Assembly passed a law appointing their own general to supersede Metellus. The *people* thus assumed charge of a great foreign enterprise, and, what was more important, *the people by this action seized control of the army.* The Senate was unable to prevent the Assembly's action from going into effect. The interests of the people were no longer dependent wholly upon civil magistrates, changing from election to election, but upon military force under a leader who might be given a long command.

The commander on whom the people relied was himself a man of the people, named Marius, who had once been a rough plowboy. He was fortunately an able soldier, and he quickly brought the war with Jugurtha to an end, after the Senate's leaders had allowed the war to drift on for six years. When the news of his victory reached Rome the people promptly elected him consul for the second time, before his return. In 104 B.C. he returned to Rome, and the people beheld the captive Numidian king led through the streets in chains. Meantime the two powerful tribes of German barbarians, the Cimbrians and the Teutons, combined with Gauls, had been shifting southward and crossing the northern frontiers of Rome. In Gaul and on the Gallic frontiers six Roman armies, one after another, had been disastrously defeated. It looked as if the Roman legions had at last met their match. There was great anxiety in Rome, and the people determined to reëlect Marius consul and send him against the terrible northern barbarians. Meeting the Teutons in southern Gaul, the people's hero not only defeated but practically destroyed the first German host (102 B.C.). Shortly afterward, when the Cimbrians had finally succeeded in crossing the Alps into the Po valley, Marius met and crushed them also. A soldier of the people had saved Rome.

Marius was not only an able soldier, but he was also a great organizer, and he introduced changes in the Roman army which were epoch-making both in the history of warfare and in the political history of Rome. In order to secure sufficient men for the legions, he abolished the old custom of allowing only citizens of property to serve in the army, and he took in the poor and the penniless. Such men soon became professional soldiers. As once in Greece (§ 629), so now in Rome, the day of the citizen-soldier had passed. The long wars had made many a Roman citizen practically a professional soldier, as we have noticed. The army of Marius was largely a professional army, and although the obligation to serve in the army still rested on every Roman citizen, it was less and less rigidly enforced.

**938.** The cohort as the tactical unit, devised by Marius

The youths who permanently took up the life of the soldier could be so well drilled that they were able to carry out maneuvers impossible for an army made up of citizens serving for a limited time. Marius therefore completely reorganized the legion. He raised its numbers from forty-five hundred to six thousand. He divided each six thousand into ten groups of six hundred each. Such a body of six hundred was called a *cohort*. It formed the unit in the shifting maneuvers, which, as we have seen, meant victory or defeat in battle (§ 874). So perfectly drilled and so fearless were these units, that the cohorts would move about the field with the precision of clockwork and with complete confidence in the plan of the commander, just as the individuals in a perfectly trained football squad respond almost automatically to the signal. The production of the cohort, as we shall see, made it possible to complete the final chapter in the development of the art of warfare in ancient times.

**939.** Failure of Marius as a statesman; the Senate regains leadership

But in spite of his ability as a soldier and as an army organizer, Marius was not a statesman. Having risen from the ranks, he was at heart a rough Roman peasant. He hated the aristocrats of the city; he did not know how to deal with them, nor did he understand the leadership of the popular party which had given him his great military commands. Elected consul for the sixth time in the year 100 B.C., he failed utterly to control the leaders of his party in the political struggles in Rome. They went to such excesses that two of them were slain in a riot. Moderate men were estranged from the cause of the people, and the Senate gained the upper hand again. Marius retired in disgrace, but his leadership had revealed to the people how they might gain control over the Senate by combining on a *military* leader, whose power, therefore, did not consist in the peaceful enforcement of the laws and usages of the Roman State, but in the illegal application of military force.

Meantime the struggle between Senate and people was complicated by the increasing discontent of the Italian allies. They had contributed as many troops to the conquering armies as had Rome herself, and now they were refused any voice in the control of the conquered territory or any share in the immense wealth which they saw the Romans drawing from it. The wise and liberal policy of the ancient Senate in freely granting citizenship to communities in newly acquired Italian territory (§ 814) had been long abandoned, reminding us of the Athenians in the later years of Pericles (§ 588). Before the different communities of Italy had had time to merge into a nation (§ 828), they had been forced into a long series of foreign wars which had made vast conquests. But the possession of these conquests had corrupted and blinded the Senate and the governing community at Rome. By this sudden wealth and power Rome had been raised above all feeling of fellowship with the other communities of Italy. The great peninsula was still filled with disunited communities (§ 829), and there now rested upon Rome the obligation to make Italy a nation.

940. Disunion in Italy and discontent of the Italian allies

There were, happily, some Roman leaders with the insight of statesmen, who perceived this great need and who planned that the Italian allies should receive citizenship. Among them was a wealthy, popular, and unselfish noble named Drusus, who gained election as tribune and began measures leading to the enfranchisement of the Italian allies. But so fierce and savage was the opposition aroused, that this great Roman statesman was stabbed in the street. The opposition to Drusus and his plans was by no means confined to the Senate. The common people of Rome were likewise jealous of their ancient privileges, and the wealthy men of the new equestrian order were equally unwilling to share their opportunities of plundering the provinces. The Italian allies therefore soon saw the hopelessness of an appeal to Rome for their rights. Immediately after the assassination of Drusus the leading Italian peoples of central and southern Italy revolted and formed a new state and

941. Blind exclusiveness of the Romans and assassination of Drusus (91 B.C)

government of their own, with a capital at a central town which they impressively renamed Italica (90 B.C.).

**942.** War with allies (Social War, 90–88 B.C.); citizenship given to all Italy

In the war which followed, the army of Rome was at first completely defeated, and although this reverse was in a measure retrieved, the strength of the allies could not be broken. Seeing the seriousness of the situation, the Roman politicians tardily took action and granted the desired citizenship. The Italian alliance then broke up, and the Italian communities reëntered the Roman State. Yet they entered it as distant wards of the city on the Tiber. The citizens residing in these distant wards could not vote or take any part in the government unless they journeyed to Rome to do so. This situation was of course an absurdity, and again illustrated the inability of an ancient city-state to furnish the machinery of government for a large nation, not to mention a world empire. Nevertheless, Italy was on the way to become a nation unified in government and in speech.

**943.** Rise of Sulla; a consul sustains the Senate and defeats the will of the people with an army

A very threatening war was now breaking out in Asia Minor. Wealthy senators and other Romans of the moneyed class who ruled Rome had many financial interests in this region, and this led them to dread a war there, and to stop it as soon as possible. Among the officers of Marius there had been a very successful soldier named Sulla, who was chosen consul for the year after the war with the allies. The Senate now selected him to command in Asia Minor. But the leaders of the people would not accept the Senate's appointment, and just as in the war against Jugurtha, they passed a law electing Marius to command in the coming Asia Minor war. Now Marius had no army at the moment, but Sulla was still at the head of the army he had been leading against the Italian allies. He therefore ignored the law passed by the people, and marched on Rome with his troops. For the first time a Roman consul took possession of the city by force. The Senate was now putting through its will with an army, as the Assembly had before done. Sulla forced through a new law by which the Assembly would always be obliged to secure the consent of the Senate before it could vote on any measure. Having thus destroyed the power of the people legally to oppose the will of the Senate, Sulla marched off to his command in Asia Minor.

The Senate had triumphed, but with the departure of Sulla and his legions the people refused to submit. There was fighting in the streets, and the senatorial troops fell upon the new Italian citizens as they voted in the Forum and slew them by hundreds. In the midst of these deeds of violence Marius, who had escaped to Africa, returned at the head of a body of cavalry. He joined the popular leaders, and, entering Rome, he began a frightful massacre of the leading men of the senatorial party. The Senate, the first to sow seeds of violence in the murder of Tiberius Gracchus (§ 932), now reaped a fearful harvest. Marius was elected consul for the seventh time, but he died a few days after his election (86 B.C.). Meantime the people ruled in Rome until the day of reckoning which was sure to come on the return of Sulla.

944. Restoration of people's control in Sulla's absence; war and murder in the streets of Rome

The war which had called Sulla to Asia Minor was due to the genius of Mithradates, the gifted young king of Pontus (see map IV, p. 552). He had prospered by taking advantage of Roman misrule in the East. He had rapidly extended his kingdom to include a large part of Asia Minor, and such was the deep-seated discontent of the Greek cities under Roman rule that he was able to induce the Greek states of Asia Minor and some in Greece to join him in a war against Rome. Even Athens, which had suffered least, supported him. The Romans, busily occupied with civil war at home, were thus suddenly confronted by a foe in the East who seemed as dangerous as Carthage had once been. Sulla besieged Athens (see description of cut, p. 425), recovered European Greece, and drove the troops of Mithradates back into Asia. Thereupon crossing to Asia Minor he finally concluded a peace with Mithradates. He laid an enormous indemnity of twenty thousand talents on the Greek cities of Asia Minor. Then leaving them to the tender

945. Sulla's campaign against Mithradates

mercies of the Roman money-lenders and to the barbarous raids of the eastern pirates, Sulla returned to Rome.

**946.** Sulla defeats the armies of the Roman people and is made Dictator (82 B.C.)

On the way thither the Roman army of Sulla defeated the Roman armies of the people, one after another. Finally, outside the gates of the city, Sulla overthrew the last army of the people and entered Rome as master of the State, without any legal power to exercise such mastery. By means of his army, however, he forced his own appointment as Dictator, with far greater powers than any Dictator had ever before possessed (82 B.C.). His first action was to begin the systematic slaughter of the leaders of the people's party and the confiscation of their property. Rome passed through another reign of terror like that which followed Marius's return. The hatreds and the many debts of revenge which Sulla's barbarities left behind were later a frequent source of disturbance and danger to the State (§ 951).

**947.** Sulla deprives the people of political power and gives the Senate supreme leadership (82–79 B.C.)

Then Sulla forced the passage of a whole series of new laws which deprived the Assembly of the people and the tribunes of their power, and gave the supreme leadership of the State to the Senate, the body which had already so disastrously failed to guide Rome wisely since the great conquests. Some lesser reforms of value Sulla did introduce, but a policy based on the supremacy of the Senate was doomed to failure. To Sulla's great credit he made no attempt to gain permanent control of the State, but on the completion of his legislation he retired to private life (79 B.C.).

### Section 85. The Overthrow of the Republic: Pompey and Cæsar

**948.** The people elect Pompey consul and regain political power (70 B.C.)

Following the death of Sulla a year after his retirement, agitation for the repeal of his hateful laws, which bound the people and the tribunes hand and foot, at once began. To accomplish this the people had now learned that they must make use of a military leader. The Senate had been ruling nine years in accordance with Sulla's laws when the popular leaders found the military commander whom they needed. He was a former officer of Sulla, named Pompey, who had recently won distinction in Spain, where he had been sent by the Senate to overthrow a still unsubdued supporter of Marius. He was elected consul (70 B.C.) chiefly because he agreed to repeal the obnoxious laws of Sulla, and he did not fail to carry out his promise. This service to the people now secured to Pompey a military command of supreme importance.

Such was the neglect of the Senate to protect shipping that the pirates of the East, chiefly from Cilicia, had overrun the whole Mediterranean (§ 915). They even appeared at the mouth of the Tiber, robbing and burning. They kidnaped Roman officials on the Appian Way, but a few miles from Rome, and they finally captured the grain supplies coming in to Rome from Egypt and Africa. In 67 B.C. the Assembly of the people passed a law giving Pompey supreme command in the Mediterranean and for fifty miles back from its shores. He was assigned two hundred ships and allowed to make his army as large as he thought necessary. No Roman commander had ever before held such far-reaching and unrepublican power.

949. Pirates of the Mediterranean and Pompey's appointment against them (67 B.C.)

In forty days Pompey cleared the western Mediterranean of pirates. He then sailed eastward, and in seven weeks after his arrival in the Ægean he had exterminated the Cilician sea robbers likewise and burned their docks and strongholds. The next year his command was enlarged to include also the leadership in a new war against Mithradates which had been going on with satisfactory results under Lucullus, a Roman commander of the greatest ability. Lucullus had already broken the power of Mithradates and also of the vast kingdom of Armenia, under its king, Tigranes. Pompey therefore had little difficulty in subduing Mithradates, and had only to accept the voluntary submission of Tigranes. He crushed the remnant of the kingdom of the Seleucids (§ 718) and made Syria a Roman province. He entered Jerusalem and brought the home of the

950. Extermination of the pirates, subjection of Mithradates, and conquests in the Orient by Pompey (67–62 B.C.)

Jews under Roman control. Before he turned back, the legions under his leadership had marched along the Euphrates and had looked down upon the Caspian. There had been no such conquests in the Orient since the Macedonian campaigns, and to the popular imagination Pompey seemed a new Alexander marching in triumph through the East.

**951.** Rise of Cæsar and his support of Catiline and Antony

FIG. 244. BUST SAID TO BE A PORTRAIT OF JULIUS CÆSAR

The ancient portraits commonly accepted as those of Julius Cæsar are really of uncertain identity

Meantime a new popular hero had arisen at Rome. He was a nephew of Marius, named Julius Cæsar (Fig. 244), born in the year 100 B.C., and thirty years old in Pompey's consulate. He had supported all the legislation against the laws of Sulla and in favor of Pompey's appointment to his great command. He took up the cause of Marius, and exalted his memory in public speeches so that he quickly gained a foremost place among the leaders of the people. The hatreds aroused by Sulla's executions and confiscations had left a great number of revengeful and dissatisfied men, who to no small extent made up the following of Cæsar. Among Cæsar's political friends was a noble named Catiline. He was the leader of a good many undesirable followers, but Cæsar was supporting him and another friend for election to the consulship.

Popular distrust of Cæsar's purposes, and Catiline's evil reputation, led to the defeat of Catiline and to the election of Cicero, a comparatively new man, but the ablest orator and the most gifted literary man of the age. By the formation of a new middle-class party from the Italian communities, which should stand between the Senate and the people, Cicero dreamed of a restoration of the old republic as it had once been. Catiline, meanwhile, burdened with debts and rendered desperate by the loss of the election, gathered about him all the dissatisfied bankrupts, landless peasants, Sullan veterans, outlaws, and slaves, the debased and lawless elements of Italy seeking an opportunity to rid themselves of debt or to better their situation. Foiled by Cicero in an attempt to seize violent control of the government, the reckless Catiline died fighting at the head of his motley following. Cicero's overthrow of Catiline brought him great power and influence and made his consulship (63 B.C.) one of brilliant success. Cæsar, on the other hand, was suspected of connection with the uprising of Catiline. This suspicion, whether just or unjust, proved to be a serious setback in his political career.

952. The overthrow of Catiline and the success of the great orator Cicero (63 B.C.)

Just at this juncture Pompey returned to Italy clothed in splendor as the great conqueror of the Orient. He made no attempt to influence the political situation by means of his army, the command of which he relinquished; but he needed political influence to secure the Senate's formal approval of his arrangements in Asia Minor, and a grant of land for his troops. For two years the Senate refused Pompey these concessions. Meantime Cæsar stepped forward in Pompey's support, and the two secured for their plans the support of a very wealthy Roman noble named Crassus. The plan was that Cæsar should run for the consulship and, if successful, secure the two things which we have seen Pompey needed. This private alliance of these three powerful men (called a " triumvirate ") gave them the control of the situation. As a result Cæsar was elected consul for the year 59 B.C.

953. Return of Pompey; the triumvirate — Pompey, Cæsar, and Crassus; Cæsar elected consul (59 B.C.)

The consulship was but a step in Cæsar's plans. Having secured for Pompey the measures which he desired, Cæsar fearlessly put through new land laws for the benefit of the

**954.** Cæsar secures the government of Gaul on both sides of the Alps

people, and then provided for his own future career. It was clear to him that he must have an important military command in order to gain an army. He saw a great opportunity in the West, like that which had been given Pompey in the Orient. Rome still held no more than a comparatively narrow strip of land along the coast of what is now southern France. On its north was a vast country occupied by the Gauls, and this region of Gaul was now sought by Cæsar. He had no difficulty in securing the passage of a law which made him for five years governor of Illyria and of Gaul on both sides of the Alps, that is, the valley of the Po in northern Italy, which we remember had been occupied by the Gauls (§ 815), and also of further Gaul beyond the Alps, as just described.

**955.** Cæsar's military skill and general plan of operations in Gaul

Cæsar took charge of his new province early in 58 B.C., and at once showed himself a military commander of surpassing skill. Not only did he possess the keenest insight into the tactical maneuvers which win victory on the field of battle itself, but he also understood at a glance the resources and abilities of a people and their armies. He knew that the greatest problem facing a commander was to keep his army in supplies and to guard against moving it to a point where it was impossible either to carry with it the supplies for feeding it or to find them on the spot. So efficient was his own great organization that he knew he could carry such supplies more successfully than could the barbarian Gauls. He perceived that no great barbarian host could be kept long together in one place, because they did not possess the organization for carrying with them, or securing later, enough food to maintain them long. When the necessity of finding provisions had forced them to separate into smaller armies, then Cæsar swiftly advanced and defeated these smaller divisions.

**956.** Cæsar's conquest of Gaul (58–50 B.C.)

By this general plan of operations in eight years of march and battle he subdued the Gauls and conquered their territory from the ocean and the English Channel eastward to the Rhine. He drove out a dangerous invasion of Gaul by the Germans, and astonishing them by the skill and speed with which he built a bridge over the Rhine, he invaded their country and established the frontier of the new Gallic province at the Rhine. He even crossed the Channel and carried an invasion of Britain as far as the Thames. He added a vast dominion to the Roman Empire, comprising in general the territory of modern France and Belgium. We should not forget that his conquest brought Latin into France, as the ancestor from which French speech has descended (see map IV, p. 552).

Cæsar had shown himself at Rome a successful politician. In Gaul he proved his ability as a brilliant soldier. Was he also a great statesman, or was he, like Pompey, merely to seek a succession of military commands and to accomplish nothing to deliver Rome from being a cat's-paw of one military commander after another? Cæsar's understanding of the situation at Rome was perfectly clear and had been so from the beginning. He was convinced that the foreign wars and the rule of the provinces had introduced into Roman government the ever-returning opportunity for a man of ability to gain military power which could not be controlled by the State. It was of no use to bring in a new political party, as Cicero hoped to do, and to pit mere *votes* against the flashing swords of the legions. For the old machinery of government furnished by the republic possessed no means of preventing the rise of one ambitious general after another to fight for control of the State as Marius and Sulla had done. The republic could therefore never again restore order and stable government for Italy and the empire. Herein Cæsar showed his superiority as a statesman over both Sulla and Cicero.

957. Cæsar's view of the situation as a statesman

The situation therefore demanded an able and patriotic commander with an army behind him who should make himself the undisputed and permanent master of the Roman government and subdue all other competitors. Consistently and steadily Cæsar pursued this aim, and it is no reflection upon him to say that it satisfied his ambition to do so. One of his cleverest

958. Cæsar publishes an account of his Gallic Wars

moves was the publication of the story of his Gallic campaigns, which he found time to write even in the midst of dangerous marches and critical battles. The tale is narrated with the most unpretentious simplicity. Although it is one of the greatest works of Latin prose, the book was really a political pamphlet, intended to convey to the Roman people an indelible impression of the vast conquests and other services which they owed to their governor in Gaul. It did not fail of its purpose. At present it is the best-known Latin reading book for beginners in that language in the whole civilized world.

**959.** Pompey at Rome takes up the cause of the Senate

When Cæsar's second term as governor of Gaul drew near its end, his supporters in Rome, instructed by him, were arranging for his second election to the consulship. The Senate was dreading his return to Italy and was putting forth every effort to prevent his reëlection as consul. The experience in the time of Marius had taught the Senate what to fear when a victorious commander returned to Rome to avenge their opposition to the people. They must have a military leader like Sulla again. Meantime Crassus, the wealthy member of the triumvirate (§ 953), had been slain in a disastrous war against the Parthians, beyond the Euphrates, and the group had broken up, thus freeing Pompey. In the midst of great confusion and political conflict in Rome, the leading senators now made offers to Pompey, in spite of the fact that he had received his great command from the Assembly of the people and had been a leader of the popular party. He was no statesman and had no plans for the future of the State. He was simply looking for a command. The result was that he undertook to defend the cause of the Senate and support the enemies of the people. What should have been a lawful political contest, again became a military struggle between two commanding generals, Cæsar and Pompey, like that of Marius and Sulla a generation earlier.

**960.** Cæsar and his army of professional soldiers

Cæsar endeavored to compromise with the Senate, but on receiving as their reply a summons to disband his army, he had no hesitation as to his future action. The professional soldiers who now made up a Roman army had no interest in political questions, felt no responsibility as citizens, and were conscious of very little obligation or attachment to the State. On the other hand, they were usually greatly attached to their commanding general. The veterans of Cæsar's Gallic campaigns were unswervingly devoted to him. When he gave the word, therefore, his troops followed him on the march to Rome without a moment's hesitation, to draw their swords against their fellow Romans forming the army of the Senate under Pompey. Cæsar and his troops at once crossed the Rubicon, the little stream which formed the boundary of his province toward Rome. Beyond this boundary Cæsar had no legal right to lead his forces, and in crossing it he had taken a step which became so memorable that we still proverbially speak of any great decision as a " crossing of the Rubicon."

The swiftness of Cæsar's lightning blows was always one of the greatest reasons for his success. Before the Senate's message had been an hour in his hands, Cæsar's legions had been on the march from the Po valley toward Rome (49 B.C.). Totally unprepared for so swift a response on Cæsar's part, the Senate turned to Pompey, who informed them that the forces at his command could not hold Rome against Cæsar. Indeed, there was at the moment no army in the Empire capable of meeting Cæsar's veteran legions with any hope of victory. Pompey retreated, and as Cæsar approached Rome, the majority of the senators and a large number of nobles fled with Pompey and his army. By skillful maneuvers Cæsar forced Pompey and his followers to forsake Italy and cross over to Greece. Cæsar's possession of Rome made it possible for him to be elected consul, and then to assume the rôle of lawful defender of Rome against the Senate and the army of Pompey.

**961.** Cæsar takes Rome, maneuvers Pompey out of Italy, and is elected consul (49 B.C.)

His position, however, was not yet secure. Pompey, in the eyes of the Orient, was the greatest man in Rome. He could muster all the peoples and kingdoms of the East against Cæsar. Furthermore, he now held the great fleet with which he had

**962.** Pompey's power. Cæsar captures Pompey's army in Spain (summer of 49 B.C.)

suppressed the pirates, and he was thus master of the sea. With all the East at his back, he was improving every moment to gather and discipline an army with which to crush Cæsar. Furthermore, Pompey's officers still held Spain since his recovery of it from the followers of Marius. Cæsar was therefore obliged to reckon with the followers of Pompey on both sides, East and West. He determined to deal with the West first. With his customary swiftness he was in Spain by June (49 B.C.). Here he met the army of Pompey's commanders with maneuvers of such surprising cleverness that in a few weeks he cut off their supplies, surrounded them and forced them to surrender without fighting a battle.

**963.** Cæsar surprises the senatorial party by crossing to Greece (winter of 49–48 B.C.)

Having heard of Cæsar's departure into Spain, Pompey and his great group of senators and nobles had been preparing at their leisure to cross over and take possession of Italy. Before they could even begin the crossing, Cæsar had returned from Spain victorious, and to their amazement, in spite of the fact that they controlled the sea, he embarked at Brundisium, evaded their warships, and landed his army on the coast of Epirus. Forced by lack of supplies to divide his army, a part of his troops suffered a dangerous reverse. In the end, however, in spite of his inferior numbers, he accepted battle with Pompey at Pharsalus, in Thessaly (48 B.C.).

**964.** Battle of Pharsalus (48 B.C.)

Pompey's plan for the battle was skillfully made, but it was not clever enough to outwit the greatest commander of the age. It consisted in drawing up his line so that a small stream would protect his right wing, in order that he might throw *all* his cavalry to the left wing. Probably twice as strong as Cæsar's right wing which it faced, it was expected to cut its way victoriously through, and then, passing around Cæsar's right end, to attack his legions in the rear. As the two armies approached each other, Cæsar perceived Pompey's plan of battle. He at once shifted six of his best cohorts, over three thousand men, to his right end, where they were screened by his cavalry from discovery by the enemy (plan, p. 593). The position of these six

cohorts may be compared to that of an unobserved football
player crouching on the right side lines to receive the ball.
Cæsar then ordered his cavalry, mostly Gauls and Germans,
to retreat as Pompey's horsemen attacked them. As they retreated, Pompey's unsuspecting cavalry followed and pushed
forward into Cæsar's cleverly devised trap. For when Cæsar's
six cohorts swiftly dropped in behind them, Pompey's horsemen
were caught between the six cohorts behind and Cæsar's cavalry in front, and they were quickly cut to pieces. Cæsar's
cavalry then swept swiftly around the enemy's now undefended

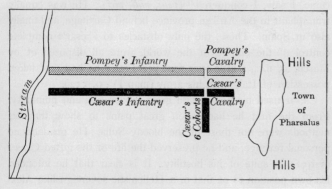

PLAN OF THE BATTLE OF PHARSALUS (§ 964)

left end and attacked Pompey's legions in the rear. As Cæsar
threw in his reserves against the hostile center at the same
moment, the whole senatorial army was driven off the field in
flight. Its remnants surrendered the next morning.

This battle represented the highest development of military
art, and it never passed beyond the masterful skill of the victor
of Pharsalus. Pompey, crushed by the first defeat of his life,
escaped into Egypt, where he was basely murdered. Cæsar,
following Pompey to Egypt, found ruling there the beautiful
Cleopatra, the seventh of the name, and the last of the Ptolemies. The charms of this remarkable queen and the political

**965.** Cæsar
completes the
conquest of
the Mediter-
ranean world
(48–45 B.C.)

advantages of her friendship met a ready response on the part of the great Roman. Here Cæsar displayed probably the most serious weakness in his career, as he tarried in Alexandria, dallying with this beautiful and gifted woman for three-quarters of a year (from October, 48, to June, 47 B.C.). In a dangerous outbreak which found Cæsar without sufficient troops, he was attacked by a mob and the great Alexandrian library (§ 750) was burned. We know little of the operations and battles by which Cæsar overthrew his opponents in Asia Minor. It was from there that he sent his famous report to the Senate: "I came, I saw, I conquered" (*veni, vidi, vici*). He was equally triumphant in the African province behind Carthage, and finally also in Spain. These, the only obstacles to Cæsar's complete control of the empire of the world, were all disposed of by March, 45 B.C., a little over four years after he had first taken possession of Italy with his army (map IV, p. 552).

**966. Cæsar's moderation and his own position**

Cæsar used his power with great moderation and humanity. From the first he had taken great pains to show that his methods were not those of the bloody Sulla. He gratified no personal revenge, and he preserved the life of the gifted Cicero (§ 952), in spite of his hostility. It is clear that he intended his own position to be that of a Hellenistic sovereign like Alexander the Great. Nevertheless, he was too wise a statesman to abolish at once the outward forms of the Republic. He possessed all the real power, and the Republic was doomed, for there was no one in Rome to gainsay this mightiest of the Romans. He had himself made Dictator for life, and assumed also the powers of the other leading offices of the State.

**967. Cæsar's reorganization of the State and Empire**

Cæsar lived only five years (49–44 B.C.) after his first conquest of Italy (49 B.C.). Of this period, as we have seen, four years were almost wholly occupied by campaigns. He was therefore left but little time for the colossal task of reshaping the Roman State and organizing the vast Roman Empire, the task in which the Roman Senate had so completely failed. Sulla had raised the membership of the Senate from three to six hundred. Cæsar did not abolish the ancient body, but he greatly increased its numbers, filled it with his own friends and adherents, and even installed former slaves and foreigners among its members. He thus destroyed the public respect for it, and it was entirely ready to do his bidding. The new Senate could not obstruct him and hence the whole projected administration of the provinces centered in him and was permanently responsible to him. The election of the officials of the Republic went on as before, but he began far-reaching reforms of the corrupt Roman administration. In all this he was launching the Roman Empire. He was in fact its first emperor, and only his untimely death continued the death struggles of the Republic for fifteen years more.

He sketched vast plans for the rebuilding of Rome, for magnificent public buildings, and for the alteration of the plan of the city, including even a change in the course of the Tiber. He laid out great roads along the important lines of communication, and he planned to cut a sea canal through the Isthmus of Corinth (Fig. 163). He completely reformed the government of cities. He put an end to centuries of inconvenience with the Greco-Roman moon-calendar (§ 564) by introducing into Europe the practical Egyptian calendar (§ 61), which we are still using, though with inconvenient Roman alterations. The imperial sweep of his plans included far-reaching conquests into new lands, like the subjugation of the Germans. Had he carried out these plans, the language of the Germans to-day would be a descendant of Latin, like the speech of the French and the Spanish. *968. Cæsar's vast plans and improvements*

The eighteenth of March, 44 B.C., was set as the date for Cæsar's departure for the Orient on a great campaign against the Parthians east of the Euphrates. But there were still men in Rome who were not ready to submit to the rule of one man. On the fifteenth of March, three days before the date arranged for his departure, and only a year after he had quelled the last disturbance in Spain, these men struck down the greatest of *969. The assassination of Cæsar (March 15, 44 B.C.) and its results* the Romans. If some of the murderers of this just and kindly statesman, who was for the first time giving the unhappy peoples of the Mediterranean world a government alike just, honest, and efficient, — if some of his murderers, like Brutus and Cassius (headpiece, p. 574), fancied themselves patriots overthrowing a tyrant, they little understood how vain were all such efforts to restore the ancient Republic. World dominion and its military power had forever demolished the Roman Republic, and the murder of Cæsar again plunged Italy and the Empire into civil war. The death of Alexander the Great interrupted in mid-career the conquest of a world empire stretching from the frontiers of India to the Atlantic Ocean. The bloody deed of the Ides of March, 44 B.C., stopped a similar conquest by Julius Cæsar — a conquest which would have subjected Orient and Occident to the rule of a single sovereign. A like opportunity never arose again, and Cæsar's successor had no such aims.

## SECTION 86. THE TRIUMPH OF AUGUSTUS AND THE END OF THE CIVIL WAR

**970.** Youth of Cæsar's nephew, Octavian (Augustus)

Over in Illyria the terrible news from Rome found the murdered statesman's grand-nephew Octavian (Fig. 245), a youth of eighteen, quietly pursuing his studies. A letter from his mother, brought by a secret messenger, bade him flee far away eastward without delay, in order to escape all danger at the hands of his uncle's murderers. The youth's reply was to proceed without a moment's hesitation to Rome. This statesmanlike decision of character reveals the quality of the young man both as he then showed it and for years to follow.

**971.** Early career of Octavian

On his arrival in Italy Octavian learned that he had been legally adopted by Cæsar and also made his sole heir. His bold claim to his legal rights was met with refusal by Mark Antony, Cæsar's fellow consul and one of his closest friends and supporters (§ 951), who had taken possession of Cæsar's

fortune and as consul could not be easily forced. By such
men Octavian was treated with patronizing indulgence at first
— a fact to which he owed his life. He was too young to be
regarded as dangerous. But his young shoulders carried a
very old head. He slowly gathered the threads of the tangled
situation in his clever fingers, not forgetting the lessons of his
adoptive father's career. The
most obvious lesson was the
necessity of military power.
He therefore rallied a force
of Cæsar's veterans, and two
legions of Antony's troops
also came over to him. Then
playing the game of politics,
with military power at his
back and none too scrupulous
a conscience, he showed himself a statesman no longer to
be ignored.

972. The
second
triumvirate

By skillful improvement of
the situation at Rome, Octavian forced his own election
as consul when only twenty
years of age (43 B.C.). He
was then able to form an

FIG. 245. PORTRAIT OF AUGUS-
TUS, NOW IN THE BOSTON MU-
SEUM OF FINE ARTS

alliance composed of himself and the other two most powerful
leaders, Antony, Cæsar's old follower, and Lepidus. This
second triumvirate (three-man-alliance) was officially recognized
by vote of the people. To obtain the money for carrying on
their wars and establishing themselves, the three began at once
a Sullan reign of terror, with confiscation of property and murder of their enemies. Among them the great orator Cicero,
who had endeavored to preserve the old Republic, was slain
by Antony's brutal soldiers. He was the last of the orator-
statesmen of Rome, as had been Demosthenes of Athens

(§ 721). But the Republic was still supported by the two leading murderers of Cæsar, Brutus, and Cassius. They were at the head of a powerful eastern army, like that of Pompey, and were encamped at Philippi in Macedonia. As soon as they could leave Rome, Octavian and Antony moved against Brutus and Cassius, and in a great battle at Philippi the last defenders of the Republic were completely defeated (42 B.C.).

**973.** Octavian gains Italy and the West (42–35 B.C.)

The two victors then divided their domains: Octavian was to return to Italy and endeavor to crush the enemies of the triumvirate in the West. Antony was to remain in the East and bring it again under full subjection to Rome. In the West a rebellious son of Pompey, who seized Sicily and held control of the sea with his fleet, was finally crushed by Octavian; and soon after Lepidus, who had been given the province of Africa behind Carthage, was also overthrown. Within ten years after Cæsar's assassination, and though only twenty-eight, Octavian had gained complete control of Italy and the West.

**974.** Octavian overthrows Antony and gains the East (31 B.C.)

Antony had meantime showed that he had no ability as a serious statesman. His prestige was also greatly dimmed by a disastrous campaign against the Parthians. Dazzled by the attractions of Cleopatra, he was now living in Alexandria and Antioch, where he ruled the East as far as the Euphrates like an oriental sovereign. With Cleopatra as his queen, he maintained a court of sumptuous splendor like that of the Persian kings in the days of their empire. Cleopatra, who had once hoped to rule Rome as Cæsar's queen, was now cherishing similar hopes as the favorite of Antony. The tales of all this made their way to Rome and did not help Antony's cause in the eyes of the Roman Senate. Octavian easily induced the Senate for this and other reasons to declare war on Cleopatra, and thus he was able to advance against Antony. As the legions of Cæsar and Pompey, representing the East and the West, had once before faced each other on a battlefield in Greece (§ 964), so now Octavian and Antony, the leaders of the East and the West, met at Actium on the west coast of Greece. A naval battle was fought, with the land forces as spectators. Before the end of the battle the soldiers of Antony saw their leader and his oriental queen forsaking them in flight, as Cleopatra's gorgeous galley, followed by her splendid royal flotilla, swept out to sea carrying the cowardly Antony to Egypt. The outcome was a sweeping victory for the heir of Cæsar.

The next year Octavian landed in Egypt without resistance worth mentioning and took possession of the ancient land. Antony, probably forsaken by Cleopatra, took his own life. The proud queen was unwilling to undergo the crushing humiliation of gracing Octavian's triumph at Rome, two of whose rulers had yielded to the power of her beauty and her personality, and she too died by her own hand. She was the last of the Ptolemies (§ 716), the rulers of Egypt for nearly three hundred years, since Alexander the Great. Octavian therefore made Egypt Roman territory (30 B.C.). To the West, which he already controlled, Octavian had now added also the East. The lands under his control girdled the Mediterranean, and the entire Mediterranean world was under the power of a single ruler. Thus at last the unity of the Roman dominions was restored and an entire century of revolution and civil war, which had begun in the days of the Gracchi (133 B.C.), was ended (30 B.C.).

**975.** Octavian makes Egypt a Roman province (30 B.C.), and ends a century of revolution and civil war (133–30 B.C.)

Octavian's success marked the final triumph of one-man power in the entire ancient world, as it had long ago triumphed in the Orient. The century of strife which Octavian's victory ended, was now followed by two centuries of profound peace, broken by only one serious interruption. These were the first two centuries of the Roman Empire, beginning in 30 B.C.[1] We shall now take up the two centuries of peace in the two following chapters.

**976.** The beginning of two centuries of peace

---

[1] It should be noticed that these two centuries of peace did not begin with the Christian Era. They began thirty years before the first year of the Christian Era, and hence the two centuries of peace do not correspond exactly with the first two centuries of our Christian Era.

## QUESTIONS

SECTION 83. What problems beset the Roman State in Italy? outside of Italy? What can you say of the ability and the legal right of the Senate to meet these problems? Who began the struggle for farm lands on behalf of the people? How did the Licinian laws attempt to aid the people? What was the condition of the government lands? What did Tiberius Gracchus tell the people? Describe his efforts to aid the people, and the result. Recount the work of Gaius Gracchus, and the result.

SECTION 84. What was the chief reason for the failure of the Gracchus brothers? Toward what kind of power did their leadership tend? How did the people gain control of the army in the war with Jugurtha? Recount the victories of Marius against Jugurtha and the Northern barbarians. Give an account of his new military measures. How did Marius succeed as a statesman? What was now the feeling of the Italian allies toward Rome? What can you say of Drusus? What happened on the death of Drusus? What was the result of the war with the allies? Describe the rise of Sulla. How did he defeat the will of the people? Was his action legal? What happened in Rome after Sulla went to Asia Minor? Recount Sulla's campaign against Mithradates. What happened on Sulla's return to Italy? What was the policy of Sulla, and how did he put it through?

SECTION 85. How did the people succeed in throwing off the rule of the Senate? What great command did they give to Pompey? Recount his operations against the pirates and in the Orient. Tell about the rise of Julius Cæsar. Recount the rise of Cicero and his defeat of Catiline. How did this prove a setback to Cæsar? How did Cæsar secure election as consul? Recount his campaigns in Gaul. What was his view of the political situation of Rome? What did the Senate do to thwart Cæsar? What was the result of Cæsar's advance on Rome? Recount his operations in Spain, and his invasion of Epirus. Describe the battle of Pharsalus. Recount briefly the achievements of Cæsar after his triumph. Tell the story of his death and its results.

SECTION 86. Tell the story of Octavian until the battle of Philippi. How did Octavian gain the West? Who was ruler of the East? How did Octavian gain the East? What great world did he then control? What kind of power had triumphed at the end of a century of revolution? What was to follow?

# PART V. THE ROMAN EMPIRE

## CHAPTER XXVII

### THE FIRST OF TWO CENTURIES OF PEACE: THE AGE OF AUGUSTUS AND THE SUCCESSORS OF HIS LINE

SECTION 87. THE RULE OF AUGUSTUS AND THE BEGIN-NING OF TWO CENTURIES OF PEACE (30 B.C.–14 A.D.)

When Octavian returned to Italy he was received with the greatest enthusiasm. A veritable hymn of thanksgiving arose among all classes at the termination of a century of revolution, civil war, and devastation. The great majority of Romans now felt that an individual ruler was necessary for the control of the vast Roman dominions. Octavian therefore entered upon forty-four years of peaceful and devoted effort to give to the

977. Octavian's moderate policy

NOTE. The above headpiece shows a restoration of a magnificent marble inclosure containing the "Altar of Augustan Peace," erected by order of the Senate in honor of Augustus. The inclosure was open to the sky, and its surrounding walls, of which portions still exist, are covered below by a broad band of ornamental plant spirals, very sumptuous in effect. Above it is a series of reliefs, of which the one on the right of the door pictures the legendary hero Æneas bringing an offering to the temple of the Roman household gods (Penates) whom he carried from Troy to Latium (footnote, p. 484).

Roman Empire the organization and government which it had so long lacked. His most difficult task was to alter the old form of government so as to make a legal place for the power he had taken by military force. Unlike Cæsar, Octavian felt a sincere respect for the institutions of the Roman Republic and did not wish to destroy them nor to gain for himself the throne of an oriental sovereign. During his struggle for the mastery heretofore, he had preserved the forms of the Republic and had been duly elected to his great position.

**978. Organization of the Roman State by Octavian**

Accordingly, on returning to Rome, Octavian did not disturb the Senate, but did much to strengthen it, and improve its membership. Indeed, he voluntarily handed over his powers to the Senate and the Roman people in January, 27 B.C. The Senate thereupon, realizing by past experience its own helplessness, and knowing that it did not possess the organization for ruling the great Roman world successfully, gave him officially the command of the army and the control of the most important frontier provinces. Besides these vast powers, he held also the important rights of a tribune (§§ 797, 810), and on this last office he chiefly based his legal claim to his power in the State.

**979. Titles of the new ruler**

At the same time the Senate conferred upon him the title of " Augustus," that is, " the august." The chief name of his office was " Princeps," that is, " the first," meaning the first of the citizens. Another title given the head of the Roman Empire was an old word for director or commander; namely, " Imperator," from which our word " emperor " is derived. Augustus, as we may now call him, regarded his position as that of an official of the Roman Republic, appointed by the Senate. Indeed, his appointment was not permanent, but for a term of years, after which he was reappointed.

**980. Dual character of the new State; waning power of the Senate**

The Roman Empire, which here emerges, was thus under a dual government of the Senate and of the Princeps, whom we commonly call the emperor. The clever Augustus had done what his great foster father, Julius Cæsar, had thought unnecessary: he had conciliated those Romans who still cherished the old Republic. The new arrangement was officially a restoration of the Republic. But this dual state in which Augustus endeavored to preserve the old Republic was not well balanced. The Princeps held too much power to remain a mere appointive official. His powers were more than once increased by the Senate during the life of Augustus; not on his demand, for he always showed the Senate the most ceremonious respect, but because the Senate could not dispense with his assistance. At the same time the old powers of the Senate could not be maintained reign after reign, when the Senate controlled no army.

The Princeps was the real ruler, because the legions were behind him, and the so-called republican State created by Augustus tended to become a military monarchy, as we shall see. All the influences from the Orient were in the same direction. Egypt was in no way controlled by the Senate, but remained a private domain of the emperor. In this the oldest State on the Mediterranean the emperor was king, in the oriental sense. He collected its huge revenues and ruled there as the Pharaohs and Ptolemies had done (§ 717). His position as absolute monarch in Egypt influenced his position as emperor and his methods of government everywhere. Indeed, the East as a whole could only understand the position of Augustus as that of a king, and this title they at once applied to him. This also had its influence in Rome.

**981.** Tendency toward military monarchy; oriental influences in this direction

The Empire which Rome now ruled consisted of the entire Mediterranean world, or a fringe of states extending entirely around the Mediterranean and including all its shores (map I, p. 636). But the frontier boundaries, left almost entirely unsettled by the Republic, were a pressing question. There was a natural boundary in the south, the Sahara, and also in the west, the Atlantic; but on the north and east further conquests might be made. In the main Augustus adopted the policy of organizing and consolidating the Empire *as he found it*, without making further conquests. In the east his boundary thus became the Euphrates, and in the north the Danube and the

**982.** Peace policy of Augustus, and the frontiers

Rhine. The angle made by the Rhine and the Danube was not favorable for defense of the border, and late in his reign Augustus seems to have made an effort to push forward to the Elbe (see map I, p. 636). This would have given the Empire a more nearly straight boundary, extending from the Black Sea to Denmark in a line from the southeast to the northwest. But whatever the intentions of Augustus may have been, the Roman army was terribly defeated by the barbarous German tribes, and the effort was abandoned. The northern boundary of the Empire was then made a line of provinces west of the Rhine and south of the Danube, extending from the North Sea to the Black Sea.[1]

**983. The army**

For the defense of these vast frontiers it was necessary to maintain a large standing army. Nevertheless the army, now carefully reorganized by Augustus, was not as large as the armies which had grown up in the civil wars. Augustus first reduced it to eighteen legions, but later raised it to twenty-five. It probably contained, on the average, about two hundred and twenty-five thousand men. The army was now recruited chiefly from the provinces, and the foreign soldier who entered the ranks received citizenship in return for his service. Thus the fiction that the army was made up of citizens was maintained. But the tramp of the legions was heard no more in Italy. Henceforth they were posted far out on the frontiers, and the citizens at home saw nothing of the troops who defended them.

**984. The sufferings of the provinces**

At the accession of Augustus the Roman Empire from Rome outward to the very frontiers of the provinces was sadly in need of restoration and opportunity to recuperate. The cost of the civil wars had been borne by the provinces. The eastern dominions, especially Greece, where the most important fighting of the long civil war had occurred, had suffered severely. For a century and a half before the great battles of the civil war, the provinces had been oppressed, excessively overtaxed or

[1] Recent study of this question is leading some historians also to the view that Augustus never really intended or attempted to conquer to the Elbe.

tacitly plundered (§ 888). Barbarian invaders had seized the undefended cities of Greece and even established robber states for plundering purposes. Greece herself never recovered from the wounds then suffered, and, in general, the eastern Mediterranean had been greatly demoralized. The civilized world was longing for peace.

Augustus therefore now undertook to do for the Mediterranean world what five hundred years earlier Darius had done for the Persian Empire (§ 267), when it was even larger than the Roman Empire. But the task of Augustus demanded the organization of a much more highly civilized world than that of the Persian Empire, including a vast network of commerce in the Mediterranean such as no earlier age had ever seen. Great peoples and nations had to be officially taken into the Empire and given honest and efficient government. Some of them had old and successful systems of government; others had no government at all. Egypt, for example, had long before possessed the most highly organized administration in the ancient world, but regions of the West, like Gaul, had not yet been given a system of government. All this Augustus endeavored to do.

**985. The great task of Augustus: the organization of the provinces**

Under the Republic the governor of a province not only served for a short term but was also without experience. His unlimited power, like that of an absolute monarch, made it impossible for the consuls changing every year at home to control him. The governor of a province was now appointed by the permanent ruler at Rome, and such a governor knew that he was responsible to that ruler for wise and honest government of his province. He also knew that if he proved successful he could hold his post for years, or be promoted to a better one. There thus grew up under the permanent control of Augustus and his successors a body of provincial governors of experience and efficiency. The small group of less important provinces still under the control of the Senate, although they continued to suffer to some extent under the old system, also felt the influence of the improved methods.

**986. The improved system of governors of the provinces**

**987.** Augustus for the first time regulates the finances of the Empire

In the days of the Republic no one had ever tried to settle how much money was needed to carry on the government, and how much of this sum each province ought justly to pay in the form of taxes. Augustus proceeded to put together huge census lists and property assessments, by which to determine the population and the total value of the property in each province. When this great piece of work was done he could determine just how much taxes each province should justly pay. He decreed that the inhabitants of the provinces were to pay two kinds of direct taxes, one on land and one on personal property, besides customs duties and various internal revenue taxes. Augustus had complete control of the vast sums which he thus received in taxes, and his use of them was wise and just. Much of this money went back to the provinces to pay for necessary public works, like roads, bridges, aqueducts, and public buildings. In making all these financial arrangements Augustus learned much from Egypt.

**988.** Beneficial effect of the new efficient government

Thus at last two centuries of Roman mismanagement of the provinces ended, and the obligation of Rome to give good government to her dependencies was finally fulfilled. The establishment of just, stable, and efficient control by the government at once produced a profound change, visible in many ways as we shall see (§§ 991–1004), but especially in business. Men of capital no longer kept their money timidly out of sight, but put it at once into business ventures. The rate of interest under the last years of the Republic had been twelve per cent. But as money now became more plentiful, the interest rate quickly sank to four per cent.

**989.** The Mediterranean *world* on the way to become a Mediterranean *nation*

The great Mediterranean world under the control of Rome now entered upon a new age of prosperity and development, unknown before, when the nations along its shores were still fighting each other in war after war. A process of unification began which was to make the Mediterranean *world* a Mediterranean *nation*. The national threads of our historical narrative have heretofore been numerous, as we have followed the stories of the oriental nations, of Athens, Sparta, Macedonia, Rome, Carthage, and others. For a long time we have followed these narratives separately like individual strands; but now they are to be twisted together into a single thread of national history, that of the Roman Empire. The great exceptions are the German barbarians in the north, and the unconquered Orient east of the Euphrates.

## Section 88. The Civilization of the Augustan Age

In the new Mediterranean nation thus growing up, it was the purpose of Augustus that Italy should occupy a superior position, as the imperial leader of all the peoples around the Mediterranean. Italy was not to sink to the level of these peoples nor to be merely one of them. We have seen the sturdy virtues of earlier Roman character undermined and corrupted by sudden wealth and power (§§ 906–922), before Italy had had a chance to become a nation. Augustus made a remarkable effort to undo all this damage and restore the fine old days of rustic Roman virtue, the good old Roman customs, the beliefs of the fathers. To meet increasing divorce, laws to protect the sanctity of marriage were passed. The oriental gods, so common for centuries in Greece (§ 657), and long widespread in Italy, were to be banished. The people were urged to awaken their declining interest in the religion of their fathers, and the old religious feasts were celebrated with increased splendor and impressiveness. At the same time the State temples, which had frequently fallen into decay, were repaired; new ones were built, especially in Rome, and the services and usages of Roman State religion were everywhere revived.

990. Augustus attempts a restoration of old Roman life, and plans preëminence of Italy

Tendencies like those which had changed the Roman people lie too deep in the life and the nature of men to be much altered by the power of a government or the pressure of new laws. It was a new world in which the Romans of the Augustan Age were living. The more Augustus applied his own power

991. The new Rome

to modify the situation, the more noticeable became the contrast between the Augustan Age and the old days before one-man power arose. Under Augustus, Rome for the first time received organized police, a fire department, a water department, and a fully organized office for the government sale of grain. Augustus himself boasted that he found Rome a city of brick and left it a city of marble. To the visitor at Rome, therefore, the new age proclaimed itself in imposing new buildings. For republican Rome had lacked the magnificent monumental theaters and gymnasia, libraries and music halls, which had long adorned the greater Hellenistic cities. It had also, of course, possessed no royal palace, like that at Alexandria. Architecturally, Alexandria was still the most splendid city of the ancient world.

**992.** Rome the greatest center of art; the Palatine buildings of Augustus

The great architectural works which Augustus now began, made Rome the leading art center of the ancient world. His building plans were in the main those which his adoptive father, the Great Dictator, had himself either laid out or already begun. On the Palatine Hill, Augustus united several dwelling houses, already there, into a palace for his residence. It was very simple, and the quiet taste of his sleeping room, which long survived the rest of the building (§ 1014), was the

* The Sacred Way (plan, p. 622) passed the little circular temple of Vesta (*A*), and reached the Forum at the Arch of Augustus (*B*), and the Temple of the Deified Julius Cæsar (*C*). On the right was the old Basilica of Æmilius (*D*) (§ 890), and on the left the magnificent new Basilica of Julius Cæsar (*E*) (§ 993). Opposite this, across the old Forum market place (*F*), was the new Senate House (*G*) planned by Julius Cæsar (§ 993). At the upper end of the Forum was the new speaker's platform (*H*); near it Septimius Severus later erected his crude arch (*I*). Beyond rises the Capitol, with the Temple of Saturn (*J*) and the Temple of Concord (*K*) at its base; above on its slope is the Tabularium (*L*), a place of public records; and on the summit of the Capitol the Temple of Jove (*M*). Julius Cæsar extended the Forum northward by laying out his new Forum (*N*) behind his Senate House (*G*). The subsequent growth of the emperors' Forums on this side may be seen in the next figure (Fig. 247), where the same lettering is repeated and continued.

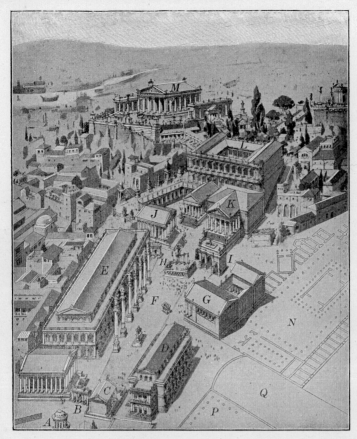

FIG. 246. THE ROMAN FORUM AND ITS PUBLIC BUILDINGS IN THE
EARLY EMPIRE. (AFTER LUCKENBACH)*

We look across the ancient market place (*F*, § 784) to the Tiber with its
ships at the head of navigation. On each side of the market place, where
we see the buildings (*E*, *J*, and *D*, *G*, *I*), were once rows of little wooden
booths for selling meat, fish, and other merchandise. Especially after the
beginning of the Carthaginian wars, these were displaced by fine buildings,
like the basilica hall *D*, built not long after 200 B.C. Note the square
ground plans (*J*, *M*) and the arches showing Etruscan influence, the Attic
roofs and colonnades and the clerestory windows (*D*, *E*) copied from the
Hellenistic cities. See complete key on opposite page, footnote

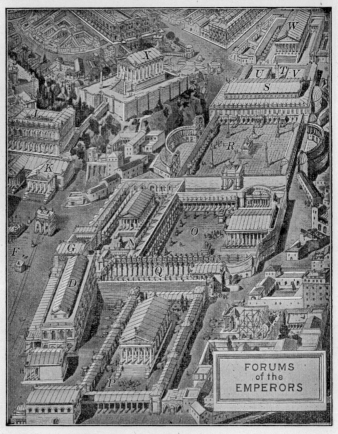

FORUMS
of the
EMPERORS

FIG. 247. THE FORUMS OF THE EMPERORS CONTINUING THE VIEW
OF THE OLD FORUM IN FIG. 246. AFTER L. LEVY (LUCKENBACH)*

The plan (p. 622) shows how the Forums of the emperors formed a
connecting link uniting the old Roman Forum (*F*) with the magnificent
new buildings of the Campus Martius, like the Theater of Pompey,
Baths of Agrippa, Pantheon, etc. In order to make this connection,
Trajan cut away the ridge joining the Capitol Hill and the Quirinal Hill
to a depth of 100 feet. The summit of his column (*T* above and Fig. 263)
still marks the former height of the ridge. Little now remains of all
this magnificence; see the ruined colonnades around the column of
Trajan (Fig. 263). See discussion of buildings on opposite page, footnote

admiration of later Romans. From this royal dwelling on the *Palatine* arose our English word "palace." A new and sumptuous temple of Apollo surrounded by colonnades, in which the emperor installed a large library (§ 1001), was erected within easy reach of his palace doors.

The palace looked down upon an imposing array of new marble buildings surrounding the ancient Forum. Nearest the palace the magnificent basilica business hall erected by Cæsar, left unfinished and then damaged by fire, was now restored and completed by Augustus (Fig. 246, *E*). He also erected a new Senate building, planned but never built by Cæsar, opposite the new basilica (Fig. 246, *G*). Facing the end of the Forum the emperor now built a temple for the worship of his deified foster father, known as the temple of the Divine Julius (Fig. 246, *C*), and facing it, at the opposite end of the Forum, Augustus placed a magnificent speaker's platform of marble (Fig. 246, *H*). Behind the ground intended by him for the new Senate building, Cæsar had built a new forum, called the Forum of Cæsar (Figs. 246 and 247, *N*); but the growing business of the city led Augustus to build a third forum, known as the Forum of Augustus (Fig. 247, *O*), which he placed next to that of Cæsar.

**993.** The new buildings in the Forum and vicinity

---

* The Senate House of Julius Cæsar (*G*) and his new Forum (*N*) extended from the old Forum northward, occupying the ground where once the Assembly of the Roman People had been accustomed to meet (*Comitium*). This northern addition to the old Forum was still further extended in the same direction by the Forum of Augustus (*O*) (§ 993). The great emperors of the first and second centuries then extended this northern addition in two directions, first on the southeast (*P, Q*), and then on the northwest (*R, S, T, U, V, W,* and plan, p. 622). In the first century Vespasian built the beautiful Forum of Peace (*P*), and the aged Nerva inserted his long, narrow Forum (*Q*); while in the second century A. D. Trajan, going to the other side of the Forum of Augustus (*O*), built the most magnificent of all the forums (*R*), with a vast basilica (*S*, called Basilica Ulpia) beside it, and beyond it his two libraries (*U, V*) (§ 1051), with his wonderful column (*T*, and Fig. 263) between them. In Trajan's honor Hadrian then built a temple (*W*), completing this line of the most magnificent buildings the ancient world ever saw.

**994. First theaters and baths; Altar of Peace**

The first stone theater in Rome had been built by Pompey about twenty-five years before the accession of Augustus (plan, p. 622). The emperor, therefore, erected a large and magnificent theater, which he named the Theater of Marcellus (§ 1007), after his deceased son-in-law Marcellus. At the same time Agrippa, the ablest of the generals and ministers of Augustus, erected the first fine public baths in Rome, for which he was given space in the Field of Mars, an old drill ground (plan, p. 622). In connection with it were other splendid public buildings added by Agrippa, and a spacious open square for the Assembly of the People. At the same time the Senate showed its appreciation of the new era of peace by erecting a large and beautiful marble Altar of Peace (headpiece, p. 601).

**995. Influence of Greece and the Orient on Roman architecture**

In this new architecture of Rome, Greek models were the controlling influence. Nevertheless, oriental influences also were very prominent. Greek architecture did not employ the arch so long used in the Orient, but the architects of Rome now gave it a place of prominence along with the colonnade, as the two leading features of their buildings. It was through these Roman buildings that the arch gained its important place in our own modern architecture. Augustus seems to have been much interested in the monuments of the ancient oriental world, which he more than once visited. His triumphal arch was arranged with three gates like the Assyrian palace front (Fig. 248). He carried away from the Nile a number of Egyptian obelisks and set them up in Rome, and in building his own family tomb he selected a design from the Orient. One of the noble families of Rome even built a pyramid as a tomb, and it still stands on the outskirts of the city (Fig. 249).

**996. Complete lack of initiative in sculpture and painting at Rome**

While architecture flourished in Rome, sculpture was less cultivated. Beautiful sculpture, following old models, might still be produced; but there were no creative sculptors in Rome like those whom we have met in Athens. Painting as an independent art had ceased to be practiced. There was not a single great painter in Rome, and the painting which was practiced

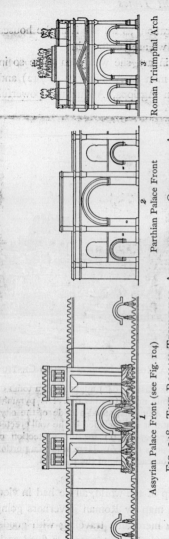

Assyrian Palace Front (see Fig. 104)     Parthian Palace Front     Roman Triumphal Arch

FIG. 248. THE ROMAN TRIUMPHAL ARCH AND ITS ORIENTAL ANCESTORS

The imposing front of the Assyrian palace (*1*), with its tall arch in the middle and a lower arch on each side (see Fig. 104), was continued by the Parthians (*2*), and at the same time they shifted the side arches nearer to the middle arch (*2*). We have seen the arch making its way slowly westward (Fig. 224), although the Greeks were very reluctant to adopt it and did not make full use of it until they were Christianized and began to employ it in their churches (headpiece, p. 688). The Romans, on the contrary, were influenced by the Etruscans, who probably brought the arch with them from Asia Minor (Fig. 224). Hence we early found it in Rome (Fig. 232), and the triumphal arch of Augustus, and other arches of this kind built by the Romans (*3*), were descendants of the Assyrian palace front, with a tall arch in the middle and lower arches on each side, just as widely traveled Romans had seen it in the East

Ancient Times

was merely that of wall decoration, as we see it in the houses
of Pompeii (Fig. 197), which we are yet to visit.

If Rome was a borrower in art, she was even more so in
science. Rome had no such men as Archimedes (§ 742) and
Eratosthenes (§ 745). When Agrippa, Augustus's powerful

**997.** Lack
of science
at Rome;
Agrippa's
map

FIG. 249. PYRAMID-TOMB OF A ROMAN NOBLE NAMED CESTIUS

Wealthy Romans familiar with the East (§ 1046) might erect a tomb of
oriental form, as the family of this noble Cestius did. His pyramid-
tomb when built (in the reign of Augustus) stood outside of the city;
but nearly three hundred years later it was included in the wall erected
around the city by Aurelian (270–275 A.D.) for the protection of
Rome against the barbarian invasions (§ 1096). Here we see a portion
of the wall of Aurelian on each side of the pyramid

minister, drew up a great map of the world, all he had in view
was the practical use of the map by Roman governors going
out to their provinces or by merchants traveling with goods.
Hence the roads were elaborately laid out, not on a fixed scale
but so that there would be space enough along each road for
the names of all the towns situated along it, and for all the

distances in miles between towns, which were inserted in figures on the map. Such a map was without doubt convenient, but it entirely lacked the network of latitude and longitude so carefully worked out by Eratosthenes (§ 748), and for this reason the shapes of the countries and seas were so distorted that none of the readers of this book would be able to find anything or recognize familiar countries.

The leading geography of the time was written by a Greek living in Rome, named Strabo. It was a delightful narrative of wide travels mingled with history, and although it sadly lacked in scientific method, it was for many centuries the world's standard geography and may still be read with great pleasure and profit as an ancient book of travel. The work of Strabo, however, is a landmark disclosing the decline of ancient science and the end of that great line of scientists whose achievements made the Hellenistic Age the greatest age of science in the early world.

**998.** Strabo and geography; decline of science

Indifference to science at Rome was in marked contrast with Roman interest in literature. The greatest of the leading Romans displayed in some cases an almost pathetic devotion to literary studies, even while weighed down with the heaviest responsibilities. Cæsar put together a treatise on Latin speech while crossing the Alps in a palanquin, when his mind must have been filled with the problems of his great wars in Gaul. He dedicated the essay to Cicero, the greatest master of Latin prose. Such men as these had studied in Athens or Rhodes, and were deeply versed in the finest works of Greek learning and literature. Cæsar and Cicero and the men of their class spoke Greek every day among themselves, perhaps more than they did Latin. In these men Hellenistic civilization and Roman character had mingled to produce the most cultivated minds of the ancient world. Among the educated men in the declining Greek communities of the East, none could rival these finest of the Romans in cultivation or in power of mind. Indeed, Greece never produced men of just this type, who exhibited

**999.** Enthusiastic interest in literature; Romans of Greco Roman culture the leading cultivated men of the ancient world

such a combination of gifts — the highest ability both in public leadership and in literary achievement.

**1000. Cicero the type of the highly educated man of the late Republic; his writings and their enduring influence**

Of literary studies Cicero said: " Such studies profit youth and rejoice old age; while they increase happiness in good fortune, they are in affliction a consolation and a refuge; they give us joy at home and they do not hamper us abroad; they tarry with us at night time and they go forth with us to the countryside." Thus spoke the most cultivated man Rome ever produced, and the ideals of the educated man which he himself personified have never ceased to exert a powerful influence upon educated men in all lands. When he failed as a statesman, a career for which he did not possess the necessary firmness and practical insight (§ 957), he devoted himself to his literary pursuits. As the greatest orator in Roman history, he had already done much to perfect and beautify Latin prose in the orations which he delivered in the course of his career as a lawyer and a statesman. But after his retirement he produced a group of remarkable essays on oratory, a series of treatises on conduct — such matters as friendship, old age, and the like; and he left behind also several hundred letters which were preserved by his friends. As one of the last sacrifices of the civil wars, Cicero had fallen by the hands of Antony's brutal soldiery (§ 972); but his writings were to exert an undying influence. They made Latin speech one of the most beautiful instruments of human expression, and as an example of the finest literary style they have influenced the best writing in all the languages of civilization ever since.

**1001. Augustan Age and literature: Livy**

Augustus and a number of the leading men about him had known Cicero. For them that commingling of Greek and Roman civilization, which might well be called Ciceronian, became the leading cultivated influence in their lives. The Ciceronian culture of the last days of the dying Republic thus became the ideal of the early Empire and the Augustan Age. Augustus had early established two libraries in Rome, and one of them contained the greatest collection of both Greek and

Latin books in the ancient world. Men steeped in this Greco-Roman culture now began to feel the influence of the great events which had built up the vast Roman Empire. As at Athens in the days of the greatest Athenian power, so the vision of the greatness of the State stirred the imagination of thinking men. Livy wrote an enormous history of Rome from the earliest times, that is to say, from the Trojan War to the reign of Augustus, in one hundred and forty-two rolls (§ 751) — a work which cost him forty years of labor. While it was beautiful literature, and the fragments which survive still form fascinating reading, it was very inaccurate history. The careful historical method that had made Thucydides (§ 667) the greatest of ancient historians had disappeared.

In the last days of the Republic, in spite of turbulence and civil war, Cicero and the men of his time had perfected Latin *prose*. On the other hand, the greatest of Latin *poetry* arose under the inspiration of the early Empire and the universal peace established by Augustus. Horace, the leading poet of the time, had been a friend of the assassins of Cæsar, and he had faced the future Augustus on the battlefield of Philippi. After a dangerous struggle he had saved himself and at last found security in the era of peace. Having lived through many dangers, to rejoice in the general peace, he gained the forgiveness and friendship of Augustus. In his youth, although only the son of a freedman of unknown race, he had studied in Greece, and he knew the old Greek lyric poets (§ 482) who had suffered danger and disaster as he himself had done. With the haunting echoes of old Greek poetry in his soul, he now found his own voice. Then he began to write of the men and the life of his own time in a body of verse which forms for us an undying picture of the Romans in the days of Augustus. The poems of Horace will always remain one of the greatest legacies from the ancient world — a treasury of Roman life as pictured by a ripe and cultivated mind, unsurpassed even in the highly developed literature of the Greeks.

1002. Rise of poetry in the Augustan Age; Horace

**1003. Virgil and the Æneid**

Virgil, the other great poet of the Augustan Age, had from the beginning been a warm admirer of the great Cæsar and the young Octavian. When the civil war had deprived Virgil of his ancestral farm under the shadow of the Alps in the North, it was restored to him by Augustus. Here, as he looked out upon his own fields, the poet began to write verses like those of Theocritus (§ 754), reflecting to us in all its poetic beauty the rustic life of his time on the green hillsides of Italy. But these imitations of Greek models would never have given Virgil his place as one of the greatest poets of the world. As time passed he gained an exalted vision of the mission of Rome, and especially of Augustus, as the restorer of world peace. More than one Latin epic was already in circulation (§ 904), but in order to give voice to his vision, Virgil now undertook the creation of another epic, in which he pictured the wanderings of the Trojan hero Æneas from Asia Minor to Italy, where in the course of many heroic adventures he founded the royal line of Latium (headpiece, p. 484). From him, according to the story, were descended the Julian family, the Cæsars, whose latest leader Augustus had saved Rome and established a world peace.

**1004. Character of the Æneid**

Unlike the Homeric epics, Virgil's Æneid, as it is called, was not the outgrowth of an heroic age. It was a tribute to Augustus, whom the poem artistically placed against a glorious background of heroic achievement in the Trojan Age, just as Alexander the Great contrived to do the same for himself (§ 689). The Æneid was therefore the product of a self-conscious, literary age — the highly finished work of a literary artist who now took his place with Horace as one of the great interpreters of his age. Hardly so penetrating a mind as his friend Horace, Virgil was perhaps an even greater master of Latin verse. Deeply admired by the age that produced it, the Æneid has ever since been one of the leading schoolbooks of the civilized world, and has had an abiding influence on the best literature of later times.

Augustus himself also left an account of his deeds. When he was over seventy-five years old, as he felt his end approaching, he put together a narrative of his career, which was engraved on bronze tablets and set up before his tomb. In the simple dignity of this impressive story we see the career of Augustus unfolding before us in one grand achievement after another, rising like a panorama of successive mountain peaks, in a vision of such grandeur as to make the document probably the most impressive brief record of a great man's life which has survived to us from the ancient world. Almost with his last breath Augustus penned the closing lines of this remarkable document, and on the nineteenth of August, the month which bears his name, in the year 14 A.D., the first of the Roman emperors died.

1005. Account of his deeds left by Augustus in the Ancyra monument

## Section 89. The Line of Augustus and the End of the First Century of Peace (14 A.D.–68 A.D.)

Augustus had been in supreme control of the great Roman world for forty-four years; that is, nearly half a century. Four descendants of his family, either by blood or adoption, were to rule for more than another half century, and thus to fill out the first century of peace. The prejudice against one-man power was still so strong that the writers of this age and their successors have transmitted to us very unfair accounts of these four rulers. Two of them were indeed deserving of the contempt in which they are still held; but the other two were in many respects able rulers, who did much to improve the developing government of the Empire.

1006. The four successors of the line of Augustus (14–68 A.D.)

Augustus had never put forward a law providing for the appointment of his successor or for later successors to his position. Any prominent Roman citizen might have aspired to the office. Augustus left no son, and one after another his male heirs had died, among them his grandsons, the sons of his daughter Julia. He had finally been obliged to ask the

1007. Question of the succession; Tiberius

Senate to associate with him his stepson Tiberius, his wife's son by an earlier marriage. Before the death of Augustus, Tiberius had therefore been given joint command of the army and also the tribune's power. The Senate, therefore, at once appointed him to all his stepfather's powers, and without any limit as to time.

**1008. The efficient reign of Tiberius (14–37 A.D.)** Tiberius was an able soldier and an experienced man of affairs. He gave the provinces wise and efficient governors, and showed himself a skilled and successful ruler. He did not, however, possess his stepfather's tact and respect for the old institutions. He found it very vexatious to carry on joint rule with a Senate whose power was in reality little more than a fiction. He felt only contempt for the Roman nobles who publicly did him homage and secretly slandered him or plotted his downfall. He likewise despised the Roman populace. Under Augustus they had continued to go through the form of electing magistrates and passing laws as in the days of the Republic, but of course both the magistrates they elected and the laws they passed had been those proposed to the assemblies by Augustus. Tiberius, however, no longer allowed the Roman rabble to go through the farce of voting on what the emperor had already decided, and even the appearance of a government by the Roman people thus finally disappeared forever. To complete his unpopularity in Rome, Tiberius also practiced strict economy in government and much reduced the funds devoted to public shows for the amusement of the people. Universally hated in Rome, greatly afflicted also by bereavements and disappointments in his private life, Tiberius left the city and spent his last years in a group of magnificent villas on the lofty island of Capri, overlooking the Bay of Naples, where he died a disappointed man (37 A.D.).

**1009. Caligula (37–41 A.D.)** As Tiberius had lost his son, the choice for his successor fell upon Gaius Cæsar, a great-grandson of Augustus, nicknamed Caligula ("little boot") by the soldiers among whom he was brought up. A young man of only twenty-five years, and at first very popular in Rome, Caligula was so transformed by his sense of vast power and by long-continued dissipation that his mind was crazed. He made his horse a consul, and the enormous wealth saved for the State by Tiberius he squandered in reckless debauchery and absurd building enterprises. In the midst of confiscation and murder, this mockery of a reign was brought to a sudden close by Caligula's own officers, who put an end to his life in his palace on the Palatine after he had reigned only four years.

The imperial guards, ransacking the palace after the death of Caligula, found in hiding the trembling figure of a nephew of Tiberius and uncle of the dead Caligula, named Claudius. He had always been merely tolerated by his family as a man both physically and mentally inferior. He was now fifty years old, and there is no doubt that he was weak-kneed both in body and in character. But the guards hailed him as emperor, and the Senate was obliged to consent. Claudius was a great improvement upon Caligula, although he was easily influenced by the women of his family and the freedmen officials whom he had around him. The palace therefore soon became a nest of plots and intrigues, in which slander, banishment, and poison played their evil parts.

Nevertheless Claudius accomplished much for the Empire and devoted himself to its affairs. He conducted in person a successful campaign in Britain, and for the first time made its southern portion a province of the Empire. It was this conquest which helped to bring so much of Latin speech into the English language, for Britain remained a Roman province for three and a half centuries. At Rome Claudius was greatly interested in buildings and practical improvements. He built two vast new aqueducts, together nearly a hundred miles in length, furnishing Rome with a plentiful supply of fresh water from the mountains (Fig. 250). At the same time his own officials, chiefly able Greek freedmen who were aiding him in his duties, were beginning to form a kind of cabinet destined finally to

1010. The accession of Claudius (41 A.D.)

1011. Achievements of Claudius: conquest of Britain; public works; creation of ministers of state (41–54 A.D.)

give the Empire for the first time a group of efficient ministers, whom we would call the Secretary of the Treasury, the Secretary of State, and others like them.

The inability of Claudius to select wisely and to control those who formed his circle was the probable cause of his death. It

Fig. 250. The Aqueduct of the Emperor Claudius

This wonderful aqueduct, built by the Emperor Claudius about the middle of the first century A. D., is over 40 miles long. About three fourths of it is subterranean, but the last 10 miles consists of tall arches of massive masonry, as seen here, supporting the channel in which the water flowed, till it reached the palace of the emperor on the Palatine (plan, p. 622). Such ancient Roman aqueducts were so well built that four of them are still in use at Rome, and they convey to the city a more plentiful supply of water than any great modern city elsewhere receives

was also the reason why Agrippina, the last of his wives, was able to push aside the son of Claudius and gain the throne for her own son Nero, as the successor of Claudius. Not only on his mother's side, but also on his father's, Nero was descended from the family of Augustus. His mother had intrusted his education to the philosopher Seneca, and for the first five years of his reign, while Seneca was his chief minister, the rule of

Nero was wise and successful. When palace plots and intrigues, in which Seneca was not without blame, had removed this able minister from the court and had also banished Nero's strong-minded mother, Agrippina, he cast aside all restraint and followed his own evil nature in a career of such vice and cruelty that the name of Nero has ever since been regarded as one of the blackest in all history.

Nero was devoted to art and wished personally to practice it. While the favorites of the palace carried on the government, he toured the principal cities of Greece as a musical composer, competing for prizes in dancing, singing, and chariot races. As the companion of actors, sportsmen, and prize fighters, he even took part in gladiatorial exhibitions. Becoming more and more entangled in the meshes of court plots, his cowardly and suspicious nature led him to condemn his old teacher, Seneca, to death, to cause the assassination of the son of Claudius and of many other innocent and deserving men. In the same way he was persuaded to take the life of his wife, and to crown his infamy even had his own mother assassinated. At the same time his wild extravagance, his excessive taxation in some of the provinces, and his murders among the rich and noble were stirring up dangerous dissatisfaction, which was to result in his fall.

**1013. The infamy of Nero's reign**

A great disaster, meantime, took place in Rome. A fire broke out among the cheap wooden buildings around the circus (see plan, p. 622). It swept over the Palatine Hill, destroying the palace of Augustus, leaving only his sleeping room (§ 992), and then passed on through the city. It burned for a week, wiping out a large portion of the city, and then breaking out again, increased the damage. Dark rumors ran through the streets that Nero himself had set fire to the city that he might rebuild it more splendidly, and gossip told how he sat watching the conflagration while giving a musical performance of his own on the destruction of Troy. There is no evidence to support these rumors. Under the circumstances, Nero himself welcomed

**1014. The great fire at Rome (64 A.D.), and Nero's palace**

another version, which accused the Christians of having started
the fire, and he executed a large number of them with horrible
tortures. At vast expense, to which much of his excessive taxation was due, he undertook the rebuilding of the city, and he
erected an enormous palace for himself called the "Golden

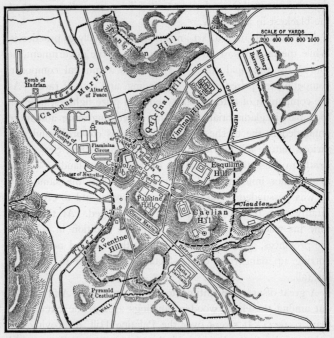

MAP OF ROME UNDER THE EMPERORS

House," extending across the ground where the Colosseum
now stands, from the east end of the Forum eastward and
northeastward across the Esquiline Hill and over a large section
of the city. At the entrance was a colossal bronze statue of
himself over a hundred feet high (Fig. 262). There can be no
doubt that Nero's interest in art was sincere and that he really
desired to make Rome a beautiful city.

The dissatisfaction at Rome and Nero's treatment of the only able men around him deprived him of support there. Then the provinces began to chafe under heavy taxation. When the discontent in the provinces finally broke out in open revolt, led especially by Galba, a Roman governor in Spain, Nero showed no ability to meet the revolt. The rebellious troops marched on Rome. Nero went into hiding, and on hearing that the Senate had voted his death, he theatrically stabbed himself, and, attitudinizing to the last, he passed away uttering the words, "What an artist dies in me!" Thus died in 68 A.D. the last ruler of the line of Augustus, and with him ended the first century of peace (31 B.C.–68 A.D.); for several Roman commanders now struggled for the throne and threatened to involve the Empire in another long civil war.

**1015.** The death of Nero, the last of the Julian line; the end of the first century of peace (68 A.D.)

In spite of the misrule which had attended the reigns of two of the line of Augustus, the good accomplished in the reigns of Tiberius and Claudius could not be wholly undone. Both at Rome and in the provinces, the government had been much improved. But, as we have seen, the Roman State was fast becoming a monarchy in which the crown was bequeathed from father to son. This process had been hastened by the fact that the Cæsars, as the emperors were now called, had gained a position of unique reverence. Beginning with Julius Cæsar, the emperors,[1] like Alexander the Great, were deified, and their worship was widely practiced throughout the Empire. It was indeed an obligation of citizenship to pay divine homage to the emperor. The supreme place which he now occupied was not to be endangered by the brief struggles which followed the death of Nero, and the wide rule of the Roman emperor, even after the fall of Julius Cæsar's line, was to maintain another century of prosperity and peace. To this second century of peace in the Roman Empire we must devote another chapter.

**1016.** Lasting progress during the rule of the Julian line; deification of the emperors

---

[1] Besides Julius Cæsar and Augustus, Claudius was the only emperor of the Julian line who was deified. Tiberius failed of it because of his unpopularity, and Caligula and Nero, of course, because of their infamous characters.

## QUESTIONS

SECTION 87. What kind of a period did the rule of Augustus begin? What was his attitude toward the Republic? What chief offices and powers did he receive? From what body? What were his titles? Had the Republic survived? What body was continuing the power of the Republic? Was this power likely to survive? Who was the real ruler? What influences tended to make him a sovereign? What was the policy of Augustus on the frontiers? What did he do with the army? How had the provinces, especially Greece, suffered? What did Augustus attempt to do about it? How did Augustus improve the rule of the provinces? Describe his financial improvements. What beneficial effects in business were observable? Was the Mediterranean world about to become a nation?

SECTION 88. What kind of life did Augustus desire for Italy? What did he want the position of Italy to be? How had Rome become a new world? What improvements did Augustus introduce in the city? on the Palatine? in the Forum? What other buildings were erected? What architectural influences prevailed? Were there any creative artists in sculpture and painting? What can you say of science in Rome? What work did Strabo produce? Tell about the attitude of educated Romans toward literature. What was Cicero's feeling about literature, and what did he write? What has been the influence of his writing? What was his influence in the Augustan Age? What was Rome's position in literature? What can you say of Livy? of Horace? of Virgil? Discuss the leading work of Virgil. What remarkable narrative did Augustus himself write?

SECTION 89. How long were Augustus and the four following rulers of his line in power? Who succeeded Augustus? Describe his rule. What became of the old power of the people under Tiberius? Who succeeded Tiberius, and what can you say of his reign? Describe the accession of Claudius. What did he accomplish? Who succeeded Claudius? How had Nero been educated? Describe his reign and character. What catastrophe overtook Rome? Describe his end and its causes. What period closed with his death? Give its date. What can you say of the results of the rule of the Julian line? What exalted station was given to the Roman emperors? What period followed the disappearance of the Julian line?

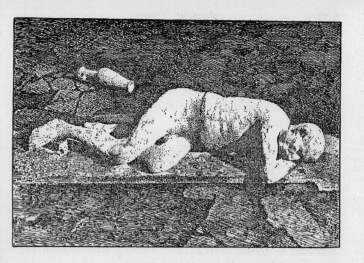

# CHAPTER XXVIII

## THE SECOND CENTURY OF PEACE AND THE CIVILIZATION OF THE EARLY ROMAN EMPIRE

SECTION 90. THE EMPERORS OF THE SECOND CENTURY OF PEACE (BEGINNING 69 A.D.)

For about a year after the death of Nero the struggle among the leading military commanders for the throne of the Cæsars threatened to involve the Empire in another long civil war. Fortunately the troops of Vespasian, a very able commander in the East, were so strong that he was easily victorious, and in 69 A.D. he was declared emperor by the Senate. With him,

**1017.** Advent of the second century of peace with the triumph of Vespasian (69 A.D.)

NOTE. The above headpiece shows us the body of a citizen of Pompeii who perished when the city was destroyed by an eruption of Vesuvius in 79 A.D. (§ 1034). The fine volcanic ashes settled around the man's body, and these rain-soaked ashes made a cast of his figure before it had perished. After the body had perished it left in the hardened mass of ashes a hollow mold, which the modern excavators poured full of plaster, and thus secured a cast of the figure of the unfortunate man just as he lay smothered by the deadly ashes which overwhelmed him over eighteen hundred years ago.

therefore, began a second century of peace under a line of able emperors who brought the Empire to the highest level of prosperity and happiness. We shall first sketch the political and military activities of these emperors and then turn to the life and civilization of the Empire as a whole during the second century of peace.

**1018. Rebellion of the Jews and destruction of Jerusalem (70 A.D.)**

Even though remote wars broke out on the frontiers or in distant provinces, they did not disturb the peace of the Empire as a whole. Before his election as emperor, Vespasian had been engaged in crushing a revolt of the fanatical Jews in Palestine, and the next year his able son Titus captured and destroyed Jerusalem amid frightful massacres which exterminated large numbers of the rebellious Jews (70 A.D.). It was later found necessary to forbid all Jews from entering their beloved city, consecrated by so many sacred memories; and it was made a Roman colony under a different name. Judea at the same time became a Roman province.

**1019. Two great tasks of the emperors: frontier defenses and efficient government organization**

Two great tasks were accomplished by the emperors of the age we are discussing: first, that of perfecting the system of defenses on the frontiers, and second, that of more fully developing the government and administration of the Empire. Let us look first at the frontiers. On the south the Empire was protected by the Sahara and on the west by the Atlantic; but on the north and east it was open to attack. The shifting German tribes constantly threatened the northern frontiers; while in the east the frontier on the Euphrates was made chronically unsafe by the Parthians, the only civilized power still unconquered by Rome (see map I, p. 636).

**1020. The Roman Empire, the bulwark of Mediterranean civilization against northern barbarism**

The pressure of the barbarians on the northern frontiers, which we recall in the time of Marius (§ 936), was the continuance of the vast movement with which we are already acquainted — the tide of migration which long before had swept the Indo-European peoples to the Mediterranean (see diagram, Fig. 112) and had carried the Greeks and the Romans into their two Mediterranean peninsulas. Mediterranean civilization was thus in constant danger of being overwhelmed from the North, just as the splendid Ægean civilization was once submerged by the incoming of the Greeks (Chap. IX). The great problem for future humanity was whether the Roman emperors would be able to hold off the barbarians long enough so that in course of time these rude Northerners might gain enough of Mediterranean civilization to respect it, and to preserve at least some of it for mankind in the future.

The Flavian family, as we call Vespasian and his two sons, did much to make the northern frontiers safe. After the mild and kindly rule of Vespasian's son, Titus (§ 1018), the latter's brother, Vespasian's second son Domitian, adopted the frontier lines laid down by Augustus and planned their fortification with walls wherever necessary. He began the protection of the exposed border between the upper Rhine and the upper Danube. In Britain, Domitian even pushed the frontier further northward and then erected a line of defenses. But on the lower Danube he failed to meet the dangerous power of the growing kingdom of Dacia. He even sent gifts to the Dacian king, intended to keep him quiet and satisfied. By this unwise policy Domitian created a difficult problem in this region, to be solved by his successors (see map I, p. 636).

1021. The strengthening of the northern frontiers by the Flavian emperors (69–96 A.D.)

The brief and quiet reign of the senator Nerva, who was selected by the Senate to succeed Domitian (96 A.D.), left the whole dangerous situation on the lower Danube to be met by the brilliant soldier Trajan, who followed Nerva in 98 A.D. He quickly discerned that there would be no safety for the Empire along the Danube frontier, except by crossing the river and crushing the Dacian kingdom. Bridging the Danube with boats and hewing his way through wild forests, Trajan led his army through obstacles never before overcome by Roman troops. He captured one stronghold of the Dacians after another, and in two wars finally destroyed their capital. Thereupon the Dacian king and his leading men took their own lives. Trajan built a massive stone bridge (Fig. 251), across the

1022. Trajan crushes the barbarians on the lower Danube and conquers Dacia (101–106 A.D.)

Danube, made Dacia a Roman province, and sprinkled plentiful Roman colonies on the north side of the great river. The descendants of these colonists in the same region still call themselves *Roumanians* and their land *Roumania*, a form of the

FIG. 251. THE EMPEROR TRAJAN SACRIFICING AT HIS NEW
BRIDGE ACROSS THE DANUBE

In the background we see the heavy stone piers of the bridge, supporting the wooden upper structure, built with strong railings. In the foreground is the altar, toward which the emperor advances from the right, with a flat dish in his right hand, from which he is pouring a libation upon the altar. At the left of the altar stands a priest, naked to the waist and leading an ox to be slain for the sacrifice. A group of the emperor's officers approach from the left, bearing army standards. The scene is sculptured with many others on the column of Trajan at Rome (Fig. 263), and is one of the best examples of Roman relief sculpture of the second century (§ 1053)

word "Roman." Trajan's vigorous policy quieted all trouble along the lower Danube for a long time.

**1023. Trajan's war with the Parthians (115–117 A.D.)**    The military glory of Rome, which had declined since the days of Cæsar, revived in splendor under this great soldier emperor. Trajan then turned his attention to the eastern frontier, extending from the east end of the Black Sea southward to the Peninsula of Sinai. In the northern section of this frontier a large portion of the boundary was formed by the upper Euphrates River. Rome thus held the western half of the Fertile Crescent, but it had never conquered the eastern half, with Assyria and Babylonia (see map I, p. 636). Here the powerful kingdom of the Parthians, kindred of the Persians, had maintained itself with ups and downs since the days of the early Seleucids, for three hundred and fifty years. Twice

FIG. 252. RESTORATION OF THE ROMAN FORTIFIED WALL ON THE GERMAN FRONTIER

This masonry wall, some three hundred miles long, protected the northern boundary of the Roman Empire between the upper Rhine and the upper Danube, where it was most exposed to German attack. At short intervals there were blockhouses along the wall, and at points of great danger strongholds and barracks (Fig. 254) for the shelter of garrisons

before they had defeated Roman expeditions against them. Trajan, however, dreamed of a great oriental empire like that of Alexander. He led an army against the Parthians and defeated them. He added Armenia, Mesopotamia, and Assyria to the Empire as new provinces. He visited the ruins of Babylon to behold the spot where, four hundred and forty years before, Alexander had died; but he said he "saw nothing worthy of such fame, but only heaps of rubbish, stones, and ruins" (Fig. 111). Then a sudden rebellion in his rear forced him to a dangerous retreat. Weakened by sickness and bitterly realizing that his great expedition was a failure, he died in Asia Minor while returning to Rome (**117** A.D.).

**1024.** Hadrian (117–138 A.D.) completes the frontier defenses

Trajan's successor, Hadrian, was another able soldier, but he had also the judgment of a statesman. He made no effort to continue Trajan's conquests in the East. On the contrary, he wisely gave them all up except the Peninsula of Sinai (see map I, p. 636) and brought the frontier back to the Euphrates. But he retained Dacia and strengthened the whole northern frontier, especially the long barrier reaching from the Rhine to the Danube, where the completion of the continuous wall (Fig. 252) was largely due

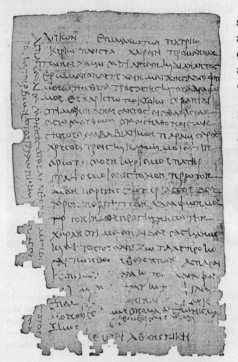

FIG. 253. LETTER OF APION, A YOUNG SOLDIER IN THE ROMAN ARMY, TO HIS FATHER, EPIMACHOS, IN EGYPT*

to him. He built a similar wall along the northern boundary across Britain. The line of both these walls is still visible. As a result of these wise measures and the impressive victories of Trajan, the frontiers were safe and quiet for a long time. Nor was there any serious disturbance until a great overflow of the northern barbarians (167 A.D.) in the reign of Marcus Aurelius brought to an end the second century of peace.

Under Trajan and Hadrian the army which defended these frontiers was the greatest and most skillfully managed organization of the kind which the ancient world had ever seen. Drawn from all parts of the Empire, the army now consisted of all

**1025. The army under Trajan and Hadrian**

---

\* This Egyptian youth, Apion, having enlisted in the Roman army in company with other boys from his little village in Egypt, bade his family good-by and embarked on a great government ship from Alexandria for Italy. After a dangerous voyage he arrived safely at Misenum, the Roman war harbor near Naples, and hastened ashore in his new uniform to have a small portrait of himself painted (§ 1054 and Plate VIII, p. 654) and to send his father the letter on the opposite page. It was written for him in Greek, on papyrus, in a beautiful hand by a hired public letter writer, and reads as follows (with the present author's explanations in brackets): " Apion to Epimachos his father and lord, many good wishes! First of all I hope that you are in good health, and that all goes well with you and with my sister and her daughter and my brother always. I thank the lord Serapis [a great Egyptian god] that he saved me at once when I was in danger in the sea. When I arrived at Misenum, I received from the emperor three gold pieces [about fifteen dollars] as road money, and I am getting on fine. I beg of you, my lord father, write me a line, first about your own well-being, second about that of my brother and sister, and third in order that I may devotedly greet your hand, because you brought me up well and I may therefore hope for rapid promotion, the gods willing. Give my regards to Capiton [some friend], and my brother and sister, and Serenilla and my friends. I send you by Euktemon my little portrait. My [new Roman] name is Antonius Maximus. I hope that it may go well with you." On the left margin, where we see two vertical lines inserted, just as we are accustomed to insert them, Apion's chums (the other village boys who enlisted with him) sent home their regards. Folded and sealed as in Fig. 210, the letter went by the great Roman military post, arrived safely, and was read by the young soldier's waiting father and family in the little village on the Nile over seventeen hundred years ago (§ 1025). Then years later, after the old father had died, it was lost in the household rubbish, and there the modern excavators found it among the crumbling walls of the house (cf. Fig. 211). The ancient letter had some holes in it, but with it was another letter written by our soldier to his sister years later, after he had long been stationed somewhere on the Roman frontier (§ 1025) and had a wife and children of his own. And that is all that the rubbish heaps of the village on the Nile have preserved of this lad who entered the army of the great Roman Empire in the second century A.D.

possible nationalities, like the British army in the Great European War. A legion of Spaniards might be stationed on the Euphrates, or a group of youths from the Nile might spend many years in sentry duty on the wall that barred out the Germans. Although far from home, such young men were enabled to communicate easily with their friends at home by a very efficient military

FIG. 254. GLIMPSES OF A ROMAN FRONTIER STRONGHOLD
(RESTORED AFTER WALTZE-SCHULZE)

Above, at the left, the main gate of the fort; the other three views show
the barracks (cf. Fig. 251)

postal system covering the whole Empire like a vast network. We are still able to hold in our hands the actual letters written from a northern post by a young Egyptian recruit in the Roman army to his father and sister in a distant little village on the Nile (Fig. 253). When not on sentry duty somewhere along the frontier line, such a young soldier lived with his comrades in one of the large garrisons maintained at the most important frontier points, with fine barracks and living quarters for officers and men (Fig. 254). The discipline necessary to keep the troops always ready to meet the barbarians outside the walls was never relaxed. Besides regular drill, the troops were also employed in making roads, building bridges, aqueducts, and public buildings or in repairing the frontier walls.

Meantime the Empire had been undergoing important changes within. The emperors developed a system of government departments already foreshadowed in the time of Claudius (§ 1011). To manage them, they appointed Roman knights. There thus grew up a body of experienced administrators as heads of departments and their helpers, who carried on the government of the Empire. It was the wise and efficient Hadrian who accomplished the most in perfecting this organization of the government business. Thus after Rome had been for more than three centuries in control of the Mediterranean world, it finally possessed a well-developed government organization such as **had** been in operation in the Orient since the days of the pyramid builders (§§ 74–75).

1026. Organization of efficient government departments

Among many changes, one of the most important was the abolition of the system of " farming " taxes, to be collected by private individuals — a system which had caused both the Greeks (§ 623) and the Romans (§ 889) much trouble. Government tax collectors now gathered in the taxes of the great Mediterranean world. It is interesting to recall that such a system had been fully organized on the Nile over three thousand years before the Romans possessed it (§ 74 and Fig. 40).

1027. Change from private tax-farmers to government tax collectors

With the complete control of these departments entirely in his own hands, the power of the emperor had much increased. From being the first citizen of the State like Augustus, ruling jointly with the Senate, the emperor had thus become a sovereign, whose power was so little limited by the Senate that he was not far from being an absolute monarch. Furthermore, the emperors of the second century of peace secured laws and regulations which made the rule of the emperor legal, although they unfortunately passed no laws providing for a successor

1028. Increased power of the emperor and decline of the Senate

on the death of an emperor, and dangerous conflict might ensue whenever an emperor died.

**1029. Italy loses its leadership and drops to the level of the provinces**

At the same time an important change in the position of Italy was taking place. The condition of the farmers was now so bad that there was danger of the complete disappearance of free population in the country districts of Italy. Two of the emperors, Nerva and Trajan, even set aside large sums as capital to be loaned at a low rate of interest to farmers needing money. This interest was to be used to support poor free children in the towns of Italy in the hope that a new body of free country population might be thus built up. This remarkable effort, one of the earliest known State charities, was, however, not successful. As Italy was furthermore not a manufacturing country, its citizenship declined. Meantime a larger idea of the Empire had displaced the conception of Augustus, who had desired to see the Empire a group of states led and dominated by Italy. Whole provinces, especially in the West, had been granted citizenship, or a modified form of it, by the emperors. Influential citizens in the provinces were often given high rank and office at Rome. As a result there had now grown up a Mediterranean nation, as we have seen it foreshadowed even in the time of Augustus, and Italy dropped to a level with the provinces.

**1030. Rise of a system of law for the whole Empire**

Not only did the subjects of this vast State pay their taxes into the same treasury, but they were now controlled by the same laws. The lawyers of Rome under the emperors we are now discussing were the most gifted legal minds the world had ever seen. They expanded the narrow *city*-law of Rome that it might meet the needs of the whole Mediterranean world. They laid the foundations for a vast imperial code of laws, the greatest work of Roman genius. In spirit, these laws of the Empire were most fair, just, and humane. Antoninus Pius, the kindly emperor who followed Hadrian, maintained that an accused person must be held innocent until proved guilty by the evidence, a principle of law which has descended to us and is still part of our own law. In the same spirit was the protection of wives and children from the arbitrary cruelty of the father of the house, who in earlier centuries held the legal right to treat the members of his family like slaves. Even slaves now enjoyed the protection of the law, and the slave could not be put to death by the master as formerly, although we should notice that in some important matters the Roman law treated a citizen according to his social rank, showing partiality to the noble in preference to the common citizen. These laws did much to unify the peoples of the Mediterranean world into a single nation; for they were now regarded by the law not as different nations but as subjects of the same great State, which extended to them all, the same protection of justice, law, and order. At the same time the earlier laws long developed by the older city-states were not interfered with by Rome, where they did not conflict with the interests of the Empire.

The Empire as a whole was still organized in provinces, which steadily increased in number. Within each province by far the large majority of the people lived in towns and cities. Such a city and its outlying communities formed a city-state like that which we found in early Greece. Each city had the right to elect its own governing officials and to carry on its own local affairs. The people still took an interest in local affairs, and there was a good deal of rivalry for election to the public offices. On the walls at Pompeii (Fig. 255) we still find the appeals of rival candidates for votes. At the same time each city was under the sovereignty of the Roman Empire and the control of the Roman governor of the province.

**1031.** Government of the provinces; survival of the people's interest in public affairs

Able and conscientious governors were now controlling affairs all over the Empire. The letters written to Trajan by the younger Pliny, governor of Bithynia in Asia Minor, regarding the interests of his province reveal to us both his own faithfulness and the enormous amount of provincial business which received the emperor's personal attention. Fig. 253 shows us how such a letter looked. Such attention by emperors like

**1032.** Close attention to the provinces by the emperors, and decline of the people's interest

Trajan and Hadrian relieved the communities of much responsibility for their own affairs. Hadrian traveled for years among the provinces and became very familiar with their needs. Hence the local communities inclined more and more to depend upon the emperor, and interest in public affairs declined. Along with growing imperial control of the provinces, there thus began a decline in the sense of responsibility for public welfare. This was eventually a serious cause of general decay, as we shall see.

## SECTION 91. THE CIVILIZATION OF THE EARLY ROMAN EMPIRE: THE PROVINCES

**1033. The peoples of the Roman Empire**

Here was a world of sixty-five to a hundred million souls girdling the entire Mediterranean. Had human vision been able to penetrate so far, we might have stood at the Strait of Gibraltar and followed these peoples as our eyes swept along the Mediterranean coasts through Africa, Asia, and Europe, and thus back to the Strait again. On our right in Africa would have been Moors, North Africans, and Egyptians; in the eastern background, Arabs, Jews, Phœnicians, Syrians, Armenians, and Hittites; and as our eyes returned through Europe, Greeks, Italians, Gauls, and Iberians (Spaniards); while north of these were the Britons and some Germans within the frontier lines. All these people were of course very different from one another in native manners, clothing, and customs, but they all enjoyed Roman protection and rejoiced in the far-reaching Roman peace. For the most part, as we have seen, they lived in cities, and the life of the age was prevailingly a city life, even though many of the cities were small.

**1034. Pompeii, a provincial city of the early Roman Empire**

Fortunately one of the provincial cities has been preserved to us with much that we might have seen there if we could have visited it nearly two thousand years ago. The little city of Pompeii, covered with volcanic ashes in the brief reign of Titus (79 A.D.), still shows us the very streets and houses, the forum and the public buildings, the shops and the markets,

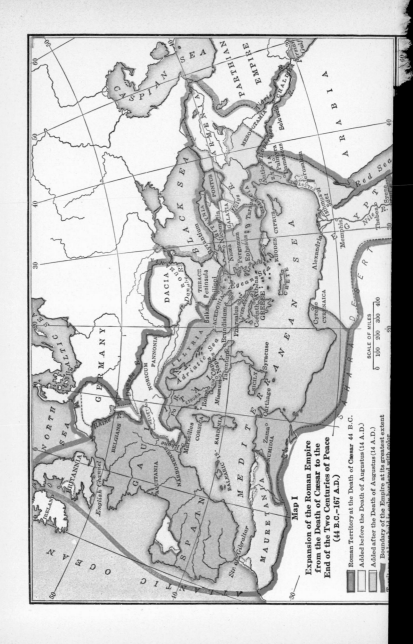

**Map I**

**Expansion of the Roman Empire
from the Death of Cæsar to the
End of the Two Centuries of Peace
(44 B.C.–167 A.D.)**

Roman Territory at the Death of Cæsar 44 B.C.

Added before the Death of Augustus (14 A.D.)

Added after the Death of Augustus (14 A.D.)

Boundary of the Empire at its greatest extent

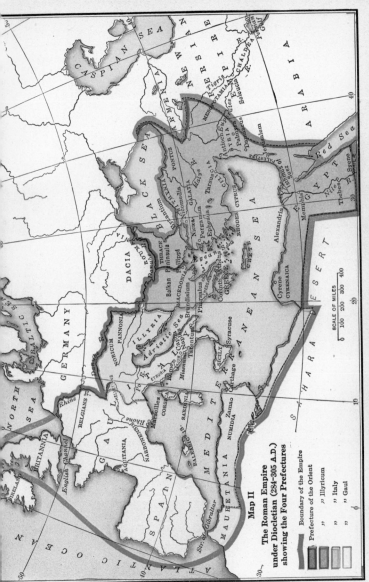

**Map II**

**The Roman Empire under Diocletian (284–305 A.D.) showing the Four Prefectures**

Boundary of the Empire
,, ,, Prefecture of the Orient
,, ,, ,, Illyricum
,, ,, ,, Italy
,, ,, ,, Gaul

SCALE OF MILES
0   100   200   300   400

SEQUENCE MAP SHOWING TERRITORIAL GAINS AND LOSSES OF THE ROMAN EMPIRE FROM THE DEATH OF CÆSAR (44 B.C.) TO THE DEATH OF DIOCLETIAN (305 A.D.)

and a host of other things very much as we might have found them if we had been able to visit the place before the disaster (Fig. 255). We can look down long streets, where the chariot wheels have worn deep ruts in the pavement; we can enter dining rooms with charming paintings still on the walls

FIG. 255. A STREET IN ANCIENT POMPEII AS IT APPEARS TO-DAY

The pavement and sidewalk are in perfect condition, as when they were first covered by the falling ashes (§ 1034). At the left is a public fountain, and in the foreground is a street crossing. Of the buildings on this street only half a story still stands, except at the left, where we see the entrances of two shops, with the tops of the doors in position and the walls preserved to the level of the second floor above

(Fig. 197); we can look into the bakers' shops with the charred bread still in the ovens and the flour mills standing silent and deserted (Fig. 256); or we can peep into kitchens with the cooking utensils still scattered about (Fig. 243) and the cooking hearth in perfect order for building another fire. The very life of the people in the early Roman Empire seems to rise before us as we tread the now silent streets (Fig. 255) of this wonderfully preserved place.

**1035.** Improved means of intercourse: Roman roads and bridges

Pompeii was close beside the Greek cities of southern Italy, and we at once discover that the place was essentially Hellenistic in its life and art. Indeed, from southern Italy eastward we should have found the life of the world controlled by Rome to be simply the natural outgrowth of Hellenistic life and civilization. In some matters there had been great progress. This was especially true of intercourse and rapid communication. Everywhere the magnificent Roman roads, massively paved with smooth stone, like a town street (Fig. 255), led straight over the hills and across the rivers by imposing bridges. Some of these bridges still stand and are in use to-day (Fig. 260). Near the cities there was much traffic on such a highway.

**1036.** Traffic on a Roman highway

One met the ponderous coach of the Roman governor, perhaps returning from his province to Rome. The curtains are drawn and the great man is comfortably reading or dictating to his stenographer. Behind him trots a peddler on a donkey, which he quickly draws to one side to make room for a cohort of Roman legionaries marching with swinging stride, their weapons gleaming through a cloud of dust. Following them rides an officer accompanied by a shackled prisoner going up to Rome for trial. He is a Christian teacher named Paul (§ 1068). A young dandy exhibiting the paces of his fine horse to two ladies riding in a palanquin, grudgingly vacates the road before a rider of the imperial post who comes clattering down the next hill at high speed. Often the road is cumbered with long lines of donkeys laden with bales of goods or caravans of heavy wagons creaking and groaning under their heavy loads of merchandise — the freight trains of the Roman Empire. As for passenger trains, the traveler must resort to the horse coach or small special carriage or ride his own horse. The speed of travel and communication was fully as high as that maintained in Europe and America a century ago, before the introduction of the steam railway, and the roads were better.

Indeed, the good Roman roads were a great advance over the Hellenistic Age. By sea, however, the chief difference was the freedom from the old-time pirates (§ 949). From the splendid harbor laid out at the mouth of the Tiber by Claudius,

FIG. 256. BAKERY WITH MILLSTONES STILL IN POSITION AT POMPEII

In a court beside the bakery we see the mills for grinding the baker's flour. Each mill is an hourglass-shaped stone, which is hollow, the upper part forming a funnel-shaped hopper into which the grain is poured. The lower part of the stone is an inverted funnel placed over a cone-shaped stone inside it. The grain drops between the inner stone and the outer, and when the outer stone is turned by a long timber inserted in its side, the grain is ground between the two

the traveler could take a large and comfortable ship for Spain and land there in a week. The Roman whose son was studying in Athens dispatched a bank draft for the youth's university expenses, and a week later the boy could be spending the money. A Roman merchant could send a letter to his agent in Alexandria in ten days. The huge government corn ships that plied regularly between the Roman harbors and Alexandria were stately vessels carrying several thousand tons. They could accommodate an Egyptian obelisk weighing from three to four hundred tons which the emperor desired to erect in Rome (§ 995), besides a large cargo of grain and several hundred passengers. Good harbors had everywhere been equipped with docks, and lighthouses modeled on that at Alexandria guided the mariners into every harbor. In winter, however, sea traffic stopped.

**1038. Commerce from the Atlantic to India and from the Baltic to the Mediterranean**

Under these circumstances business flourished as never before. The good roads led merchants to trade beyond the frontiers and to find new markets. Goods found their way from Italy even to the northern shores of Europe and Britain, whence great quantities of tin passed up the Seine and down the Rhone to Marseilles. At the other end of the Empire the discovery of the seasonal winds in the Indian Ocean led to a great increase of trade with India, and there was a fleet of a hundred and twenty ships plying regularly across the Indian Ocean between the Red Sea and the harbors of India. The wares which they brought crossed the desert by caravan from the Red Sea to the Nile and were then shipped west from the docks of Alexandria, which still remained the greatest commercial city on the Mediterranean, the Liverpool of the Roman Empire. It shipped besides East Indian luxuries (§ 733) Egyptian paper (papyrus), linen, rich embroideries, the finest of glassware (§ 83), great quantities of grain for Rome, and a host of other things. There was a proverb that you could get everything at Alexandria except snow. Along the northern roads of the Eastern world was the caravan connection with China which continued to bring silk goods to the Mediterranean. It will be seen then that a vast network of commerce covered the ancient world from the frontiers of China and the coast of India on the east to Britain and the harbors of the Atlantic on the west.

Both business and pleasure now made travel very common, and a wide acquaintance with the world was not unusual. The Roman citizen of means and education made his tour of the Mediterranean much as the modern sight-seer does. Having arrived in the provincial town, however, he found no good hotels, and if he did not sleep in his own roomy coach or a tent carried by his servants, he was obliged to pass the night in untidy rooms over some shop, the keeper of which entertained travelers. More often, however, the traveler of birth and means brought with him letters of introduction, which procured him entertainment at some wealthy private house.

1039. Frequency of travel but lack of hotels

For even in the provincial town the traveler found a group of successful men of business and public affairs who had gained wealth and had been given the rank of Roman knights. Among them now and again was one of especial prominence who had been given senatorial rank by the emperor. Below the Senators and knights there was a free population of merchants, shopkeepers, artisans, and craftsmen. Following a custom as old as the end of the Athenian Empire, these men were organized into numerous guilds, societies, and clubs, each trade or calling by itself. These societies were in some ways much like our labor unions. They were chiefly intended for mutual benefit of the members in their occupations; some of them also aided in social life, in the celebration of popular holidays, and the society treasury paid the funeral expenses when a member died, just as some societies among us do. As likely as not the richest and most influential man of the place was a freedman. There was in every large town a great number of freedmen, and they carried on an important share of the business of the Empire.

1040. Society in the provinces

As the traveler walked about such a town he found everywhere impressive evidences of the generous interest of the citizens. There were fountains, theaters, music halls, baths, gymnasiums, and schools, erected by wealthy men and given to the community. The most famous among such men was

1041. Public benefactions and schools in the provinces

FIG. 257. SCRIBBLINGS OF SICILIAN SCHOOLBOYS ON A BRICK IN THE DAYS OF THE ROMAN EMPIRE

In passing a brickyard, these schoolboys of seventeen hundred years ago amused themselves in scribbling school exercises *in Greek* on the soft clay bricks before they were baked. At the top a little boy who was still making capitals carefully wrote the capital letter *S* (Greek Σ) ten times, and under it the similar letter *K*, also ten times. These he followed by the words "turtle" (ΧΕΛΩΝΑ), "mill" (ΜΤΛΑ), and "pail" (ΚΑΔΟΣ), all in capitals. Then an older boy, who could do more than write capitals, has pushed the little chap aside and proudly demonstrated his superiority by writing in two lines an exercise in tongue gymnastics (like "Peter Piper picked a peck of pickled peppers," etc.) which in our letters is as follows:

Nai neai nea naia neoi temon, hōs neoi ha naus

This means: "Boys cut new planks for a new ship, that the ship might float." A third boy then added two lines at the bottom. The brick illustrates the spread of Greek (§ 727) as well as provincial education under the Roman Empire (§ 1041)

Herodes Atticus, who built a magnificent concert hall (Fig. 183, *I*) for Athens. He has been called the "Andrew Carnegie" of his time. In the market place were statues of such donors, with inscriptions expressing the gratitude of the people. The boys and girls of these towns found open to them schools with teachers paid by the government, where all those ordinary branches of study which we have found in the Hellenistic Age were taught (Fig. 257). The boy who turned to business could engage a stenographer to teach him shorthand, and the young man who wished higher instruction could still find university teachers at Alexandria and Athens, and also at a number of younger universities in both East and West, especially the new university established by Hadrian at Rome and called the Athenæum. Thus the cultivated traveler found men of education and literary culture wherever he went.

To such a traveler wandering in Greece and looking back some six hundred years to the Age of Pericles or the Persian Wars of Athens, Greece seemed to belong to a distant and ancient world, of which he had read in the histories of Thucydides and Herodotus (§§ 567, 667). Dreaming of those ancient days when Rome was a little market town on the Tiber, he might wander along the foot of the Acropolis and catch a vision of vanished greatness as it was in the days of Themistocles and Pericles. He could stroll through the porch of the Stoics (§ 761) and renew pleasant memories of his own student days when as a youth his father had permitted him to study there; or he might take a walk out to the Academy, where he had once listened to the teachings of Plato's successors.

1042. The Roman traveler in the East: Greece and Athens

At Delphi too he found a vivid story of the victories of Hellas in the days of her greatness — a story told in marble treasuries and votive monuments, the thanksgiving gifts of the Greeks to Apollo (§ 490 and Fig. 172). As the Roman visitor stood there among the thickly clustered monuments, he noticed many an empty pedestal, and he recalled how the villas of his friends at home were now adorned with the statues which had once occupied those empty pedestals. The Greek cities which had brought forth such things were now poor and helpless, commercially and politically, in spite of the rich heritage of civilization which they had bequeathed to the Romans.

1043. The Roman traveler in the East: Delphi

As the traveler passed eastward through the flourishing cities of Asia Minor and Syria, he might feel justifiable pride in what Roman rule was accomplishing. In the western half of the Fertile Crescent, especially on the east of the Jordan, where there had formerly been only a nomad wilderness (§ 135), there were now prosperous towns, with long aqueducts, with baths, theaters, basilicas, and imposing public buildings, of which the ruins even at the present day are astonishing. All

1044. The Roman traveler in the East: Asia Minor and Syria

these towns were not only linked together by the fine roads we have mentioned, but they were likewise connected with Rome by other fine roads leading entirely across Asia Minor and the Balkan Peninsula.

**1045. The Roman traveler in the East: Parthia, Assyria, and Babylonia**

Beyond the desert behind these towns lay the troublesome Parthian Empire. The educated Roman had read how over five hundred years earlier Xenophon, and later Alexander the Great,

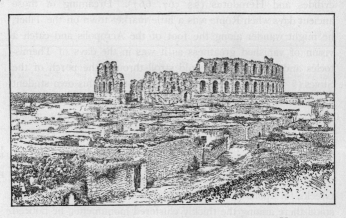

FIG. 258. ROMAN AMPHITHEATER SEEN ACROSS THE HUTS OF A MODERN NORTH AFRICAN VILLAGE

The town which once supported a public place of amusement like this has given way to a squalid village, and the whole region west of Carthage has to a large extent relapsed into barbarism

had passed by the heaps of ruins which were once Nineveh out yonder on the Tigris (Fig. 203), and he knew from several Greek histories and the report of Trajan (§ 1023) that the ruinous buildings of Babylon lay still farther down toward the sea on the Euphrates. Trajan's effort to conquer all that country having failed (§ 1023), the Roman traveler made no effort to extend his tour beyond the frontier out into these foreign lands.

But he could take a great Roman galley at Antioch and cross over to Alexandria, where a still more ancient world awaited him. In the vast lighthouse (§ 733), over four hundred years old and visible for hours before he reached the harbor, he recognized the model of the Roman lighthouses he had seen. Here our traveler found himself among a group of wealthy Greek and Roman tourists on the Nile. As they left the magnificent buildings of Hellenistic Alexandria, their voyage up the river carried them at once into

**1046. The Roman traveler in the East: Egypt**

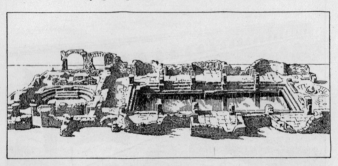

FIG. 259. RUINS OF ROMAN BATHS AT BATH, ENGLAND

There are hot springs at Bath, England, and here the Roman colonists in Britain developed a fashionable watering place. In recent years the soil and rubbish which, through the centuries, had collected over the old Roman buildings have been removed, and we can get some idea of how they were arranged. The picture represents a model of a part of the ruins. To the right is a large quadrangular pool, 83 by 40 feet in size, and to the left a circular bath. Over the whole a fine hall was built, with recesses on either side of the big pool where one might sit and talk with his friends

the midst of an earlier world — the earliest world of which they knew. All about them were buildings which were thousands of years old before Rome was founded. Like our modern fellow citizens touring the same land, many of them were merely curious idlers of the fashionable world. They berated the slow mails, languidly discussed the latest news from Rome, while with indolent curiosity they visited the Pyramids of Gizeh, lounged along the temple lakes and fed the sacred crocodiles, or spent a lazy afternoon carving their names on the colossal statues which overshadowed the plain of Egyptian Thebes (Fig. 69), where Hadrian himself listened to the divine voice which issued from one of the statues every morning when the sun smote upon it. And here we still find their scribblings at the present day. But the thoughtful Roman, while he found not a little pleasure in the sights, took

Fig. 260. Roman Bridge and Aqueduct at Nîmes, France

This structure was built by the Romans about the year 20 A.D. to supply the Roman colony of Nemausus (now called Nîmes) in southern France with water from two excellent springs 25 miles distant. It is nearly 900 feet long and 160 feet high, and carried the water over the valley of the river Gard. The channel for the water is at the very top, and one can still walk through it. The miles of aqueduct on either side of this bridge and leading to it have almost disappeared

note also that this land of ancient wonders was filled as of old with flocks and herds and vast stretches of luxuriant grainfields, which made it the granary of Rome and an inexhaustible source of wealth for the emperor's private purse.

**1047.** Ancient civilization in the East; later Roman in the West The eastern Mediterranean then was regarded by the Romans as *their* ancient world, long possessed of its own ancient civilization, Greek and oriental. There the Roman traveler found Greek everywhere, and spoke it as he traveled. But when he turned away from the East and entered the western Mediterranean, he found a much more modern world, with vast regions where civilization was a recent matter, just as it is in America. Thus throughout North Africa, west of Carthage, throughout Spain, Gaul, and Britain, the Romans had at first found only rough settlements, but no cities and no real architecture. Indeed, these Western lands, the America of the ancients, when first conquered by Rome had not much advanced beyond the stage of the Late Stone Age settlements of several thousand years earlier (§ 325), except here and there, where they had come into contact with the Greeks or Carthaginians.

Seneca, one of the wisest of the Romans, said, "Wherever a Roman has conquered, there he also lives." This was especially true of the West. Roman merchants and Roman officials were everywhere, and many of the cities were Roman colonies. The language of civilized intercourse in all the West was Latin, the language of Rome, whereas east of Sicily the traveler heard only Greek. In this age western Europe had for the first time been building cities; but it was under the guidance of Roman architects, and their buildings looked like those at Rome. In North Africa between the desert and the sea, west of Carthage, the ruins of whole cities with magnificent public buildings still survive (Fig. 258) to show us how Roman civilization reclaimed regions little better than barbarous before the Roman conquest. Similar imposing remains survive in western Europe, especially southern France. We can still visit and study massive bridges, spacious theaters, imposing public monuments, sumptuous villas, and luxurious public baths — a line of ruins stretching from Britain through southern France and Germany to the northern Balkans (Figs. 259–261). <sub>1048. The Roman cities of the West and their surviving buildings</sub>

1048. The Roman cities of the West and their surviving buildings

Just as the communities of Roman subjects once girdled the Mediterranean, so the surviving monuments and buildings which they used, still envelop the great sea from Britain eastward to Jerusalem, and from Jerusalem westward to Morocco. They reveal to us the fact that as a result of all the ages of

1049. The whole Mediterranean world at last highly civilized

FIG. 261. RESTORATION OF ROMAN TRIUMPHAL ARCH AT
ORANGE, FRANCE

Having once adopted this form of monument (Fig. 248), the Romans
built many such handsome arches to commemorate important victories.
There were a number at Rome, naturally (see Fig. 246, *B* and *I*); of
those built in the chief cities of the Empire, several still remain. The
one pictured above was built at the Roman colony of Arausio (now
called Orange), on the river Rhone, to celebrate a victory over the
Gauls in 21 A.D. Modern cities have erected similar arches; for example, Paris, Berlin, London, and New York

human development which we have studied, the whole Mediterranean world, West as well as East, had now gained a high
civilization. Such was the picture which the Roman traveler
gained of that great world which his countrymen ruled: in the
center the vast midland sea, and around it a fringe of civilized

countries surrounded and protected by the encircling line of legions. They too stretched from Britain to Jerusalem, and from Jerusalem to Morocco, like a dike restraining the stormy sea of barbarians outside, which would otherwise have poured in and overwhelmed the results of centuries of civilized development. Meantime we must return from the provinces to the great controlling center of this Mediterranean world, to Rome itself, and endeavor to learn what had been the course of civilization there since the Augustan Age — that is, for the last three quarters of the two centuries of peace.

## Section 92. The Civilization of the Early Roman Empire: Rome

The visitor in Rome at the close of the reign of Hadrian found it the most magnificent monumental city in the world of that day. It had by that time quite surpassed Alexandria in size and in the number and splendor of its public buildings. At the eastern end of the Forum, on ground once occupied by Nero's Golden House (§ 1014), Vespasian erected a vast amphitheater for gladiatorial combats, now known as the Colosseum (Fig. 262). It was completed and dedicated by his son Titus, who arranged for the forty-five thousand spectators which it held, a series of bloody spectacles lasting a hundred days. Although now much damaged, it still stands as one of the greatest buildings in the world. At the same time Vespasian completed the rebuilding of the city, after the great fire of Nero's reign (§ 1014).

1050. Public buildings of Rome: the Colosseum

It was especially in and alongside the old Forum that the grandest buildings of the Empire thus far had grown up. The business of the great world capital led Vespasian and Nerva to erect two more magnificent forums (Fig. 247, *P, Q*). These two, with the two of Cæsar and Augustus (Fig. 247, *N, O*), formed a group of four new forums along the north side of the old Forum. At the northwest end of this group of four Trajan built another,

1051. The new forums of the emperors

that is, a fifth new forum (Fig. 247, *R*), which surpassed in magnificence anything which the Mediterranean world had ever seen before. On one side was a vast new business basilica, and beyond this rose a mighty column (Fig. 263) richly carved with scenes picturing Trajan's brilliant campaigns (Fig. 251). On each side of the column was a library building, one for

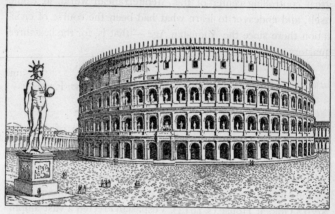

Fig. 262. The Vast Flavian Amphitheater at Rome now called the Colosseum. (Restored after Luckenbach)

This enormous building, one of the greatest in the world, was an oval arena surrounded by the rising tiers of seats, accommodating nearly fifty thousand people. We see here only the outside wall, as restored. It was built by the emperors Vespasian and Titus, and was completed in 80 A.D. (§ 1050). At the left is the colossal bronze statue of Nero, about 100 feet high, which originally stood in this vicinity, near the entrance of his famous " Golden House," just east of the Forum (§ 1014)

Greek and one for Latin literature. The column still stands beside one of the busy streets of modern Rome, but little of the other magnificent buildings has survived.

**1052. Roman concrete: Pantheon and Hadrian's tomb** In the buildings of Trajan and Hadrian the architecture of Rome reached its highest level both of splendor and beauty, and also of workmanship. Sometime in the Hellenistic Age architects had begun to employ increasing quantities of cement concrete, though it is still uncertain where or by whom the hardening properties of cement were discovered. Under Hadrian and his successors the Roman builders completely mastered the art of making colossal casts of concrete. The domed roof of Hadrian's Pantheon (Fig. 264) is a single enormous concrete cast, over a hundred and forty feet across. The Romans, therefore, eighteen hundred years ago were employing concrete on a scale which we have only recently learned to imitate, and after all this lapse of time the roof of the Pantheon seems to be as safe and stanch as it was when Hadrian's architects first knocked away the posts which supported the wooden form for the great cast. The mausoleum erected by Hadrian is the greatest of all Roman tombs

FIG. 263. THE COLUMN OF TRAJAN

This remarkable monument was erected beyond Trajan's Forum in the court between his two libraries (Fig. 247, *T*). It is of Parian marble and stands 100 feet high. Around it winds a spiral band of one hundred and fifty-four relief scenes, passing twenty-two times around the shaft. This band contains twenty-five hundred human figures, and if it could be unrolled it would be over 650 feet long. An examination of one of these reliefs (Fig. 251) shows us that they are very interesting works of art, wrought with much skill. They record Trajan's great campaigns (§ 1022). The broken columns belonged to the magnificent Basilica Ulpia (Fig. 247, *S*), next to Trajan's Forum (Fig. 247, *R*) and for several generations was the burial place of the emperors. It survives as one of the great buildings of Rome.

The *relief* sculpture adorning all these monuments (Fig. 251) is the greatest of Roman art. The reliefs covering Trajan's

FIG. 264. INTERIOR VIEW OF THE DOME OF THE PANTHEON
BUILT AT ROME BY AGRIPPA AND HADRIAN

The first building on this spot was erected by Agrippa, Augustus's great minister. But it was completely rebuilt, as we see it here, by Hadrian. The circular hole in the ceiling is 30 feet across; it is 142 feet above the pavement, and the diameter of the huge dome is also 142 feet. This is the only ancient building in Rome which is still standing with walls and roof in a perfectly preserved state. It is thus a remarkable example of Roman skill in the use of concrete (§ 1052). At the same time it is one of the most beautiful and impressive domed interiors ever designed. Compare the church of St. Sophia, p. 688

column are a wonderful picture book of his campaigns, displaying greater power of invention than Roman art ever showed elsewhere. Of *statue* sculpture, however, the vast majority of the works now produced were copies of the masterpieces of the great Greek sculptors. Many such famous Greek works, which perished long ago, are now known to us only in the form of surviving copies made by the Roman sculptors of this age and discovered in modern excavations in Italy (Fig. 218). The portrait sculptors followed the tendencies which they had inherited from the Hellenistic Age. Their portraits of the leading Romans are among the finest works of the kind ever wrought (Fig. 265).

In painting, the wall decorators were almost the only surviving practicers of the art. They merely copied the works of the great Greek masters of the Hellenistic Age over and over again on the walls of Roman houses (Fig. 197). Portrait painting, however, flourished, and the hack portrait painter at the street corner, who did your portrait quickly for you on a tablet of wood, was almost as common as our own portrait photographer. A young soldier in the Roman army, proud of his new uniform, would for a few cents have his portrait painted to send home in a letter to his parents

1054. Roman painting

FIG. 265. PORTRAIT OF AN UNKNOWN ROMAN

This terra-cotta head is one of the finest portraits ever made. It represents one of the masterful Roman lords of the world, and shows clearly in the features those qualities of power and leadership which so long maintained the supremacy of the Roman Empire

in Egypt (Fig. 253, descriptive matter), and perfectly preserved examples of such work have been excavated in the Nile valley (Plate VIII, p. 654).

There was now a larger educated public at Rome than ever before, and the splendid libraries maintained by the State were open to all. Authors and literary men were also liberally

**1055. Leadership in literature passes from Rome back to Athens**

supported by the emperors. Nevertheless, even under these favorable circumstances not a single genius of great creative imagination arose. Just as in sculpture and painting, so now in literature, the leaders were content to imitate or copy the great works of the past. Real progress in literature therefore ceased. The leadership in such matters, held for a brief time by Rome in the Augustan Age, had now returned to Athens, where the emperors had endowed the four schools of philosophy (§ 762) as a government university. Nevertheless, Rome was still a great influence in literature; the leading literary men of the Empire desired to play a part there, and when a philosopher or teacher of rhetoric published his lectures in book form, he was proud to place under the title the words, " delivered at Rome."

**1056. Latin prose writers: Seneca, Tacitus, and the younger Pliny**

While poetry had declined, prose writers were still productive. Nero's able minister Seneca (§ 1012) wrote very attractive essays and letters on personal character and conduct. They show so fine an appreciation of the noblest human traits that many have thought he had secretly adopted Christianity. His style became so influential that it displaced that of Cicero for a long time. The new freedom of speech which arose under the liberal emperors after the death of Domitian permitted Tacitus to write a frank history of the Empire from the death of Augustus to the death of Domitian (from 14 A.D. down to 96 A.D.). Although he allowed his personal prejudices to sway him, so that he has given us a very dark picture of the Julian emperors, his tremendous power as a writer resulted in the greatest history ever put together by a Roman. Among his other writings was

---

\* Quite a number of such portraits have been preserved in Egypt attached to mummies of the second century A.D. The portrait was painted on a thin board, laid over the face of the mummy, and bound down with the wrappings. The method of painting is interesting. No oil colors were known in the ancient world. The painter mixed his colors in melted wax, which he then applied while hot to the board. While this method was old Egyptian, the artist's skill in painting light was Greek (§ 650; cf. Fig. 197). It was common in Italy, and even poor people had their portraits painted in this way. The portrait of Apion, the young Roman soldier (§ 1054), must have looked like this.

PLATE VIII. ONE OF THE OLDEST SURVIVING
PORTRAIT PAINTINGS*

a brief account of Germany, which furnishes us our first full glimpse into the life of the peoples of northern Europe. The letters which at this time passed between the younger Pliny and the emperor Trajan (§ 1032) are among the most interesting literature of the ancient world. They remind us of the letters of Hammurapi of Babylon some twenty-two hundred years earlier (§§ 178–182).

With these writers in Latin we should also associate several immortal works by Greeks of the same age, though they did not live at Rome. In the little village of Chæronea in Bœotia, where Philip of Macedon crushed the Greeks (§ 685), Plutarch at this time wrote his remarkable series of lives of the greatest men of Greece and Rome, placing them in pairs, a Greek and a Roman together, and comparing them. Although they contain much that belongs in the world of romance, they form an imperishable gallery of heroes which has held the interest and the admiration of the world for eighteen centuries. At the same time another Greek, named Arrian, who was serving as a Roman governor in Asia Minor, collected the surviving accounts of the life of Alexander the Great. He called his book the Anabasis of Alexander, after the Anabasis of Xenophon (§ 631), whom he was imitating in accordance with the imitative spirit of the age. Arrian was only a passable writer of prose and certainly not a great historian, but without his compilation we would know very little about Alexander the Great. A huge guidebook through Greece, telling the reader all about the buildings and monuments still standing at that time in the leading Greek towns, like Athens, Delphi, and Olympia, was now put together by Pausanias. It furnishes us an immortal picture book in words of ancient Greece in all its splendor of statues and temples, theaters and public buildings.

**1057. Greek prose writers: Plutarch, Arrian, and Pausanias**

In science the Romans continued to be collectors of the knowledge gained by the Greeks. During a long and successful official career the elder Pliny devoted himself with incredible industry to scientific studies. He made a vast collection of the

**1058. Lack of scientific attainments at Rome: Pliny's "Natural History"**

facts then known in science, to be found in books, chiefly Greek. He put them all together in a huge work which he called "Natural History" — really an encyclopedia. He was so deeply interested in science that he lost his life in the great eruption of Vesuvius, as he was trying both to study the tremendous event at short range, and (as admiral of the fleet) to save the fleeing people of Pompeii (§ 1034). But Pliny's "Natural History" did not contain any new facts of importance discovered by the author himself, and it was marred by many errors in matters which Pliny misunderstood. Nevertheless, for hundreds of years, until the revival of science in modern times Pliny's work was, next to Aristotle, the standard authority referred to by all educated Europeans. Thus men fell into an indolent attitude of mind and were satisfied merely to learn what earlier discoverers had found out. This attitude never would have led to the discovery of the size of the earth as determined by Eratosthenes (§ 745), or in modern times to X-ray photographs or wireless telegraphy.

**1059. End of investigative science at Alexandria; Ptolemy**   A great astronomer and geographer of Alexandria, who flourished under Hadrian and the Antonines, was the last of the famous scientists of the ancient world. He wrote among other works a handbook on astronomy, for the most part a compilation from the works of earlier astronomers. In it he unfortunately adopted the conclusion that the sun revolved around the earth as a center. His book became a standard work, and hence this mistaken view of the solar system, called the Ptolemaic system, was everywhere accepted by the later world. It was not until four hundred years ago that the real truth, already long before discovered by the Greek astronomer Aristarchus of Samos (§ 744), was rediscovered by the Polish astronomer Copernicus. It was a further sign of the decline of science that Ptolemy even wrote a book on Babylonian astrology (§ 192). Knowledge of the spherical form of the earth as shown by Ptolemy and earlier Greek astronomers reached the travelers and navigators of later Europe, and finally led Columbus to undertake the voyage to India and the East *westward* — the voyage which resulted in the discovery of America.

The position of educated Greeks at Rome was very different from what it had been under the Republic, when such men were slaves or teachers in private households. Now they were holding important positions in the government or as teachers and professors paid by the government. The city was no longer Roman or Italian; it had become Mediterranean, and

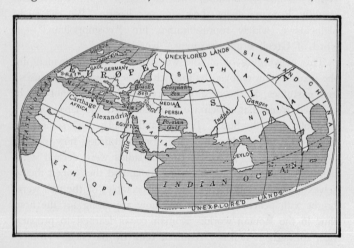

MAP OF THE WORLD BY THE ASTRONOMER AND GEOGRAPHER PTOLEMY (SECOND CENTURY A.D.)

many worthy families from the provinces, settling in Rome, had greatly bettered the decadent society of the city. Leading men whose homes in youth had looked out from the hills of Spain upon the Atlantic mingled at Rome with influential citizens who had been born within a stone's throw of the Euphrates. Men of all the world elbowed each other and talked business in the banks and countinghouses of the magnificent new forums; they filled the public offices and administrative departments of the government, and discussed the hand-copied daily paper published by the State; they sat in the libraries and lecture halls of the university and they crowded the lounging places of the public baths and the vast amphitheater. They largely made up the brilliant social life which ebbed and flowed through the streets, as the wealthy and the wise gathered at sumptuous dinners and convivial winter evenings in the city itself, or indolently killed time loafing about the statue-filled gardens and magnificent country villas overlooking the Bay of Naples, where the wealthy Romans spent their summer leisure. We call such all-inclusive, widely representative life "cosmopolitan"—a word of Greek origin meaning "world-cityish."

**1061. Incoming of oriental luxuries** This converging of all the world at Rome was evident in the luxuries now enjoyed by the rich. The outward life, houses, and costumes of the wealthy were on the whole not much changed from that which we found toward the close of the Republic (§§ 889–898). Luxury and display had somewhat increased, and in this direction oriental rarities now played a noticeable part (§ 1038). Roman ladies were decked with diamonds, pearls, and rubies from India, and they robed themselves in shining silks from China. The tables of the rich were bright with peaches and apricots, now appearing for the first time in the Roman world. Roman cooks learned to prepare rice, formerly a delicacy required only by the sick. Horace had amusingly pictured the distress of a miserly Roman when he learned the price of a dish of rice prescribed by his physician. Instead of sweetening their dishes with honey as formerly, Roman households began to find a new product in the market place known as "sakari"; for so the report of a venturesome oriental sailor of the first century A.D. calls the sirup of sugar cane, which he brought by water from India into the Mediterranean for the first time. This is the earliest mention of sugar in history. These new things from the Orient were beginning to appear in Roman life just as the potatoes, tobacco, and Indian corn of America found their way into Europe after the voyages of Columbus had disclosed a new Western world.

## SECTION 93. POPULARITY OF ORIENTAL RELIGIONS AND THE SPREAD OF EARLY CHRISTIANITY

The life of the Orient was at the same time continuing to bring into the Mediterranean other things less easily traced than rice or sugar, but much more important in their influence on the Roman world. The intellectual life of the Empire was steadily declining, as we have seen indicated by literature and science. Philosophy was no longer occupied with new thoughts and the discovery of new truths. Such philosophy had given way to the semireligious systems of living and ideas of right conduct taught by the Stoics and Epicureans (§ 761). Thoughtful Romans read Greek philosophy of this kind in the charming treatises of Cicero (§ 1000) or the discussions of Seneca (§ 1056). Such readers had given up the old Roman gods and accepted these philosophical precepts of daily conduct as their religion. But such teaching was only for the highly educated and the intellectual class.

*1062. Decline of intellectual life and Roman religion*

Nevertheless, such men sometimes followed the multitude and yielded to the fascination of the mysterious religions coming in from the East. Even in Augustus's time the Roman poet Tibullus, absent on a military campaign which sickness had interrupted, wrote to his fiancée Delia in Rome: " What does your Isis for me now, Delia? What avail me those brazen sistra [1] of hers, so often shaken by your hand? . . . Now, now, goddess, help me; for it is proved by many a picture in thy temples that man may be healed by thee." Tibullus and his fiancée belonged to the most cultivated class, but they had taken refuge in the faith of the Egyptian Isis. When Hadrian's handsome young Greek friend Antinoüs was drowned in the Nile, the emperor erected an obelisk at Rome in his memory, with a hieroglyphic inscription announcing the beautiful youth's divinity and his union with Osiris. Attached to

*1063. Egyptian religion in Europe*

---

[1] Egyptian musical instruments played by shaking in the hand.

Hadrian's magnificent villa near Rome was an Egyptian garden, chiefly sacred to Isis and Osiris and filled with their monuments. Plutarch wrote an essay on Isis and Osiris which he dedicated to a priestess of Isis at Delphi. Since the days of the early Empire, multitudes had taken up this Egyptian faith, and temples of Isis were to be found in all the larger

FIG. 266. THE TEMPLE OF ISIS AT POMPEII

Even the little town of Pompeii had its temple of Isis (§ 1063), as did also the little Hellenistic city of Priene (Fig. 212). It has here been restored after Mau

cities (Fig. 266). To-day tiny statuettes and other symbols of the Egyptian goddess are found even along the Seine, the Rhine, and the Danube.

**1064. The Great Mother goddess of Asia Minor; Persian Mithras; popularity of the oriental "mysteries"** The Great Mother goddess of Asia Minor (§ 357), with her consort Attis, gained the devotion of many Romans, also. In the army the Persian Mithras, a god of light (§ 287), was a great favorite, and many a legion had its underground chapel where its members celebrated his triumph. All these faiths had their "mysteries," consisting chiefly of dramatic presentations of the career of the god, especially his submission to death, his triumph over it, and ascent to everlasting life (§ 117). It was believed that to witness these things and to undergo certain holy ceremonies of initiation would bring to those initiated deliverance from evil, the power to share in the endless life of the god and to dwell with him forever.

The old Roman faith had little to do with conduct and held out to the worshiper no such hopes of future blessedness. Throughout the great Roman world men were longing for some assurance regarding the life beyond the grave, and in the midst of the trials and burdens of this life they wistfully sought the support and strength of a divine protector. Little wonder that the multitudes were irresistibly attracted by the comforting assurances of these oriental faiths and the blessed future insured by their "mysteries." At the same time it was believed possible to learn the future of every individual by the use of Babylonian astrology (§ 192). Even the astronomer Ptolemy wrote a book on it (§ 1059). The Orientals who practiced it were called Chaldeans (§ 238), or Magi, whence our words "magic" and "magician," and everyone consulted them.

1065. Decline of Roman religion and the old gods

The Jews too, now that their temple in Jerusalem had been destroyed by the Romans (§ 1018), were to be found in increasing numbers in all the larger cities. Strabo, the geographer, said of them, "This people has already made its way into every city, and it would be hard to find a place in the habitable world which has not admitted this race and been dominated by it." The Roman world was becoming accustomed to their synagogues; but the Jews refused to acknowledge any god besides their own, and their exclusiveness brought them disfavor and trouble with the government (cf. Fig. 267).

1066. Judaism

Among all these faiths of the East, the common people were more and more inclining toward one, whose teachers told how their Master, Jesus, a Hebrew, was born in Palestine, the land of the Jews, in the days of Augustus. Everywhere they told the people of his vision of human brotherhood and of divine

1067. Rise of Christianity

fatherhood, surpassing even that which the Hebrew prophets had once discerned (§ 304). This faith he had preached for a few years in the Aramaic language of his countrymen (§ 207) — till he incurred their hatred, and in the reign of Tiberius, they had put him to death.

**1068.** Paul and the foundation of the earliest churches; the New Testament

FIG. 267. CERTIFICATE SHOWING THAT A ROMAN CITIZEN HAD SACRIFICED TO THE EMPEROR AS A GOD*

A Jewish tentmaker of Tarsus named Paul, a man of passionate eloquence and unquenchable love for his Master, passed far and wide through the cities of Asia Minor and Greece, and even to Rome (§ 1036), proclaiming his Master's teaching. He left behind him a line of devoted communities stretching from Palestine to Rome. Certain letters (cf. Fig. 253) which he wrote in Greek to his followers were circulating widely among them and were read with eagerness. At the same time a narrative of the Master's life had also been written in Aramaic (Fig. 131), the language in which he had preached. This perished, but Greek accounts drawing upon the Aramaic narrative also appeared, and were now widely read by the common people. There were finally *four* leading biographies of Jesus in Greek, which came to be regarded as authoritative, and these we call the Four Gospels. Along with the letters of Paul and some other writings they were later put together in a Greek book now known in the English translation as the New Testament.

The other oriental faiths, in spite of their attractiveness, could not offer to their followers the consolation and fellowship of a life so exalted and beautiful, so full of brotherly appeal and human sympathy as that of the new Hebrew Teacher. In the hearts of the toiling millions of the Roman Empire his simple summons, "Come unto me all ye that labor and are heavy laden," proved a mightier power than all the edicts of the Roman emperors. The slave and the freedman, the artisan and craftsman, the humble and the despised in the huge barracks which sheltered the poor in Rome, listened to this new "mystery" from the East, as they thought it to be, and as time passed, multitudes responded and found joy in the hopes which it awakened. In the second century of peace it was rapidly outstripping the other religions of the Roman Empire.

1069. Superiority of Christianity over the other oriental religions

The officers of government often found these early converts not only refusing to sacrifice to the emperor as a god (§ 1016) but also openly prophesying the downfall of the Roman State. The early Christians were therefore more than once called upon to endure cruel persecution (Fig. 267). Their religion seemed incompatible with good citizenship, since it forbade them to show the usual respect for the emperor and the government.

1070. Rome persecutes the early Christians

---

* Excavators in the ruins of Egyptian villages like Fig. 211 have discovered over a score of such certificates, each written on a strip of papyrus. This specimen states that a citizen named Aurelius Horion, living in the village of Theadelphia in Egypt, appeared before a government commission, and not only affirmed that he had always been faithful in the worship of the gods but that he also in the presence of the commission and of witnesses offered sacrifice (a slaughtered animal), presented a drink offering, and likewise consumed a portion of these offerings. In the middle we see the heavy black signature of the presiding official, and at the bottom in four lines the date, corresponding to our 250 A.D. Every Roman citizen at this time, no matter what his religion might be, was obliged to possess such a certificate and to show it on demand. It was called a *libellus*, and the owner of it was called a *libellaticus*. A Christian who would resort to such a means of escaping persecution by the government was greatly despised by the faithful, who refused to comply. Compare our word "libel."

**1071.** Organization of churches and revival of popular leadership

Nevertheless, their numbers steadily grew, and each new Christian group or community organized itself into an assembly of members called an "ecclesia," or as *we* say, a church. " Ecclesia " was the old Greek word for Assembly of the People, and in these new assemblies, or churches, men of ability were now beginning to find those opportunities for leadership and power which the decline of citizenship in the old city republics no longer offered. The leaders of the *churches* were soon to be the strong men of the people, and to play a *political* as well as a *religious* rôle.

## SECTION 94. THE END OF THE SECOND CENTURY OF PEACE

**1072.** Beginning of decline: Antoninus Pius (138–161 A.D.) and Marcus Aurelius (161–180 A.D)

In spite of outward prosperity, especially suggested by the magnificent buildings of the Empire, Mediterranean civilization was declining in the second century of peace. The decline became noticeable in the reign of Hadrian. The just and kindly Antoninus, who followed Hadrian in 138 A.D., was called by the Romans " the Pius," but he hardly showed energy enough to maintain the foreign prestige of the Empire, even though he strengthened the northern frontier walls. His successor, the noble Marcus Aurelius, therefore had to face a very serious situation (161 A.D.). The Parthians, encouraged by the easygoing reign of Antoninus Pius, made trouble on the eastern frontier, and Marcus Aurelius was obliged to fight them in a four years' war before the frontier was safe again.

**1073.** Marcus Aurelius stops the barbarian invasion (167–180 A.D.)

When the Roman troops returned from this war, they brought back with them a terrible plague which destroyed multitudes of men at the very moment when the Empire most needed them. For at this juncture the barbarian hordes in the German North broke through the frontier defenses (Fig. 252), and for the first time in two centuries they poured down into Italy (167 A.D.). The two centuries of peace were ended. At the same time the finances of the Empire were so low that the emperor was obliged to sell the crown jewels to raise the money necessary for equipping and supporting the army. With little intermission, until his death in 180 A.D., Marcus Aurelius maintained the struggle against the Germans in the region later forming Bohemia. Indeed, death overtook him while still engaged in the war. But in spite of victory over the barbarians, Marcus Aurelius was unable to sweep them entirely out of the northern regions of the Empire. He finally took the very dangerous step of allowing some of them to remain as farmer colonists on lands assigned to them inside of the frontier. This policy later resulted in very serious consequences to the Empire.

Nevertheless, the ability and enlightened statesmanship of Marcus Aurelius are undoubted. Indeed, they were only equaled by the purity and beauty of his personal life. He regarded his exalted office as a sacred trust to which he must be true, in spite of the fact that he would have greatly preferred to devote himself to reading, study, and philosophy, which he deeply loved. Amid the growing anxieties of his position, even as he sat in his tent and guided the operations of the legions among the forests of Bohemia in the heart of the barbarous North, he found time to record his thoughts and leave to the world a little volume of meditations written in Greek. As the aspirations of a gentle and chivalrous heart toward pure and noble living, these meditations are among the most precious legacies of the past. Marcus Aurelius was the last of a noble succession, the finest spirit among all the Roman emperors, and there was never another like him on the imperial throne. But no ruler, however pure and unselfish his purposes, could stop the processes of decline going on in the midst of the great Roman world. Following the two centuries of peace, therefore, was to come a fearful century of revolution, civil war, and anarchy, from which a very different Roman world was to emerge.

1074. Character of Marcus Aurelius

## QUESTIONS

SECTION 90. Did the struggle at the death of Nero long endanger the peace of the Empire? Who triumphed? What were the two great tasks awaiting the emperors? Describe the dangers on the frontiers. What did Domitian do for the frontiers? Recount the achievements of Trajan on the lower Danube; in the Orient. How did Hadrian treat the conquests of Trajan? What can you say of the Roman army under Trajan and Hadrian? How was the management of the government improved? How did this affect tax collecting? What can you say of agricultural conditions in Italy? How were the laws improved? Tell about the people's interest in public affairs in the provinces.

SECTION 91. Give an imaginary bird's-eye view of the Roman Empire from Gibraltar. Describe Pompeii. Describe Roman roads and their traffic. Tell something of sea travel; of commerce; of hotels; of society in the provinces. What did a Roman traveler find in Athens and Delphi? in Asia Minor and Syria? in Egypt? Where did the Roman's ancient world lie? Where was his modern world? What can you say of Roman buildings surviving in the West?

SECTION 92. How had Rome now improved? Describe the Colosseum; the forums of the emperors. What can you say of Roman use of cement in architecture? of Roman sculpture? of Roman painting? What had happened to literature in Rome since Augustus? Tell about the Latin prose writers; the Greek prose writers. What can you say of science at Rome? at Alexandria? Tell about the cosmopolitan life of Rome. What can you say of incoming luxuries of the Orient?

SECTION 93. What can you say of intellectual life at Rome? of religious life? of incoming oriental religions? What was the feeling of the common people toward the oriental religions? What can you say of the Jews at this time? Describe the rise of Christianity and the work of Paul. What can you say of the superiority of Christianity? What practical difficulty did the Christians meet in their relations with the Roman government? What certificate did a citizen have to possess?

SECTION 94. What people first caused Marcus Aurelius trouble? What event ended the second century of peace? What did Marcus Aurelius do to subdue the barbarians? What can you say of the mind and character of Marcus Aurelius?

# CHAPTER XXIX

## A CENTURY OF REVOLUTION AND THE DIVISION OF THE EMPIRE

### SECTION 95. INTERNAL DECLINE OF THE ROMAN EMPIRE

We have seen good government, fine buildings, education, and other evidences of civilization more widespread in the second century of peace than ever before. Nevertheless, the great

**1075. Signs of inner decay: former decline of farming continues**

NOTE. The above headpiece shows us the surviving ruins of the royal palace at Ctesiphon on the Tigris (see map, p. 709), once the capital of New Persia. The tiny human figure in one doorway will indicate to us the vast size of the building. The huge vault on the right was built over the enormous hall below, without any supporting timbers during the course of construction. It is 84 feet across and is the largest masonry vault of its age still standing in Asia. Here the magnificent kings of New Persia held their splendid court, imitated by the weak Roman emperors at Constantinople (§ 1099). Note the situation of Babylon as a river station on the great highway between Asia Minor and the East (map, p. 434). Ctesiphon, situated almost within sight of Babylon, was but one in a succession of powerful capitals, occupying this great river crossing: Akkad (§ 166), Babylon (§ 175), Ctesiphon (§ 1094), and, finally, Bagdad (§ 1153). A British expedition, after fighting several battles under the shadow of these ruins of Ctesiphon, captured Bagdad in 1917.

Empire which we have been studying, although in a condition seemingly so favorable, was suffering from an inner decay, whose symptoms at first hidden were fast becoming more and more evident. In the first place, the decline of farming, so noticeable before the fall of the Republic (§§ 918 f.), had gone steadily on.

**1076. Spread of the oriental domain system of landownership; villas**

In spite of the heavy taxes imposed upon it, land had continued to pass over into the hands of the rich and powerful. The oriental system of confining landownership to large domains held by the State and a few individuals had also a strong influence. From Asia Minor, where it was widespread under the Persians, this system had passed to Greece (§ 626). The Romans had found it also in Africa, the province behind Carthage. Already in Nero's time half of this province was made up of six domains, held by only six great landlords. Such a great estate was called a *villa*, and the system of villa estates, having destroyed the small farmers of Italy (§§ 918–920), was likewise now destroying them in the provinces also. Villas now covered not only Italy but also Gaul, Britain, Spain, and other leading provinces.

**1077. Rise of *coloni***

Unable to compete with the great villas, and finding the burden of taxes unbearable, most of the small farmers gave up the struggle. Such a man would often enter upon an arrangement which made him the *colonus* of some wealthy villa owner. By this arrangement the farmer and his descendants were forever bound by law to the land which they worked, and they passed with it from owner to owner when it changed hands. While not actually slaves, they were not free to leave or go where they pleased; and without any prospect of bettering themselves, or any opportunity for their children ever to possess their own lands, these men lost all energy and independence and were very different from the hardy farmers of early Rome. As we shall see, many Northern barbarians also became *coloni* within the frontiers of the Empire.

The great villas once worked by slaves were now cultivated chiefly by these *coloni*. With the end of the long wars the captives who had been sold as slaves were no longer obtainable, and slaves had steadily diminished in numbers. Their condition had also much improved, and the law now protected them from the worst forms of cruelty once inflicted upon them (§ 915). We have already noticed the growing practice of freeing slaves, which made freedmen so common throughout the Empire that they were playing an important part in manufactures and business (§ 1040).

1078. Decline of slavery and improvement in the condition of slaves

Multitudes of the country people, unwilling to become *coloni*, forsook their fields and turned to the city for relief. Many did this because neglect of fertilization and long-continued cultivation had exhausted their land and it would no longer produce crops. Great stretches of unworked and weed-grown fields were no uncommon sight. As a result the amount of land under cultivation continually decreased, and the ancient world was no longer raising enough food to feed itself properly. The scarcity was felt most severely in the great centers of population like Rome, where prices had rapidly gone up. Our own generation, afflicted in the same way, is not the first to complain of the " high cost of living."

1079. Decrease in extent of cultivated lands and diminishing food supply

Offers by the emperor to give land to anyone who would undertake to cultivate it failed to increase the amount of land under the plow. Even under the wisest emperors the government was therefore entirely unable to restore to the country districts the hardy yeomen, the brave and independent farmers, who had once formed the basis of Italian prosperity — the men who, in the ranks of the legion, had laid the foundation of Roman power. The destruction of the small farmers and the inability of Rome to restore them formed the leading cause among a whole group of causes which brought about the decline and fall of this great Empire.

1080. Disappearance of the farmers and Rome's inability to restore them

The country people who moved to Rome were only bringing about their own extermination as a class. The large families which country life favors were no longer reared, the number of marriages decreased, and the population of the Empire shrank.

1081. Debasing influences of city life

Debased by the life of the city, the former sturdy yeoman lost his independence in an eager scramble for a place in the waiting line of city poor, to whom the government distributed free grain, wine, and meat. The time which should have been spent in breadwinning was worse than wasted among the cheering multitudes at the chariot races, bloody games, and barbarous spectacles. Notwithstanding the fine families who moved to Rome from the provinces under the liberal emperors of the second century A.D., the city became a great hive of shiftless population supported by the State, with money which the struggling agriculturist was taxed to provide. The same situation was in the main to be found in all the leading cities.

**1082. Decline of citizenship in the cities**

In spite of outward splendor, therefore, these cities too were declining. They had now learned to depend upon Rome to care for them even in their own local affairs, and their citizens had rapidly lost all sense of public responsibility. The helpful rivalry between neighboring city-states too had long ago ceased. Everywhere the leading men of the cities were indifferently turning away from public life. Moreover, Rome was beginning to lay financial obligations upon the leading men of such cities, and it was becoming increasingly difficult to find men willing to assume these burdens. Responsible citizenship, which does so much to develop the best among the citizens in any community and which had earlier so sadly declined in Greece (§ 767), was passing away, never to reappear in the ancient world.

**1083. Decline of business**

At the same time the financial and business life of the cities was also declining. The country communities no longer possessed a numerous purchasing population. Hence the country market for the goods manufactured in the cities was so seriously reduced that city industries could no longer dispose of their products. They rapidly declined. The industrial classes were thrown out of work and went to increase the multitudes of the city poor. City business was also much hurt by a serious lack of precious metals for coining money.

Many of the old silver and gold mines around the Mediterranean now seem to have been worked out. Wear in circulation, loss by shipwreck, private hoards, and considerable sums which went to pay for goods in India and China, or as gifts to the German barbarians, — all these causes aided in diminishing the supply of the precious metals. The government was therefore unable to secure enough to coin the money necessary for the transaction of business. The emperors were obliged to begin mixing in an increasing amount of less valuable metals and coining this cheaper alloy. The Roman coin collections in the European museums show us that the coins of Augustus were pure, while those of Marcus Aurelius contain twenty-five per cent of alloy. Two generations after Marcus Aurelius there was only five per cent of silver in a government coin. A *denarius*, the common small coin worth nearly twenty cents under Augustus, a century after the death of Marcus Aurelius was worth only half a cent.

**1084.** Lack of precious metals for coinage and debasement of coins

Even Marcus Aurelius had trouble in finding enough money to pay his army. As soon as this difficulty became serious it paralyzed the government and demoralized the army. It was impossible to maintain a paid army without money. As it became quite impossible to collect taxes in money, the government was obliged to accept grain and produce as payment of taxes, and great granaries and storehouses began to take the place of the treasury as in ancient Egypt (§ 75). Here and there the army was paid in grain. On the frontiers, for lack of other pay the troops were assigned lands, which of course did them no good unless they could cultivate them. Then they were allowed to marry and to live with their families in little huts on their lands near the frontier. Called out only occasionally for drill or to repel a barbarian raid, they soon lost all discipline, became merely feeble militia, called by the Roman government "frontiersmen" (*limitanei*).

**1085.** Decline of the army; the frontier legions become militia

Even under Marcus Aurelius, a governor of a province had started a serious rebellion. Hence the emperor was now

**1086. Standing army in Italy, and its decline**

obliged to keep a standing army in Italy. These legions had become much smaller, and they were made up increasingly of barbarians, especially Germans and the uncivilized natives of the northern Balkan, among whom the Illyrians took the lead. The Roman citizen was now a rarity in the ranks, and it soon became necessary to allow the barbarians to fight in their own massed formations, to which they were accustomed (§ 1120). The discipline of the legion, and the legion itself, disappeared, and with it the superior military power of Rome was gone. The native ferocity and reckless bravery of uncivilized hordes, before which the unmilitary Roman townsmen trembled, were now the power upon which the Empire relied for its protection.

**1087. Demoralization of army and State caused by lack of a law of succession**

This degeneration of the army was much hastened by a serious imperfection in the organization of the Roman State, left there by Augustus. This was the lack of a legal and long-practiced method of choosing a new emperor and transferring the power from one emperor to the next and thus maintaining from reign to reign without a break the supreme authority in the Roman State. The troops found that they could make a new emperor whenever the old emperor's death gave them an opportunity. For an emperor so made they had very little respect, and if he attempted to enforce discipline among them, they put him out of the way and appointed another. Rude and barbarous mercenary soldiery thus became the highest authority in the State.

**1088. Rise of the provinces to a level with Italy and resulting competition**

Finally, the spread of civilization to the provinces had made them feel that they were the equals of Rome and Italy itself. Even under the Republic there was much foreign blood in the peninsula. Horace himself had been the son of a freedman, of nobody-knows-what race. Italy was now largely foreign in population. Trajan and Hadrian had been Spaniards, and more than one province furnished the Empire with its ruler. When, in 212 A.D., citizenship was granted to all free men within the Empire, in whatever province they lived, the leveling of distinctions gave the provinces more and more opportunity to compete for leadership.

## SECTION 96. A CENTURY OF REVOLUTION

These forces of decline were bringing swiftly on a century of revolution which was to shipwreck the civilization of the early world. This fatal century began with the death of Marcus Aurelius in 180 A.D. The assassination of his unworthy son Commodus, who reminds us of Nero, was the opportunity for a struggle among a group of military usurpers. From this struggle a rough but successful soldier named Septimius Severus emerged triumphant. It was he who found himself obliged to settle the frontier troops on their own lands, with resulting demoralization of the army (§ 1085). He systematically filled the highest posts in the government with military leaders of low origin. Thus, both in the army (§ 1086) and in the government, the ignorant and often foreign masses were gaining control. Nevertheless, the energy of Severus was such that he led his forces with success against the Parthians in the East, and even recovered Mesopotamia. But the arch which he erected to commemorate his victories, and which still stands in the Forum at Rome (Fig. 246, *1*), reveals in its barbarous sculptures the fearful decline of culture in Italy. The Roman artists who wrought these rude reliefs were the grandsons of the men who had so skillfully sculptured the column of Trajan (Fig. 251).

*1089. Beginning of a century of revolution; decline under Septimius Severus (193-211 A.D.)*

The family of Septimius Severus maintained itself for a time, and it was his son Caracalla who conferred citizenship on all freemen in the Empire in 212 A.D. (§ 1088). But when the line of Severus ended (235 A.D.), the storm broke. The barbaric troops in one province after another set up their puppet emperors to fight among themselves for the throne of the Mediterranean world. The proclamation of a new emperor would be followed again and again by news of his assassination. From the leaders of the barbaric soldier class, after the death of Commodus, the Roman Empire received eighty rulers in ninety years. One of these rulers of a day, in 248 A.D., went

*1090. End of the line of Severus (235 A.D.) and the ensuing civil wars among provincial emperors*

through the mockery of celebrating the thousand years' jubilee of the traditional founding of Rome.

**1091. Fifty years of anarchy and the collapse of higher civilization**

Most of these so-called emperors were not unlike the revolutionary bandits who proclaim themselves presidents of Mexico. For fifty years there was no public order, as the plundering troops tossed the scepter of Rome from one soldier emperor to another. Life and property were nowhere safe; turbulence, robbery, and murder were everywhere. The tumult and fighting between rival emperors hastened the ruin of all business, and as the affairs of the nation passed from bad to worse, national bankruptcy ensued. In this tempest of anarchy during the third century A.D. the civilization of the ancient world suffered final collapse. The supremacy of mind and of scientific knowledge won by the Greeks in the third century B.C. (§ 743) yielded to the reign of ignorance and superstition in these social disasters of the third century A.D.

**1092. Barbarian raids**

As the Roman army weakened, the Northern barbarians were quick to perceive the helplessness of the Empire (§ 1086). In the East the Goths, one of the strongest German tribes, took to the water, and their fleet passed out of the Black Sea into the Mediterranean. While they devastated the coast cities far and wide, other bands pushed down through the Balkan Peninsula and laid waste Greece as far as the Peloponnese. Even Athens was plundered. The barbarians penetrated far into Italy; in the West they overran Gaul and Spain, and some of them even crossed to Africa. In Gaul they burned city after city, and their leaders stood by and laughed in exultation as they saw the flames devouring the beautiful buildings of the Roman cities (Figs. 258–261).

**1093. Temporary independence of Gaul and evidences of rebuilding of its cities**

Under these circumstances, when the people of the plundered lands saw that the Empire could no longer defend them, they organized for their own defense. In this way Gaul, for example, became an independent nation under its own rulers for years in this terrible century. Its people repulsed the barbarians and slowly rebuilt their burned cities. They dared not spread out the city, as before, but grouping all the buildings close together, the town was built compactly and surrounded by a massive wall, made largely of blackened blocks of stone taken from the ruined buildings burned by the barbarians. In no less than sixty cities of France to-day sections of these heavy walls, when taken down to make room for modern improvements, are found to contain these smoke-blackened blocks. Far outside the city walls containing these blocks, excavation has revealed to us the foundations of the splendid Roman structures from which the blocks came and which formed the once larger city destroyed by the barbarians.

At the same time a new danger had arisen in the East. A revival of patriotism among the old Persian population had resulted in a vigorous restoration of their national life. Their leaders, a family called Sassanians (or Sassanids), overthrew the Parthians (226 A.D.) and furnished a new line of enlightened Persian kings. As they took possession of the Fertile Crescent and established their capital at Ctesiphon on the Tigris, not far north of Babylon, a new Orient arose on the ruins of seemingly dead and forgotten ages. Fine buildings of Persian architecture (headpiece, p. 667), though influenced by Greek art, again looked down upon the Tigris and Euphrates, beautiful works of the Persian artist and craftsman again began to appear, and the revered religion of Zoroaster took on new life. We have in this movement a last revival of that old Iranian race which produced the religion of Zoroaster and built up the vast Persian Empire. The Sassanian kings organized a much more powerful State than that of the Parthians which they overthrew, and they regarded themselves as the rivals of the Romans for the Empire of the world. The old rivalry between the Orient and the West, as in the days of Greece and Persia, was now continued, with Rome as the champion of the West, and this New Persia as the leader of the East (see map II, p. 636).

Just as the family of Severus was declining, this empire of New Persia rose into power as a dangerous foe of the Roman

1094. Rise of New Persia (226 A.D.) under her Sassanian kings

**1095.** Palmyra a buffer state against New Persia; Zenobia

Empire on the eastern frontier. From this time on the Empire was seriously threatened on two fronts, on north and east. As in Gaul, so in the East, the rise of a usurper within the Roman Empire for a time saved the region from absorption by the outside enemy. One of the eastern governors, using Palmyra as a center, gained his independence and defended the eastern frontier on his own account. After his death his widow, the beautiful Zenobia, ruled at Palmyra as queen of the East, over a realm which included Asia Minor, Syria, and Egypt. Her kingdom served for a time as a buffer state, protecting the Roman Empire from attack by New Persia.

**1096.** Aurelian (270–275 A.D.) recovers the East and Gaul; Diocletian restores order (284 A.D.)

With a powerful oriental state under Zenobia holding the eastern Mediterranean lands, and an able senator named Tetricus, master of Gaul, Britain, and northern Spain, ruling the West as an independent emperor (§ 1093), it looked as if the Roman Empire were about to fall to pieces. The anarchy which we have already noticed within the Empire was at its worst, when one of the soldier emperors, named Aurelian (270 to 275 A.D.), advanced against Zenobia, defeated her army, captured Palmyra and took the queen prisoner. Similar success in Gaul enabled him to celebrate a gorgeous triumph in Rome, with Zenobia and Tetricus led through the streets of the city along with the other captives who adorned his triumph. Aurelian restored some measure of order and safety. But, in order to protect Rome from the future raids of the barbarians, he built entirely around the great city the massive wall (Fig. 249, and plan, p. 622) which still stands, — a confession of the dangerous situation of Rome in the third century A.D. It was a little over a century after the death of Marcus Aurelius, when the emperor Diocletian restored what looked like a lasting peace (284 A.D.).

If at this point we look back some four hundred years over the history of Rome since she became mistress of the world, we discern three great periods.[1] With the foundation of the

---

[1] Periods of history do not end or begin abruptly. There is always a gradual transition from one to the next, and the dates in this paragraph merely suggest the points at which the transition was very evident.

Empire by Augustus there began two centuries of peace, and this period of peace was both preceded and followed by a century of revolution. We have thus had a century of revolution, two centuries of peace, and then a second century of revolution. The first century of revolution led from the Gracchus brothers to the triumph of one-man power and the foundation of the Empire by Augustus (that is, about 133 to 30 B.C.). The two centuries of peace beginning with the foundation of the Empire by Augustus continued into the reign of Marcus Aurelius (that is, about 30 B.C. to nearly 170 A.D.). The second century of revolution led from the enlightened reign of Marcus Aurelius to oriental despotism under Diocletian (that is, about 180 to about 284 A.D.). Thus four centuries of Roman imperialism, after bringing forth such masterful men as Sulla and Julius Cæsar, had passed through various stages of one-man power, to end in despotism. We are now first to examine that despotism and then to see how it was overwhelmed by two centuries of barbarian invasions from the North, while at the same time it was also crushed by the reviving power of the Orient, whose assaults were to last many centuries more (study map, p. 678).

1097. Summary of four centuries of Roman imperialism culminating in Diocletian (284 A.D.)

## Section 97. The Roman Empire an Oriental Despotism

The world which issued from the disasters of this second revolution toward the end of the third century A.D. under Diocletian was a totally different one from that which Augustus and the Roman Senate had ruled three centuries before. Diocletian deprived the shadowy Senate of all power, except for the municipal government of the city of Rome. The Roman Senate, now reduced to a mere City Council, a Board of Aldermen, disappeared from the stage of history. The emperor thus became for the whole Roman world what he had always been in Egypt, — an absolute monarch with none to limit his power.

1098. Diocletian (284–305 A.D.); the Roman Empire an oriental despotism

The State had been completely militarized and orientalized. With the unlimited power of the oriental despot the emperor now assumed also its outward symbols — the diadem, the gorgeous robe embroidered with pearls and precious stones, the throne and footstool, before which all who came into his presence must bow down to the dust.

**1099. New Persian influence; triumph of oriental influences**

Recent discovery has shown that the gorgeous costume in which the Roman emperor now decked himself was copied from that of the Sassanian kings of New Persia. The Roman leaders had seen much of this new empire of the East for two generations, and from its brilliant oriental court these outward matters of royal costume, court symbols, and customs were adopted. Oriental influence on Roman beliefs, such as we have seen in the spread of the worship of the Persian god Mithras (§ 1064), was now also affecting the notion of the divinity of the emperor (§ 1016). In these things we recognize a further stage in that commingling of the East and West, begun by Alexander the Great over six hundred years before (§ 703). Indeed, the Roman Empire had now become like a vast sponge absorbing the life and civilization of the Orient.

**1100. Emperor an oriental Sun-god; triumph of despotism, end of democracy**

As a divinity, the emperor had now become an oriental Sun-god and he was officially called the "Invincible Sun." His birthday was on the twenty-fifth of December; that is, about the date when the sun each year begins to turn northward after he has reached his southernmost limit. The inhabitants of each province might revere their particular gods, undisturbed by the government, but all were obliged as good citizens to join in the official sacrifices to the head of the State as a god. With the incoming of this oriental attitude toward the emperor, the long struggle for democracy, which we have followed through so many centuries of the history of early man, ended in the triumph of oriental despotism.

The necessity of leading the army against New Persia, the new oriental enemy, carried the emperor much to the East. The result was that Diocletian resided most of the time at

ROMAN EMPIRE
AS ORGANIZED BY DIOCLETIAN AND CONSTANTINE

Boundary Line of the Empire
Line of Division between the Eastern and Western Empires
Prefecture of the Orient
Prefecture of Illyricum
Prefecture of Italy
Prefecture of Gaul

Scale of Statute Miles
0   100   200   300   400   500   600

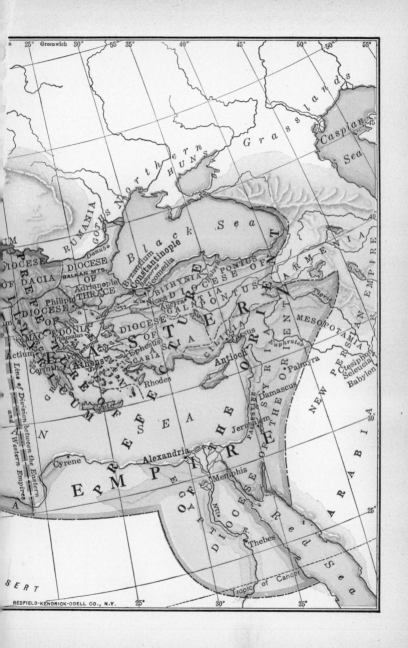

Greenwich 25° 30° 35° 40° 45° 50° 50° 55°

Northern Grasslands

GOTHS HUNS

RUMANIA

Caspian Sea

Danube

Black Sea

DIOCESE OF DACIA

BALKAN MTS.

Byzantium
Bosphorus
Constantinople
Nicomedia

DIOCESE OF THRACE

Adrianople

Philippi

DIOCESE OF MACEDONIA

Pharsalus

Nicaea
Ancyra
BITHYNIA
PONTUS

DIOCESE OF PONTUS

ARMENIA

NEW PERSIAN EMPIRE

MESOPOTAMIA

Tigris

DIOCESE OF ASIA

GALATIA

Ephesus
CARIA

CILICIA
Tarsus

Euphrates

Ctesiphon
Seleucia
Babylon

Actium

GREECE

Corinth
Athens

Antioch

SYRIA

Palmyra

Line of Division between the Eastern and Western Empires

Rhodes

Crete

SEA

Damascus

THE ORIENT

DIOCESE OF THE ORIENT

PALESTINE

ARABIA

Jerusalem

Cyrene

Alexandria

EMPIRE

Memphis

DIOCESE OF EGYPT

Nile

Red Sea

Thebes

Tropic of Cancer

DESERT

REDFIELD-KENDRICK-ODELL CO., N.Y.     25°     30°     35°

Nicomedia in Asia Minor (see map, p. 678). As a natural consequence the emperor was unable to give close attention to the West. Following some earlier examples, and perhaps remembering the two consuls of the old Republic, Diocletian therefore appointed another emperor to rule jointly with himself, to give his attention to the West. The second emperor was to live at Milan in the Po valley, really the most important region of Italy. All government edicts, whether issued in the East or the West, were signed by both emperors, and it was not Diocletian's intention to divide the Roman Empire, any more than it had been the purpose to divide the Republic in electing two consuls. The final result was nevertheless the division of the Roman Empire into East and West, just as it had once been divided by the war between Cæsar in the West and Pompey in the East, or the similar conflict between Octavian in the West and Antony in the East.

**1101.** Diocletian resides in the East and appoints an emperor of the West

In order to avoid the recurrence of civil war at the death of an emperor, Diocletian endeavored to arrange the transfer of power from one emperor to the next. He and his fellow emperor each bore the title of Augustus. The two Augustuses appointed two subordinates, to be called Cæsars. There were thus two emperors, or Augustuses, and two subordinate emperors, or Cæsars, intended to be something like vice presidents. For it was provided that at the death or resignation of either Augustus one of the Cæsars should at once take his place as Augustus, and another Cæsar was then to be appointed. These arrangements display little statesmanship, and there was no possibility of their permanence.

**1102.** Diocletian's arrangements for the succession

In accordance with this organization, involving four rulers, the provinces of the Empire, over a hundred in number, were divided into four great groups, or prefectures (see map, p. 678), with a prefect over each. Still smaller groups of provinces, twelve in number, were called *dioceses*, mostly ruled by *vicars*, the subordinates of the prefects; while under the vicars were the governors of the separate provinces. The business of each

**1103.** Diocletian's administrative organization

province was organized in the hands of a great number of local officials graded into many successive ranks and classes from high to low. There was an unbroken chain of connection from the lowest of these up through various ranks to the governor, the vicar, and the prefect, and finally to the emperor himself.

**1104. Oppressive taxation**

The financial burden of this vast organization, begun under Diocletian and completed under his successors, was enormous. For this multitude of government officials and the clamorous army had all to be paid and supported. It was a great expense also to maintain the luxurious oriental court of the emperor, surrounded by his innumerable palace officials and servants. But now there were *four* such imperial courts, instead of one. At the same time it was still necessary to supply "bread and circuses" for the populace of the towns (§ 1081). In regard to taxation, the situation had grown steadily worse since the reign of Marcus Aurelius. The amount of a citizen's taxes therefore continued to increase, and finally little that he possessed was free from taxation.

**1105. Bad methods of tax collection**

When the scarcity of coin forced the government to accept grain and produce from the delinquent taxpayer, taxes had become a mere share in the yield of the lands. The Roman Empire thus sank to a primitive system of taxation already thousands of years old in the Orient. It was now customary to oblige a group of wealthy men in each city to become responsible for the payment of the entire taxes of the district each year, and if there was a deficit, these men were forced to make up the lacking balance out of their own wealth. The penalty of wealth seemed to be ruin, and there was no motive for success in business when such prosperity meant ruinous overtaxation.

**1106. Loss of both farmers and middle-class business men; obligatory practice of occupations**

Many a worthy man secretly fled from his lands to become a wandering beggar, or even to take up a life of robbery and violence. The Roman Empire had already lost, and had never been able to restore, its prosperous *farming class*. It now lost likewise the enterprising and successful *business men* of the middle class. Diocletian therefore endeavored to force these

classes to continue their occupations. He enacted laws forbidding any man to forsake his lands or occupation. The
societies, guilds, and unions in which the men of various occupations had long been organized (§ 1040) were now gradually
made obligatory, so that no one could follow any calling or
occupation without belonging to such a society. Once a
member he must always remain in the occupation it implied.

Thus under this oriental despotism the liberty, for which
men had striven so long, disappeared in Europe, and the once
free Roman citizen had no independent life of his own. For
the will of the emperor had now become law, and as such his
decrees were dispatched throughout the length and breadth of
the Roman dominions. Even the citizen's wages and the prices
of the goods he bought or sold were as far as possible fixed for
him by the State. The emperor's innumerable officials kept an
eye upon even the humblest citizen. They watched the grain
dealers, butchers, and bakers, and saw to it that they properly
supplied the public and never deserted their occupation. In
some cases the State even forced the son to follow the profession of his father. In a word, the Roman government now
attempted to regulate almost every interest in life, and where-
ever the citizen turned he felt the control and oppression of
the State.

1107. Disap-
pearance of
liberty and
free citizen-
ship

Staggering under his crushing burden of taxes, in a State
which was practically bankrupt, the citizen of every class had
now become a mere cog in the vast machinery of the government. He had no other function than to toil for the State,
which exacted so much of the fruit of his labor that he was
fortunate if it proved barely possible for him to survive on what
was left. As a mere toiler for the State, he was finally where
the peasant on the Nile had been for thousands of years. The
emperor had become a Pharaoh, and the Roman Empire a
colossal Egypt of ancient days.

1108. The
citizen a
toiler for the
State

The century of revolution which ended in the despotic reorganization by Diocletian completely destroyed the creative ability

of ancient men in art and literature, as it likewise crushed all progress in business and affairs. In so far as the ancient world was one of progress in civilization, its history was ended with the accession of Diocletian. Nevertheless, the Roman Empire had still a great mission before it, in the preservation of at least something of the heritage of civilization, which it was to hand down the centuries to us of to-day. Moreover, it was out of the fragments of the Roman Empire that the nations of modern Europe grew up. We are now to watch it then as it falls to pieces, still mechanically maintaining its hold upon its mighty heritage from the past, and furnishing the materials, as it were, out of which our world of to-day has been built up.

## SECTION 98. THE DIVISION OF THE EMPIRE AND THE TRIUMPH OF CHRISTIANITY

Under Diocletian Italy had been reduced to the position of a taxed province, and had thus lost the last vestige of superiority over the other provinces of the Empire. The dangerous flood of German barbarians along the lower Danube and the threatening rise of New Persia had drawn the emperor into the northeast corner of the Empire. During the century of revolution just past, the Illyrian soldiers of the Balkan Peninsula had filled the army with the best troops and furnished more than one emperor. An emperor who had risen from the ranks of provincial troops in the Balkans felt little attachment to Rome. Rome had not only ceased to be the residence of an emperor, but the center of power had clearly shifted from Italy to the Balkan Peninsula. The movement was the outcome of a reviving respect for the East and a long growing interest in the Balkan Peninsula, observable even as early as Hadrian, who spent vast sums in the beautification of Athens. After the struggles following Diocletian's death, — struggles which his arrangements for the succession (§ 1102) failed to prevent,— the emperor Constantine the Great emerged victorious (324 A.D.).

He did not hesitate to turn to the eastern edge of the Balkan Peninsula and establish there a New Rome as his residence.

The spot which he selected showed him to be a far-seeing statesman. He chose the ancient Greek town of Byzantium,

**1111. Constantine (324 –337 A.D.) makes Constantinople his residence and seat of government (330 A.D.)**

FIG. 268. VIEW ACROSS THE BOSPORUS FROM EUROPE TO ASIA

This view places us on the *European* shore of the Bosporus, and we look eastward to the *Asiatic* shore, with the mountains behind, rising to the table-land of central Asia Minor (§ 351). Just south of us (at the right) on the same shore is Constantinople; a little to the north (the left) is the place where Darius the Great probably built his bridge when he first invaded Europe to conquer the Scythians (§ 500). The towers and walls before us are part of a fortress built by the Turkish conquerors when they crossed from Asia for the conquest of Constantinople in 1453 A.D. (§ 1158). For ages this intercontinental crossing has been the commercial and military link between Europe and Asia, and as the author writes (May, 1916) the greatest nations of the world are fighting for its possession

on the European side of the Bosporus (Fig. 268), — a magnificent situation overlooking both Europe and Asia, and fitted to be a center of power in both. In placing his new capital here, Constantine established a city, the importance of which was only equaled by the foundation of Alexandria in Egypt. The emperor stripped many an ancient city of its great monuments in order to secure materials for the beautification of his splendid residence (Fig. 269). By 330 A.D. the new capital on the

FIG. 269. ANCIENT MONUMENTS IN CONSTANTINOPLE

The obelisk in the foreground (nearly 100 feet high) was first set up in Thebes, Egypt, by the conqueror Thutmose III (§ 111); it was erected here by the Roman emperor Theodosius (§ 1125). The small spiral column at the right is the base of a bronze tripod set up by the Greeks at Delphi (Fig. 172) in commemoration of their victory over the Persians at Platæa (§ 517). The names of thirty-one Greek cities which took part in the battle are still to be read, engraved on this base. These monuments of ancient oriental and Greek supremacy stand in what was the Roman horse-race course when the earlier Greek city of Byzantium became the Eastern capital of Rome (§ 1111). Finally, the great mosque behind the obelisk, with its slender minarets, represents the triumph of Islam under the Turks, who took the city in 1453 A.D.

Bosporus was a magnificent monumental city, worthy to be the successor of Rome as the seat of the Mediterranean Empire. It was named Constantinople ("Constantine's city") after its founder.

The transfer of the capital of the Roman Empire to the east side of the Balkan Peninsula was a decided triumph for the older civilization of the eastern Mediterranean. But it meant the separation of east and west — the cutting of the Roman Empire in two. Although the separation did not take place abruptly, yet within a generation after Constantinople was founded, the Roman Empire had in fact if not in name become two states, and they were never more than temporarily united again. Thus the founding of Constantinople sealed the doom of Rome and the western Mediterranean lands of the Empire. For a time the eastern half of the Empire, ruled by Constantinople, was greatly strengthened by Diocletian's reorganization. Nevertheless, it too was doomed to steady decline. We have seen that citizenship in the Roman Empire no longer meant a share in the control of public affairs. Able men of affairs were no longer arising among such citizens, except as the army raised one of its commanders to the position of emperor. Peaceful civil life was no longer producing statesmen to control government affairs as in the days of the Roman and Greek republics.

> 1112. Constantinople and the separation of East and West; continuance of decline

In this situation, as the Christian churches steadily increased in numbers, and their influence grew, they more and more needed the guidance of able men. The management of the great Christian communities and their churches called for increasing ability and experience. Public discussion and disputes in the Church assemblies enabled gifted men to stand forth, and their ability brought them position and influence. The Christian Church thus became a new arena for the development of statesmanship, and Church statesmen were soon to be the leading influential men of the age, when civil democracy had long since ceased to produce such men.

> 1113. The churches a new arena for the rise of able men

These officers of the Church gradually devoted themselves more and more to Church duties until they had no time for anything else. They thus came to be distinguished from the other members and were called the *clergy*, while the people who made up the membership were called the *laymen*, or the *laity*. The

> 1114. The Church a powerful organization: priests, bishops, and archbishops

old men who cared for the smaller country congregations were finally called merely *presbyters*, a Greek word meaning "old men," and our word "priest" is derived from this Greek term. Over the group of churches in each city, a leading priest gained authority as bishop. In the larger cities these bishops had such influence that they became archbishops, or head bishops, having authority over the bishops in the surrounding cities of the province. These church arrangements were modeled to a large extent on those of the Roman government, from which such terms as "diocese" (§ 1103) were borrowed. Thus Christianity, once the faith of the weak and the despised, became a powerful organization, strong enough to cope with the government.

**1115.** Christianity placed on a legal basis with other religions (311 A.D.)

The Roman government therefore began to see the uselessness of persecuting the Christians. The struggle to suppress them was one which decidedly weakened the Roman State, at a time when the long disorders of the century of revolution made the emperors feel their weakness. After the retirement of Diocletian, his "Cæsar" Galerius, feeling the dangers threatening Rome from *without* and the uselessness of the struggle against the Christians *within*, issued a decree, in 311 A.D., by which Christianity was legally recognized. Its followers received the same legal position granted to the worshipers of the old gods. This decree was also maintained by Constantine, and under his direction the first great assembly, or council, of all the churches of the Roman world was held at Nicæa, in northeastern Asia Minor.

**1116.** Julian "the Apostate" (361–363 A.D.)

The victory of Christianity was not yet final however. After Constantine's sons and nephews had spent years in fighting for the crown, which one of the sons held for a time, the survivor among the group was Constantine's nephew Julian, the ablest emperor since the second century of peace. Like Marcus Aurelius, he was a philosopher on the throne; for he was devoted to the old literature and philosophy of the Greeks. He therefore renounced Christianity and did all that he could to retard its progress and to restore Hellenistic religion and civilization. He was an able general also. He defeated the German barbarians in the West, but while leading his army in the East against the New Persians he died. The Church called him Julian "the Apostate"; he was the last of the Roman emperors to oppose Christianity.

## QUESTIONS

SECTION 95. In spite of seeming prosperity, what was now the real condition of the Roman Empire? What can you say of the decline of farming? Describe the system of *coloni*. What was now the condition of slavery? What can you say of the extent of cultivated lands and the food supply? What was happening to the farming class? Discuss city life; the decline of business. Discuss the supply of precious metals and money. How did this difficulty affect the army? What was the effect of the lack of a law of succession on the army? What was now Italy's situation in the Empire?

SECTION 96. Tell what happened after the death of Marcus Aurelius. Describe the conditions following the time of the family of Septimius Severus. What did the Northern barbarians do? What happened in Gaul? Describe the rise of New Persia. Tell about Palmyra and Zenobia. How were Gaul and Palmyra subdued? How did Aurelian protect Rome? Who ended the century of revolution, and when? How can we summarize the four centuries of Roman imperialism which ended with the advent of Diocletian (284 B.C.)?

SECTION 97. How did Diocletian treat the Roman Senate? What did the Roman emperor become? What influences triumphed? What became of democracy? What can you say about the emperor's place of residence? What arrangements for the succession did Diocletian make? Tell about his administrative organization. What can you say of taxation under Diocletian? How did this affect men of means? What two classes of men had the Empire now lost? What can you say of liberty and free citizenship? What was the result?

SECTION 98. Where had the center of power shifted? Who triumphed in the struggles following Diocletian's death? Where did he establish the new eastern Rome? What was the effect upon old Rome? upon the Empire? What can you say of the opportunities offered by the Church to able men? Tell about its organization. How did Christianity gain legal recognition? When? Tell about Julian the Apostate.

# CHAPTER XXX

## THE TRIUMPH OF THE BARBARIANS AND THE END OF THE ANCIENT WORLD

### SECTION 99. THE BARBARIAN INVASIONS AND THE FALL OF THE WESTERN EMPIRE [1]

**1117. The barbarian danger**

We have often met the Indo-European barbarians who occupied northern Europe, behind the civilized belt on the north of the Mediterranean. Since the days of the Stone Age men this

[1] This account of the absorption of the western part of the ancient world by the barbarians is here necessarily very brief. A fuller presentation of this period will be found in Robinson's *Medieval and Modern Times* (chaps. ii–v), a book which continues this *Ancient Times*.

NOTE. The above headpiece shows us the interior of the famous church of St. Sophia, built at Constantinople by Justinian from 532 to 537 A.D. (§ 1149). The first church on this spot was of the usual basilica form (Fig. 271, 5), but Justinian's architects preferred an oriental dome. They therefore roofed the great church with a gigantic dome 183 feet high at the center, sweeping clear across the audience room and producing the most imposing vaulted interior now surviving from

688

northern region had never advanced to a high civilization. Its barbarian peoples had been a frequent danger to the fringe of civilized nations along the Mediterranean. We recall how the Gauls overwhelmed northern Italy, even capturing Rome, and how they then overflowed into the Balkan Peninsula and Asia Minor (§§ 722,813,815). We remember the terror at Rome when the Germans first came down, and how they were only defeated by a supreme effort under the skillful soldier Marius (§ 936).

By superior organization the Romans had been able to feed and to keep together at a given point for a long time a larger number of troops than the barbarians. This was the secret of Cæsar's success against them (§ 955). During the century of revolution after the reign of Marcus Aurelius, Roman army organization had gone to pieces and the barbarians raided the lands of the Empire without hindrance. After such raids the barbarians commonly withdrew. By the time of Diocletian, however, the barbarians were beginning to form permanent settlements within the limits of the Empire, and there followed two centuries of barbarian migration, in the course of which they took possession of the entire western Mediterranean world. *1118. Former Roman superiority, and later inferiority to barbarian armies*

The Germans were a fair-haired, blue-eyed race of men of towering stature and terrible strength. In their native forests of the North each German people or nation occupied a very limited area, probably not over forty miles across, and in numbers such a people had not usually more than twenty-five or thirty thousand souls. They lived in villages, each of about a hundred families, and there was a head man over each village. Their homes were but slight huts, easily moved. They had little interest in farming the fringe of fields around the village, much preferring their herds, and they shifted their homes often. *1119. The German peoples at home*

the ancient world. Justinian is said to have expended 18 tons of gold and the labor of ten thousand men in the erection of the building. Since the capture of Constantinople by the Turks (1453 A.D.), the vast church has served as a Mohammedan mosque. The Turks have whitewashed the gorgeous mosaics with which the magnificent interior is adorned, and large circular shields bearing the monogram of the Sultan have been hung against the walls.

They possessed no writing and very little in the way of industries, manufactures, or commerce. A group of noble families furnished the leaders (dukes) or sometimes kings, governing the whole people.

**1120. The German peoples in migration and war**

Hardened to wind and weather in their raw Northern climate, their native fearlessness and love of war and plunder often led them to wander, followed by their wives and families in heavy wagons. An entire people might comprise some fifty villages, but each village group remained together, protected by its body of about a hundred warriors, the heads of the village families. When combined, these hundreds made up an army of five to six thousand men. Each hundred held together in battle, as a fighting unit. They all knew each other; the village head man, the leader of the group, had always lived with them; the warrior in the tumult of battle saw all about him his friends and relatives, the sons of his brothers, the husbands of his daughters. In spite of lack of discipline, these fighting groups of a hundred men, united by such ties of blood and daily association, formed battle units as terrible as any ever seen in the ancient world. Their eager joy in battle and the untamed fierceness of their onset made them irresistible.

**1121. Admission of whole German peoples to settle in the Empire and serve in the army**

The highly organized and carefully disciplined Roman legions, which had gained for Rome the leadership of the world, were now no more. Legions made up of the peace-softened townsmen of Diocletian's time, even if they had existed, would have given way before the German fighting groups, as chaff is driven before the wind. Hopeless of being able to drive the Germans back, the emperors had allowed them to settle within the frontiers (§ 1073). Even Augustus had permitted this. Indeed, the lack of men for the army had long since led the emperors to hire the Germans as soldiers, and Julius Cæsar's cavalry had been largely barbarian. A more serious step was the admission of *entire* German peoples to live in the Empire in their accustomed manner. The men were then received into the Roman army, but they remained under their own German leaders

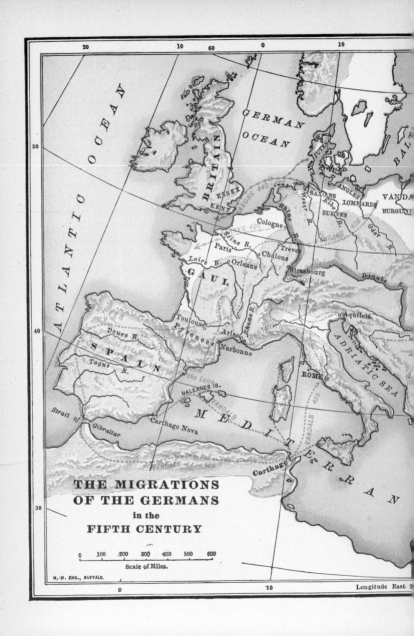

THE MIGRATIONS
OF THE GERMANS
in the
FIFTH CENTURY

0   100   200   300   400   500   600
Scale of Miles.

M.-N. ENG., BUFFALO.

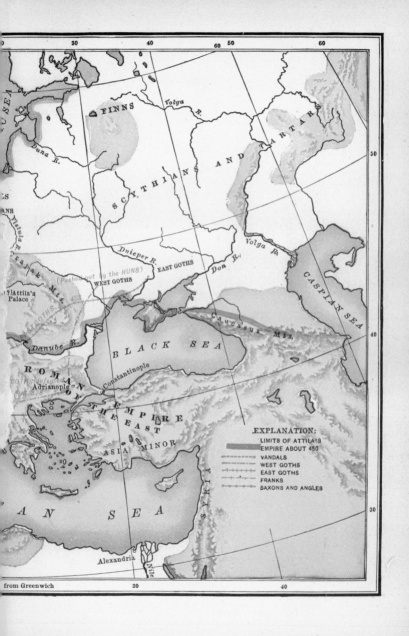

SCYTHIANS AND TARTARS

FINNS

*Volga R.*

*Duna R.*

*Vistula R.*

*Dnieper R.*

EAST GOTHS

(Pushed out by the HUNS)

WEST GOTHS

*Don R.*

*Volga R.*

CASPIAN SEA

(?) Attila's Palace

*Carpak Mts.*

*VISIGOTHS*   453

*OSTROGOTHS*

*Danube R.*

Caucasus Mts.

ROMAN

B L A C K    S E A

*GOTHS defeated*

Constantinople

Adrianople

EMPIRE

THE EAST

ASIA    MINOR

EXPLANATION:

LIMITS OF ATTILA'S
EMPIRE ABOUT 450

VANDALS

WEST GOTHS

EAST GOTHS

FRANKS

SAXONS AND ANGLES

A N    S E A

Alexandria

*Nile*

from Greenwich

and they fought in their old village units. For it was only as the Roman army was made up of the German fighting units that it had any effectiveness. Barbarian life, customs, and manners were thus introduced into the Empire, and the Roman army as a whole was barbarian. At the same time the German leaders of such troops were recognized as Roman officers.

Along the lower Rhine there lived under a king a powerful group of German peoples, called the Franks. The Vandals, also in the North, had long borne an evil reputation for their destructive raids. South of them, the Alemanni had frequently moved over the frontiers, and on the lower Danube the Goths were a constant danger. Constantine's nephew Julian (§ 1116) had gained a fierce battle against the Germans at Strassburg (357 A.D.), and had thus stopped the Franks and Alemanni at the Rhine. He established his headquarters at Paris, where he still continued to read his beloved books in the midst of the campaign. The philosopher emperor's stay at Paris fifteen and a half centuries ago, for the first time brought clearly into history that important city of future Europe.

**1122. The chief German peoples; Julian's defeat of Franks and Alemanni at Strassburg (357 A.D.)**

This constant commingling of the German peoples with the civilized communities of the Empire was gradually softening their Northern wildness and giving them not only familiarity with civilization but also a respect for it. Their leaders, who held office under the Roman government, came to have friends among highborn Romans. Such leaders sometimes married educated Roman women of rank, even close relations of the emperors. Some of them too were converted to Christianity. An educated German of the Goths, a man named Ulfilas, translated the New Testament into Gothic, a dialect akin to German. As the Germanic peoples possessed no writing, he was obliged to devise an alphabet from Greek and Latin for writing Gothic. He thus produced the earliest surviving example of a written Germanic tongue and aided in converting the Northern peoples to Christianity.

**1123. German peoples gain some civilization, including writing and Christianity**

**1124.** West Goths pushed across the Danube by the Huns; battle of Adrianople (378 A.D.) the beginning of a century of continuous barbaric migration

At this juncture barbarians of another race, having no Indo-European blood in their veins, had been penetrating Europe from Asia. These people were the Huns. They were the most destructive of all the barbarian invaders. They pushed down upon the lower Danube, and the West Goths (often called Visigoths), fleeing before them, begged the Romans for permission to cross the Danube and settle in the Empire. Valens, who had followed Julian as emperor of the East, gave them permission to do so. Thereupon friction between them and the Roman officials caused them to revolt. In the battle which ensued at Adrianople (378 A.D.), although the Goths could not have had an army of over fifteen thousand men, the Romans, or rather the Germans fighting for them, were defeated, and the emperor Valens himself was killed. Henceforth the helplessness of the Roman Empire was evident to all the world. This movement of the West Goths and the battle of Adrianople were the beginning of a century of continuous migration in which the Western Empire was slowly absorbed by the barbarians and broken up into German kingdoms under German military leaders.

**1125.** Theodosius (379–395 A.D.) restores the Empire

Theodosius, who succeeded Valens at Constantinople, was the last of the great emperors to unite and rule the whole Roman Empire. He came to an understanding with the West Goths, allowing them to settle where they were, taking them into his army, and giving their leaders important posts in the government. But it was only by using the able and energetic Germans themselves as his ministers and commanders that he was able to maintain his empire. He even gave his niece in marriage to his leading military commander, a Vandal named Stilicho, and at his death, in 395 A.D., Theodosius intrusted to this able German the care of his two young sons Honorius and Arcadius.

**1126.** Division of the Empire at death of Theodosius (395 A.D.)

Theodosius divided the Empire between these two youths, giving to Arcadius the East and to Honorius the West. The Empire was never to be united again. Indeed, after the appearance of these two young emperors, the dismemberment of the Western Empire went rapidly forward, and in two generations resulted in the disappearance of both the Western emperor and his empire (see map, p. 678).

From both the Danube and the Rhine the movement of the barbarians southward and westward went on. Led by their king Alaric, the West Goths first pushed down from the Danube into the Balkan Peninsula and advanced plundering into Greece, where they even took Athens. Here the German Stilicho, leading German troops, confronted the German invasion and forced it back. Driving their wagons piled high with the plunder of Greece, Alaric led his West Goths into Illyricum, where Arcadius made him official commander. When the faithful Stilicho had been executed on a charge of treason by Honorius, there was no one to oppose Alaric in his invasion of Italy. In 410 A.D. the emperor of the West was thus obliged to look on helplessly while the Gothic host captured and plundered Rome itself.[1] Indeed, when the West Goths, after the death of Alaric, retired from Italy into southwestern Gaul, and later into Spain, Honorius was obliged to recognize the West Gothic kingdom which they set up there (see map, p. 690).

1127. West Goths invade Greece and Italy (400 A.D.), take Rome (410 A.D.), and establish a kingdom in Gaul

While these movements of the West Goths were going on after 400 A.D., the Vandals and two other German peoples had crossed the Rhine, and, advancing through Gaul, they had penetrated into Spain, where these three peoples set up three German kingdoms. These kingdoms, like that of the West Goths in Gaul, acknowledged that they were vassals of Honorius as emperor of the West. Not long after their settlement in Spain, the Vandals sailed across the Strait of Gibraltar and seized the Roman province of Africa (429 A.D.). The African kingdom of the Vandals was likewise recognized by the Western emperor. A little later the German Burgundians had pushed in beside the West Goths and set up a kingdom in southeastern Gaul.

1128. Establishment of Vandal kingdoms in Spain and Africa; Burgundians in Gaul (400-450 A.D.)

---

[1] Not long after 400 B.C. Rome was captured by the *Gauls* (§ 815), and a few years after 400 A.D. it was captured by the *Goths*.

**1129. Western Empire loses Britain and dwindles to Italy**

Meantime German peoples located along the North Sea had taken to the water and were landing in the Island of Britain. While Alaric was sacking Rome, the last Roman soldiers were being withdrawn from the island, and within a generation afterward the German tribes of the Angles and Saxons were setting up kingdoms there, which did not acknowledge the sovereignty of Rome. A rival emperor in Gaul was obliged to let the island go, nor could the feeble emperor of the West, in Italy, ever recover it. He was equally helpless as far as any real power over the western German kingdoms was concerned. Within a generation after 400 A.D. the Western Empire had therefore dwindled to Italy itself, and even there the emperor of the West was entirely in the hands of his German officials and commanders.

**1130. Italy and the West invaded by the Huns (450–453 A.D.); Rome taken by the Vandals (455 A.D.)**

In this condition of weakness Italy was subjected to two more serious invasions. The Eastern Empire had not been able to control the Huns who had forced the West Goths across the Danube (§ 1124). For two generations since then the kingdom of the Huns had steadily grown in power, until their king Attila governed an empire extending from southern Russia to the Rhine. He laid the Eastern Empire under tribute, and by 450 A.D. he and his terrible barbarian host were sweeping down upon Italy in the most destructive invasion which the South ever suffered. The West Goths, with other western Germans, however, rallied to the assistance of the Western emperor against the common enemy, and in a terrible battle at Chalons, in France, Attila was defeated in 451 A.D. He retreated eastward, and two years later, as he was invading Italy, he died. The Hunnish empire fell to pieces, never to trouble Europe again. Hardly had Rome thus escaped when the Vandals crossed over from Carthage to Sicily and Italy, and in 455 A.D. they captured Rome. Although they carried off great quantities of spoil, they spared the magnificent buildings of the city, as Alaric and his West Goths had also done forty-five years earlier (see map, p. 690).

In Italy, all that was left of the Western Empire, the German military leaders possessed all the power and made and unmade emperors as they pleased. But these *seeming* emperors of the West were now to disappear. By a remarkable coincidence the last to bear the title was called Romulus Augustulus; that is, Romulus, "the little Augustus." He thus bore the names both of the legendary founder of Rome itself and of the founder of the Roman Empire. He was quietly set aside by the German soldiery, who put Odoacer, one of their number, in his place. Thus in 476 A.D., two generations after Theodosius, the last of the Western emperors disappeared. The line of emperors at Rome thus ended a little over five hundred years after it had been established by Augustus. The German leaders in Italy sent word to the Eastern emperor at Constantinople that they acknowledged the sovereignty of the Eastern emperor, who then authorized Odoacer to rule with the title of "patrician."

1131. Last of the emperors at Rome, Romulus Augustulus, displaced by a German leader, Odoacer (476 A.D.)

Meantime another great migration of the barbarians again altered the situation in the West. An eastern branch of the Goths, whom we call, therefore, the East Goths (Ostro-Goths), had remained along the Danube for two generations after their kindred, the West Goths, had departed (§ 1124). Then they also shifted westward and southward into Italy, where, in 493 A.D., their king Theodoric the Great displaced Odoacer and made himself king of a strong East Gothic kingdom in Italy. Although he was unable even to read, Theodoric was a wise and highly civilized ruler, and under him Italy began to recover from her misfortunes. His power finally included, besides Italy and Sicily, part of Gaul and Spain, and it at one time seemed that the Western Empire was about to be restored under a German emperor. This restoration of the West was prevented, however, by the rise of Justinian, the last great emperor of the East at Constantinople.

1132. Establishment of an East Gothic kingdom in Italy by Theodoric (493 A.D.)

After the death of Theodosius (395 A.D.) the Eastern Empire had been ruled by weaklings. Justinian, however, who was crowned at Constantinople in 527 A.D., only a generation after

1133. Justinian's partial reconquest of the West

the rise of Theodoric, was a gifted and energetic ruler. His dream was the restoration of the united Empire. Under his able general Belisarius, he therefore endeavored to reconquer the West. Belisarius overthrew the Vandal kingdom in the province of Africa and then passed over into Italy, where he finally crushed the kingdom of the East Goths. Although disturbed by a serious revolt in Italy, the Eastern emperor's authority was restored in Italy, Sicily, Africa, and southern Spain. But Justinian showed very poor judgment in supposing that the Eastern Empire

Fig. 270. Hall of an Egyptian Temple altered into a Christian Church

Over fifteen hundred years ago, in the reign of Theodosius (379–395 A.D.), not many years before 400 A.D., the temples of the old gods all around the Mediterranean were closed by edict of the emperor. They were then gradually forsaken, as we find them now, or the huts and sun-dried-brick hovels of the poor crowded into them. In some cases a temple hall, once devoted to the worship of the gods, was then converted into a Christian church. In such a hall of the Luxor Temple at Thebes in Egypt, the arched niche we see here was cut into the wall for the pulpit of the preacher, and Greek columns were set up to support a canopy over his head. The pagan relief scenes on the walls were covered with plaster on which Christian saints were painted. This Christian plaster, visible just at the left of the left-hand column, has now largely fallen off and revealed the old pagan pictures, as we see them here still further to the left, where the pictures of the old Egyptian gods have emerged again, to find their former worshipers all vanished

possessed the power again to rule the whole Mediterranean world. His destruction of the East Gothic kingdom in Italy left the peninsula helpless before the next wave of barbaric migration, nor were his successors able to maintain his conquests.

But if political unity failed, the emperor's large plans did succeed in establishing a great judicial or legal unity. He employed a very able lawyer named Tribonian to gather together all the numerous laws which had grown up in the career of Rome since the age of the Twelve Tablets (§ 802) a thousand years before. Justinian was the Hammurapi of the Roman Empire, and the vast body of laws which he collected represented the administrative experience of the most successful rulers of the ancient world. Almost every situation and every difficulty arising in social life, in business transactions, or in legal proceedings had been met and settled by Roman judges. The collection of their decisions arranged by Justinian in brief form was called a digest. Justinian's Digest became the foundation of law for later ages, and still remains so to a large extent in the government of the civilized peoples of to-day.

**1134.** Justinian's code compiled

Under Justinian Constantinople enjoyed wide recognition and the emperor gave lavishly for its beautification. But it was no longer for building the old temples of the gods or basilicas and amphitheaters that the ruler gave his wealth. The old world of Greek civilization had received its last support from Julian, two centuries earlier (§ 1116). Theodosius, the last emperor to rule the entire Empire, had forbidden the worship of the old gods and issued a decree closing all their temples. Since 400 A.D. the splendid temples of the gods, which fringed the Mediterranean (Fig. 219) and extended far up the Nile (Fig. 64), were left more and more forsaken by their worshipers, till finally they were deserted and desolate as they are to-day, or they were altered for use as Christian churches (Fig. 270). The last blow to what the Church regarded as Greek paganism was now struck by Justinian, who closed the schools of philosophy forming the university at Athens. The buildings to which the

**1135.** End of the old temples

emperor now devoted his wealth were churches. The vast church of Saint Sophia which he built at Constantinople still stands to-day, the most magnificent of the early churches of the East (headpiece, p. 688).

**1136.** Division of the Church into East and West

Just as this building shows its oriental origin in its architecture, so did the teachings of the Church in the Eastern Empire. The efforts of Justinian to unite East and West failed to a large extent because of the jealousy of the oriental churches and the power of the Western Church. A division was therefore steadily developing between the Eastern (Greek) Church and the Western (Latin) Church. For while the dismemberment of the Western Empire, which we have followed, was still going on, there was arising at Rome an emperor of the Church, who was in no small degree the heir to the lost power of the Western emperor. As there had been an Empire of the East and an Empire of the West, so there were to be also a Church of the East and a Church of the West. To the Western Church we must now turn.

## Section 100. The Triumph of the Roman Church and its Power over the Western Nations

**1137.** Unique position of Rome, and the bishop of Rome

The venerable city of Rome, with its long centuries as mistress of the world behind it, had gained a position of unique respect and veneration, even among the barbarians. The Goths and the Vandals had stood in awe and reverence under the shadow of its magnificent public buildings. They had left them uninjured, and in all its monumental splendor, Rome was still the greatest city of the world, rivaled only by Constantinople and Alexandria, the two other imperial cities. It was natural that the bishop of Rome should occupy a position of unusual power and respect. When the West Goths were threatening the city, and also in other important crises caused by the incoming of the barbarians, the bishop of Rome had more than once showed an ability which made him the leading statesman of Italy, if not of the West. There is no doubt that his influence had much to do with the respect which the West Goths and the Vandals had shown toward the city in sparing its buildings.

At the same time the Church throughout the West had early produced able men. This was especially true in Africa, the province behind Carthage, where the leading early Christian writers had appeared. The bishop of Carthage was soon a serious rival of the bishop of Rome, and their rivalry in Christian times curiously reminds us of the long past struggle between the two cities. Here in Africa in the days of Theodosius, Augustine, the greatest of the thinkers of the early Church, had arisen. Not at first a Christian, the young Augustine had been devoted to Greek philosophy and learning. At the same time he gave way to evil habits and uncontrolled self-indulgence. As he gained a vision of spiritual self-denial, his faithful Christian mother, Monica, followed him through all the tremendous struggle and distress of mind, from which he emerged at last into a triumphant conquest of his lower nature, and the devotion of his whole soul to Christianity. In a volume of "Confessions" he told the story, which soon became the never-failing guide of the tempted in the Christian Church. Along with the *Meditations* of Marcus Aurelius, it belongs among the most precious revelations of the inner life of a great man which we have inherited.

1138. Early rise of influential men in the African Church: Augustine (354–430 A.D.)

In the days after Alaric had plundered Rome, and earthly government seemed to totter, Augustine also wrote a great treatise which he called "The City of God," meaning the government of God. Opposed to the governments of this world and superior to them, he pictured an invisible kingdom of God, to which all Christian believers belonged. But this invisible kingdom was after all hardly distinguished by Augustine from the visible organized Church with its bishops and priests. To the authority of this eternal kingdom—that is, to the authority of the Church—all believers were urged by Augustine to submit without reservation. In the teaching of Augustine, therefore, the

1139. Augustine's "City of God," and the power of Church and State over the beliefs of men

Church gained complete control over the beliefs of men. This was at the very same time when the Edict of Theodosius was closing the temples of the old gods. The State was thus assuming the power to suppress all other beliefs, and henceforth it maintained its power over both the bodies and the minds of its subjects. In accordance with this idea Justinian had closed the university at Athens in order to stop freedom of thought and the teaching of the old philosophy (§ 1135). To the authority of the State over the beliefs of its people, Augustine added the authority of the Church. Thus ended all intellectual liberty in the ancient world.

**1140.** Growing power of Church of Rome

Augustine, moreover, recognized the leadership of the Church at Rome, and thus added his influence to a tendency already long felt by all (§ 1137). For it was widely believed that Christ had conferred great power in the Church upon the Apostle Peter. Although it was known that Paul had also worked in Rome, early tradition told how Peter had founded the Church at Rome and become bishop there. It was also widely held that Peter had transferred his authority to his successors as bishops at Rome. Tradition thus aided in establishing the supremacy of the bishop of Rome.

**1141.** Rise of missionary monks and spread of regard for the Roman Church in the North

As increasing numbers of men withdrew from worldly occupations and gathered in communities, called monasteries, to lead holy lives or to help carry the Christian faith to the Northern barbarians, these beliefs regarding the Church of Rome went with them. Such monks, as they were called, taught the barbarians that the Church also had power over the life hereafter. Dreading frightful punishments beyond the grave, the superstitious peoples of the North submitted readily to such influences, and the Church gained enormous power over the barbarians. It was a power wielded more and more exclusively by the bishop of Rome.

When the power of the Roman Empire was no longer able to restrain the barbarians, the influence of the Church held them in check. The Church gradually softened and modified the fierce

instincts of barbarian kings ruling over barbarian peoples. The barrier of Roman organization and of Roman legions which had protected Mediterranean civilization had given way, but the Church, taking its place, made possible the transference of power from the Roman Empire to the barbarians in the West, without the complete destruction of our heritage of civilization bequeathed us by Greece and Rome.

1142. Value of the influence of the Church over the barbarians

Less than a generation after the death of Justinian, a gifted bishop of Rome named Gregory, commonly called Gregory the Great, showed himself a statesman of such wisdom and ability that he firmly established the leadership of the Roman Church. Italy, left defenseless by Justinian's destruction of the East Gothic kingdom (§ 1133), was thereupon invaded by the Lombards ("Longbeards"), the least civilized of all the German barbarians, who easily took possession of the Po valley. The Lombards were divided into small and rather weak communities. Thus the fallen Western Empire was not followed by a powerful and enduring nation in Italy, and this gave to the bishops of Rome the opportunity so well used by Gregory, to make themselves the leaders of Italy. It was this great Church ruler who also sent missionary monks to Britain, and thus established Christianity in England two centuries after the Roman legions had left it.

1143. Gregory the Great, bishop of Rome (590–604 A.D.)

The influence of the Roman Church was likewise extended among the powerful Franks (§ 1122), a group of German tribes on the lower Rhine. Their king, Clovis, accepted Christianity not long before 500 A.D. He succeeded in welding together the Frankish tribes, and the kingdom he left had been steadily growing for over a century before Gregory's time. After Gregory's death this Frankish kingdom included a large part of western Europe, embracing, besides western Germany, the countries which we now call Holland, Belgium, and France. By the middle of the sixth century the Frankish kings had fallen under the influence of a family of their own powerful household stewards called "Mayors of the Palace," who at last

1144. Rise of the Franks and the "Mayors of the Palace"

really held the ruling power, though in the name of the king. After 700 A.D. the Mayor of the Palace, who actually governed the great Frankish kingdom, was Charles Martel. He saved Europe from being overrun by the Moslems (732 A.D.) (see § 1154), and his descendants became the greatest kings of the Franks.

**1145.** Alliance of Charlemagne and the Pope; Charlemagne's coronation by the Pope (800 A.D.)

By combining with the bishop of Rome, whom we may now call the Pope, the new Frankish kings gained the dominion of western Europe. They assisted the Pope by subduing the unruly Lombards in Italy and conquered a large part of modern Germany, besides northern Spain. Charlemagne, the grandson of Charles Martel, ruled an empire consisting of western Germany, France, Italy, and northern Spain. He was the most powerful European sovereign of his time, and in 800 A.D. he was crowned by the Pope at Rome as Roman emperor, theoretically supposed to succeed the line of emperors headed by Augustus. The emperor Charlemagne was an enlightened ruler who desired to do all that he could for the education and well-being of his people. The civilization which he tried to spread, although it was very limited, was what was left of old Roman life and organization, which had been preserved largely through the influence of the Church.

**1146.** Church gains literary culture; preservation of Latin literature by the Church

The Church had been founded in the beginning chiefly among the lowly and the ignorant (§ 1069). It had originally been without higher Greek civilization, learning, and art. Gradually it gained also these things, as men like Augustine arose. It is chiefly to the libraries of the monks in the monasteries, and to their practice of copying ancient literary works, that we owe the preservation of such Latin literature as has survived. To-day our oldest and most important copies of such things as Virgil's Æneid (§ 1004) are manuscripts written on parchment, preserved in the libraries of the Christian monks.

**1147.** The basilica church and its oriental ancestor

Art was slow to rise among early Christians, and for a thousand years or more there were no Christian painters or sculptors to be compared with those of Greece. On the other hand, the need for places of assembly led to the rise of great

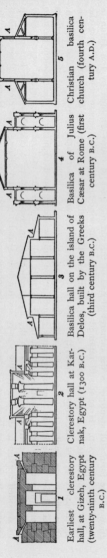

1. Earliest clerestory hall, at Gizeh, Egypt (twenty-ninth century B.C.)

2. Clerestory hall at Karnak (1300 B.C.)

3. Basilica hall on the island of Delos, built by the Greeks (third century B.C.)

4. Basilica of Julius Cæsar at Rome (first century B.C.)

5. Christian basilica church (fourth century A.D.)

FIG. 271. THE BASILICA CHURCH AND ITS ORIENTAL ANCESTORS

A central aisle with roof windows (A) in the side walls, forming a clerestory and occupying the difference in level between the higher roof over the central aisle (nave) and the lower roof over the side aisles, with a resulting division of the building into three aisles — this arrangement is the chief characteristic of the basilica cathedral. We found the earliest hint of such an arrangement at the Pyramids of Gizeh (Fig. 55), shown in cross section above (1). Its clerestory windows (AA), built in the twenty-ninth century B.C., were mere light chutes. In the course of fifteen hundred years these light chutes were developed by the Egyptian architects into tall stately clerestory windows, at Karnak (2, AA). In the Hellenistic Age the Greeks adopted the form and combined it with their sloping roofs, as shown here in a business hall excavated by the French on the island of Delos (3, AA). It was the Greeks who gave this form of hall its name "basilica" (§ 732). In Rome it was in use in the second century B.C. in the Forum (Fig. 246, D), and we have put in the above series (4) the great Basilica of Julius Cæsar (Fig. 246, E). Finally, these business basilica halls of the Greeks and Romans influenced the early Christian architects to adopt a similar form for their churches (5). We thus have an architectural development of some thirty-four hundred years leading from the early Orient, nearly 3000 B.C., to the Christian churches of the fourth century A.D.

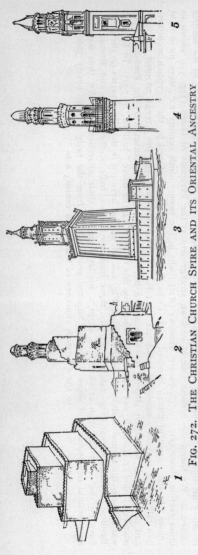

FIG. 272. THE CHRISTIAN CHURCH SPIRE AND ITS ORIENTAL ANCESTRY

The tower as an architectural form first appeared alongside the early Babylonian temples (probably not long after 3000 B.C.) (§ 152). It was adopted by the Assyrians (tailpiece, p. 170), and its earliest form in Assyria has been reconstructed by the German expedition at Assur, as shown above (1). A very noticeable example of the continuation of the form still standing is the minaret of one of the old mosques of Cairo (2), built by Ibn Tulun in the ninth century A.D. Here it still retained the outside ascent winding about the square tower. Above the tower the top of the building was formed of round sections. This addition was in imitation of the ancient Pharos lighthouse tower of Alexandria (Fig. 213), in which the square tower was surmounted by a six-sided section, upon which was built a round section as the final top of the tower (3). This arrangement of three sections (square below, six-sided in the middle, and round at the top) was continued in many of the Moslem mosque towers (minarets), like the one above, in the Nile Delta (4). The Moslem minarets themselves were greatly influenced by the early church towers in the East, especially in Syria. Many a church spire of Europe, with its six-sided section in the middle, the square section below, and the round above, show clearly their oriental origin, as in the example above (5), the spire of the church of St. John at Parma, Italy. Here again, as in the clerestory (Fig. 271), we have an architectural development from the Orient to the West, beginning nearly 3000 B.C. and covering from three to four thousand years

704

architects among the early Christians. Influenced chiefly by the old business basilica, they devised noble and impressive assembly rooms for the early congregations in the days of Constantine. We still call such a church a basilica, to indicate its form. In the basilica churches we find the outcome of that long architectural development of thirty-five hundred years, from the earliest known clerestory at the Pyramids of Gizeh to the Christian cathedral (Fig. 271).

The church tower also, at first not a part of the church building, was a descendant of the old Babylonian temple tower (Fig. 272). Thus the faith of Jesus, an oriental teacher, was sheltered in beautiful buildings which likewise showed their oriental ancestry. These Christian buildings, the church and its tower, like the faith they sheltered, are a striking example of how the world of later Europe reached back into that early Orient with which we began the story of civilization, when Europe was still in the Stone Age. And that ancient Orient, whose civilization thus survived in the life of Europe, was yet to rise once more, to dominate the Mediterranean as it had so often done before. To this final revival of the Orient we must now turn.

**1148.** The church tower and its oriental ancestor

## SECTION 101. THE FINAL REVIVAL OF THE ORIENT AND THE FORERUNNERS OF THE NATIONS OF MODERN EUROPE

Justinian, whose reign covered the middle years of the sixth century A.D., was, as we have already said, the last great ruler of the Eastern Empire. His endeavors to reunite the Empire and to adorn his capital both proved very disastrous. He spent the strength of his Empire in trying to regain the West, when he needed all his resources to defend himself against the New Persians, who assailed the eastern frontier in war after war. His great buildings, especially the magnificent church of Saint Sophia (headpiece, p. 688), required so much money that his

**1149.** The decline of the Eastern Empire after Justinian

treasury was emptied and the government was bankrupt. From the mistakes of Justinian the Eastern Empire never recovered, and at his death it entered upon an age of steady decline.

**1150. Invasion of the Slavs; Eastern Empire no longer Roman**

Meantime a new invasion of barbarians was bringing in the Slavs, a non-German group of Indo-European peoples. They poured into the Balkan Peninsula to the gates of Constantinople and even down into Greece. They were soon holding the territory in these regions which they still occupy. Under these circumstances the Eastern Empire at Constantinople, although it was without interruption the direct descendant of the Roman Empire, was no longer Roman, any more than was the Empire of Charlemagne in the West. The Eastern Empire became what it was in population and civilization, a mixed Greek-Slavic-Oriental State.

**1151. Mohammed (570–632 A.D.) and the founding of Islam**

Moreover, a vast section of the Eastern emperor's dominions lay in the Orient. Of these eastern dominions a large part was now about to be invaded and seized by a great Semitic migration like those which we have repeatedly seen as the nomads of the Arabian desert were led by Sargon or the rulers of Hammurapi's line into Babylonia; or as the Hebrews swept in from the desert and seized the towns of Palestine (§§ 135, 166, 175, 293). The last and the greatest movement of the Semitic barbarians was now about to take place. Not long after the death of Justinian, there was born in Mecca (Fig. 273) in Arabia a remarkably gifted lad named Mohammed. As he grew up he believed, like so many Semitic teachers, that a commanding voice spoke within him as he wandered in the wilderness. This voice within him brought him messages which he felt compelled to communicate to his people as teachings from God, whom he called Allah. After much persecution and great danger to his life, he gathered a group of faithful followers about him, and when he died, in 632 A.D., he had established a new religion among the Arabs, which he had called Islam, meaning "reconciliation"; that is, reconciliation to Allah, the sole God. The new believers he had called Muslims, or, as we spell it,

Moslems, meaning "the reconciled." By us they are often called Mohammedans, after their prophet. After Mohammed's death the Moslem leaders gathered together his teachings, till

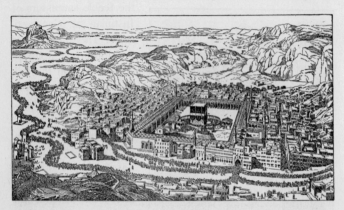

FIG. 273. A BIRD'S-EYE VIEW OF MECCA AND ITS MOSQUE

Mecca is one of the few towns in the barren Arabian peninsula; for by far the great majority of the Arabs live as roving shepherds (§ 134) and not in towns. Mecca had been a sacred place long before the time of Mohammed, and the people had been accustomed to come there as pilgrims, to do homage to a sacred black stone called the Kaaba. Mohammed did not interfere with these customs. After his death the Moslems built a large court modeled on a colonnaded Greek market place (Fig. 212, *M*), around the Kaaba. Such a structure was the simplest form of a mosque. Over the Kaaba they erected a square shelter, which we see in the middle of the mosque court. To this place the Moslem believers still come in great numbers as pilgrims every year. Our sketch shows an exaggerated representation of the procession of pilgrims. In his later years Mohammed lived at Medina, over 200 miles north of Mecca, and the pilgrims also visit his tomb there

then uncollected, and copied them to form a book called the Koran (Fig. 274), now the Bible of the Moslems.

The Moslem leaders who inherited Mohammed's power were called caliphs, a word meaning "substitute." As rulers, they proved to be men of the greatest ability. They organized the untamed desert nomads, who now added a burning religious

**1152.** Rise of the oriental Empire of the Moslems

zeal to the wild courage of barbarian Arabs. This combination made the Arab armies of the caliphs irresistible. Within a few years after Mohammed's death they took Egypt and Syria from the feeble successors of Justinian at Constantinople. They thus reduced the Eastern Empire to little more than the Balkan Peninsula and Asia Minor. At the same time the Arabs crushed the empire of the New Persians and brought the Sassanian line of kings to an end (640 A.D.), after it had lasted a little over four hundred years. Thus the Moslems built up a great oriental empire, with its center at the east end of the Fertile Crescent.

**1153.** The nomad Arabs learn city civilization along the Fertile Crescent

FIG. 274. A PAGE OF A MANUSCRIPT COPY OF THE KORAN, THE BIBLE OF THE MOSLEMS

Just as the people of Sargon and Hammurapi took over the city civilization which they found along the lower

This writing has descended from the ancient alphabet of the Phœnicians (Fig. 160), and, like the Phœnician writing, it is still written and read from right to left. The Arab writers love to give it decorative flourishes, producing a handsome page. The rich, decorative border is a good example of Moslem art. The whole page was done by hand. In such hand-written books as these the educated Moslems wrote out translations of the books of the great Greek philosophers and scientists, like Aristotle; for example, one of the most valuable of the books of Ptolemy, the Greek astronomer (§ 1059), we now possess only in an Arabic translation. At the same time the Moslems wrote their own treatises on algebra, astronomy, grammar, and other sciences (§ 1155) in similar books to which the West owes much

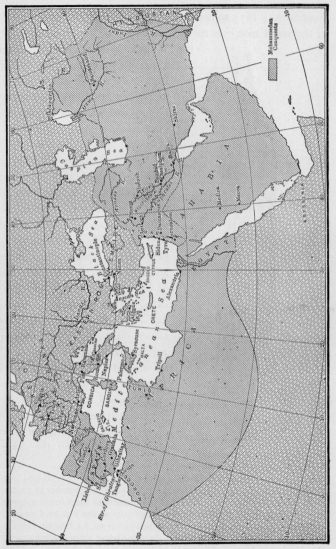

THE MOHAMMEDAN CONQUESTS AT THEIR GREATEST EXTENT, ABOUT THE YEAR 750 (INDICATED BY OBLIQUE SHADING, UNBROKEN LINES)

Euphrates (§ 167), so now in the same region the Moslem Arabs of the desert took over the city civilization of the New Persians.

With the ruins of Babylon looking down upon them, the Moslems built their splendid capital at Bagdad beside the New Persian royal residence of Ctesiphon (headpiece, p. 667). They built of course under the influence of the ancient structures of Egypt, Babylon, Persia, and Assyria. The Babylonian temple towers or Christian-church towers of similar character showed them the first models of the minarets (Fig. 272, 2) with which they adorned their mosques, as the Moslem houses of prayer are called. Here, as Sargon's people and as the Persians had so long before done, the once wandering Arabs learned to read and write, and could thus put the Koran into writing. Here too they learned the business of government and became experienced rulers. Thus beside the shapeless mounds of the older

FIG. 275. MOORISH MOSQUE TOWER, OR MINARET, IN SPAIN

It was built, not long before 1200 A.D., out of the ruins of Roman and West Gothic buildings found here by the Moors, and blocks bearing Latin inscriptions are to be seen in a number of places in its walls. The Moors erected it as the minaret of their finest mosque at Seville, Spain. After extensive alterations at the top by Christian architects, it was converted into the bell tower of a Christian church. While the Christian-church towers in the Orient strongly influenced the Moslem minarets, we see how the reverse was the case in some buildings of the West where Moslem minarets became church spires

capitals, Akkad, Babylon, and Ctesiphon, the power and civilization of the Orient rose into new life again for the last time.

Bagdad became the finest city of the East and one of the most splendid in the world. The caliphs extended their power eastward to the frontiers of India. Westward the Moslems pushed along the African coast of the Mediterranean, as their Phœnician kindred had done before them (§ 397). It was the Moslem overthrow of Carthage and its bishop, which now relieved the bishop of Rome (the Pope) of his only dangerous rival in the West. Only two generations after the death of Mohammed the Arabs crossed over from Africa into Spain (711 A.D.). As they moved on into France they threatened to girdle the entire Mediterranean. At the battle of Tours (732 A.D.), however, just a hundred years after the death of Mohammed, the Moslems were unable to crush the Frankish army under Charles Martel (§ 1144). They withdrew permanently from France into Spain, where they established a western Moslem kingdom, which we call Moorish. The magnificent buildings which it left behind are the most splendid in Spain to-day (Fig. 275).

**1154. Caliphs of Bagdad and the Moslem advance to the West; the battle of Tours (732 A.D.)**

The Moorish kingdom developed a civilization far higher than that of the Franks, and indeed the highest in Europe of that age. Thus while Europe was sinking into the ignorance of the Middle Ages, the Moslems were the leading students of science, astronomy, mathematics, and grammar. There was soon much greater knowledge of these matters among the Moslems than in Christian Europe. Such Arabic words as *algebra* and our numerals, which we received from the Arabs, suggest to us how much we owe to them.

**1155. Leadership of Moslem civilization**

As we look out over this final world situation, we see lying in the middle the remnant of the Roman Empire ruled by Constantinople, and holding little more than the Balkan Peninsula and Asia Minor; while on one side was the lost West, made up of the German kingdoms of the former Northern barbarians; and on the other side was the lost East, now part

**1156. Emergence of the forerunners of the nations of modern Europe**

of the great oriental empire of the caliphs of Bagdad. Looking at Europe without the East, we discover that there was at its western end a *Moslem* oriental kingdom (the Moors), while at its eastern end there was a *Christian* oriental state (Constantinople). Between these lay chiefly the German Empire of Charlemagne, with vast masses of Slavs on the east of it, and detached German peoples in the outlying island of Britain. Out of these fragments of the Roman Empire and the newly formed nations of the North, the nations of modern Europe came forth. In France, and the two southern peninsulas of Spain and Italy, Latin speech survived among the people, to become French, Spanish, and Italian. While in the island of Britain the German language spoken by the invading Angles and Saxons (§ 1129), mingled with much Latin and French to form our own English speech, written with Roman letters inherited from Greece, Phœnicia, and Egypt (Fig. 160).

**1157.** Surviving influences of Rome in later Europe

Thus Rome left her stamp on the peoples of Europe, still evident, not only in the languages they use, but also in many other important matters of life, and especially in law and government. In Roman law, still a power in modern government, we have the great creation of Roman genius, which has more profoundly affected the later world than any other Roman institution. Another great achievement of Rome was the universal spread of that international civilization brought forth by Greece under contact with the Orient. Rome gave to that civilization the far-reaching organization which under the Greeks it had lacked. That organization, though completely transformed into oriental despotism, endured for five centuries and long withstood the barbarian invasions from the North, which would otherwise have overwhelmed the disorganized Greek world long before. The Roman State was the last bulwark of civilization intrenched on the Mediterranean against the Indo-European barbarians. But the bulwark, though shaken, did not fall because of hostile assaults from without. It fell because of decay within.

Nor did it fall everywhere. For, as we have seen, a fragment of the vast Empire still survived in the East. The emperors ruling at Constantinople traced their predecessors back in an unbroken line to Augustus, and they ruled as his successors. Founded on the site of an ancient Greek city, lying in the midst of the Greek East, Constantinople had always been Greek in both language and civilization. But at the same time, as we have seen, it was largely oriental also. Notwithstanding this, it never wholly lost the tradition of old Greek culture. Learning, even though of a mechanical type, never died out there, as it did so completely in the West; nor did art ever fall so low. As Rome declined, Constantinople became the greatest and most splendid city of Europe, exciting the admiration and surprise of all visitors from the less civilized West. Thus the last surviving fragment of the Empire, which by right of succession might still continue to call itself Roman, lived on for a thousand years after the Germans had completely conquered the West. Nor did the Germans ever gain Constantinople, but in 1453 this last remnant of the Roman Empire fell into the hands of the Turks, who have held it ever since.

1158. Survival of a fragment of the Empire at Constantinople, and its fall in 1453 A.D.

## Section 102. Retrospect

Besides the internal decay of Rome and the triumph of the Christian Church, the other great outstanding feature of the last centuries of the Roman Empire was the incoming of the barbarians, with the result that while Mediterranean civilization steadily declined, it nevertheless slowly spread northward, especially under the influence of the Church, till it transformed the ruder life of the North. At this point then we have returned to the region of western and northern Europe, where we first took up the career of man, and there, among the crumbling monuments of the Stone Age, Christian churches now began to rise. Books and civilized government, once found only along the Mediterranean, reached the northern shores of Europe, where

1159. From the fist-hatchet to the Christian civilization of northern Europe in fifty thousand years

grass and great forest trees were growing over the shell heaps of the Stone Age Norsemen (Fig. 13). What a vast sweep of the human career rises before our imagination as we picture the first church spires among the massive tombs of Stone Age man (Fig. 20)!

**1160. The long struggle of civilization and barbarism**

We have watched the men of Europe struggling upward through thousands of years of Stone Age barbarism, while toward the end of that struggle, civilization was arising in the Orient. Then on the borders of the Orient we saw the Stone Age Europeans of the Ægean receiving civilization from the Nile and thus developing a wonderful civilized world of their own. This remarkable Ægean civilization, the earliest in Europe, was overwhelmed and destroyed by the incoming of those Indo-European barbarians whom we call the Greeks (§ 380). Writing, art, architecture, and shipbuilding, which had arisen on the borders of southeastern Europe, passed away, and civilization in Europe perished at the hands of the Greek nomads from the Danube. Civilization would have been lost entirely, had not the Orient, where it was born, now preserved it. Southeastern Europe, controlled by the Greeks, was therefore able to make another start, and from the Orient it again received writing, art, architecture, shipbuilding, and many other things which make up civilization. After having thus halted civilization in Europe for over a thousand years, the Greeks left behind their early barbarism (cf. Fig. 155), and, developing a noble and beautiful culture of their own, they carried civilization to the highest level it ever attained. Then, as the Indo-European barbarians from the North again descended to the Mediterranean (Section 99), Roman organization prevented civilization from being destroyed for the second time. Thus enough of the civilization which the Orient and the Greeks had built up was preserved, so that after long delay it rose again in Europe to become what we find it to-day. Such has been the long struggle of civilization and barbarism which we have been following.

To-day, marking the various stages of that long career, the stone fist-hatchets lie deep in the river gravels of France; the furniture of the pile-villages sleeps at the bottom of the Swiss lakes; the majestic pyramids and temples announcing the dawn of civilization rise along the Nile; the silent and deserted city-mounds by the Tigris and Euphrates shelter their myriads of clay tablets; the palaces of Crete look out toward the sea they once ruled; the noble temples and sculptures of Greece still proclaim the new world of beauty and freedom first revealed by the Greeks; the splendid Roman roads and aqueducts assert the supremacy and organized control of Rome; and the Christian churches proclaim the new ideal of human brotherhood. These things still reveal the fascinating trail along which our ancestors came, and in following that trail we have recovered the earliest chapters in the wonderful human story which we call Ancient History.

**1161.** The trail which we have followed to recover ancient history

## QUESTIONS

SECTION 99. Describe the German peoples at home; in migration and war. Describe the incoming of the West Goths and the results. What chief movements of the barbarians took place after the death of Theodosius? What was the effect upon the Western Empire? Describe the two great barbarian invasions of Italy in the middle of the fifth century A.D. and the end of the line of emperors at Rome. Describe Justinian's Digest. What had happened to the old religions? What did Justinian do about Greek philosophy? Describe the division of the Church.

SECTION 100. Tell about Augustine and his writings. Describe the growing power of the Church at Rome. Sketch the story of the Franks and their alliance with the bishop of Rome. What elements of culture had the church now gained? What forms did early church architecture have, and whence did they come?

SECTION 101. Tell the story of Mohammed. What did his successors accomplish in civilization? in conquest? Describe briefly the world situation which resulted. How long did the Roman Empire last? What influences did it leave behind?

SECTION 102. Where did mankind first gain civilization? Where did civilization first arise in Europe? What happened when the Greeks came in? Where was civilization then preserved? Who carried it to its highest level? By whom was it almost destroyed for the second time? What organization saved it for the second time?

NOTE. The scene below shows us the condition of Europe at least fifty thousand years ago, in the Early Stone Age (§§ 6–12), when man began the long upward climb which carried him through all the ages of developing and declining civilization which we have been following.

# BIBLIOGRAPHY

It is not the aim of this bibliography to mention all of even the important books in various languages that relate to the periods in question. The writer is well aware that teachers are busy people, and that high-school libraries and local public libraries usually furnish at best only a few historical works. It is therefore most important that those books should be given prominence in this list which the teacher has some chance of procuring and finding the time to use. It not infrequently happens that the best account of a particular period or topic is in a foreign language or in a rare publication, such as a doctor's dissertation, which could only be found in one of our largest libraries. All such titles, however valuable, are omitted from this list. They can be found mentioned in all the more scholarly works in the various fields.

A small high-school library on the ancient world, of moderate cost, including a standard book or two on each main period or topic, has been indicated in the following list by a dagger (†) before each title. From these a selection can be made. The price will *average* not more than $1.50 per volume. Preference is sometimes indicated by double dagger (††). All books with a star (*) are suited chiefly for the teacher and are rather advanced for the high-school student. Where a book is referred to often, the star or dagger usually appears only with the first mention.

## CHAPTER I

*SOLLAS, *Ancient Hunters*. †TYLOR, *Primitive Culture*. †HOERNES, *Primitive Man*. †MYRES, *The Dawn of History*, chaps. i–ii, vii–xi. An excellent little book in which only the traditional Babylonian chronology needs revision. *SIR JOHN LUBBOCK (LORD AVEBURY), *Prehistoric Times*. *OSBORN, *Men of the Old Stone Age*. A very valuable and sumptuously illustrated presentation of Early Stone Age life.

## CHAPTERS II AND III

BREASTED, *History of Egypt*. †BREASTED, *History of the Ancient Egyptians*. *HALL, *The Ancient History of the Near East*, chaps. ii–iv, vi–viii.

B. Art and archæology

†MASPERO, *Art in Egypt.* A useful little manual in *Ars una — species mille.* (Hachette & Cᵢₑ, and Scribner's, New York.) *MASPERO, *Manual of Egyptian Archæology.* (Last edition, 1914. Putnam's.) †HEDWIG FECHHEIMER, *Die Plastik der Aegypter* (156 beautiful plates showing the finest examples of Egyptian sculpture. The best series to be had, and very low priced).

C. Mythology and religion

*BREASTED, *The Development of Religion and Thought in Ancient Egypt.*

D. Social life

†ERMAN, *Life in Ancient Egypt.*

E. Excavation and discovery

†EDWARDS, *Pharaohs, Fellahs, and Explorers.* *PETRIE, *Ten Years' Digging in Egypt.* WEIGALL, *Treasury of the Nile.* Two quarterly journals begun in 1914, called *Ancient Egypt* (edited by Petrie; $2.00 a year; subscriptions taken by Dr. W. C. Winslow, 525 Beacon Street, Boston, Mass.) and *Journal of Egyptian Archæology* (published by the Egypt Exploration Fund). Both report discoveries in Egypt as fast as made.

F. Original sources in English

*BREASTED, *Ancient Records of Egypt,* Vols. I–V. †PETRIE, *Egyptian Tales.* †MASPERO, *Popular Stories of Ancient Egypt* (translated from the French by Mrs. C. H. W. Johns).

G. The monuments as they are to-day

The Underwood & Underwood series of Egyptian views, edited by †BREASTED, *Egypt through the Stereoscope: a Journey through the Land of the Pharaohs* (100 views with explanatory volume and set of maps). See remarks above, p. viii. †(Selected views, with explanations printed on the backs, may be secured at moderate cost. The most useful fifteen on Egypt are Nos. 17, 27, 29, 30, 31, 42, 48, 52, 57, 60, 62, 69, 82, 89, 97.)

## CHAPTER IV

A. Histories

*KING, *History of Sumer and Akkad* and *History of Babylonia.* †GOODSPEED, *History of the Babylonians and Assyrians.* Recent discoveries have greatly altered the chronology. †C. H. W. JOHNS, *Ancient Babylonia* (Cambridge Manuals). *HALL, *The Ancient History of the Near East,* chaps. v, x, xii. *OLMSTEAD, *Sargon of Assyria.* *ROGERS, *A History of Babylonia and Assyria.*

B. Art and archæology

There is no handbook corresponding to Maspero's *Art in Egypt.* *HANDCOCK, *Mesopotamian Archæology.* *HALL, *The Ancient History of the Near East.* *JASTROW, *Civilization of the Babylonians and Assyrians.*

C. Mythology and religion

*JASTROW, *Aspects of Religious Belief and Practice in Babylonia and Assyria.* See also his *Civilization.*

D. Social life

†SAYCE, *Babylonian and Assyrian Life and Customs.* *JASTROW, *Civilization.*

*ROGERS, *A History of Babylonia and Assyria*, Vol. I. There is no journal reporting discoveries in Babylonia and Assyria (like *Ancient Egypt* above), but see the new journal of the American Archæological Institute, called *Art and Archæology* ($2.00 a year; subscriptions taken by The Macmillan Company, 64–66 Fifth Avenue, New York), which reports discovery in the whole field of ancient man. — *E.* Excavation and discovery

*R. F. HARPER (Ed.), *Assyrian and Babylonian Literature.* †BOTSFORD, *A Source Book of Ancient History*, chap. iii. *SAYCE (Ed.), *Records of the Past* (First Series, 12 vols.; Second Series, 6 vols.). †C. H. W. JOHNS, *Oldest Code of Laws in the World* (Laws of Hammurapi). *KING, *Letters of Hammurapi.* — *F.* Original sources in English

The buildings surviving in Babylonia and Assyria are in a very ruinous state. Photographs are now available in the excellent series by Underwood & Underwood on Mesopotamia. — *G.* The monuments as they are to-day

## CHAPTER V

†GOODSPEED, *History of the Babylonians and Assyrians.* †C. H. W. JOHNS, *Ancient Assyria* (Cambridge Manuals). *KING, *History of Babylonia.* *HALL, *Ancient History of the Near East.* *OLMSTEAD, *Sargon of Assyria.* *ROGERS, *A History of Babylonia and Assyria.* — *A.* Histories

There is no handbook of Assyrian art. The Patterson-Kleinmann series of photographs contains the most important Assyrian sculptures. See also *JASTROW, *Civilization.* — *B.* Art and archæology

On religion, social life, excavation and discovery, and original sources, see the books mentioned under Chapter IV, above.

## CHAPTER VI

There is no good modern history of Persia in English based on the sources, but see especially : †BENJAMIN, *Story of Persia* (Story of the Nations Series). MEYER, " Persia," in *Encyclopædia Britannica.* RAWLINSON, *Five Great Monarchies : Persia.* *HALL, *The Ancient History of the Near East*, chap. xii. — *A.* Histories

*PERROT and CHIPIEZ, *History of Art : Persia.* RAWLINSON, *Monarchies.* — *B.* Art and archæology

MEYER, " Persia," in *Encyclopædia Britannica.* RAWLINSON, *Monarchies.* — *C.* Mythology and religion

*JACKSON, *Zoroaster.* RAWLINSON, *Monarchies.* — *D.* Social life

†JACKSON, *Persia, Past and Present.* This valuable book is the best introduction to the subject of Persia as a whole, and contains much information on all the above subjects. †MICHAELIS, *A Century of Archæological Discovery.* — *E.* Exploration and discovery

F. Original sources in English

†TOLMAN, *The Behistan Inscription of King Darius.* The Persian monuments are not numerous, and this inscription of Behistun is the most important. A considerable part of it will be found quoted in BOTSFORD, *A Source Book of Ancient History*, pp. 57–59. The *Avesta* will be found in the series called Sacred Books of the East.

## CHAPTER VII

A. Histories

*GEORGE ADAM SMITH, *The Historical Geography of the Holy Land.* The most valuable of the many books on Palestine, but a little advanced for high-school pupils. *HENRY PRESERVED SMITH, *Old Testament History.* *CORNILL, *History of the People of Israel.* †KENT, *History of the Hebrew People.* †KENT, *History of the Jewish People.* *HALL, *The Ancient History of the Near East*, chap. ix. †MACALISTER, *A History of Civilization in Palestine* (Cambridge Manuals).

B. Mythology and religion

*BUDDE, *The Religion of Israel to the Exile.* *CHEYNE, *Jewish Religious Life after the Exile.* †J. M. POWIS SMITH, *The Prophet and his Problems* (Scribner's).

C. Excavation and discovery

HILPRECHT, *Recent Research in Bible Lands.* †MACALISTER, *A History of Civilization in Palestine* (Cambridge Manuals). Current reports will be found in *Journal of the Palestine Exploration Fund*, and in *Art and Archæology* (see above).

D. Social life

DAY, *Social Life of the Hebrews.*

E. Original sources in English

The *Old Testament* in the Revised Version. †MOORE, *The Literature of the Old Testament.* *CORNILL, *Introduction to the Canonical Books of the Old Testament.* *ROGERS, *Cuneiform Parallels to the Old Testament.* †BOTSFORD, *A Source Book of Ancient History*, chap. iv.

F. Palestine, its people and monuments as they are to-day

The Underwood & Underwood stereoscopic photographs (edited by HURLBUT), *Traveling in the Holy Land through the Stereoscope* (100 views with guidebook and maps). †(A selection of the best ten would include Nos. 8, 9, 18, 25, 39, 40, 41, 47, 61, 71.) SMITH, GEORGE ADAM, *The Historical Geography of the Holy Land.* PATON, *Guide to Jerusalem.*

## CHAPTER VIII

A. Histories

†BOTSFORD, *Hellenic History*, chap. i. †WESTERMANN, *Ancient Nations*, pp. 43–50. †GOODSPEED, *Ancient World*, pp. 65–71. ††MYRES, *Dawn of History*, chap. viii. †KIMBALL-BURY, *Students' Greece*, chap. i. †BURY, *History of Greece* (second edition), pp. 1–43. ††REINACH, *Story of Art*, pp. 26–32. ††HAWES, *Crete the Forerunner of Greece.* †BAIKIE, *Sea Kings of Crete.* †ZIMMERN, *Greek Commonwealth*, Pt. I (second edition).

The surviving documents are here almost wholly archæological, but a few selections bearing on this chapter are to be found in Botsford and Sihler's *Hellenic Civilization*, chap. ii.

*B. Sources and source selections*

## CHAPTER IX

Botsford, *Hellenic History*, chap. ii. Westermann, *Ancient Nations*, chap. vii. Goodspeed, *Ancient World*, pp. 65–77. Myres, *Dawn*, chap. ix. Kimball-Bury, *Students' Greece*, chap. ii. Bury, *Greece*, chap. i. *Hall, *Ancient History of the Near East*, pp. 31–72. Hawes, *Crete*. Baikie, *Sea Kings*. *Mosso, *Dawn of Mediterranean Civilization*.

*A. Histories*

See note under preceding chapter, also †Botsford, *Source Book of Ancient History*, chap. vii.

*B. Sources and source selections*

## CHAPTER X

Botsford, *Hellenic History*, chap. iii. Westermann, *Ancient Nations*, chap. viii. Goodspeed, *Ancient World*, pp. 83–87, 91–99. Kimball-Bury, *Students' Greece*, chap. ii. Bury, *Greece*, chap. i. †Greenidge, *Greek Constitutional History*, chap. ii. ††Capps, *Homer to Theocritus*, pp. 14–128. †Keller, *Homeric Life*. *Seymour, *Homeric Age*. Zimmern, *Greek Commonwealth*.

*A. Histories*

††Botsford and Sihler, *Hellenic Civilization*, chap. ii. Botsford, *Source Book of Ancient History*, chaps. viii–ix. †Thallon, *Readings in Greek History*, chap. i. Selections from the Iliad and Odyssey.

*B. Sources and source selection*

## CHAPTER XI

Botsford, *Hellenic History*, chap. iv. Westermann, *Ancient Nations*, chap. ix. Goodspeed, *Ancient World*, pp. 79–82, 87–92, 100–101. Kimball-Bury, *Students' Greece*, chap. iii. Bury, *Greece*, chap. ii. †Allcroft, *History of Sicily*, chaps. i–ii. Greenidge, *Greek Constitutional History*, chaps. ii–iii. Capps, *Homer to Theocritus*, pp. 129–140. Keller, *Colonization*, pp. 26–50. Zimmern, *Greek Commonwealth*.

*A. Histories*

Botsford and Sihler, *Hellenic Civilization*, chap. iii. Botsford, *Source Book*, chap. xi. *Herodotus* (Rawlinson), IV, 150–159. *Hesiod and Theognis* (Collins). *Hesiod* (Mair). Thallon, *Readings*, chaps. ii–iv.

*B. Sources and source selections*

## CHAPTER XII

Botsford, *Hellenic History*, chaps. vi–ix. Westermann, *Ancient Nations*, chap. x. Goodspeed, *Ancient World*, pp. 101–108, 115–125. Kimball-Bury, *Students' Greece*, pp. 79–89, and chaps. v–vi.

*A. Histories*

GREENIDGE, *Greek Constitutional History*, pp. 135–187. BURY, *Greece*, pp. 144–162 and chaps. iv–v. CAPPS, *Homer to Theocritus*, chaps. vi–vii. ††BENN, *Ancient Philosophy*, chaps. i–ii. REINACH, *Story of Art*, pp. 33–41. †MAHAFFY, *Social Life in Greece*, chaps. iv–v. ZIMMERN, *Greek Commonwealth*.

*B.* Sources and source selections

BOTSFORD and SIHLER, chap. iv. BOTSFORD, *Source Book*, chaps. x, xii–xiv. †*Aristotle's Constitution of Athens* (KENYON or POSTE), chaps. i–xxii. †*Plutarch's Lives of Theseus and Solon.* †*Herodotus*, I, 29–33, 59–64; III, 39–46, 120–125. THALLON, *Readings*, chaps. iv and vi.

## CHAPTER XIII

*A.* Histories

BOTSFORD, *Hellenic History*, chaps. x–xi. WESTERMANN, *Ancient Nations*, chap. xii. GOODSPEED, *Ancient World*, pp. 126–144. KIMBALL-BURY, *Students' Greece*, chaps. vii–viii. ALLCROFT, *History of Sicily*, chaps. iii ff. BURY, *Greece*, chaps. vi–vii. HALL, *Near East*, chap. xii. †HOGARTH, *Ancient East*, pp. 120–186. *ABBOTT, *Pericles*, chap. iii. *GRUNDY, *Great Persian War*.

*B.* Sources and source selections

BOTSFORD and SIHLER, pp. 162–172. †FLING, *Source Book of Greek History*, chap. v. BOTSFORD, *Source Book*, chaps. xv–xvi. *Herodotus*, Bks. VI–IX, especially VII, 140–233. *Plutarch's Lives of Aristides, Themistocles, Pausanias.* †*Æschylus' Persians*, especially lines 355–520. THALLON, *Readings*, chaps. vii–viii.

## CHAPTER XIV

*A.* Histories

BOTSFORD, *Hellenic History*. WESTERMANN, *Ancient Nations*, chaps. xi and xiii. GOODSPEED, *Ancient World*, pp. 109–115, 144–155, 168–173. KIMBALL-BURY, *Students' Greece*, pp. 64–74 and chaps. ix–x. BURY, *Greece*, pp. 120–143 and chap. viii. †SEIGNOBOS, *Ancient Civilization*, chap. xi. GREENIDGE, *Greek Constitutional History*, pp. 78–120, 189–207. †GRANT, *Greece in the Age of Pericles*, chaps. v–vii. *ABBOTT, *Pericles*, chaps. iv–viii. ZIMMERN, *Greek Commonwealth*.

*B.* Sources and source selections

BOTSFORD and SIHLER, chaps. vi–vii. BOTSFORD, *Source Book*, chap. xvii. *Plutarch's Lives of Aristides, Cimon, Lycurgus. Xenophon's State of the Lacedæmonians. Aristotle's Athenian Constitution*, chaps. xxiii–xxvii. †*Thucydides* (JOWETT), I, 98–103, 127–139. THALLON, *Readings*, chaps. v and ix.

## CHAPTER XV

*A.* Histories

BOTSFORD, *Hellenic History*. WESTERMANN, *Ancient Nations*, chaps. xiv–xv. GOODSPEED, *Ancient World*, 156–169. KIMBALL-BURY, *Students' Greece*, chap. xi. SEIGNOBOS, *Ancient Civilization*, chap. xiv.

BURY, *Greece*, chap. ix. GRANT, *Age of Pericles*, chaps. vii–x, xii. BENN, *Ancient Philosophy*, chap. iii. ††TARBELL, *History of Greek Art*, chaps. iii, vii, and viii. CAPPS, *Homer to Theocritus*, chaps. viii–xii. †MONROE, *History of Education*, pp. 28–59. MAHAFFY, *Social Life in Greece*, chaps. vi ff. ABBOTT, *Pericles*, chaps. xvi–xviii. ZIMMERN, *Greek Commonwealth*.

BOTSFORD and SIHLER, chaps. viii–xi. BOTSFORD, *Source Book*, chap. xviii. *Plutarch's Pericles*. THALLON, *Readings*, chap. ix.   *B. Sources and source selections*

## CHAPTER XVI

BOTSFORD, *Hellenic History*. WESTERMANN, *Ancient Nations*, chap. xvi. GOODSPEED, *Ancient World*, pp. 174–199. KIMBALL-BURY, *Students' Greece*, chaps. xii and xiv. BURY, *Greece*, chaps. x–xi. ALLCROFT, *Sicily*. GRANT, *Age of Pericles*, chap. xi. ABBOTT, *Pericles*, chaps. xiv–xv. *FERGUSON, *Greek Imperialism*, Lect. II. *WHIBLEY, *Political Parties in Athens*. ZIMMERN, *Greek Commonwealth*.   *A. Histories*

BOTSFORD and SIHLER, chap. vi. BOTSFORD, *Source Book*, chaps. xix–xx. FLING, *Source Book*, chap. vii. *Plutarch's Lives of Alcibiades, Nicias, Lysander*. Thucydides (JOWETT), Selections. THALLON, *Readings*, chaps. x–xii.   *B. Sources and source selections*

## CHAPTER XVII

BOTSFORD, *Hellenic History*. WESTERMANN, *Ancient Nations*, chap. xvii. GOODSPEED, *Ancient World*, pp. 200–215. KIMBALL-BURY, *Students' Greece*, chaps. xv–xvii. ALLCROFT, *History of Greece, 404–362 B.C.* BURY, *Greece*, chaps. xii–xiv. ALLCROFT, *Sicily*. CAPPS, *Homer to Theocritus*, pp. 330–338. †SANKEY, *Spartan and Theban Supremacies*.   *A. Histories*

BOTSFORD, *Source Book*, chaps. xxii–xxiii. †*Xenophon's Anabasis*, IV, 7 ff.; *Agesilaos* (DAKYNS). *Nepos' Epaminondas*. *Plutarch's Lives of Pelopidas and Timoleon*. THALLON, *Readings*, chaps. xiii–xiv.   *B. Sources and source selections*

## CHAPTER XVIII

BOTSFORD, *Hellenic History*. WESTERMANN, *Ancient Nations*, pp. 193–198. GOODSPEED, *Ancient World*, pp. 184–189, 215–220. BURY, *Greece* (see Index). ALLCROFT, *History of Greece, 404–362 B.C.*, chap. xi. CAPPS, *Homer to Theocritus*, chaps. xv–xvii. MAHAFFY, *Social Life in Greece*, chaps. vi ff. BENN, *Ancient Philosophy*, chaps. iv–vi. REINACH, *Story of Art*, pp. 50–58, 66–74. MONROE, *History of Education*, pp. 59–72. TARBELL, *Greek Art*, chap. ix. FERGUSON, *Greek Imperialism*, Lect. III. †TAYLOR, *Plato*. *MAUTHNER, *Aristotle*.   *A. Histories*

*B. Sources and source selections*

BOTSFORD and SIHLER, chaps. xii–xv. FLING, *Source Book*, chap. viii. THALLON, *Readings*, pp. 513–516, 532–558. *Xenophon's Economics* (DAKYNS). *Plato's Apology.* Selections from *Euripides* in †APPLETON, *Greek Poets*, and in †GOLDWIN SMITH, *Specimens of Greek Tragedy.* *Aristophanes' Acharnians and Birds* (FRERE in Everyman's).

## CHAPTER XIX

*A. Histories*

BOTSFORD, *Hellenic History.* WESTERMANN, *Ancient Nations*, pp. 187–193 and chap. xix. GOODSPEED, *Ancient World*, pp. 220–247. KIMBALL-BURY, *Students' Greece*, chaps. xviii–xx. ALLCROFT, *History of Greece, 362–323 B.C.* BURY, *Greece*, chaps. xvi–xviii. †HOGARTH, *Ancient East*, pp. 186–217. FERGUSON, *Greek Imperialism*, Lect. IV. CAPPS, *Homer to Theocritus*, chap. xiv. †CURTEIS, *Macedonian Empire.* †WHEELER, *Alexander.*

*B. Sources and source selections*

BOTSFORD and SIHLER, chap. xvi, passim. BOTSFORD, *Source Book*, chaps. xxiv–xxv. *Plutarch's Lives of Demosthenes, Phocion, Alexander.* †*Arrian's Anabasis* (selections). JUSTIN, *History*, Bk. IX (Bohn). *Demosthenes' Crown and Third Philippic.* THALLON, *Readings*, chap. xv. DAVIS, *Readings*, I, chap. ix.

## CHAPTER XX

*A. Histories*

BOTSFORD, *Hellenic History.* WESTERMANN, *Ancient Nations*, chap. xx. GOODSPEED, *Ancient World*, pp. 248–256, 258–269. *GARDNER, New Chapters in Greek History*, chap. xv. FERGUSON, *Greek Imperialism*, Lects. V–VII. †SHUCKBURGH, *Greek History*, pp. 235–310. GREENIDGE, *Greek Constitutional History*, chap. vii. MAHAFFY, *Problems in Greek History*, chap. ix. †MAHAFFY, *Progress of Hellenism*, Lects. II–IV. *Greek Life and Thought*, chaps. iii–v, xvi.

*B. Sources and source selections*

JUSTIN, *History*, Bk. IX. *Plutarch's Lives of Aratus, Demetrius, Pyrrhus, Agis, Cleomenes, Eumenes.* FLING, *Source Book*, chap. xiii. †*Polybius' Histories.* SHUCKBURGH, Selections, especially on the Achæan League.

## CHAPTER XXI

*A. Histories*

BOTSFORD, *Hellenic History.* WESTERMANN, *Ancient Nations*, chaps. xxi–xxii. GOODSPEED, *Ancient World*, pp. 256–262, 265–267. HOGARTH, *Ancient East*, pp. 218–251. MAHAFFY, *Alexander's Empire*, chaps. xiv, xx, and xxiii; *Progress of Hellenism*, Lect. V; *Greek Life and Thought*, chaps. i–ii, vi–xv. MONROE, *History of Education*, pp. 73–78. †TUCKER, *Life in Ancient Athens*, chap. ix. TARBELL, *Greek Art*, chap. x. CAPPS, *Homer to Theocritus*, chap. xviii.

## CHAPTER XXV

**Histories** BOTSFORD, *History of Rome*, pp. 116–150. WESTERMANN, *Ancient Nations*, chaps. xxix–xl. GOODSPEED, *Ancient World*, pp. 354–363, 365–392. BRYANT, *Short History*, chaps. xii–xiv. FOWLER, *Rome*, pp. 110–135. †MASOM, *Rome, 133–78 B.C.*, chap. i. †ALLCROFT and MASOM, *Rome, 202–133 B.C.*, chaps. x–xiv. †DAVIS, *Influence of Wealth in Imperial Rome*, chap. ii. ABBOTT, *Roman Political Institutions*, chap. v. GREENIDGE, *Roman Public Life*, chap. viii; *Roman History*, Vol. I, chap. i. *DUFF, *Literary History of Rome*, pp. 92–117. PELHAM, *Outlines*, pp. 149–198. HEITLAND, *Short History*, pp. 146–248. †ABBOTT, *Society and Politics in Ancient Rome*, pp. 22–40.

**Sources and source selections** BOTSFORD, *Story of Rome*, pp. 125–126 and chap. vi; *Source Book*, chaps. xxxiv–xxxv. DAVIS, *Source Readings*, II, pp. 85–104. MUNRO, *Source Book*, chaps. vii and xii. *Livy*, xxxiv, 1–8; xlv, 10–12. *Plutarch's Lives of Cato the Censor, Flaminius, Æmilius Paulus*.

## CHAPTER XXVI

**Histories** BOTSFORD, *History of Rome*, chaps. vii–viii. WESTERMANN, *Ancient Nations*, chaps. xxxi–xxxiv and pp. 379–382. GOODSPEED, *Ancient World*, pp. 392–428. BRYANT, *Short History*, chaps. xv–xxvi. FOWLER, *Rome*, pp. 136–186. HEITLAND, *Short History*, pp. 249–512. †ABBOTT, *Common People of Ancient Rome*, pp. 235–286. PELHAM, *Outlines*, pp. 201–258, 398–469. ABBOTT, *Roman Political Institutions*, chaps. vi–vii. HOW and LEIGH, *Rome*, pp. 331–551. †PRESTON and DODGE, *Private Life of the Romans*, chap. v. †ALLCROFT, *Rome, 78–31 B.C.* FRANK, *Roman Imperialism*. *JONES, *Companion to Roman History*.

**Sources and source selections** BOTSFORD, *Story of Rome*, chaps. vii–viii; *Source Book*, chaps. xxxvi–xxxvii. MUNRO, *Source Book*, pp. 180–185 and chap. viii. DAVIS, *Source Readings*, II, pp. 105–162. *Plutarch's Lives of Tiberius and Gaius Gracchus, Marius, Sulla, Crassus, Pompey, Cicero, Cæsar, Sertorius.* † *Cæsar's Gallic War*, I, 42–47. *Sallust's Jugurthine War* (Bohn).

## CHAPTER XXVII

**A. Histories** BOTSFORD, *History of Rome*, pp. 204–232. WESTERMANN, *Ancient Nations*, pp. 382–403. FOWLER, *Rome*, pp. 187–211. GOODSPEED, *Ancient World*, pp. 428–451. *JONES, *Roman Empire*, chaps. i–iii. †BURY, *Student's Roman Empire*, chaps. i–xii. ABBOTT, *Roman Political Institutions*, chap. xii. DAVIS, *Influence of Wealth*, chap. vii. PELHAM, *Outlines*, pp. 357–509. *FIRTH, *Augustus*. †FOWLER, *History of Roman*

# Bibliography

BOTSFORD and SIHLER, chaps. xvi–xix. BOTSFORD, *Source* chaps. xxvi–xxvii. †DAVIS, *Readings*, I, chap. x.

## CHAPTER XXII

BOTSFORD, *History of Rome*, chaps. i–iv. WESTERMANN, *Ancient Nations*, chaps. xxiii–xxv. GOODSPEED, *Ancient World*, pp. 276–325, 331–342. †BRYANT, *Short History of Rome*, chaps. i–vii. †FOWLER, *Rome*, pp. 7–54. ††MYRES, *Dawn*, chap. x. MOSSO, *Dawn of Civilization*, chaps. xxi–xxii, xxiv–xxv. JONES, *Companion to Roman History*, pp. 1–12. †HEITLAND, *Short History of the Roman Republic*, pp. 1–82. †HOW and LEIGH, *History of Rome*, pp. 1–131. †PELHAM, *Outlines*, pp. 45–67. ††ABBOTT, *Roman Political Institutions*, chap. iv. †CARTER, *Religion of Numa*. *FRANK, *Roman Imperialism*.

BOTSFORD, *Story of Rome*, chaps. i–iv; *Source Book*, chaps. xxix–xxxi. MUNRO, *Source Book*, chaps. i, ii, iv, and v. *Plutarch's Lives of Romulus, Numa, Pyrrhus, Camillus*. DAVIS, *Source Readings*, II, pp. 1–40.

## CHAPTER XXIII

BOTSFORD, *History of Rome*, chap. v. WESTERMANN, *Ancient Nations*, pp. 275–276, 279–284. GOODSPEED, *Ancient World*, pp. 326–331, 343–346. BRYANT, *Short History*, pp. 67–74. FOWLER, *Rome*, pp. 55–83. HEITLAND, *Short History*, pp. 82–97. †LIDDELL, *Student's Rome*, pp. 218–229. *GREENIDGE, *Roman Public Life*, chap. vii. HOW and LEIGH, *Rome*, pp. 131–148. †SMITH, *Carthage and the Carthaginians*. FRANK, *Roman Imperialism*.

BOTSFORD, *Story of Rome*, pp. 101–104; *Source Book*, chap. xxxii. MUNRO, *Source Book*, chap. iii. DAVIS, *Source Readings*, II, pp. 41–50.

## CHAPTER XXIV

BOTSFORD, *History of Rome*, chap. v. WESTERMANN, *Ancient Nations*, chaps. xxvi–xxvii. GOODSPEED, *Ancient World*, pp. 346–354. FOWLER, *Rome*, pp. 84–110. BRYANT, *Short History*, pp. 73–79 and chaps. ix–xi. HOW and LEIGH, pp. 169–244. LIDDELL, *Rome*, pp. 256–320. *HAVELL, *Republican Rome*, pp. 156–274. HEITLAND, *Short History*, pp. 98–145. *MORRIS, *Hannibal*. FRANK, *Roman Imperialism*.

BOTSFORD, *Story of Rome*, pp. 104–124; *Source Book*, chap. xxxiii. MUNRO, *Source Book*, chap. vi. DAVIS, *Source Readings*, II, chap. iii. *Polybius*, I, 56–62; III, 49–56. †*Livy*, xxi, 32–38. *Plutarch's Lives of Fabius and Marcellus*.

*Literature,* Bk. II. ††MACKAIL, *Roman Literature,* Bk. II, chaps. i–v.
†TUCKER, *Life in the Roman World,* chap. v.

BOTSFORD, *Story of Rome,* chaps. ix–x; *Source Book,* chaps. xxxviii–
xxxix. MUNRO, *Source Book,* chaps. ix and xi. DAVIS, *Source Readings,*
pp. 163–196. †LAING, *Masterpieces of Latin Literature* (selections);
†*The Deeds of Augustus* (Fairley's translation in the *Pennsylvania
Translations and Reprints*), Vol. V, No. 1. *Suetonius' Lives of the
Cæsars* (selections). †*Tacitus' Annals,* XV, 38–45, 60–65.

*B. Sources
and source
selections*

## CHAPTER XXVIII

BOTSFORD, *History of Rome,* pp. 232–266. WESTERMANN, *Ancient
Nations,* pp. 403–435. FOWLER, *Rome,* pp. 211–251. GOODSPEED, *Ancient
World,* pp. 451–482. PELHAM, *Outlines,* pp. 509–541. REINACH,
*Story of Art,* pp. 75–83. †PELLISON, *Roman Life in Pliny's Time,* chap. ix.
*MAU and KELSEY, *Pompeii,* chaps. vii–viii, xii–xxii, xlvi–xlviii, lvi–lix.
TUCKER, *Roman Life,* chaps. i–iii, xix–xxi. GREENIDGE, *Roman Public
Life,* chap. xi. *HARDY, *Studies in Roman History,* Series I, chaps. i–v.
JONES, *Roman Empire,* chaps. iv–vi. DAVIS, *Influence of Wealth,* chaps.
iii–vi. BURY, *Students' Roman Empire.* *CUMONT, *Oriental Religions in
Roman Paganism* (an epoch-making work).

*A. Histories*

BOTSFORD, *Story of Rome,* chap. xi; *Source Book,* chap. xl. DAVIS,
*Source Readings,* II, pp. 196–287. MUNRO, *Source Book,* pp. 162–171, 176–
179. *Letters of Pliny* (FIRTH). New Testament, The Acts.

*B. Sources
and source
selections*

## CHAPTER XXIX

BOTSFORD, *History of Rome,* chap. xii. WESTERMANN, *Ancient
Nations,* chaps. xl–xli. GOODSPEED, *Ancient World,* pp. 483–501. JONES,
*Roman Empire,* chaps. vii–xi. OMAN, *Byzantine Empire,* chap. ii.
ABBOTT, *Roman Political Institutions,* chap. xvi. *WRIGHT, *Palmyra
and Zenobia,* chaps. xi–xv. SEIGNOBOS, *Ancient Civilization,* pp. 332–
346. DAVIS, *Outline History,* pp. 130–183. PELHAM, *Outlines,* pp.
577–586. †CUTTS, *St. Jerome.* JONES, *Companion to Roman History.*
*COTTERILL, *Medieval Italy,* pp. 21–54. DAVIS, *Influence of Wealth,*
chap. viii. *UHLHORN, *Conflict of Christianity with Heathenism,*
pp. 420–479.

*A. Histories*

BOTSFORD, *Source Book,* chaps. xli–xliii, xlv. DAVIS, *Source Readings,*
II, pp. 287–389. MUNRO, *Source Book,* pp. 171–174. †ROBINSON, *Readings in European History,* Vol. I, pp. 14–27. *The Notitia Dignitatum
(Pennsylvania Translations and Reprints).*

*B. Sources
and source
selections*

## CHAPTER XXX

*A.* Histories  BOTSFORD, *History of Rome*, chaps. xiii–xiv. WESTERMANN, *Ancient Nations*, chaps. xlii–xlv. GOODSPEED, *Ancient World*, pp. 502–521. †OMAN, *Byzantine Empire*, chaps. iii, vi, ix, xi–xii. COTTERILL, *Medieval Italy*, pp. 55–116, 159–185, 194, 205, 251–283. †HODGKIN, *Dynasty of Theodosius*, pp. 55–72, 134–203. †H. W. C. DAVIS, *Medieval Europe*, chap. i. REINACH, *Story of Art*, pp. 84–91. JONES, *Roman Empire*, pp. 410–446. \*HUTTON, *Church and the Barbarians*, chaps. iv–x. \*EMERTON, *Introduction to the Middle Ages*. \*MOREY, *Outlines of Roman Law*.

*B.* Sources and source and selections *selectic*  BOTSFORD, *Source Book*, chaps. xliv–xlvi. DAVIS, *Source Readings*, II, chaps. x–xi. †ROBINSON, *Readings in European History*, Vol. I, pp. 19–27, 97–100 and chaps. iii–vi. *Tacitus' Germania. Cæsar's Gallic War*, VI, pp. 21–28. †*Eugippus' Life of St. Severinus* (ROBINSON). *Jordanes' Gothic History* (MIEROW). *English Correspondence of St. Boniface* (KYLIE).

*A.* Hi

# ADDITIONAL WORKS OF REFERENCE ON THE GREEK AND HELLENISTIC AGE, TOPICALLY ARRANGED

*A.* General and political histories  The histories of Greece by Grote, Curtius, Holm, Abbott. †FREEMAN, *Story of Sicily* ; \**History of Federal Government*. \*DENIKER, *Races of Man*. \*FERGUSON, *Hellenistic Athens*. \*BEVAN, *House of Seleucus*, \*RAWLINSON, *Bactria*. \*HOGARTH, *Philipp and Alexander*. \*DODGE, *Alexander*. \*GRUNDY, *Thucydides and the History of his Age*. \*TARN, *Antigonos Gonatas*. †TILLYARD, *Agathocles*. \*MAHAFFY, *Silver Age of the Greek World*.

*B.* Constitutional and institutional history  \*GILBERT, *Greek Constitutional Antiquities*. \*PHILLIPSON, *International Law and Custom of Ancient Greece and Rome*. †CALHOUN, *Athenian Clubs in Politics and Litigation*. \*TOD, *International Arbitration amongst the Greeks*. \*WHIBLEY, *Greek Oligarchies*. †HAMMOND, *Political Institutions of the Ancient Greeks*.

*C.* Life and society  ††GULICK, *Life of the Ancient Greeks*. \*GUHL and KONER, *Life of the Greeks and Romans*. †GARDNER, *Greek Athletic Sports and Festivals*. †BLUEMNER, *Home Life of the Ancient Greeks*. †DAVIS, *A Day in Ancient Athens*. \*DAVIDSON, *Education of the Greek People*. \*MAHAFFY, *What have the Greeks done for Modern Civilization ?* \*BALL, *Short History of Mathematics*. \*JONES, *Greek Morality*. \*WARD, *The Ancient Lowly*. †DONALDSON, *Woman ; her Position and Influence in Greece and Rome*. \*ABRAHAMS, *Greek Dress*.

*FARNELL, *Higher Aspects of Greek Religion*. *MURRAY, *Four Stages in Greek Religion*. *HARRISON, *Religion of Ancient Greece*. *ADAM, *Religious Teachers of Greece*. *HALLIDAY, *Greek Divination*. *FAIRBANKS, *Mythology of the Greeks and Romans*. †BULFINCH, *Age of Fable*.

*D. Religion and mythology*

*GARDNER, *Ancient Athens* ; *Handbook of Greek Sculpture*. †FOWLER and WHEELER, *Greek Archæology*. †RICHARDSON, *Vacation Days in Greece*. *SCHREIBER, *Atlas of Classical Antiquities* (illustrated).

*E. Art and archæology*

†FOWLER, *Ancient Greek Literature*. †CROISET, *Greek Literature*. †JEVONS, *Greek Literature*. *MACKAIL, *Lectures on Greek Poetry*. *JEBB, *Greek Literature* ; *Classical Greek Poetry* ; *Attic Orators*. *LANG, *Homer and the Epic*. *MURRAY, *Rise of the Greek Epic*. *MOULTON, *Ancient Classical Drama*. *HAIGH, *Attic Theatre*. †BURT, *Brief History of Greek Philosophy*. †MAYOR, *Sketch of Ancient Philosophy*. *SANDYS, *Classical Greek Scholarship*.

*F. Literature and philosophy*

There is no cheap dictionary of classical antiquities. †HARPER, *Dictionary of Classical Literature and Antiquities*. *WHIBLEY, *Companion to Greek Studies*. *HALL, *Companion to Classical Texts*. †TOZER, *Ancient Geography*. †SHEPHERD, *Atlas of Ancient History*. The new series of individual maps of the ancient world by †MURRAY are very valuable. †PUTZGER, *Schulatlas*. †SIEGLIN, *Schulatlas*. A new series of classroom wall maps for ancient history (edited by †BREASTED & HUTH) is being published by the Denoyer Geppert Company, Chicago.

*G. Handbooks, atlases, etc.*

†MICHAELIS, *A Century of Archæological Discoveries*. *SCHUCHARDT, *Schliemann's Excavations*. †BURROWS, *Discoveries in Crete*. *MOSSO, *The Palaces of Crete*. *GARSTANG, *Asia Minor*. ††HAWES, *Crete the Forerunner of Greece*.

*H. Exploration and discovery*

The Underwood & Underwood series of stereoscopic photographs of Greece and its monuments (edited by RICHARDSON), *Greece through the Stereoscope* (100 views with guidebook and maps). A short description is also printed on the back of each view. See remarks above, p. viii. †(A selection of fifteen of the most useful views comprises Nos. 1, 8, 21, 35, 39, 42, 48, 54, 62, 64, 77, 80, 87, 96, 97.)

## GREEK AUTHORS IN TRANSLATION

*Æschylus* (CAMPBELL, verse). *Alcæus* (EASBY-SMITH). *Aristophanes* (FRERE ; ROGERS). *Aristotle* (KENYON ; POSTE). *Demosthenes* (KENNEDY). *Euripides* (MURRAY ; WAY). *Herodotus* (RAWLINSON). *Hesiod* (with *Callimachus* and *Theognis*, by BANKS ; with *Theognis*, COLLINS ; best translation of *Hesiod* alone, MAIR). *Homer: Iliad* (LANG, LEAF, MYERS ; BRYANT) ; *Odyssey* (BUTCHER and LANG ; BRYANT). *Isocrates*

(FREESE). *Pausanias* (FRAZER). *Pindar* (MYERS). *Plato* (JOWETT). *Plutarch* (CLOUGH; selected *Lives*, by PERRIN). *Polybius* (SHUCK-BURGH). *Strabo* (HAMILTON and FALCONER). *Thucydides* (JOWETT; CRAWLEY). *Xenophon* (DAKYNS).

## ADDITIONAL WORKS OF REFERENCE ON THE ROMAN AGE, TOPICALLY ARRANGED

*A*. General and political histories

For a detailed criticism of the tradition about earliest Rome (p. 497, note), see †IHNE, *History of Rome*. Other more extended and valuable histories are those of Mommsen, Heitland, Duruy, Long, Ferrero, Merivale, Gibbons. See also *MOMMSEN, *Provinces*. *BUSSELL, *Roman Empire*. Other special works are *DODGE, *Hannibal*. *HOW, *Hannibal and the Great War*. †STRACHAN-DAVIDSON, *Cicero*. †BOISSIER, *Cicero and his Friends*. †FOWLER, *Cæsar*. *SIHLER, *Julius Cæsar*. *HOLMES, *Cæsar's Conquest of Gaul*. *SHUCKBURGH, *Augustus*. *TARVER, *Tiberius*. *BARING-GOULD, *Tragedy of the Cæsars*. †CAPES, *Early Empire*. *WATSON, *Marcus Aurelius*. *BRYANT, *Antoninus Pius*. *GREGOROVIUS, *Hadrian*. *HENDERSON, *Life and Principate of the Emperor Nero*. *HOPKINS, *Alexander Severus*. *HAY, *Heliogabalus*. *FIRTH, *Constantine*. †CUTTS, *Constantine*. *BOISSIER, *Roman Africa*. †BOUCHIER, *Life and Letters in Roman Africa*; *Roman Spain*. *GLOVER, *Life and Letters in the Fourth Century*.

*B*. Constitutional and institutional history

†TAYLOR, *Constitutional and Political History of Rome*. *MATTINGLY, *Imperial Civil Service*. *BOTSFORD, *Roman Assemblies*. *ARNOLD, *Roman Provincial Administration*. *REID, *Municipalities of the Roman Empire*. *GREENIDGE, *Legal Procedure in Cicero's Time*. *HADLEY, *Introduction to Roman Law*. *FOWLER, *City State of the Greeks and Romans*. †BRYCE, *The Roman and British Empires*.

*C*. Life and society

*DILL, *Roman Society from Nero to Marcus Aurelius*; *Roman Society in the Last Century of the Western Empire*. †BECKER, *Gallus*. *BUCKLAND, *Roman Law of Slavery*. †INGE, *Society at Rome under the Cæsars*. †JOHNSTON, *Private Life of the Romans*. *INGRAM, *History of Slavery*. *FRIEDLAENDER, *Roman Life and Manners*. †CHURCH, *Roman Life in the Days of Cicero*. *OLIVER, *Roman Economic Conditions*. †*Roman Farm Management*, by a Virginia farmer (FAIRFAX HARRISON).

*D*. Religion and mythology

*CARTER, *Religious Life of Ancient Rome*. *FOWLER, *Religious Experience of the Roman People*. †GRANGER, *Worship of the Romans*. †GUERBER, *Myths of Greece and Rome*. †MURRAY, *Manual of Mythology*. *GLOVER, *Conflict of Religions*. *FISHER, *Beginnings of Christianity*. *HATCH, *Organization of the Early Christian Churches*. *CUMONT, *Mysteries of Mithra*.

*E. R. Barker, Buried Herculaneum. *T. B. Platner, Topography and Monuments of Ancient Rome. †C. Huelsen, The Roman Forum. *H. B. Walters, Art of the Romans. *R. Lanciani, Ruins and Excavations of Ancient Rome; *Pagan and Christian Rome. *J. Fergusson, History of Architecture. †Ramsay and Lanciani, Manual of Roman Antiquities.

E. Art and archæology

††J. W. Mackail, Latin Literature. *Lawton, Classical Latin Literature. *C. T. Crutwell, History of Roman Literature. *Teuffel and Schwabe, History of Roman Literature. *W. Sellar, Roman Poets of the Republic; *Roman Poets of the Augustan Age. *E. V. Arnold, Roman Stoicism. See works on ancient philosophy under Greece.

F. Literature and philosophy

†Michaelis, A Century of Archæological Discoveries. *Mau and Kelsey, Pompeii, its Life and Art. Barker, Buried Herculaneum. *Peet, Stone and Bronze Ages in Italy. Lanciani, Ruins and Excavations of Ancient Rome.

G. Exploration and discovery

The Underwood & Underwood series of stereoscopic photographs of Rome and Italy (edited by Ellison and Egbert), *Italy through the Stereoscope* (100 views with explanatory volume and set of maps). See above, p. viii. †(A selection of the most useful fifteen views comprises Nos. 21, 23, 25, 27, 30, 33, 34, 43, 45, 46, 47, 58, 60, 62, 91.)

H. The monuments as they are to-day

## ROMAN AUTHORS AND OTHER SOURCES FOR ROMAN HISTORY IN TRANSLATION

*Ammianus Marcellinus* (Bohn Ed.). *Appian* (White). *Cæsar* (Bohn Ed.). *Cassiodorus' Letters* (Hodgkin). *Cicero's Letters* (Shuckburgh); *Works* (Bohn Ed.). *Dio Cassius* (Foster or Carey). *Eugippus' St. Severinus* (Robinson). *Horace* (Martin; Lonsdale and Lee; Wickham). *Jordanes* (Mierow). *Josephus* (Whiston). *Justin, Nepos,* and *Eutropius* (Bohn Ed.). *Juvenal* (Gifford). *Livy* (Spillan; Brodribb). *Lucretius* (Munro). *Marcus Aurelius* (Rendall or Long). *Monumentum Ancyranum* (Fairley). *Ovid* (Riley). *Pliny's Letters* (Firth). *Propertius* (Moore). *Sallust,* with *Florus* and *Paterculus* (Bohn Ed.). *Strabo* (Falconer). *Suetonius* (Forester). *Tacitus* (Church and Brodribb). *Virgil* (Bryce; Crane).

# INDEX

## KEY TO PRONUNCIATION